YALE UNIVERSITY PRESS
PELICAN HISTORY OF ART

FOUNDING EDITOR: NIKOLAUS PEVSNER

SHEILA S. BLAIR AND JONATHAN M. BLOOM

THE ART AND ARCHITECTURE OF ISLAM
1250–1800

Sheila S. Blair and Jonathan M. Bloom

The Art and Architecture of Islam
1250–1800

Yale University Press
New Haven and London

For Felicity and Oliver

First published 1994

Reprinted with corrections 1995
10 9 8 7 6 5 4 3 2

Typeset in Linotron Ehrhardt by Best-set Typesetter Ltd., Hong Kong
and printed by CS Graphics Pte, Singapore

Designed by Mary Carruthers

Library of Congress Cataloging-in-Publication Data

Blair, Sheila.
    The art and architecture of Islam 1250–1800 / Sheila S. Blair
and Jonathan M. Bloom.
        p.   cm. – (Yale University Press Pelican history of art)
    Continuation of: The art and architecture of Islam 650–1250 /
Richard Ettinghausen and Oleg Grabar. Harmondsworth,
Middlesex, England; New York, N.Y.: Penguin Books, 1987.
(The Pelican history of art).
    Includes bibliographical references and index.
    ISBN 0-300-05888-8 (cloth)
        0-300-06465-9 (paper)
1. Art, Islamic.   2. Architecture, Islamic.   I. Bloom, Jonathan
(Jonathan M.).   II. Ettinghausen, Richard. The art and architecture
of Islam 650–1250.   III. Title.   IV. Series.
N6260.B56   1994
709'.17'671 – dc20   93-49561
                                                          CIP

Titlepage illustration: detail of *Mahmud of Ghazna Crossing the Ganges* from Rashid al-Din, *Jāmiʿ al-tawārīkh*, plate 34

Contents

Preface

When *The Pelican History of Art* first commissioned a work on Islamic art, Sir Nikolaus Pevsner envisioned a single volume covering the 1400 years and forty-odd countries where Islamic art and architecture were produced. Richard Ettinghausen asked Oleg Grabar to collaborate on the project in 1959, and they began to write it together, with Grabar writing largely about architecture and Ettinghausen about the "minor" arts. Within twenty years, however, interest in and knowledge about Islam in general and Islamic art and architecture in particular had grown so enormously that Ettinghausen and Grabar felt that the first half of its history was sufficient to fill a single volume (which Grabar finished after Ettinghausen's death in 1979). The first volume was published in 1987, but other commitments made it impossible for Grabar to continue the project and he suggested that Pelican approach us, a team of independent scholars, to write Volume II. We enthusiastically agreed to undertake the project in 1987 and met with the two editors of the series, Peter Lasko and Judy Nairn, who provided encouragement and advice about how to approach such a large and complex project. Susan Rose-Smith, the indefatigable picture researcher responsible for the images illustrating the first volume, agreed to take on the task for the second. In early 1992, a year after the death of Judy Nairn (who had been the mainstay of the series), Penguin Books, for decades its publisher, announced that *The Pelican History of Art* had been acquired by Yale University Press in London. We are pleased that our volume is one of the first to appear in Yale's new and expanded format, and Susan Rose-Smith has cheerfully and ably expanded her search for color photographs to illustrate it.

When Yale University Press announced that it would continue to publish the *Pelican* series, some critics wondered about the value of surveys and handbooks in an age of multiple and competing critical approaches to the history of art. In the half-century since the series was conceived as the first comprehensive history of art in English, the study of the history of art has evolved enormously from such formalist concerns as the description of works of art, their attribution to masters, and the delineation of careers to broader questions not only about the roles the arts play in the societies in which they are made and exhibited but also about the nature of the investigation itself. Once the purview of a handful of rich collectors and connoisseurs, the study of the history of art has expanded to become a staple of college curricula everywhere and its popularity has exploded the numbers of museum-goers.

In the thirty-five years since Pevsner commissioned a book on the subject, the study of Islamic art has metamorphosed, not only because of new approaches to the history of art in general and discoveries in Islamic art in particular, but also because of the changed political and economic positions of many lands where Islam is the dominant religion. Thirty-five years ago the study of Islamic art was almost exclusively the bailiwick of Europeans and Americans interested in a somewhat alien and exotic world; today Islamic art is increasingly studied by scholars from that very world, who quite naturally see it in a different light and ask of it different questions. Unlike some critics who see any approach by European and American "Orientalists" as a vestige of nineteenth-century colonialism and an attempt at domination, we do not question the validity of one culture trying, however inadequately, to "understand" or "explain" the other. We do, however, realize that our position and method are relative and take note that ours is but one possible approach of many.

Paradoxically, while much of the Islamic world has been intent on rediscovering and validating a tradition of Islamic art, equivalent in the grand scheme of things to, say, Chinese or Greek art, other scholars, particularly in the West, have come to question the validity of such concepts as "Islamic" art. In their view, the concept of an Islamic art is the equivalent not of Chinese or Greek art, but of a Christian or Buddhist art, and the study of Islamic art, which is supposed to explain not only Morocco but Malaysia, makes as much sense as the combined study of Ravenna and Raphael or the Kushans and Kyoto. The concept of a unified "Islamic" art or culture is largely a creation of the nineteenth and twentieth centuries in the West, when scholars looked back to a golden age in the eighth and ninth centuries and projected it onto the kaleidoscopic contemporary world. This appealing idea has been accepted somewhat uncritically by newly empowered countries seeking to validate their position in the twentieth century and create connections with past glories. Scholars have recently begun to look at continuities and discontinuities in the arts of such well-defined entities as the Mediterranean or the fifteenth century, without prejudice to the confessional or political allegiances of the participants.

The nature of the *Pelican* series and the desire to continue the story begun in the first volume have prevented us from addressing such issues. Constraints on the size of this book have forced us to omit discussion, let alone illustration, of Islamic art and architecture in sub-Saharan Africa, both west and east, the Balkans, China, and south-east Asia. We have limited our coverage to the traditional Islamic belt stretching from Spain across North Africa and Egypt to Syria, Arabia, and Turkey, and across Iran to Central Asia, Afghanistan, and India. We have also continued the arbitrary and somewhat old-fashioned method of treating architecture separately from the other arts. We believe, nevertheless, that this methodology and type of book are still valuable, for the study of Islamic art is comparatively young, and there are few accessible sources to which the interested reader or student may turn. Even for experienced scholars in other fields, it is often difficult to distinguish the forest from the trees, and we hope that this book will provide a balanced overview for a wide audience, including art historians in many fields, students of the Middle East and Islam, and the general public.

No project of this size could be accomplished without outside support. We would like to acknowledge financial support from the National Endowment for the Humanities, an independent federal agency; the Aga Khan Program for Islamic Art and Architecture at Harvard University and the Massachusetts Institute of Technology; and the Getty Grant Program. The unparalleled resources of the Harvard University Library were made available through the Center for Middle Eastern Studies at Harvard and its Director, William Graham. The American Institute for Indian Studies provided hospitality, accommodation, and assistance for our travels in India. We have also benefitted from much recent scholarship made available as a result of our editorial work for *The Dictionary of Art*. In addition many colleagues and friends contributed to the completion of this project in various ways; in particular we would like to thank Mohammad Al-Asad, James Allan, Tulay Artan, Catherine and Frederick Asher, Michael Bates, Maureen Blackledge, Mary and Bill Blair, Hal Bloom, Richard Born, Mary Carruthers, Walter Denny, Kevin Duval, Massumeh Farhad, H.-O. Feistel, Annette Fern, Leonor Fernandes, Carol Fisher, Kjeld von Folsach, Lisa Golombek, Oleg Grabar, Ernst Grube, Klaus Herdeg, Renata Holod, Anatol Ivanov, Dickran Kouymjian, Thomas Lentz, Judith Lerner, Robert McChesney, Michael and Viktoria Meinecke, Elizabeth Merklinger, Gülru Necipoğlu, Pen and Courtney Nelson, Amy Newhall, John Nicoll, Bernard O'Kane, Richard Parker, Julian Raby, András Riedelmeyer, Sally Salvesen, Barbara Schmitz, Margaret Ševčenko, John Seyller, Eleanor Sims, Abolala Soudavar, Jeff Spurr, Tim Stanley, Wheeler Thackston, Daniel Walker, Cary Welch, Estelle Whelan, Caroline Williams, Robert Williams, David Wise, Filiz and Şahin Yenişehirlioğlu, and Karen Zitta.

Richmond, New Hampshire
12 January 1993

Photographic Acknowledgements

The publishers are grateful to the following persons and institutions for providing photographic material:

J. Allan Cash Photo Library: 194, 348, 393; American Numismatic Society, New York: 358; Antikvarisk-Topografiska Arkivat, Stockholm: 189; Archivi Alinari: 165; Catherine B. Asher: 198, 199, 203; Ashmolean Museum, Oxford (Creswell Archive): 97; Benaki Museum, Athens: 310; The British Library, London: 38, 76, 131, 206, 207, 213, 226, 364; The British Museum, London: 129, 208, 302, 303, 373; The Burrell Collection, Glasgow: 369; The Chester Beatty Library, Dublin, Courtesy of the Trustees: 41, 92, 143, 266, 267, 366; Bibliothèque Nationale, Paris: 81, 147, 148; The Brooklyn Museum: 42, 362 (Ella C. Woodward Fund); Bulloz, Paris: 388; The Cleveland Museum of Art: 82, 139 (Purchase from the J. H. Wade Fund, 39.40), 166, 379; Colnaghi Collection, London: 218; K. A. C. Creswell Archive: 98; David Collection, Copenhagen: 227, 382; Walter Denny: 168, 180, 184, 186, 286, 291; Douglas Dickins: 231, 356, 358; Edinburgh University Library: 32, 33, 34; Erkin Emiroglu: 176, 182; Erzbischöfliche Dom- und Diozesanmuseum (Gerhard Sokol), Vienna: 23; Gemeentemuseum, The Hague: 295; Gulbenkian Foundation, Lisbon: 89; Harvard University, Cambridge, MA: 22 (Aga Khan Program); Courtesy of the Arthur M. Sackler Museum: 36, 211 (Promised gift of Mr. & Mrs. Stuart Cary Welch, Jr.), 222 (Sarah C. Sears collection), 223 (Bequest of the estate of Abby Aldrich Rockefeller), 331 (Gift of John Goelet); Her Majesty the Queen © 1992 Royal Library, Windsor Castle: 371; Robert Hillenbrand: 125; Johns Hopkins University, Garrett Collection, Baltimore: 84; A. Hutt: 63; Institut Royal du Patrimoine Artistique: 27; The India Office Library and Records, London: 386; The Jewish Museum, New York: 395 (Gift of Dr. Harry G. Friedman, F3615); A. F. Kersting: 53, 101, 117, 178, 387; Kuwait National Museum, the Al Sabah Collection, Dar al-Athar al-Islamiyyah: 137, 294; Leiden University Library: 272; London University, School of Oriental and African Studies: 363; Los Angeles County Museum of Art: 85, 374; Mas: 159, 162; Robert McChesney: 255; Michael Meinecke: 110; The Metropolitan Museum of Art, New York: 2, 28 (The Rogers Fund, 1910.10.218), 221 (91.1.579), 248, 367 (13.228.29); Museum für islamische Kunst, Berlin: 219, 293, 312, 332; Museum of Fine Arts, Boston: 26 (Holmes collection), 212 (Francis Bartlett donation), 215 (by purchase and gift of John Goelet), 217 (Gift of Mrs. Walter Scott Fitz), 224 (Francis Bartlett donation); Museum of Islamic Art, Cairo: 126, 138, 140; National Gallery of Art, Washington, DC: 292 (Samuel H. Kress collection); National Trust, Powis Castle: 378, 381; New York Public Library: 187 (Spencer collection); Christine Osborne: 200; Österreichisches Museum für angewandte Kunst, Vienna: 299; Österreichische Nationalbibliothek, Vienna: 133; Bernard O'Kane: 8, 15, 56, 71, 78, 94, 99, 118, 123, 152, 167, 193, 252, 262, 315, 394; The Pierpont Morgan Library, New York: 31; Josephine Powell: 4, 6, 50, 66, 68, 69, 157, 158, 191, 195, 201, 202, 234, 250, 270, 276, 280, 281, 282, 287, 289, 327, 335, 336, 344, 353, 355, 399; B. W. Robinson: 228; The Royal Asiatic Society, London: 83; Arthur M. Sackler Gallery, Smithsonian Institution, Washington, DC: 25, 35, 40, 80, 132, 216, 264, 265, 370, 371, 372; Prince Sadruddin Aga Khan, Geneva: 204, 209; Saltykov-Shchedrin State Public Library, St Petersburg: 43, 383; Service Photographique de la Reunion des Musées Nationaux, Paris: 24, 127, 128; State Hermitage Museum, St Petersburg: 19, 73, 74, 90; The Textile Museum, Washington, DC: 144; Thyssen-Bornemisza Collection, Lugano: 376; Topkapı Sarayı Müzesi Müdürlügü, Istanbul: 29, 39, 44, 77, 91, 296, 300, 301, 305, 306, 307, 308, 314, Türk ve Islam Eserleri Müzesi, Istanbul: 86, 87, 142, 188, 297; Board of Trustees of the Victoria & Albert Museum, London: 10, 88, 108, 141, 214, 304, 365, 377, 380, 390, 397; S. C. Welch: 210; The Whitworth Art Gallery, University of Manchester: 313; Caroline Williams: 145; Roger Wood: 230, 236

Line Drawing Credits

E. Akurgal, ed., *Art and Architecture of Turkey*: 283; R. Andrews: 51, 149, 181, 235; N. Ardalan and L. Bakhtiar, *The Sense of Unity*: 229; C. B. Asher, *Architecture of Mughal India*: 337, 340; M. Barrucand, *Urbanisme princier en Islam*: 328; D. Behrens-Abouseif: *Islamic architecture in Cairo*: 112; J. M. Bloom: 93, 95, 96, 160, 242, 242, 251, 269, 271; K. A. C. Creswell, *The Muslim Architecture of Egypt*: 102; L. Golombek and D. Wilber, *The Timurid Architecture of Iran and Turan*: 47, 54, 55, 59, 62, 67; G. Goodwin, *A History of Ottoman Architecture*: 273, 279; J. C. Harle, *Art and Architecture of the Indian Subcontinent*: 192; K. Herdeg, *Formal Structure in Islamic Architecture*: 260; R. Hillenbrand, "Political Symbolism in the Early Indo-Islamic Mosque", *Iran* 26 (1988): 190; A. Kuran, *Sinan*: 275; A. Kuran, *The Mosque in Early Ottoman Architecture*: 171, 175, 183; E. La Roche, *Indische Baukunst*: 352; R. B. Lewcock and G. R. Smith, "Three Medieval Mosques in the Yemen," *Oriental Art*, 20 (1974): 124; G. Marçais, *L'Architecture musulmane d'occident*: 323; R. D. McChesney, "Economic and Social Aspects of the Public Architecture of Bukhara," *Islamic Art* 2 (1987): 254, 256; Michael Meinecke: 116; E. Merklinger, "Gulbarga", *Islamic Heritage of the Deccan*: 197; Rudolf Naumann, *Die Ruinen von Tacht-e Suleiman und Zendan-e Suleiman*: 1; Reginald Piggott: maps; S. N. Polupanov, *Arkhitekturniyye pamyatniki Samarkanda*: 57; A. U. Pope and P. Ackerman, eds., *A Survey of Persian Art*: 59; J. M. Rogers, *The Spread of Islam*: 106; P. Sanpaolesi, *Ta'thīr-i mi'mārī-yi gunbad-i sultānīya-yi īrān*: 5; F. Sarre, *Denkmäler persischer Baukunst*: 14; C. Terrasse, *Medersas du Maroc*: 156, 321; A. Volwahsen, *Living Architecture: Islamic Indian*: 349; A. G. Walls, *Geometry and Architecture in Islamic Jerusalem*: 120; G. Zander, ed., *Travaux de restauration de monuments historiques en Iran*: 240

All other photographs by the authors.

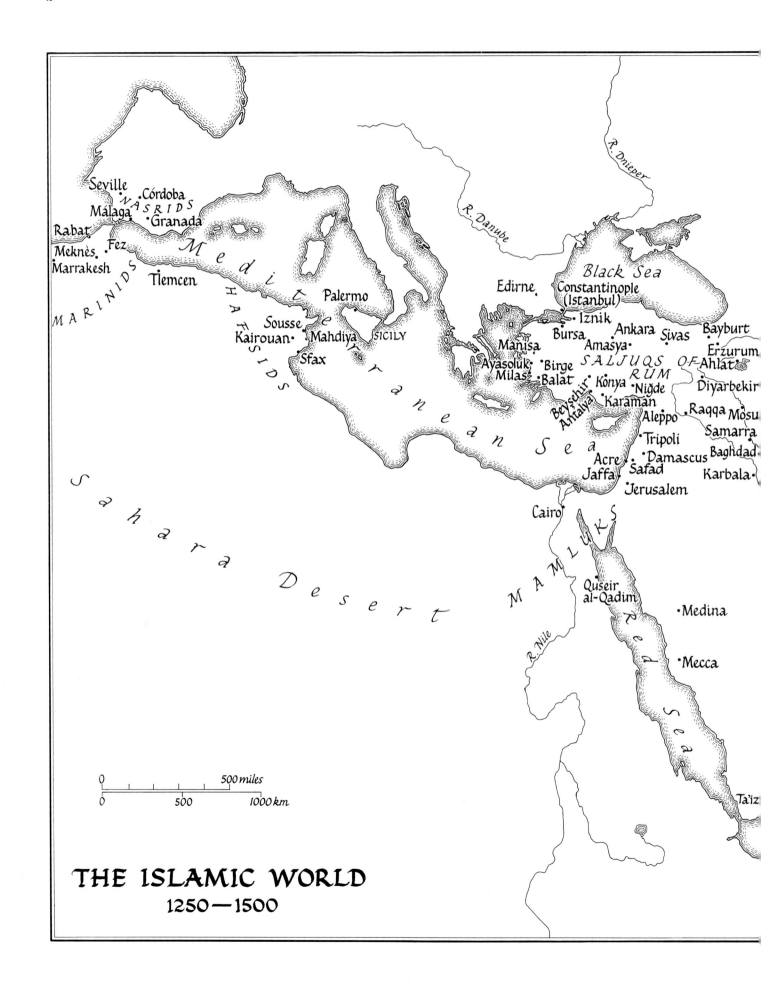

x

Seville
Córdoba
NASRIDS
Málaga
Granada
Rabat
Meknès
Fez
Marrakesh
MARINIDS
Tlemcen

Mediterranean Sea

HAFSIDS

Sousse
Kairouan
Mahdiya
Sfax
Palermo
SICILY

R. Dnieper

R. Danube

Black Sea

Edirne
Constantinople
(Istanbul)
Iznik
Bursa
Ankara
Sivas
Bayburt
Manisa
Amasya
Erzurum
Ayasoluk
Birge
SALJUQS OF
Ahlat
Milas
Balat
RUM
Beyşehir
Konya
Niğde
Diyarbekir
Antalya
Karaman
Aleppo
Raqqa
Mosu
Samarra
Tripoli
Acre
Damascus
Baghdad
Jaffa
Safad
Karbala
Jerusalem

Cairo

Sahara Desert

MAMLUKS

R. Nile

Quseir
al-Qadim

Red Sea

Medina

Mecca

0   500 miles
0   500   1000 km

Ta'iz

THE ISLAMIC WORLD
1250—1500

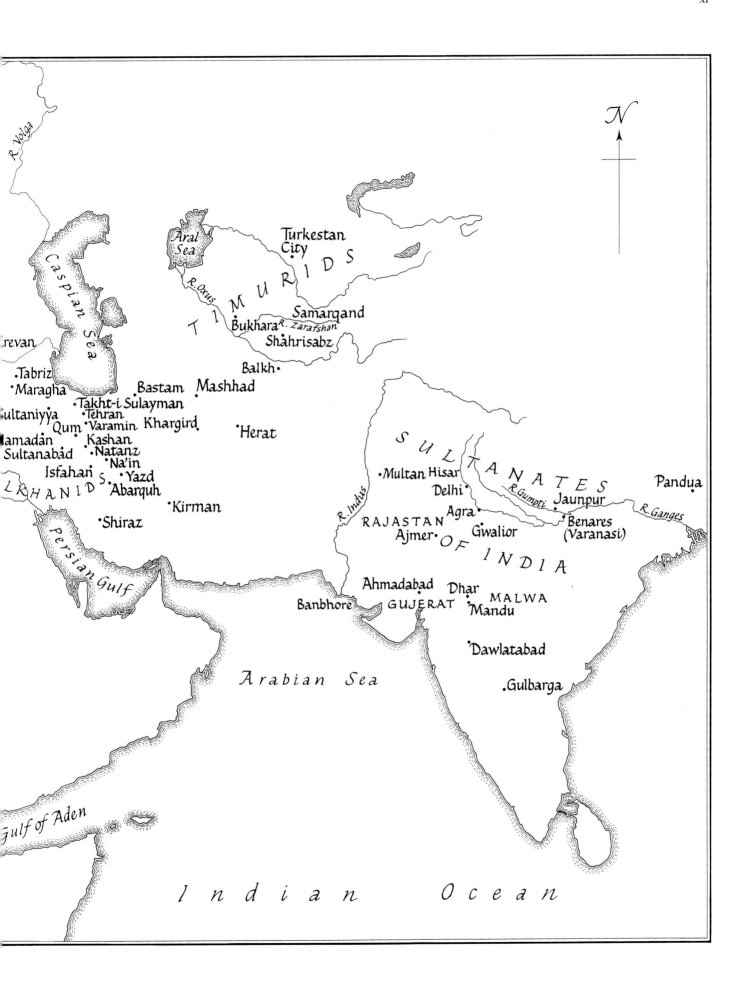

THE ISLAMIC WORLD
1500 – 1800

brilliant center of diversity under the Norman rulers in the twelfth century, ceased to be part of the Islamic world. In contrast, Anatolia, which had only been opened to Muslim settlement after the battle of Manzikert in 1071, developed in the years following 1250 as a new center of Islamic art and culture and served as the staging-post for the expansion of Islam into the Balkans and southern Russia. Similarly India, which had had a sporadic and limited Muslim presence from the eighth century, began to develop distinctive forms of Islamic art with the establishment of the Delhi sultanates in the thirteenth century.

Although the chronological and geographical scope of this book is roughly equivalent to that covered in the first volume, far more buildings and objects have survived from the later period, and there is far more documentation for them. This wealth of information has required several changes in approach. First, the importance of archaeology as an adjunct to the traditional techniques of art history has been superseded for the later period by an increased reliance on textual and archival sources, such as endowment deeds, registers, and notebooks. Second, the survival of greater amounts of evidence, both monumental and textual, has meant that only a fraction of the surviving works can be considered in a survey of this size. In the early period, a particular building or object may have been considered because it was the only one of its kind to survive. This is rarely the case for the later period, where myriad examples of a particular type have survived. In Cairo, for example, literally hundreds of standing buildings attest to architectural activity at all levels of society after 1250, and thousands more buildings there are known through texts and legal documents. Similarly, a recent survey of glazed ceramic tablewares from Iznik in Turkey includes hundreds of examples from museums and private collections, without enumerating the even vaster quantity of related tile revetments which remain *in situ*.

The large amount of information and the greater number of examples mean that stylistic groupings can be worked out with greater refinement in the later period. It is often possible to distinguish not only regional but also local styles. In the architecture of fifteenth-century Iran, for example, buildings from central Iran use an idiom quite different from the metropolitan style used in the provinces of Khurasan and Transoxiana where the capitals were located. Sometimes stylistic groups can be assigned to different levels of patronage. A group of carpets known as the Ottoman court type [311], for example, is distinguishable from another contemporary group made for the market. These distinctions are, of course, easier to make in media and regions that have been better studied. The art of the Persian illustrated book, for example, has long been appreciated in the West, although it should be said that more attention has been paid to styles of painting than to styles of writing, with the result that the hands of painters are more familiar than those of calligraphers, who probably enjoyed greater status in their own time. Similarly, the scholarship of Indian art has a long history and many buildings in India have been precisely measured and recorded, while in comparison the artistic traditions of North Africa are poorly documented and many buildings remain inaccessible to outsiders.

Readers may be surprised to find that favorite examples of particular types are missing from this book. Apart from the sheer impossibility of including every beautiful and well-known object from the period, we have often given preference to works with specific dates or signatures, even if a more beautiful example of the same type exists. Signed and dated works are the fixed points around which undated works can be clustered and from which the history of art is written. Our reliance on signed and dated works, however, should not give a false impression: as in the earlier period, only a tiny minority of the works of art produced in the period contain such information. Ignoring this fact can lead one to inflate the importance of the role of the individual, a concept which is largely a creation of the West in modern times. Nevertheless, the period after 1500 in the Islamic world, particularly in Iran, India, and Turkey, is notable for the emergence of distinct artistic personalities, such as the Persian painter Sultan-Muhammad and the Ottoman architect Sinan.

Although artists may have tended to sign and date the works they themselves held in greater esteem, these may also have been the works produced on commission for more important or munificent patrons. We have tended to focus, therefore and somewhat unfashionably, on the arts of the court rather than on those made for broad strata of society. Quite apart from the difficulty of finding evidence for vernacular architecture and art before, say, 1800, we believe that in the period between 1250 and 1800 imperial and royal courts provided the primary patronage and inspiration for significant artistic creation, the styles of which may have been followed at other levels of society. We have, therefore, used such dynastic rubrics as Timurid, Mamluk, or Mughal to refer to the arts produced in the periods during which the individual dynasties held sway. Yet not all art produced in fifteenth-century Iran and Central Asia can be connected directly, or even indirectly, with the patronage of the Timurid dynasty, and much "Timurid" art may have had little to do with the actual descendants of Timur.

It will be no surprise to specialists of Islamic art that many of the works covered in this book, as in the previous volume, belong to the category known as the decorative, or minor, arts. One of the features that distinguishes the Islamic artistic tradition is the transformation of utilitarian objects into works of art, and hence the hierarchies traditionally used in Western art do not pertain. Although architecture is equally important in East and West, there are few if any sculptures or panel paintings in this volume, but many ceramics, metalwares, and textiles. Representational painting was practiced, but in general it was but one aspect of the arts of the book. It is easy to find the cultural equivalent for such an illustrated manuscript as the fine copy of Nizami's *Khamsa* [213] made ca. 1540 for Tahmasp in the *Très riches heures du Duc de Berry*. It may be more difficult to perceive that such works as the blue-and-white ceramic charger [295], the inlaid brass basin made for al-Nasir Muhammad [129], and the garden carpet [220] are equivalents to the paintings and sculptures that figure so prominently in the artistic history of Europe.

The esthetic appeal of many of the works of art illustrated and discussed in this book is self-evident, but we have also tried to set them in their historical and cultural contexts, for

Introduction

This book surveys the art and architecture of the traditional Islamic lands between the Atlantic and Indian oceans and the Eurasian steppe and the Sahara in the period from the Mongol conquests in the early thirteenth century to the European conquests in the early nineteenth. It is conceived as a sequel to *The Art and Architecture of Islam: 650–1250*, written by Richard Ettinghausen and Oleg Grabar and published by Penguin Books in 1987. Like Ettinghausen and Grabar's volume, ours is designed as a survey and a manual, not as a vehicle for speculation and broad cultural interpretation. These are perennially popular and important topics, and there is ample literature on them, to which we have tried to provide adequate but not ponderous references for the interested reader. We have followed the general format of the first volume, with chronological and regional divisions and the separation of architecture from the other arts, so that the two volumes may be used together profitably.

Already in the early period, Iran and the eastern Islamic lands had begun to play an increased role in the history of the Islamic world, but the old Arabo-centric order was definitively disrupted by the Mongol invasions, which effectively ended the Abbasid caliphate (although a puppet caliph was maintained in Cairo until 1517, when the Ottoman sultans assumed the caliphate). For architecture and the arts, the Mongol conquests resulted in the Iranian world becoming the undisputed center of artistic and cultural innovation in the Islamic world, and the visual arts in most Islamic lands after 1250 can be understood in terms of their reliance on or reaction to Iranian models and ideas. In architecture, for example, the arrangement of four iwans around an open court that had been introduced for the design of Iranian mosques in the twelfth century was adopted in Egypt, which had continued to favor the traditional hypostyle plan, and the echo of the four-iwan plan was soon heard as far as Morocco and India. Similarly, the illustrated book, although known in the Arab lands before the Mongol conquests, was transformed after them into a major medium of royal patronage in Iran, whence it was adopted elsewhere. Iranian art was also the channel through which Chinese decorative motifs were disseminated throughout the Islamic world. Although Chinese wares, most notably ceramics, had long been prized imports in the Islamic lands, it was only after 1250 that chinoiserie motifs were incorporated into the decorative repertory, where they became major elements of design. We have therefore given the arts of Iran prominence by considering them first in each of the two chronological sections of this book.

For the first two and a half centuries Iranian ideas were paramount among the regional powers, while after ca. 1500

the preeminence of Iran was challenged by new imperial powers, the Ottomans in the eastern Mediterranean and the Mughals in northern India. Nevertheless, Persian culture and language remained the standard against which achievements were measured. Only gradually did Turkish replace Persian as the literary language at the Ottoman court and new Ottoman artistic formulas replace traditional Persian ones. Similarly Iranian artists emigrated in the mid-sixteenth century to the Mughal court in India, where Persian manuscript traditions were avidly adopted, but only late in the century did the distinctive Mughal idiom of book illustration and decoration emerge, although Persian remained the literary language there for centuries.

We have ended our survey ca. 1800, when the European imperialistic presence began to be felt increasingly in such countries as Egypt, Algeria, and India. Although neither Turkey nor Iran was colonized directly, in the nineteenth century European industrial manufactures replaced native goods and European styles of architecture were grafted onto indigenous ones, with greater or lesser degrees of success. The story of European interaction with North Africa and the Middle East is long and involved: one need think only of Hannibal (a North African) crossing the Alps or Crusader ventures into the Levant. Within the period covered in this book, European paper supplanted the local product in Egypt, while ceramics from Islamic Spain were highly prized in England (in 1289 Eleanor of Castile, wife of Edward I, had fifty-six pieces of lusterware brought from Málaga). Perhaps the most intriguing period for the artistic interaction between the lands of the East and West is the reign of the Ottoman sultan Mehmed II (r. 1444–81, with interruption; see Chapters 15 and 16), when Italian painters, medalists, and perhaps even architects attended the court of this quintessential Renaissance patron, while Bursa silks were prized in Italy. Most of the interchange between Europe and the Islamic lands took place in the nineteenth century, but the limitations of space and the nature of the experience have prevented us from devoting more than a cursory glance (Chapter 20) in this direction. Given the media introduced, such as photography and printing, the wealth of information available staggers the imagination, as do the questions that can be answered, and these fascinating and challenging subjects demand separate and fuller treatment.

The two periods covered here are subdivided geographically, and these divisions largely correspond to long-established regions of Islamic art: Iran and Central Asia, Syria and Egypt, and North Africa. Nevertheless there are several changes from the earlier period: Spain, after the catastrophic defeat at Las Navas in 1212, ceased to be a major Muslim power, although the court of the Nasrids remained a splendid cultural center until 1492. North Africa became increasingly isolated from the central and eastern Islamic lands and developed its own distinctive and introspective forms. Sicily, which had flourished briefly as a

Detail of plate 85

many of these works were created and displayed to affirm the patron's power. Sinan's work as chief court architect for the Ottoman sultans did not just provide attractive or even brilliant designs for buildings; his buildings with their distinctive domes and minarets also provided a means of visually marking the broad extent of Ottoman dominion. Rashid al-Din's *Jāmiʿ al-tawārīkh* [33, 34] was not just a lavishly illustrated book, but also a vehicle to justify Mongol hegemony over Iran. Inlaid metal vessels of the Mamluk court [126] were not just pleasing wares to grace the sultan's table but important accessories in court ceremonies which reaffirmed the relationships between the sultan and his entourage.

Later Islamic works of architecture and art continue to use most of the favorite forms, techniques, and motifs found in the earlier period. Much of the previous volume was devoted to the development of typical forms and types, notably the mosque, madrasa, minbar, mihrab, and muqarnas (the **M** words memorized by beginning students). All these continue to be used in the later period, although several new variants emerged. For example, the large mosque covered with a single dome, which had been unknown in earlier times, became a characteristic feature of Ottoman architecture and has come to represent, for much of the Muslim and non-Muslim world, the stereotype of what a mosque should be. Similarly such decorative techniques as carved stucco and glazed brick and tile, introduced long before 1250, continued to be characteristic, while such new techniques as cuerda seca also became popular. Geometric patterns, arabesques, and inscriptions, which had long been the subject-matter of much Islamic art, remained important despite the new role played by chinoiserie decoration.

In the later period these established forms, techniques, and motifs were understood, elaborated, and combined in new ways. Buildings and art objects from the early period were still in use, and these were often restored, refurbished, or re-used in new styles and for new purposes. The Friday mosque of Isfahan, which had set the style for a generation of mosques in Iran in the twelfth and thirteenth centuries, continued to be redecorated in contemporary taste throughout the later period [12, 69]. Manuscripts of the Koran penned by the renowned calligrapher Yaqut al-Mustaʿsimi, for example, were often embellished with splendid decoration under the Safavids and Ottomans. Manuscripts of historical and literary works are known to have been illustrated in earlier centuries, but in the later period the illustrated manuscript was transformed into a major art form which enjoyed widespread and enduring popularity. The monumental tomb had already been introduced at the end of the preceding period, but examples from the later period were usually incorporated into architectural ensembles, comprising charitable and educational foundations and gardens. The complex of Hasan in Cairo [106–8] or the Taj Mahal [349–51] are familiar examples. The Blue Mosque in Tabriz [67–8] is a virtual museum of contemporary ceramic techniques, with examples of tile mosaic, luster, and under- and overglaze-painted tiles, all combined in a glittering web which envelops the building. In all media, once discrete motifs were increasingly layered, whether in cursive inscriptions written on arabesque grounds [12] or intertwined lattices of vegetal ornament [219].

One of the most characteristic features of all Islamic art is the exuberant use of color, be it in the shining revetments on buildings or the minute inlay of silver, gold, and bitumen on metalware. The nature of the surviving evidence, not to speak of the economics of publishing, has often led to an inadvertent distinction between an earlier period in black-and-white followed by a later one in technicolor. This is by no means true, as buildings from the earlier period were often brightly decorated with mosaic or paint and contemporary ceramics were equally flashy. Nevertheless the works of art from the later period show an extraordinary, sophisticated, and expanded use of color. This can be seen in a single building, such as the Friday mosque at Isfahan, where the original structure and early additions employ a minimal amount of color which is designed to emphasize the structure, while the fifteenth- and sixteenth-century additions employ an exuberant palette which serves to conceal the underlying building. Greater sophistication in the use of color can also be seen in illustrated books: in early illustrations the colors were applied rather haphazardly, but those from the later period show a modulated palette designed to evoke specific emotions and lead the eye through the image. The pigments themselves are finer and more carefully prepared. Color reproductions are all the more essential for understanding the art of this period, and we are indeed gratified that our publisher has made them available.

Another feature that distinguishes the art of the later period is the increased exchange of ideas and motifs among media. The same leaves and flowers were used to decorate a caftan [301], a ceramic dish [302], or a carpet [311], and the same artist might have designed the decoration of a manuscript of the Koran [29] or the interior of a building [6]. Motifs had long been transferred from one material to another, primarily through the medium of textiles, but the ready availability and use of paper in the later period made this transfer easier. Paper had, of course, been known in the Islamic world since the middle of the eighth century and the Islamic world was responsible for its diffusion to the West, but it remained relatively expensive until the period following the Mongol conquests. In the fourteenth century sheets of paper were made in larger sizes (the Baghdadi sheet specified by Rashid al-Din was indeed imperial in scale), leading not only to larger books with larger and more detailed illustrations, but also to the use of cartoons and pattern books.

Not surprisingly, the first true architectural plans and drawings in the Islamic world date from this time. In the earlier period, the perpetuation of a style relied on individual experience and visual memory, but the dissemination of plans from a central source allowed the creation of distinct dynastic styles of architecture in the later period. For example, Abbasid architecture is characterized by the decorative styles associated with the palaces at Samarra, which were developed in the ninth century in Iraq and disseminated from the capital to such regional centers as Cairo, Naʾin, and Balkh. The organizational principles, materials, and techniques are reasonably consistent from one example to another, but the exact repetition of motifs is rare. In contrast, the use of architectural drawings and the concomitant creation of a language of architectural representation allowed a degree of uniformity over a broad area unknown (and virtually impossible) earlier. It was not necessary for Sinan to personally supervise the construction of the Sulaymaniyya mosque in Damascus [278]; he could design the building at the imperial studio in Istanbul and be reasonably sure that his intentions would be carried out on the site, although some details, particularly the elevation and materials of construction, may have been realized *in situ*.

Similarly, the imperial design studios of the Timurid and Ottoman courts, in contrast to royal ateliers of the earlier period, produced paper cartoons which could be used in the capital or abroad and realized in varying materials, colors, and scales. The same pattern sheet could have been used to design a small leather bookbinding, a set of glazed tiles, or an immense knotted carpet. A pounced drawing could be turned over to create compositions in mirror-reverse. Thus, the later period of Islamic art may be said to be characterized by an increasing separation between the medium and the decoration applied to it.

A final characteristic of many of the works considered in this volume is their superb technical finish. While some of the works of art from the earlier period, such as the mosaics of the Dome of the Rock or the ivories from Córdoba, are undeniably masterpieces of craftsmanship, the level of workmanship seen in objects from the later period is often technically superior. The finest silk carpets [215] produced under the Safavids, for example, sometimes have as many as 125 knots per square centimeter, and the carved hardstones of the Timurids [89] and Mughals [377] show an apparently effortless technical perfection rarely matched elsewhere. The flawless intricacy of Persian book illustrations from the fifteenth and sixteenth centuries is breathtaking. Some of this refinement may be due to the greater resources available to patrons in the later Islamic period, although the Abbasid caliphs had been by no means poor. The degree of intricacy and high quality of finish was also a cultivated taste, for it increasingly came to represent the triumph of sedentary civilization over a perceived nomadic past. In the words of Ibn Khaldun, the great fourteenth-century philosopher and historian:

The crafts and sciences are the result of man's ability to think, through which he is distinguished from the animals . . . [The sciences and crafts] come after the necessities. The [susceptibility] of the crafts to refinement, and the quality of [the purposes] they are to serve in view of the demands made by luxury and wealth, then correspond to the civilization of a given country.[1]

CHAPTER 2

Architecture in Iran and Central Asia under the Ilkhanids and their Successors

In the fall of 1253 the Great Khan Mongke, grandson of Chingiz Khan and supreme ruler of the Mongols in China, dispatched his brother Hulagu at the head of an army against the Isma'ilis in northern Iran and the Abbasid caliph in Baghdad. Hulagu moved speedily across Iran, conquering and devastating whatever areas did not capitulate, and took Baghdad in 1258. This date marks the official establishment of the Mongol rulers in Persia known as *Il-khāns* or subordinates to the great khan in China. Hulagu and his immediate successors continued the nomadic practices of the steppe, wintering in the warmer lands of Mesopotamia and summering on the grassy plains of north-western Iran. They preferred living in tents, and only a few monuments of secular architecture remain from the second half of the thirteenth century. The Ilkhanids controlled the lands from the Oxus almost to the Mediterranean and from the Caucasus to the Indian Ocean, territory that is now western Afghanistan, Iran, southern Russia, eastern Turkey, and Iraq. Earthquakes, invasions, and subsequent occupations have destroyed all but the odd building from their capitals at Maragha, Tabriz, Baghdad, and Sultaniyya; and their urban infrastructure can hardly be gleaned from textual descriptions. Instead, it is provincial buildings in central and western Iran that have survived to provide an idea of the magnificence of architectural patronage under the Ilkhanids.[1]

The Ilkhanids inherited a repertory of building types, forms, materials, and techniques of construction which had been developed in Iran in the previous period. The congregational mosque had evolved its classical form of a court with iwans on the four sides and a domed chamber on the qibla, and this plan was standard for other types of religious buildings such as madrasas and khanaqahs and for secular ones such as caravanserais. Graves were marked by tomb towers or by square or polygonal canopy-like mausoleums. The standard vocabulary of forms included iwans, domes, squinches, and minarets, and these were usually combined in predictable ways. The standard elevation in a dome chamber, for example, was tripartite; a zone of transition with squinches bridged the gap from a square or polygonal room to the circular base of a dome. The main façade was usually marked by a *pīshtāq*, the high and formal gateway composed of an arch set within a rectangular frame and functioning like a shallow iwan. Minarets were often used as framing devices, either at the ends of the façade or at the sides of an iwan. High-quality baked brick was the preeminent medium of construction, and bricks were often laid in decorative patterns, although stucco revetment was also popular and inserts of terracotta and glazed tiles were used to enliven surfaces.[2]

In this period the traditional vocabulary would be modified in several ways. Individual buildings were grouped in monumental complexes, often centered around the grave of the patron or a revered figure. The earliest complexes were haphazardly arranged, although a *pīshtāq* and elaborate decoration were used to draw attention to the main façade. Proportions were altered as rooms became taller, arches more pointed, and minarets more attenuated. The new taste for verticality is combined with a refined sense of form, seen in monumental portals with soaring double minarets. Baked brick remained the major medium of construction, but new methods were developed for enlivening surfaces. Color became increasingly important: glazed bricks were added to exteriors, and interiors were decorated with tile revetments and carved and painted plaster. Muqarnas units were no longer structural elements constructed of brick, but decorative ones made of plaster and suspended from vaults or walls.

ARCHITECTURE UNDER THE ILKHANIDS

One of the first actions by the Ilkhanid rulers after conquering Baghdad was to construct an observatory in their summer capital at Maragha in north-western Iran. Located on a hill five hundred meters north of the town, the building was begun in 1259. Excavations have uncovered sixteen units, including a central tower containing a quadrant (forty-five meters in diameter), a foundry for the manufacture of astronomical instruments, five round towers, and several large buildings. The large site and the quality of the materials, which included stone, baked brick, and glazed and luster tiles, show how important astronomy and astrology were to the shamanist Mongols.[3]

Many structures from the early Ilkhanid period were built of degradable materials, for contemporary accounts state that the Ilkhanids used tents of horsehair and felt. The sole surviving example of Ilkhanid palatial architecture is the summer palace begun by Abaqa ca. 1275 and continued by his son Arghun a decade later [1]. The site, now known as Takht-i Sulayman, stands south-east of Lake Urmiya in Azerbayjan on the foundations of the Sasanian sanctuary of Shiz. A huge courtyard (125 by 150 meters), oriented north–south, encompassed an artificial lake and was surrounded by porticoes with four iwans. Behind the north iwan was a domed room, which occupied the site of the Sasanian fire temple and probably served as Abaqa's audience hall. Behind the west iwan was a transverse hall flanked by two octagonal kiosks; it had served as the throne-room of Khusraw and became the living quarters of the Ilkhanid sovereign. Plaster fragments on the ground indicate that the southern octagonal kiosk was covered with a muqarnas vault, composed of many individual plaster units. The excavations also uncovered a stucco plaque fifty centimeters on a side; the incised drawing on it represents one-quarter of the dome

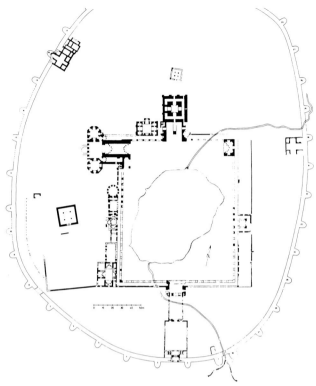

1. Takht-i Sulayman, plan of the site, ca. 1275

and was evidently used to guide the workmen in assembling the pre-cast units. This unique document is one of the earliest pieces of evidence for the use of architectural plans in the Islamic world and confirms the historical sources, which state that plans were sent from the capital to the provinces.[4] The walls of the northern octagonal kiosk were revetted with a superb dado. The lower two meters were covered with star- and cross-shaped tiles overglazed in a technique known as *lājvardīna*, from the Persian word for lapis lazuli (see Chapter 3 and plate 24). This dado was surmounted by a frieze of square tiles, thirty-five centimeters on a side, depicting simurghs and dragons among other heroic subjects. The wall was crowned with a wide band of painted plaster. The quality and abundance of the architectural decoration, particularly the marble capitals, the luster [2] and *lājvardīna* tiles, and the muqarnas dome, show that the Mongol sultans lavishly decorated their own homes. Both the placement, considered by the Ilkhanids to be the site where the Sasanian emperors had been crowned, and the decoration, luster tiles with verses and scenes illustrating the themes of the *Shāhnāma*, the Persian national epic composed by the poet Firdawsi ca. 1010 at the court of Mahmud of Ghazna, were deliberately chosen to affirm Mongol connections to pre-Islamic Iranian kingship.[5]

Ghazan Khan's accession in 1295 marked a change in both Ilkhanid society and architectural patronage. He severed links with the Great Khan in China, thereby accelerating acceptance of the culture of the sedentary Persians over that of the nomadic Mongols. He converted to Islam, taking the Muslim name of Mahmud. He and his prime minister Rashid al-Din (d. 1318) also inaugurated a vast program of reforms which revitalized the economy and provided an economic basis for significant amounts of new construction, particularly religious buildings. He ordered caravanserais built along the major trade routes and bath houses in every city; the revenues from these buildings could support the mosques he also ordered. The effects of Ghazan's reforms continued through the reigns of his two successors, his brother Uljaytu (r. 1304–16) and his nephew Abu Sa'id (r. 1317–35), and the major works of Ilkhanid religious architecture thus date from the period 1295–1335.

Ghazan's single greatest project was his tomb complex in a western suburb of Tabriz. Earlier Ilkhanid rulers had followed Mongol burial practice and concealed gravesites, but Ghazan adopted the traditions of Islamic Iran and ordered a charitable foundation to surround his "lofty" tomb. The complex included a hospice, hospital, library, observatory, academy of philosophy, fountain, pavilion, and two madrasas for students of Hanafi and Shafi'i law. Only fragments of brick and tile remain, but texts describe the mausoleum as a twelve-sided structure containing a semi-subterranean crypt, a chamber for the cenotaph, and a crowning dome. Rashid al-Din followed royal precedent and ordered his own funerary complex in an eastern suburb of Tabriz. It too has disappeared, but the surviving endowment deed allows a reconstruction of the buildings and enumeration of the personnel and services provided.[6] Four structures were enclosed within a sturdy wall behind a monumental portal: a hospice, khanaqah, hospital, and tomb with winter and summer mosques. The deed also specified that copies of the Koran, collections of prophetic traditions, and Arabic and Persian copies of Rashid al-Din's own works were to be commissioned annually by the supervisor of the endowment and distributed throughout the realm (see Chapter 3). Tile fragments glazed in light and dark blue and similar to those found at Ghazan's tomb complex litter the site.

2. Luster-painted frieze tile with Bahram Gur, probably from Takht-i Sulayman, ca. 1275. W 33 cm. New York, Metropolitan Museum of Art

3. *View of Sultaniyya* from Matrakci Nasuh, *Bayān-i manāzil*, Istanbul, 1537–8. Istanbul, University Library, MS. 5964, ff. 31v–32r

4. Sultaniyya, Tomb of Uljaytu, 1307–13

The imperial scale of Ilkhanid architecture can best be seen in the magnificent tomb of Uljaytu at Sultaniyya. Arghun had chosen the site, some one hundred and twenty kilometers north-west of Qazvin on the road to Tabriz, as his summer residence, and Uljaytu transformed it into the capital of the empire, hence its name "Imperial." Like most Iranian cities, it had an outer wall and an inner citadel. The outer ramparts measured thirty thousand paces around; the inner citadel was protected by a moat, sixteen round towers, and a single gate in a machicolated wall broad enough for four horsemen to ride abreast. These features are visible in the earliest representation of the site [3], contained in Matrakci Nasuh's account, made in 1537–8, of the Ottoman sultan Süleyman's campaigns in Iraq and Iran. The largest monument within the citadel was the sultan's tomb complex, which included a mosque, madrasa, hospice, hospital, guesthouse, and other buildings.[7]

Uljaytu's tomb [4] is the only part of the complex at Sultaniyya to survive. It is an enormous octagon, some thirty-eight meters in diameter, which is oriented almost cardinally [5]. The north wall projects to meet the lateral walls, thereby creating triangular compartments which house stairs to the upper stories. To the south, a rectangular hall measuring fifteen by twenty meters is attached to the central

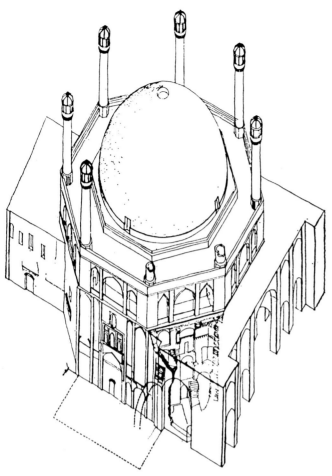

5. Sultaniyya, Tomb of Uljaytu, axonometric view

conversion to Shi'ism and to a spurious tale of his desire to transfer the bodies of 'Ali and Husayn, the two most revered Shi'ite martyrs, from Iraq. Inscriptions provide three fixed poles for the history of the building. The exterior decoration was complete in 1310; the interior decoration in brick and tile was finished in 1313, when the building was dedicated with much celebration, including the issuing of commemorative copper coins. The redecoration in painted plaster was ordered within the next three years, before the sultan's death in December 1316. These dates cannot be correlated with any shift in piety or taste, and the redecoration was probably ordered to commemorate the brief period when Uljaytu was recognized as protector of the Holy Cities of Arabia.[8]

Not only did Ilkhanid sultans and viziers erect charitable foundations around their own tombs, but the same patrons also commemorated the graves of Sufi shaykhs with monumental tomb complexes. Some were built around the graves of renowned historical figures. In northern Iran, the grave of Bayazid Bastami (d. 874 or 877), one of the most celebrated mystics in Islam, was a focus for much Ilkhanid work, including superb decoration in cut and painted plaster and a large, flanged tomb tower [6] dedicated to Uljaytu's infant

6. Bastam, flanged tower, 1308–9

octagonal space, which measures twenty-five meters in diameter and is surmounted by a fifty-meter high dome ringed by eight minarets. The interior of the octagonal hall has eight arched openings with balconies. Above them, on the exterior, a ring of galleries overlooks the surrounding plain and provides a visual transition from the flat walls (which probably abutted subsidiary structures on several sides) to the ethereal blue-glazed dome. The subtle design of interpenetrating volumes is complemented by the sophisticated gallery vaults [7]. The two dozen vaults display a wide variety of carved and plaster motifs, painted in red, yellow, green, and white. Many of the strapwork panels closely resemble contemporary manuscript illumination, suggesting that Ilkhanid designers provided patterns used on different scales in architecture and manuscripts. The lofty interior, one of the largest uninterrupted spaces of medieval times, comes as an awesome surprise after the stately exterior. The spatial elegance and grandeur attest to the abilities of the designer(s), who were able to realize the sultan's desire for monumentality with sophistication and grace.

The interior of Uljaytu's tomb was decorated in two phases: a first phase in brick and tile and a second one over it in painted plaster. This redecoration has provoked the wildest speculation. At first, scholars attributed the redecoration to the Safavid period; then it was linked to Uljaytu's

7. Sultaniyya, Tomb of Uljaytu, vaults of the exterior galleries

son. With an interior diameter measuring just over six meters, the tower is articulated with twenty-five flanges whose verticality makes the tower seem more lofty than its actual height (it measures only 13.58 meters from base to top of the cornice). Iran had a long tradition of tomb towers, but the placement of the Bastam tower represents a new development. Standing behind the qibla wall of the town's congregational mosque, the tomb became the focus of all prayers uttered there, a development also seen in contemporary Mamluk architecture (see Chapter 6).[9] Although the sultan was the major patron at Bastam, lesser individuals might donate furnishings, as for example the candlestick donated to the shrine in 1308–9 by the vizier Karim al-Din Shugani [26].[10]

Other shrines honored contemporary mystics. At Natanz in central Iran, the grave of 'Abd al-Samad (d. 1299), the leading Suhrawardi shaykh of the day, developed into a major shrine complex in the decade following his death. The vizier Zayn al-Din Mastari (put to death in 1312 with his associate Karim al-Din Shugani) refurbished the town's congregational mosque and built a tomb, minaret, and hospice adjacent to it. The builders attempted to unify these disparate structures behind a single slightly curved façade [8]. Decorated in glazed tile, stucco, and terracotta and flickering in the shadow of an immense plane tree, it has often been compared to an illustration from a contemporary Persian manuscript. The irregular depth of the iwans in the mosque, the uneven floor levels, and the haphazard organization of the interior [9] show that the builders were constrained both by the topography of the site and by the structures already built on it. The tomb is a chamber approximately six meters square erected on the site of 'Abd al-Samad's residence across a lane from the mosque. As at Bastam, the shape is traditional, but the interior is decorated with the finest fittings Zayn al-Din could procure. The walls were once revetted with a 1.35-meter dado of luster tiles, now dispersed in museums throughout the world, and often recognizable by a frieze of paired birds whose heads were later defaced by some zealous iconoclast [10]. Large, specially ordered luster tiles also decorated the mihrab and the cenotaph, but the glory of the room is still a spectacular twelve-tier muqarnas vault [11]. Eight screened windows admit a subdued light which plays across the faceted surfaces to reveal the sculptural richness of the vault and illuminates the superbly designed and carved stucco inscription band that encircles the base of the dome.[11] Traces of an equally fine inscription band in the north iwan of the mosque are signed by Haydar, the master carver who executed the finest sculptural achievement of the age, the mihrab added to Isfahan's congregational mosque in 1310.

Over six meters high and three broad, the Isfahan mihrab exhibits the typical arrangement of concentric niches within rectangular frames [12]. It is distinguished from other examples, such as that at the small shrine known as Pir-i Bakran at Linjan outside Isfahan, by the crispness of its carving. Each area of the composition is worked in a distinct pattern; each pattern is worked simultaneously on several levels. The outer rectangular frame, for example, has a ground of double arabesque scrolls sprouting carved and stippled palmettes which supports an elegant inscription in

8. Natanz, Shrine of 'Abd al-Samad, 1299–1312

9. Natanz, Shrine of 'Abd al-Samad, plan

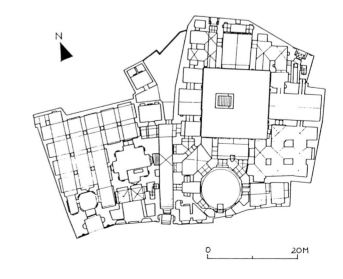

N

0   20M

10. Luster-painted frieze tile with paired birds from the Shrine of ʿAbd al-Samad at Natanz, 1308. H 36 cm. London, Victoria and Albert Museum

thuluth script. The inscriptions include praise on the twelve imams revered by the Shiʿites and traditions of ʿAli, the Prophet's successor,[12] and the choice of texts suggests that the mihrab was commissioned to commemorate Uljaytu's conversion to Shiʿism at the end of 1309. Haydar, who signed the work beside the foundation inscription in the tympanum, was one of the most famous calligraphers of the day. He was one of the six pupils of Yaqut al-Mustaʿsimi, the "cynosure of calligraphers" (see Chapter 3), and was himself the teacher of such calligraphers as ʿAbdallah Sayrafi and such viziers as Taj al-Din ʿAlishah and Rashid al-Din's son, Ghiyath al-Din Muhammad.

Taj al-Din was a wily nouveau-riche cloth merchant who rose meteorically to the head of the vizierate, arranging Rashid al-Din's downfall in the process. He curried favor by presenting the sultan with such gifts as an elaborate jeweled barge to float along the Tigris and underwriting such projects as a cloth bazaar for Sultaniyya. The vizier's ambition is evident in the new congregational mosque he ordered in Tabriz ca. 1315. A large forecourt with a central pool one hundred and fifty cubits square preceded an elephantine brick iwan [13]. The vault, which subsequently collapsed, originally spanned thirty meters and sprang from walls ten meters thick and twenty-five meters high. In its own day it was lauded as larger than the iwan at Ctesiphon, the Sasanian palace outside of Baghdad considered to be one of the wonders of the world, and visitors marveled at its rich revetment in marble and tile, although only the baked brick walls remain.

Other Ilkhanid mosques had two iwans. That at Ashtarjan, thirty-three kilometers south-west of Isfahan, was ordered in 1315 by an accountant in the Ilkhanid administration for his

11. Natanz, Shrine of ʿAbd al-Samad, muqarnas dome over tomb, 1307

13. Tabriz, Mosque of 'Alishah, ca. 1315, view from the south

15. Varamin, Congregational Mosque

home town. The indifferent construction is covered with showy stucco and tile revetments.[13] The most common mosque plan, however, continued to have four iwans and a dome as developed in Iran several centuries earlier. It can best be seen in the now restored congregational mosque at Varamin, forty-two kilometers south of Tehran. The mosque, ordered in 1322 during the reign of Uljaytu's son and successor Abu Sa'id, is a freestanding rectangle sixty-six by forty-three meters. Lateral entrances lead to iwans on the court, but the major entrance is from the north [14]. Its elaborate portal, probably once flanked by minarets, prefigures the façade of the sanctuary iwan which leads from the court to the dome chamber [15]. The dome chamber, just over ten meters in diameter, also presents the classic elevation developed in the Saljuq period. A square chamber supports an octagonal zone of four squinches alternating with four blind arches. This in turn supports a sixteen-sided zone on which rests the dome [16]. The building is distinguished from its Saljuq prototypes by its attenuated pro-

12. Stucco mihrab in the Congregational Mosque at Isfahan, 1310

16. Varamin, Congregational Mosque, interior of dome chamber

14. Varamin, Congregational Mosque, begun 1322, plan

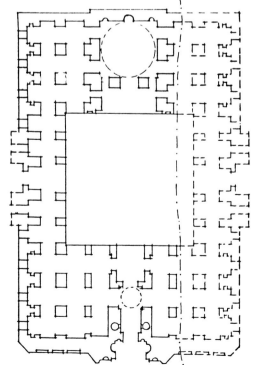

17. Yazd, Congregational Mosque, begun 1325, portal

portions, its small court, and its extensive but routine use of tile mosaic.

A distinctive type of congregational mosque developed in Yazd. Between 1325 and 1334 a local notable, Shams al-Din Nizami, ordered a new courtyard mosque in which the dome chamber and iwan were flanked by halls. This arrangement became standard for mosques in the region. A much restored monumental portal [17] provided a link between the old mosque and the new. Shams al-Din had spent much time in Tabriz, as he had married Rashid al-Din's daughter, and such new features of the Yazd mosque as tribunes and the easy flow of space between the sanctuary and the side halls were probably copied from now lost buildings in the capitals in north-west Iran.[14] The prosperity of central Iran can be seen in the other mosques built in the Isfahan basin along the Ziyanda river at Dashti, Kaj, and Aziran. In plan, each comprises a square dome chamber flanked by subsidiary structures including corridors, a monumental entrance, and a forecourt, and together they testify to the urban expansion of Isfahan under the Ilkhanids.[15]

Not all Ilkhanid buildings were monumental in scale. The tradition of freestanding tomb towers continued. A good example is the Imamzada Ja'far in Isfahan [18], built for an 'Alid shaykh and descendant of the fifth imam who died in 1325. The octagonal tomb measures seven meters in diameter and eleven meters high and is more refined in proportion than earlier examples. The terracotta and three colors of tile that decorate the exterior have been heavily restored, but the attenuated proportions of the blind arcading on the exterior show the elegance and grace of Ilkhanid architecture at its prime. Its general appearance and architectural details are so close to the tomb known as Chelebi Oglu at Sultaniyya, built for the Sufi shaykh Buraq (d. 1308), that the workers probably came to Isfahan from Sultaniyya. In this period teams of the finest artisans are known to have moved from site to site: those who made the tile revetments for Natanz in the first decade of the fourteenth century, for example, then made those for Sultaniyya in the second. Typically, the interiors of these small Ilkhanid shrines were decorated with luster tiles, and pieces could be added by different patrons at different times. Most luster tiles have been preserved in Shi'ite shrines because these tombs continued to be venerated over the centuries. As late as the nineteenth century, the Imamzada Yahya at Varamin, for example, had splendid tiles on the mihrab, dado, and tomb. Over one hundred and fifty star and cross tiles decorated with arabesque, geometric, or floral designs, now dispersed in some two dozen collections, were produced between October and December 1262. The main mihrab was made by 'Ali b. Muhammad b. Abu Tahir in May 1265; forty years later his son Yusuf and a partner 'Ali b. Ahmad made a cover for the cenotaph in the shape of a mihrab [19]. The frieze, unusually made of carved plaster rather than luster tile, is dated 1307. The interiors of other tombs from the Ilkhanid period in Qum and Kashan indicate that the one hundred and forty years of continuous production of luster tiles ceased in 1339–40, to be replaced by revetments of carved and painted plaster.

18. Isfahan, Imamzada Ja'far, 1325 (restored)

19. Luster-painted tiles from the Imamzada Yahya at Varamin, 1305. St. Petersburg, Hermitage

20. Kirman, Congregational Mosque, portal with tile mosaic, 1350

ARCHITECTURE UNDER THE ILKHANIDS' SUCCESSORS

After Abu Sa'id's death in 1335, political power became so fragmented and squabbling for the throne so intense that the pace of architectural endeavor slackened, although sporadic work continued through the middle of the fourteenth century under the patronage of amirs who had broken with the Ilkhanids to found their own dynasties. The most important were the Muzaffarids (1314–93), who controlled central Iran, and the Jalayirids (1336–1432), who controlled north-western Iran and Iraq. Muzaffarid architecture is best seen in the large congregational mosque at Kirman (1350). The plan exhibits many of the features introduced at Yazd, such as the tall portal and the integration of the prayer halls behind the court arcades with the four iwans of the court. A notable feature is the extensive four-color tile mosaic decoration found throughout the mosque, and especially on the portal [20], which it envelops in a sparkling web of exquisite color. Buildings from the beginning of the four-teenth century had a continuous surface of tile mosaic only in restricted areas and a limited number of colors. The tomb at Sultaniyya, for example, had complete tile mosaic in light and dark blue only on the muqarnas cornice and in the spandrels of the gallery arcade. Fifteen years later, on the Imamzada Ja'far at Isfahan, white had been added to the traditional palette and the surfaces were completely covered with tile mosaic. By the middle of the century, the evolution was complete and tile mosaic covered broad surfaces and entire units. Geometric designs also evolved into increasingly naturalistic vegetal and floral arabesques.

In the last quarter of the fourteenth century, work was resumed on the new congregational mosque in Yazd: covered halls connected the new portal to the south iwan and much of the present tile revetment was added, for example in the sanctuary chamber and on the façade of the south iwan [21]. Here, too, the building was draped in a many-colored cloak of tile mosaic. Interlocking arabesques are exactly fitted to the reveals and the spandrels, and inscriptions frame the main spaces, clearly displaying the high quality of the tilecutter's art. The similarities between work at Kirman and Yazd suggest once again that teams of specialized workmen moved from one important job to another.

The most important surviving Jalayirid building is the caravanserai built by the governor of Baghdad, Mirjan b. 'Abdallah, in 1359 to support the endowment of his funerary-religious complex nearby. Constructed in brick, the rectangular building comprises two stories surrounding a long central hall. The hall, measuring fourteen meters high, is spanned by eight transverse arches which support stepped vaults crowned with domes on squinches [22]. The sophisticated roofing system allows light to reach the interior and shows that the governor must have considered this commercial construction on a par with the other parts of his complex, which have not survived.

Transverse vaulting was one of the most important in-novations in fourteenth-century architecture. In the period before the Mongol conquest, architects had been interested in structural experimentation, developing innovative ways of using ribs over bays or of breaking up the squinch and

elaborating the zone of transition. After the Mongol invasions, architects shifted their interest to space, particularly the problem of covering rectangular areas. The simplest masonry covering for a rectangular space is a barrel vault, but its continuous walls create a dark interior often unacceptable for a public space. The continuous barrel vault can be interrupted by a series of cross-arches which in turn support transverse filler vaults. This scheme was used in south-western Iran and Iraq in such early Islamic buildings as the palace at Ukhaydir, the congregational mosque of Shiraz, and the fire temple at Sarvistan.[16] In all these early examples the crown of the vault is horizontal along its entire length. Fourteenth-century architects developed this system by introducing rampant transverse vaults in which the springing lines of the vaults curve upward parallel to the profile of the cross-arches. A rampant transverse vault appears already in the south iwan of the mosque at Natanz. The barrel vaults in the galleries at Sultaniyya have shoulder-arched profiles; varying vaults on pendentives connect the cross-vaults. Other examples appear in south-western Iran, including Yazd, Abarquh, and Isfahan. From there the technique would be adopted in north-eastern Iran, where Timurid architects developed its decorative possibilities by reducing the load-bearing elements and opening the room to increased light and applied decoration (see Chapter 4).

21. Yazd, Congregational Mosque, tilework on the interior of the south iwan, late fourteenth century

22. Baghdad, Khan al-Mirjan, 1359, interior

م ولادة النبي عليه الصلوة والسلم ه

ى فى ذلك الوقت روايات اصحها انه عليه الصلوة والسلم

سنة من ملك انوشروان العادل واثنين وثمانين وثمانيه

CHAPTER 3

The Arts in Iran and Central Asia under the Ilkhanids and their Successors

The Mongol conquest in the mid-thirteenth century changed the balance of artistic production in Iran. In the preceding century the decorative arts – textiles, pottery, metalwork, jewelry, and manuscript illumination – were "perhaps at their most inventive and brilliant."[1] These "basic" crafts continued to be produced after the Mongol conquest, but the arts of the book took on a new role as the central focus of artistic production and the means by which new ideas and motifs were introduced to the other arts. The pivotal role of the arts of the book, particularly illustration, is one of the most important developments of Islamic art after 1250, as it characterizes the later history of the arts not only of Iran, but also of Turkey and India. The widespread availability of paper was one of the primary reasons for this development; paper had been known for centuries, but it seems to have become available more readily and in larger sizes. Designs executed on paper were easily transferred from one medium to another, and professional designers (*naqqāsh*) signed works in such other media as inlaid metal, carved stucco and wood, and glazed tile.[2]

THE DECORATIVE ARTS

Textiles continued to be a major industry and underpinning of the economy, but only one gold and silk textile can be attributed with certainty to Ilkhanid Iran [23].[3] It bears the name and the titles that the Ilkhanid sovereign Abu Saʿid (r. 1317–35) assumed after 1319. This sumptuous textile is woven in lampas, with areas of compound weave in tan and red silk with gold wefts made of strips of gilded silver wound around a yellow silk core. The striped pattern consists of a wide band of staggered polylobed medallions and ornamental diamonds with peacocks in the interstices, flanked by narrow bands of running animals and wide epigraphic bands. The official inscription indicates that it was woven in a state factory, probably in Tabriz, and was not a commercial trade good produced for export. The clear provenance of this textile allows a group of related silk and gold lampas textiles to be attributed to Iran in the period from before the Mongol conquests to the fourteenth century. Carpets are also depicted in contemporary manuscript paintings under enthroned sovereigns, but these floor coverings must have been quite rare and no Ilkhanid examples have survived.[4]

Ceramics from the late thirteenth and fourteenth centuries are far less varied in technique than earlier examples. All works of artistic pretension have bodies of a white paste whose softness precluded the subtlety of shapes used earlier. Overglaze decoration was generally replaced by the cheaper technique of underglaze painting which did not require repeated and complex firings. Lusterwares continued to be produced, but the quality of the decoration declined as painting was simplified and stylized. Designs were less detailed and drawing was cruder, although new Chinese motifs such

as simurghs and lotuses were added to the repertory. The few luster-painted vessels made in the second half of the thirteenth century have somber and heavy decoration. Although luster tiles for architectural revetment were produced until 1340 (see Chapter 2), the production of luster vessels declined after 1261 and ceased after 1284.[5]

Kashan remained the major center of luster production, where the traditional craft was handed down in families. The best-known potters belonged to the family descended from Abu Tahir. One member, Yusuf b. ʿAli b. Muhammad b. Abi Tahir, signed a mihrab dated 1305 from the Imamzada Yahya at Varamin [19], frieze tiles dated 1309–10 in the British Museum and Cairo, and a large mihrab dated 1334 taken from the Dar-i Bihisht in Qum to the Archaeological Museum in Tehran. He and his fellow luster potters worked in other ceramic techniques as well, for he signed a molded blue-and-black underglaze tile containing the foundation inscription of the Qalʿa Mosque in the village of Quhrud outside Kashan. Yusuf learned his craft from his father, who had signed luster mihrabs between 1242 and 1265, but his brothers chose other professions. One brother, ʿIzz al-Din Mahmud, became a mystic at the Suhrawardi khanaqah attached to the tomb complex of ʿAbd al-Samad at Natanz [8–11]. Another brother, Jamal al-Din Abuʾl-Qasim ʿAbdallah, became a scribe and accountant in the imperial bureaucracy; he composed a biography of Sultan Uljaytu and a treatise on gems and minerals, which is the major source

23. Lampas and compound-woven textile with the name of Abu Saʿid, probably Tabriz, 1319–35. Silk with gold wefts. Vienna, Erzbischöfliche Dom- und Diocezan Museum

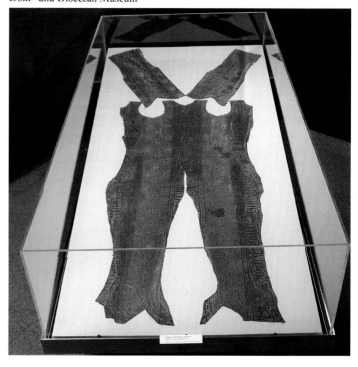

24. Overglaze-painted *lājvardīna* bowl, Iran, early fourteenth century. Diameter 21.2 cm. Paris, Louvre

25. Underglaze-painted "Sultanabad" bowl, Iran, early fourteenth century. Diameter 27 cm. Washington, DC, Freer Gallery of Art

for the art of making ceramics in medieval Iran. It gives information on where potters' materials were found, how they were prepared, and how vessels were fired, glazed, gilded, and enameled.[6]

A group of enameled and gilded bowls and tiles attributed to the late thirteenth and fourteenth centuries is known as *lājvardīna* ware, from the Persian word for lapis lazuli, because of the deep blue glaze that characterizes many of them. Some are glazed in a lighter turquoise, blue color. The pieces are leaf-gilded and overglaze-painted in red, black, and white. These wares, which apparently replaced the *mina'i* wares of the pre-Mongol period, must have been extremely expensive because they use costly materials and require a second firing in a special kiln. They were produced for some time: Abu'l-Qasim describes the technique in his treatise, and a fragmentary star tile is dated 1315.[7] A bowl dated 1374–5 is à late piece which must been made near the end of production.[8] Vessels have a coarse grayish body and clumsy shapes. Bowls [24] often have radial patterns decorated with scrolls, circles, and dots. Dadoes of star and cross tiles in alternating dark and light blues were set below a frieze of rectangular tiles with inscriptions and borders of phoenixes and dragons, designs that may have been copied from Chinese silks.

During this period potters shifted their production to underglaze-painted wares. The major type is known as "Sultanabad" ware after the city on the road from Hamadan to Isfahan where many pieces were found, but as it was founded only in 1808 and no kiln sites have been discovered there, the name is only a convenient, if misleading, label.[9] A few of the more finely potted pieces transfer luster designs into the underglaze technique and have been attributed to Kashan, but most of the pieces have coarse and clumsy potting with a thick glassy glaze which forms greenish pools and drops. The typical shape [25] is a deep conical bowl with a wide rim overhanging the interior and exterior. The rim is decorated with a pearl border, while the interior has a

design of animals or birds with spotted bodies on a ground of thick-leaved foliage. The greenish or grayish-brown slip gives the surface a bumpy texture.[10] A similar interest in texture is apparent in a group of molded monochrome wares, including large jars, bowls with vertical sides, jugs, figurines, and models. They are glazed in either cobalt blue or turquoise and molded in relief with vegetal, epigraphic, and figural motifs.

As with textiles, the surviving pieces of metalwork that can be attributed clearly to Ilkhanid Iran cannot adequately reflect contemporary production. Mahmud b. Sunqur's penbox inlaid with silver and gold of 1281 shows that earlier styles and techniques continued, although he replaced the copper inlay used earlier with gold.[11] Contemporary authors,

26. Candlestick base, north-west Iran, 1308–9. Bronze inlaid with silver. H 32.5 cm; diameter 47.3 cm. Boston, Museum of Fine Arts

27. Bowl made for Shaykh Abu Ishaq, Shiraz, 1343–53. Brass inlaid with silver and gold. Brussels, Musées Royaux d'Art et d'Histoire

such as Hamdullah Mustawfi Qazwini, mention many centers of metalwork production, and metalwares and architectural fittings are represented in contemporary manuscript painting [35]. One of the most common objects depicted is a large candlestick meant to stand on the floor. An example in Boston, which is missing its socket and neck, was given in 1308–9 to the shrine of Bayazid Bastami by a Karim al-Din Shugani, a vizier of Sultan Uljaytu [26].[12] Its size makes it the largest candlestick to survive from Islamic Iran. The truncated conical base has narrow vegetal bands at top and bottom which have lost most of their silver inlay. The body is decorated with four roundels inlaid with floral designs alternating with four cartouches inlaid with the dedicatory inscription, but is otherwise plain. The complex arabesque cartouche on a plain ground recalls the decoration painted on the interior of Uljaytu's tomb at Sultaniyya and may ultimately be traced to contemporary manuscript illumination. The presence of peony and lotus motifs on the candle-stick is one indication of the close diplomatic and commercial relations in the Ilkhanid period which led Iranian artists to look at the arts of Yüan China.[13] Although the place of manufacture is not stated, the candlestick reflects the highest level of patronage and may well have been made in the capital, Tabriz.

Most of the other candlesticks attributed to the period have all-over decoration, and many bear figural representations. A group of about fifty candlesticks with concave sides and decorated with princely themes and the labors of the month were traditionally attributed to north-western Iran under Ilkhanid rule, but an attribution to Anatolia under the Saljuqs is more likely.[14] The only other pieces clearly attributable to the region in this period are bronze ball-joints for window-grilles (diameter 13 cm), inlaid with gold, silver, and a bituminous material. Three bear the name of Uljaytu and may well have come from his tomb at Sultaniyya [4–6]; they are decorated with cartouches, arabesque scrolls, and T-fret designs.[15] A related piece (diameter 9 cm) bears a

representation of a mounted falconer set against arabesque scrolls in the central medallion and peony scrolls outside it.[16] Common stylistic features allow the attribution of several basins, caskets, and boxes to workshops active in the orbit of the Ilkhanid court.

The city of Shiraz in south-western Iran was another center of production of brasses inlaid with gold, silver, and a black bituminous material. A key piece is a bucket (height 48.7 cm) made in 1332–3 by Muhammad Shah al-Shirazi, who identifies himself as the servant of the Injuid ruler of Shiraz, Sharaf al-Din Mahmud, during the reign of an anonymous sultan who carries the title "heir to Solomon's kingdom" (Pers. *vārith-i mulk-i sulaymān*).[17] The title refers to the Achaemenid monuments of Fars province (which were considered to be inhabited by the spirit of Solomon) and was adopted by rulers of Fars. The pear-shaped bucket has a bail handle, and decorative zones on the body and neck contain epigraphic cartouches alternating with roundels filled with geometric and arabesque ornament. Triangular- and T-fret patterns fill the ground and interstices. The distinctive titulature, script, and stylistic features are characteristic of the school of Shirazi metalwork that flourished in the fourteenth century.[18]

The most characteristic type of metalware produced at Shiraz in the fourteenth century is a low, rounded bowl decorated with epigraphic cartouches, including the title "heir to Solomon's kingdom," alternating with polylobed medallions with figures of hunters, riders, or enthroned figures. Many examples are decorated on the neck with a band of running animals and on the base with a radiating sun on the exterior and a fish pond around a sun on the interior. These solar symbols were deliberately placed so that when the bowl was filled, the celestial light in the center was evident and when the bowl was tilted for drinking, the image of the sun in the heavens was visible to the viewer. The bowls were made as early as 1305, to judge from an example in Modena signed by 'Abd al-Qadir Shirazi.[19] Pro-

28. Koran stand, Iran or Central Asia, 1359. Wood. 130.2 cm × 41 cm. New York, Metropolitan Museum of Art

duction increased in the second quarter of the century, when Shiraz was in the hands of the Injuid dynasty, a family who had been assigned to supervise the royal estates (Arab. *injū*) of the Ilkhanids, but who by ca. 1325 had become virtually independent rulers of Fars province. The Injuids were great patrons of the arts, and under their auspices in the 1330s and 1340s a number of illustrated manuscripts were produced in a distinctive local style (see below). A good example of the type of bowl produced in Shiraz is the large one made for the Injuid ruler Shaykh Abu Ishaq (r. 1343–53), with mounted figures in the roundels [27]. Bowls made later in the century become increasingly straight-sided and higher in proportion to their width. The figures become taller and slimmer, as in contemporary manuscript painting, and the tricornered Mongol hat is replaced by a small rounded cap set on the back of the head. Inscriptions similarly become more attentuated and a second line of writing in a stylized angular script is often superimposed on the stems of the first.[20]

Wood continued to be used in the Ilkhanid period for architectural fittings as well as portable objects. Minbars in the congregational mosques of Nayin and Isfahan in central Iran are the most important pieces to survive from the early fourteenth century. They are both similar in form, but the one in Nayin has a canopy.[21] It was ordered in 1311 by a merchant and was signed by Mahmud Shah b. Muhammad, the designer (*naqqāsh*) from Kirman. The triangular sides are composed of rectangular panels with shallow Beveled style arabesques within a mortised frame. The minbar from Isfahan has complex designs of octagonal tracery and intaglio carving. The carving on the geometric panels resembles that on the minbar from Nayin, but the decoration includes two new elements found in contemporary carved stucco: inscriptions in a stylized square script and naturalistic leaves in high relief. Many of these features can be found on other contemporary pieces of woodwork, such as the doors to the mosque in the shrine of Bayazid at Bastam (1307–9), a group of cenotaphs from the area around Sultaniyya, and a folding Koran stand made by Hasan b. Sulayman al-Isfahani for an unidentified madrasa in 1359 [28].[22] They all show great technical ability and a rich decorative repertory; the Koran stand in particular has deeply undercut naturalistic flowers, inscriptions, and arabesques worked on several levels. Perhaps the most unusual piece is the Cenotaph of Esther from the Mausoleum of Esther and Mordecai at Hamadan. All its decorative motifs and forms are typical of early fourteenth-century Persian woodwork except for the Hebrew inscription.[23]

ARTS OF THE BOOK

Illuminated and illustrated books had been produced for centuries in the Islamic world, but following the Mongol conquests in Iran they became more numerous and larger. Surviving examples from the period show that the book was conceived as a complete work of art, with every step – transcription, illumination, illustration, and binding – an integral part of the whole. It is possible that books had been conceived in this way somewhat earlier, but no examples have survived. Surviving works also show that larger, more heavily illustrated books were produced at the beginning of the fourteenth century and intended to comment visually on contemporary society.[24] Few details about production practices of this major art form are known, and it is only in the fifteenth and sixteenth centuries that the steps of production are clear (see Chapters 5 and 12).

Bookbinding was still relatively straightforward, to judge from one of the earliest surviving Iranian examples. It conforms to the standard arrangement of Islamic books, with the spine on the right and foredge and envelope flaps attached to the back cover on the left. It covers a text of Ibn Bakhtishu's *Manāfiʿ al-ḥayawān* ("Benefits of animals") which was copied at Maragha, one of the Ilkhanid capitals in north-western Iran, in 1297 or 1299 (the last digit of the date is unclear) and seems to be contemporary with the text.[25] Measuring 33.9 by 25 centimeters, the dark reddish-brown leather covers are decorated with blind tooling applied with a small number of punches. The front and back covers have almond-shaped medallions with three different radiating elements. All the patterns are symmetrical, excepting two graceful arabesques on the flap. The total effect is of austere dignity.

The greatest calligrapher of the thirteenth century, and perhaps the greatest of all times, was Jamal al-Din Abu Majd b. ʿAbdallah al-Mawsuli, known as Yaqut al-Mustaʿsimi (1221–98). He was secretary to the last ʿAbbasid caliph of Baghdad, al-Mustaʿsim, hence the sobriquet. Yaqut perfected the proportioned script developed by Ibn Muqla (d. 940) and refined by Ibn al-Bawwab (d. 1042) in which letters were measured in dots, circles, and semicircles formed by the nib of the reed pen. By cutting the pen at an angle, Yaqut created a more elegant ductus, for which he earned the epithets "sultan," "cynosure," and "qibla" of calligraphers. He was a master of the six canonical scripts (*naskh, rayḥān, muḥaqqaq, thuluth, tawqīʿ,* and *riqāʿ*). Although he reportedly copied two Koran manuscripts per month, surviving examples of his work are rare.[26] It was prized by later collectors and calligraphers, and many fine calligraphic specimens have been attributed to him.[27] He had six famous pupils, from whom most later calligraphers in Iran and Turkey traced their descent. These six not only executed works on paper, but designed inscriptions in other media: Haydar, for example, designed the stucco inscriptions at Natanz and Isfahan [12].

Under Ilkhanid patronage at the beginning of the fourteenth century, a group of some two dozen monumental Koran manuscripts was produced whose size, format, and magnificence surpassed all previous examples known. The most impresssive are five manuscripts made in Mesopotamia and north-western Iran for Sultan Uljaytu or his vizier Rashid al-Din.[28] Each is a thirty-volume set, with five lines of writing on large-format folios. Four of them measure approximately 54 by 38 centimeters, and one, made at Baghdad and endowed to the sultan's mausoleum at Sultaniyya [29], is significantly larger (72 by 50 cm). Colophons on one of the smaller manuscripts, also made at Baghdad, show that Ahmad b. al-Suhrawardi, one of the six pupils of Yaqut, took four years to calligraph it and Muhammad b. Aybak eight years to decorate it.[29] The same team was probably responsible for the enormous manuscript made for the mausoleum at Sultaniyya. This copy may well have taken a

29. Page from a 30-volume manuscript of the Koran, Baghdad, 1306–13. Istanbul, Topkapı Palace Museum, MS. E.H. 234, f. 10r

few years longer to produce (1306–13), as it is not only larger but each folio has three lines of majestic *muḥaqqaq* script in gold outlined in black alternating with two lines of a more fluid *thuluth/muḥaqqaq* script in black outlined in gold, one of the most spectacular examples of monumental Koranic calligraphy. The illumination, executed in a wide range of colors, is equally elaborate, although perhaps not as successful. Verses are marked by rosettes, and groups of five and ten verses are marked in the margin by medallions decorated with arabesque scrolls. Chapter headings are written in a contrasting cursive script on a ground of arabesque scrolls framed by a gold braid and marked by a marginal palmette. All of these imperial Koran manuscripts have magnificent double frontispieces with self-contained geometric designs that often recall contemporary architectural decoration. The frontispiece in a manuscript done for Rashid al-Din in 1315 has a pattern of alternating stars and crosses like the one used in tile revetment, and the frontispieces to a multi-volume manuscript done at Hamadan in 1313 have often been compared to the patterns painted in the vaults of the sultan's mausoleum at Sultaniyya [7].

Illustrated manuscripts had been produced in Baghdad before the Mongol invasions, and despite the political interruption, they continued to be produced there in the same style. The double frontispiece to a manuscript of the *Rasāʾil ikhwān al-ṣafāʾ* ("Epistles of the sincere brethren"),

30. Double frontispiece to *Rasā'il ikhwān al-ṣafa'*, Baghdad, 1287. Istanbul, Suleymaniye Mosque Library, MS. Esad Effendi 3638, fols. 3v–4r

completed in Baghdad in 1287, depicts the five authors seated in a brick arcade and surrounded by scribes, students, and servants [30].[30] The painting follows the tradition known since classical antiquity of inserting author portraits at the beginning of the text and represents the full maturity of the style developed in Mesopotamia before the Mongol invasions, without any hint of Far Eastern motifs or pictorial concepts.

These new motifs and concepts begin to appear in the illustrations of the manuscript of Ibn Bakhtishu's *Manāfi' al-ḥayawān* done in the late 1290s. According to the preface, the text was translated from Arabic to Persian on the orders of the Ilkhanid sultan Ghazan. It describes the nature and habits of man, animals, birds, reptiles, insects, and aquatic creatures. It was embellished with ninety-four paintings of varying size, which are set off from the text and show the various species in naturalistic landscape settings. Those on the first folios follow the conservative Baghdad style of large-scale figures set in a simple landscape of grassy turf and stylized plants. The plain paper serves as ground, and there is no attempt to depict illusionistic space. Other paintings later in the manuscript [31] have smaller figures integrated into more developed landscapes, with gnarled trees, convoluted clouds, and rocky mountains; these features add a new sense of atmosphere and space and show an awareness of Chinese painting. In the later paintings figures at the edge of the picture are sometimes cropped, thereby suggesting a world beyond the small picture plane.[31]

The same mixture of traditional and new pictorial devices is seen in a manuscript of al-Biruni's *Āthār al-bāqiya*

("Vestiges of the past") copied by Ibn al-Kutbi in 1307–8.[32] Composed around the year 1000, the text discusses various calendrical systems used by pre-Islamic peoples, and twenty-four paintings, framed with gold rulings and patterned borders, illustrate some of the historical events that occurred in connection with these calendars. Simple symmetrical compositions, haloed figures with turbans and robes, and patterned drapery are typical of the earlier Mesopotamian style, but such motifs as convoluted clouds and colored ground are new. The image of *The Investiture of 'Ali at Ghadir Khumm* [32] shows three figures flanking the Prophet, who raises his hand to 'Ali's shoulder. The static figures derive from earlier Near Eastern painting, but the drama is enhanced by direct eye contact and the swirling red and gold clouds set against a dark sky. The unusually large size, the complexity of the pictorial conception, and the fine quality of this painting distinguish it from others in the manuscript and reflect contemporary interest in a variety of religious movements, most notably Shi'ism.[33]

The quality and style of these manuscripts indicate that they were produced for discerning patrons associated with the Ilkhanid court, but the identity of the individual patrons remains a mystery. Matters of patronage, provenance, and production become much clearer in the second decade of the fourteenth century, when the vizier Rashid al-Din established a scriptorium at his charitable foundation in

31. *Two Gazelles* from Ibn Bakhtishu, *Manāfi' al-ḥayawān*, Maragha, 1290s. 16.8 × 14.8 cm. New York, Pierpont Morgan Library, MS. M. 500

32. *The Investiture of ʿAli at Ghadir Khumm* from Biruni, *Āthār al-bāqiya*, north-west Iran, 1307–8. Edinburgh, University Library, MS. Arab 161, f. 162r

the suburbs of Tabriz. The foundation's endowment deed provided for the annual transcription of the Koran and religious manuscripts, and an addendum provided for annual copies of the vizier's collected works in Arabic and Persian. Some of the two hundred and twenty slaves attached to the complex were assigned to the tasks of calligraphy, painting, and gilding, and all manuscripts were to be done on good Baghdadi paper in a neat hand, collated with the originals in the library, and bound in fine leather. The bound copies were displayed in the mosque, registered at the judiciary, and then sent to different cities throughout the realm.[34]

Despite these precautions, only a handful of the works commissioned by Rashid al-Din have survived: one volume of a thirty-volume Koran manuscript, part of a collection of tracts, and fragments of the author's *Jāmiʿ al-tawārīkh* ("Compendium of histories"), a multi-volume history of the world, covering the reigns of Ghazan and his forebears, the non-Mongol Eurasian peoples, the genealogy of ruling houses, and geography.[35] The major surviving fragment of the world history forms about one-half of the Arabic version of the second volume about the Eurasian peoples.[36] It originally comprised some three hundred folios (written surface 37 by 25 cm, with thirty-five lines of text on each page), with one hundred and ten illustrations and eighty portraits of Chinese emperors. Although the colophon to the manuscript has not been preserved, the date 1314–15 later added to the manuscript can be regarded as plausible.

In contrast to illustrations in earlier manuscripts, which are generally square, most of the illustrations to the historical text are horizontal strips occupying about one-third of the written surface. One possible source for this unusual format was Chinese pictorial handscrolls, which would have been available in Ilkhanid Iran.[37] Only certain kinds of compositions were effective in these strongly horizontal frames: the most common for indoor scenes is a tripartite one with a central figure or group flanked by other figures, often separated by columns or other architectural devices [33]. Outdoor scenes are more varied in composition [34] and extend the space beyond the picture plane with a variety of pictorial devices. Figures at the sides are often cropped, lances and hooves project beyond the frame into the text area, and figures occasionally turn directly toward or away from the viewer. Such landscape elements as clouds, trees, mountains, and water (depicted as imbrications) are frankly inspired by Chinese prototypes, but occasionally a model from European or Byzantine manuscript painting was used, particularly if the subject was new to the Islamic tradition.[38] The representation of *The Birth of the Prophet Muhammad* [33], for example, is broadly based on a depiction of the Nativity of Christ, but on the left three women have replaced the Magi and on the right ʿAbd al-Muttalib, the Prophet's grandfather, has replaced Joseph. Whereas earlier Islamic manuscripts had paintings executed in opaque pigments, the paintings in this manuscript are done in black ink heightened with colored washes, also a Chinese technique. Another new feature is the selection of certain narrative cycles for illustration so that the illustrations are a visual commentary on the text. The section on the Ghaznavid dynasty of Afghanistan (977–1186), for example, has the most, the largest, and some of the most inventive and dynamic illustrations in the manuscript [34], while the long section dealing with the history of the Abbasid caliphate of Baghdad (749–1258) has no illustrations at all. The decided preference for the Ghaznavids, who in the larger scheme of things were less important than the Abbasids, was undoubtedly due to the way the Mongols saw themselves as heirs to the great Turkish tradition of military conquest exemplified by the Ghaznavids. Finally, the sheer number of illustrations in the volume shows the increased importance of the art of the book as a means of expressing concepts not necessarily inherent in the text itself.

This interest in expanding the potential of the illustrated book culminated in the most magnificent manuscript of the fourteenth century, a monumental copy of the *Shāhnāma* ("Book of kings"). The manuscript originally had some three hundred folios in large format (written surface 41 by 29 cm) with six columns of thirty-one lines each. It was bound in two volumes and was planned to have nearly two hundred illustrations, although it is unlikely that all were completed. It seems to have remained in Tabriz at least until the early sixteenth century: at the beginning of the twentieth century, what remained of the manuscript was broken up for sale by the Parisian dealer Georges Demotte, after whom the manuscript is often known. The remaining fifty-eight

ولادة النبي صلى الله عليه الصلاة والسلام ۞

33. *The Birth of the Prophet Muhammad* from Rashid al-Din, *Jāmiʿ
al-tawārīkh*, Tabriz, ca. 1315. H 10 cm; W 25 cm. Edinburgh, University
Library, MS. Arab 20

34. *Mahmud of Ghazna Crossing the Ganges* from Rashid al-Din, *Jāmiʿ
al-tawārīkh*, Tabriz, ca. 1315. H 12 cm; W 25 cm. Edinburgh, University
Library, MS. Arab 20

35. *The Bier of Alexander* from the Great Mongol *Shāhnāma*, north-west Iran, 1328–36. H 25 cm; W 29 cm. Washington, DC, Freer Gallery of Art

illustrated folios and a handful of text pages are scattered in museums and private collections in Europe and North America.[39]

The Great Mongol *Shāhnāma* is even larger than the manuscripts made for Rashid al-Din, and its illustrations are taller and squarer in format. Most of them occupy four or six columns of text, and a few have stepped or shaped compositions which emphasize the action more effectively than in other manuscripts. Several figural types, such as that of *Mahmud of Ghazna Crossing the Ganges*, and landscape elements, such as gnarled tree trunks and imbricated designs for water, are derived directly from the Rashidiyya illustrations, but the compositions have been expanded to include more figures and more space. The greater size of the illustration seems to have encouraged artists to integrate larger figures into more developed landscapes than are found in earlier illustrations. For example, the representation of the *Bier of Alexander* [35] is still based on a tripartite scheme, but the central space dominates the composition, which is united by the figures arranged in a circle around the bier. Some of the figures, particularly the veiled mourners in the foreground and Alexander's mother lamenting over the coffin in the center, are inspired by figures in Western represen-

tations of the Lamentation, but the artist has recombined individual elements to create a dramatic sense of pictorial space unknown in the earlier Rashidiyya illustrations.

Outdoor scenes are even more inventive. In the depiction of *Bahram Gur Killing a Wolf* [36], the protagonist, who is barely contained by the picture plane, is mounted to one side; on the other the vanquished beast sprawls on its back, gushing blood and writhing in agony around the gnarled trees. This sense of emotion and drama is unique to this manuscript. Surviving evidence suggests that it was an experiment which was rarely repeated in Iranian book-painting. The experimental nature of the manuscript is also apparent in the wide variation in the quality of conception and execution of the illustrations. Some of the compositions are quite prosaic, and the quality of the drawing varies. Figures wear a wide range of costumes, including some thirty-seven types of hat and eight different styles of lapel.[40] Some paintings are executed in line and colored wash; others use opaque colors, but these range from cool greens and muddy browns to bright reds and vivid blues. The choice of pigments also seems to have been experimental, for in some cases they have flaked or deteriorated badly. The range of painting styles has led some scholars to suggest that many artists were involved in the project, but their attempts to identify individual hands have not met universal agreement.

Such experimentation may have been due to the historical situation leading up to the creation of this manuscript and to the role it was expected to play. It may have been commissioned by Rashid al-Din's son, Ghiyath al-Din, who became vizier to Abu Sa'id in 1328, engineered the appointment of Arpa as sultan, and was himself put to death in May 1336.[41] It would have been meant to commemorate Ghiyath al-Din's power as a kingmaker, with the illustrations chosen with reference to contemporary events. As in the *Jāmi' al-tawārīkh*, the rate of illustration was extremely variable, with some episodes, such as the Alexander sequence, illustrated on almost every folio, and others, even such famous ones as the Rustam cycle, less well represented. The images were chosen to emphasize several themes, such as the enthronement of minor kings, dynastic legitimacy, and the role of women as kingmakers, that would have been particularly appropriate in the unsettled political circumstances. The illustrations were designed not only to visually enliven a magnificent manuscript but also, and more importantly, to glorify a moribund dynasty and to connect it with the glorious rulers of the Iranian past. The formerly private art of the book thereby took on a more public and rhetorical function.

It is not surprising that this new role grew directly out of the experiments of the Rashidiyya school some decades earlier, for in the eyes of the Ilkhanids the *Shāhnāma* was history as was Rashid al-Din's *Jāmi' al-tawārīkh*. Many of the novel features of the later manuscript, such as the interest in space, the emotionalism, and the emphasis on death and mourning, were not continued in later Persian painting, but the illustrated manuscript continued to play its new public role as important figures deemed it essential to commission illustrated manuscripts to affirm their status. Later generations looked back on this period as a watershed in the history of Persian painting. When Dust Muhammad (fl. 1510–64) was asked to compile an account of past and present artists for the album of calligraphy and painting that

36. *Bahram Gur killing a Wolf* from the Great Mongol *Shāhnāma*, northwest Iran, 1328–36. H 21 cm; W 29 cm. Cambridge, MA, Harvard University Art Museums

he compiled for Bahram Mirza, brother of the Safavid shah Tahmasp, the painter, calligrapher, and chronicler wrote that during the reign of Abu Sa'id, "Master Ahmad Musa . . . lifted the veil from the face of depiction and the [style of depiction] that is now current was invented by him."[42] This moment marked the beginning of a continuous tradition of manuscript painting which was passed from master to pupil.

This monumental style of manuscript illustration continued despite the chaos that ensued with the dissolution of Ilkhanid power. As with the Mongol conquest of Baghdad nearly a century before, political upheaval was not reflected immediately in the arts. Features that characterize the Great Mongol *Shāhnāma*, such as spatial complexity, large figures, and integrated Chinese motifs, are also seen in several fragmentary manuscripts produced in the middle decades of the fourteenth century. In his album Dust Muhammad included paintings from a dismembered *Mi'rājnāma* ("Book of the [Prophet's] Ascension") and assigned them to the hand of Ahmad Musa.[43] Whether or not one accepts the attribution, the style of the paintings is consistent with a date in the second quarter of the fourteenth century. Illustrations from another fourteenth-century manuscript, a copy of the animal fables *Kalīla and Dimna*, were included in another album prepared for Tahmasp I and probably date from the middle

of the fourteenth century.[44] The interior scenes, especially enthronements, are comparable in composition, spatial interest, figural groups, and sartorial detail to the *Shāhnāma* illustrations, but the exterior scenes [37] show an interest in the representation of landscape only latent in the earlier manuscript. Landscape elements spill out of the confines of the picture frame into the margin. In indoor scenes, the vertical ruling between text and border marks the division between interior and exterior space; in outdoor scenes the ruling dissolves beneath a riot of landscape details which engulf the image. As befitting the subject of the manuscript, animals are represented with extraordinary naturalism, sensitivity, and skill. The clearest evidence for the continuation of this court style of painting after the fall of the Ilkhanids is a manuscript of the *Garshāspnāma* dated July 1354, which has space for many more illustrations than the five that were completed.[45] They are similar to, albeit less refined than, those in the Great Mongol *Shāhnāma*, but the smaller, more stilted and formal figures and the projection of the images into the margin anticipate later developments.

The history of Persian manuscript illustration in the third quarter of the fourteenth century is extremely speculative and controversial. According to Dust Muhammad, the mantle passed from Ahmad Musa to Amir Dawlat Yar, a slave of Abu Sa'id, who specialized in ink drawing (Pers. *qalamsiyāhī*). One of his students, in turn, was Shams al-Din, who trained

37. *Kardana and the Tortoise become Friends* from a dismembered *Kalila and Dimna*, probably Tabriz, mid-fourteenth century. 20.3 × 19.7 cm. Istanbul, University Library, MS F. 1422, f. 19v

38. *Humay on the Day After his Wedding Has Gold Coins Poured over Him as
he leaves Humayun's Room* from Khwaju Kirmani, *Dīvān*, Baghdad, 1396.
32 × 19 cm. London, British Library, MS. Add. 18113, f. 45v

during the reign of the Jalayirid sultan 'Uvays (1356–74) and who made scenes in a square-format *Shāhnāma*. Shams al-Din was followed in turn by two pupils: 'Abd al-Hayy, who worked under and instructed 'Uvays's son Ahmad (r. 1382–1410), and Junayd of Baghdad. Manuscript paintings later mounted in albums have often been attributed on stylistic grounds to this period, but their identification and exact chronology remain matters of debate.[46] Only with the reign of Ahmad Jalayir at Baghdad does the evolution of Persian illustrated manuscripts become clear, because there are complete, dated manuscripts, and they contain paintings that can be linked to the names mentioned by Dust Muhammad.

The earliest illustrated manuscripts from the library of Ahmad Jalayir are a copy of Nizami's *Khamsa* ("Five poems") dated 1386–8 and a cosmological manuscript adapted from al-Qazwini's *Ajā'ib al-makhlūqāt* ("The wonders of creation") dated 1388.[47] The titles show the increased range of manuscripts chosen for illustration in a royal library. The slanting calligraphy of the text, the high horizons, the semé ground scattered with vegetation, and the smaller figures in the illustrations are distinctly new features which would later characterize the Jalayirid style, but the general conception and execution are somewhat rough, particularly in contrast to the superb polish and refined elegance of the acknowledged masterpiece of the style, a copy of Khwaju Kirmani's *Dīvān* ("Collected poems"), made at Baghdad in 1396.[48] This manuscript, which measures 32 by 24 centimeters, now contains nine illustrations. The one illustrating *Humay on the Day after his Wedding* [38] shows the princess seated in her bed on the left; the window-grille above her head bears the signature of Junayd, "the royal painter," the first unquestionably genuine signature in Persian manuscript painting.[49]

All the paintings of the Khwaju Kirmani manuscript are executed in the same style. The images engulf the text, spilling from the text block into the margins and filling the entire page. The picture plane is conceived as a flat backdrop against which the small and slender figures are posed in a circle. The depiction of architecture is particularly elaborate, with geometric tile dadoes, floral arabesque archways, compartment carpets, and carved plaster grilles displayed in a dazzling array of brilliant blues, oranges, and reds. The illustrations are some of the most romantic in Persian manuscript painting and contrast sharply with the big figures, emotionalism, and drama in the illustrations to the Great Mongol *Shāhnāma*. This world of eternal lyricism in which flowers bloom and birds sing forever is one of the most characteristic features of Persian manuscript painting in the following century.

One illustrated folio depicting an *Angel Seen in a Dream* [39] was removed from the *Dīvān*, probably in the early sixteenth century, and included in the album prepared by Dust Muhammad.[50] Although the painting is executed in the same style as the others in the manuscript, Dust Muhammad's elaborate heading at the top paradoxically attributes the work to 'Abd al-Hayy, the other pupil of Shams al-Din active during the reign of Ahmad Jalayir. Dust Muhammad's attribution may well be due to one feature not found in the other paintings: the wall at the rear contains a line drawing of a woman and an infant standing in a rocky landscape studded with plants and trees. Later generations

39. *An Angel Seen in a Dream*, detached page mounted in an album, Baghdad, 1396. 28.5 × 19.5 cm. Istanbul, Topkapı Palace Library, MS. H. 2154, f. 20v

associated 'Abd al-Hayy's name with the techniques of line drawing and wall painting, so Dust Muhammad may have been led to conclude that this illustration was his work.[51] It is more probable that the painting is, like all the others in the manuscript, by Junayd, who included in it a witty visual quotation of the work of his contemporary.

'Abd al-Hayy's renown as a master of drawing may well make him the artist responsible for the other masterpiece surviving from the reign of Ahmad Jalayir, a manuscript of the sultan's own *Dīvān*.[52] Eight of the 337 folios (17a, 18a, 19a, 21b, 22b, 23a, 24a, and 25b) have marginal drawings exquisitely rendered with fine brushwork in black ink and slight touches of blue and gold. The first [40] shows a pastoral scene with a flock of geese flying overhead. On the left an old man leaning on a staff accompanies a woman carrying an infant; below are several pairs of water buffalo and a herdsman. These drawings are unusual in technique, location, and meaning. Unlike earlier and contemporary paintings executed in opaque pigments, they are executed exclusively in line, without the washes of the Rashidiyya school, and they were conceived independently of the text-block: the mystical poems exalt love and praise the Creator, but the images seem to have little to do with the ostensible meaning of the poetry. The images may parallel the mystical themes of the poems by depicting the seven stages in the

40. *Pastoral Scene* from Sultan Ahmad Jalayir, *Dīwān*, Baghdad, 1403. Washington, DC, Freer Gallery of Art

mystic's search for God, best exemplified in Farid al-Din 'Attar's poem *Manṭiq al-ṭayr* ("Language of the birds"), in which thirty birds, symbolizing mankind, search for the Divine through seven valleys only to discover it in themselves.[53] Timur reportedly dragged 'Abd al-Hayy from Baghdad to his capital in Samarqand, and it is easy to see how this refined and lyrical style of the Jalayirids became the foundation for the classical style of Persian painting that developed under the Timurids (see Chapter 5).

The continuous tradition of court patronage of large-format luxury manuscripts for royal libraries was accompanied by commercial production for the marketplace. In general these manuscripts are smaller, less ambitious, and less polished in execution than the royal manuscripts. A group of three dispersed manuscripts of the *Shāhnāma* lack dedications, colophons, or dates, but can be grouped together on stylistic grounds.[54] All are small in format (the written surface on the largest measures 24.5 by 17.5 cm), and each has approximately three hundred folios, with six columns of text and about thirty lines to the page. Each includes more than one hundred paintings carefully executed in bright, thickly applied colors and lavish amounts of gold for background and secondary motifs. Patterned designs crowd the

compositions, and the small, vivacious figures seem to burst from the picture frame. A representation of *Bahram Gur Kills the Dragon* [41] shows the hero confronting his foe head-on, with none of the compositional complexity and sophisticated use of landscape found in the representation of the same subject from the Great Mongol *Shāhnāma* [36]. The figures in the depiction of *Bahram Gur in the Peasant's House* [42] are arranged in a simple tripartite composition divided by pillars, an archaic arrangement reminiscent of the interior scenes of the Rashidiyya school [33]. The small figures and low or non-existent horizon indicate a date in the first half of the fourteenth century, but the place of production is still a matter of lively debate, with attributions ranging from Baghdad to India. None of these attributions has been universally accepted, but the good quality of the pigments, extensive use of gold, meticulous painting, and awareness of such stylistic innovations of the court school as stepped compositions used to emphasize the action point to Tabriz in the 1330s and 1340s. The close similarity between two of the three manuscripts suggests that they were not individual commissions but commercial products made in expectation of sale to a rich merchant or minor courtier.

South-western Iran, particularly the city of Shiraz, was another center for illustrated manuscripts in a distinctive regional style. Production flourished in the 1330s and 1340s under the Injuid governors, to judge from a group of manuscripts, including three dated copies of the *Shāhnāma*.[55]

41. *Bahram Gur Kills the Dragon* from the First Small *Shāhnāma*, north-west Iran, first half of the fourteenth century. Dublin, Chester Beatty Library, MS. Pers. 104.61

These manuscripts are neither as large as those of the Rashidiyya school nor as small as the small *Shāhnāma*s (the written surface is typically about thirty centimeters high). The illustrations are vibrant, energetic, and even slapdash [43]. The paint is often unevenly applied and reveals the underdrawing. The palette is broad, but red and ochre backgrounds are common. The landscape is imaginatively depicted, but is strictly planar and uses a limited range of conventions, the most distinctive being pointed, cone-shaped hills. Like metalwork, this school seems to have flourished under Injuid economic prosperity, but its origins can be traced as far back as 1307–8, the date of a tiny *Kalīla and Dimna* manuscript in the British Library, and beyond that to the older Mesopotamian style of the thirteenth century.[56]

Shiraz continued to be the center of commercial manuscript production in the second half of the fourteenth century under the Muzaffarid dynasty, who controlled most of southwest Iran. The distinctive new style is first evident in a *Shāhnāma* copied there in 1371.[57] The wasp-waisted figures with egg-shaped heads set on long necks are the most distinctive feature of the twelve illustrations in the manuscript. Men wear thin moustaches and fringed beards. Landscapes are uniformly simple, with high horizons, large rounded hills outlined with spongy rocks, and semé grounds. An image such as *Bahram Gur Killing the Dragon* [44] shows how stylized paintings have become: the dragon no longer breathes fire and smoke, but is coiled in carefully arranged arabesque curls. Color, as in the blue dragon with gold

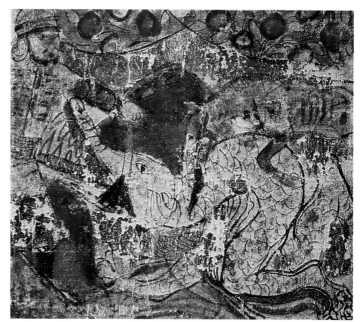

43. *Rustam Fighting a Dragon* from Firdawsi, *Shāhnāma*, Shiraz, 1333. 10 × 11.2 cm. St. Petersburg, Saltykov-Shchedrin State Public Library, MS. Dorn 329, f. 45v

scales, is used for its formal qualities rather than for representation. As with contemporary painting at the Jalayirid court, the earlier interest in pictorial space has been abandoned, and the picture plane has become a flat backdrop against which dolls are posed. This style continued to the end of the century, to judge from another illustrated copy of the *Shāhnāma* dated 1393–4, and was the basis for illustrated manuscripts produced in Shiraz in the early fifteenth century.[58]

42. *Bahram Gur in the Peasant's House* from the Second Small *Shāhnāma*, north-west Iran, first half of the fourteenth century. Brooklyn Museum,

44. *Bahram Gur Kills the Dragon* from Firdawsi, *Shāhnāma*, south-west Iran, 1371. Istanbul, Topkapı Palace Library, MS. H. 1511, f. 203v

Architecture in Iran and Central Asia under the Timurids and their Contemporaries

By the 1370s the last remnants of the Ilkhanid empire in Iran had disappeared, but a new power emerged in Central Asia which revitalized the power of the descendants of Chingiz Khan over much of Eurasia. Timur, known to the West as Tamerlane, was a nomadic chieftain who transformed his tribal organization into a world empire. The capital cities of the Timurid dynasty in Central Asia and Afghanistan – Shahr-i Sabz, Samarqand, Bukhara, and Herat – were centers of art and culture intended to display the greatness of Timurid power. The finest craftsmen of the day were recruited, often forcibly, from east and west to realize Timurid aspirations. Much of this splendor has not survived, as earthquakes, invasions, and neglect have all taken their toll. The architecture of this period falls neatly into four phases: building under Timur (r. 1370–1405); that of his son Shahrukh (r. 1405–47) and his wife Gawharshad; that of the sultan Husayn Bayqara (r. 1470–1506) and his confidant, the bureaucrat 'Alishir Nava'i; and that of the Timurids' Turkoman rivals in western Iran, the Qaraqoyunlu (Black Sheep; 1380–1468) and the Aqqoyunlu (White Sheep; 1378–1508).[1]

Timur's campaigns were decisive: he quickly conquered Iran, Anatolia, and Mesopotamia. His attack on Anatolia forced the Ottomans to postpone their conquest of Byzantium. Baghdad, which had remained the Mongols' winter capital, received the coup de grace and never recovered its former glory. Timur moved east into India and saw the wonders of the Delhi sultanate, but just as he was about to set off against China and complete his dream of restoring the empire of his predecessor Genghiz Khan, he died unexpectedly. His new capitals and commissions reflected his world-conquering aspirations, and the colossal scale and profusion of expensive materials, especially for decoration, attest to his unlimited access to resources which he marshaled to create an impression of dominance and wealth.[2]

Timur's first major architectural undertaking was to transform his birthplace, Kish, into his capital. He named it Shahr-i Sabz ("the green city") to celebrate the verdant metropolis in the midst of the barren steppe south of Samarqand on the other side of the Zarafshan mountains.[3] Only the shattered portal remains from his palace, called Aqsaray (White Palace; 1379–96; 45). It consists of a mammoth twenty-two-meter-wide iwan flanked by bastions. Built of brick, it was embellished with the finest tile decoration: large surfaces are covered with brick mosaic, while smaller ones are bejeweled with elaborate multicolored tile panels signed by Muhammad Yusuf from Tabriz. They are done in the cuerda seca technique, in which glazes of different colors were combined on a single tile within areas

outlined by a greasy substance which prevented the liquid colors from running together during firing and then burned away.

Similarly, Timur used the prodigious booty he gained by defeating the Golden Horde to construct a massive tomb over the grave of the Sufi shaykh Ahmad Yasavi (d. 1166). Yasi, now Turkestan City in Kazakhstan, was an oasis on the trade route north of Tashkent. A disciple of the great Bukharan shaykh Yusuf Hamadhani, Ahmad founded the Yasavi order, and after his death his tomb became a focus of pilgrimage for the Turks of Central Asia and the Volga.[4] From afar, the silhouette of the massive domes and vaults [46] surfaces above the flat steppe like a whale rising from the sea. A rectangular structure measuring 65.5 by 46.5 meters, its exterior walls are decorated with brick mosaic inscriptions. On the south a huge vaulted iwan soars some 37.5 meters and beckons the visitor to enter. Elaborately inlaid and carved wooden doors [72] lead into a square room covered by a muqarnas dome as high as the entrance iwan [47]. The room must have been for Sufi gatherings, because it contained an elephantine bronze basin [73], once used to serve porridge to pilgrims on 'Ashura, the commemoration of the martyrdom of Husayn. The central axis leads towards the tomb itself, which projects from the building's rear wall and is covered by a stunning muqarnas vault [48], protected by a blue-tiled melon-shaped dome. Subsidiary service and residential rooms, including a mosque, kitchen, bath, library, and meditation room, occupy the lateral spaces of the building. Often rectangular or irregular in plan, these rooms are covered by some of the most inventive vaults in early Timurid architecture. Several are especially noteworthy for the transverse arches that support stellate vaults, for transverse vaulting had been used earlier in buildings in Central Iran (see Chapter 2). The parapet at the shrine of Ahmad Yasavi is inscribed "the work of Hajji Hasan ... Shirazi;" and a tile on the drum of the tomb chamber is signed by Shams [b.] 'Abd al-Vahhab Shirazi, the builder. The references to Shiraz, a city in south-western Iran where few monuments from the period have survived, suggests that Shirazi architects abducted by Timur introduced advanced vaulting techniques to Central Asia.[5] Once resident in Central Asia, these builders would have passed on their knowledge and techniques to others, and transverse vaulting became a standard feature in the repertory of later Timurid architecture. Several other architects in the Timurid period bear the epithet Shirazi (see below), but it may have come to identify a group of master architects in Central Asia who traced their lineage back to émigrés from Shiraz rather than the émigrés themselves.

Another measure of the increased standardization and professionalism in Timurid architecture is the use of standard units to generate plans. Scholars have hypothesized that the shrine of Ahmad Yasavi was laid out on a grid using a cubit

45. Shahr-i Sabz, Aqsaray Palace, 1379–96, portal

46. Turkestan City, Shrine of Ahmad Yasavi, 1394–99

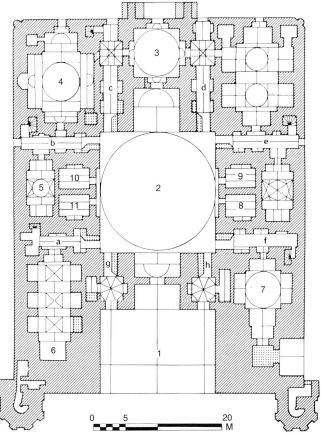

47. Turkestan City, Shrine of Ahmad Yasavi, plan. 1) iwan; 2) central hall;
3) tomb; 4) mosque; 5) library; 6) kitchen; 7) room with a well; 8–11)
meditation rooms

48. Turkestan City, Shrine of Ahmad Yasavi, muqarnas dome over tomb

(*gaz*) of 60.6 centimeters.[6] The first room to be designed
must have been the central hall, and this thirty-*gaz* square
and its diagonal provided the scale for all the surrounding
spaces. The standardization of measurements seems to have
coincided with the development of systems of architectural
notation, which facilitated the use of plans.[7] The architect
used muqarnas vaults to mark significant spaces in the
complex: a multi-tiered muqarnas vault covers the central
meeting space; even more elaborate ones cover the tomb and
mosque. Muqarnas vaults had long been used to cover
important spaces, such as the tomb of ʿAbd al-Samad at
Natanz [11], but the shrine of Ahmad Yasavi is one of the
first examples on an enormous scale. Their use in early
Timurid architecture represents the culmination of the
Iranian tradition in which muqarnas elements are assembled
to form a vault; later they would be used as subsidiary
elements within squinch-net vaults, found on a smaller scale
in the Turkestan shrine.

Shahr-i Sabz soon became too remote a capital for the
aspirations of the world-conquering Timur, and he decided
to move to Samarqand. Ruy Gonzáles de Clavijo, ambassador
from the court of Henry III of Castile and Leon, visited
Timur's capital in 1404 and glowingly described its splendor.
Huge tent pavilions made of bejeweled golden cloth and
tiled multistoried kiosks stood amidst verdant gardens
watered by rivulets.[8] In 1399 Timur had ordered a new
congregational mosque whose size and magnificence were
appropriately immense for his capital [49]. Completed
in 1404, the mosque, commonly called the Mosque of Bibi

49. Samarqand, Mosque of Bibi Khanum, 1399–1404

Khanum in memory of Timur's wife, is a huge rectangle (109 by 167 meters); minarets flank an enormous portal whose nineteen-meter vault rivals the Aqsaray. Within, hypostyle halls surround the courtyard and link the iwans in the middle of each of the four sides. The shallow iwans on the sides lead to square chambers surmounted by high and bulbous domes; the iwan on the qibla side, like the portal, is flanked by minarets and leads to a third, especially large and elaborate dome. The domes, which had already collapsed in the fifteenth century, were double, with a high cylindrical drum concealing the low sphericonical dome on the interior.[9] Walls were covered with tile and brick mosaic in several colors; domes were covered with blue-glazed tiles which display the rich variety of Timurid decoration. Although the four-iwan plan had been traditional in Iranian mosques since the twelfth century, the dome chambers beyond the lateral iwans are new. The scale of the building was in keeping with the rest of Timur's architecture; the plan also copied the last great imperial mosque built in Iran, the one ordered by the Ilkhanid sultan Uljaytu at Sultaniyya, now destroyed.[10] Timur's mosque was designed not only to continue Iranian imperial tradition, but also to symbolize his conquest of the world. According to the contemporary chronicler Sharaf al-Din 'Ali Yazdi, masons were brought from Iran and India and materials for construction were hauled on the backs of ninety-five elephants.[11] The process of constructing the building was so important that it was illustrated almost a century later, probably by Bihzad, the most famous Persian painter [84].

A large madrasa stood opposite the entrance to the mosque, but all that remains of it is the domed tomb of Bibi Khanum. Most female members of Timur's family, however, were buried in the necropolis on the hill outside the walls of Samarqand [50]. Known as the Shah-i Zinda (The Living King), the cemetery arose around the grave of Qutham b.

50. Samarqand, Shah-i Zinda, eleventh to fifteenth centuries

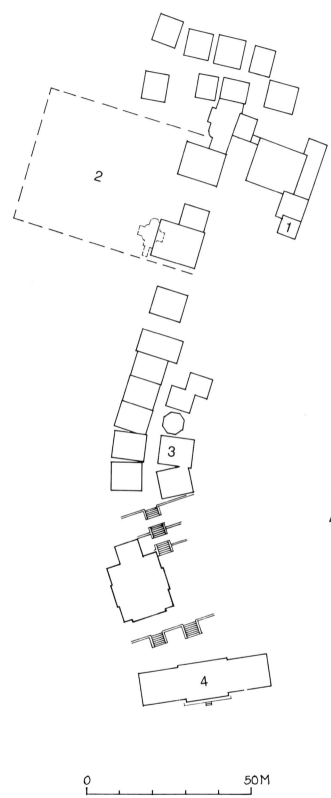

N ▲

0   50 M

51. Samarqand, Shah-i Zinda, plan. 1) mausoleum of Qutham b. ʿAbbas; 2) 11th-century madrasa; 3) tomb of Shirin Bik Aga; 4) Ulughbeg's portal

ʿAbbas, a cousin of the Prophet Muhammad, who was purportedly martyred on the site in 677.[12] Already by the eleventh century a sizable mausoleum and madrasa had marked an east–west axis, but the string of some thirty mausoleums running along a north–south street was substantially the work of the fourteenth and fifteenth centuries [51]. The earliest mausoleums were built nearest Qutham's tomb at the top of the hill, while later ones cascaded down it. Between 1370 and 1405 twenty mausoleums were erected, and in 1434–5 Ulughbeg connected the ensemble to the city with a monumental gateway. The typical building [52] is a small domed square. The side facing the street has an elaborate portal, but the other sides are left plain. Apart from the tiled cenotaph in the center, interiors were generally painted, although some had tile revetments.[13] Elaborate inscription bands framing the portals give the names and dates of the deceased.[14] The techniques of tile decoration reflect the latest fashions available to these wealthy patrons: the earliest ones were done in cuerda seca, but this technique eventually gave way to tile mosaic in an increased number of colors.

Timur himself was buried elsewhere. He had planned to be buried in his birthplace, Shahr-i Sabz, but after his unexpected death in 1405, he was interred in the building now called the Gur-i Mir (Tomb of the Amir) within the city of Samarqand itself [53]. It was built before 1401 as a madrasa, and when Timur's grandson and heir-presumptive Muhammad Sultan died in 1403, he was temporarily buried there. When Timur returned to Samarqand in 1404, he ordered the present tomb built. After his death his son Shahrukh buried him there, and his grandson Ulughbeg made it the dynastic mausoleum of the Timurids. The plan of the original complex [54] has been reconstructed as a courtyard with a madrasa on the east and a khanaqah on the west. The most significant remains, however, are the tomb and its adjacent structures on the south. On the exterior, the brilliantly blue, bulbous, and ribbed dome over the tomb glitters in the light and typifies the Timurid profile: the swelling silhouette is gathered into the wide band of the drum at the base by several courses of muqarnas. On the interior, however, a hemispheric dome springs from the base of the drum. The two shells are connected by invisible vertical flanges which rest on the inner dome and support the fantastic corbeled outer profile. This ingenious system satisfied the need for high visibility and exterior monumentality on the one hand and a harmonious interior space on the other. The fact that the dome has survived in a land of earthquakes testifies to the technical abilities of Timur's architects.

After Timur's death authority passed to his son Shahrukh, who ruled Khurasan from Herat; Shahrukh's sons Ulughbeg and Ibrahim Sultan ruled Transoxiana from Samarqand and western Iran from Shiraz respectively. With his formidable wife Gawharshad (d. 1457), Shahrukh made Khurasan the center for architectural innovation in the first half of the fifteenth century. To appease the increasingly powerful Shiʿite element in Iranian society, Gawharshad ordered extensive renovations to the shrine of Imam Riza at Mashhad between 1416 and 1418 [55, 56]. Riza was the eighth imam, or lineal descendant of the Prophet Muhammad, who

53. Samarqand, Gur-i Mir, ca. 1400–4

54. Samarqand, Gur-i Mir, plan and section. A) Madrasa; B) Khanaqah;
C) Entrance to court; D) Mausoleum; E) Gallery of Ulughbeg; F) Later
addition

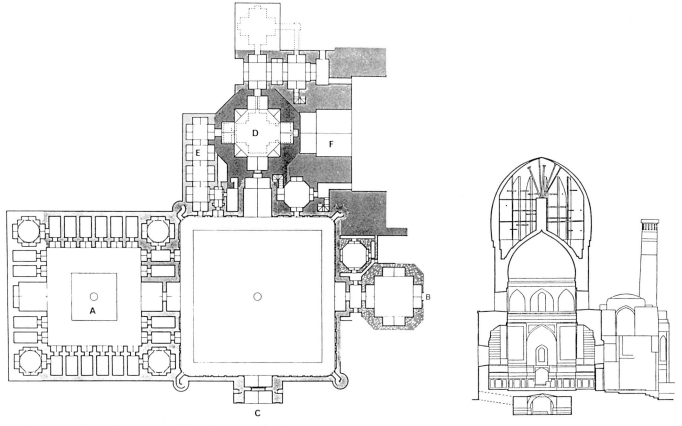

52. Samarqand, Shah-i Zinda, tomb of Shirin Bika Aga, 1385–6

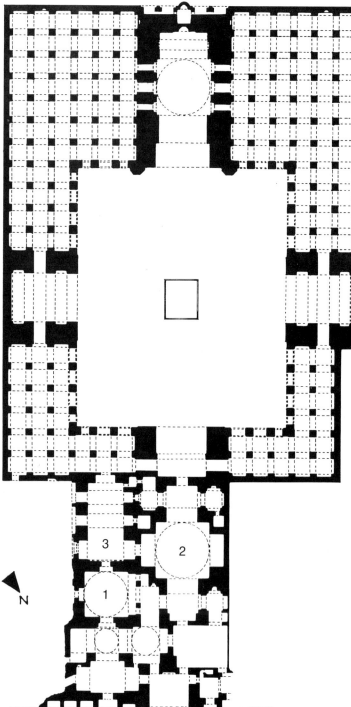

55. Mashhad, Shrine of Imam Riza, Congregational Mosque, plan.
1) mausoleum of Imam Riza; 2) dār al-siyadā'; 3) dār al-ḥuffāẓ

56. Mashhad, Shrine of Imam Riza, restored 1416–18, qibla iwan of the Congregational Mosque

had been martyred in the early ninth century near Tus in eastern Iran. The site became known as *mashhad* (martyrium) and was the most venerated Shi'ite shrine in Iran. Over the centuries many subsidiary buildings had been added around the mausoleum, which was embellished with luxurious decorative revetments in carved marble and luster tiles. To accommodate the growing number of pilgrims, Gawharshad added a large congregational mosque and two assembly halls (*dār al-siyadā'* [house for sayyids] and *dār al-ḥuffāẓ* [house for Koran-reciters]). The architect Qavam al-Din Shirazi appended the mosque to the tomb chamber and wedged the two halls into the available space. For the mosque he used the traditional four-iwan plan, but ingeniously placed a dome over, not beyond, the qibla iwan. The iwan opposite led to the assembly halls. He covered the rectangular *dār al-ḥuffāẓ* with transverse vaulting, already used at the shrine of Ahmad Yasavi.

Decorating the building also took much time and money. Since the mosque was appended to the shrine, it had no exterior façade and the most lavish work was concentrated around the courtyard. The two-storied tilework panels continue uninterruptedly around the corners of the courtyard so that the elevation wraps the space. The mosque's qibla iwan was distinguished by flanking minarets with lozenge decoration and a broad inscription band in tile mosaic, personally designed by Gawharshad's son Baysunghur, a renowned calligrapher and the leading bibliophile of the day (see Chapter 5). The huge tile mosaic mihrab at the rear of the qibla iwan stands under a semidome of cascading muqarnas elements. The overall effect has stunned pilgrims for centuries.[15]

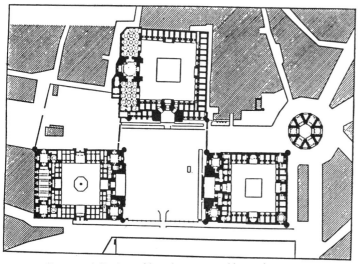

57. Samarqand, Registan, fifteenth century and later, plan

Between 1417 and 1421, Shahrukh's son Ulughbeg built a royal madrasa and khanaqah facing the Registan, the town square of Samarqand [57, 58]. Nothing is known about the khanaqah, since the site is now occupied by the seventeenth-century Shirdar madrasa [261]. Ulughbeg's madrasa, however, is the largest and most complex of all Timurid examples, measuring fifty-six by eighty-one meters. Minarets stand at each of the four corners, and an imposing

façade faces the square. The thirty-five-meter-high central *pīshṭāq* may once have been flanked by tall double domes, but only low cupolas remain. The thirty-meter-square court has iwans in the middle of each side and fifty rooms which once housed one hundred students. A broad shallow mosque stands along the rear wall between cruciform domed chambers. All exterior surfaces were covered: marble dadoes were surmounted with areas revetted in brick mosaic, tile mosaic, and cuerda seca tiles. In monumentality and scale, Ulughbeg deliberately emulated such works of his grandfather Timur as the Mosque of Bibi Khanum, but as a seat of learning, the madrasa reflected the governor's personal interest in science. It attracted some of the greatest minds of the age, who designed the observatory that Ulughbeg built on the northern outskirts of the city. Excavations there have uncovered three colossal astronomical instruments: a sextant, a solar clock, and a quadrant sector.

At the same time Gawharshad ordered work begun on a large complex in Herat.[16] She used the same architect she had hired to work at Mashhad, Qavam al-Din Shirazi. He took two decades (1417–38) to complete the work, probably because he was repeatedly interrupted by other commissions. The complex included a large rectangular congregational mosque and a madrasa with a dynastic mausoleum [59], but only two minarets and the tomb, covered with the typical Timurid high double dome, survive. Time and earthquake have taken their toll, but the worst damage was inflicted in 1885, when the complex was mined at British insistence lest

58. Samarqand, Registan

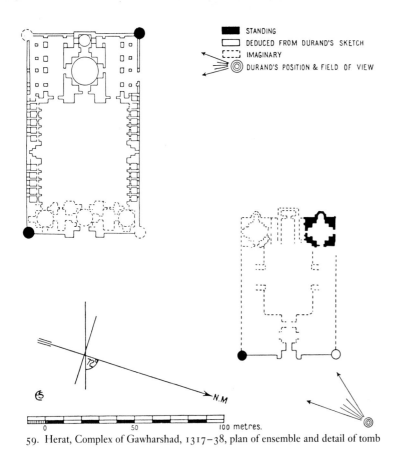

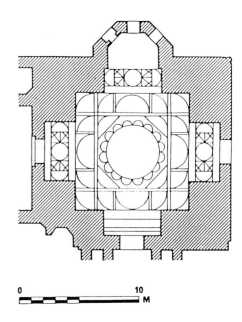

59. Herat, Complex of Gawharshad, 1317–38, plan of ensemble and detail of tomb

it harbor enemy Russians. The fragmentary remains show the high level of Gawharshad's taste and resources, for the complex was at the forefront of architectural innovation in the early fifteenth century. The minarets were clad in brilliant tile mosaic with intricate geometric patterns and inscriptions, but the interior vaulting of the tomb [60] is where Qavam al-Din's genius is best displayed. Whereas the Gur-i Mir had a relatively simple hemispherical dome covering the interior of the tomb, the mausoleum in Herat uses an elaborate system of squinch-net vaulting which integrates the interior space into a unified vertical composition.

Squinch-net vaulting is the most important innovation in Timurid architecture and seems to develop from earlier experiments with transverse vaulting over rectangular spaces. Here, the traditional square room (9.5 meters to a side) is expanded into a cruciform chamber with broad niches on all sides. Four broad arches span the recesses; four other arches spring simultaneously across the central square. Their intersection creates a smaller square which supports the traditional arrangement of four squinches, an octagon, a sixteen-sided zone, and the dome. The interstices between the ribs and squinches are filled with faceted and painted plaster, hence the name "squinch net." The advantages of this system are manifold: the vault itself is significantly smaller than the square room it covers; it is relatively light in weight; the loads are concentrated on points rather than walls, as in Gothic architecture, allowing the walls to be opened up with windows or filled with staircases and subsidiary rooms.

This new trend of opening up the interior space through the dissolution of walls and piers is also found at the shrine Shahrukh ordered at the grave of the Sufi shaykh 'Abdallah Ansari at Gazargah (1425–7), a few kilometers north-east of

Herat. This may have been one of the projects that drew Qavam al-Din away from his work for Gawharshad. The shrine consists of a large rectangular courtyard with an iwan in the middle of each of its sides. The largest is on the qibla, or western, side of the complex, and overlooks the saint's grave [61]. The entrance stands opposite and is flanked by large rectangular rooms covered with transverse vaulting and small rooms covered with squinch nets. This plan has been called a *ḥazīra*, or funerary enclosure, and may have been chosen as a compromise between the traditional Muslim reluctance to cover the grave and the patron's desire to monumentalize a sacred spot.[17]

The culmination of these new types of vaults in early Timurid architecture is found at the Ghiyathiyya madrasa at Khargird, Qavam al-Din's last work, finished by Ghiyath al-Din Shirazi in 1442–3. It was built for the vizier Pir Ahmad Khwafi, who came from Khwaf, a once flourishing town in a now desolate region on the Iranian-Afghan border. The building uses a standard plan [62] like that of Gazargah, with an entrance complex leading to a courtyard with four iwans. Here, however, the distribution of space is far more complex and sophisticated: the courtyard [63], for example, is square. Its corners are beveled to unify the four façades, taking the experiment of the Mashhad mosque one step further. Its four iwans are equal in size, the result of moving the mosque to the entrance complex. The elaboration of the entrance complex as an architectural unit is a hallmark of Timurid architecture and a feature that attracted the attention of architects in later periods. The rooms that flank the entrance are cruciform, one covered with spectacular squinch-net vaulting, as in the tomb of Gawharshad. The one to the right, which has a mihrab, has been identified as a mosque; the other [64] is believed to have been an

60. Herat, Complex of Gawharshad, tomb

61. Gazargah, 1425–27, Shrine of 'Abdallah Ansari, view of iwan

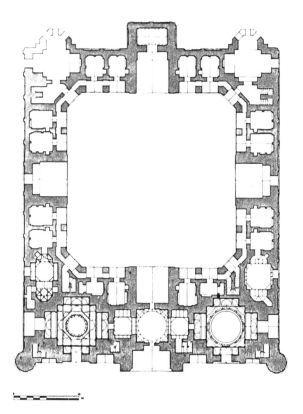

62. Khargird, Ghiyathiyya Madrasa, 1442–45, plan

63. Khargird, Ghiyathiyya Madrasa, courtyard

assembly hall. Instead of the shallow dome found at Herat, it has an octagonal lantern that allows light to suffuse the chamber and to lead the eye along the arches from the dome to the ground. Today, the building lacks the height typical of earlier Timurid monuments, since the original exterior treatment of the assembly hall dome is unknown, but its horizontal mass is emphasized by the decoration of the side walls with monumental inscriptions in brick mosaic. The brilliant colors of the tilework (blue, turquoise, black, and white) contrast sharply against the dun-colored plain. The foundation inscription on the portal gives the date 1444–5, suggesting that it took several years to complete the elaborate tile decoration.[18]

Timurid prosperity extended to central Iran, and many towns in the hinterland of Isfahan and Yazd were embellished with restored and new buildings. Some twenty buildings have survived in the region of Yazd alone, and dozens more are attested in the sources. The largest was the complex (1437) founded by Shahrukh's governor Mir Chaqmaq and his wife; it included a four-iwan mosque, khanaqah, qanat, cistern, and well, supported by a nearby bath and caravanserai. A regional style of architecture emerged which was related to but distinct from the metropolitan style of north-eastern Iran. In contrast to the light and airy quality of the finest metropolitan buildings, these provincial examples are heavier and never vaulted with intersecting arches. Walls are usually whitewashed; decoration is confined to tiled dadoes and minbars [65].[19]

64. Khargird, Ghiyathiyya Madrasa, interior vault

65. Yazd, Mosque of Mir Chaqmaq, 1437, interior

restorations and foundations in Herat and its environs was the madrasa he built ca. 1492–3. Only four minarets, towering some fifty-five meters above the ruins, remain, but the shafts, decorated with spectacular tile mosaic panels in seven colors (light and dark blue, black, white, buff, yellow, and green), are more elaborate than the two remaining from Gawharshad's complex nearby. In the debris at the base of the minarets, a black tombstone [66] inscribed with the name of Mansur, Husayn Bayqara's father, was found. Exquisite allover carving with vegetal arabesques on several levels, punctuated with peony and lotus blossoms, gives this tombstone a sense of lushness and movement. It and a related group of tombstones represent the finest Timurid stone-carving and show that stone-carvers were well aware of contemporary innovations in manuscript illumination, carpets, and woodwork (see Chapter 5).[21]

The works of Husayn Bayqara's companion and confidant, ʿAlishir Navaʾi, were as important as those of the ruler. The historian Khwandamir counted fifty-two caravanserais, twenty mosques, nineteen cisterns, fourteen bridges, ten khanaqahs and related buildings, nine baths, five soup kitchens, four madrasas, one hospital, and one room for readers of the Koran. Some of these were only repairs to existing buildings, but at least two were major projects in Herat: the foundation of the Ikhlasiyya, a charitable complex (1475), and a complete restoration of the congregational mosque (1498–1500). Nothing remains of the Ikhlasiyya, which may have stood opposite the sultan's madrasa on the east side of Khiyaban, the main street north of the city. It included a congregational mosque, a madrasa, a khanaqah, a hospital, a Koran-readers' room, and a bath, and the magnitude of the work was undoubtedly inspired by the great foundation of the Ilkhanid vizier Rashid al-Din outside Tabriz (see Chapter 2). More remains of ʿAlishir's work on Herat's congregational mosque: the vaulting of the portal and the tilework in the south-east corner. Both, however, are of mediocre quality and show a decline from work produced in mid-century.

*

After Shahrukh's death in 1447, his son Ulughbeg took over the realm, but within two years he was murdered by his own son. His nephew Abu Saʿid (r. 1461–59) managed to overcome depredations by rivals on the east and west and reunited Transoxiana, present-day Afghanistan, and northern Iran. The most famous building from his reign is the building erected by his wife (ca. 1465) known as Ishrat-Khana, a burial place for women and children of the Timurid family. Its complex vaulting continues the imperial Timurid style seen at Gawharshad's mausoleum and the madrasa at Khargird.[20]

The most remarkable patron of the age, however, was Husayn Bayqara (r. 1470–1506) who ruled Khurasan from Herat, where the final flowering of Timurid culture took place. Stars in his constellation included the poet ʿAbd al-Rahman Jami (1414–92), the painter Bihzad (see Chapter 5), and the polymath ʿAlishir Navaʾi (1440–1501), himself another famous patron. Among Husayn Bayqara's numerous

While the Timurids were ruling in eastern Iran, two Turkoman confederations, the Qaraqoyunlu (Black Sheep; r. 1380–1468) and the Aqqoyunlu (White Sheep; r. 1378–1508), controled western Iran. They arose in the late fourteenth century in eastern Anatolia and northern Iraq and expanded into western Iran in the fifteenth century. Their principal center was Tabriz. Jahanshah (r. 1438–67), the most famous Qaraqoyunlu ruler, controlled all of Iran and was even enthroned at Herat. The few Turkoman buildings that survive are scattered over a wide area, from Isfahan and Tabriz in Iran to Hisnkayfa in Turkey, but even such paltry material remains attest to the importance of Turkoman architecture in the westward transmission of Timurid architectural innovations and the internationalization of the Timurid style, particularly in Turkey under Ottoman rule.

The only building remaining from the Qaraqoyunlu capital at Tabriz is the Blue Mosque (Pers. *masjid-i kabūd* or *firūz-i islām*, "The Turquoise of Islam," 1465), which takes its name from the superb tile revetment, never surpassed

66. Herat, Tombstone of Ghiyath al-Din Mansur, father of Husayn Bayqara, late fifteenth century

in later monuments. It originally formed part of a multi-functional complex, known as the Muzaffariyya after its patron Abu'l-Muzaffar Jahanshah. It included a cistern, library, tomb, and khanaqah for Sufis, but the identification of the surviving part is unclear. The building now consists of a domed central room (fifteen meters on a side), surrounded

67. Tabriz, Blue Mosque, 1465, plan

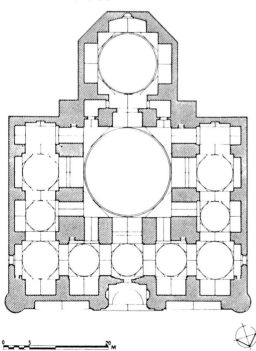

on three sides by a U-shaped vestibule of nine domed bays and on the fourth (qibla) side by a domed sanctuary. Its unusual plan [67] has been compared to the so-called Masjid-i Shah in Mashhad, which was built in 1451 by Ahmad b. Shams al-Din Muhammad, "the builder from Tabriz." Some scholars have also noted the similarities between the Blue Mosque and the Yeşil or Green Mosque in Bursa [181], whose tile decoration is signed by workmen from Tabriz. It has been suggested that the builder of the Masjid-i Shah at Mashhad also designed the Blue Mosque in Tabriz and was familiar with the Green Mosque at Bursa, but a simpler and more likely explanation is that all these buildings were modeled on the early-fourteenth-century Rashidiyya complex that once stood outside Tabriz, one of the greatest multi-functional complexes of its day.[22] The Blue Mosque may have been designed to serve a commemorative function as Jahanshah's tomb, but no burial has been found; it may have been designed as a mosque, since an inscription around the iwan screen contains Koranic verses (9:18–19) referring to mosques.[23] The inscription ends with the date (4 Rabi' I 870/26 October 1465) and the signature of Ni'mat Allah b. Muhammad al-Bawwab ("the Doorkeeper"), whose role in the work is yet to be determined.

The exterior and interior surfaces of the Blue Mosque are ruined, but they still display an unusual variety of tile decoration of superb quality [68]. Tile mosaic in six colors covers the exterior and much of the interior walls, above a marble dado carved with an elegant inscription against a vegetal scroll. Particularly striking are the fluid arabesque motifs and the inscriptions, often set out in white or gold

68. Tabriz, Blue Mosque, interior with tilework decoration

69. Isfahan, Congregational Mosque, south iwan, restored 1475–76

against a deep blue or green ground. The upper surfaces and vaults of the main chamber were covered with hexagonal dark-blue glazed tiles, while those of the sanctuary were purple overpainted in gold. At the base of the cable molding on the entrance portal, luster tiles were used in one of the very rare instances of this technique in fifteenth-century architecture. Highly embossed molded fragments of underglaze-painted tile remain on the corner buttresses.

Other buildings in Tabriz were even more splendid than the Muzaffariyya, according to contemporary accounts. The Nasriyya complex, begun by the Aqqoyunlu Uzun Hasan (r. 1453–78) and enlarged by his son Ya´qub (r. 1478–90), comprised a mosque, a madrasa in which the patron was buried, a kitchen serving meals to the poor, and a bazaar. Ya´qub's palace, known as the Hasht Bihisht ("Eight Paradises"), is known only from the description of a Venetian merchant who saw it in 1507. He described the palace as having four corner rooms, four antechambers before the entrances, a dome, and upper rooms. These elements correspond to a type of building described in Timurid sources and found in many later examples from Istanbul to Agra (see Chapters 15 and 18).[24] The plan of eight rooms surrounding a central domed hall undoubtedly inspired the name. This pavilion was set within a garden and attached to a maidan, mosque, and hospital.

Turkoman buildings in Isfahan show the same awareness of color seen at the Blue Mosque in Tabriz and ultimately in Timurid buildings in Central Asia. Thirteen years earlier, in 1453–4, Jahanshah, the Qaraqoyunlu patron of the Blue Mosque, had built the Darb-i Imam there. This shrine for two imams has a magnificent tile mosaic portal [70] with symmetrically displayed panels containing arabesques, vases,

70. Isfahan, Darb-i Imam, 1453–4, north portal

and inscriptions. Persian verses on the portal and in the vestibule describe the building with mystical images. Uzun Hasan, the Aqqoyunlu ruler who held Isfahan between 1469 and 1477, also embellished the city with superb tile mosaic: he ordered extensive repairs to the south, or qibla, iwan of the congregational mosque [69]. Its revetment displays a variety of motifs, including raised polygons on a strapwork ground and geometric patterns similar to those used earlier at the Darb-i Imam. The hospice built under his son Yaʿqub for the Sufi shaykh Abu Masʿud (1490) has an entrance portal decorated with elaborate tile paterns, including vase panels similar to those on the Darb-i Imam.

The region around Yazd also continued to prosper under Turkoman rule. In 1457, during the reign of Jahanshah, the arch over the portal of the congregational mosque was repaired and its revetment of tile mosaic restored. In the surrounding towns and villages, mosques were built or repaired, most with plans based on the distinctive disposition of the congregational mosque in Yazd. The typical plan comprised a court with low arcade on three sides and a large single iwan and dome chamber flanked by closed prayer halls on the qibla side. The mosque at Bundarabad (1473–4) is a good example and is remarkable for its fine tile mosaic minbar.[25]

The Timurid architectural vocabulary penetrated further west. One example is the tomb at Hisnkayfa (Hasan Keyf, Turkey) [71], for Zayn al-Mirza, Uzun Hasan's son killed in battle against the Ottomans in 1473. Prototypes for its cylindrical shape can be found in earlier buildings from Anatolia, but the bulbous dome and decoration in-brick and tile mosaic are frankly Timurid in style and technique. Another example is the Çinili Kiosk ("Tiled Pavilion") built in 1472 by the Ottoman sultan Mehmed II (r. 1444–81, with interruption) in the Topkapı Palace in Istanbul [270]. The centralized and symmetrical plan, squinch-net vaulting, and tile decoration are standard elements in the Timurid architectural vocabulary, but again, it is much more likely that the immediate source was now vanished Turkoman buildings in western Iran and eastern Anatolia, also the model for Yaʿqub's Hasht Bihisht palace in Tabriz.

The importance of Timurid architecture lies not only in the magnificent buildings in Central Asia, but also in the

inspiration it provided throughout the eastern Islamic lands, from Turkey to India. The model of Timurid architecture was disseminated through direct knowledge of the buildings themselves, plans and drawings of them, and the emigration of architects and craftsmen who worked on them. The concatenation of talent and resources in the Timurid capitals made it possible to create a dynastic style of architecture, and such subsequent imperial powers as the Safavids, Ottomans, and Mughals emulated not only Timurid forms, but also the Timurid ideal, whatever they identified it to be.

71. Hisnkayfa, Mausoleum of Zayn al-Mirza, ca. 1473

CHAPTER 5

The Arts in Iran and Central Asia under the Timurids and their Contemporaries

As with architecture, the decorative arts created under the Timurids and their contemporaries set the standards of excellence for generations in Iran, as well as India and Turkey. Not only were Timurid models emulated, compositions repeated, and techniques followed, but works of art that had belonged to Timur's followers were avidly collected by discerning connoisseurs. The Timurid style can be seen in a variety of media, but the arts of the book were preeminent, and the Timurids witnessed the classical moment of the Persian illustrated book. The atelier (Pers. *kitābkhāna*), an institution which can be traced to the scriptorium established by Rashid al-Din at Tabriz in the early fourteenth century, was not only the center of book production but also the center of design from which motifs and compositions were disseminated to other workshops. As well as being exquisite objects, beautifully calligraphed, illustrated, decorated, and bound books were commissioned for political and propagandistic purposes.[1]

EARLY PERIOD

The major evidence for Timur's own patronage of the arts are fittings and furnishings for the shrine of Ahmad Yasavi at Turkestan. Virtually no illustrated manuscripts have survived from his reign,[2] and few other objects can be attributed to his patronage. The size and superb quality of the Turkestan objects, however, testifies that his patronage of architecture was accompanied by patronage of the other arts. Two pairs of wooden doors survive *in situ* at the shrine, one at the main portal [72] and another at the entrance to the mausoleum. Each valve maintains the traditional tripartite division into three rectangular panels: a larger vertical one sandwiched between smaller ones. The upper panels are inscribed and the lower ones contain a geometric medallion, but the glory of the doors is the superb carving of the central panels. Those on the main portal contain arched cartouches of arabesque tracery and palmettes on a delicate scrolling ground. The spandrels are filled with an even finer naturalistic vegetal tracery of peonies, flowers, and leaves. The panels contrast with the framework of the valves, which is decorated with a strapwork pattern based on eight-pointed stars, filled and bordered with delicate arabesques. Many of these motifs developed from earlier woodcarving in Central Asia and Iran, such as those found on a cenotaph made in the mid-fourteenth century for the grandson of the celebrated mystic Sayf al-Din Bakharzi[3] and the folding Koran stand dated 1359 [28], but the integration of disparate elements into a harmonious composition is a distinctly new feature. Both sets of doors have bronze doorknockers inlaid with silver and gold and inscribed with verses from Sa'di's *Gulistān* ("Rose-garden"):

> May this door always be open to the Sincere;
> May it always be open to friends and closed to enemies.

72. Doors to the main portal at the Shrine of Ahmad Yasavi, Turkestan City, 1396–97

73. Cauldron from the Shrine of Ahmad Yasavi, Turkestan City, 1395. Bronze. H 1.58 m; diameter 2.43 m. St. Petersburg, Hermitage

74. Oil lamp, from the Shrine of Ahmad Yasavi, Turkestan City, ca. 1396. Brass inlaid with silver and gold. H 84.5 cm; diameter 58 cm. St. Petersburg, Hermitage

Both are signed by 'Izz al-Din b. Taj al-Din Isfahani, and those on the main portal are dated 1396–7.[4]

Several metal objects also survive from the shrine. The most impressive is an elephantine bronze basin [73], which originally held ritual porridge to mark the end of 'Ashura. The basin consists of an almost hemispherical bowl on a slender high foot. The top half of the exterior is decorated with two horizontal bands of cursive and angular inscriptions punctuated by bosses and pendant handles. The upper inscription in *thuluth* script says that Timur ordered it for the tomb on 20 Shawwal 801 (25 June 1399). Below, a smaller inscription states that it was the work of the master 'Abd al-'Aziz b. Sharaf al-Din Tabrizi. The bottom half has pendant triangular cartouches of arabesque tracery. While the vessel's size is unprecedented, its form and decoration were undoubtedly inspired by a somewhat smaller bronze basin ordered in 1373–4 by the Kart ruler of Herat for the congregational mosque there.[5] The effort involved in assembling the necessary materials, fuel, and labor in this remote and desolate region is staggering to contemplate; indeed, to bring it to Leningrad in 1935 required the construction of a special railway.

Six inlaid brass oil lamps [74] are also associated with Timur's patronage at the shrine of Ahmad Yasavi. They too are remarkable for their size (they average ninety centimeters high) and bear inscriptions with Timur's name and titles. Essentially of similar baluster shape, three have cylindrical oil reservoirs and three have globular ones. All present a deeply indented profile which offers a variety of flat, concave, and convex surfaces for decoration. Bands with inscriptions set on a dense arabesque ground contrast with plain surfaces engraved with palmettes, knots, and cartouches.[6]

Elephantine manuscripts were also produced at the beginning of the fifteenth century, although they cannot be directly

75. Page from a dismembered manuscript of the Koran, Khurasan or Transoxiana, first quarter of the fifteenth century. 1.77 × 1.01 m. London, Fatema Farmanfarmaian private collection

associated with Timur. Huge pages (177 by 101 cm) from a seven-line Koran [75] are in keeping with the other enormous works commissioned by the sovereign, although later marginal notations on some folios attribute them to the hand of Timur's grandson Baysunghur, the noted calligrapher and bibliophile. The manuscript may well have been housed in the congregational mosque that Timur ordered in Samarqand, for a large stone Koran stand (230 by 200 cm), originally in the domed sanctuary chamber and now in the court, was ordered by another of Timur's grandsons, Ulughbeg, perhaps to hold this very manuscript. The folios are so large that the lines of *jalāl al-muḥaqqaq* script are on separate sheets of paper which have been pasted together.[7] The majestic hastae of the vertical letters are counterbalanced by the sweeping tails of the horizontals. The tails, which often nest inside each other, have the pointed terminals characteristic of *muḥaqqaq* script.

According to contemporary travelers and panegyrists, the walls of Timurid palaces and garden pavilions were decorated with paintings of Timur, his family, his courtiers, and his campaigns, but only manuscript painting has survived from the period. In western Iran, luxury manuscripts had been produced for the Jalayirid court and other patrons (see Chapter 3); this refined and lyrical style provided the foundation for the origins of Timurid painting under Timur's grandson Iskandar Sultan (1384–1415). Appointed governor of Shiraz in 1409, he is known to have commissioned eighteen manuscripts dated between 1410 and 1413.[8] The manuscripts seem to be pedagogical tools to provide a member of the Timurid family with a basic introduction to Iranian Islamic culture, but they also reveal an interest in astrology which could reflect the taste of the patron or his advisers. The combination of multiple works and small format meant that one text was often written in the central field of each page while another was written diagonally in the margins [76]. In order to maintain lines of equal length and to have the text read continuously from the top of the page to the bottom, a triangular illuminated space was placed in the middle of the vertical margins. On other pages, particularly those from the astrological sections, this illuminated

76. *Shirin examines the portrait of Khusraw* from an *Anthology* made for Iskandar Sultan, Shiraz, 1410–11. 18.1 × 12.5 cm. London, British Library, MS. Add. 27261, f. 38r

thumbrest is retained but illustrations replace the marginal text. This interest in the decorative potential of the margin, which developed out of earlier Jalayirid manuscript illumination [40], is typical of the period. The paintings combine the attenuated figures and high horizon already used in the late fourteenth century by Junayd and other Jalayirid and Muzaffarid painters, but faces have become oval and are often tilted to one side. Figures are larger in proportion to the setting and involve the viewer more immediately in the actions depicted. Landscapes continue to spill over the borders of the text-block, and the illustration often engulfs the text. These elaborate compositions with multiple figures were so appreciated by later generations that they were repeated again and again.[9] Other manuscripts, such as an *Anthology* copied in Yazd in 1407, share many of these stylistic and technical features and show that manuscripts were produced for a wide clientele.[10]

The first extant illustrated manuscripts produced in northeastern Iran and Transoxiana were made for Timur's son Shahrukh (r. 1405–47). All but a few are historical manuscripts and show the ruler's preoccupation with his place in history and his dynasty's right to rule. The earliest is a *Kulliyāt-i tārīkhī* ("Compendium of histories"), dated 1415–16; the manuscript combines Bal'ami's translation of Tabari's lives of the Prophets; Rashid al-Din's world history, *Jāmi' al-tawārīkh*; and Sharaf al-Din Yazdi's panegyric history of Timur, *Zafarnāma* ("Book of victory"), with additions and supplements by Hafiz-i Abru, Shahrukh's court historian.[11] The twenty paintings illustrate the lives of the Prophets. Their large square pictures with large figures use many of the features, such as compositions and tilted heads, found in slightly earlier illustrated manuscripts produced in southwestern Iran. The so-called Historical style of Shahrukh is, however, far more typical of manuscript painting under his patronage.[12] It is most clearly seen in a volume in Istanbul dated 1425 combining holograph sections of Hafiz-i Abru's parts of a copy of Rashid al-Din's *Jāmi' al-tawārīkh*.[13] Shahrukh apparently owned an incomplete manuscript of Rashid al-Din's world history and asked his historian to complete it for him. Hafiz-i Abru proposed using the text he had prepared for Baysunghur and inserted it into the Ilkhanid manuscript.[14] Having the fourteenth-century manuscript before his eyes undoubtedly led the historian to copy many of its features, such as the large format and thirty-five long lines of prose per page. The illustrators, too, must have had the older manuscript in mind, for they used simple horizontal compositions, which had long been out of fashion for manuscript illustration [77]. Some illustrations in the Historical Style use the old technique of line and wash. Despite the deliberate archaizing, the artists were unable to avoid using many features of contemporary manuscript painting, such as bright and opaque colors, high horizons, and Timurid dress.

The Historical style was apparently short-lived and was soon supplanted by the classical style of Persian painting as formulated by artists working under the patronage of prince Baysunghur (1397–1433). Baysunghur served as regent under his father, Shahrukh, and in 1420 was sent to take Tabriz from the Aqqoyunlu Turkoman, who also ruled in south-western Iran and Baghdad. There the Jalayirid tradi-

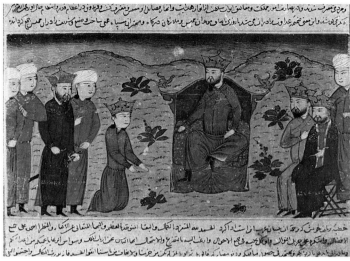

77. *Faridun Enthroned* from Hafiz-i Abru, *Majm'a-al-tawārīkh*, Herat, 1425. Istanbul, Topkapı Palace Library, MS. H. 1653, f. 21v

tion of manuscript painting had continued despite political upheavals, as shown by the five illustrations to a manuscript of Nizami's *Khamsa* ("Five poems") "done in the capital Tabriz," probably between 1405 and 1410.[15] Baysunghur returned to Herat with manuscripts, painters, and calli-

78. *The Fox and the Drum* from *Kalīla and Dimna*, Herat, 1429. 28.7 × 19.7 cm. Istanbul, Topkapı Palace Library, MS. R. 1022, f. 28v

graphers and established a workshop which became the preeminent center of book production in the Iranian world. A unique document in Istanbul, a report to Baysunghur presumably by the renowned calligrapher Ja'far b. 'Ali Tabrizi, director of the workshop, details progress on twenty-two projects including manuscripts, designs, objects, tents, and architectural work. It mentions twenty-three artists, painters, illuminators, calligraphers, binders, rulers, and chest-makers, who worked individually and in teams.[16] Baysunghur is associated with more than twenty manuscripts and numerous drawings. Of the ten illustrated manuscripts, seven dating between 1426 and 1431 are dedicated to the prince and suggest that he himself was actively involved in their planning and preparation.[17] In contrast to his father's taste for historical works, Baysunghur commissioned copies of the classics of Persian literature. Each volume shows the extraordinary taste of this discriminating bibliophile: the heavy creamy paper was specially prepared for the renowned calligraphers, and superb paintings and illuminations adorn the text, which was encased in elegant bindings of leather and cut and gilded paper. Each individual aspect was carefully planned to contribute to the creation of a total work of art.

The twenty-five illustrations to a *Kalīla and Dimna* produced for Baysunghur and dated October 1429 epitomize the classical style of Persian manuscript painting: the illustrations are integrated into the page; text and image are intertwined. In the scene depicting *The Fox and the Drum* [78] the landscape spills over the right ruling into the margin, while the tree on the left grows behind the upper text-block and ruling to reappear in the upper margin. This sophisticated arrangement creates a strong three-dimensional space.[18] Within the painting, figures and landscape elements are balanced: the intricate landscape never overwhelms the subject. The palette is vibrant and rich, with a particular use of violet, coral, and a range of blues carefully modulated to draw the eye across the composition.

The *Shāhnāma* prepared for the prince several months later shares all of the features of the Baysunghuri style, although it is quite different. The manuscript is larger (38 by 26 cm) and so are its twenty-one illustrations: in addition to the double-page frontispiece, several of them occupy the full height of the page. Baysunghur's interest in the epic is well known; a few years earlier he had ordered a new recension of Firdawsi's text and commissioned a new preface for it, but the first copy of this new edition is no longer extant. For this copy Baysunghur enlisted the services of Ja'far, the greatest calligrapher of the day, and much of the text is embellished with cloud bands reserved against a gold ground. The splendid illumination underscores the princely vision: the book opens to a large rosette bearing the dedication in green and gold:

> I adorned the beauties and rarities of these verses, and arranged the pearls and jewels of these sentiments, for the library of the most mighty Sultan, Lord of the necks of the peoples, Defender of the weak places of Islam, the greatest of the Sultans of the time, Protector of the Sultanate and of things temporal and spiritual, Baysunghur Bahadur Khan; may God perpetuate his power.

These exalted titles are far more appropriate to Baysunghur's father than to the young prince, who would never rule. His aspirations to the royal line appear again on the dazzling double page of illumination following the introduction, which includes the names and titles of the kings of Persia.

Baysunghur seems to have selected the scenes for illustration himself. Several of them, such as *Bahram Gur Entrusted to the Care of Munzir, the King of Yemen* and *Luhrasp Hearing of the Disappearance of Kaykhusraw*, are unique or rare representations of incidents in the text and would have had special resonance to a young prince eager to succeed his father.[19] Even the frontispiece, which normally depicts the ruler enthroned, has been adapted to the prince's taste, for it shows a figure in green with a small moustache, probably a portrait of the prince himself, accompanied by musicians and servants, watching an elaborate battu of horsemen attacking wolves, foxes, and other animals. The stiff figures are somewhat larger than in other Baysunghuri manuscripts, but they still easily inhabit their spacious surroundings. The typical landscape is a semé field encompassed by spongy rocks in fantastic colors, particularly purple. Architectural settings are often elaborate, reflecting contemporary practice and Baysunghur's personal role in designing monumental inscriptions (see Chapter 4). In a scene such as *Mourning for Rustam* [79], the potential emotional impact of the subject

79. *Mourning for Rustam* from the Baysunghur *Shāhnāma*, Herat, 1430. Teheran, Gulistan Palace Library, MS. 61

80. *Timur Granting an Audience at Balkh on the Occasion of his Accession to Power in 1370* from a dispersed *Ẓafarnāma*, Shiraz, 1436. Each page 35 × 24.5 cm. Washington, DC, Sackler Gallery

has been subsumed by the balanced composition, crystalline clarity, and technical brilliance. It is hard to imagine a greater contrast than with a comparable scene produced less than a century earlier [35].

Although the court workshops of Herat attracted the finest artists of the day, Shiraz remained a center of manuscript production, at first under the auspices of Ibrahim Sultan, second son of Shahrukh, who served as governor there from 1414 to his death in 1435. Ibrahim Sultan, also a calligrapher, maintained close relations with his younger brother in Herat, and even sent him gifts of illustrated manuscripts. An *Anthology* penned in Shiraz in 1420 by Mahmud al-Husayni, the calligrapher who had copied the *Anthology* for Iskandar Sultan six years earlier, was presumably offered by Ibrahim Sultan to his younger brother in Herat, for the dedication says that the volume was made for the Baysunghur's library.[20] The format continues the traditions of earlier Shirazi manuscripts, for it too has a second text in the margin with a triangular thumbrest, and the twenty-nine rather simple paintings have high horizons and semé fields. The empty landscapes serve as backdrops for a few tall, slender, and rather awkward figures. While the style of the paintings from the *Anthology* looks backwards, manuscripts produced later in the reign of Ibrahim Sultan develop

many of the same elements into a new and distinctive style.

The full-blown style of painting identified with Ibrahim Sultan can be seen in two manuscripts dedicated to him. A *Shāhnāma* datable about 1435 has forty-seven illustrations, of which four are double-page, and five tinted drawings.[21] The first illustrated copy of the *Ẓafarnāma*, Sharaf al-Din 'Ali Yazdi's panegyric life of Timur, was completed in 1436 after Ibrahim's death. This dispersed manuscript has been reconstructed as having 355 folios, with thirty-seven paintings, of which at least twenty were double-page and all occupy almost the full page.[22] The compositions have been reduced to include only the essential figures, which are large and vigorous. Landscape consists of a series of hills defined by spongy outlines. The wasp-waisted and broad-shouldered figures inhabit their space uneasily. Distinctive costume includes a cock's comb-like headdress for ladies and a neatly tied turban for men. Timur appears throughout the manuscript, in battle, on campaign, under a parasol, and feasting. The palette is rich but subdued; pigments, however, are of poorer quality than those used in Herat: a particularly acid green has a tendency to eat away at the paper and has consequently destroyed many paintings [80]. The style associated with Ibrahim's patronage continued in such manuscripts as a *Shāhnāma* dated 1444.[23] Its detached double-

81. *The Torment of Those Who Squander the Inheritance of Orphans* from a
Mir'ājnāma, Herat, 1436. Paris, Bibliothèque nationale, MS. Supp. Turc
190, f. 61r

page frontispiece is based on the composition of the earlier *Zafarnāma* frontispiece [80] and copies many of the details of composition, landscape, and figural motifs.[24] By the middle of the century, the style was superseded by the less ambitious production of the Turkoman Commercial style (see below).

Despite the individual style associated with Shiraz, Herat remained the center of luxury book production. One of the most magnificent and unusual manuscripts of the mid-fifteenth century is a copy of the *Mi'rājnāma*, recounting the mystical night journey of the Prophet Muhammad from Jerusalem to Heaven and Hell on Buraq, his human-headed steed.[25] The large-format manuscript (34.3 by 25.4 cm) was copied in Arabic and Uighur (Eastern Turkish) by Hari-Malik Bakhshi. Although it lacks a colophon, it is bound together with another manuscript penned by the same scribe and dated 1436, so it can be attributed to Herat in the same period. Some of the sixty-one illustrations depict the calm world familiar from contemporary painting. A scene such as *Muhammad and Gabriel in the Gardens of Paradise* (fol. 45b) is set in a flat tripartite architectural composition whose illuminated patterns bring to mind the background in the earlier *Mourning for Rustam* [79], and the depictions of the *Houris in Paradise* (fol. 49a and b) use most of the conventions of contemporary landscape painting. Much more startling, however, are the scenes depicting Muhammad visiting Hell. Distinguished by their black grounds, the images always show Muhammad, Buraq, and Gabriel on the right against a gold cloud. But the artist reserved his greatest imagination for the left side, where he depicted sinners suffering a variety of ingenious torments for their misdeeds. The Koran (18:28) says that those who squander the inheritance of orphans will be encompassed by fire, and if they cry for relief they will be scalded with water like molten copper. The image of those evildoers [81] shows red demons pouring molten metal down the throats of the damned, while a guardian devil makes sure the job is done well. In other images adulterous women, misers, and other wrongdoers are similarly punished. To create these startling images of Hell and torment, the artist had to search for models beyond the conventions of Persian painting to the imagery of Central Asia and the nomadic shamanistic life.

This world is best known through a group of individual leaves [82] depicting nomads, dervishes, shamans, and monsters, many of which are inscribed as the work of Siyah Qalam ("Black Pen").[26] Painted in somber colors, predominantly blue and brown, the fantastic figures are set against the coarse unpolished paper without any indication of landscape or setting. They have dramatic gestures and expressive faces, and their garments are rendered with thick and heavy folds, but the meaning of any individual image is open to question. The consistency from one image to another suggests that many, if not all, were produced in one atelier, if not by one hand; but the localization of this production is still a matter of vigorous dispute. The most likely attribution of the Siyah Qalam paintings is a Central Asian milieu in the early fifteenth century, but other scholars ascribe them to Turkoman patronage in western Iran in the late fifteenth century.

A manuscript much more typical of the mainstream metropolitan style of Herat is the copy of the *Shāhnāma* made ca.

82. *Demon in Chains*, Transoxiana, early fifteenth century. Opaque watercolor and gold on paper. 25.4 × 33.7 cm. Cleveland Museum of Art

83. *Tahmina Entering Rustam's Bedchamber* from the *Shāhnāma* made for Muhammad Juki, Herat, ca. 1450. London, Royal Asiatic Society, MS. Morley 239, f. 56r

1450 for another of Shahrukh's sons, Muhammad Juki.[27] Like those in the copy made for his brother Baysunghur, the thirty-three images in Muhammad Juki's manuscript seem to belong to a consistent cycle, but whereas Baysunghur's manuscript projected his regal aspirations, Muhammad Juki's is romantic, magical, and lighthearted. An image such as *Tahmina Entering Rustam's Bedchamber* [83] continues the compositional balance and enamel-like colors of the school of Baysunghur, but in other images, particularly the large battle scenes, the small figures are overwhelmed by the setting. In some images, castles perch precariously on precipices, and the spongy rocks of the landscapes invoke a fantasy world of make-believe. The manuscript was a prized possession of the Mughal court, and seals of the emperors from Babur to Awrangzib were added, along with an autograph note by Shahjahan and two paintings. The manuscript displays the technical skill of Timurid painting from the first half of the fifteenth century, but the paintings lack the brilliance of the earlier works commissioned by Baysunghur or the later ones associated with the painter Bihzad.

LATE PERIOD

The history of book production in Herat during the period of political confusion between the death of Shahrukh in 1447 and the accession of Husayn Bayqara in 1470 remains obscure. Few, if any, manuscripts can be attributed with certainty, and painters as well as books may have been moved west to the Turkoman courts when the Qaraqoyunlu Jahanshah occupied Herat in 1458. Under the munificent patronage of Husayn Bayqara (r. 1470–1506), however, Herat once again became the center of literature and book production in the Iranian world.[28]

Husayn Bayqara, a minor Timurid princeling (he was a great-great-grandson of Timur through his son 'Umar Shaykh), took advantage of the struggles between the Turkoman rulers in the west and the Timurid princes in the east and left his refuge in Khwarazm to take Herat unopposed in the spring of 1469. Although the Aqqoyunlu briefly retook the city in the following year, Husayn Bayqara was able to dislodge them and established a brilliant court which flourished for the next thirty-six years. It attracted many of the leading literary and artistic figures of the day, including the poet Nur al-Din 'Abd al-Rahman Jami and the statesman and poet 'Alishir Nava'i. The earliest illustrated text that the sultan is known to have commissioned is a copy of the *Zafarnama* penned by Shir'Ali in 1467–8.[29] The early date of completion indicates that even before his conquest of Herat, Husayn Bayqara already aspired to connect himself with his ancestor Timur, the subject of the epic. Space was left for six double-page illustrations, an unusual arrangement that suggests a link to the earlier illustrated *Zafarnama* made for Ibrahim Sultan in 1436 [80]. That manuscript also has an unusually large number of full- and double-page compositions and is known to have been in Herat at the time. The illustrations to Husayn Bayqara's *Zafarnama* feature either Timur or 'Umar Shaykh. They illustrate Timur's accession, four decisive battles, and the building of the mosque of Samarqand [84]. The choice of subjects suggests that the patron wished the manuscript to underscore his direct descent from Timur, who founded the dynasty, established its territory, and championed Islam. There can be no doubt that the manuscript was created in anticipation of Husayn Bayqara's victorious campaigns in Khurasan and establishment of his capital in Herat. It later became a symbol of Timurid legitimacy, as it too was taken to the Mughal court in India, where it became a prized possession of the emperors Akbar, Jahangir, and Shahjahan (see Chapter 19).

The illustrations to this manuscript are often attributed to Bihzad, the most renowned Persian manuscript painter, but as they are not signed, the attribution rests on comparison to Bihzad's known work.[30] Born sometime in the 1450s, Bihzad came to Herat thirty years later where he worked first for 'Alishir Nava'i, Husayn Bayqara's boon companion, and then for the sultan himself. After the sultan's death, Bihzad may have worked for the Shibanid ruler of Herat, but he then moved to Tabriz where, as head of the royal library of the Safavid sultans, he was placed in charge of librarians, calligraphers, painters, gilders, marginal draftsmen, gold-mixers, gold-beaters, and lapis lazuli washers. According to a chronogram, he died in 1536–7. The illustrations to a *Bustan* ("Orchard") of Sa'di written for the library of Husayn Bayqara in 1488 provide the best evidence for Bihzad's style. Of the five illustrations, the double-page frontispiece has a defaced signature, two paintings are signed in the architectural decoration, and two others are signed so inconspicuously (on a quiver and on a book) that the signatures are usually regarded as genuine. All of the paintings are of the same style and high quality: the colors are jewel-like and carefully modulated, blues and greens predominate but are tempered by complementary warm colors, especially a bright orange. The figures are lively, often humorous, and engage in such everyday activities as building, eating, and drinking. Actions are depicted more realistically than in earlier paintings: the superviser in the upper left of ill. 84, for example, does not spare the rod. They are no longer types, but individualized personalities.

Perhaps the most brilliant of Bihzad's compositions is the *Seduction of Yusuf* from the Cairo *Bustan* [85].[31] Sa'di's text, written on uncolored paper in cloud bands at the top, middle, and bottom of the illustration, mentions the seduction of Yusuf, the Biblical Joseph, by Zulaykha, Potiphar's wife, but does not require Bihzad's elaborate architectural setting. Instead, this setting is described in the mystical poem *Yusuf and Zulaykha*, written by the Timurid poet Jami five years earlier. Four hemistiches from it are inscribed around the iwan in the center of the painting. According to Jami, Zulaykha built a palace with seven splendid rooms decorated with erotic paintings of herself with Yusuf. She led the unwary Yusuf from one room to the next locking the doors behind her until they reached the innermost chamber. There she threw herself at Yusuf, but he fled from her grasp through the seven locked doors, which miraculously opened before him. Bihzad has chosen to illustrate the most dramatic moment of the story, when the desperate Zulaykha grabs for Yusuf. The illustration works on several levels simultaneously. It literally depicts the elaborately decorated palace with its many locked doors and convincingly conveys Yusuf's

84. Bihzad: *Building the Mosque of Samarqand*, added to the *Ẓafarnāma*
made for Husayn Bayqara, Herat, ca. 1480. Baltimore, Johns Hopkins
University, John Work Garrett Collection, ff. 359v–360r

sense of isolation and entrapment in it. Although based on a
story recounted in Chapter 12 of the Koran, the event is
depicted here, as in all Persian manuscript painting, in contemporary terms. The empty palace is built of baked brick
and sumptuously decorated with tiles, tile mosaic, wooden
screens, and carpets, like Timurid architecture. Jami's text is
also an allegory of the soul's search for divine love and
beauty, and Bihzad's image is an appropriate starting point
for mystical contemplation.[32] The splendid palace represents
the material world, the seven rooms represent the seven
climes, and the beauty of Yusuf is a metaphor for the beauty
of God. Sequestered with the lovely and eager Zulaykha,
Yusuf could have yielded to her passion, since there was no
witness. Yet he realized that the all-seeing and all-knowing
God was ever present. The doors, which are so prominently
displayed and lead the eye through the composition, are
tightly shut and can be opened only by God. This brilliant
image transcends the literal requirements of the text to
evoke the mystical themes so prominent in contemporary

literature and society. Bihzad was obviously proud of his
creation, for he signed it on the architectural panel over the
window in the room on the upper left and dated it 1488 on
the cartouche to the left of the iwan.

None of the other manuscripts attributed to Bihzad is
so securely signed as the images in the Cairo *Būstān*, but
similarities of figural type, composition, and style – "the
perfectly executed combination of the decorative and the
realistic" – can serve as a guide to other Bihzadian paintings.[33] This raises the complicated question of the distinction
between an individual's hand and a group style. Traditionally, the calligrapher's greatest achievement was to flawlessly
copy the work of past masters, and it is logical to assume that
painters, who were often considered second to calligraphers,
worked in the same manner.[34] Thus, while scholars will
continue to debate individual attributions and dates, a group
of pictures can reasonably be considered the work of the
master himself or of his close associates.[35] The illustrations to the *Ẓafarnāma* made for Husayn Bayqara are a

85. Bihzad: *The Seduction of Yusuf* from Saʿdi, *Būstān*, Herat, 1488. 30.5 ×
21.5 cm. Cairo, National Library, MS. Arab Farsi 908, f. 52v

86. Binding to the copy of Jalal al-Din Rumi, *Mathnavi*, made for Husyan
Bayqara, Herat, 1483. Pasteboard covered with varnish. 25.8 × 17.5 cm.
Istanbul, Türk ve Islam Eserleri Müzesi

good example of the Bihzadian style. The Mughal emperor
Jahangir, a noted connoisseur, considered eight of them to
be the early work of Bihzad, but for modern scholars, the
attribution is complicated by the retouching of the illustrations, probably in the Mughal period. An image such as
Building the Mosque of Samarqand [84] displays the typical
Bihzadian interest in daily activities, variety of figure types,
intricate composition, humor, and wit, as well as the sure
draughtsmanship, carefully modulated cool palette punctuated with jolts of bright color, and jewel-like finish associated with the Cairo *Būstān*. While most scholars agree
that the paintings in the *Zafarnāma* are the work of Bihzad,
they disagree about when they were added to the manuscript, some putting them before the *Būstān* and some after.

All the arts of the book – papermaking, calligraphy, illumination, and binding – flourished under the patronage of
Husayn Bayqara. One of the most exquisite examples of
bookbinding to survive covers the copy of Jalal al-Din Rumi's
Mathnavī made for the sultan at Herat in 1483.[36] The
exterior [86] has a rectangular field containing a central
cartouche with small pendants above and below and quarter-
cartouches in the four corners. Peonies and spiral arabesques
decorate everything. The rectangular frame, the quarter-
cartouches, and the central cartouche and pendants are re-

cessed and painted with embossed gold; the field and the
outer border are painted in black. The composition is typical
of fifteenth-century bindings and was transferred to carpets.
The technique of covering pasteboard with varnish, commonly but misleadingly known as Islamic lacquer, is an
innovation that would become increasingly popular under
the Safavids. Equally splendid are the doublures, made of
leather filigree pasted over a royal blue ground [87]. While
the lower cover maintains the traditional composition, the
upper one and the flap depict deer, monkeys, wild geese,
foxes, and birds sitting in a tree. The border is filled with
flying geese; a serpentine dragon of Chinese inspiration art-
fully fills the triangular flap. Exquisite detail, including the
fur and veins on the leaves, makes this one of the masterpieces of fifteenth-century art. Filigree had been used for
bookbinding in Iraq and western Iran since the beginning of
the century, as demonstrated by the inside covers of a copy
of Ahmad Jalayir's *Dīvān* ("Collected poems") made for the
author in Baghdad in 1406–7.[37] According to the sixteenth-
century biographer Dust Muhammad, the technique
(*munabbatkārī*) was introduced to Herat by Qavam al-Din,
the bookbinder from Tabriz, who was commissioned by
Baysunghur to prepare a *Miscellany* just like the one that
had been produced for Ahmad Jalayir.[38]

87. Doublure to a copy of Jalal al-Din Rumi, *Mathnavī*, Herat, 1483.
Leather filigree. 25.8 × 17.5 cm. Istanbul, Türk ve Islam Eserleri Müzesi

88. Jug, Herat, 1461–2. Brass inlaid with gold and silver. H 13 cm.
London, Victoria and Albert Museum

known, such jugs were princely accoutrements, for another example was made for Husayn Bayqara in April 1498 by Muhammad b. Shams al-Din al-Ghuri.[41] The shape can be traced in metal to the early thirteenth century,[42] but it is known also in jade and ceramics. A white nephrite jug in Lisbon inscribed around the neck with the name and titles of Ulughbeg [89] is strikingly similar, even to the S-shaped

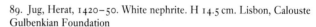

89. Jug, Herat, 1420–50. White nephrite. H 14.5 cm. Lisbon, Calouste Gulbenkian Foundation

Most of the accoutrements of everyday life in the Timurid period have disappeared over the centuries, but some can be reconstructed through illustrations. The double frontispiece to the Cairo *Būstān*, for example, depicts the court of Husayn Bayqara. On the left side the prince is seated on a geometric medallion carpet beneath a canopy. Before him are Chinese blue-and-white ceramics and metal jugs on a low table. On the right, servants and courtiers fill bottles and flasks and carry dishes to and fro. Almost no textiles or rugs have survived from the period, and they can only be reconstructed from manuscript illustration.[39] We are, however, better informed about metalwork. Almost one hundred objects made of brass, either inlaid or engraved and tinned, have survived. One of the most characteristic fifteenth-century shapes is the pot-bellied jug (average height 13.5 cm) with an S-curved dragon handle [88]. An early example was made by Habib Allah b. 'Ali Baharjani and dated 1461–2.[40] Every surface has been ornamented, mostly with epigraphy. A broad band encircles the neck and invokes good wishes to its owner. Arabesque friezes enclose two mystic odes in praise of wine by the fourteenth-century poet Hafiz. Even the underside of the foot is inscribed with good wishes and the artist's signature. Although the owner of this vessel remains un-

90. Underglaze-painted blue-and-white ceramic dish, Mashhad, 1473–4. Diameter 35.2 cm. St. Petersburg, Hermitage

91. Shaykhi: *Bahram Gur in the Green Pavilion* from Nizami, *Khamsa*, Tabriz, 1480s. Istanbul, Topkapı Palace Library, MS. H. 762, f. 170b

dragon handle. The form was also imitated by Chinese potters, for a blue-and-white example of the Xuand period (1426–35) was made perhaps for the export market.[43]

Chinese blue-and-white ceramics were highly valued in fifteenth-century Iran, to judge from their appearance in manuscript illustration and the frequent copies of them by Iranian potters.[44] Timurid blue-and-white wares, however, rarely equaled the achievements of their Chinese models: the potting is coarse and heavy, the glazes are thick, the drawing is often uninspired. One of the few dated pieces is a plate made at Mashhad in 1473 [90].[45] The well has three chrysanthemum flowers displayed on loose tendrils, the cavetto is inscribed with Persian verses, and the rim is decorated with a rather crude variant of the Chinese wave and rock pattern that was to become extremely popular in later Iznik wares (see Chapter 16).

Many of the splendid works of art produced in fifteenth-century Iran were made for descendants of Timur and can correctly be called Timurid, but in other cases dynastic labels are inappropriate. An example is the well-known copy of Nizami's *Khamsa* which was commissioned by the Timurid prince Abu'l-Qasim Babur (r. 1449–57) from the calligrapher Azhar, but was unfinished at the prince's death.[46] After the Qaraqoyunlu Jahanshah sacked Herat a year later, the manuscript passed to Jahanshah's son Pir Budak. It then went to the Aqqoyunlu ruler Khalil Sultan, who commissioned the calligrapher 'Abd al-Rahman al-Khwarazmi, known as Anisi, to finish copying the text and two artists, Shaykhi and Darvish Muhammad, to illustrate it. Still unfinished at Khalil Sultan's death in 1478, the manuscript passed to his brother Ya'qub (d. 1490). He, too, died before the book was completed; it finally passed to Isma'il I (r. 1501–24), founder of the Safavid dynasty, under whose patronage it was finished.[47] The illustration of *Bahram Gur*

in the Green Pavilion [91] is probably the work of Shaykhi, an artist of Herati origin. Added during Sultan Ya'qub's possession of the manuscript, this example of the Aqqoyunlu Court style contrasts markedly with the Herat style exemplified by Bihzad, especially in its palette and the fantastic vegetation. The carefully modulated colors of Bihzad have given way to acid greens set against brilliant blues. Nature has exuberantly burst from the frame's constraints to engulf the nominal subject, the prince in the pavilion, in a riot of anthropomorphic rocks among which grow lollypop trees with imbricated leaves.

The Istanbul *Khamsa* represents the finest in court patronage, but over one hundred manuscripts were illustrated in related but more prosaic styles, apparently for sale in the marketplace. One style, the Turkoman Commercial style, has been localized in the city of Shiraz during the last quarter of the fifteenth century. The style crystalized in the dispersed illustrations to a manuscript of the *Khavarnāma*, a folk rendition of the story of 'Ali in imitation of the *Shāhnāma*, the Persian national epic.[48] An illustration signed by the artist Farhad in 1476–7 [92] shows the general Sa'd defeating the divs. The painting shares the exuberance of the Istanbul *Khamsa*, but landscape has been simplified to a pale ground with grassy tufts and the occasional zoomorphic rocky outcrop. The high horizon is indicated by a white eyelet border below puffy comma-shaped clouds in white or gold. Other outdoor illustrations have a lush green or ocher ground with large masses of vegetation; indoor scenes have schematic, but meticulously detailed settings. The stocky figures, often wearing large lopsided turbans, are drawn with an extraordinarily fine line. Another twenty-six manuscripts with facial features and hair drawn in brown can be grouped in a related, but more delicate, style dubbed the Brownish (Turk. *kumral*) style.[49]

The legacy of the decorative arts in Iran and Central Asia during the fifteenth century passed not only through the splendid objects made for Timurid patrons but also through artists and artisans who carried the Timurid style elsewhere. The Timurid visual vocabulary which had been developed in Iran and Central Asia in the fifteenth century came to permeate the visual arts of other regions, notably Turkey and Muslim India, and there developed what has come to be called an International Timurid style. This style, characterized by chinoiserie floral motifs integrated into languid arabesques, became particularly important in the development of a distinct Ottoman style in the sixteenth century (see Chapter 16).

92. Farhad: *Sa'd Defeating the Divs* from Muhammad b. Husam al-Din, *Khwarnāma*, Shiraz, 1476–7. Dublin, Chester Beatty Library, MS. Pers. 293, no. 1, f. 104

CHAPTER 6

Architecture in Egypt under the Bahri Mamluks (1260–1389)

After the death of the last effective Ayyubid sultan of Egypt, Salih Najm al-Din Ayyub (r. 1240–49), his former concubine, Shajarat al-Durr, led a junta of his trusted advisers and generals until his son Turanshah could be brought back from abroad; but Turanshah was so hated that he was assassinated two months later and Shajarat al-Durr elected queen. For the next decade, a conspiratorial elite maneuvered for control of Egypt. In 1260 an army of former slaves (Arab. *mamlūk*) defeated the Mongols at ʿAyn Jalut in Syria, and Baybars I al-Bunduqdari, one of the former mamluks of Salih, emerged as the most powerful of the conspirators and assumed the title of sultan. The sequence of sultans he initiated ruled from Cairo over Egypt, Syria, western Arabia, and parts of Anatolia for the next two hundred and fifty years.[1] They are, somewhat artificially, divided into two lines. The first, mainly Kipchak Turks from southern Russia, are often called the Bahris, since they originally had their barracks on the island of Rawda in the Nile (*al-bahr*). The second, mainly Circassians from the Caucasus, are known as the Burjis, since they were quartered in the citadel (Arab. *burj*).

The Mamluks had a peculiar political system in which the governing class was recruited largely from Turkish slaves who were converted to Islam, educated in the arts of war and peace, and attached to the service of the sultan or other high notables. These slaves rose in the ranks, were manumitted, and eventually one among them was elected sultan. The sons of Mamluks occupied a lesser social status: as they were free-born Muslims they were excluded from the Mamluk corps and were consequently unable (at least in theory) to inherit their fathers' high political rank, although the descendants of Qalaʾun (r. 1280–90) reigned for much of the fourteenth century. The system was inherently unstable; many sultans, particularly in the fifteenth century, reigned only months, while others reigned several times successively. Family fortunes were always subject to confiscation by the state, and many Mamluks turned to architectural patronage to insure the survival of their wealth and perpetuate their names.

Money and property established in trust for a pious foundation (Arab. *waqf*) were protected by religious law from confiscation, so many Mamluks established such trusts in which their descendants were executors and beneficiaries. Usually the foundation centered on the tomb of the founder and incorporated other religious and charitable elements, such as a mosque, theological college (Arab. *madrasa*), hospital (*maristān*), hospice (*khānaqāh*), drinking-water dispensary (*sabīl*) and elementary school (*kuttāb*), as conservative ulema continued to disapprove of such impious display. These charitable functions were combined in large and impressive ensembles in order to glorify the founder's memory through architecture. The complexes were prominently sited on increasingly small and irregular plots along the main streets of Mamluk cities, particularly Cairo,

Damascus, and Aleppo. Any space intended for prayer had to be oriented towards the qibla, and patrons required that such elements as tombs, minarets, and portals be displayed on the street façade, which was usually at some variance to the direction of Mecca.[2] These three conflicting constraints of irregular sites, internal orientation, and desire for exteriorization led to the creation of an astonishing range of ingenious plans, one of the most characteristic features of Mamluk architecture. Familiar types of buildings and forms were combined behind ashlar-clad rubble walls in novel ways which give Cairo and other Mamluk cities their distinctive urban aspects. The preeminence of Cairo made it the most important locus of Mamluk patronage, but distinct regional styles were developed in other cities where lesser Mamluk amirs were assigned.[3]

The first Mamluk sultan, Baybars al-Bunduqdari (r. 1260–77), repaired a great many fortresses in Palestine and Syria, but only a handful of the many buildings he commissioned in Egypt has survived. The largest is his congregational mosque in Cairo, which is located north of the Fatimid city in the new suburb of al-Husayniyya [93]. The building measures some one hundred meters square internally; three sharply projecting, monumental entrances in the middle of the north-east, north-west, and south-west walls give access to the interior, an open courtyard some sixty by seventy-five meters surrounded by covered arcades. The two arcades on the sides are three bays deep, that in the direction of the

93. Cairo, Mosque of Baybars al-Bunduqdari, 1266–69, axonometric view

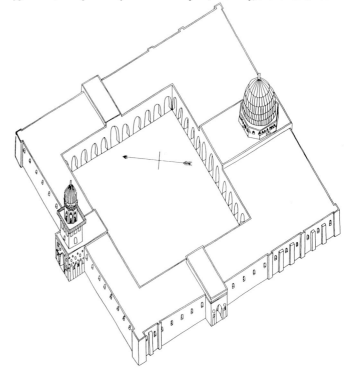

qibla is six bays deep, and that opposite is only two bays deep. Although much of the exterior remains in reasonably good condition, the interior is largely destroyed and only fragments of its stucco decoration remain. In most respects – the general plan, proportions, projecting portals, corner bastions, and support systems – the mosque repeats the Mosque of al-Hakim, built some two hundred and fifty years before. The Mamluk mosque differs, however, in three significant ways: the single minaret that originally stood over the main portal opposite the mihrab, the enormous dome covering the nine bays in front of the mihrab, and the axial bays leading from the three monumental entrances to the court. The arrangement of a single minaret opposite the mihrab hearkened back to the great Abbasid mosques of the ninth century, most notably that of Ahmad ibn Tulun, also in Cairo. The huge dome (diameter 15.5 meters), built of wood taken from the Crusader fortress at Jaffa, is the first example of a monumental dome in a Cairene mosque. Slightly larger than the largest dome then existing in Cairo, that over the tomb of the noted jurisconsult Imam al-Shafiʿ (d. 820), it signaled both Baybars' affiliation with the rival Hanafi sect and his victory over the Crusaders. The dome and the emphasis on cross-axiality were a local interpretation of the type of mosque fashionable in the Islamic east at that time, which had four iwans arranged around the court and a dome over the bays in front of the mihrab (see Chapter 2). This type of plan was probably brought to Cairo by Iranian immigrants who settled in the region.[4]

This freestanding congregational mosque is something of an anomaly in Mamluk architecture, for most other Mamluk buildings were multi-purpose structures wedged into the dense urban fabric. Baybars himself erected a madrasa (largely destroyed) on an irregular site facing the qaṣaba, the main street of the former Fatimid city. Once occupied by two halls of the great Fatimid palace, the site was adjacent to the madrasa and tomb of the Ayyubid sultan Salih Najm al-Din, Baybars' former master. By following the example of the building next door, Baybars linked himself with the previous regime and established a precedent that would be followed throughout the Mamluk period. Choice sites along the qaṣaba were snatched up by the most powerful individuals, usually sultans, for pious foundations to perpetuate their names. Baybars may have also intended to be buried in a tomb to be erected beside his madrasa, but he died suddenly in Damascus and was buried there. Of this building, all that survives is the portal with a muqarnas hood, and the square tomb chamber (nine by nine meters) immediately to its right was erected between 1277 and 1281 by Ibrahim ibn Ghanim al-muhandis (the engineer).[5] The decoration of the tomb [94] is particularly fine, with a marble dado sur-

94. Damascus, Mausoleum of Baybars al-Bunduqdari (Zahiriyya Madrasa), 1277–81, mosaic frieze

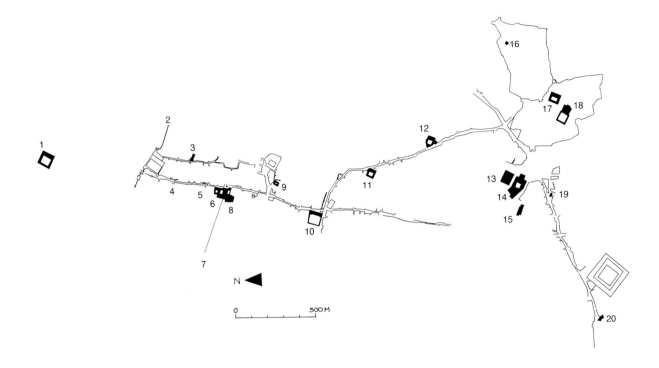

95. Map of central Cairo: 1) Mosque of Baybars I; 2) North Wall;
3) Khanaqah of Baybars al-Jashankir; 4) *qaṣaba*; 5) Fountain of 'Abd
al-Rahman Katkhuda; 6) Complex of Barquq; 7) Complex of al-Nasir
Muhammad; 8) Complex of Qala'un; 9) *Wakāla* of al-Ghuri; 10) Mosque of
Mu'ayyad Shaykh; 11) Mosque of al-Maridani; 12) Mosque of Aqsunghur;
13) Mosque of al-Rifa'i; 14) Complex of Hasan; 15) Palace of Amir
Yashbak; 16) Mosque of Sulayman Pasha; 17) Mosque of al-Nasir
Muhammad; 18) Mosque of Muhammad 'Ali; 19) *sabīl-kuttāb* of Qa'itbay;
20) Complex of Salar and Sanjar al-Jawli

mounted by an unusual frieze of glass mosaic. The frieze,
depicting architectural vignettes and acanthus scrolls framed
by trees, imitates the splendid eighth-century mosaics of the
nearby Great Mosque, although the Mamluk mosaics are
coarser and bolder in execution.[6] Both the marble dadoes
and, to a much lesser degree, the glass mosaics are features
that would be continued in the decorative repertory of
Mamluk builders in Cairo.

Baybars' eventual successor Qala'un, also one of Salih's
former mamluks, incorporated his own tomb within his complex located on the west side of the *qaṣaba* opposite the
madrasa of his former master [95, 96]. The west side of the
street may have been favored because the mihrab wall coincided with the street façade; windows flanking the mihrab
could have been opened to let passers-by hear recitations
and prayers from within. The imposing scale and lavish
decoration of this building, which combines a madrasa and a
mausoleum with a hospital, is the earliest example of the
new Mamluk style of architecture to survive in something
like its original state. Having once been treated by drugs
supplied by the hospital of Nur al-Din in Damascus, Qala'un
had vowed to build a similar institution in Cairo should he
ever come to the throne. In December 1283 he used monies
from his private purse to buy the land and buildings from
the occupants of the site, once part of the western, or
smaller, Fatimid palace. The site is shaped like a great L
measuring roughly one hundred meters in each direction.
The building was completed by July – August 1285, an
unusually short time: after preparation of the site, the hospital was completed in five months, the mausoleum in four,
and the madrasa in another four.[7] Although little remains
of the hospital, which continued to operate until the mid-
nineteenth century, its plan was recorded in the early
twentieth century, when much more of it still stood. The
hospital occupied the base of the L; its major feature
is a court with iwans in the centers of each of the four
sides. On the east and west were deep iwans with fountains
(*shādirwāns*) at their ends, and on the north was a T-shaped
iwan with a triple-arched façade; the largest iwan lay on the
south. In the corners between the iwans were wards for the
sick and convalescent, storerooms, latrines, and mortuaries,
with separate quarters for men and women. Fragments of
carved stucco decoration around the windows and exquisite
marble mosaic from the fountain show that no expense was
spared in the building.

To the east of the hospital (at the top of the L) lie the
mausoleum and the madrasa, which face each other across a
great corridor leading from the street to all three buildings.
The long street façade (67 meters) [97] is divided by the
entrance to the great corridor. To its left the exterior wall of
the madrasa projects 10.15 meters into the street; to its right
the exterior wall of the mausoleum is extended across the
base of the minaret, a tower of three receding stories. The
lower two are cubic and of fine masonry; the cylindrical
upper story of brick was added by Qala'un's son al-Nasir
after the earthquake of July 1303. The façade, constructed

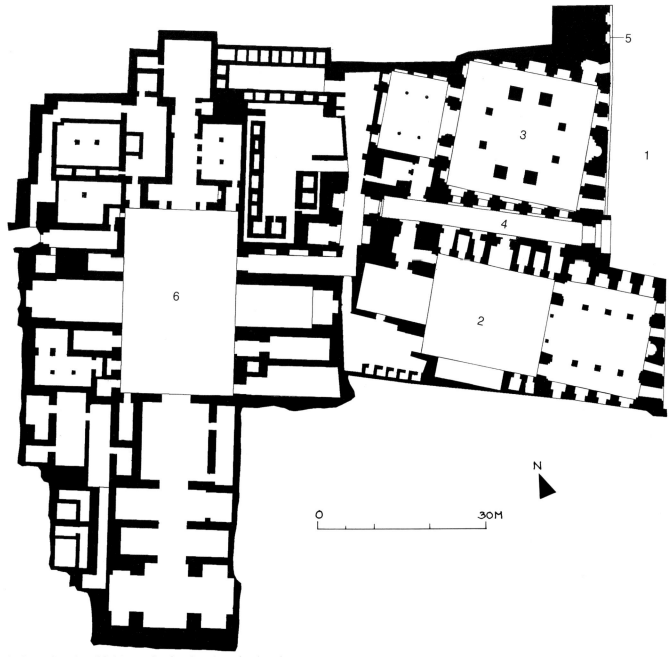

96. Cairo, Complex of Qala'un, 1283–85, plan: 1) *qaṣaba*; 2) madrasa;
3) mausoleum; 4) great corridor; 5) minaret; 6) maristan

97. Cairo, Complex of Qala'un, street façade of the mausoleum

98. Cairo, Complex of Qala'un, interior of mausoleum

in fine ashlar, consists of blind, pointed-arched panels of varying sizes enclosing single windows and coupled windows surmounted by an oculus. Subtle variations distinguish the façade of the madrasa from that of the mausoleum, but the entire expanse is unified by crenellated cresting along the top and by a magnificent inscription band which runs at the level of the first story. The inscription, which was once gilded, prominently displays the names and lofty titles of the founder and the dates of the inauguration and completion of the work. The inscription band jumps over the tall and narrow entrance bay, which consists of two superposed horseshoe arches over the doorway itself. The upper arch is rounded, the first of its type in Egypt, while the lower arch is slightly pointed. The arch has joggled voussoirs of alternating black and buff; the spandrels above it are revetted with geometric knot-like motifs in the same colors of marble. It encloses a coupled window and an oculus, whose iron grilles are Crusader spoils. The valves of the door are covered with bronze plates magnificently decorated with a geometric interlace pattern based on eight-pointed stars. They open onto a lofty corridor (four by ten by thirty-five meters) with a carved and painted wooden ceiling. The paneled recesses of the exterior façade are repeated along the walls of the corridor.

Since the tomb had to be sited behind the street façade, which also served as the qibla wall of the tomb, the architect was forced to place the main entrance to it on the opposite (west) side. The visitor thus passes along the corridor, turns right up three steps, and passes through a domed vestibule to enter an arcaded court. The center of the court is open to the sky, and medieval sources state that it contained a basin with a richly decorated fountain. On the east side of the court is the main entrance to the mausoleum, a (largely restored) grille of turned wooden spoolwork (*mashrabiyya*) surmounted by one of the finest stucco ensembles surviving in Egypt [99]. Its composition incorporates many of the elements of the façade, such as coupled windows surmounted by an oculus and interlacing based on star patterns. Other elements, such as the lobed cartouches enclosing arabesque motifs, are logical developments of earlier work, for example the fragmentary stuccoes of the Mosque of Baybars. The interior of the tomb [98] consists of a great rectangle (21 by 23 meters) in the midst of which four piers and four columns are arranged to form an octagon and support a high drum surmounted by a dome. A *mashrabiyya* grille connecting the four piers encloses the sultan's cenotaph. The grille was donated by Qala'un's son Muhammad in 1303–4. The rich interior decoration includes marble mosaic and carved stucco on the walls, painted and gilded wooden coffers on the ceilings, *opus sectile* on the floors, and glass mosaic in the mihrab.[8]

99. Cairo, Complex of Qala'un, entrance to mausoleum

The madrasa, which is poorly preserved, lies opposite the tomb; entrances opposite those to the tomb lead from the great corridor to a rectangular court (20.5 by 16.78 meters). On the east, a triple-arched façade screens the prayer hall, divided into three aisles by two arcades of four arches each. On the opposite side is a deep iwan which has also lost its original ceiling; the exigencies of the site left space for only the shallowest of recesses on the south. The surviving decoration in the prayer hall is simpler than that of the mausoleum, but the wall over the mihrab is encrusted with stucco finely carved with strapwork and arabesques.

The ensemble is one of the finest and most complex erected under the Mamluks. The speed with which it was constructed necessitated the assembly of a large corps of workmen. Although some of the features, such as the paneled façade, derive from a long tradition of architecture in Cairo, many others are more typical of Syria. Planimetric and decorative features are paralleled in the earlier monuments of Jerusalem, Damascus, and Aleppo. The plan and elevation of the mausoleum, for example, are loose quotations from the Dome of the Rock in Jerusalem, and the plan of the hospital is indebted to that of Nur al-Din in Damascus. The arcading in the mihrabs, the marble mosaic, the glass mosaic, the marble knotwork on the façade, and the square Kufic inscriptions on the interior of the mausoleum are all typical of the Syrian tradition. It was once believed that the Mongol destruction of Syria sent craftsmen scurrying to safety in Cairo, but it now seems more likely that the Mamluk campaigns in Syria and south-eastern Anatolia familiarized Mamluk patrons with the rich architectural heritage of the region, and their wealth and power enabled them to attract to Cairo the finest craftsmen available.

In the two decades following Qala'un's death on 10 November 1290, the Mamluk amirs fought viciously for power, while rival factions installed the sons of Qala'un on the throne. Al-Ashraf Khalil (r. 1290–4) was murdered and succeeded by Qala'un's last surviving son, the eight-year-old Muhammad, who took the name al-Nasir. In the following year Kitbugha (r. 1295–7), a Mongol who had been Qala'un's mamluk, usurped the throne from al-Nasir Muhammad and ordered that the bath to the north of Qala'un's tomb be replaced with a madrasa and mausoleum for himself. Work was begun, foundations were laid, and the building rose to the level of the inscription band on the façade when the sultan was removed from power by another claimant. When al-Nasir Muhammad returned to the throne in 1299, he ordered that the madrasa be completed in his own name, and it was finished five years later. He buried his mother and son in the mausoleum and intended to be buried there as well, although he was actually interred in his father's mausoleum next door. The plot is a rectangle some thirty-one by fifty-three meters, but the madrasa is inscribed in it at an angle so as to be correctly oriented toward the qibla. Like the complex next door, this complex has a central corridor leading to the madrasa on the south and the tomb on the north. Although the tomb is far smaller and the complex much less ambitious than that of Qala'un, the

101. Cairo, Complex of al-Nasir Muhammad, portal

madrasa is approximately the same size as the one next door. It has four iwans arranged around an open court and is the first example of a cruciform madrasa intended for teaching the four orthodox schools of law. The interior is largely ruined except for some marvelous stucco work over the mihrab [100]. The high relief, particularly in the conch over the mihrab, the multiple levels of arabesque, and the techniques of punching and stamping clearly belong to the Iranian tradition of stucco carving that culminated in the mihrab Uljaytu added to the Friday mosque in Isfahan in 1310 [12].[9]

The exterior of the complex of al-Nasir Muhammad preserves more of its original aspect: the Gothic portal of white marble inserted in the middle of the façade [101] had been removed from a Crusader church at Acre, transported by sea to Cairo, and eventually installed. Above the portal rises the minaret, whose square lower shaft of brick is decorated with superb stucco ornament much like that at the top of Qala'un's minaret next door. Some features, such as the keel-shaped blind arches with ribbed hoods, clearly belong to the local tradition, while others, such as the arcade of cusped blind arches on paired colonnettes, the intricate geometric patterns within them, and the interlaced arches at the top of Qala'un's minaret, resemble contemporary work in North Africa (see Chapter 9). The successes of the Christian reconquest of Spain meant that craftsmen from the Islamic west were also available for work in the Mamluk capital.

100. Cairo, Complex of al-Nasir Muhammad, 1295–1304, stucco panel over the mihrab

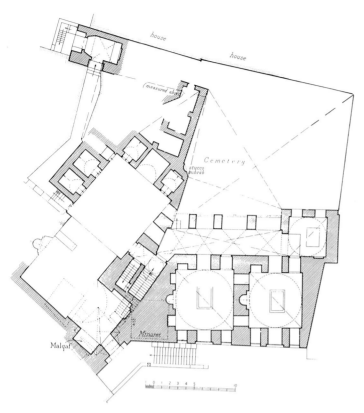

102. Cairo, Complex of Salar and Sanjar al-Jawli, begun 1303, plan

Other powerful mamluks also ordered funerary complexes in Cairo, but these patrons were not able to secure the prime sites along the *qaṣaba* available to those at the pinnacle of power. The amirs Salar (d. 1310) and Sanjar al-Jawli (d. 1344–5), for example, obtained a site for their funerary complex adjacent to Salar's palace near the Mosque of Ibn Tulun on an outcropping of the Muqattam hills. The two amirs had undoubtedly met while in the service of Qala'un and his sons.[10] Despite their different backgrounds, many mamluks who served the same masters developed strong bonds of loyalty (Arab. *khushdāshiyya*), which often explain actions in these turbulent and bloody decades, although this *esprit de corps* was often honored more in the breach than in reality.[11] In 1299, at the beginning of al-Nasir Muhammad's second reign as puppet of the powerful amirs, Salar was viceroy of Egypt, sharing power with Baybars al-Jashangir, and Sanjar was major-domo (*ūstādār*) for al-Nasir Muhammad. Salar built the complex in 1303 at the height of his power, but when al-Nasir Muhammad returned to the throne for his third reign in 1310, Salar was sent to prison, where he died of starvation. Sanjar, however, became governor of Palestine and a major patron of architecture there, until he fell out of favor in the 1320s and was imprisoned, dying in 1344–5. The historian al-Maqrizi (d. 1441) credits Sanjar with the foundation of the building, although at the time the complex was built Salar was more important and was accorded a bigger and more lavishly decorated tomb.

While the complexes of Qala'un and Kitbugha/al-Nasir Muhammad are regular buildings wedged into irregular but flat plots within the already dense urban fabric, the complex for Salar and Sanjar had to overcome the steep terrain of the site [102].[12] By ingeniously terracing the complex on several levels, the designer turned the problematic site into an advantage. A flight of steps leads from the street to an elevated portal, to the right of which stands a minaret of three stories separated by muqarnas cornices. The first is a tall square shaft of stone decorated on the south and west with mock balconies supported on muqarnas corbels and surmounted by horseshoe arches with cushion voussoirs. The upper shaft is of brick; the octagonal second story has eight keel-shaped arches with fluted hoods, and the cylindrical third story is crowned with a fluted dome. The harmonious composition of the façade [103] masks the complexity of the interior. From the portal one passes into a cruciform vestibule and ascends an internal staircase to a small domed vestibule at the center of the complex. A short cross-vaulted passage on the left leads to an interior court (now roofed over) with two stories of alcoves and small chambers; on its east is a slightly raised large room with a tunnel-vaulted iwan lit by a window overlooking the portal. The court was also accessible from the street above via a stair and bent corridor. The portal there is crowned with an elaborate muqarnas hood and may have marked the entrance from Salar's palace. The domed vestibule at the center of the complex also gives access to a long cross-vaulted corridor leading to a small mausoleum (diameter 4.63 meters) containing a ruined cenotaph and covered with a stone dome, the first of its kind in Cairo. On the left of the corridor, three arched openings into a courtyard are screened with exquisite pierced and carved stone grilles. On the right of the corridor lie the mausoleums of the founders: the first, which is slightly larger (diameter 7.06 meters), bears an inscription to Salar. It has carved wooden closet doors and cenotaph panels, muqarnas squinches, and fine marble paneling on the qibla wall. The second mausoleum (diameter 6.47 meters) is inscribed to Sanjar; its decoration is simpler. Both tombs are crowned with fluted brick domes covered with stucco.

The foundation inscription only identifies the building as a "place" (Arab. *makān*), and the function of the rooms to the left of the vestibule is unclear. Unlike other major complexes of the time, only the tombs are oriented to the qibla; the rooms to the left of the vestibule are at a 45° angle to it, an extremely unusual arrangement which necessitated the addition of ungainly mihrabs. Given the ingenuity of the architects in dealing with the site, it is hard to explain why this is so. Al-Maqrizi, writing more than a century later, identifies the complex as a madrasa for Shafi'is and a hospice for Sufis (Arab. *khānaqāh*), and some scholars have designated the interior court as the center of the hospice and the large room as the madrasa, with an iwan for teaching and possibly another iwan opposite for prayer.

Contemporary khanaqahs commissioned by high-ranking Mamluk amirs and sultans, however, are significantly larger. The institution of the khanaqah had been introduced into Egypt by Salah al-Din in 1173, and under the Mamluks Sufism was integrated into Egyptian society. Salar's colleague Baybars al-Jashangir, while still an amir, began a khanaqah, tomb, and residence on the site of the former

103. Cairo, Complex of Salar and Sanjar al-Jawli

palace of the Fatimid viziers; it was completed in 1310 during Baybars' brief sultanate after he had triumphed over Salar and before al-Nasir Muhammad definitively regained the throne. Baybars' complex is much larger than that of Salar, occupying a rectangular block over thirty meters wide and seventy meters deep. Its endowment deed provides information about the number and kind of personnel attached to a charitable foundation of the period. When completed, four hundred Sufis were appointed to the khanaqah, of whom one hundred were resident, and one hundred soldiers and elderly sons of amirs were selected to live in the residence. Other personnel of the khanaqah included the shaykh, Hanafi and Shafi'i prayer leaders, two repeaters, an attendant, a water-distributor, lamplighter, janitor, doorman, water-sprinkler, cook, housekeeper, bread-attendant, two broth-attendants, a weigher, an ophthalmologist, and a washer of the dead, and there were further personnel for the residence and the tomb. Their salaries and board were provided by the revenues of endowed properties.[13]

Al-Nasir Muhammad's third reign (1310–40) was marked by great growth and monumental construction in Cairo. The sultan undertook a vast building program on the citadel, and the huge domes of the palace and mosque there (respectively 18 and 15 meters in diameter) dominated the Cairo skyline until the nineteenth century, when Muhammad 'Ali erected a mosque on the site [394]. While the palace, the Qasr al-Ablaq, can be partially reconstructed from descriptions and nineteenth-century engravings,[14] the only part that survives is the congregational mosque (1318–35). It is a freestanding rectangle (53 by 59 meters) with a central courtyard surrounded by two-storied arcades and hypostyle halls. The prayer hall is four bays deep, the other three are two bays deep. The nine bays in front of the mihrab are covered by a large dome, originally of wood but restored several times. The outer walls are dressed ashlar; many of the columns and capitals inside were taken from Ptolemaic, Roman, and Christian buildings. The interior was once richly decorated with a high marble dado, but it was removed and shipped off to Istanbul in the sixteenth century (see Chapter 15, Note 16). The stone minarets [104], which stand at the northeast corner and over the north-west portal, are the most unusual feature of the mosque. The former has a rectangular base, a cylindrical second story, and an open hexagonal third story; the latter has a cylindrical lower shaft decorated with vertical zig-zags carved in deep relief, a cylindrical second story decorated with horizontal zig-zags, and a deeply fluted third story. Both are crowned with fluted bulbous cupolas and decorated above the third story with glazed tiles in light blue, manganese purple, and white. This unusual decoration was part of the second campaign on the mosque when the walls were heightened, the roof rebuilt, and the upper shafts of the minarets clad in brick and glazed tile. The techniques of brick and glazed tile, as well as the shape of the bulbous finials, are clearly foreign to the Cairene tradition. Al-Maqrizi reports that a builder from Tabriz worked on the mosque of Qawsun in Cairo (1330) and modeled the minarets there on those of the mosque of 'Alishah at Tabriz [13]; and traces of glazed decoration on several buildings in Cairo indicate that Tabrizi tileworkers had a

104. Cairo, Citadel, Mosque of al-Nasir Muhammad, 1318–35, minarets

workshop there during the 1330s and 1340s.[15] The taste for brightly colored decoration was already evident in Cairo in the late thirteenth century. Qala'un's tomb, for example, had been lavishly decorated with multicolored marble paneling, marble mosaic, and turquoise blue glass colonnettes in the arcades of the mihrab. The prosperity of Cairo during the reign of al-Nasir Muhammad encouraged craftsmen to emigrate there; Persian techniques and motifs became more accessible with the rapprochement in Mamluk-Mongol relations in the 1320s.[16]

Whereas Baybars I had encouraged the extension of Cairo towards the new north-eastern suburb of al-Husayniyya, al-Nasir Muhammad encouraged his amirs to build south of the city between the Fatimid walls and the citadel in an area that had been a cemetery and was to become a major processional route. He provided many of the amirs, who in some cases were his sons-in-law, with building materials and the necessary funds for construction. Many of these amiral foundations were congregational mosques, built to meet the needs of a burgeoning population. As strict Shafi'is, the Ayyubids had allowed only one congregational mosque in any urban entity, but this restriction was relaxed under the Mamluks, who often favored the Hanafi rite, which put no

105. Cairo, Mosque of al-Maridani, 1339–40, courtyard with *mashrabiyya* grille

limit on the number of congregational mosques. Some of these mosques were modeled on the example built by the sultan on the citadel, but they vary considerably in size. The grandest is the mosque built in 1339–40 on the Darb al-Ahmar by Altinbugha al-Maridani, cup-bearer and son-in-law of al-Nasir Muhammad and later governor of Aleppo.[17] The plan of the mosque closely follows that of al-Nasir Muhammad on the citadel; the similarity is not surprising as Altinbugha's mosque was designed by the court architect, master (Arab. *mu'allim*) Ibn al-Suyufi.[18] The mosque measures approximately forty-three meters on a side, but the eastern corner has been inset to adjust the façade to the angle of the street. Shallow panels with muqarnas hoods enliven the exterior. The octagonal minaret next to the entrance is crowned by a little dome supported on slender columns. The interior decoration of the mosque is particularly fine and displays most of the contemporary decorative repertory, such as marble paneling, carved stucco and wood, and tiled windows. A splendid *mashrabiyya* grille screens the prayer hall from the court [105]. The mihrab is particularly colorful with its mosaic of colored stone and mother-of-pearl, turquoise glass colonnettes, and joggled voussoirs in

contrasting colors, and the qibla wall is decorated with stucco unusually carved to represent trees.

The forty years following al-Nasir Muhammad's death in 1341 marked a return to the turbulence of the previous era. Egypt and Syria were ravaged by severe economic and social problems, while Mamluk amirs vied for power under Qala'unid epigons. In just seven years, the sultanate passed to seven of al-Nasir Muhammad's sons. The seventh was Hasan, an eleven-year-old who was installed as sultan in the summer of 1347, although a junta of amirs controlled the administration and treasury. The financial reserves accumulated by al-Nasir Muhammad had already been depleted, and the economic problems of the regime were exacerbated by the arrival of the Black Death in Alexandria in the autumn of that year. Approximately one-third of the population, estimated at two-hundred to two-hundred-fifty thousand, is thought to have died, and subsequent epidemics of pneumonic plague kept the population from regaining its earlier level.[19] After four years Hasan was deposed, and Salih, yet another young son of al-Nasir Muhammad, was put on the throne. Salih was himself deposed three years later and Hasan retrieved from the harem where he had

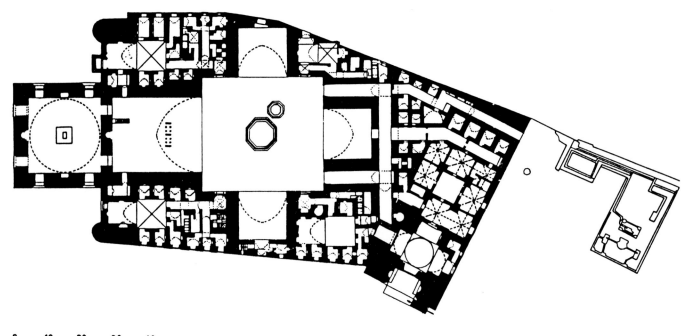

0 10 20 30 40 m.

106. Cairo, Complex of Hasan, begun 1356, plan

been imprisoned. During his second reign from 1354 to
1361, Hasan became increasingly unpopular, as he was stingy
to his mamluks and siphoned money from the state treasury
to pay for his massive funerary complex.

This colossal project, probably the greatest of all Mamluk
buildings, was built at the western foot of the citadel on a
site adjacent to the large maidan. Begun in 1356, it was still
unfinished when the sultan was deposed five years later.
Specialists (Arab. *muhandisūn*) were invited from all over the
Islamic world to assist in this most ambitious construction
project of the period.[20] Measuring some one hundred fifty
meters long and sixty-eight meters wide, it covers an area of
nearly eight thousand square meters and contained a cruciform congregational mosque with four madrasas and a mausoleum of imperial scale, as well as an orphanage, a hospital,
covered bazaar with shops, water tower, baths and kitchens.
The plan [106] is oriented in two directions: the service
block, including the entrance, ablution facility, and water
tower, is set at an oblique angle to the mosque, madrasas,
and tomb, which are all oriented to the qibla and raised on a
high plinth.

The exterior façade is articulated with regularly spaced,
shallow vertical niches and crowned by a deep muqarnas
cornice once surmounted by crenellations. The extraordinary
portal [107], rising thirty-seven meters above the current
street level, is crowned by a superb muqarnas semidome and
flanked by spiral-cut pilasters and vertical panels. The unfinished state of the carving on many of the panels shows
that large decorative elements were cut to size before they
were erected, while small ones were carved in place. The
portal's height would have been accentuated by the two
minarets that were intended to surmount it, but three months
before the patron died, one of them collapsed, killing three
hundred people in its fall. This event was seen as an augury
of the collapse of the sultan's power, and construction was
halted. The carved stone decoration around the portal is of
the highest quality and includes such Chinese motifs as
chrysanthemums and lotus flowers.

107. Cairo, Complex of Hasan, portal

108. Cairo, Complex of Hasan, view of courtyard

Superb bronze doors, illegally removed by sultan Mu'ayyad to his mosque at Bab Zuwayla [114, 115], opened to a cruciform vestibule with a raised platform at the rear and a stunning muqarnas vault above. The vestibule gives access to a long double-bent passageway which leads to the center of the complex, a magnificent court paved in marble with a decorative fountain in the center [108]. On each side of the court is a soaring iwan, and the corners of the building between the arms of the iwans house madrasas for the four orthodox schools of law. Each has its own smaller court surrounded by four or five stories of rooms for students. The south-east iwan is spanned by an enormous vault which contemporaries believed surpassed the Sasanian arch at Ctesiphon, considered one of the wonders of the world.[21] Just the wood used to construct the centering for this arch cost one hundred thousand dirhams, or more than the cost of an ordinary mosque. The iwan served as the prayer hall of the complex, and the mihrab and surrounding qibla wall are paneled in marble slabs of contrasting colors. To the right of the mihrab is a marble minbar, much praised by contemporaries, and in front of it is an equally fine *dikka*, or tribune, for the official charged with repeating the daily prayers so that all worshippers could hear and follow the service. Around the iwan at the springing of the vault is a superb stucco band with a large Koranic inscription carved in monumental Kufic against a floral arabesque ground. Doors flanking the mihrab lead to the tomb beyond the qibla

iwan; that on the right is original and of exceptional workmanship, plated with bronze and inlaid with silver and gold. The tomb chamber, a simple square, is the largest domed mausoleum in Cairo, measuring twenty-one meters on a side and thirty meters to the top of the walls. At its center is a wooden screen enclosing a raised marble cenotaph, but only Hasan's two young sons were buried there; the sultan's body was never recovered after his assassination. All four walls are paneled with marble; above is a wooden band carved and painted with the Throne Verse (2:225), the well-known Koranic passage dealing with God's majesty.[22] Wooden muqarnas pendentives, lavishly painted and gilded, once supported a bulbous wooden dome, but the present dome is a restoration. This lofty chamber was once illuminated by hundreds of glass lamps, specially commissioned for the building [138].

The architect of this building ingeniously resolved the problem of maximum urban visibility and religious orientation toward Mecca. On the exterior the tomb's visibility from the citadel, seat of Mamluk power, was maximized by having three sides of it project from the main building and by framing it with two other minarets, of which only the southern one retains its original form. Putting the tomb behind the sanctuary meant that worshippers had to pray directly toward the tomb. The complex of Hasan represents a culmination of many elements in earlier Cairene architecture, but its size and largely freestanding position made it

109. Cairo, "Sultaniyya" complex in the Southern Cemetery, 1350s

exceptional. Other features, such as the four-iwan plan with dome behind the qibla iwan, the portal framed by minarets, and the domed vestibule, are innovations in Cairene architecture. Some scholars have traced these features to particular monuments in Central Asia and Anatolia, but it seems far more likely that the immediate models were the now lost imperial constructions of the Ilkhanids in north-western Iran, such as Ghazan's funerary complex at Tabriz and Uljaytu's complex at Sultaniyya, where many of these same features were found in one building (see Chapter 2). The Ilkhanids had been the major power in the early fourteenth century and their monuments still represented the imperial ideal. With the collapse of the Ilkhanid state in 1335, the imperial building tradition there came to a halt. In the ensuing turmoil and plague throughout the Middle East, artisans would have gravitated to Cairo, bringing with them techniques and motifs, such as muqarnas vaults, square Kufic inscriptions, and chinoiserie, already popular elsewhere. Ibn Khaldun, the great philosopher of history who arrived in Cairo in 1382, twenty years after Hasan's death, wrote that large cities and high monuments were built only by strong royal authority, and he cited the examples of the pyramids and the iwan at Ctesiphon.[23] Sultan Hasan, the weak and ineffectual ruler of Egypt, sought to make his mark with an equivalent monumental construction; his stunning architectural achievement belies his political ignomiy.

Had the Cairene builders been able to erect a stone dome over the intended tomb of the sultan, they undoubtedly would have done so, but its enormous size must have forced them to use wood. Its bulbous profile, however, is common to several other funerary domes erected in Cairo in the middle of the fourteenth century. The one over the tomb of

Amir Sarghatmish (1356), for example, has a smooth profile, but the more common type has ribs rising from a muqarnas cornice around a high drum. The best examples are found in an anonymous mausoleum in the Southern Cemetery known as the Sultaniyya, which probably dates to the 1350s.[24] It consists of two ribbed bulbous domes on high drums flanking a vaulted iwan [109]. The iwan originally opened onto a court, of which only a minaret in one corner remains. Each dome had a ribbed stone shell cemented onto a brick shell, and the whole is buttressed by a system of interior supports hidden in the space behind the drum and above the low inner dome. This system attempts to translate the structural requirements of a brick dome into limestone; it clearly shows that this was a foreign type of construction imported to Egypt from the Iranian world. The earliest examples there, however, such as the Gur-i Mir in Samarqand [53–54] date from the early fifteenth century, but there must have been earlier ones that have not survived, and the Iranian tradition of double domes constructed in brick can be traced back as far as the eleventh century.[25] The carved low-relief decoration on the drum of the eastern tomb – floral arabesques between the windows and a band of square Kufic above – is another translation of Iranian tile motifs into carved stone. The increasing congestion in the metropolis of Cairo meant that choice sites were harder to obtain, and enhancing the visibility of a building from afar, whether by increased height or distinctive profiles, became all the more important. The tendency toward extreme height is exemplified in the small mausoleum of Yunus al-Dawadar (1382) near the citadel.[26] Its dome and drum are so elongated that the building has often been mistaken for a minaret.

Architecture in Egypt, Syria, and Arabia under the Circassian Mamluks (1389–1517)

After the death of Sultan Hasan in 1361, the supply of al-Nasir Muhammad's sons was exhausted, so one of his grandsons, al-Mansur Muhammad, was enthroned, continuing the old pattern of a series of brief reigns by epigons of Qala'un manipulated by strong Mamluk amirs. Even this system collapsed by the 1380s when intense strife within the Mamluk corps brought Barquq b. Anas (r. 1382–99, with interruption) to the sultanate. Barquq inaugurated the line of Circassian (or Burji) Mamluks, who were related not by blood, like the Qala'unids, but by clientage, for the great majority of Barquq's successors were his mamluks, mamluks of his mamluks, and so on. If the history of the Turkish Mamluks was violent, that of the Circassian Mamluks was tumultuous. Yet despite a ruined economy, plague, drought, and the European discovery of a sea-route to India bypassing Egypt, this period was one of unparalleled building activity; 133 monuments survive in Cairo alone.

Architecture of the Circassian period is distinguished by several notable developments, some already present at the end of the earlier period. As space became increasingly scarce, buildings became taller in relation to their area. Funerary complexes remained the major building type, but as orthodox opinion against the construction of tombs moderated, tomb chambers became increasingly important and central in the plan. Stone continued to be the major material of construction, but as wood and marble became increasingly scarce, inventive techniques had to be found to use the limited supplies to greatest advantage. Surface ornament, both on the exterior and the interior, became increasingly elaborate and shows the impact of designs developed and used in the other arts. Moldings are particularly fine, and their subtle sequencing around portals, windows, zones of transition, and domes is a hallmark of the Circassian style.

Syria recovered slowly from the Mongol invasions, owing to plague, governors' revolts, and internal strife. With the fall of Cilicia to the Mamluks in 1375 and the destruction of Genoese factories on the Black Sea, the fortunes of Aleppo began to revive, as it became the entrepot for caravans bringing silk from Iran to be traded with Venetian merchants. New souks with very large caravanserais were erected, as were vast and populous suburbs along the caravan routes into the city.[1] These suburbs needed such amenities as congregational mosques with minarets, baths, and hospices for Sufis. The Utrush mosque (1399–1410), for example [110], is located two hundred meters south-east of Aleppo's citadel.[2] The amir Aqbugha al-Utrush, a mamluk of Barquq who was successively governor of Safad, Tripoli, Aleppo, and Damascus, began it as his final resting-place, but he died before it was finished, and it was only completed some years later by his successor Demirdash. The building is a rectangle (20 by 36 meters) with an open courtyard sur-rounded by single arcades except on the qibla side, where the prayer hall is two bays deep. At the north-west corner stand the entrance, the minaret, and the tomb. The mosque is of a standard Aleppan type, for it follows the plan of the mosque that Zahir Ghazi had built in the Upper Maqam of the Citadel some two centuries earlier and that of the mosque of Altinbugha (1318), but the way the tomb of the founder has been added is noteworthy. Whereas Cairene architects would have had to insert the building in an already dense urban fabric and would have juggled the elements of the plan to put the mausoleum on the qibla side, Aleppan builders were able to secure a largely open site and were content to integrate the tomb behind a continuous façade. The presence of the tomb is indicated only by the dome, whose plain profile rises behind the façade. Typical Aleppan features are the fine bichrome (Arab. *ablaq*) masonry, exquisitely detailed carved moldings, octagonal minaret, and groined vaults.

Syria, which had been ravaged by the rivalries of warring Mamluk amirs, fell an easy prey to Timur, who attacked such major cities as Aleppo, Homs, and Damascus in the winter of 1400–1. His brief campaign was not aimed at annexation but was meant to collect booty and demonstrate his superior power and prestige. Although Aleppo submitted without a struggle and was spared, Damascus was pillaged and burned to set an example of Timur's might.[3] Timur left Syria in the spring, sending any artisans and qualified workmen who were left in the city to Samarqand. This mass deportation was one of the greatest catastrophes in the history of Damascus, and fifteenth-century buildings there, such as the al-Qali minaret (1470), are more ostentatious

110. Aleppo, Mosque of Aqbugha al-Utrush, 1399–1410, façade

than innovative. Damascene patrons desired showy façades, loaded with polychromy and carving and dripping with muqarnas to conceal uninspired structures.[4]

Safe from the Timurid raids, Cairo remained the center of Mamluk power and display. Sultan Barquq was an upstart: he had no Kipchak Turkish ancestry nor had he begun his career in the service of the old royal family. To consolidate his uneasy social position, he married a widow of sultan Sha'ban, one of the last of Qala'un's descendants, and to further establish his legitimacy, he built his family mausoleum on the *qaṣaba* of Cairo.[5] Few sites there were still available, but he somehow acquired a caravanserai which was one of the charitable foundations dependent upon the adjacent madrasa of al-Nasir Muhammad. The site provided some forty-five meters of street frontage, and the complex of mosque, madrasa, khanaqah, and mausoleum was made all the more prominent by projecting the façade three meters into the street. The plan is similar to that of the nearby madrasa built by Qala'un a century earlier [96], but the building incorporates features developed in Hasan's complex such as the monumental entrance and vestibule, cruciform plan, and court façade. The materials and decoration, however, differ significantly from those of the earlier foundation and set the style for Cairene architecture in the first half of the fifteenth century. Bronze, marble, wood, and even stucco had become dearer and scarcer, and techniques were developed to use them sparingly for the greatest effect. The doors inside Barquq's complex are not faced with bronze, but decorated with a central bronze medallion and quarter-medallions in the corners, in a design reminiscent of contemporary leather bookbindings. Thin strips and chips of colored marbles made up the requisite marble paneling, which was sometimes replaced by stone for crenellations, moldings, and vaults. For screenwork, turned wood was often replaced by "matchwood," grooved splinters jointed together, as on the windows of the façade. The mihrab [111] is framed by prismatic columns which have been trimmed to provide thin marble strips for paneling; the blue Pharaonic or Ptolemaic votive colonnettes, Egyptian faience bosses, mother-of-pearl, bitumen, and glass paste in the niche stand in for the marble mosaic of earlier times.

Barquq's family mausoleum was only the final resting-place for one of his daughters; he himself had requested in his will that he be buried in Cairo's Northern Cemetery near the tombs of his father, whom he had invited to Egypt, and revered Sufis. Accordingly, Barquq's son Faraj (r. 1399–1412, with interruption) erected an enormous complex in the desert to the east of the Fatimid city walls.[6] The site, which had been used as a hippodrome in early Mamluk times, began to be used as a cemetery in the early fourteenth century, but under Faraj major efforts were made towards integrating the area into Cairo's urban fabric. For example, the procession beginning the pilgrimage to Mecca was rerouted through this district. The sultan ordered a large residential area constructed; it included baths, bakeries, grain mills, lodgings for travelers, and a marketplace, but all that survives is the khanaqah. The open site in an outlying

111. Cairo, Complex of Barquq, 1384–86, mihrab

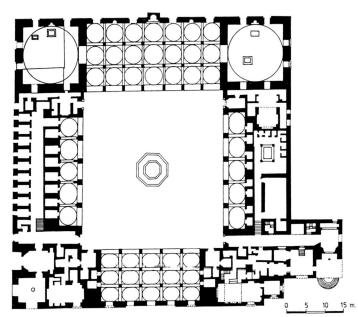

112. Cairo, Complex of Faraj b. Barquq in the Northern Cemetery, 1400–11, plan

district allowed for a large, freestanding, and symmetrical building [112] like the Mosque of Baybars [93]. The building is an open square, measuring seventy-three meters to a side. The main façade on the north-west has twin entrances, twin drinking-water dispensaries and elementary schools (Arab. *sabīl-kuttāb*), and twin minarets at either end. Corridors lead to a spacious open court, whose sides are occupied by porticoes with four stories of cells and dependencies behind. Hypostyle halls three bays deep stand on the north-west and south-east, the latter serving as the prayer hall. The small dome over the bay in front of the mihrab is flanked by the twin domes of the mausoleums. Measuring just over fourteen meters in diameter, they are the largest stone domes in Cairo and masterpieces of Mamluk engineering. On the exterior they are decorated with horizontal bands of zig-zags which are exactly coordinated to the structure and contract as the stones diminish in size toward the top. This system replaced the arbitrary ribs of earlier examples [109] and became the most popular type of decoration for Cairene domes. The enormous thrusts of the domes are absorbed by massive masonry zones of transition, which are visually lightened by an ingenious arrangement of concave and convex moldings [113]. On the interior the domes are painted in red and black with patterns simulating marble, which would have been too heavy and too expensive to use. Matchwood grilles in geometric patterns screen the entrances. The northern tomb contains the bodies of Barquq, Faraj, and his son, while that on the south contains the bodies of Barquq's daughters and their nurse. An arcade to the north connected the modest tomb of Barquq's father, Sharaf al-Din Anas, to the complex.

Faraj's reign was notable for the uninterrupted struggles between the sultan and his amirs; he was deposed in May 1412 and killed several weeks later. After a brief reign by an Abbasid caliph, whose line had been reestablished in Cairo by Baybars I in an attempt to add prestige to the new Mamluk regime, the sultanate passed to the former viceroy

113. Cairo, Complex of Faraj b. Barquq, court

114. Cairo, Mosque of Mu'ayyad Shaykh, begun 1415, groined vault over the vestibule

of Damascus, Shaykh al-Mahmudi, who took the regnal name al-Mu'ayyad (r. 1412–21). This pattern of a usurper followed briefly by his son who was overthrown within a few years was repeated throughout the Circassian period. According to the contemporary historian al-Maqrizi, al-Mu'ayyad had been imprisoned in Cairo while still an amir, and he vowed to transform the infested prison into a place of prayer and study.[7] This vow also provided a good excuse to acquire a valuable piece of downtown real estate. The large pious foundation, which included a congregational mosque, three minarets, two mausoleums, and a madrasa for the four rites dedicated to Sufi students, was begun in 1415; it remained unfinished at the sultan's death.

Al-Mu'ayyad's mosque, measuring eighty-five by eighty-two meters, stands at the southern end of the *qasaba* adjacent to the Fatimid gate, Bab Zuwayla, which supports two of the three minarets the building originally had. The main portal opens at the north end of the principal façade on the *qasaba*. Revetted in alternating courses of black and white marble, it consists of a deep recess crowned by a trilobed muqarnas vault, the whole inset in a rectangular frame rising above the cornice. Known in Persian as a *pīshṭāq* (see Chapter 2), this feature was ubiquitous in Iranian architecture and had already been used on the north portal of the complex of Faraj in the northern cemetery. The doorjambs and lintel (a Pharaonic block of pink granite) are framed with a white interlaced band inset with red and turquoise paste. The portal leads to a rectangular vestibule, with two recesses on the axis covered with trilobed muqarnas hoods, like that of the portal. The center is covered with a folded groined vault rising to a recessed cross [114]. This elaborate type of vault probably originated in Syrian military architecture, but its decorative possibilities were developed in the religious archi-

115. Cairo, Mosque of Mu'ayyad Shaykh, qibla wall

tecture of Jerusalem and particularly Cairo in the fifteenth century.[8] The vestibule leads to the courtyard, which was originally surrounded by four halls, an arrangement much like that of the complex of Faraj, but only the hypostyle prayer hall on the qibla side survives. Three rows of eight marble columns support a lavishly decorated wooden ceiling, but the major decorative emphasis was reserved for the qibla wall [115]: a high dado of two registers of white and black marble and porphyry is surmounted by a frieze of paired colonnettes made of turquoise blue glass. The window surrounds are inlaid with patterns of joggled voussoirs and arabesques; the area around the mihrab is decorated in the same manner but with particularly fine detail. To its right stands the original wooden minbar inlaid with ivory, a fine example of the richness of contemporary woodwork. As in the complex of Faraj, the prayer hall was designed to be flanked by two domed mausoleums, but only the one on the north, containing the cenotaphs of the sultan and his son, is domed. The deeply articulated zone of transition and the chevron pattern on the shell are virtually identical to those at the complex of Faraj, although the dome is somewhat smaller. The cenotaphs have splendid decoration in foliated Kufic, a deliberate revival of an earlier style.

The sultan spent enormous sums on the construction and endowment of the complex; according to contemporaries the figure approached one hundred thousand dinars. When costly materials were unavailable, the sultan expropriated elements of earlier foundations. Although he payed into their endowments, the practice was still illegal, for once endowed the buildings and their fittings could not change owners. Nevertheless, against payment of five hundred dinars, the magnificent bronze doors and chandelier were taken from the complex of Hasan, which was by then largely abandoned. The large plaques of marble on the qibla wall were expropriated from old houses in Alexandria and shipped upriver, for no marble had been quarried in Egypt since Antiquity, and marbles were already scarce in Barquq's time. Decoration of such richness or rapacity would not be possible again. Similarly, borrowing the towers of Bab Zuwayla for the bases of the minarets gave them a prominence they might not otherwise have had: they are clearly visible from a great distance along the *qasaba* and soar over fifty meters above the street.[9] It may be their prominence that led the builder Muhammad b. al-Qazzaz to sign and date his work, a rare example of an architect's signature in medieval Cairo.[10] The expropriation of the past extended to motifs as well: the court façade above the arcade is decorated with blind keel arches alternating with rosettes in the manner of the Mosque of al-Maridani [105]. The ample endowment and large library made the complex one of the most prominent academic institutions of the fifteenth century. Its professorial chairs were filled by the most eminent scholars, such as Ibn Hajar al-Asqalani (1372–1449), the expert in Koranic exegisis.

Most of the fifteenth century was a period of political turmoil and economic decline, although sultans such as Barsbay (r. 1422–37) and Inal (r. 1453–61) continued the tradition established by Faraj of erecting magnificent

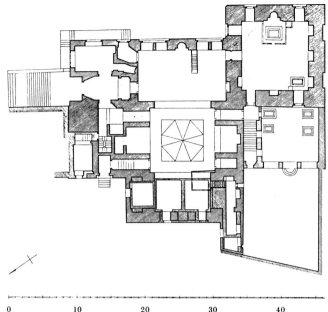

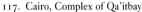

0   10   20   30   40

116. Cairo, Complex of Qa'itbay in the Northern Cemetery, 1472–4, plan

117. Cairo, Complex of Qa'itbay

funerary complexes in the Northern Cemetery. The authority of the sultanate was reestablished by al-Ashraf Qa'itbay (r. 1468–96), who stabilized the economy and inaugurated an unprecedented revival of the arts. He was responsible for some sixty-five projects, many encompassing several buildings, in every quarter of Cairo and in Mecca, Medina, Damascus, and Jerusalem. The buildings of his reign are notable not for their size, but for their elegance and harmonious style. Furnished with the products of revived craft industries, particularly metalwork and manuscripts (see Chapter 8), they came to represent the paradigm of Mamluk architecture.[11]

The largest and best-preserved of Qa'itbay's buildings is his funerary complex (1472–4) in the Northern Cemetery of Cairo. The irregular plan [116] reveals that the building is an agglutination of self-contained units connected only by corridors. A flight of steps on the north rises to the tall portal [117], crowned with a groined vault in bichrome masonry. To the left is a water dispensary (Arab. *sabīl*) on the ground floor with the open loggia of a Koran school (Arab. *kuttāb*) above. To the right the slender and elegant minaret rises forty meters from a square base in a succession of octagonal, cylindrical, and open stories separated by balconies on muqarnas cornices and crowned by a bulbous finial. Passing through the portal, one enters a groined vaulted vestibule with a raised bench opposite, a vestige of the tradition inaugurated in the complex of Hasan. A door on the left of the vestibule leads into the water dispensary; one on the right leads to a stair ascending to the Koran school and minaret and a bent passage leading to the madrasa and tomb. The madrasa [118] consists of a square court with a wooden roof having a central lantern; there are shallow iwans on two sides and rectangular halls on the two ends, the larger one at the qibla end serving as a prayer hall. The roofing of the court and the truncation of the side iwans are features adopted from domestic architecture, particularly the reception room of Cairene great houses (Arab. *qā'a*; see below), and the impact of the *qā'a* on Cairene religious architecture can already be seen in the madrasa of Amir Mithqal (1384–6), which nevertheless has an open court.[12] The richly decorated interior, with marble paving, painted and gilded wood, bichrome masonry, and colored glass, is heavily restored, but gives a good indication of the harmonious opulence of the Mamluk style.

To the right of the prayer hall lies the tomb, with the sultan's cenotaph within a wooden screen in front of the marble mihrab. The chamber is a square, measuring 9.25 meters to a side and 31 meters high. The lower walls are over two meters thick to support the weight and absorb the thrusts of the enormous dome. Inside, the zone of transition consists of pendentives with nine tiers of shallow muqarnas between triple narrow windows surmounted by three oculi. A narrow drum with sixteen windows supports the dome, which is quite plain. The exterior [117], however, is the masterpiece of carved masonry domes, comprising two networks of contrasting arabesque and geometrical interlace perfectly fitted to the decreasing domical surface. While the

118. Cairo, Complex of Qa'itbay, interior of madrasa

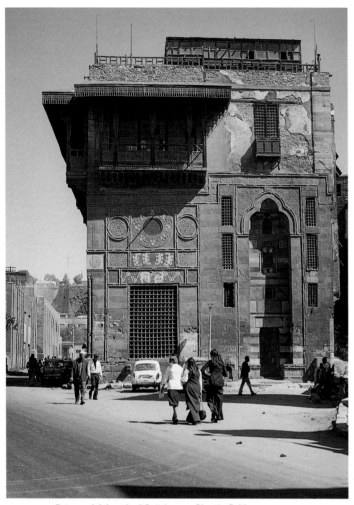

119. Cairo, *sabīl-kuttāb* of Qa'itbay on Shari'a Saliba, 1477

two systems evolve from common centers, the contrast between the two is heightened by the differing surface treatment: the geometric interlace is left plain while the surface of tendrils, trefoils, and split leaves is grooved with a beveled cut. Such intricacy of design, refinement of execution, and elegance were attempted again only on the other dome to the west in the complex. The treatment of the zone of transition derives directly from that inaugurated at the nearby complex of Faraj b. Barquq, but the sequence of concave and convex moldings is more intricate, and many of the surfaces are carved. The triangular spaces on either side of the windows are filled with roundels carved with Qa'itbay's distinctive epigraphic emblem.

According to its endowment deed, this building formed the centerpiece of a large walled compound comprising a mausoleum, madrasa, mosque, hospice for sufis, loggia for receptions (Arab. *maq'ad*), water-trough, monumental gate, and tenement (Arab. *rab'*), supported by the revenues from an urban caravanserai (Arab. *wakāla*) and a house elsewhere in Cairo.[13] The compound measured at least two hundred and fifty meters from south to north, from the remains of the gate to the tenement, which had street-level shops and upper apartments reached by communal stairs.

The most notable of Qa'itbay's other buildings in Cairo is

the drinking-water dispensary and elementary school he erected on the Saliba, the street leading west from the maidan below the Citadel [119].[14] This building is the first example of a freestanding *sabīl-kuttāb* in Cairo, for earlier ones had been attached to religious or commercial structures. The type became a favorite for patrons with limited resources, particularly in the Ottoman period, when nearly one hundred were built [316]. Qa'itbay's structure has the fountain house at the north-west corner and the main portal facing a small square on the west. Although the upper story has been restored and the interior adapted for use as a center of instruction, the exterior preserves some of the finest architectural detail of the later Mamluk period. Its unusually extravagant polychromy has been obscured by grime, but the effect is still striking. A raised double fillet interrupted by circular knots divides the exterior into variously shaped panels. An inscription band wraps around the top of the portal and the fountain. Below it, the tall and narrow portal, with a characteristic trilobed hood, is revetted with black, white, and red striped masonry. The spandrels contain Qa'itbay's epigraphic emblem, set off against a ground of arabesque worked in low relief. Perhaps the finest decoration is found in the nine panels above the fountain grille, which are arranged in three rows of three. The lintel is decorated with interlocking trefoils inlaid in black and white; it is flanked by arabesques in shallow beveled relief. The relieving arch has intricately joggled voussoirs in black and white and is flanked by geometric interlaces inlaid in blue and white paste and red stone. The oculus was inlaid with arabesques in various colors, of which only the white has survived. The central panel is flanked by medallions inlaid with blue and white paste in a geometric interlace generated from a red hexagon. The lavishness of the exterior is unusual, even in late Mamluk architecture, and seems to be explained by the nature of the building, which was meant to be appreciated from the exterior, and the prominent site on an important Cairene thoroughfare. The compartmentalized design of the façade is reminiscent of contemporary book illumination [143] and suggests that in late Mamluk Egypt, as in the contemporary Iranian world, designs were freely exchanged from one medium to another. These designs were undoubtedly worked out first on paper, which by this point was readily available and reasonably cheap, and then realized in carved stone, inlaid metal, or paint and ink on paper.

Qa'itbay built extensively in the holy cities of Mecca and Medina. After the Mosque of the Prophet in Medina was seriously damaged by fire in 1481, Qa'itbay ordered it rebuilt, and the materials and construction are described in detail by contemporary historians.[15] Qa'itbay's activities in Mecca and Medina were motivated by more than piety: with the rising power of the Ottomans and Turkoman to the north of the Mamluk domains, sovereignty over the Holy Cities became an increasingly important symbol of power within the Islamic lands of the eastern Mediterranean region. Jerusalem, the third holiest city in Islam, was also important to Qa'itbay. It had special significance not only for its associations with the Prophet, but also as the city won back from the Franks. Between 1480 and 1482 Qa'itbay ordered a large madrasa, known as the Ashrafiyya after its founder's

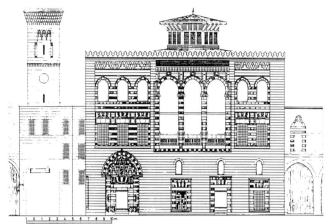

120. Jerusalem, Ashrafiyya Madrasa, 1480–82, reconstructed elevation of east façade

121. Jerusalem, Qa'itbay's fountain on the Haram al-Sharif, 1482

epithet, for an extremely prominent site on the western enclosure of the Haram al-Sharif facing the Dome of the Rock.[16] The site had been occupied by an earlier madrasa, begun for the Mamluk sultan Khushqadam in 1465, but when Qa'itbay saw the building in 1475, he found it unsuitable and had it replaced with another construction. Only parts of the lower stories have survived, but the extensive contemporary documentation of the building and careful investigation of the remains allow its original disposition to be imagined [120].[17]

The most striking feature of the building is the façade, some twenty-five meters wide, which projects in front of the arcade that forms the western boundary of the Haram. This unique encroachment was undoubtedly a result of royal prerogative, for it is the only royal foundation of the Circassian period in Jerusalem and recalls Barquq's usurpation of the street for his complex in Cairo. Less prominent patrons had to vie for sites as close as possible to the Haram, or, less preferably, along the thoroughfares leading to it. The doorway flanked by two windows on the right side of the ground floor belongs to a large rectangular assembly hall which incorporates three bays of the west portico. The bay on the left comprises an elaborate entrance porch with access to a vestibule and staircase leading to the upper stories. The madrasa proper lies upstairs. It had a large rectangular hall whose disposition was quite similar to that of Qa'itbay's foundation in Cairo, except that the east iwan had a three-bay loggia giving an uninterrupted view of the Dome of the Rock. Residential cells were disposed around an open court built over the adjacent Baladiyya madrasa.

The contemporary historian Mujir al-Din said that the earlier madrasa on the site did not live up to Qa'itbay's expectations, being "built after the fashion of Jerusalem madrasas, which are not up to much."[18] Consequently he sent a team of stone-cutters and builders from Cairo to work on the new madrasa, and many of its features, such as the folded groined vaults, raised double fillets with circular knots, intricately joggled voussoirs, and arabesques inlaid in white, black, red, and blue, are found in Qa'itbay's earlier buildings in Cairo. As the most important city in the Mamluk realm, Cairo had attracted artisans from provincial capitals, and the

metropolitan Mamluk style of architecture incorporated the best features of the provincial styles. This is a rare example of a building ordered by a sultan outside of Cairo, for most buildings in provincial centers were founded by local figures, either powerful ones or ones out of power who had been "retired" to the provinces to be kept under surveillance.

Three months after the completion of the madrasa, the fountain house to its north-east was rebuilt.[19] Qa'itbay had already ordered extensive repairs to the water-supply system of Mecca, Medina, and Jerusalem, as signs of his sovereignty over the Holy Places, following the example of al-Nasir Muhammad in the early fourteenth century.[20] This charming building [121] is 13.28 meters high and has a small, nearly square (4.60 by 4.80 meters) base supporting a stepped zone of transition, a short drum, and a pointed dome. The arabesque carving of the dome, while quintessentially Egyptian in style, is hardly Egyptian in execution, for it is inconsistent and ambiguous. Compared to the dome over Qa'itbay's tomb, the pattern is poorly adapted to the domical surface and there is no consistent relationship between the rising masonry joints and the vertical axes of the pattern. Given its date and Cairene features, it has been suggested that the fountain was begun by the same team of Egyptian craftsmen who had recently completed the nearby madrasa. As the madrasa had no tomb, and therefore no dome, there had been no need to import a Cairene specialist in dome design from Cairo, and the dome over the fountain is an amateur attempt at a highly specialized job.

122. Cairo, Palace of Amir Yashbak, fourteenth and fifteenth centuries, portal

Religious architecture constitutes the largest group of buildings surviving from the Mamluk period, but an unusually good idea of domestic architecture can also be gleaned from the remarkably large number of surviving buildings, descriptions, and endowment deeds. While none of the royal palaces remains, several residences of the amirs have survived from the late fourteenth century.[21] These are often rambling structures of many stories, as earlier buildings were frequently incorporated by successive owners. They often had shops along the street and stables and service areas on the ground floor. The main reception areas were elevated and surmounted by living quarters which had *mashrabiyya* screens to provide privacy, light, and ventilation. The best-preserved is the palace of Yashbak min Mahdi (d. 1482), located to the west of the complex of Hasan.[22] It was once a princely residence erected for Qawsun, cup-bearer and son-in-law of al-Nasir Muhammad.[23] It eventually passed to Yashbak, the powerful amir who was first secretary, regent of the realm, and commander-in-chief under his crony

Qaʾitbay. No Mamluk before him had amassed so many positions simultaneously. A magnificent portal [122], surpassed only by that of the mosque of Hasan [107], opens to the north-east. A deep porch crowned with an extraordinary muqarnas hood supporting a gadrooned dome was added by Yashbak to the front of Qawsun's already elaborate entry.[24] The earlier entrance had a tall portal worked in bichrome masonry and crowned with a muqarnas hood leading to a square domed vestibule with muqarnas hoods on the axis. The massive vaulted halls on the ground floor served as stables and storerooms and supported the sumptuous reception hall above. It followed the typical form of a large roofed court (Arab. *durqāʿa*), measuring approximately twelve meters on a side, with broad iwans on the longitudinal axis and recesses on the transverse axis. Despite its ruined condition, the importance of this residence can be determined from the quality and size of the pointed horseshoe arches worked in *ablaq* masonry that define its major lines. One has to imagine the splendid marble pavements, carved, painted, and gilded wooden ceiling, central fountain, stained glass windows, and turned wooden grilles which once adorned the interior.

Most of the middle-class population of Cairo lived in more modest multi-unit buildings, where living quarters rented by the month were arranged above commercial structures, such as caravanserais and shops. In general, each apartment was a duplex; the lower floor had a latrine, niche for water jugs, and reception hall, while the upper floor included the sleeping areas. Usually there was no kitchen, for food was bought already prepared.[25] A good example is the urban caravanserai (Arab. *wakāla*) and tenement (Arab. *rabʿ*) of the sultan Qansuh al-Ghawri (r. 1501–17) near al-Azhar. It was an income-producing property for his funerary complex (1503–4), whose two buildings were erected on either side of the *qaṣaba* nearby.[26] A monumental entrance on the north leads to a rectangular court [123], with two stories of storerooms for merchandise behind an arcade. A separate entrance from the street leads to the three stories of triplex apartments above. Similar tenements are known from Cairo, Aleppo, and Damascus, but in general the Cairene examples are higher in proportion to their area, and the street façades have windows in their upper stories. These urban caravanserais were normally organized according to trade and nationality.[27]

While Egypt, Syria, and the Hijaz were under the direct control of the Mamluks, most of the Yemen was governed by the Rasulid dynasty (1229–1454), who descended from an ambassador (Arab. *rasūl*) sent by the Abbasid caliph in the twelfth century. The close relations that the Rasulids maintained with Mamluk Egypt can be seen in their architecture as well as the other arts (see Chapter 8). Sultans and their families, officials, scholars, and mystics commissioned mosques, madrasas, fountain houses, hospices, palaces, and pavilions in Taʿizz, the capital and primary residence of the court, as well as Zabid, Hays, Jibla, Ibb, and other centers. The three buildings to survive from the Rasulid period in Taʿizz were all madrasas, although the Muzaffariyya complex (1249–95) has lost its teaching rooms and appears to be a mosque. The Muʿtabiyya (1392), founded by the wife and mother of sultans, preserves exquisite painted decoration on

123. Cairo, *Wakāla* of al-Ghawri, 1504–5, courtyard

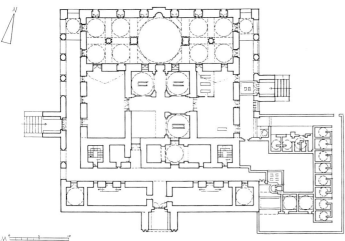

124. Ta'izz, Ashrafiyya Mosque, 1397–1401, plan

the interior,[28] but the largest and most complex is the Ashrafiyya (1397–1401).[29] It is a large square (34.7 by 33.7 meters) with projecting portals on three sides leading to an open-roofed loggia which runs around three sides of an inner square [124]. The inner square, measuring twenty-seven meters to a side, is divided into three zones. The southern one contains two multistoried minarets flanking a domed vestibule and rooms for teaching. In the center is a small square courtyard (ten by eleven meters) flanked by rectangular vaulted halls. One serves as a tomb chamber, and three other tombs covered with lobed domes have been added in the court itself. To the north lies the prayer hall, which, like a typical Rasulid mosque, consists of a large domed bay flanked by two pairs of smaller domed units. The exterior of the qibla wall, which faces the town, is enlivened with superimposed blind arcades and cresting, and much of the interior is sumptuously decorated with carved and painted stucco. The large dome over the prayer hall [125] is supported on muqarnas squinches and a sixteen-sided zone in which eight scalloped niches alternate with eight windows. The cupola itself is decorated with magnificent calligraphic friezes in white and gold around the base and a white calligraphic rosette in the center. The two zones of calligraphy are linked by an exquisite floral arabesque in dark blue, gold, brown, and white. The tomb chambers, although

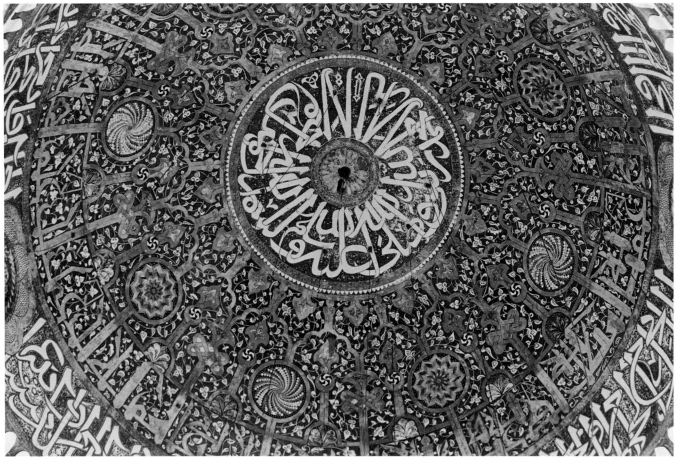

125. Ta'izz, Ashrafiyya Mosque, interior of main dome

less well preserved, were equally decorated with delicately carved and painted stucco and pierced wooden screens.

Mamluk architecture represents the last great flowering of the architectural tradition that had developed in the Arab lands of the eastern Mediterranean since the late tenth century. An important, prolific, and vibrant tradition, it nevertheless had limited impact in succeeding centuries. Unlike the Timurid and early Ottoman styles, which were the foundations for the imperial styles of the period after 1500, Mamluk architecture had a restricted impact outside of Cairo, where traditional formulas were repeated in an uneasy balance with new Ottoman ones (see Chapter 17). Only in the nineteenth century, when the wonders of Mamluk architecture were rediscovered, did it become a source for a new orientalist style, one that was accepted even in the Ottoman capital itself [399].

CHAPTER 8

The Arts in Egypt and Syria under the Mamluks

Architecture was the preeminent art of the Mamluk period and the Mamluks' patronage of architecture defined many of the other arts, which produced fittings and furnishings for their charitable foundations. Such diverse objects as glass lamps, brass candlesticks, paper Koran manuscripts, and wooden minbars can all be understood within the continuous traditions of individual media as well as patronage by an individual or the furnishing of a particular building. Except for manuscripts of the Koran, luxury books were not as important as in the Iranian world, and, other than manuals of horsemanship, illustrated books were rarely enjoyed by members of the court, probably because the Mamluks were of Turkish origin and did not grow up in the Arabic literary culture. Without the model provided by the ruling class, the production of illustrated books never enjoyed widespread commercial popularity, although large numbers of unillustrated histories and chronicles were commissioned. As self-made men, the Mamluks were extremely conscious of their status: elaborate ceremonial punctuated their daily life, and an individual's rank was immediately visible in his dress. Many of the wares produced for the Mamluks therefore were marked with prominent emblems of ownership.

The two greatest periods of Mamluk art coincide with the reigns of al-Nasir Muhammad (1294–1340, with interruptions) and al-Ashraf Qa'itbay (1468–96), when a variety of crafts was patronized by the sultans and their entourages. The period between the two is often considered one of decline, attributable to the ravages of the Black Death and subsequent plagues, mismanagement of the agricultural and commercial sectors, and the growth of European mercantilism. While it was undeniably a period of depopulation and economic upheaval, luxury goods continued to be produced, albeit on a more limited scale as the cost of labor and materials increased. The price of an astrolabe, for example, doubled following the Black Death.[1] Indeed, the most luxurious manuscripts of the Koran and the most sumptuous silk textiles belong to this intermediate period.

The individual media varied in importance over time. Enameled glassware, for example, was produced in the first half of the period, but the industry seems to have died out in the fifteenth century. All known examples of Mamluk carpets, in contrast, are attributed to the very end of the period. Despite the grand tradition of ceramic production in Egypt, ceramics played a relatively minor role, probably because fine Chinese porcelains were easily available. The preeminent medium throughout the period was metalware. Unlike the Iranian world, where royal patrons had silver and gold plate which was later melted down in times of financial crisis, Mamluk patrons had inlaid brasses and bronzes, and large numbers of these pieces have survived.[2] Metal utensils, such as ewers, basins, and candlesticks, played an important role in court ceremonial, and Koran stands and boxes were endowed to charitable foundations. The extraordinary inlaid brasses of the first half of the period generally gave way in the later years to simpler engraved pieces. Throughout the period the designs and motifs developed on metalwares were copied in the other arts. The typical layout of bands of alternating cartouches and roundels, for example, was copied on glass lamps and later used for carpet borders.

Cairo, Damascus, and Aleppo, the principal cities of the Mamluk realm, were important entrepots for trade between the Mediterranean world and the East. The prosperous cities of southern Europe had an apparently insatiable demand for the textiles, spices (particularly pepper and ginger), and drugs available in Mamluk bazaars; these goods were traded for wood, metals (particularly silver and copper), woolens, and eventually glass and paper. The Mediterranean trade is particularly well documented in European archives, but maritime and overland trade with Iran, India, and China was even more extensive. The prosperous dwellers in Mamluk cities were not only merchants but also consumers, who showed a decided taste for oriental fabrics and ceramics, the designs and motifs of which were often incorporated into the local vocabulary. Thus by the middle of the fourteenth century such Chinese motifs as chrysanthemum, peony, and lotus flowers were used to decorate architecture and most of the portable arts.

EARLY PERIOD

The earliest dated example of metalwork produced under Mamluk rule in Egypt is a brass candlestick made by Muhammad b. Hasan al-Mawsuli (from Mosul) at Cairo in 1269–70 [126].[3] It has the typical form of a truncated conical base supporting a cylindrical neck and truncated conical socket, but its profile is distinctively squat. The surface, once impeccably inlaid in silver and gold, is divided into horizontal bands. The largest has roundels containing arabesque friezes around a geometric interlace alternating with concave-ended cartouches containing knotted pseudo-Kufic inscriptions. Above and below are friezes of running animals. The neck is covered with latticework interrupted by five quatrefoils with figures holding tambourines, lutes, and cymbals. These figural compositions are executed with extremely fine detail. The organization of the decoration in horizontal bands of roundels and cartouches, the superb craftsmanship, and the figural compositions follow the earlier style of metalwork made in Mosul and Damascus.[4] This is not surprising since Muhammad b. Hasan identifies himself as al-mawṣulī, "from Mosul," in the inscription on the shoulder.[5]

A great many candlesticks survive from the Mamluk period, and their importance is clear from the descriptions of Mamluk ceremonies preserved by the historian al-Maqrizi. On 7 Jumada I 733/14 January 1334 the sultan al-Nasir Muhammad sat at the palace gate while his amirs approached him according to rank, presenting 3030 candles weighing 3060 qintars (hundredweight) in elaborately decorated candlesticks. The finest were those of Sanjar al-Jawli,

126. Candlestick, Cairo, 1269–70. Brass inlaid with silver and gold. H 22.5 cm; diameter of base 25.0 cm. Cairo, Museum of Islamic Art

128. Baptistère of Saint-Louis, detail showing interior. Paris, Louvre

127. Baptistère of Saint-Louis, Egypt or Syria, 1290–1310. Brass inlaid with silver and gold. H 22.2 cm; diameter 50.2 cm. Paris, Louvre

who had had them made in Damascus. Seven months later on the eve of the marriage of al-Nasir's favourite son Anuk, the amirs again presented candles throughout the night; in the morning the amirs' wives presented their gifts and danced while musicians beat on tambourines.[6] With its decoration of musicians, the candlestick by Muhammad b. Hasan could well have been made for a similar occasion during the reign of Baybars I. This Mamluk candlestick differs from earlier examples in the importance of the inscription band over the figural panels. With a few notable exceptions, this epigraphic style would come to characterize Mamluk metalwork for the next two and a half centuries.

The most notable exception and the most famous example of Mamluk metalwork is a large inlaid basin known as the "Baptistère de Saint-Louis" [127, 128].[7] The name is totally spurious: the basin can have no connection with Louis IX of France, who died well before it was made, and its first recorded use for baptism dates from the seventeenth century. In shape it belongs to a well-known type of basin with incurving sides and flaring rim, such as the D'Arenberg Basin in Washington made for the last Ayyubid sultan.[8] Such basins were used for the ceremonial washing of hands and were usually made in sets with matching ewers [e.g. 136 below].[9] The organization of the decoration on the Baptistère follows the Ayyubid precedent of horizontal registers with roundels alternating with cartouches. It differs from the candlestick and most other pieces of Mamluk metalwork in the absence of epigraphic bands and the total reliance on the extraordinarily detailed and superbly executed figural compositions that cover most of the exterior and interior surfaces. On the exterior, the central band is framed by friezes of varied running animals interrupted by roundels, now filled with fleurs-de-lys. The four cartouches of the main band alternate with four roundels depicting mounted figures. Two wear hats and cloaks and spear a dragon or a bear, while the two in the alternating roundels wear turbans, robes, and boots. One attacks a lion with a sword; the other carries a polo stick. Twenty other figures are depicted in the rectangular panels. They can be similarly divided into two groups on the basis of their dress and facial features: huntsmen or servants, and sword-bearing figures with Mongolian features. The former wear hats and are unarmed; the latter wear turbans and carry swords. The hair of the former hangs free, while that of the latter is tied. The interior of the basin has a similar arrangement alternating roundels and panels between animal friezes. Two of the roundels have been covered with pointed escutcheons, while the other two depict enthroned figures, each flanked by a sword-bearer and secretary. The panels show two hunting scenes and two battle scenes, in which figures wear a third type of headgear. The distinctive physiognomy and dress distinguish three types of figures: indigenous servants and hunters, Mamluk amirs, and Mongol enemies. The base is covered with a fantastic fishpond inhabited by crabs, eels, tortoises, frogs, a lizard, wild duck, pelican, crocodile, and two harpies. The superb craftsmanship, precision of detail, and specificity of figural type make this the masterpiece of all Mamluk and perhaps all Islamic metalwork. The maker was justly proud of his work, for the master (Arab. mu'allim) Muhammad b. al-Zayn signed it in six different places: one formal signature under the rim and five more informal signatures on representations of metal objects and thrones within the scenes.

The basin bears no date or identification of a specific patron, yet the brilliance of the conception, quality of the execution, and specificity of the detail make it impossible to believe that it was made to be sold on the open market. The specificity of the representations led D. S. Rice to identify the bearded figure wearing a short-sleeved tunic and carrying a mace as the amir Salar (d. 1310; see Chapter 6). His boots, unlike those of all the other figures, are decorated with a tripartite circular shield, which corresponds exactly to Salar's emblem: a three-fielded shield of which the central field is black and the other two white. Salar was somewhat of a dandy, and favored a distinctive short-sleeved or sleeveless tunic which was named after him (Arab. qabā' salārī).[10] This identification has led to the conventional dating of the basin (1290–1310). Although it is unlikely that Salar was the intended recipient of the basin, for he would then have been the focus of the decoration, his role as one of the attendant amirs makes it plausible that Salar commissioned it as a gift for the sultan. The specificity of the representations has also led scholars to suggest that the scenes depict actual events and have narrative content, as do works from the contemporary Iranian world.[11] It is far more likely, however, that the images substitute for the laudatory inscriptions that give the names, titles, and attributes of the patron normally found on contemporary Mamluk metalwork. An aniconic basin made for al-Nasir Muhammad [129], for example, has much the same arrangement of panels interrupted by roundels as on Ibn al-Zayn's basin.[12] The roundels, however, bear the sultan's epigraphic emblems and the panels bear the dedicatory inscription: "Glory to our master the sultan, al-Malik al-Nasir, the devout, the warrior, the defender of the faith, nāṣir al-dunyā wa'l-dīn, Muhammad b. Qala'un." Such formulaic inscriptions, which invoke glory and prosperity on the owner, are exactly paralleled by the representations on Ibn al-Zayn's basin, which depict the good Mamluk life.[13] The medallions of enthroned figures are understandable as rulers' emblems; so too must be the hunters and riders. Everything and everybody in Mamluk society was identified by signs and emblems: buildings, metalwork, glassware, ceramics, animals, and people were marked with signs of ownership.

Although the patron of the Baptistère cannot be identified, other work of Ibn al-Zayn can. The Vasselot bowl, a small bowl (diameter 17.2 cm) with figural decoration is signed by him on a tazza carried by a seated amir, just like the informal signatures on the Baptistère.[14] A stunning mirror with personifications of signs of the zodiac is signed "the work of the master Muhammad" (Arab. 'amal al-mu'allim muḥammad), using the same formula as the formal signature on the Baptistère.[15] A unfinished brass basin prepared for silver and gold inlay with figural scenes and animal bands is a virtual twin to the Baptistère and must also be the work of Ibn al-Zayn.[16] The style of Muhammad b. al-Zayn on these pieces is characterized by witty and ingenious figural compositions, fluid draughtsmanship, and impeccable execution, with particular emphasis on facial expressions and details of

129. Basin, Egypt or Syria, ca. 1330. Brass inlaid with silver and gold.
H 22.7 cm; diameter of rim 54.0 cm. London, British Museum

dress. Several other pieces in this style have been attributed to him or his workshop, such as an incense-burner found at Qus.[17]

Production of metalwork at the court of al-Nasir Muhammad was particularly prolific, and nearly thirty pieces are extant that can be assigned to the patronage of the sultan or his amirs. In addition to the basin [129], they include a ewer, lampstand, vase, penbox, Koran box, incense-burner, cylindrical box, and hexagonal stand.[18] They are characterized by an extremely high level of finish, an increased preference for epigraphy over figural decoration, and the incorporation of emblems into the decorative vocabulary. Other typical motifs include a ring of flying ducks and small whirling rosettes. Vegetal motifs include a scroll enclosing three triangular leaves whose veins are delineated by parallel lines. Such chinoiserie motifs as lotus and peony flowers point to increased contact with the arts of the Iranian world. The standard decorative layout consists of registers of cartouches alternating with roundels containing the emblem of the patron: pieces for the sultan are identified by his epigraphic emblem, but those for his amirs bear pictorial emblems, often called blazons. A pear-shaped vase, for example, made for the gentle and pious Tuquztimur, who was cup-bearer to al-Nasir Muhammad and one of his favourite amirs, has a teardrop-shaped shield bearing an eagle with outstretched wings, with a bar above and a cup below.[19]

In addition to objects for court ceremonial, elaborate metal furnishings were also commissioned for Mamluk charitable foundations. These include splendid doors, window-grilles, chandeliers, and boxes for multi-part manuscripts of the Koran. Two such boxes in Cairo and one in Berlin can be dated to the reign of al-Nasir Muhammad, when Koran manuscripts in thirty volumes were first introduced into Egypt.[20] They are square wooden boxes on four short legs [130]; covered with plates of brass, inlaid with silver and gold, bound with bands, and attached to the wooden core with studs, they all measure over forty centimeters to a side and nearly thirty centimeters high. An angular lid is attached with hinges and fastens in front with a hasp. The interior is divided into two compartments, each partitioned to hold fifteen small, slender volumes. All three boxes are decorated with large *thuluth* inscriptions on the body and stylized Kufic inscriptions on the lid against a ground of floral arabesques. Other decorative motifs include rosettes, lotus and peony flowers and, singularly, bunches of grapes on the lid of the example in the Cairo Museum. The artists' signatures are modestly placed under the clasp so that they are invisible when the box is closed. The main inscription on the box from al-Azhar [130] asks God to prolong the reign of al-Nasir Muhammad; the other two are inscribed with well-known Koranic verses. Although the hasp has been replaced on the box in the Cairo Museum, the al-Azhar box was signed by Ahmad b. Bara al-Mawsuli (from Mosul) in 1322–3, and the one in Berlin was made by Muhammad b. Sunqur and inlaid by Hajji Yusuf al-Ghawabi. Five years later Muhammad b. Sunqur also made a large hexagonal taboret.[21] All these pieces represent the finest of Mamluk

130. Chest for a 30-volume manuscript of the Koran, Egypt or Syria, 1322–23. Wood plated with brass inlaid with silver. Cairo, Library of al-Azhar Mosque

metalwork, with the harmonious combination of epigraphic and vegetal motifs highlighted by the contrasting colors of the metals.

Thirty-part manuscripts of the Koran were made in the 1320s for public readings in the khanaqahs patronized by the Mamluk elite. The Moroccan traveler Ibn Battuta, who visited Cairo in 1325, attended a Sufi ritual in a khanaqah and described how copies of Korans in thirty volumes were brought out so that each Sufi could read a section.[22] Perhaps the most remarkable example of a multi-volume manuscript of the Koran commissioned by a Mamluk for his khanaqah is that made for the khanaqah of Baybars al-Jashangir in 1304–6.[23] The manuscript is unusually large (48 by 32 cm) and comprises seven volumes, each with 155 folios, a unique format for Mamluk Koran manuscripts. Such a grand format, totaling well over one thousand folios, was remarkable in its time, and this very manuscript is mentioned in the endowment deed of the khanaqah of Baybars (see Chapter 6), where "a reader of the main Koran [is] in charge of reading from the special Koran consisting of seven parts written in gold and made *waqf* by the founder."[24] The Mamluk historian Ibn Iyas (1448–ca. 1524) also preserves an unusually complete account of this manuscript. "In 705 [1305–6] the *atabeg* Baybars al-Jashankir began to build his khanaqah . . . It is said that when the building was completed, shaykh Sharaf al-Din b. al-Wahid wrote a copy of the Koran in seven parts for the *atabeg* Baybars. It was written on Baghdadi paper in *ash'ar* script. It is said that Baybars spent 1600 dinars on these volumes so that they could be written

in gold. It was placed in the khanaqah and is one of the beauties of the age."[25] A project of this scale had to have been a collaborative effort, and it is no surprise that a team of artists was assembled. The team was headed by the calligrapher Sharaf al-Din Muhammad b. Sharaf b. Yusuf al-Katib al-Zar'i al-Misri, known as Ibn al-Wahid, one of the outstanding practitioners of the art in the early fourteenth century. Born in Damascus in 1249, he trained in Baghdad under Yaqut al-Musta'simi (see Chapter 3) and others, before removing to Cairo, where he died in 1311. Ibn al-Wahid was assisted by three illuminators, the two masters Abu Bakr (known as Sandal) and Muhammad b. Mubadir, and their assistant, Aydughdi b. 'Abdallah al-Badri. The overall design of each volume is the same, showing that the project had a single director. Each volume opens with a double frontispiece [131], containing the number of the volume within an elaborate trellis pattern. The six lines of script on the text pages are written in gold *thuluth* and outlined with a black hair-like line that gives the script its name (*ash'ar*, or "hairs"). Chapter headings are written in red, and marginal markers indicate groups of five and ten verses. The opening pages of each volume are distinguished by four lines of a slightly larger script surrounded by reserve panels on a ground drawn finely in red, arabesques in the case of Sandal and geometric patterns in the case of Ibn Mubadir. The design of the colophon pages in Ibn Mubadir's volumes repeats the opening folios, while those of Sandal differ. The signatures in the colophons allow the work of Sandal and Ibn Mubadir to be distinguished, but it is

131. Left half of the frontispiece to the 7th volume of a manuscript of the Koran, Cairo, 1304–6. 47 × 32 cm. London, British Library, MS. Add. 22412, f. 2r

132. *Hand-washing Machine* from al-Jazari, *Automata*, Egypt or Syria, 1315. 31.4 cm × 21.9 cm. Washington, DC, Freer Gallery of Art

unclear what the contribution of Aydughdi was. He is said to have "illuminated" (Arab. *zammaka*) all the volumes, which may mean that he painted in the gold or polychrome.

Although it stands at the head of a tradition, the Baybars Koran manuscript differs in size, format, and script from all the others produced in the first decades of the fourteenth century.[26] Ten other dated manuscripts, some of which are connected directly with important Mamluks or their intimates, make it possible to delineate the style with precision and examine the individual contributions of calligraphers and illuminators.[27] The likes of the Baybars Koran was not seen for another fifty years, although Sandal and his associates illuminated at least ten other manuscripts of the Koran in the first three decades of the fourteenth century in Cairo. They share many of the decorative motifs found in the Baybars Koran, but they are all single volumes and much smaller in size, averaging some 35 by 26 centimeters, and, with one exception, are written in a robust small or medium *naskh* (cursive) script.

Such features of the Baybars Koran as the unusually large size, rectangular blocks of repeat patterns, the prominence of hexagons and octagons, the borders surrounding each half of a double frontispiece, and the exploding compositions clearly show the impact of manuscripts made in the Ilkhanid domains, particularly those by Yaqut al-Musta'simi and his circle in Baghdad. The impact of Iranian models on Mamluk manuscripts of the Koran has long been recognized, but it was usually attributed to the impact of a single Iranian

manuscript, a thirty-part manuscript of the Koran copied at Hamadan in 1313, which was endowed by an amir of al-Nasir Muhammad to the amir's mausoleum at Cairo in 1326.[28] The investigation of these early Mamluk manuscripts of the Koran shows that calligraphers and illuminators trained in the Baghdad tradition, like other artists, had already migrated to Cairo at the beginning of the fourteenth century. There they worked for wealthy patrons, particularly those Mamluks who were establishing large charitable foundations of the type discussed in Chapter 6. This school of manuscript production appears to have ceased production about 1330, and the following twenty-five years is an obscure period in the production of Koran manuscripts in Cairo, although the followers of Yaqut continued to produce large, multi-volumed, and magnificently illuminated manuscripts of the Koran in such cities of the Iranian world as Baghdad, Shiraz, and possibly Tabriz.

In contrast to the contemporary Iranian world (see Chapter 3), the illustrated book played a minor role in the Mamluk domains, and only about sixty illustrated manuscripts can be ascribed to the period as a whole. Most of them were produced in the late thirteenth century and first half of the fourteenth, although a few point to a revival of illustrated manuscripts at the very end of the Mamluk period.[29] The same types of scientific treatises and works of belles-lettres popular in earlier periods, such as al-Jazari's *Automata*, al-Hariri's *Maqāmāt* ("Assemblies"), and the animal fables *Kalīla and Dimna*, continued to be popular, and the illus-

varying width. Typical motifs include inscriptions, pseudo-inscriptions, and large birds and animals on a vegetal background. Many of these same features appear on jars and albarelli decorated in the cheaper technique of underglaze blue and black on a white slip. The production of luster vessels appears to have ceased in the fifteenth century, either as a result of Timur's destruction of Damascus or, more likely, increased competition from Spain.

The Mamluks inherited a rich tradition of glass manufacturing in Egypt and Syria. Coloristic effects had long been a speciality of glass produced in the region, and the wide range of colored glass used in the Ayyubid period decreased under the Mamluks, when the techniques of enameling and gilding predominated. Decorative elements were outlined in red enamel and filled with white, yellow, green, blue, purple, and pink. The enamel was applied cold and fixed by firing at a low temperature, the same technique used in the production of enameled metalware and ceramics.[50] These techniques, which had been invented earlier, were fully exploited in the thirteenth and fourteenth centuries in glasswares destined for domestic consumption and export. Excavations at such sites as Fustat and Quseir al-Qadim on the Red Sea have produced examples of simple wares intended for domestic use or as shipping containers. Luxury wares have been found in European church treasuries; others were commissioned by the Rasulid sultans of the Yemen, and some are even said to have been found in China, all testifying to the high esteem in which these products were held.[51] Almost any shape could be produced, including goblets, tall bottles, pilgrim flasks, perfume-bottles, vases, footed bowls, and basins, but Mamluk glass-makers are best known for lamps.

The most characteristic type of lamp is about forty centimeters high and has a wide and flaring neck, sloping shoulders with six applied handles, bulbous body, and prominent foot or footring. A small glass container for water and oil with a floating wick would have been inserted inside the lamp, and the lamp itself would have been suspended by chains from the ceiling. Sometimes an egg-shaped object of glass would have held the chains together above the lamp. Thousands of such lamps must have been commissioned to illuminate the mosques and charitable foundations established by the Mamluks. The fifty lamps bearing the name of Hasan, for example, can be only a fraction of the number originally commissioned for the sultan's enormous complex in Cairo. Although Damascus is traditionally considered to have been the preeminent center of glass production, Cairo may also have been important. In general, decorative developments on glasswares follow those of inlaid metal: figural compositions common in the early Mamluk period increasingly gave way to bands of cartouches and roundels filled with inscriptions and arabesques.

The decoration on lamps of Hasan's reign show the full repertory of motifs developed by Mamluk artists. Some pieces have lozenge-shaped panels with floral motifs or

138. Mosque lamp, Egypt or Syria, ca. 1363. Glass, gilded and enameled in green, blue, yellow, red, and white with applied handles. H 40.5 cm. Cairo, Museum of Islamic Art

overall decoration with chinoiserie lotus and peony flowers amidst lush vegetal arabesques, but more typically they have bold inscriptions, such as the Light Verse (Koran 24:35) on the neck and a dedication to the sultan on the upper part of the body [138].[52] The inscription on the neck is written a tall cursive script in blue enamel outlined in red. In contrast, the inscription on the body is written in a thick cursive script in reserve against a blue ground. The letters, which are piled one on top of the other, are outlined in red. When the lamp was lit, the sultan's name and titles would have glowed with divine light, a stunning visual realization of the beautiful Koranic metaphor inscribed above:

> God is the Light of the heavens and the earth;
> the likeness of His Light is as a wick-holder
> [wherein is a light
> (the light in a glass
> the glass as it were a glittering star)].[53]

137. Luster-painted ceramic jar, Damascus, second half of the thirteenth century. H 29 cm. Kuwait, Dar al-Athar al-Islamiyya

139. Damask made into a mantle for a figure of the Virgin, Egypt, early fourteenth century. Silk with gold. L 70.5 cm; W 111.1 cm. Cleveland Museum of Art

In the fifteenth century there was a significant decline in the quality of glass manufactures, although its exact cause, whether plague, deportation of workers, or foreign competition, has yet to be determined. Enameled tablewares, such as goblets and bowls, seem to have gone out of production, and the few surviving lamps suggest that the quality of painting had declined substantially. A European visitor to the Holy Land in 1480 tells how vessels from Murano were sent to Jaffa and Damascus for one of Qa'itbay's functionaries. The Renaissance decorative motifs and the inept inscription on the one enameled lamp from Qa'itbay's foundation in Cairo show that it was of European manufacture.[54]

Despite the esteem in which textiles were held, comparatively few survive from the Mamluk period, probably because textiles are inherently fragile and were cherished to shreds. Those that do survive illustrate the privatization of the textile industry in Egypt over the years of Mamluk rule: the Black Death and recurrent plagues are known to have decimated skilled workers in Alexandria's cloth factory and vitally affected production. The number of weavers in Alexandria is reported to have fallen from about twelve or fourteen thousand in 1394 to eight hundred in 1434. Furthermore, disruptions in trade wrought by the Mongol conquests made Iraqi and Iranian raw materials, particularly dyestuffs, very scarce. Egypt had always been famous for its textiles, particularly tapestry-woven woolens and linens, but loom technology had changed markedly, probably in the thirteenth century, when experienced weavers fleeing either the Mongols in Iraq and Iran or the Christian reconquest of Spain brought the drawloom to Egypt.[55] Apart from the introduction of the drawloom, which was already in use in the fourteenth century,[56] the period is characterized by technological stagnation. European woolens were cheaper and better. The dumping of European textiles, which had begun already at the beginning of the Mamluk period, became a major fact in the economic life of the Near East.[57] It has long been thought that government tiraz factories were the only ones with the potential resources to adapt to new competition, but those of Cairo and Alexandria were closed in the early fifteenth century, and private manufacturers lacked sufficient patronage and risked government confiscation. The closure of the state tiraz factory at Alexandria during the reign of Barsbay, however, did not indicate Egypt's penury and decay; rather production was shifted to Cairo and privatized. The reasons for this are unclear; perhaps it was due to the vulnerability of the Delta to pirates. Mamluk chronicles make it abundantly clear that the sultan continued to distribute precious cloths and imported furs to his subjects until the end of the regime.[58]

The richness of Mamluk silks can be seen in a splendid blue textile with a gilt pattern highlighted with white, which was eventually made into a mantle [139] for a statue of the Virgin in Spain. The ground is satin and the pattern worked in plain-weave with gilt membrane wrapped around silk thread. The complex ogival layout is composed of large peony blossoms and small eight-lobed medallions on a vine trellis which frames tear-shaped lotus blossoms. The lotuses have Arabic inscriptions in mirror reverse; the medallions are inscribed in a horizontal band. A related textile in London has the same pattern in green and the medallions are inscribed with the title *al-ashrāf*.[59] This pattern was depicted ca. 1430 in an *Enthroned Madonna with Saints* by the Master of the Bambino Vispo, suggesting that the textile dates to the reign of al-Ashraf Barsbay (r. 1422–37).[60] The ogival patterns on Mamluk silks were undoubtedly inspired by those on Yüan silks, which were highly prized in Islamic lands, but it is still unclear whether these ogival patterns on Chinese textiles were themselves made specifically to cater to the taste of the Islamic world. In any event, the delicate and naturalistic patterns of Chinese originals were transformed into bold and abstract ones in the Mamluk derivations. In addition to ogival patterns, striped silks became increasingly popular in Mamluk times, and their prestige led them to be copied in textiles produced under the Nasrids in Spain (see Chapter 9).

Reasonably fine examples of Koran manuscripts were produced at the turn of the fifteenth century, but then the quality of illumination suffered a marked change for the worse, although calligraphy remained fine. Illumination was heavily dependent on earlier styles; the palette was more limited, pigments declined in quality, and colors became muddy, chipped, and easily faded. All this was probably the result of the high cost of imported materials. The shortage of materials also seems to have affected the production of metalwork, for few pieces have survived and those that do are of beaten brass. Openwork revetments for wooden doors replaced cast bronze or brass plaques (see Chapter 7). The contemporary historian al-Maqrizi lamented the absence of metalworkers in the markets, and numismatic evidence attests to the shortage of silver and copper.[61] The shortage of silver in Egypt may have been the result of increased demand for it in Italy, and henceforth copper falus and dirhams were the principal currency. The currency was devalued and inflation rampant.

140. Candlestick, Cairo, 1482–3. Engraved brass. H 48 cm, diameter of base 40.0 cm. Cairo, Museum of Islamic Art

LATE PERIOD

Many of the economic problems of the first half of the fifteenth century were overcome during the long and prosperous reign of Qa'itbay, who promoted the economic interests of his realm and was well disposed to international trade. His financial resources, however, were swallowed up by the almost incessant wars he was forced to fight with his neighbors to the north, the Aqqoyunlu Turkoman and the Ottomans. Under Qa'itbay there was a distinct revival in many of the arts, including metalwork, manuscript illumination, and carpet-weaving. In metalwork, such types and techniques as brasses and inlaid pieces, which had not been produced for some fifty years, were revived, perhaps spurred by the sultan's need for prestigious furnishings for the holy shrines of Arabia.[62]

Five candlesticks made for the Prophet's tomb in Medina have survived.[63] They are of traditional form [140] with a truncated conical base, cylindrical neck, and tapering socket; the whole measures just under fifty centimeters high. The organization of the decoration is traditional, with horizontal bands interrupted by large medallions bearing the sultan's epigraphic emblem. The traditional inlay, however, has been replaced by engraving and the addition of a black bituminous paste in the sunken areas to contrast with the polished brass. Apart from some narrow bands of foliage, the decoration is entirely epigraphic and written in a distinctive script, in which the pairs of vertical shafts of the thick *thuluth* letters rise up and cross each other to form pincers enclosing lotus buds. Pincer-topped *thuluth* is a characteristic feature of metalwork made for Qa'itbay.[64] Although many of the pieces inscribed with his name are only incised, a few of the finest are inlaid with gold and silver, showing that Egyptian craftsmen could still equal the quality of work produced a century and a half earlier. A large lobed brass bowl inlaid with silver and gold is perhaps the finest piece surviving from the period [142].[65] There are several other bowls of similar shape with faceted sides and engraved and inlaid decoration attributable to the period.[66]

A magnificent minbar in London [141] bears inscriptions

141. Minbar, Egypt, ca. 1470. Wood with carved ivory insets. H 7.3 cm. London, Victoria and Albert Museum

with the name of Qa'itbay on the entrance and on the backs of the doors.[67] It was presumably made for Qa'itbay's madrasa at Qal'at al-Kabsh in Cairo (1468–9), but it may have come from another foundation, for the sultan was a prolific builder and restorer of religious monuments, and an unusually large number of minbars and religious furnishings

survive from his reign. Most minbars, including the one made for his funerary complex [116–18] in Cairo, were made of wood, but several were also of marble, such as the one sent to Medina after the fire of 1481, or stone, such as the one prepared in 1483 for the complex of Faraj b. Barquq in the Northern Cemetery of Cairo. Fine wooden minbars had been produced in Cairo throughout the fifteenth century, and woodcarvers were accorded high status. The career of Ahmad b. 'Isa, for example, is particularly long: around 1446 he signed the minbar made for the Mosque of al-Ghamri, which was later transferred to the complex of al-Ashraf Barsbay, and nearly thirty years later (879/ 1474), at Qa'itbay's request, Ahmad made a high wooden minbar for the Masjid al-Haram in Mecca.[68] In 1480–1 Ahmad also signed a minbar made for the madrasa of Abu Bakr b. Muzhir in Cairo. Minbars of the period have the triangular shape, elaborate portal, and speaker's seat that had been typical for centuries, but they are distinguished by the projecting muqarnas cornice over the portal and the bulbous dome over the seat.

The London minbar is remarkable for its superb condition. The frame, which divides the surface into several architectural panels, is composed of large planks decorated with scrolls in shallow relief. The triangular flanks are decorated with a pattern of grooved strapwork radiating from sixteen-pointed stars; the intersticial star-shaped and polygonal fields are filled with ivory panels delicately carved with arabesques and inlaid into wood. Similar panels from either a door or minbar are preserved in New York.[69] The balustrades and the vertical panels below the seat are filled with similar strapwork patterns on a smaller scale. The juxtaposition of the bold geometric patterns of the strapwork and the minute arabesque carving of the ivory inlays makes this piece visually striking from near as well as far. The sheer size of this and similar minbars forced designers to adopt architectural solutions for the overall conception, but the minute detail of the carving relates it to the other decorative arts of the period. Inlaid wooden minbars had already been made under the Ayyubids, but under the Mamluks, ivory was added to the varicolored woods, such as ebony and redwood, used for inlays. By the late Mamluk period, ivory seems to have become too expensive for all but the most elevated patrons; in a minbar made in 1480–1 for Qajmas al-Ishaqi, one of Qa'itbay's amirs, it is replaced by bone.[70] Typical compositions were based on strapwork radiating from a central star and are comparable to the astral designs on the frontispieces to earlier manuscripts of the Koran [131, 135].

Historical and religious manuscripts and manuals are known to have been made for Qa'itbay, but the finest are manuscripts of the Koran and of *Al-kawākib al-durriyya* ("The pearly stars"), also called *Qasīdat al-burda* ("Ode to the mantle"), a laudatory poem composed by al-Busiri (d. 1296). The poem concerns the incident when the Prophet Muhammad placed his mantle on the shoulders of Ka'b b. Zuhayr, a poet who had composed an ode in praise of Muhammad and recited it to him. No other Arabic poem attained such renown, and it became traditional in the Mamluk period to embellish the text with a *takhmis* (lit. "making of five"), a poetic form in which each line of the

142. Bowl, Cairo, last quarter of the fifteenth century. Brass inlaid with silver and gold. Istanbul, Türk ve Islam Eserleri Müzesi

143. Double frontispiece from al-Busiri, *al-Kawākib al-durriyya*, Cairo, ca. 1470. 40.5 × 30 cm. Dublin, Chester Beatty Library, MS. 4168, ff. 1v–2r

text was elaborated with four rhyming lines of commentary. Busiri's text was copied in a large hand in one color; the four additional lines were usually copied in smaller scripts in other colors, such as red, blue, green, and gold. An example in Dublin [143] exemplifies the art of illumination under

144. Carpet, Cairo, late 15th century. Wool with red, green, blue pile.
1.86 × 1.37 m. Washington, DC, Textile Museum

Qa'itbay. Although undated, an identical manuscript, also in Dublin, was made for Qa'itbay's crony Yashbak min Mahdi (see Chapter 7) in 1472–3.[71] The double-page frontispiece of the Qa'itbay manuscript shows how manuscript illumination had changed since the late fourteenth century: the typical astral panel in the center has been replaced by large lobed medallions bearing the name of the sultan (right) and a blessing on him (left). The traditional tripartite arrangement has been maintained, but the design has been simplified, with fewer border bands and less contrast between the size of panels, although there is greater contrast between epigraphic and arabesque motifs. The restricted palette comprises somewhat muddy tones of red, blue, green, and dull gold. The poor colors are typical of late-fifteenth-century work.

One of the most distinctive products associated with the patronage of the later Mamluks is the knotted carpet, and a group of several dozen carpets with a distinct technical structure and design are commonly called "Mamluk."[72] They are all wool, with the exception of one stunning example in silk.[73] They have S-spun warps, usually three or four plied with a Z twist; alternate warps are depressed. The asymmetrical knots are open to the left, normally with three weft passes between rows of knots. The traditional palette includes a lac-dyed red, rich blue, and green, to which yellow and ivory are occasionally added. The design is always based on a field of one or more large octagonal motifs within a border of alternating cartouches and roundels. Typical smaller carpets (2.0 by 1.5 meters) have a field with a single octagon flanked by two narrow rectangular strips; larger carpets (up to 11 by 4 meters) have three or uniquely five octagons in a line filling the field.[74] Filler motifs, such as octagons, hexagons, triangles, umbrella-shaped leaves, cypress trees, and cups, create a dense, almost kaleidoscopic effect [144].

The localization of these "Mamluk" carpets has been a matter of lively scholarly debate, and at one time or another they have been assigned to Damascus, Rhodes, Syracuse, Spain, Cairo, and the Maghrib, but Cairo seems the most likely. Historical sources show that already by the fourteenth century carpets were used in Cairo and made there. For example, when the palace of the wealthy amir and sugar industrialist Sayf al-Din Qawsun was pillaged in 1341, the booty included carpets from Anatolia, Diyarbakir, Shiraz, sixteen pairs from the royal factories at Cairo, and four pairs of priceless silk carpets.[75] In 1474 the Venetian traveler Giuseppe Barbaro mentioned that the carpets produced in Cairo were inferior to those of Tabriz. Two Mamluk carpets, furthermore, bear emblems directly associated with amirs in the court of Qa'itbay. Production of Mamluk carpets in the fifteenth century may have been encouraged by virtually continuous warfare in eastern Anatolia, where the domains of the Ottomans, Mamluks, and Aqqoyunlu Turkoman converged: this was a major center of carpet production, and workmen may have emigrated to the safer haven of Cairo. Another reason for attributing these carpets to Egypt is that Italian inventories of the sixteenth century refer to them as "Cairino." Finally, Cairo continued to be an important center of carpet manufacture in the sixteenth century, for in 1585 the Ottoman sultan Murad III ordered eleven weavers from Cairo to move to the court in Istanbul, bringing with them almost two tons of dyed wool. Three other types of carpets technically related to the "Mamluk" group, "Para-Mamluks," "Chessboard," and "Ottoman Court," may have been produced virtually anywhere in the eastern Mediterranean during the sixteenth century (see Chapter 16).

Architecture and the Arts in the Maghrib under the Hafsids, Marinids, and Nasrids

The collapse of the Almohad empire following its catastrophic defeat in 1212 at Las Navas de Tolosa led to the emergence of four regional powers in the Maghrib: three rival Berber dynasties in North Africa – the Hafsids of Tunis (1235–1554), the 'Abd al-Wadids or Zayyanids of Tlemcen (1236–1554), and the Marinids and Wattasids of Fez (1229–1549) – and the Nasrids of Granada (1230–1492) in southern Spain. Power in North Africa was balanced between the Hafsids in the east and the Marinids in the west, for both claimed to be the rightful heirs of the Almohads. The 'Abd al-Wadids were often caught between their more powerful neighbors and had hardly the opportunity or the money to be major patrons of the arts. The Muslim cities of Spain, such as Córdoba and Seville, fell to the Christians following the Almohad retreat to North Africa, but the mountainous province of Granada came under the control of the Nasrids, who tried to maintain a balance between their powerful neighbors, Christians to the north and Muslims to the South.

The arts of this period in North Africa are best-known through religious buildings and their fittings, not only because court life was less splendid than in Granada, but also because, in the usual fashion, charitable endowments ensured the perpetual upkeep of religious foundations while buildings for secular purposes were often abandoned by succeeding patrons. In Spain, by contrast, succeeding generations destroyed virtually all evidence for the arts associated with the Muslim faith, and knowledge about the arts of this period there rests mainly on monuments identified with the splendid court life. The palaces and furnishings of the Nasrid court were easily adopted by the international culture of princes, appealing to Muslims and Christians alike.

THE HAFSIDS

The Hafsids took their name from Shaykh Abu Hafs 'Umar (d. 1176), a disciple of the founder of the Almohads, whose descendants served as governors in the province of Ifriqiya (modern Tunisia). One of them, Abu Zakariya Yahya I (r. 1228–49), declared his independence and established his capital at Tunis. Under the Hafsids, Kairouan, the traditional capital, lost its political preeminence, and such coastal cities as Tunis, Sousse, and Sfax were reinvigorated by trade and diplomatic relations which flourished across the Mediterranean. The population was swelled by the influx of refugees from Spain, who brought many of their artistic traditions with them and made Tunis a great artistic and intellectual center. The close relations the Hafsids maintained with the Mamluks of Egypt brought artistic ideas from the eastern Islamic lands as well, and Hafsid art represents a meeting of east and west.

The Mosque of the Qasba in Tunis (1231–5) was begun several years before the Hafsid governor declared his independence from the Almohads. The building stands squarely in the long tradition of Islamic architecture in the region, with stone construction and a prayer hall roofed with groin vaults resting on columns. The new impact of decorative features from further west, whether Morocco or Spain, can be seen in the muqarnas and the elaborately carved stucco used in the dome over the bay in front of the mihrab. The square stone minaret [145], which is decorated with lozenge-net panels and crowned by a lantern roofed with a pyramid of green tiles, is distinctly Almohad in inspiration and evidently another import from the west. The closest parallel is the minaret of the Mosque of the Qasba in Marrakesh, built some fifty years before.[1]

Although Kairouan, once capital of the Muslim west, had been relegated to a provincial city, the Hafsids refurbished its congregational mosque in recognition of its revered status as one of the oldest mosques in Islam. They reconstructed the galleries surrounding the courtyard and remodeled some of the portals. The Bab Lalla Rihana [146] on the east was constructed on the order of Abu Hafs 'Umar in 1294. Known after a local female saint buried nearby, it is a projecting rectangular pavilion covered with a fluted dome. The general form and technique of construction are undoubtedly inspired by the projecting portal at the mosque in the nearby coastal town of Mahdiya (917),[2] but the blind arcading, crowning merlons, and carved plaster arabesques on the soffits of the arches are again derived from Hispano-Moresque models.

In addition to constructing mosques, the Hafsids were also responsible for introducing the madrasa into the Maghrib.[3] Established under official or private sponsorship in the Islamic east in the eleventh and twelfth centuries to combat the spread of heterodoxy and strengthen orthodoxy, these theological colleges had become particularly popular in the central and eastern Islamic lands when housing the mausoleum of the founder, thereby combining pious works with the perpetuation of the patron's name. In the Islamic west, however, the funerary madrasa was almost unknown, for according to Maliki law, which was prevalent there, an individual was prohibited from appointing himself administrator of a pious endowment. Most Maghribi madrasas were consequently sponsored by the government, for only the ruler could afford to spend such large sums for purely spiritual rewards.

145. Tunis, Qasba Mosque, Minaret, March 1233

146. Kairouan, Great Mosque, Bab Lalla Rihana, 1294

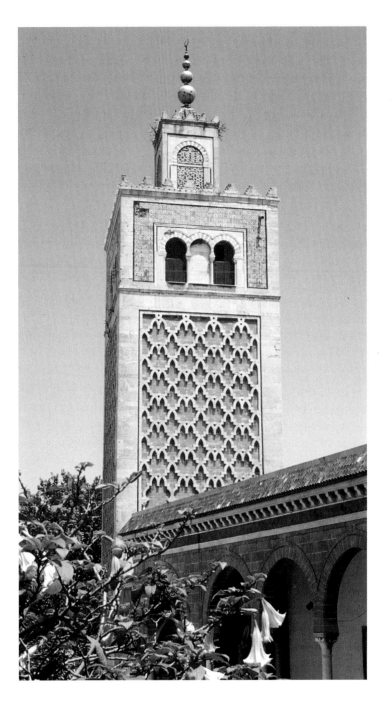

The first person to introduce the madrasa in the Islamic west was the founder of the Hafsid dynasty, Abu Zakariya Yahya, who established the Shamma'iyya madrasa at Tunis in 1249. It was a simple urban house reworked to accommodate students and offer them a place of instruction and prayer. Other madrasas, such as the Muntasiriyya, begun by the caliph al-Muntasir (r. 1434–5), were built expressly for the purpose. It had a modified four-iwan plan, which was undoubtedly adopted from eastern models, probably those of Mamluk Egypt (see Chapter 6), with which the Hafsids maintained close relations. All of these buildings have been so transformed by restoration, particularly in the seventeenth century, that much of their original aspect is obscured.

The Hafsids' claim to be champions of the faith can be seen not only in buildings they commissioned but also in objects. A good example is a five-volume manuscript of the Koran [147, 148], which was endowed to the Mosque of the Qasba in Tunis in March 1405 during the reign of al-Mutawakkil (r. 1394–1434).[4] The manuscript was copied on small folios (24 × 16 cm); the paper was dyed in a range of colors from light brown to purple. Each page has thirteen lines penned in silver ink with gold chapter headings, verse markers, and marginal illumination. The script used is a typical Maghribi hand, which is distinguished from eastern Islamic scripts by the uniform thickness of the ductus, the rounded bowls of the descenders, and the peculiar dotting of the letters *fā'* and *qāf*. This script had developed in the western Islamic lands during the eleventh century as a

147. Page from a 5-volume manuscript of the Koran, Tunis, ca. 1405. 24.2 × 15.8 cm. Paris, Bibliothèque nationale, MS. Arabe 392, f. 25v

148. Binding to a 5-volume manuscript of the Koran, Tunis, ca. 1405. Blind-tooled leather. Paris, Bibliothèque nationale, MS. Arabe 392

regional variant of the new style of calligraphy favored in the eastern Islamic lands. The manuscript is unusual in several ways. It is an early example of a Maghribi manuscript of the Koran written on paper, for in the Islamic west parchment continued to be used for copying the Koran long after it had been supplanted by paper in the Islamic east. Its format is vertical, while most earlier manuscripts of the Koran in Maghribi script tend to have a square format. Finally its color scheme of silver and gold on tinted paper recalls one of the most famous early Koran manuscripts from the Maghrib, the so-called Blue Koran. Produced at Kairouan in the middle of the tenth century, it was a seven-volume set with gold writing on parchment dyed a deep blue.[5] According to an early Hafsid document, the Blue Koran was in the library of the Great Mosque of Kairouan ca. 1300, and its unusual color scheme might well have provided the model for the Hafsid manuscript a century later.[6]

The binding of the Hafsid manuscript is made of blind-tooled leather. The spine connecting the upper and lower covers is modern, but the rest, including the foredge flap, is original. The upper flap has a carpet format, with several borders enclosing a rectangular field with a central octagram. The central star and the borders are filled with a braided pattern created by blind tooling. The lower and foredge flaps have the same format, but the field is entirely filled with the braided pattern. The use of blind tooling, the central octagram, and the braided pattern are all features found on earlier bindings in the library of the mosque at Kairouan, but in order to adapt the traditional elements of a squarer binding to the rectangular shape of these volumes, corner-pieces have been added to create the carpet format already standard in the Islamic east.[7]

THE MARINIDS

After the Almohads were defeated at Las Navas in 1212, they withdrew to North Africa, but their rule there lasted only for a few years, as the Marinids, a tribe of nomadic Zenata Berbers, began to invade Morocco from the Sahara in 1216. They took the Almohad capital of Marrakesh in 1269 and relegated it to second place after the foundation of their new capital, Fas al-Jadid (New Fez), on 21 March 1276. Marinid history falls into two periods. The first, from 1269 to 1358, is marked by military exploits, urban expansion, and government stability. Most of the major Marinid foundations date from this period. The second, from 1358 to 1465, is a period of slow erosion of the political structure, territorial regression, and internal division. The material prosperity of the Marinid state was based on agriculture, urban industry, and trade, particularly the gold trade with Mali. This prosperity and the image that the Marinids adopted as successors to the Almohads and champions of Maghribi Islam explain the large number of their pious foundations, many of which have survived intact, unlike those of their Hafsid rivals.

One of the first Marinid building projects (1294) was the enlargement of the congregational mosque of Taza, which had been founded by the Almohads in 1142. This eastern Moroccan town had long been of strategic importance, as it commanded the gap between the Rif mountains and the

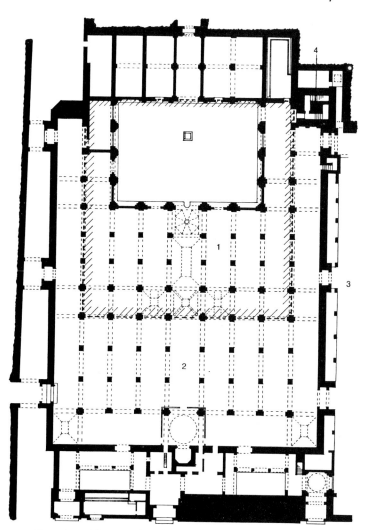

149. Taza, Great Mosque, enlarged 1294, plan: 1) original mosque (shaded); 2) extension; 3) side court; 4) minaret

Middle Atlas, thereby controlling the major artery between Morocco and points east. One of the first towns taken by the Marinids, Taza became a base for their expansion throughout Morocco. Once in control, they lavished special attention on this provincial town, rebuilding the fortifications, endowing madrasas and a hospital, and, most importantly, enlarging the congregational mosque. According to an inscription there, the sultan Abu Ya'qub Yusuf (r. 1286–1307) expanded it by four bays (Arab. *balāt*) in the direction of the qibla and two more bays on the east and the west [149], thereby doubling the area of the prayer hall.[8] The Marinid additions are clearly distinguishable from the Almohad originals on the interior by the greater width of the arches and their rounder horseshoe shape and on the exterior by a distinct break in the gabled tile roofs. The Marinids also added an enormous new court to the east of the mosque, which is virtually the same size as the mosque itself, some 72 by 44 meters. Like the expansion of the Great Mosque of Córdoba in the ninth and tenth centuries, the enlargement of the mosque testifies to the growth of the town's population and its increased importance under the Marinids.[9]

Following Almohad tradition, the aisle in front of the qibla wall in the mosque at Taza is punctuated by three vaulted units: wooden vaults in the corners flank a superb pierced plaster vault in front of the mihrab [150], itself elaborately carved in stucco. Supported by lambrequin arches, the bay is entirely revetted in intricately carved plaster. An eight-sided zone of transition, with muqarnas squinches alternating with triangular windows which repeat the shape of the squinch, supports the sixteen-sided cupola. The cupola itself is formed of thirty-two ribs which interlace to form a star in the center. The space between the ribs is filled with pierced arabesque and epigraphic decoration on several levels. The elaborate ribbed dome in the bay in front of the mihrab is a North African feature which can be traced back to the tenth-century restorations to the mosque at Córdoba, but the immediate prototype was the Almohad dome in the Great Mosque of Tlemcen dated 1136.[10] To the right of the mihrab at Taza is a closet for the wooden minbar, which in North Africa was usually rolled out of storage when needed for the Friday sermon. The minbar follows the classic Almoravid form, with marquetry decoration made of precious woods and ivory and assembled in octagonal patterns exactly coordinated to the risers of the stairs.[11]

In the center of the prayer hall, the three bays in front of and flanking the old mihrab were marked on the exterior by pyramidal roofs and on the interior by lambrequin arches and elaborate decoration in carved stucco. An enormous bronze chandelier (diameter 2.5 meters) [151] is suspended from the bay in the center. Composed of nine circular tiers of diminishing size arranged like a wedding-cake, it could hold 514 glass oil lamps and is the largest extant example of a type of chandelier found throughout North Africa. Its arabesque and epigraphic ornament is pierced and engraved with great delicacy, and the underside is decorated with sixteen intersecting ribs which repeat the design of the dome in front of the mihrab. A poem inscribed on the interior states that it was offered to the mosque by Abu Ya'qub in AH 694 (1294). According to a medieval account, the chandelier cost eight thousand dinars to make and weighed 32 qintars. The minbar and the chandelier are the most spectacular of the contemporary furnishings preserved in the mosque, which also include several other lamps and an 'anaza, or wooden screen in the form of a mihrab, placed on the court façade of the prayer hall.

The importance of Taza lay in its position controlling access to and from Tlemcen, the capital of the 'Abd al-Wadids or Zayyanids, another Berber dynasty, related to but usually in conflict with the Marinids.[12] The Marinid sultan Abu Ya'qub attacked Tlemcen four times and laid siege to the city for eight years, establishing a fortified camp to its west. Known as *al-maḥalla al-manṣūra* (the victorious camp) or more simply Mansura, it contained baths, caravanserais, a hospital, and a congregational mosque within its four kilometers of walls. All that survives are the ruins of the mosque built in 1303; its pisé walls measure 60 by 85 meters. In plan, it hearkens back to such Almohad congregational mosques as the one at Rabat,[13] also built to serve a large army garrison. Several stone portals give access to the interior, which had a square court surrounded by arcades. The prayer hall had thirteen aisles of six bays perpendicular to the qibla wall, with three additional aisles parallel to it, all

150. Taza, Great Mosque, dome over mihrab, 1291–94

151. Taza, Great Mosque, bronze chandelier, 1294

carried on onyx columns. The nine bays in front of and surrounding the mihrab formed a large (fourteen-meter) square, whose piers must have supported a dome or pyramidal wooden roof. Opposite the mihrab stands the minaret, thirty-eight meters high and ten meters to a side [152]. Built of dressed stone, like the portals, the tower would have been crowned with a cubic domed lantern, but half of its exterior and all of the interior has fallen. Relief carving and string-courses divide the exterior into four stories of unequal height. The lowest, which contains the principal entrance to the mosque, is particularly elaborate. Concentric arches are set within an inscribed rectangular frame, the whole decorated with arabesques and interlaced and cusped arches. The light blue tile insets that heighten the design are an unusual feature in stone construction. Shell motifs carved in high relief are set in the spandrels. The whole arrangement derives from such Almohad models as the Oudaia Gate at Rabat.[14] Above the portal is a series of muqarnas corbels which may have supported a balcony or awning. The second story is relatively plain, with windows or blind arches within larger lambrequin frames. The tall third story is covered with lozenge-net panels, while the fourth has cusped-arch arcades, much like the earlier minaret at the congregational mosque of Tlemcen. Although many of the individual features have precedents in Almohad minarets, the overall conception is more harmonious, making this, even in its ruined state, one of the most pleasing monuments built by the Marinids.

Abu Ya'qub's siege of Tlemcen was unsuccessful; he was assassinated in 1307, and work on Mansura was left unfinished. Three decades later his grandson, Abu'l-Hasan 'Ali (r. 1331–48), finally took Tlemcen and incorporated it into the Marinid domains. The mosque at Mansura was apparently finished at this time (the foundation inscription on the minaret refers to Abu Ya'qub as deceased), and the congregational mosque in Tlemcen itself was restored. The most spectacular of Abu'l-Hasan's works in the area, however, is the shrine complex perched on the northern slope of Mafrush Mountain in the village of al-'Ubbad, two kilometers east of Tlemcen. The shrine centers around the grave of the well-known Andalusian mystic Abu Madyan Shu'ayb (d. 1197), known popularly as Sidi Bu Medine. Soon after his death, during the reign of the Almohad ruler Muhammad al-Nasir (1199–1214), the mystic's grave was marked by a tomb, but only under the Marinids in the fourteenth century was it converted into a shrine complex, which included a residence, mosque, ablution facility, and madrasa. The mystic's tomb, heavily restored in the eighteenth century, is a small square covered by a tiled pyramidal roof; the forecourt (5.4 meters square) is a tetrastyle atrium whose onyx columns and capitals were brought from Mansura. Below the tomb is a ruined multi-room structure which may have served as a residence for rich pilgrims.

A narrow court separates the tomb from the congregational mosque, built on the site of a garden purchased by the Marinid sultan for the new construction. The glory of the mosque is its extraordinarily richly decorated portal [153], although the constricted approach makes it somewhat difficult to appreciate. The portal is laid out in much the same

152. Tlemcen, Mosque at Mansura, begun 1303, minaret and portal

way as the lower story of the minaret at Mansura, with concentric, cusped arches set within a rectangular frame, but the cusped arches and frame are worked in brick inset with pieces of glazed tile, and their matte surface contrasts with the tile mosaic covering the rest of the portal. Known in North Africa as *zallīj*, the tile mosaic is laid out in arabesque patterns in light blue, brown, and black set against a white ground. The portal is crowned with an inscription band mentioning the patron of the mosque, Abu'l-Hasan ʿAli, and the date 739 (1338–9). A flight of eleven steps leads to an elaborately decorated vestibule [154]. Above a plain dado, the sides are revetted with carved stucco panels of blind arches filled with vegetal ornament and cartouches filled with inscriptions set on an arabesque ground. The ceiling is covered by a stunning muqarnas vault. These matte surfaces contrast with the tile mosaic on the intrados and back side of the portal. Doors on the sides give access to small rooms for a Koran school and shelter for pilgrims, and magnificent bronze doors at the head of the stairs open to the interior.

The mosque is a small rectangle (19 by 29 meters), with the standard arrangement of a court surrounded by arcades and a prayer hall with five aisles perpendicular to the qibla.

153. Tlemcen, Mosque of Abu Madyan, portal, 1338–9

154. Tlemcen, Mosque of Abu Madyan, vestibule

155. Tlemcen, Complex of Abu Madyan, Madrasa, 1346, view of courtyard

The arcades in the prayer hall stop one bay short of the qibla wall, and the bay in front of the mihrab is covered by a stucco dome. Above a plain dado, most of the interior surfaces are revetted in richly carved stucco. A minaret (27.5 meters high) decorated with lozenge-net panels soars above the north-west corner of the court. Inscriptions throughout the mosque invoke God's help and show that the building was intended as a monument to commemorate the sultan's taking of Tlemcen two years earlier.

To the east of the mosque across a small alley lies the ablution facility, with well-preserved latrines and baths. The madrasa lies on the west side at the top of the hill. Like the mosque, it has an elaborate tiled façade, which is reached by a flight of steps on the north-east. A block of latrines projects from the north-west corner. The doorway opens to a court surrounded by arcades [155]. The lateral sides have small cells (2.85 by 2 meters) for the students, twelve on the ground floor and twelve more on the upper story, accessible by a stair to the left of the entrance. In the south-east corner of the ground floor is a suite of four additional cells, probably for the teacher. Opposite the entrance, the square prayer hall is covered by a wooden dome whose base is inscribed with a poem lauding the patron, Abu'l-Hasan 'Ali, and giving the date Rabi' II 747 (July–August 1346). This date,

eight years after the foundation of the mosque, may mark the completion of the work. A marble slab encased in the column to the left of the mihrab enumerates the gardens, orchards, houses, windmills, baths, and land bought by the sultan and endowed to the madrasa and mosque.

Constructed in brick, the buildings at 'Ubbad are richly decorated in the techniques and styles typical of Marinid architecture: glazed tile is played off against stucco, and wood, more abundant than in many other areas of the Islamic world, is used for awnings, ceilings, and vaults. The high level of patronage allowed for particularly lavish fittings, such as the bronze doors to the mosque and the onyx columns and capitals. The remarkable state of preservation gives a good sense of how the complex was used by residents and visitors. The rural site allowed for the construction of separate buildings, of which the madrasa was clearly one of the most important. It was almost as large in area as the mosque, and it remained an important center for instruction in the Maghrib.[15]

Madrasas were a particularly significant focus of Marinid patronage, for they were erected to combat both the apparent heresy of the Almohads and the decentralizing tendencies inherent in the Sufism that had helped bring the Marinids to power. Notable examples remain in Meknes, Marrakesh,

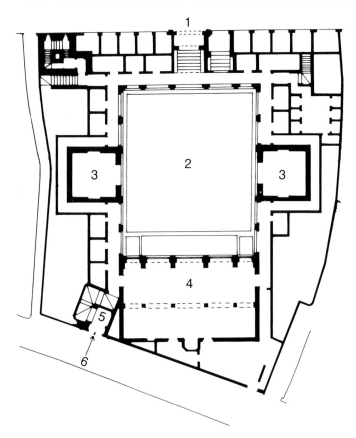

and Salé, but the largest number are still found in Fez.[16] The most elaborate there is the Bu 'Inaniya madrasa [156], built between 1350 and 1355 for the sultan Abu 'Inan Faris (r. 1348–59). Set on a trapezoidal site between two branches of the main artery that connect New Fez with the heart of the old city, the complex also straddles a channel of the Wadi Fez. The principal street façade is lined with shops, which provided income for the foundation, and its right end is a tall minaret, from which one could see all the other minarets of the city. It is the only madrasa in Fez with a minaret, indicating from afar the additional function of the complex as a congregational mosque. On the other side of the street is an extensive latrine, whose size indicates that it was intended for public use. Its façade preserves the remains of an extraordinary water-clock, with thirteen consoles, some of which still support bronze bowls which were rung to mark the hours. This unique device, built by Abu Sa'id (r. 1310–31) in 1317 and restored by Abu 'Inan Faris, was a mechanical wonder in its day.

The entrance to the Bu 'Inaniya madrasa lies in the center

156. Fez, Bu 'Inaniya Madrasa, 1350–55, plan: 1) Main entrance;
2) Courtyard; 3) Halls; 4) Mosque; 5) Minaret; 6) Back entrance

157. Fez, Bu 'Inaniya Madrasa, courtyard

of the principal façade and is marked by an arched bridge connecting the two buildings. A stair roofed with an elaborate wooden muqarnas vault gives access to a large paved court [157]. On the sides, lambrequin arches led to two-story square (five-meter) halls surmounted by wooden domes. These halls, intended for instruction, recall the lateral iwans in madrasas of the east. On the fourth side of the court and separated from it by the channel of the Wadi Fez stands the prayer hall. It has two aisles parallel to the qibla separated by four onyx columns. Each aisle is covered by an elaborate wooden vault, decorated with complex star patterns. Narrow corridors and staircases lead from the entrance vestibule to the cells for students, some of which have small windows overlooking the court. The Bu 'Inaniya madrasa is remarkable for its size, integration of diverse elements into a harmonious plan, and lavish decoration, although the details are somewhat less inventive than in earlier Marinid madrasas. Nevertheless, the decorative formula developed by the Marinids, with tile mosaic dadoes surmounted by carved plaster walls and wooden cornices and eaves, was so successful that it was maintained virtually unchanged into the sixteenth century (see Chapter 17).

The strength of Marinid piety can be seen in the large dynastic necropolis at Chella (Arab. Shillah). Located on the outskirts of Rabat and once the Roman town of Sala Colonia, the site is one of the most picturesque in Morocco, with lush gardens cascading down the hillside to the Bou Regreg estuary below. Much of the site fell into ruins after the great earthquake of 1755, and while the remains are of limited artistic interest, the total effect is memorable and unusually evocative.[17] An imposing portal [158] set within massive walls was begun by Abu Sa'id and completed by Abu'l-Hasan, enclosing a cemetery already in use in the mid-thirteenth century. The heart of the complex is a rectangular block (44 by 29 meters) erected near a spring at the foot of the hill. It comprises a mosque, a minaret, several tombs, and a hospice for Sufis (Arab. zāwiya). The tombs house the remains of the early Marinid sultans and their family up to Abu'l-Hasan (d. 1351), after whom they were buried on a hilltop overlooking Fez. Some idea of the once lavish decoration can be gleaned from the exterior of Abu'l-Hasan's tomb, with a relief panel in which colonnettes support three cusped arches, themselves supporting shorter colonnettes and a lozenge-net panel, an arrangement recalling the decoration of the minaret at the Almohad mosque of Hasan (1199) in nearby Rabat.

158. Rabat, Chella, portal, 1351

159. Granada, Alhambra

THE NASRIDS

The Nasrid court at Granada remained a brilliant center of Islamic civilization, despite its precarious position between the Christian kingdoms to the north and the Marinids to the south, until all of the Iberian peninsula was brought under Christian control in 1492, and nearly eight centuries of Islamic civilization there came to an end. The Alhambra, the royal city of the Nasrids, dominates Granada from the south [159]. It comprises the most extensive remains of a medieval Islamic palace anywhere and is one of the most famous monuments in all Islamic art. Like all Nasrid buildings, those of the Alhambra are structurally simple, with trabeate construction and heavy stone walls supporting light wooden roofs, the whole concealed behind a glittering façade. A virtual encyclopedia of Nasrid architecture and decoration in glazed tile, carved and painted stucco, and carved and joined wood, the Alhambra is particularly notable for several superb muqarnas vaults. As early as the ninth century the site contained a citadel called al-hamrā' (the red), probably because of the color of its walls. In the eleventh century the citadel was linked with the town's defenses to the north, and between 1052 and 1056 Yusuf b. Naghrallah, the Jewish vizier to the Zirid rulers of Granada, built his palace there. Two centuries later, Muhammad I (r. 1230–72), founder of the Nasrid dynasty, made the Alhambra his residence. Over the next two centuries his descendants continued to enlarge and embellish it. Most of the work was done by Yusuf I (r. 1333–54) and Muhammad V (r. 1354–91, with interrup-

tions), although Charles V (r. 1516–56) added a palace in the Renaissance style, and Philip V (r. 1700–46) redecorated some rooms in an Italianate style. The site subsequently fell into ruin but was rediscovered in the early nineteenth century by the Romantics, who supplied the buildings with the names commonly used today.[18]

The Alhambra is contained with a walled enclosure (740 by 220 meters) punctuated with twenty-three towers and gates [160]. At its western end is the Alcazaba (Arab. al-qaṣaba, fortress); to the east are the remains of several palaces, a mosque, baths, and an industrial zone with a mint, tanneries, and ovens. Across a ravine to the east of the enclosure are the palace and gardens of the Generalife (Arab. jinān al-ʿarīf, gardens of the overseer). The Alcazaba, the oldest part, is a double-walled fortress of solid and vaulted towers containing barracks, cisterns, baths, houses, storerooms, and a dungeon. Access from the north was controlled by the Armas gate; access from the south was controlled by the Gate of Justice (Arab. sharīʿa, erroneously for shurayyaʿa, esplanade), which is decorated with carved stone, cut brick, marble, and glazed tile. The Puerta del Vino, framed with ceramic spandrels and stucco panels, is a ceremonial portal to the main street of the royal quarter.

The core of the Alhambra, the so-called Casa Real Vieja (to distinguish it from the addition of Charles V), consists of several palaces arranged along the northern curtain wall and incorporating several of its towers. The palaces follow the traditions of palace design in the western Islamic world, with rooms arranged symmetrically around rectangular courts.

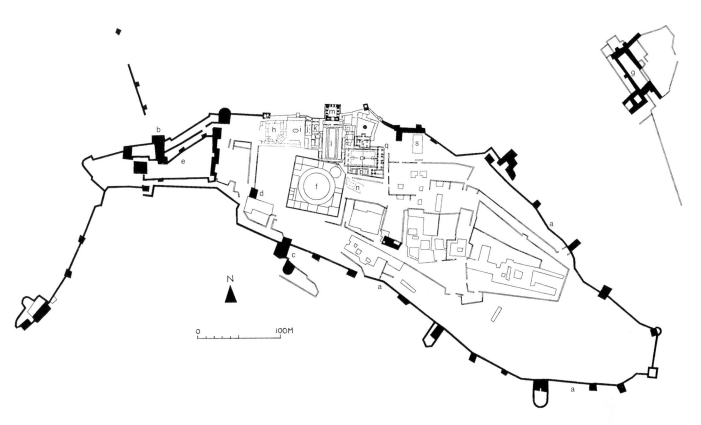

160. Granada, Alhambra, plan: a) walls, b) Armas gate, c) 'Justice' gate, d) Puerta del Vino, e) Alcazaba, f) Palace of Charles V, g) Generalife, (h–m) Palace of the Myrtles: h) first court, i) Machuca court, j) Mexuar, k) Cuarto Dorado, l) Court of the Myrtles, m) Hall of the Ambassadors, n) Rawda, (o–r) Palace of the Lions: o) Court of the Lions, p) Hall of the Abencerrajes, q) Hall of the Kings, r) Hall of the Two Sisters, s) Portal

161. Granada, Alhambra, Cuarto Dorado, south façade

One entered the Palace of the Myrtles from the large square facing the Alcazaba and passed through the first court, whose foundations indicate that it had an oratory and minaret, into the second or Machuca court. Only its northern portico and a tower survive; from it passages lead to a dwelling, another oratory, and the façade of the Mexuar (Arab. *mashwar*, place of the royal audience), the present public entrance. The Mexuar is a rectangular room with a flat roof supported on six columns; from it one passes through a narrow doorway into the Cuarto Dorado, whose plain lateral walls emphasize and illuminate the splendid carved stucco façade at its south [161].[19]

This internal façade, crowned by windows which allowed women to watch the activities unobserved and a muqarnas cornice supporting deep eaves, presents the visitor with two identical doors: that on the right leads back to the Mexuar, while that on the left leads via a bent passage to the Court of the Myrtles. The court (36.6 by 23.5 meters) contains a long pool bordered by low hedges. Doors along the side walls open to rooms for the sovereign's wives, service areas, and the palace bath. At either end porticoes of seven arches on slender marble columns protect lavish tile and stucco decoration on the walls. A door in the center of the northern portico opens to the Sala de la Barca, which has a magnificent joined wooden ceiling in the shape of a ship's hull, giving the room its name. It was once the sovereign's bed- and sitting-room. Beyond is the Hall of the Ambas-

162. Granada, Alhambra, Hall of the Ambassadors, interior

sadors [162], a large (11.30-meter) square room contained within one of the massive towers of the enclosure walls. Deep alcoves in its walls overlook the city; the one opposite the entrance is the most richly decorated, and the poem inscribed on its walls indicates that it was the throne recess. The floor and walls are superbly decorated with tile and carved plaster; the ceiling, composed of many thousands of individual wooden elements joined into a pyramidal vault, depicts a starry sky and may well symbolize the seven heavens of Paradise.

The area to the south of the Comares court was modified when Charles V constructed his palace there, but a street once led from the Mexuar past the royal mausoleum (rawda), a square building with a central lantern, to the Palace of the Lions. One passed from its entrance through a bent passage to the relatively intimate Court of the Lions (28.5 by 15.7 meters) [163]. An arcade supported on slender columns arranged singly or in groups of two, three, and four surrounds the court and the kiosks projecting at either end. At its center a fountain with twelve white marble lions (perhaps preserved from Yusuf b. Naghrallah's eleventh-century palace) spouts around an elevated polygonal basin inscribed with verses by the Andalusian poet Ibn Zamrak (1333–ca. 1393). To the south is the square hall of the Abencerrajes; squinches support a stellate drum and superb

muqarnas vault, which may also represent the dome of Heaven. On the east of the court is the Hall of the Kings: it comprises alternately square and rectangular spaces, with subsidiary side chambers separated by elaborate muqarnas arches and covered with muqarnas and painted vaults. The paintings, which are on gesso over leather, portray men in Arab dress and romantic fables of chivalric deeds.[20] To the north of the court is the Hall of the Two Sisters, a square hall with alcoves on its ground and first floors. Muqarnas squinches support an octagonal drum with eight paired windows and another superb muqarnas vault [164]. From the hall one passes through another vaulted room to the exquisitely decorated belvedere of Lindaraxa overlooking the gardens below.

This splendid architectural setting was embellished with the finest products of local workshops. Among them is a group of large wing-handled vases overglaze-decorated in luster [165]. They are known as Alhambra vases because several were found in the palace in the eighteenth century. At least eight have survived more or less intact, in addition to several large fragments.[21] The many thick-walled vase

163. Granada, Alhambra, Court of the Lions

shards excavated at the Alhambra itself suggest that many more were made. They are all shaped like amphoras with narrow bases, swelling bodies, sloping shoulders, ribbed necks, and broad flat handles shaped like wings. They are the largest lusterware pots ever produced and average 125 centimeters high. The surviving examples fall into two stylistic groups. The first, characterized by a bulbous shape, short neck, bold angular inscriptions, and monochrome luster, can be dated to the late thirteenth or early fourteenth century. The second group, more elongated and elegant in shape, with less conspicuous inscriptions, a narrow band of cursive script instead of a central wide register, and additional decoration in cobalt blue or gilding, can be dated to the late fourteenth century or early fifteenth. Several of the earlier examples have depictions of a stylized hand on the handles, an apotropaic device. Two of the later examples include the depiction of confronted gazelles on the body.

These large jars, which are unstable and would have been supported on tripods or set into holes in the floor, might have been put in front of small niches in the jambs between the rooms of the palace. One pair of such recesses, flanking the entrance to the Sala de la Barca at the Alhambra, is inscribed with a poem:

> I am a bride in her nuptial attire, endowed with beauty and
>   perfection.
> Contemplate [this] ewer to understand the full truth of my
>   statement:
> Look as well at my crown and you will find it similar to the
>   crown of the new moon;
> Ibn Nasr [Muhammad V] is the sun of this heaven in
>   splendour and in beauty;
> May he remain forever in [this] high position without
>   fearing the time of sunset.

The poem continues on the left side with the statement that the niche held a jar of water; when in use, the jar was like a man in prayer. It ends with the standard praise of the prince.[22] It is not known whether these luxury objects were actually used for storing and serving water in the palace. In shape they represent the culmination of a long tradition of large jars for the storage and serving of water; they were normally made of unglazed earthenware, sometimes decorated in the barbotine technique, to allow evaporation to naturally cool the contents. The Alhambra vases, by sheer dint of their size and glittering glazed decoration, are removed from this mundane function: their imposing bulk, which approaches human proportions, suggests that they functioned very much like sculpture, a metaphor underscored by the poem which compares the ewer to a bride or a man in prayer.

All of these vessels were probably made in Málaga, to the south-west of Granada on the Mediterranean coast, where cuerda seca ceramics had been produced from the tenth century and lusterwares from the early thirteenth. It was once believed that the appearance of the luster technique in Spain owed something to Iranian craftsmen fleeing the Mongol invasions, but the Andalusian tin-glazed earthenwares are quite unlike Iranian ceramics, which have a fritted paste and colored alkaline glazes and use different shapes and designs. It is much more likely that the development of lusterware in Spain was due to the emigration of craftsmen

165. 'Alhambra' Vase, Granada, late thirteenth century. Luster-painted earthenware. H 1.28 m. Palermo, Museo Nazionale

164. Granada, Alhambra, Hall of the Two Sisters, muqarnas ceiling

from Egypt after the fall of the Fatimids in 1171.[23] Málaga became a major center of ceramic production, and its products were exported throughout Europe. Nasrid lusterwares are characterized by a yellowish amber luster with a pronounced iridescence and a limited repertory of designs. The Málagan technique of using fluxed pigments has a tendency to overfiring, in which the clay medium adheres to the glaze and dulls the metallic film. Compared to the finest Kashan lusterwares, the painting is coarse and loose, although the finest specimens are more elegant and their great size shows enormous skill in firing. The Fortuny Tablet, for example, is a single slab measuring 90 by 44 centimeters. Its carpet-like design consists of a rectangular border with cartouches inscribed with the name of Yusuf III (r. 1408–17) and a central field with arabesques and the heads of swans, peacocks, and dragons.[24] Production at Málaga ceased abruptly sometime before the mid-fifteenth century, but continued elsewhere under Christian patronage. The memory of Málaga persisted, however, in the common European term majolica, the original Italian name for lusterware.[25]

The carved stucco walls on the interior of the Alhambra have often been likened to textiles, for their square fields and endless repeats are characteristic of textile designs, a resemblance that could only have been heightened by the bright colors with which they were originally painted. Surviving contemporary wall hangings indicate that the resemblance is not fortuitous. The most splendid textiles of the period are three more or less complete silk curtains, of which the finest [166] measures some 4.38 by 2.72 meters.[26] It consists of two loom-width panels joined by a narrow central strip; each panel has a main field decorated with three compositions of squares and elaborate borders at either end. Executed in lampas weave on a drawloom, the curtain has a deep rose-red ground and pattern worked predominantly in yellow, with details in dark blue, green, and white. In size and complexity this stunning piece has few if any rivals in medieval textiles. Its splendid condition gives an unusually vivid sense of the luxury and richness of Nasrid palace interiors. The design is sure and sophisticated, juxtaposing the rich but plain red ground with intricate geometric patterns in one, two, three, or four colors.

The place and date of production of these pieces have been widely disputed, but a Nasrid attribution is certain, as many of the patterns have exact parallels in the mural decoration of the Alhambra. Cartouches on the Cleveland curtain are inscribed with *lā ghālib ilā'llah* ("There is no victor save God"), the motto of the Nasrid dynasty, inscribed on many of their commissions. The use of yellow silk instead of gold thread confirms a fifteenth-century date, for a letter to Fernando I, King of Aragon, dated 4 June 1414 mentions that Muslim weavers had ceased using gold. There was a long tradition of fine silk-weaving in Spain, and monumental curtains are known there from the thirteenth century. A dispersed tapestry-woven textile from the tomb of Bishop Gurb (d. 1284) in Barcelona Cathedral can be reconstructed as pictorial roundels spaced in rows against a dark red ground set between borders, an arrangement prefiguring that of the Cleveland curtain.[27] The technique of producing hangings in tapestry-weave was exported from Spain to North Africa, for two military banners in Toledo Cathedral of tapestry inwoven in a tabby ground are inscribed with the names of the Marinid sultans of Fez, Abu Sa'id and Abu'l-Hasan. Like the ceramics of Málaga, Nasrid textiles were appreciated in the Christian courts of Europe, and similar types continued to be produced under Christian patronage after the fall of the Nasrid kingdom in 1492.

166. Curtain, Granada, fifteenth century. Silk. 4.38 × 2.72 cm. Cleveland Museum of Art

Architecture and the Arts in Anatolia under the Beyliks and Early Ottomans

In 1243 the Saljuqs of Rum were defeated by the Ilkhanids at the battle of Kösedağ and forced to pay a huge tribute. During the next decades the Saljuqs were weakened by internal squabbling, and after an abortive attempt to overthrow the Mongol protectorate in 1277, eastern Anatolia came under direct Mongol rule, although a powerless Saljuq dynasty reigned in name until the early fourteenth century. Eastern Anatolia continued to be linked closely to Iran after the fall of the Ilkhanids and came under the power of two Turkoman confederations, the Qaraqoyunlu (1380–1468) and the Aqqoyunlu (1378–1508; see Chapters 4–5). In western Anatolia, dozens of independent regional principalities, usually known collectively as the Beyliks, replaced the relative unity of Saljuq rule and became particularly important after the fall of the Ilkhanids in 1335. Some of them, such as the Eşrefoğlu of Beyşehir in central Anatolia (late thirteenth century to 1328), had brief periods of glory, while others, such as the Karamanids of Karaman and Konya (ca. 1256–1483), the Menteşids of Milas, Muğla, and Pecin (ca. 1270–1426), and the Aydinids of Selçuk and Birge (1307–1426), lasted longer. In the end the most successful was the Osmanlı or Ottoman dynasty (1281–1924): they rose to power as warriors on the Byzantine frontier in northwest Anatolia and expanded their realm to include much of Anatolia and all of Thrace before they eventually defeated the Byzantines at Constantinople in 1453.

ARCHITECTURE

In central and eastern Anatolia, which had been the heart of the Saljuq realm, Saljuq traditions ran deeper and the Saljuq style continued under the emirates. The type of wooden columnar mosque typical of the Saljuq period continued to be built.[1] The example at Beyşehir constructed in 1299 by the Eşrefoğlu Süleyman Bey (r. 1296–1301) is the largest and most original of the type. The mosque is a rectangle (26 by 39 meters) with a beveled north-east corner containing the richly carved main façade, consisting of a portal flanked by a fountain and a minaret. The conical mausoleum for the Eşrefoğlu abuts the mosque on the center of the east side. In the interior [167] forty-eight columns with muqarnas capitals create seven aisles perpendicular to the qibla. The central aisle leading to the mihrab is wider and higher, and the center bay was originally open over a pool. A raised platform on the right provided the ruler with a private place for prayer, much like the *maqṣūra* of early Islamic times. The mihrab is decorated with tile mosaic in dark and light blues and purple, and the rafters, brackets, and capitals are painted. Like the plan, the decorative elements, such as the stone carving, tile mosaic, and painted woodwork, are the culmination of the Saljuq style.

In eastern Anatolia the patronage of architecture dwindled after the Saljuq defeat at Kösedağ, but eventually revived with the intervention of Ilkhanid authority. In Sivas, for

example, no major structures were erected from 1243 to 1271, when three buildings were endowed in the same year: the Çifte Minare madrasa ordered by the Ilkhanid vizier Shams al-Din Muhammad Juvayni, the Gök madrasa ordered by the Saljuq vizier Fakhr al-Din 'Ali Sahib Ata, and the madrasa ordered by the otherwise unidentified Muzaffar Barujirdi. The revival of architectural patronage then proceeded unabated in Amasya, Tokat, Ahlat, and Erzurum.[2] In Amasya a hospital (1308–9) was ordered by Anbar b. 'Abdallah, a freedman of the Ilkhanid sultan Uljaytu; it follows the plan of a traditional Saljuq madrasa with an arcaded court and two iwans. In Erzurum a madrasa (1310) was commissioned by Khwaja Yaqut, a freedman of the Ilkhanid Sultan Ghazan and amir of the region of Erzurum and Bayburt.[3] The Yakutiye (Yaqutiyya) madrasa includes the amir's tomb, and to insure its upkeep, he endowed to it the revenues from several villages in the district, their immovable property, and buildings in them, including khans, shops, a windmill, and baths.[4] The building is similar to Saljuq domed madrasas but the court has a central muqarnas vault with an oculus flanked by transverse vaults and supported on four piers [168]. Three iwans and fourteen cells open onto the court. The disposition of the twin minarets flanking the portal and the domed mausoleum behind the main iwan are features modeled on the Çifte Minare madrasa built in 1243 in the same city,[5] but the slightly projecting portal is a new feature. The rich stone carving on the façade was also inspired by that on the earlier building, but the motif of a double-headed eagle atop a palm tree issuing from a double-headed dragon has been transposed into a single-headed eagle facing left or right atop a palm tree set over confronted lions, and the motif, whose significance has yet to be determined, has been moved from the main façade directly below the minarets to the jambs flanking the doorway.

A final example showing how the Saljuq style continued into the early fourteenth century is the mausoleum of the Saljuq princess Hudavend Hatun (Khudavand Khatun), daughter of Qilij Arslan IV (r. 1259–65), at Niğde (1312). The entrance portal on the east side of the octagonal tomb [169] is richly carved with geometric interlacing; the other seven sides are capped by muqarnas corbels supporting an elaborately carved, sixteen-sided zone of transition; and the whole is crowned by a pyramidal roof. The tomb's rich decoration is the last flowering of the Saljuq style of stone carving, but the traditional repertory is enriched by profuse figural carving of double-headed eagles, harpies, panthers or lions, and heads concealed in the lush vegetation.

167. Beyşehir, Eşrefoğlu Mosque, 1299, interior

168. Erzurum, Yaqutiye Madrasa, 1310, interior

169. Niğde, Hudavend Hatun mausoleum, 1312

Architecture was more experimental on the western frontier as architects encountered new ideas, particularly features of Byzantine architecture, and a trove of ancient and medieval materials. Buildings had a new emphasis on entire façades, which were often composed with windows and two-storied porticos. Beginning in the second quarter of the fourteenth century, cities such as Iznik, Bursa, Selçuk, and Milas acquired architectural ensembles of distinction. The architecture of the period is often considered either under dynastic rubrics or by strictly formal types, but the inter-mingling of individuals and ideas was so pronounced that it is equally valid to consider the material in a single chronology.[6] The longevity of the Ottomans led to a comparatively clear and consistent stylistic development; their political successes and territorial expansion led to the gradual imposition of their style throughout Anatolia and the Balkans and eventually much of the Mediterranean Islamic lands (see Chapter 15).

The Mosque of Haci Özbek (1333) at Iznik, the Byzantine Nicaea, was built two years after the Ottoman leader Orhan (ca. 1324–1360) took the city in a prolonged siege.[7] The city's cathedral, the Church of Hagia Sophia, which stood at

its center, was converted into the congregational mosque, but Haci Özbek built his small private foundation several blocks away on the main east–west artery. The building [170] consists of a room 7.92 meters square, covered by a hemispheric dome resting on an octagonal zone of transition. Originally it had an entrance portico on the west side with a barrel vault covering two bays and a cross-vault covering the third bay in front of the door. The portico was destroyed during road-widening operations in 1959 and replaced with a glassed-in porch on the north. There was no minaret. The building has courses of stone ashlars separated by two to four courses of bricks laid in common bond. Within the ashlar course, each stone is separated by a soldier brick. The dome is covered with terracotta tiles molded to face a spherical surface. They are typical of early Ottoman buildings, although in most cases the roof tiles have been replaced by lead sheets. The interior is rather plain, with eight windows and three simple niches in the south wall, the central one serving as the mihrab. The dome sits on a band of Turkish triangles, a structural belt of broken prismatic surfaces. Features such as its modest scale, size, and zone of transition with Turkish triangles are typical of the Saljuq monuments of thirteenth-century Konya, such as the Karatay and Ince Minareli madrasas.[8] The technique of construction, using alternating courses of brick and stone, however, is distinctly Byzantine.

Orhan himself ordered yet another kind of mosque 400 meters outside Iznik's Yenişehir (south) gate in 1334–5. Excavation of the site revealed a porch preceding a long rectangular space (ca. 8 by 18 meters) divided in half by two steps and flanked by two rectangular rooms.[9] The rectangular space probably comprised a covered court and a mosque; the side rooms were probably used as hostels (Arab. *zāwiya*; Turk. *zaviye*) for traveling dervishes.[10] The plan seems to have been a logical development of the enclosed type of madrasa that had four iwans opening onto a closed court (e.g. the Yakutiye in Erzurum [168]), but the iwans and the

170. Iznik, Haci Özbek mosque, 1333, view from south-west

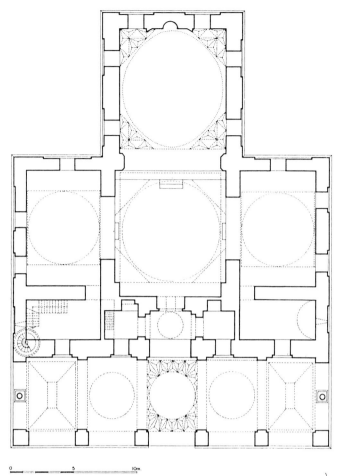

171. Bursa, Mosque of Orhan Gazi, 1339, plan

steps, is the main iwan, covered with an elliptical vault; two other iwans, also raised and vaulted, stand to either side of the central hall. The iwans may well have been hostels for traveling dervishes and the religious brotherhoods (Turk. *ahi*) who provided much of the support for Ottoman expansion. The pyramidal massing of domes around the central court when seen from the exterior is a feature that would become a hallmark of later Ottoman architecture.

While the early Ottomans typically built zaviye-type mosques, congregational mosques in the other principalities had different kinds of spatial organization whose innovative features were then incorporated into the Ottoman repertory. In Selçuk (formerly Ayasoluk and ancient Ephesus) a congregational mosque was built in 1375. According to an inscription over the main portal, it was the work of 'Ali b. al-Dimishqi for 'Isa b. Muhammad b. Aydin (r. 1360–90), the Aydinid sultan whose domain extended from western Anatolia to the Greek islands.[13] Measuring some 53 by 57 meters, it has high walls constructed of rough-cut ashlars enclosing a spacious courtyard (27 by 35 meters) which is bordered on three sides by two-storied porticoes [172]. On the south side, a triple-arched gateway in the center of the façade opens into the prayer hall, which consists of two parallel aisles, now covered with gabled roofs but originally flat, intersected by a transept of two domes resting on triangular pendentives and monolithic stone columns. The pendentives are faced with glazed tiles in geometric patterns. Monumental entrances and minarets with cylindrical brick shafts flank the façade. Much of the building material was undoubtedly salvaged from the ruins of Ephesus, to judge from the many spolia used, but other pieces were made specifically for the mosque. Of particular note is the monumental western façade [173], constructed of stone and brick faced with marble. It is enlivened with windows whose frames are delicately carved with muqarnas, joggled voussoirs, and inscriptions. Two flights of steps lead to a portal which projects from the wall surface and is crowned with a muqarnas hood. The surface above is inlaid with black and white marble in an intricate knot pattern, a technique also used on the windows of the façade and around the mihrab (restored). Many features of the mosque, from its plan and elevation to the decoration with marble inlay, relate to earlier Syrian buildings, most notably the Umayyad mosque of Damascus.[14] This Syrian connection is no surprise, given the origins of 'Ali b. al-Dimishqi ("'Ali the son of the Damascene"). An unusual feature of the building is the integrated courtyard, which appears in contemporary Anatolian architecture only in a smaller version at the congregational mosque in Manisa built in 1367 for the Saruhanid Ishaq Beg [174],[15] but it would be picked up some sixty years later by Ottoman architects and incorporated into the standard repertory.

The Ottoman sultan Murad I (r. 1360–89), later known by the epithet Hüdavendigar ("Lord," "Master"), captured Edirne and extended the Ottoman empire into Europe, adding Thrace, Macedonia, and Bulgaria. His major preoccupations were military: he founded the Janissaries, the highly trained corps of infantry recruited from the tribute children. His main architectural commission was a complex at Çekirge,

court have become virtually the same size. The building differs, however, in the emphasis accorded the exterior, particularly the massing of domes it must have had in its original state. It is the earliest example of a type that would remain characteristic of Ottoman architecture for at least another century. It is known variously as the zaviye- (zawiya-), eyvan- (iwan-), T-plan, Bursa-type or multi-function mosque, for many of the finest and earliest examples were royal foundations in and around Bursa, the Ottoman capital from 1326 to 1403.[11]

After Timur's army burned and plundered Bursa (ancient Prusa), a splendid site on the northern slopes of Ulu Dağ, the capital was moved to Edirne (Adrianople) in Thrace and then in 1453 to Istanbul (Constantinople). Bursa nevertheless retained much of its prestige, for Osman (d. 1324), the founder of the dynasty, and five of his successors were buried there, and it was an important center for the silk industry. Orhan built a palace in the citadel, a public soup kitchen (Turk. *imaret*), a bath, a caravanserai, and several mosques, including one near the main market.[12] Although repeatedly restored, the essential features of the 1339 plan can still be determined [171]. It continues the type seen earlier at Iznik: a five-bay porch precedes a domed vestibule and the central hall, which is covered with a dome 8.45 meters in diameter. Beyond, on the qibla axis and up two

172. Selçuk, Isa Bey Mosque, 1375, view from north-east

173. Selçuk, Isa Bey Mosque, west façade

174. Manisa, Congregational Mosque, 1367, courtyard

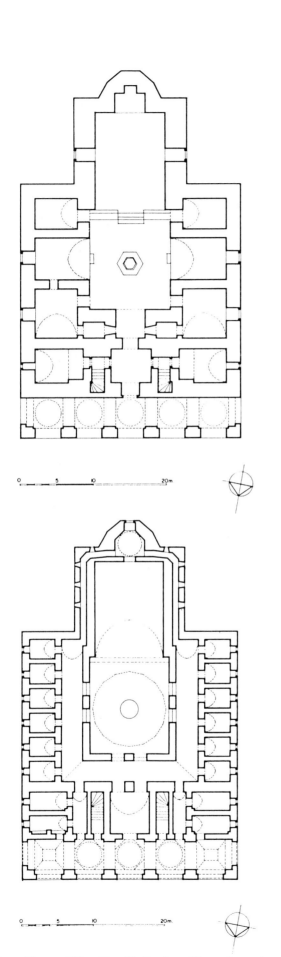

175. Bursa, Mosque of Murad I, 1366–85, plans of first and second stories

176. Bursa, Mosque of Murad I

a hilltop site a bit west of Bursa. The mosque, built in the traditional Byzantine technique of alternating courses of brick and stone, was begun in 1366 but not completed until 1385. It is unusual in combining a zaviye-type mosque on the ground floor with a madrasa on the second [175]. The ground floor has a five-bay porch on the north leading to a vestibule; the main interior space consists of a domed court (diameter 11 meters; height 23 meters) surrounded by four iwans; six other rooms fill the corner spaces. Staircases flanking the vestibule lead to the second floor, which has a five-bay gallery over the portico and a large room over the vestibule. Small cells (2.5 by 3.5 meters) open onto a barrel-vaulted corridor which runs around three sides of the central domed hall; a narrow passage in the thickness of the wall around the main iwan leads to a small domed room (perhaps an oratory) over the mihrab below. The plan is a more complex variant of the early zaviye type and combines two functions which are logically reflected in the two-storied façade [176]. It has slightly pointed arches enclosing pairs of smaller arches carried on re-used Byzantine columns and capitals. The openness and airiness are reminiscent of the façade of a Venetian palazzo and have led to the unsupported speculation that the architect was an Italian in Ottoman service.

Bayezid I (r. 1389–1403), known as Yıldırım ("Thunderbolt"), expanded the empire with impetuous military exploits. In the winter of 1389–90 he annexed several of the emirates in western Anatolia, including that of the Menteşids, and the mosque at Milas (ancient Mylasa), built in 1394 by Firuz Beg, the Menteşid he appointed governor of the region, is

177. Milas, Mosque of Firuz Beg, 1394, façade

transitional between the local Menteşid and the emerging Ottoman styles [177]. It is one of the few non-Ottoman mosques to use the zaviye-type plan, and, like Orhan's mosque at Bursa [171], it has a five-bay portico with pointed arches resting on piers. Some of the decorative motifs, such as the zig-zag lobes on the three central arches of the portico, were also used at Bursa, but the decoration at Milas is much richer. The side bays of the portico, for example, have muqarnas brackets on the piers and pierced marble balustrades decorated with stars and interlaced motifs. The building is faced with blocks of colored marble, and the windows have muqarnas hoods and bi-colored joggled voussoirs. The decoration of the mihrab is equally rich, including embossed arabesques and palmettes in the spandrels, porphyry columns, a muqarnas hood, an inscription band, and a representation of a mosque lamp hanging in a niche. Perpendicular to the corner of the mihrab are the signatures of the builder Musa b. 'Abdallah and the

178. Bursa, Ulu Cami, 1396–1400, interior

decorator Musa b. 'Adil.[16] Beside the mosque is a simple madrasa with twelve rooms in a row covered with domes and transverse and barrel vaults.

Bayezid I was a prodigious builder. He began his own complex in Bursa a few years after his accession, and it was completed by 1395. Like the complex built by his father at Çekirge, it was located on a hilltop outside the city walls, this time to its east. It consisted of seven separate buildings: a zaviye-type mosque, a madrasa, a tomb, a bath, a soup kitchen, a hospital, and a palace. The mosque, which was the center of the complex and placed at the top of the hill, is similar to that of Murad I. More unusual is the new congregational mosque (Turk. *ulu cami*) that Bayezid I ordered for Bursa's central business district [178]. Funds for the mosque came from the considerable booty he seized when he defeated Sigismund of Hungary on 25 September 1396 at Nicopolis on the lower Danube. The mosque was completed by 1399–1400, remarkably quickly considering

180. Niğde, Aq madrasa, 1409, façade

its size (68 by 56 meters). Twelve piers divide the interior into twenty domed bays of equal size, arranged in a four-by-five grid. The main entrance lies in the middle of the north façade, opposite the mihrab. The second bay along the axis from portal to mihrab is a vestigial court: it is two steps lower than the rest of the mosque, paved with marble, and has an open oculus over the pool. Like the zaviye-type mosque, this type of hypostyle mosque with multi-domed bays is mainly associated with the Ottomans (another example is the Eski Cami at Edirne, 1402–14) but is known in other principalities as well. The earliest example is the Yivli Minare Mosque in Antalya (1373), built by the Hamidids on the foundations of a Byzantine church, and others were constructed in eastern Anatolia by the Aqqoyunlu and the Qaraqoyunlu.

Despite the increasing importance of the Ottomans and the imposition of their style of architecture, some principalities maintained their independence and continued distinctive local styles of building. The fine stone carving and rich revetment typical of Menteşid buildings, such as the Mosque of Firuz Beg at Milas [177], is found again at the mosque at Balat (ancient Miletus). It was built in 1404 by Ilyas Beg, the Menteşid ruler who reestablished the emirate when Bayezid I was captured by Timur. Like the early Ottoman Mosque of Haci Özbek [170], it is a traditional Anatolian type of small mosque, with a square base, octagonal zone of transition, and hemispheric dome, but is almost twice as large (interior diameter 14 meters) and has a minaret in the north-west corner. The traditional portico has been replaced by an entrance block. It projects slightly from

the façade and contains a large pointed arch which itself encloses three smaller arches [179]. The central one is the door; those on the side are windows with marble balustrades. All three arches are decorated with bi-colored joggled voussoirs, used a decade earlier on the mosque at Milas, and are surmounted by relieving arches with a flat-topped profile. Although the interior is a single unified space like that found in many small Saljuq mosques, two tiers of two windows on each side provide generous illumination. The south wall is dominated by the magnificent mihrab, a large marble panel (7.35 by 5.2 meters). The mosque once formed part of a larger complex, with a tomb to the north and madrasa rooms at the sides arranged around a courtyard with arcades, but little of this remains.

The impact of the emerging Ottoman style on local building traditions outside the Ottoman domains can be seen in the Aq (White) madrasa at Niğde, built by the Karamanid ruler ʿAli Beg in 1409. After the Ottomans, the Karamanids were the most powerful and longest-lasting of the Turkoman emirates. They considered themselves the rightful successors of the Saljuqs, the last major power in central Anatolia, and their architecture reflected their political claim by adhering to the canons of Saljuq style. The Aq madrasa follows the plan formulated in the Saljuq period and used for the early-fourteenth-century hospital at Amasya: an open court with two iwans flanked by rooms on two stories. Its fine masonry construction and elaborate carved decoration are typical of other buildings erected by the Karamanids, such as the Hatuniye (Khatuniyya) madrasa at Karaman (1382). The façade [180], however, is remarkable, not only for its high,

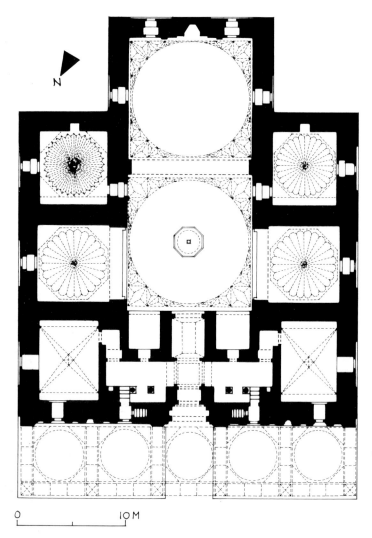

181. Bursa, Yeşil Mosque, 1412–24, plan

tomb, which was placed unusually on a higher level than the mosque. Begun in 1412, the mosque is of the typical zaviye type, and its plan [181] follows that of Bayezid's mosque in the same city, but there is no porch, although arch springs visible on the façade indicate that one was planned. On either side of the central domed fountain court are raised iwans covered with ribbed domes; beyond it and four steps higher is a smaller domed iwan (diameter ca. 11 meters) which serves as the prayer hall. Smaller domed rooms for dervishes were inserted on either side of the main iwan. The entrance itself has been elaborated with two stories of rooms: passages on either side of the vestibule lead to vaulted chambers and stairs ascend to a royal balcony (Turk. *hünkâr mahfili*) overlooking the central hall. Lavishly paneled with cuerda seca tiles, it has a gilded ceiling and a pierced tile balustrade. The elaboration of the space reserved for the sultan is unprecedented in Ottoman architecture, although the idea is another reworking of the *maqsūra* like that of Beyşehir. The spectacular tile decoration [182] includes a dado of hexagonal monochrome tiles with stencilled gold patterns and an elaborate mihrab (height 10 meters) with a molded frame and pyramidal muqarnas hood executed in a combination of tile mosaic and cuerda seca, the latter a cheaper alternative to the former.

Inscriptions provide much information about the building and its construction. The inscription over the portal states that the sultan funded the project and ordered construction, which was finished in Dhu'l-Hijja 822 (December 1419–January 1420). Above the niches flanking the portal is the signature of Hajji 'Iwad b. Akhi Bayazid, who "designed the building, oversaw its construction, and fixed its proportions." An inscription above the loggia states that 'Ali b. Ilyas 'Ali finished the decoration at the end of Ramadan 827 (late August 1424), some four and a half years later. On each of the lateral walls of the loggia is the signature of Muhammad (Mehmed) the Crazy. On the colonnette to the right of the mihrab is another signature, "work of the masters of Tabriz," complemented on the left by a couplet by the Persian poet Sa'di about tyranny and injustice.[17]

This ambitious programme of tile decoration is a first in Ottoman architecture and marks the reappearance of a feature last seen over a century earlier in the mosque at Beyşehir. It can be explained, in part, as a result of the Timurid invasion. 'Ali b. Ilyas 'Ali, better known as Naqqash 'Ali ('Ali the Designer), had been carted off to Samarqand and must have been inspired by Timurid buildings there, which were extensively decorated with tile. Indeed, the peculiar combination of tile mosaic and cuerda seca tiles is characteristic of late-fourteenth-century buildings in Samarqand. Local Anatolian potters would have been unable to produce either type of tile, since the techniques were otherwise unknown in the region, and foreign workers must have been brought in. The simplest explanation is that the

projecting portal enclosing an ogee arch with an elaborate muqarnas half-dome, but also for the lateral loggias with large, slightly pointed arches enclosing pairs of smaller, ogival arches carried on columns. The striking resemblance to the façade of the Mosque of Murad I at Çekirge [176] may be explained by contemporary events, for 'Ali Beg had been imprisoned in Bursa from 1397–8, when Bayezid had killed his brother-in-law, 'Ali Beg's father, until 1402, when Timur defeated the Ottomans and restored the Karamanid territories to 'Ali Beg.

In the decade following Timur's devastating defeat of Bayezid at Ankara in 1402, Bayezid's son Mehmed I Çelebi (r. 1403–21) recovered the Anatolian provinces and emerged victorious from a long fratricidal civil war, so that in 1413 he was acknowledged as sultan over the unified empire in Europe and Anatolia. Although Edirne was his political capital, he, like his father and grandfather, ordered a funerary mosque complex on a hilltop in Bursa, the traditional burial site for the early Ottoman sultans. Because of its splendid tile revetment, it is usually known as the Yeşil (Green) complex. It included a madrasa, soup kitchen, bath, and

182. Bursa, Yeşil Mosque, interior looking toward mihrab

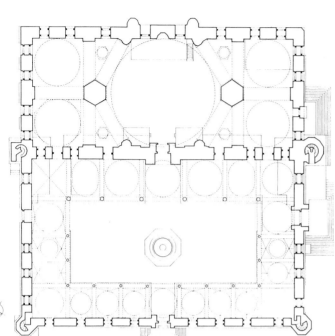

183. Edirne, Üç Şerefeli Mosque, 1437–47, plan and section

"masters of Tabriz" brought cuerda seca to Bursa. Hajji 'Iwad, the vizier responsible for the project, is said to have imported craftsmen from western Iran. Cuerda seca, however, was unknown in western Iran at this point, although it was used in the east. This has led several scholars to suggest that the "masters of Tabriz" may have come from Central Asia.[18] An artist bearing the epithet "from Tabriz" signed the cuerda seca panels at Timur's palace at Shahr-i Sabz, the Aqsaray [45], and "Tabrizi" may have come to mean master tile-maker much as the epithet "Shirazi" had come to mean master builder (see Chapter 4).

Mehmed's tomb in the Yeşil complex shows many of the same decorative innovations as the mosque, although its octagonal form can be traced back to Saljuq examples [169]. While the tiles on the exterior are modern replacements, those on the interior, particularly the mihrab and the cenotaph, are as fine as those in the mosque. This is no surprise, since the same Hajji 'Iwad supervised the work, and the wooden doors are signed by yet another craftsman with the epithet "Tabrizi," 'Ali b. Hajji Ahmad.[19]

Mehmed's successor, Murad II (r. 1421–44 and 1446–51), continued the family tradition of building a funerary complex in Bursa (1424–6). His mosque is similar in spatial organization to that of his father, but the two main domes are of equal size (diameter 10.6 meters) and height. Although the qibla dome is six steps higher than the central domed court, the side iwans are on the same level and form one continuous lateral space. Murad II's constructions in the capital Edirne were more innovative. In 1435 he ordered a convent for Mevlevi dervishes outside the city; later in his reign the building was converted into a mosque. It has a simple T-plan but is notable for its tile decoration, including

a gigantic mihrab and a dado of 479 hexagonal tiles.[20] The mihrab is mainly done in cuerda seca, and the designs are so similar to the work in Bursa by the "Masters of Tabriz" that they must have been responsible for the work at Edirne as well. The molded prisms of the muqarnas hood and the hexagonal tiles, however, are done in a new technique of underglaze blue-and-white on an alkaline frit body. The tiles exhibit a variety of chinoiserie motifs, their first appearance under the Ottomans. They are similar to other blue-and-white tiles produced at the same time in Syria and Egypt by artists bearing the epithet "Tabrizi."[21]

Murad II's major commission, however, was another congregational mosque for Edirne. Begun in 1437 and finished a decade later, it is usually known as the Üç Şerefeli ("Three Balcony") Mosque after the three galleries for muezzins on its south-western minaret, the tallest (67.65 meters) in Ottoman architecture until that time. The mosque is a monumental, nearly square building (66.50 by 64.50 meters) comprising an arcaded court with minarets at its four corners and an oblong prayer hall [183]. The prayer hall is dominated by a huge dome (24.10 meters in diameter) which covers over one-half the interior space. It is supported on the north and south by the exterior walls and on the east and west by massive hexagonal piers. The four corners of the prayer hall are covered with domes, and the small triangular spaces between the corner units and the central dome are covered with tripartite vaults decorated with muqarnas and supporting tiny domes in their centers. The exterior [184] is a cascade of domes descending from the central dome to those over the court arcades. The arched buttresses around the drum of the central dome are the first in Ottoman architecture.

184. Edirne, Üç Şerefeli Mosque

The mosque's integral fountain court and monumental dome are new features in Ottoman religious architecture.[22] The congregational mosque built in Edirne at the beginning of the fifteenth century, now known as the Eski Cami (Old Mosque), is, like the Ulu Cami in Bursa, a hypostyle building of equal domed bays, in this case nine units of approximately thirteen meters each. The inspiration for the integral fountain court and monumental dome must lie elsewhere. Although the mosque at Selçuk [172] has a court, a more likely source for both features is the Saruhanid congregational mosque in Manisa [174], a town which Murad II knew well and to which he would retire in late 1444. The copy surpasses the model in size, scale, and sophistication, and it charts a new course for Ottoman architecture. The architect wanted to create a monumental exterior, but was not always able to achieve his goal. The cascade of domes is interrupted by the tiny domes nestled in the lee of the main dome and by the uneven height of the domes over the court arcade. The elevation of the court arcade is also awkward, for the arches at the corners spring from different levels. The interior is dark. The Üç Şerefeli Mosque stands at the crossroads of Ottoman architecture: it is the culmination of spatial experiments in Beylik and early Ottoman architecture, and many of its novel features, such as its splendid portal, would be continued in later Ottoman architecture on a grander scale and in a more coherent fashion after the conquest of Constantinople.

The tile decoration that remains at the Üç Şerefeli Mosque is the culmination of the "Masters of Tabriz" style begun at Bursa. The lunette panels above the windows of the court are painted underglaze with the sultan's name against a foliate ground [185]. The earlier blue-and-white has been abandoned in favor of a palette of dark blue, light blue, purple, and white, outlined in black (verging on dark purple).

After Edirne, the "Masters of Tabriz" workshop is thought to have executed only two more commissions, tile decoration for the Mosque of Mehmed Fatih in Istanbul (1463–70), where yellow was added to the palette, and the tomb of Cem Sultan in Bursa (1479), both of significantly lower quality. Active for fifty-five years, the workshop was probably centered in Iznik, as a rare fragment from a vessel in the same technique and style was discovered there. At the end

185. Edirne, Uc Şerefeli Mosque, underglaze-painted lunette panel

of the fifteenth century Iznik would become the center of production for the superb finewares produced for the Ottoman court (see Chapter 16), and one might easily imagine that it was a continuation of the "Masters of Tabriz" workshop. But the significant technical differences between the "Masters of Tabriz" ceramics, which have a alkaline-frit body and a polychrome palette, and later Iznik wares, which have a lead-frit body and were initially decorated in blue and white, indicate that the two traditions were quite distinct.[23]

THE ARTS

Whereas architecture under the Beyliks is varied and shows a lively interplay between traditional and innovative elements, the portable arts produced then, with the exception of those directly related to architecture, seem to have been less important. This phenomenon was not unique to Anatolia during the period, but the political fragmentation that defines this period seems to have limited the patronage of the luxury arts, such as manuscripts and fine metalwares. The ceramic arts clearly demonstrate that more attention was paid to architectural commissions than to objects. Foreign craftsmen were brought to create magnificent ensembles and no expense was spared to produce revetments in the new techniques of underglaze painting and cuerda seca, but these craftsmen rarely made vessels, and the typical ceramics produced under the Beyliks are unpretentious earthenwares. The most widespread type is known as "Miletus ware" since quantities of it were excavated at Balat, the site of ancient Miletus.[24] Subsequent excavations have shown that Iznik was the major site of production.[25] Produced over the course of the fifteenth century, these wares were made of a coarse red clay with a white slip and painted in blue or green with black outlines and touches of purple under a clear lead glaze. The typical convex bowl or deep dish has a radiating design decorated with spirals.[26] These humble provincial wares provide no hint, in either technique or decoration, of the splendid ceramics that Iznik would begin to produce later in the century.

Wooden fittings for architecture were particularly important in Anatolia, due no doubt to the rich resources of timber available there, and a large number of elaborately decorated examples produced under the Beyliks survive. Earlier woodwork had been executed in the tongue-and-groove technique in which octagonal, stellate, and lozenge-shaped panels carved with arabesque decoration were joined without pins or glue in grooved frames. Widely dispersed throughout the Islamic world by the twelfth century, this technique (Turk. *kündekari*) continued in the Beylik period, when the carving became finer, more intricate, and shallower, and boss-like rosettes were added to the repertory. Since it was so time-consuming, however, it was often replaced by a cheaper technique, "false *kündekari*," in which large boards were carved with strapwork networks containing octagonal, stellate, and lozenge-shaped panels. Although mounted in frames, the boards eventually warped and split because they were less able than true *kündekari* work to adjust to changing humidity by expanding and contracting. Doors and windows were often done in "false *kündekari*," but the most elaborate examples are minbars, such as the one made for the Arslanhane Mosque in Ankara in 688/1289–90 [186].[27] Inlay,

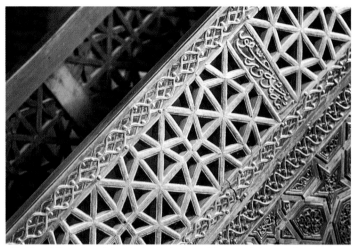

186. Detail from the minbar in the Arslanhane Mosque, Ankara, 1289–90

introduced in the fourteenth century, also became more popular in the fifteenth century. The panels from the doors to the Hajji Bayram Mosque in Ankara, for example, are inlaid with ivory.[28]

The art of metalwork during this period is still largely unexplored and a matter of much speculation. It is likely that some metalwares of artistic merit were produced, as significant metal objects, such as gilded bronze lamps, had been produced under Saljuq patronage in Konya during the thirteenth century,[29] but the only dated pieces from the period of the Beyliks are a few metal objects identified with the early Ottomans. They are more important for historical than artistic reasons.[30]

Much the same situation pertains to illustrated manuscripts. Illustrated manuscripts had been produced under Saljuq patronage in the thirteenth century.[31] Luxury books continued to be produced in Anatolia in the fourteenth century, for a section of a Koran manuscript can be attributed there.[32] The forty folios contain the thirtieth section of the Koran, and the colophon states that it was copied in Rabi' I 734 (November 1333) by Husayn b. Hasan, known as Husam, the poor (*al-faqīr*), al-Mawlawi. The scribe's epithets suggest that he was a member of the Mevlevi order of dervishes, who originated in Konya in the thirteenth century, and the manuscript probably remained in Anatolia, for it later belonged to an *ahi*, or member of one of the brotherhoods that flourished there in the fourteenth century. Each folio has three lines of large black *muḥaqqaq* script, and chapter headings are done in gold *thuluth*. The opening lines of the section [187] are surrounded by contour panels and a red crosshatched ground decorated with four exuberant vine scrolls with large palmettes and sinuous arabesque leaves. The script and illumination resemble some of the Koran manuscripts produced for Ilkhanid patrons in Iran at the beginning of the fourteenth century [29]. By the 1330s these features were known to artists in provincial Anatolia.

There may have been some demand for illustrated books under the Beyliks, but qualified painters must have been scarce in early-fifteenth-century Anatolia, to judge from a copy of the *Iskandarnāma* of Ahmedi done at Amaysa in 1416.[33] The manuscript contains twenty illustrations, but only three are contemporary with the text. They are simple in execution and composition, with three or four riders

187. Right half to the frontispiece from the 30th section of a manuscript of the Koran, probably Konya, 1333. New York Public Library, Spencer Collection, MS. Arab. 3, f. 1v

placed on blue or green grounds speckled with gold. The other seventeen illustrations have been cut from fourteenth-century Persian *Shāhnāma* manuscripts and pasted in. The manuscript was completed three years after the author's death, and it seems that no prototypes were available, so the painter was forced to cut out related images from other manuscripts. When he ran out of suitable material for pasting, he turned to his own limited talents. Literary sources mention that a court school of painting existed under Murad II and praise the skill of the artist Husamzada Sunullah, a painter of Bursa, but none of his work has survived.[34] The double frontispiece to a manuscript on music theory, the *Maqāsid al-Alhān* by ʿAbd al-Qadir al-Maraghi, however, shows the high quality of contemporary work at Edirne.[35] Painted in black, blue, and gold, with touches of orange, green, and white, the illuminated frontispieces show large central medallions decorated with delicate arabesques and floral sprays. Although details show that contemporary styles of Shiraz and Cairo were known to the artist, the composition and proportions are distinct, with oversize medallions and corner quadrants. The oval medallion on the left-hand page is inscribed with the dedication, which states that the manuscript was made in 1435 for the treasury of Murad II.

The most important development in the portable arts was the increased production of carpets. Scattered examples, such as the carpet unearthed at Pazyryk, indicate that the craft had been known in the Near East for millennia, but only from this period can a continuous tradition of carpet-making be traced to modern times. The few surviving carpet fragments are complemented by representations, primarily in

188. Fragment of a carpet from the ʿAla' al-Din Mosque, Konya, Anatolia, first half of the fourteenth century. Wool pile. 1.83 × 1.30 m. Istanbul, Türk ve Islam Eserleri Müzesi

contemporary Italian paintings, but also in Persian illustrated manuscripts. Two groups of carpets have been identified. The earlier group, known as "Konya carpets" because they were first discovered in 1903 in the ʿAla al-Din Mosque at Konya, are relatively coarse, with 5.6 to 7.8 symmetrical knots per square centimeter.[36] They show a relatively limited range of strong colors (medium and dark red, medium and dark blue, yellow, brown, and ivory). The typical layout consists of a central field with small, angular motifs arranged in staggered rows with a contrasting border of large pseudo-Kufic designs or stars. The size of the carpets (the largest measures 2.58 by 5.50 meters) suggests that their production was organized on a commercial scale rather than on the small scale of village or nomad weaving. Because they were found at the mosque at Konya, they were initially attributed to the patronage of the Saljuq sultans there, but at least one [188] has an asymmetrical motif derived from the cloud pattern on Chinese silks woven under the Yüan dynasty (1279–1368), and the group has been reattributed to the

189. Marby carpet, Anatolia, ca. 1400. Wool pile. 1.45 × 1.09 m. Stockholm, Statens Historiska Museum

first half of the fourteenth century.[37] As these carpets are not depicted in Italian paintings and only a few fragments of them have been found outside Anatolia, they seem to have been made for local consumption.[38]

Animal carpets are slightly later in date. Three examples survive: the Marby Carpet [189], found in the Swedish village of Marby in 1925, another found in a church in central Italy and now in Berlin, and a third acquired by the Metropolitan Museum of Art in New York in 1990.[39] In

contrast to the Konya carpets, animal carpets are relatively small (the Marby Carpet measures 1.45 by 1.09 meters; the Berlin carpet 1.72 by 0.90 meters; and the New York carpet 1.26 by 1.53 m). They all show confronted and stylized animals set within octagons or squares, but differ in color: the Marby Carpet has red birds flanking a tree on an ivory ground, the Berlin piece has a blue dragon attacking a blue phoenix on a yellow ground, and the New York piece has blue dragons on a red ground. The sources of the designs are also different: the birds and tree is a motif long known in Central Asia, while the dragon and phoenix is a Chinese motif which was probably brought to the Near East by the Mongols. The pieces can be attributed to ca. 1400, as animal carpets appear in early-fifteenth-century Italian paintings. The closest parallels are found in Domenico di Bartolo's fresco *The Wedding of the Foundlings*, painted between 1440 and 1444 for an orphanage in Siena, and a Sienese painting of *The Marriage of the Virgin* from the early fifteenth century.[40] Animal carpets must have been made already in the fourteenth century, as they are depicted in the Great Mongol *Shāhnāma*, made in Tabriz ca. 1335 (see Chapter 3). The illustration of *Zahhak Enthroned* shows the king seated on a throne below which is spread an carpet with octagons enclosing stylized quadrupeds.[41] Another illustration, *King Faridun Mourning his Son Iraj*, shows the king seated on a carpet depicting a dragon within a rectangular field.[42] While other carpets are depicted in contemporary manuscripts, these are the only two depictions of animal carpets in manuscripts from the early fourteenth century. Animal carpets must have been extremely rare at this time and reserved for royalty, as they are depicted under the royal figure. By the fifteenth century, however, there must have been many more of them and they must have had a much wider circulation, to judge from their appearances in Italian painting.

Other carpets and flat-weaves (Turk. *kilim*) may have been produced under the Beyliks, but their identification and dating are still a matter of lively debate. With the Ottoman unification of Anatolia and the conquest of Constantinople, the production of carpets must have increased dramatically, as did their export to Europe and their regular appearance in European painting. It is only in the later fifteenth century that the repeated depiction of Turkish carpets allows the definition of more types and the precise dating of surviving examples.

CHAPTER II

Architecture and the Arts in India¹ under the Sultanates

Muslims had founded trading settlements in Sind at the mouth of the Indus river as early as the eighth century, and excavations at such sites as Banbhore have revealed hypostyle mosques of a type common in central Islamic lands in the eighth and ninth centuries.² But a distinctive tradition of Indian Islamic architecture began to emerge only at the end of the twelfth century, when the Ghurid sultan of Khurasan, Muhammad b. Sam, conquered northern India, and his commander Qutb al-Din Aybak established his capital at Delhi in the plain to the west of the Yamuna (Jumna) river. Delhi remained the seat of several dynasties, collectively known as the Delhi sultanates, which ruled successively until the middle of the sixteenth century, and was often the capital of the Mughal emperors (see Chapter 18). The city quickly became an important center of Muslim learning and culture, as many intellectuals sought refuge there from the depredations of the Mongol conquests further west. The Chishti and Suhrawardi Sufi orders were particularly active in India, where they won many converts to Islam among lower-caste Hindus, although at no time did more than a quarter of the population ever convert to Islam.

Indigenous building techniques were adapted for the new types of buildings required by Muslims, particularly mosques and tombs. Unlike other areas of the Muslim world, which already had a large stock of congregational mosques, leading patrons to found such institutions as madrasas and khanaqahs, India was a clean slate and needed the entire range of Islamic institutions, virtually all of which were fundamentally different in spatial concept from most Hindu and Jain structures. The principal type of religious building in India was the temple, the dwelling place of the god envisioned as an architectural facsimile of the world-mountain. This largely solid mass of masonry, with its carefully regulated proportions and exuberant figural decoration, might be embellished with porches, pillared halls, and gates and set within a temenos, but it was never designed for congregational worship, the sole requirement of the mosque. In regions where stone had been the primary material of construction, temple spolia, particularly columns from porches and enclosures, were used extensively. The indigenous tradition of trabeate stone architecture, in which posts and corbels support beams and slab roofs, was modified by the introduction of the arcuate system typical of Islamic brick architecture in Afghanistan, Iran, and western Central Asia. At first, the form of an arch was imitated with corbeling and trabeate hypostyle halls were concealed by arched screens, but soon architects learned techniques of constructing arches and vaults which allowed the creation of large interior spaces, a necessity for congregational architecture.

ARCHITECTURE UNDER THE SULTANATES

Architectural developments under the Delhi sultanates are epitomized by the congregational mosque in the capital, now known as the Quwwat al-Islam Mosque, begun in the 1190s immediately after the Muslim conquest.³ Arches and domes were initially simulated with corbeling, as in the Aybak screen (1198), but by the time of the Khaljis (r. 1290–1320) true arches with voussoirs became the rule and true domes on squinches were often used. The Qutb Minar (1199 and 1368; height 72.5 meters), like minarets erected earlier by the Ghaznavids in Afghanistan, has superimposed flanged and cylindrical shafts separated by muqarnas cornices and decorated with inscriptions; unlike them it is built of sandstone. Congregational mosques survive in several other centers in northern India, such as Ajmer, some 350 kilometers to the south-west of Delhi in the heart of Rajasthan, where a mosque was built in 595/1199, six years after the region was conquered.⁴ The mosque is known as the Arhai-din-ka-jhonpra (Two and a half day) Mosque, as a fair of that duration was formerly held on the spot.⁵ According to an inscription on the mihrab, the mosque was erected during the reign of Qutb al-Din Aybak in Delhi, in Jumada II 595/March–April 1199. The building [190, 191], which sits on a high plinth set halfway up one of Ajmer's hills, comprises a large quadrangle, seventy-nine meters to a side. The plinth, a feature borrowed from temple architecture, became characteristic of Indian mosques for centuries. All corners but the north-west, which abuts a rocky outcrop, have projecting towers with deeply molded sides. On the east the main approach is up a steep stair of thirty-four steps in four flights. One passes through an arched gateway, flanked by pavilions, into the enclosure; all that remains of the interior is a hypostyle hall on the west roofed with five large and five small corbeled domes, masked by a great screen of seven corbeled and cusped arches probably added ca. 627/1229–30 by order of Iltutmish. Hypostyle halls were probably planned, if not built, for the other three sides of the quadrangle. The mihrab, which is also cusped, is exuberantly carved with vegetal and epigraphic ornament in rather flat relief.

At the mosque at Ajmer, as at the Quwwat al-Islam Mosque in Delhi, indigenous materials and techniques of construction are combined with a foreign plan and function. The plinth and staircase entrance are typical of west Indian temples, as is the trabeate construction in stone. Indeed, the structure was largely built of spolia from earlier temples: column shafts were superposed in threes to achieve sufficient height and create an effect of spaciousness unknown in indigenous types of buildings. The arched screen added to the court façade of the prayer hall is modeled on that added by Qutb al-Din Aybak to the Quwwat al-Islam Mosque in Delhi, but its carved relief decoration is a reworking in stone of brick decoration typical of Ghurid architecture in Afghanistan. The central arch, which is

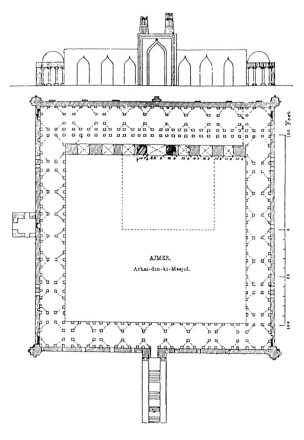

raised above the others in frank imitation of the *pīshṭāq* in front of an iwan, is surmounted by the stubs of two flanged towers, which were undoubtedly erected on the model of mosques further west.[6]

In 1290 the Mu'izzi dynasty, the descendants of Qutb al-Din Aybak, was succeeded by the Khaljis. The outstanding figure of the second line of Delhi sultans is 'Ala' al-Din Muhammad (r. 1296–1316), who considered himself a second Alexander and dreamed of assembling a vast empire. He repeatedly repulsed Mongol invasions from the north and annexed central and south India, using the stupendous booty collected there for grandiose schemes at home. In 1303, as a defense against Mongol incursions, he established a new encampment at Siri, on the plain about four kilometers north-east of the old center [192]. This foundation inaugurated the tradition of the lateral expansion of Delhi that would continue until the seventeenth century. Delhi's history is thus often told as a tale of seven cities (or eight if one includes New Delhi, inaugurated as capital of British India in 1931). The walls of Siri enclosed an irregular oval; they are said to have had seven gates, but major destruction in the sixteenth century has left few remains. Under 'Ala' al-Din and his son the area near the residence of the Chishti saint, Nizam al-Din Awliya' (1236–1325), began to be

190. Ajmer, Arhai-din-ka-jhonpra, 1199, plan

191. Ajmer, Arhai-din-ka-jhonpra, courtyard façade

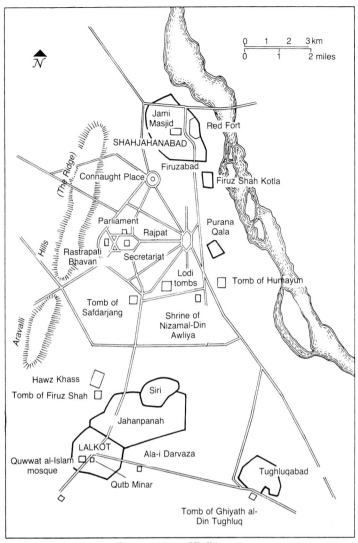

192. Map showing the seven cities of Delhi

square building measuring 10.5 meters to a side internally. It stands outside the enclosure wall of the mosque, in much the same relationship to it as the tomb of Iltutmish to the west, and serves to mark the transition between the low-lying exterior and the high interior of the mosque. The walls of the gatehouse are 3.2 meters thick and support a shallow dome carried on squinches. The unusual thickness of the walls and shallowness of the dome show the builders' unfamiliarity with the tradition of erecting small domed structures that had existed for centuries in Iran and Afghanistan. The building is faced with red sandstone inlaid with contrasting bands of white marble, all richly carved with arabesques and inscriptions in shallow relief. Lofty pointed arches with a slight return at the springing open on the three outer sides of the gateway; a moulding of conventionalized spearheads lines the arch. The arches are flanked by two stories of reveals; all are blind except for the inner pair on the lower story, which contain grilles opening to the interior. Many of these features, such as the contrasting colors of masonry, the spearhead corbels, and the pierced stone screens, later became hallmarks of Indo-Islamic architecture.

After 'Ala' al-Din's death the Khalji line fell into desuetude and was replaced by the Tughluqs (1320–1414), the third line of Delhi sultans. Descended from Ghazi Malik Tughluq, a Turco-Indian commander who had been governor of Multan for the Khaljis since 1305, the Tughluqs established the strongest and most creative state in the history of the Delhi sultanate. They were great patrons of literature, learning, and Islamic institutions. Responsible for three of Delhi's cities – Tughluqabad, Jahanpanah, and Firuzabad – the Tughluqs produced a rich and varied architecture in Delhi and in Multan in the Punjab. Materials and techniques of building were standardized and royal involvement was systematized through a bureaucracy of architects and engineers. The significant number of Tughluq buildings surviving allows a dynastic style to be defined for the first time in Indian Islamic architecture.[8]

The earliest example of Tughluq architecture is not, however, in Delhi but in Multan, now in Pakistan. It is the tomb of the Sufi saint Rukn-i 'Alam at Multan (1320), which was built by Ghazi Malik Tughluq when he was provincial governor there [194].[9] The octagonal lower story (27.4 meters in diameter and 15.5 meters high) has battered walls and tapering turrets at the angles. An octagonal second story with perpendicular walls supports a large dome, 35.1 meters high including the finial. The region of Multan and Sind had strong links to Afghanistan and eastern Iran, and its distinctive architectural style, like theirs, used bricks and glazed tile, with the addition of wood for roofs and tie beams. The tomb of Rukn-i 'Alam is built of brick, like such earlier buildings in the region as the so-called tomb of Khalid b. Walid built by the Ghurid governor 'Ali b. Karmakh in the last quarter of the twelfth century at nearby Kabirwala.[10] Bands of timber run through the brickwork of the lower octagonal level, and the exterior and interior are decorated with cut and molded bricks, which are left unglazed or glazed with light and dark blue and white. Although an octagonal second story is traditional in Multan, the octagonal lower story of the mausoleum of Rukn-i 'Alam is unusual, for three earlier tombs in Multan, those of

developed. Nizam al-Din's prayers were said to have protected the city from Mongol attack. A congregational mosque was built there, and after the saint's death the area, known as Nizamuddin, became a shrine center, following a pattern common in other regions of the Islamic world in the fourteenth century.

Between 1295 and 1315, 'Ala' al-Din attempted to expand the Quwwat al-Islam Mosque, which had already been expanded once by Iltutmish in 1210–29. The new mosque was to measure some 228 by 135 meters, and the arched screen in front of the new prayer hall was intended to be twice as long as the two previous screens combined. In the courtyard of the mosque, work was begun on a second tower, whose base is twice the diameter of the Qutb Minar and which was intended to be a stupendous 145 meters high.[7] The patron's death prevented this vast project from being completed, but it can be reconstructed from the foundations laid. Of the four major gates planned for the north, east, and south sides of the mosque, only that on the south, the 'Ala'-i Darvaza [193], was erected.

The 'Ala'-i Darvaza (Gate of 'Ala' [al-Din]; 1311) is a

193. Delhi, Quwwat al-Islam mosque, 'Ala'i Darvaza, 1311

194. Multan, Tomb of Rukn-i 'Alam, 1320

Shaykh Baha' al-Din Zakariya (d. 1262), Shadna Shahid (d. 1270), and Shah Shams Sabzavari (d. 1276), all have square lower stories. The wooden mihrab is the only one of its kind to survive in India.

Like the congregational mosque, the monumental tomb was a new form in India introduced by Muslims. The Muslim practice of inhumation of the dead was significantly different from the ritual cremation normally practiced in India. Although pious Muslims might cite the disapproval of the Prophet Muhammad for any monumentalization of graves, by the thirteenth century the construction of tombs over the graves of important and holy individuals had become a standard practice throughout the lands of Islam. The most widespread type was a square or octagonal structure supporting a dome, and the numerous examples surviving in Iran and Afghanistan undoubtedly provided models for the first Muslim tombs in India.[11]

Ghazi Malik Tughluq (r. 1320–5), who assumed the regnal name Ghiyath al-Din (Vivifier of the Faith), took large numbers of Hindus into government and military service, with a marked effect on Tughluq culture. He ordered the construction of Tughluqabad, which encompassed a royal quarter housing the court, army, and administration. Unlike Siri, which was close to Qutb al-Din's original foundation of Delhi, Tughluqabad was located seven kilometers east of the first city, in a massive fortified enclosure surrounded by a shallow lake fed by drainage from the surrounding plain. Covering a roughly trapezoidal area of 120 hectares, Tughluqabad was enclosed within battered stone walls reinforced with mighty semicircular bastions and breached by thirteen gates. The south-west quadrant was occupied by the palace, and the eastern sector contained an even more strongly fortified citadel. A causeway led from the main enclosure to another containing the founder's tomb and madrasa.

Set in an irregular court with cells along the interior of the enclosure walls, the mausoleum of Ghiyath al-Din [195] has a square lower story with walls battered 25° from the vertical, a rather short octagonal drum, and a prominent hemispheric dome surmounted by an ornate bulbous finial. Measuring sixteen meters on a side, the tomb is constructed of rubble faced with red sandstone and white marble. In the middle of all but the west, or qibla, sides are recessed arches with a slight ogee curve at the apex. They have spearhead voussoirs and are outlined in white marble. While the battering of the walls and prominent dome capped by a finial are features which seem to have been brought from Multan, where the patron had been governor, the articulation of the façades and the details of decoration show a conscious imitation of the 'Ala'-i Darvaza, perhaps to give monumental expression to the Tughluqs' succession to the Khalji line. In one respect, however, the building differs from its Mu'izzi and Khalji antecedents: whereas earlier buildings, such as the tomb of Iltutmish, were lavishly decorated with inscriptions, the tomb of Ghiyath al-Din completely lacks epigraphs. The first generation of Muslim builders in India had replaced the exuberant figural decoration of Hindu and Jain architecture with equally exuberant geometric, vegetal, and epigraphic ornament stylistically derived from Ghurid architecture in Afghanistan. A taste for more restrained surface ornament developed under the Tughluqs, where the surface was articulated by such architectural elements as doors and windows.

Ghiyath al-Din's successor, Muhammad b. Tughluq (r. 1325–51), was also a great builder; he built and then abandoned a subsidiary fort ('Adilabad) next to Tughluqabad, transferred the capital to Dawlatabad in central India, and walled the suburbs that had grown up between the first city of Delhi and Siri and called it Jahanpanah. His successor, Firuz Shah (r. 1351–88), had the longest rule of the line, probably because he left matters of state in the hands of his capable viziers. He is said to have designed many buildings himself. In 1356, to protect the Punjab against attacks from the north-west, he founded the city of Hisar-i Firuza, now Hisar in Haryana state.[12] In 1359, to control the Gumti river and counteract the importance of the Hindu holy city of Varanasi (Benares), he founded the city of Jaunpur. In 1354 in his capital, Delhi, he had begun construction of the city of Firuzabad about ten kilometers north of Jahanpanah along the old course of the Yamuna. Now largely covered and quarried for its materials to build the later city of Shahjahanabad, all that remains is the citadel, known as Firuz Shah Kotla, which contains the ruins of a palace complex, a congregational mosque, and the adjacent Lat Pyramid.

The Lat Pyramid, a three-storied stepped pyramid, fourteen meters high, of vaulted cells around a solid core, was built in the typical Tughluq rubble masonry covered with plaster and whitewash. Staircases at the corners led to the upper level on which stood an open colonnade 4.9 meters high enclosing an Ashokan (third century B.C.) sandstone pillar (lat) thirteen meters high. The pillar had been taken in 1367 from its original site near Ambala in Meerut District, 192 kilometers north of Delhi, transported down the Yamuna, and erected on the site. Contemporary sources refer to the structure as the manar (marker) of the congregational mosque, and the pillar itself was called the manar-i zarrin ("golden marker"), either because of the color of its stone, its gilded paint, or its polished surface.[13] The biography of Firuz Shah states that it was a visible statement of Muslim convictions: "After it [the lat] had remained an object of worship of the polytheists and infidels for so many thousands of years, through the efforts of Sultan Firuz Shah and by the grace of God, it became the marker of a place of worship for the faithful."[14] Although the Lat Pyramid is conceptually related to Qutb al-Din Aybak's placement of a Gupta-period (fourth-century) iron pillar from a temple of Vishnu in the court of the Quwwat al-Islam Mosque, it differs from it in form.[15] It is the first Muslim building in north India to depart from basic canons of Islamic architecture.

Although Firuz Shah commissioned many madrasas, only one survives, that founded in 1352 along the eastern and southern sides of the great tank known as Hawz Khass in Delhi [196]. The largest and most complex madrasa of this period to have survived anywhere, it was partly constructed over an earlier foundation by 'Ala' al-Din Khalji, and the tank was the gathering place for musicians, according to the Moroccan globe-trotter Ibn Battuta, who visited Delhi in the 1330s.[16] The complex comprises two long blocks perched on the sides of the tank and rivetted together by the founder's tomb, a domed square. The interior of the tomb is decorated

195. Delhi, Tomb of Ghiyath al-Din Tughluq, 1325

196. Delhi, Hawz Khass, begun 1352

in the Iranian mode with painted and carved stucco. Each of the madrasa's two stories comprises interconnecting blocks of long, narrow pillared halls and dome chambers. Cells on the lower story presumably served as residential quarters, while the more open rooms on the upper story were used for assembly and teaching. Several pavilions, domed tombs, and other structures stand in the spacious and carefully planted gardens between the madrasa and outer walls.[17] The unusual layout of the complex and its reliance on pillared halls distinguish it from madrasas elsewhere in the Islamic lands, where a court with vaulted iwans and chambers had quickly become the ubiquitous plan for this type of building [e.g. 156, 157].

Tughluq architecture is the first Islamic architecture in India to have attempted to integrate such indigenous elements as pillars, beams, and brackets, and such techniques as the control of temperature by water, with features identified with Islamic architecture elsewhere, such as arches, vaults, and domes. The exuberant carved surface decoration of earlier times was abandoned in favor of a greater interest in the massing of architectural form and its emphasis by a juxtaposition of surfaces and restrained use of color. The relatively large number of surviving buildings of various types – mosques, tombs, a madrasa, reservoirs, and fortifications – shows that patrons and builders were ready to experiment with new forms and combinations of them. This rich period of creativity came to an end following the death of Firuz Shah in 1388. A decade of internecine warfare between rival claimants to the throne climaxed in Timur's invasion of northern India and sack of Delhi in 1398, although weakling Tughluq rulers held on for another sixteen years.

After the Timurid sack of Delhi and the dissolution of the Tughluqs, the patronage of monumental architecture was restricted under the fourth and fifth Delhi sultanates. The city enjoyed little prestige under the Sayyids (1414–1451) but was revived under the Lodis (1451–1526), when several mosques and domed tombs were erected. Construction of the type of large congregational mosque that had been popular in the earlier sultanates was abandoned in favor of a new, smaller type of mosque, comprising a single aisle of three or five domed bays arranged along the qibla wall. The first extant example is the Bara Gumbad Mosque, built by Sikandar Lodi in 1494 as a ceremonial entrance to the Bagh-i Jud, once the dynastic burial ground and now the Lodi Gardens. This new type of mosque hearkens back to early Sultanate models and displays a renewed interest in the monumental façade, which was often marked by a *pīshṭāq* and decorated with inlaid colored stones and inscriptions. These Lodi buildings provided inspiration for later patrons, notably the Surs and Mughals in the sixteenth century.[18]

The most impressive architectural patronage in the late fourteenth and fifteenth centuries took place in the other Muslim states of India, where distinctive regional styles developed with greater or lesser dependence on the architectural precedents of the Delhi region. Muhammad b. Tughluq had conquered large portions of the Deccan and temporarily moved the capital to the newly founded site of Dawlatabad, but as his authority waned, independent sultanates were founded there. The most enduring was that of the Bah-

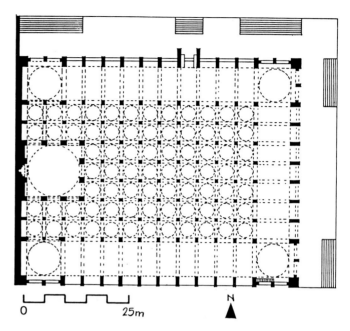

197. Gulbarga, Congregational Mosque, 1367, plan

manids (r. 1347–1527) on the table-land in the northern Deccan. The founder of the dynasty, Hasan Gangu, who assumed the regnal name Bahman Shah, moved the capital south from Dawlatabad to Gulbarga (now in Karnataka state). The Bahmanids' aggressive confrontation with the two main Hindu kingdoms of the southern Deccan, Warangal and Vijayanagar, made them renowned throughout the Muslim world as warriors for the faith, and they were the first power in the subcontinent to exchange ambassadors with the Ottomans. The Bahmanids had a well-organized administrative system and recruited skilled personnel among Turks, Persians, and Arabs. Their court became an important center of learning and culture, and a distinct style of architecture emerged.[19]

The most important building to survive in Gulbarga is the congregational mosque, built, according to an inscription, by Rafiʿ b. Shams b. Mansur al-Qazvini in 1367 during the reign of Muhammad I.[20] The building, which measures 66 by 53 meters, is a rare example of a mosque with no courtyard [197, 198]. It is a covered rectangle with large domes in each of the four corners and a dome covering the equivalent of nine bays in front of the mihrab. Transverse-vaulted aisles connect the corner domes and enclose on three sides the central hypostyle hall covered with seventy-five domes. The aisles have unusually wide spans and low imposts; this arch pattern was repeated in other buildings at Gulbarga. The use of transverse vaulting parallels its use in such fourteenth-century Iranian buildings as the congregational mosque at Abarquh, but the low imposts and distinctive profile of the arches are quite different. This unusual vaulting may be explained by the Iranian origin of the patron and perhaps by the presence of Iranian builders in the region. The tombs of the Bahmanid sultans at Gulbarga reflect the impact of the Tughluq style, whether via now lost buildings of Dawlatabad or Delhi, in their battered walls and low domes. After conquering Warangal in 1425, Ahmad

198. Gulbarga, Congregational Mosque, side aisle

I moved the capital east to the more central site of Bidar. There such features as domes raised on tall drums, glazed tilework, and the four-iwan plan show the increased role of architectural models from contemporary Iran and Central Asia under the Timurids (see Chapter 4).

Although indigenous architectural traditions seem to have played little role in the evolution of the Bahmanid style, they were stronger elsewhere in the subcontinent, where the new styles of Islamic architecture combined local traditions with the style of the Delhi sultanate and ideas from the Islamic lands to the west. The Islamic architecture of Bengal is primarily a continuation of the indigenous tradition of brick construction, although stone spolia from Hindu buildings were also used. As in Iraq, where the Tigris and Euphrates rivers have deposited the silt and clay from which brick is made, the Ganges and Brahmaputra rivers, which empty into the Bay of Bengal, have left rich deposits of silt and clay in Bengal. Bengal had been part of the Delhi sultanate, but its rich resources and distance from the capital tempted its governors to declare their independence, and already

by 1287 parts of it were virtually independent. The Ilyas Shahi dynasty (1345–1487, with an interruption 1414–37) united all Bengal under one crown, with capitals at Gaur (Lakhnawati) and Pandua, now in the Indian state of West Bengal. Commerce in textiles and foodstuffs was encouraged, and the arts and sciences flourished. Sikandar Shah (r. 1358–89) moved the capital from Gaur, on the old course of the Ganges, to Pandua, thirty-two kilometers to the northeast, after the river shifted its course.[21]

The Adina Mosque there (1374–5) is one of largest mosques in India, measuring 155 by 87 meters. It consists of a series of hypostyle halls arranged around a courtyard; that on the qibla side is five bays deep, while those on the other three sides are three bays deep. The courtyard façade is a screen of eighty-eight arches supported on piers and surmounted by a parapet. In the center of the prayer hall was a massive iwan-like barrel-vaulted hall [199] leading from the court to the mihrab and minbar. Now roofless and shattered, the vault was framed by a screen some eighteen meters high, undoubtedly modeled on the Iranian *pīshṭāq*. Stone spolia from the temples of Lakhnawati were used for the lower parts of the building, but brick was used above the imposts for the arches and the three hundred and seventy brick domes. The bays of the prayer hall terminate in mihrabs in the qibla wall, except where the wall has been pierced for doors. Three bays to the north of the mihrab is a raised platform (Pers. *takht*) which occupies six bays in the back three aisles. It was originally screened and surmounted by eighteen domes higher than those over the other bays of the prayer halls. At the level of the platform the qibla wall has three mihrabs, superbly carved of basalt, and two doors. This type of platform is found in several large congregational mosques of the sultanate period, and some scholars have argued that it was for ladies of the court; but it is more likely that it was an elevated *maqṣūra*. The two doorways are more impressive than the ground-floor entrance to the mosque on the west wall just north of the iwan, and outside the mosque behind the area of the platform is a square structure with an L-shaped ramp to the north. This was probably the original royal entrance to the mosque, but after the death of the patron, Sikander Shah, it was converted into his tomb on the model of Iltutmish's tomb in the Quwwat al-Islam Mosque at Delhi.[22] Although the size and plan of the Adina Mosque are atypical of other Bengali mosques, which are much more modest in scale, the multiplicity of mihrabs is a distinct feature that had appeared as early as the mosque of Zafar Khan Ghazi in Tribeni (1298), which has five. The grandiose quality of the Adina Mosque and the similarities to buildings in Islamic lands further west can be explained by the ambitions of the patron, who, in the foundation inscription, called himself "the most perfect of the sultans of Arabia and Persia."[23]

Similar use of the iwan motif is found at the mosques of Jaunpur, a city on the Gumti River to the north of Varanasi, now in the state of Uttar Pradesh in northern India. The city became the center of a powerful Muslim state wedged between the sultanates of Delhi and Bengal, and under the Sharqi sultans of Jaunpur (1394–1479) it was known as the "Shiraz of Hind" for its culture and learning. The Atala Mosque (1408) was built by Ibrahim Sharqi on the founda-

199. Hazrat Pandua, Adina Mosque, 1374–5, qibla iwan

200. Jaunpur, Atala Mosque, 1408, central pylon

tions of and with stones taken from a Hindu temple dedicated to Atala Devi, although the mosque is unusual among contemporary and later Indian examples in not being raised on a plinth. The mosque consists of a square enclosure (78.7 meters on a side), with hypostyle halls three bays deep surrounding the central court. Monumental entrances on the north, south, and east sides are flanked on the exterior by rows of shops and lead via domed bays (except on the east) to the court. The west or qibla side has a screen with a central pylon [200]. Battered towers 22.9 meters high frame a large arched recess pierced with windows and fringed with stylized spearheads. Behind stands a large dome (diameter 16.8 meters), and on either side smaller versions of the central unit ease the transition from the roof of the hypostyle prayer hall to the summit of the screen. The mosque is designed to be seen from particular spots, especially the court; in this it conforms to contemporary esthetics in the rest of the Islamic world (e.g. the Mosque of Bibi Khanum at Samarqand [49]), but this approach to design was still foreign to the indigenous tradition, where buildings were meant to be viewed from the exterior and designed in the round. When viewed from the exterior, particularly from the rear, the masses of the Atala Mosque are often ungainly.[24] Such features as the battered elevation of the towers and the spearhead molding are clearly derived from Khalji and Tughluq buildings in Delhi, but the mosque presents a somewhat retardataire aspect in the juxtaposition of domed chambers and hypostyle halls for the prayer hall. The overall conception is distinctly local and would be repeated on a larger scale at the congregational mosque built there by Husayn Shah (r. 1458–79).

201. Ahmadabad, Congregational Mosque, 1423, court façade

The most distinctive regional style of architecture was developed in Gujerat in western India. This region, with a rich heritage of Hindu and Jain buildings, became independent under the Tughluq governor Zafar Khan, who founded a sultanate in 1407, assuming the regnal name Muzaffar Shah. His grandson Ahmad I (r. 1411–42) consolidated the realm and moved the capital to the old Hindu town of Asaval, which he renamed Ahmadabad. He inaugurated an era of unparalleled architectural activity, when at least fifty mosques were erected in the capital alone. The finest is the congregational mosque (1423).[25] It consists of a large flagged court (75 by 66 meters), lined with a single arcade on three sides. On the fourth, or qibla, side is an exquisitely carved façade [201], with a large central arch flanked by the bases of towers (now destroyed) and smaller arches, which effect a visual transition between the height of the hall and the central arch. The façade is intensely scuptural: the horizontal bands of the tower shafts contrast with the verticality of the towers, the richly carved masses of masonry contrast with the shadowy voids behind, and the massive masonry contrasts with the slender shafts of the hypostyle prayer hall

behind. The prayer hall (64 by 29 meters) contains over three hundred closely set slender columns, which support fifteen large domes surrounded by clusters of smaller ones. The large dome immediately behind the central arch is the tallest, rising to a height of three stories, while those behind the smaller arches are two stories high. The arches are linked on the interior by an ingenious system of mezzanines. This harmonious composition, which successfully integrates trabeate and arcuate construction and combines the volumetrics of Islamic architecture with the sculptural quality of Indian architecture, is far more successful than the rather awkward arrangement of the Atala Mosque in Jaunpur.

The congregational mosque was only part of Ahmad Shah's master plan for his capital, which covered an area of about five hundred hectares on the east bank of the Sabarmati river. On the other three sides the city was protected by walls with towers at regular intervals. The main processional way led from the east wall, passing along the north side of the congregational mosque, to the citadel, a square enclosure for the palaces overlooking the river. At the foot of the citadel lay the royal grounds (Maydan-i Shah),

202. Ahmadabad, Tin Darvaza, 1423

which were entered on the east through a great triple-arched gateway, the Tin Darvaza, constructed in 1423 [202]. The wider central arch flanked by projecting buttresses and crowned with a parapet of merlons is typical of mosque architecture and echoes the qibla façade of the mosque some 150 meters to the east.

The region of Malwa, located at the crossroads between north India and the Deccan, between the central provinces and the ports of Gujerat, became independent of Delhi in the wake of the Timurid invasions. In 1405 Alp Khan Hushang, the second of the sultans of Malwa (1401–1531), transferred the capital from Dhar, the ancient stronghold of the Paramara dynasty, to Mandu, an inaccessible and heavily defended fortress. He and his successors erected an imposing new capital to emulate and compete with those of his contemporaries and adorned it with many splendid buildings which show the strong impact of the Delhi tradition. Among

203. Mandu, Jahaz-mahal, fifteenth and sixteenth centuries

the buildings erected are several gates, a congregational mosque, and several palaces and pleasure pavilions, which illustrate yet another facet of Indo-Islamic architecture. The Jahaz Mahal ("Ship Palace"), for example, extends on two levels for about 115 meters between two lakes [203]. Its roof is punctuated with several pillared and domed pavilions to take advantage of the view and cooling breezes off the water, much as at the Hawz Khass in Delhi [196]. Another palace on the Munja Talao included a special well with adjacent underground rooms to combat the summer heat. Everything was built of red ocher sandstone, and color was used extensively in tile revetments and polychrome inlay of marble and stone.[26]

THE ARTS IN THE SULTANATES

While the Muslim faith required new and distinctive kinds of buildings in India, there was no immediate reason to change the esthetic in most of the decorative arts produced in the sultanates, and traditional techniques and forms were continued. A superbly carved ivory chessman in the form of a nobleman riding in a howdah on the back of an elephant encircled by armed footmen is clearly the work of a Muslim, for it is inscribed in Arabic "the work of Yusuf al-Bahili," a Muslim name. Its iconography and style suggest an Indian provenance, but suggested dates have ranged from the eighth century to the fifteenth.[27] Virtually no object of metalwork has been identified as having been produced under the sultanates.[28] The only medium besides architecture in which a distinctive tradition evolved was the art of the book, for copies of the Koran and other books were required by mosques and pious Muslims, and indigenous traditions were inadequate and unsuitable. Few manuscripts survive from the first two centuries of Muslim rule in India, probably because many were destroyed with Timur's sack of Dehli in 1398, and the first steps in the development of a distinctive tradition of Indian Islamic book production can be traced only under the independent sultanates.

A new style of calligraphy emerges in manuscripts of the Koran. Known for unknown reasons as *khaṭṭ-i bīhārī* ("the script from Bihar"), it is a stylized script like Maghribi and has wedge-shaped letters, thick round bowls for endings, and wide spaces between words. The script is first documented in a small (24 by 17 cm) single-volume manuscript of the Koran which was completed on 21 July 1399 by Mahmud Sha'ban, described in the colophon as a resident of the fort of Galyur (modern Gwalior).[29] Each of the 550 folios has five lines of Arabic in an early Bihari script with a Persian interlinear translation in a smaller and rounder *naskh*. Chapter headings and double pages [204] marking the divisions into thirty sections (*juz'*) are illuminated with lush floral and vegetal patterns in gold, black, red, brown, yellow, blue, and white. This colorful decoration, some of which may have been repainted between 1399 and the nineteenth century, when the manuscript was restored, enlivens the somewhat static and cumbersome script. The manuscript is the finest as well as earliest of a group of manuscripts produced in northern India with similar script and decoration.[30]

In the fifteenth century Bihari script became standard in India for copying manuscripts of the Koran, and one

204. Left half of the frontispiece from a manuscript of the Koran, Gwalior, 1399. 24 × 17 cm. Geneva, Sadruddin Aga Khan, MS. 32, f. 2r

205. Double page from a manuscript of the Koran, Deccan, 1483. 47.6 × 31.1 cm. Bijapur, Archaeological Museum, MS 912

dated 1483 shows the fully developed script, with sweeping horizontal curves [205], only incipient in the earlier example.[31] The manuscript belongs to a group of Koran manuscripts of medium size (it measures 47.6 by 31.1 cm), written on rough paper which has been eaten by the acidic pigments of the illumination. Double pages at the beginning of the thirty *juz´* have four panels of illumination; the upper and lower panels project into the margin to flank large projecting *ansae*. The crude materials suggest that these manuscripts were produced not for royal patrons, but for the open market.[32]

A distinctive tradition of illustrated manuscripts, in which Indian motifs and themes were added to traditional Iranian models, also emerged in fifteenth-century India. The style was first identified in the illustrations to a group of eight manuscripts dated between 1417 and 1440, as well as illustrations in other undated manuscripts and detached illustrated leaves.[33] The illustrations share such features of Timurid provincial work done in Shiraz as a high horizon, landscape with a semé of leaves and flowers, and coral-like hills (see Chapter 5), but they are drier and simpler, includ-

ing such archaisms as horizontal formats depicting shallow space, stepping along the upper frame, and cross-hatching to indicate the ground plane. Typical Indian features include large groups of figures in serried rows and identical poses, and bright and unusual colors instead of the modulated palette typical of Timurid painting. Narrow decorated bands run across the width of the picture, a feature also found in Jain manuscripts from western India. Even more important are calligraphic peculiarities, such as a rhythmic parallelism in which the bowls of the letters are nested inside each other.

This identification of a sultanate style of painting is still controversial, and not all the manuscripts ascribed to the group are universally accepted as Indian work.[34] A copy of the *Shāhnāma* dated 1438, however, contains two pieces of indisputable evidence proving that it was produced in India.[35] First, the text contains the old preface to the *Shāhnāma*, rather than the one prepared in 1430 for Baysunghur that became standard in Iran, and includes a unique passage saying that when Firdawsi fled from his patron Mahmud of Ghazna, he took refuge at the court of the King of Delhi, who eventually sent him with rich gifts back to Tus, his birthplace in north-eastern Iran. Second, the yellow used in the illustrations throughout the manuscript is *peori* or Indian yellow, a pigment prepared from the urine of cows fed on mango leaves. In the eighteenth century the pigment was made only in a village near Munger in Bengal; while it was probably prepared and used over a larger area in earlier centuries, it was never used in Iran. The small (27 by 16.5 cm) manuscript has 513 folios of thin light-brown paper with a double frontispiece and 93 small (ca. 7–8.5 by 12 cm) paintings [206]. The basic vocabulary of figures, trellises, rolled curtains, and clouds in aerial shape belongs to a Shiraz tradition, but such features as illuminations with broad straps of blue and a heavy crimson belong to the Indian tradition. The delicate curvilinear arabesques typical of Iranian work under the Timurids and Safavids are missing, and the artist generally fails to take advantage of the high

206. *The Drunk Cobbler Riding one of Bahram Gur's Lions* from the Mohl *Shāhnāma*, India, 1438. London, British Library, MS. Or 1403, f. 368v

horizon, except in the double frontispiece, which may be by another hand.[36]

Another group of four manuscripts produced in Mandu at the turn of the fifteenth century shows the direct impact of contemporary Iranian painting in the Turkoman style of Shiraz and the classical style of Herat. The most famous is a copy of *Ni'matnāma*, a cookbook with recipes for delicacies, aphrodisiacs, and other epicurean delights.[37] Begun for the Khalji sultan of Malwa, Ghiyath Shah (r. 1469–1500), and expanded by his son Nasir Shah (r. 1500–10), the manuscript can be attributed to the decade 1495–1505. The 196 folios (each measuring some 30 by 20 cm) are copied in a large and bold *naskh* script with red headings and contain fifty paintings illustrating the preparation of the recipes. Most use a set iconographic formula showing an enthroned prince surrounded by attendants and servants, all within an architectural or landscape setting. The basic Turkoman style has been embellished with such elements from daily life in India as cooking pots and patterned textiles. Women are usually shown in profile wearing local dress, and buildings often have such features common to the vernacular tradition of Mandu as domes and heavy projecting eaves carried on carved brackets [e.g., 207]. Many of the conventions of Persian painting have been altered. In the outdoor scenes, for example, the convention of dividing the sky into a gold lower section and a blue upper one has been reinterpreted so that the gold half continues the ground and is sprinkled with clumps of flowers.

The *Ni'matnāma* was probably executed by local artists who had learned the Turkoman style from imported manuscripts or from émigrés. These Mandu artists were able to work in various styles, for a manuscript of Sa'di's *Būstān*

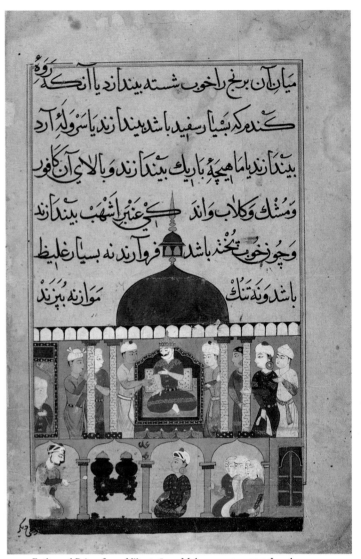

207. *Enthroned Prince* from *Ni'matnāma*, Malwa, 1495–1505. London, India Office Library, MS. 149, f. 6v

("Orchard") penned by Shahsavur al-Katib, illustrated by Hajji Mahmud, and datable to Mandu 1500 to 1503, has forty-three paintings in a provincial version of the Timurid style of Herat.[38] Features such as the extensive use of the profile, the horizontal decorative bands, and the patterned fabrics are derived from the local school of painting seen in the Mandu *Kalpasutra*, copied in 1439–40 at the fort of Mandapadurga (Mandu) in the reign of Sultan Mahmud for a Jain monk,[39] and some of the sartorial details, such as the heavy gold ring around a woman's neck and the local Malwa dress of a long gown fastened up the middle and tied with a sash at the waist, as well as the bright clashing palette, are repeated in paintings done some fifty years later in the Deccani school (see Chapter 19).

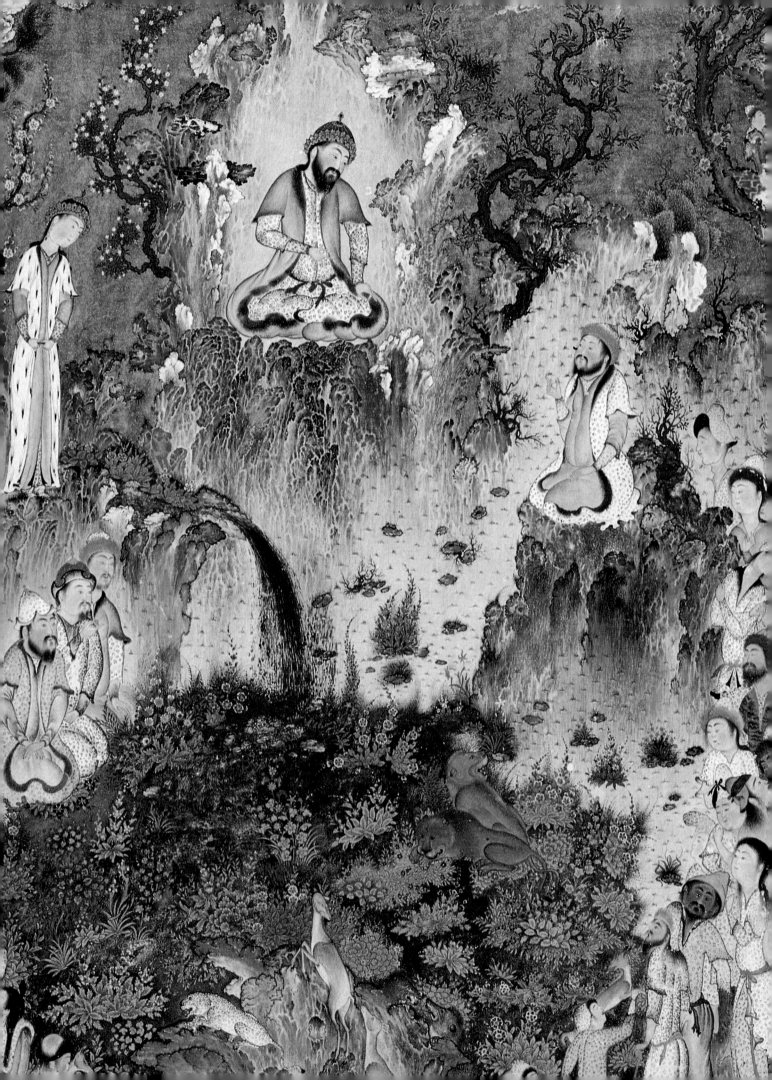

CHAPTER 12

The Arts in Iran under the Safavids and Zands

The Safavids claimed descent from Shaykh Safi al-Din (1252–1334), who established a dervish order at Ardabil in north-west Iran.[1] In the late fifteenth century his descendants worked to subvert the Turkoman in western Iran and eastern Anatolia, and in 1501 Isma'il b. Haydar seized Azerbayjan from the Aqqoyunlu and established the Safavid monarchy. Within a decade, the shah had subdued all of Iran. The Safavid state was a theocracy, for Isma'il and his successors also traced their descent from 'Ali b. Abu Talib, the son-in-law and successor to the Prophet Muhammad, and claimed semi-divine status as reincarnations of the Shi'ite imams. Their Turkoman supporters, the Qizilbash (or Redheads, from the distinctive color of their caps), owed them both political and spiritual allegiance. Shi'ism, which had enjoyed sporadic importance in earlier times, was imposed as the state religion, and, in so distinguishing itself from its Sunni neighbors, the country acquired the sense of national identity that has survived to the present. On the east, the Safavids held their own against the Uzbeks, although such frontier towns as Herat and Mashhad frequently changed hands. On the west, they were less successful against the Ottomans, who defeated them at the battle of Chaldiran outside Tabriz in 1514. The continuous insecurity of the border region led the Safavids to move their capital from vulnerable Tabriz, first to Qazvin (1555) and then to Isfahan (1591).

Most of the architecture from the early Safavid period has been destroyed, and the decorative arts are the major source for reconstructing the esthetic of the period. The arts of the book took on an extraordinary significance during the first half of the sixteenth century under Safavid patronage. The manuscripts produced were of the highest quality ever known in Islamic art, and designs for such other arts as textiles, carpets, and architectural decoration were prepared in the royal manuscript workshops. In addition, as the art of the book became a self-conscious art form, a new awareness of its history developed and individual artists took on increased importance.

THE ARTS UNDER THE EARLY SAFAVIDS (1501–76)

The importance and quality of book-painting during the reign of Isma'il I (1501–24) can be seen in three manuscripts. The first is the magnificent copy of Nizami's *Khamsa* ("Five poems") [see 91] that had been begun for Baysunghur's son Babur, continued for several Turkoman princes, and, still unfinished, passed into the hands of one of the amirs of Shah Isma'il, Najm al-Din Mas'ud Zargar Rashti, at which time several illustrations were added. One of the illustrations bears the date 910/1504–5.[2] As the illustrations added

in Safavid times have the same lush vegetation, elaborate architecture, and brilliant coloring as the Turkoman ones, the Turkoman royal workshop in Tabriz must have continued production under the new regime. The Safavid illustrations can be distinguished from the earlier ones, however, by the distinctive headgear of the figures: a tall red cap often wrapped with a voluminous turban. The same style can be seen in another peripatetic manuscript, a copy of Muhammad 'Asafi's *Dāstān-i Jamāl u Jalāl* ("Story of Jamal and Jalal") in Uppsala.[3] The copying of the text was completed at Herat in 1502–3, when the city was still in the control of the Timurids. Of the thirty-four illustrations two are dated to 1503–4 and one to 1504–5, but none is done in the classical Bihzadian style associated with Herat. Rather, they all show the distinctive exuberance and lush foliage of Turkoman painting from Tabriz and the characteristic Safavid headgear. The unillustrated manuscript was probably brought from Herat to Tabriz, where its illustrations were added.[4]

The third manuscript associated with Isma'il, a *Shāhnāma* ("Book of kings"), was the most spectacular, for in this instance he did not order the completion of an unfinished manuscript begun by others but undertook one of his own. The manuscript is known only from four detached paintings, of which three have been lost. The illustrations can be dated to Isma'il's reign by the style of headgear, which is identical to that shown in his other two manuscripts.[5] The surviving image of *The Sleeping Rustam* [208] shows the scale and quality of the manuscript from which it was taken and is the undisputed masterpiece of the Turkoman style of painting as continued under Isma'il's patronage.[6] The image depicts the great hero Rustam, who unsuspectingly falls asleep in a lion's lair. He is protected, however, from the returning lion by his trusty chestnut-colored steed Rakhsh. The artist has effectively isolated the sleeping hero with green and yellow vegetation which suggests the peaceful detachment of dreamland, and the violent confrontation between horse and lion has been transformed into a stylized ballet in the lower right. The vivid colors, sure draughtsmanship, and brilliant design indicate that no expense was spared to produce this image, but the absence of rulings between columns of text and between text and image show that the manuscript itself was never completed. The idea of commissioning a large (31.8 by 20.8 cm), illustrated copy of the Persian national epic, however, set the precedent for the biggest book project of the sixteenth century, the copy of the *Shāhnāma* produced for Isma'il's son and successor Tahmasp I (r. 1524–76).[7]

As Isma'il's oldest son, the infant Tahmasp had been sent to be governor of Herat. There he was trained in calligraphy and drawing; a manuscript was penned by him when he was eleven.[8] He returned to Tabriz in 1522, and many calligraphers and painters of Herat who had continued the Timurid traditions there probably accompanied him, although some may have come earlier. The renowned painter Bihzad was purportedly named head of the royal library in

208. *Rustam Sleeping While Rakhsh Fights the Lion*, detached page from an
unfinished copy of the *Shāhnāma*, Tabriz, 1515–22. 31.8 × 20.8 cm.
London, British Museum

209. *The Court of Gayumars*, f. 20v, from the Tahmasp *Shāhnāma*, Tabriz,
1525–35. 34.2 × 23.1 cm. Geneva, Sadruddin Aga Khan

Tabriz at this time; whether or not he actually came, the story accurately reflects the great change Persian manuscript painting underwent during the reign of Shah Tahmasp: the integration of the refined, cool, and classical Bihzadian style of Herat with the exuberant, vibrant, and brash style practiced in Tabriz under the Turkomans and Isma'il.

The *Shāhnāma* made for Tahmasp was an enormous project: a manuscript of 742 large folios (47.0 by 31.8 cm), with superb gold-flecked margins around a ruled area 26.9 by 17.7 cm. Innumerable illuminations and 258 large illustrations grace the text. Although the manuscript lacks a colophon, it bears a dedicatory rosette (fol. 16r) which says that the book was prepared for the library of Sultan Shah Tahmasp. Only one of the paintings in the manuscript is dated: that of *Ardashir and the slave-girl Gulnar* (fol. 516v), which bears a date of 934/1527–8. Tahmasp would have been fourteen years old in that year, and the romantic depiction of the young lovers may well have commemorated his coming of age. A project of this magnitude must have taken several years to complete, perhaps as much as a decade, so the manuscript can be attributed to 1525–35. Nothing of this scale is known from the fifteenth century; its size and scale suggest comparison with the Great Mongol *Shāhnāma* (see Chapter 3), which was planned to have some 200 illustrations in two volumes.[9] In 1567 the Safavid manuscript was presented by Tahmasp to the Ottoman sultan Selim II [308], and it remained in the Ottoman imperial collections at least until 1801, when Mehmed 'Arif, keeper of the guns in the palace treasury, wrote synopses of the stories on the pages protecting the paintings. By 1903 it had entered the collection of Baron Edmond de Rothschild, whose family sold it to an American collector in 1959. The manuscript, which had survived intact for over four hundred years, was subsequently dismembered. Individual folios were sold at auction like so many slices of pizza, and the integrity of one of the masterpieces of Islamic art was ignominiously destroyed.

The most brilliant painting in the manuscript, considered by many to be the greatest of all Persian manuscript paintings, represents *The Court of Gayumars* [209].[10] The first king of Iran, the benevolent Gayumars, ruled from a mountaintop; during his reign men learned how to prepare food and how to clothe themselves in leopard skins. In his presence the wild animals became meek as lambs. The painter has placed the king at the apex of the composition: he looks mournfully at his son Siyamak, seated below him on the right, who will be killed in battle with the Black Div. Opposite Siyamak stands his son, the willowy young prince Hushang, who will revenge his father's death and save the Iranian throne. The members of Gayumars' retinue, each distinguished by gesture, facial feature, mien, and pose, gather in a circle before him. The fantastic landscape repeats many of the features found in *The Sleeping Rustam* [208] such as the lush green and yellow vegetation, flowering trees silhouetted against a gold sky, and chinoiserie clouds, but the spongy rock forms have grown even more exuberant in color and conceal innumerable grotesques. It can easily be imagined that this image, like the image of the young Ardashir, was composed with particular reference to contemporary history and that the young Tahmasp saw himself as Hushang.

Already in the sixteenth century this painting was recognized for its greatness. Writing in 1544, the painter and chronicler Dust Muhammad, who himself is credited with having added the painting of *Haftvad and the Worm* (fol. 521v) to this manuscript, described the portraitists and painters in Tahmasp's library:

> First is the rarity of the age, Master Nizamuddin Sultan-Muhammad, who has developed depiction to such a degree that, although it has a thousand eyes, the celestial sphere has not seen his like. Among his creations, depicted in His Majesty's *Shāhnāma*, is a scene of people wearing leopard skins: it is such that the lion-hearted of the jungle of depiction and the leopards and crocodiles of the workshop of ornamentation quail at the fangs of his pen and bend their necks before the awesomeness of his pictures.[11]

The specificity of his description leaves no doubt that Dust Muhammad was describing this very picture.

The 258 paintings in the manuscript show a remarkable diversity of imagination, composition, draughtsmanship, and color, although they share the same technique and jewel-like finish. There can be no doubt that many hands trained in both the classical Timurid and Turkoman idioms were involved in the project. If *The Court of Gayumars* represents the culmination of the Turkoman style of Tabriz, an image such as *The Nightmare of Zahhak* [210] is the culmination of the Bihzadian tradition associated with Herat. Prince Zahhak had been lured by Iblis, the Devil, into killing his father and usurping his throne. Disguised, Iblis then demanded to kiss the new king on the shoulders, whereupon two serpents sprang from the spots where he had been kissed. The snakes demanded a daily diet of human brains, and under this evil influence the fortunes of Iran began to wane. One night, Zahhak dreamt of his impending death at the hands of a great hero wielding an ox-headed mace. The painting depicts the moment when Zahhak awakes from his dream. The white-bearded king sits behind a balcony on the upper left, but most of the visual interest is concentrated on the ways his courtiers react to his shouts. Some on the ground floor are too far away and continue to sleep unaware, while the ladies of his harem on the second floor pass the news from one to the other and raise their forefingers to their lips in gestures of surprise. Guardsmen peer down from the roof to see what has happened. The only indication of night is the narrow strip of deep blue sky with a crescent moon between the two wings of the palace. The artist has used his virtuosity to differentiate the individual courtiers by facial features, gesture, and dress and to display the rich array of tile patterns and architectural details. The intricately detailed representation of architecture stems directly from the Bihzadian tradition [85] and provides the only evidence for what the now destroyed Safavid palaces of Tabriz must have looked like.

This painting has been attributed to Mir Musavvir, one of the two other painters mentioned by Dust Muhammad as working on the royal *Shāhnāma*.[12] The only place in the manuscript where Mir Musavvir's name appears, however, is on the visor of a cap worn by an attendant in the painting of *Manuchihr Enthroned* (fol. 60v). It is also the only place in the

210. *The Nightmare of Zahhak*, f. 28v, from the Tahmasp *Shāhnāma*, Tabriz, 1525–35. 34.2 × 27.6 cm. Private collection USA

manuscript where any painter's name appears in a painting, but it is unclear whether this is a signature or the identification of an individual. It is hard to see the connection between the pedestrian quality of the painting of *Manuchihr Enthroned* and the inspired depiction of *The Nightmare of Zahhak*; furthermore, very little is known about the nature and extent of an individual artist's oeuvre at this moment. Chroniclers such as Dust Muhammad and Qazi Ahmad (ca. 1606) give the names of many contemporary and past artists, but it is rarely possible to attach a name to a particular painting. The names of individual artists are sometimes written in the margins around paintings in manuscripts, but these are ascriptions, not signatures, and may have been added at any time.

Genuine signatures are rare and are placed within the painting, on the architecture, on a book, or in another inconspicuous place, such as beneath the foot of the king, and usually contain the phrase "the work of..." (Pers. *´amal-i...*). In the late fourteenth century, the painter Junayd signed the painting of *Humay and Humayun on the Day after their Wedding* [38] and in the late fifteenth century Bihzad signed the paintings in the Cairo *Būstān* [85]. In the early sixteenth century Sultan-Muhammad, the painter of *The Court of Gayumars*, signed two paintings in a copy of the *Dīvān* ("Collected poems") of Hafiz made for Sam Mirza,

211. Sultan Muhammad: *Allegory of Drunkenness*, f. 135r, from Hafiz, *Dīvān*, Tabriz, ca. 1525. 21.5 × 15.0 cm. Jointly owned by the Harvard University Art Museums, Cambridge, MA, the Metropolitan Museum of Art and S. C. Welch

Tahmasp's brother.[13] *The Allegory of Drunkenness* [211] is signed "The work of Sultan-Muhammad" in a panel above the doorway. Hafiz's couplet at the top says

The angel of mercy took the reveling cup and tossed it down
  As rosewater on the cheeks of houris and angels.

To illustrate this mystical verse, Sultan-Muhammad depicted a wine-shop. In the upper window lolls the boozy-eyed poet, while angels tipple above him on the roof. A drunken customer staggers out the door, and a thirsty youth hauls a jug up to his balcony. In the front garden courtiers (identified by their turbans with tall batons) and mystics (identified by their long-sleeved cloaks) cavort to music and the shrieks and clangs of three fur-clad wandering dervishes. As in *The Nightmare of Zahhak*, architecture organizes the composition, landscape plays a minor role, and individuals are distinguished by gesture and physiognomy and are united by gaze into small genre scenes. This painting and the other signed painting in this manuscript are different in style from *The Court of Gayumars*, the *Shāhnāma* painting identifiable as the work of

212. *Bahram Gur and the Shepherd Who Hanged His Dog for Allowing a Wolf to Steal the Sheep*, probably prepared for the *Khamsa* made for Tahmasp, Tabriz, ca. 1540. 45.0 × 29 cm with borders. Boston, Museum of Fine Arts

213. *Nushirwan Listening to Owls in the Ruined Palace* from the *Khamsa* made for Tahmasp, Tabriz, 1539–43. 30.4 × 19.4 cm. London, British Museum, MS. Or. 2265, f. 15v

Sultan-Muhammad, but all three show the same imaginative brilliance. Nevertheless, these three paintings hardly provide the basis for reconstructing an artist's career, especially since so little is known about what an individual's role actually was in the production of an illustrated manuscript.

Close scrutiny of surviving manuscripts delineates the broad steps in the production of an illustration. The painter was given a sheet of paper on which the text had been copied, leaving a space for the illustration. In many cases the illustrations of a manuscript were never completed, and in other cases some or all of the illustrations were added significantly later, as was the case with the *Khamsa* begun for the Timurid prince Babur (see Chapter 5). The next step was to prepare the paintings. Beginning with a brush and thin black ink, the artist sketched in a composition, sometimes using models or pounces for the general composition and individual details. The composition was built up in darker strokes, and errors were corrected with opaque white pigment. The unfinished painting of *Bahram Gur and the Shepherd who Hanged his Dog for Allowing a Wolf to Steal the Sheep* [212] shows this stage of production.[14] The next stage was to color the drawing. Silver and gold were added first, then came the plain ground colors of landscape and the body colors of animals and textiles. Finishing touches included

painting vegetation, clouds, architectural details, trappings and fittings, and faces. The painting of *The Sleeping Rustam* [208] has been completed to this point, but the final stage of adding the rulings between columns of text and text and image has not been accomplished.[15]

Whether one artist worked sequentially on the various steps of a painting or each step was assigned to a different artist is unknown. Practice undoubtedly varied depending on the level of patronage and the size of the atelier. Tahmasp, for example, had many painters working for him who may well have been specialists, but in other cases a single person may have been responsible for the calligraphy, painting, illumination, and even the binding. Through the middle of the sixteenth century the book, not the painting, continued to be the work of art, and the individual artist's role was subordinated to the overall conception. Calligraphy, illumination, painting, drawing, gilding, and binding by many individuals were perfectly integrated in the books produced at the court of Tabriz. No single element overwhelmed another, and all components were equally splendid. These are some of the most magnificent products of Persian art.

The splendid copy of Nizami's *Khamsa* made for Tahmasp between 1539 and 1543 epitomizes luxury book production under the early Safavids.[16] The text was copied at Tabriz by the renowned calligrapher Shah Mahmud al-Nishapuri, and the margins of each folio were splendidly decorated in silver and several tones of gold, with animals and birds among flowers and trees. Space was left in the text for illustrations, and the manuscript now contains fourteen contemporary paintings.[17] The images are larger than the text-block and spill out into the margins on three sides. Eleven of the paintings bear later ascriptions to such masters as Aqa Mirak, Muzaffar 'Ali, and Sultan-Muhammad. The image of *Nushirvan in the Ruined Palace* [213] bears a faint inscription on the wall of the iwan:

> Build up the desert heart of those deprived of bliss;
> There is no better building in this ruined world than this.
> Mir Musavvir penned it in the year 946 [1539–40].[18]

While out riding with his vizier, the Sasanian monarch Nushirvan, who preferred sport to affairs of state, came upon a ruined palace in which two owls were hooting. The king asked what the owls were saying, and the vizier replied that one owl was demanding this ruined village and one or two others as a bride-price for his daughter. The other owl agreed, saying that if the king continued on his present course of leaving his people in misery and neglect, he would give not two or three but a hundred thousand ruined villages. To illustrate this moralistic tale, the artist has created a haunting image in a desolate landscape. The two owls perch on the top left above the ruined palace, whose decay is illustrated by the broken walls and fallen tiles and suggested by the snakes, lizards, and dog that inhabit the ruins. At the bottom, two woodsmen chop down old willow trees, undoubtedly an allusion to the misery and neglect of the people. A silver stream, now tarnished to black, cascades between rocks and exquisitely painted flowers on the right. Two deer drink from another stream behind the palace, and storks and quail nest nearby.

The manuscript was not finished in Tahmasp's lifetime. The dedicatory rosette (fol. 1v) was never inscribed and several blank spaces for paintings were completed in 1675–6 by Muhammad Zaman [226].[19] One explanation for the unfinished state of the manuscript is that ca. 1545 Tahmasp grew tired of the arts of the book. According to later chroniclers, the shah used to relax by practicing calligraphy and painting, but towards the end of his life affairs of state became pressing and his favorite artists were no longer alive, so he devoted less time to these arts.[20] Indeed, no royal illustrated manuscripts survive from the second half of Tahmasp's reign, although patronage on a large scale continued elsewhere.

The extraordinary attention given to the arts of the book during the first half of the sixteenth century spilled over into the other arts, particularly carpets and textiles. Pile carpets had long been manufactured in the Middle East and Central Asia, but the earliest complete pieces of Iranian manufacture to survive are dated to the sixteenth century. Earlier carpets are known only through their depiction in illustrated manuscripts of the fourteenth and fifteenth centuries. Although one painting from the monumental *Shāhnāma* made for the Mongols ca. 1335 depicts an animal carpet, most early examples feature inner fields of small repeat patterns edged with Kufesque borders [35].[21] In the second half of the

fifteenth century, to judge again from manuscript paintings, the geometric field was gradually transformed with arabesque designs, in which medallions and cartouches were surrounded by blossoms and leafy scrolls [85].[22] These designs are similar to those used in book illumination and binding and suggest that patterns from books were transferred to carpets. This revolution in design meant that some weavers began to work not from memory but from cartoons. Tahmasp established royal factories (Pers. *kārkhāna*) for carpets and textiles at Tabriz, Kashan, Isfahan, and Kirman. Designs became increasingly complex and included representations of flowers, trees, animals, and figures as well as calligraphy. By using a fine asymmetrical knot and silk for the warp, weft, and ultimately the pile, extraordinarily complex patterns could be produced with amazing detail.

Only three signed and dated carpets survive from this period. The most famous is the once matched pair known as the Ardabil carpets in London [214] and Los Angeles.[23] Nineteenth-century carpet traders reported that the carpets came from the shrine of Shaykh Safi at Ardabil, but their reports are notoriously inaccurate and the attribution is spurious. Both carpets are knotted in wool on silk warps and wefts; three shoots of silk weft follow each row of knots. They differ, however, in knot count, texture, and pile length. The London Ardabil has approximately 46 knots per square centimeter; the Los Angeles carpet 62. The London carpet, therefore, has some 25 million knots; when intact, the Los Angeles one had over 34 million knots! The design is the same on both carpets: a central sunburst surrounded by sixteen pendants, and two mosque lamps hanging from the pendants on the longitudinal axis. Each corner of the field repeats a quarter of the central composition. Worked in ten colors – black, three blues, green, three reds, white, and yellow – these elements seem to float above a deep blue ground strewn with arabesques. Cartouches on both carpets contain a couplet from an ode of Hafiz:

> I have no refuge in the world other than thy threshold;
> My head has no resting-place other than this doorway

followed by the signature, "Work of a servant of the court, Maqsud of Kashan, in the year 946 [1539–40]." Kashan may have been Maqsud's birthplace, his home, or his family seat. The inscription indicates that he was a royal retainer, and the size and the quality of design and manufacture of the carpets show that they were royal commissions woven in royal workshops. As it is inconceivable that a single individual wove the carpet, it is likely that Maqsud was the designer responsible for preparing the paper cartoons from which the carpets were woven in two workshops supplied with similar materials. This would explain the differences in execution despite the similarities of materials, design, and scale.

The other signed and dated contemporary carpet, a medallion carpet with hunting scenes, is much smaller (5.70 by 3.65 meters) and very different in style, although similar in technique.[24] The central medallion with cranes and cloud bands is surrounded by a lively hunting scene, in which figures wearing the distinctive Safavid turban fight lions, deer, and other animals. The medallion is red, the field dark blue, and the pattern is worked in a wide range of brilliant colors. The inscription gives the name Ghiyath al-Din Jami

214. Ardabil carpet, Tabriz?, 1539–40 Wool pile on undyed silk warps and wefts. 10.51 × 5.35 m. London, Victoria and Albert Museum

and the date 949 (1542–3).[25] Similar hunting scenes appear on three other silk carpets ascribed to the sixteenth century. The one in Boston [215] measures 4.8 by 2.55 meters and has about 125 knots per square centimeter.[26] It has the typical medallion composition with dependent cartouches. In the central medallion dragons and phoenixes enriched by brocading in silver and silver-gilt thread are set against a salmon-colored ground. In each quarter panel are six horses and riders, who again wear the distinctive Safavid turban. The border shows richly dressed men sitting before pools in a garden amidst flowering trees. The style of drawing shows close similarities to contemporary book illustration, and cartoons for this carpet were undoubtedly supplied from the royal manuscript studio.

When Tahmasp moved the capital to Qazvin in 1555, he built a new palace there. Some of the painters in his workshop came with him, for they worked on decorating the palace with wall paintings depicting famous scenes from literature, especially the works of Nizami.[27] Other artists were released to work for other patrons, of whom one of the most important was Tahmasp's nephew, Ibrahim Mirza (1543–1577), himself a noted calligrapher and artist.[28] The major record of his patronage is the copy of the *Haft Awrang* ("Seven thrones") by the mystical poet 'Abd al-Rahman Jami (1414–92). Close scrutiny of the manuscript has revealed the many steps in producing a deluxe codex in the mid-sixteenth century.[29] The text was copied onto 304 sheets of single-ply ivory paper which had been pressed against a four-column grid of twenty-one lines. According to the eight surviving colophons, the text was copied in three cities (Mashhad, Qazvin, and Herat) by five scribes – Shah Mahmud al-Nishapuri (the scribe of Tahmasp's *Khamsa*), Malik al-Daylami, Muhibb 'Ali, 'Ayshi b. Ishrati, and Rustam 'Ali – between 1556 and 1565, but the complex mail-order arrangement of the transcription is somewhat unusual. In two cases (fols. 10v and 207r) the scribes followed the traditional method and left empty rectangular blocks within the text for illustrations, but the other twenty-six illustrations were handled differently: the scribe omitted a few verses and left a whole side of the paper blank, and the full-page illustrations were prepared separately on sheets of cream-colored paper. The manuscript was then assembled: the calligraphed sheets were inserted into double-ply colored borders, and text pages were pasted, where appropriate, to the blank backs of the illustrated sheets. Thousands of rubrics, column dividers, triangular corner pieces, and colophons were then added and the margins decorated with floral designs painted in gold. The missing verses were penned onto the illustrated sides. The folios were joined into bifolios and then sewn into quires, and finally the manuscript was inserted into its binding. The process was so elaborate that a few omissions were inevitable.[30]

In the image of *Majnun Eavesdrops on Layla's Camp* [216], the logical depiction of space has given way to a confused welter of detail. Individual scenes, such as the hag conversing with Layla beneath the tent in the upper left or the woodsman and groom beneath the text-block in the upper right, make sense, but it is difficult to find the half-naked Majnun, the subject of the painting, who talks to the cameleer at the left edge of the painting or to integrate the

215. Hunt Carpet, Tabriz?, second quarter of the sixteenth century. Silk. 4.8 × 2.55 m. Boston, Museum of Fine Arts

scenes into a coherent whole. The people depicted have become more eccentric, and the vignettes are sometimes salacious. Beneath the tent on the lower right, for example, a turbaned figure fondles the arm of a youth sitting in the doorway of the tent, while his leg in turn is caressed by another youth. All twenty-eight paintings in the *Haft Awrang* continue the style developed under Tahmasp, but they are more dynamic and mannered.[31] Undoubtedly many hands worked on this manuscript, but attributions of single paintings to individual artists are yet to be established with certainty.[32]

The unified aspect of the manuscript may be due to the important role of the patron, Ibrahim Mirza. His name appears five times in the colophons, where it is sometimes highlighted in gold or colored ink, and three times in architectural decoration in the paintings. In two of the architectural inscriptions, the prince's name is inscribed below that of his uncle, Tahmasp, clearly reflecting contemporary politics. The illustrations also refer to contemporary events. The depiction of *The Wedding of Yusuf and Zulaykha* (fol. 132r) probably alludes to Ibrahim Mirza's marriage to Tahmasp's daughter, Gawhar Sultan Khanum, in 963/1556, particularly as Ibrahim Mirza's titles are inscribed on the architecture above Yusuf's nimbed head.

In many ways this copy of the *Haft Awrang* stands at the crossroads between earlier and later traditions of Persian book-painting. The work of art is still the illustrated book, which was conceived as an assemblage of calligraphy, illumination, illustration, gilding, and binding, but the illustrations have begun to play a separate role. They were executed outside the physical matrix of the book and inserted into it only at a later stage. It was a short step for artists to produce paintings independent of texts as discrete works of art, and they did so increasingly in the second half of the sixteenth century. These single-page drawings and paintings responded to changes in patronage and the artist's role, for the resources necessary to produce a single page were far less than to produce a deluxe manuscript. Indeed, many of the single pages did not even require a patron, but were made for sale on the open market and for collection by discerning connoisseurs. At the same time, signatures began to proliferate on single drawings and paintings as the importance of an individual style grew. Signatures were no longer concealed in the architectural setting, as in the work of Junayd [38] or Bihzad [85], but are calligraphed prominently beside the subject.

The new importance given to the style of an individual artist in the sixteenth century is also shown by the addition of attributions to older manuscripts and images and by a new interest in collecting specimens of signed or attributed works for inclusion in albums. Two kinds of albums had already been known in the fifteenth century: calligraphic albums and "scrapbook" albums, in which dissimilar pieces of painting, calligraphy, pounces, and designs were randomly pasted together.[33] In the mid-sixteenth century a new kind of album was developed, in which pictures and calligraphy were carefully juxtaposed, and it was albums of this kind that became particularly popular at the Mughal court [371, 374].[34] As Mir Sayyid-Ahmad wrote in his introduction to the album he prepared in 1564–5 for Amir Ghayb Beg Ostalju, one of

216. *Majnun Eavesdrops on Layla's Camp*, f. 253r, from Jami, *Haft Awrang*
Iran, 1556–65. 34.2 × 23.2 cm. Washington, DC, Freer Gallery of Art

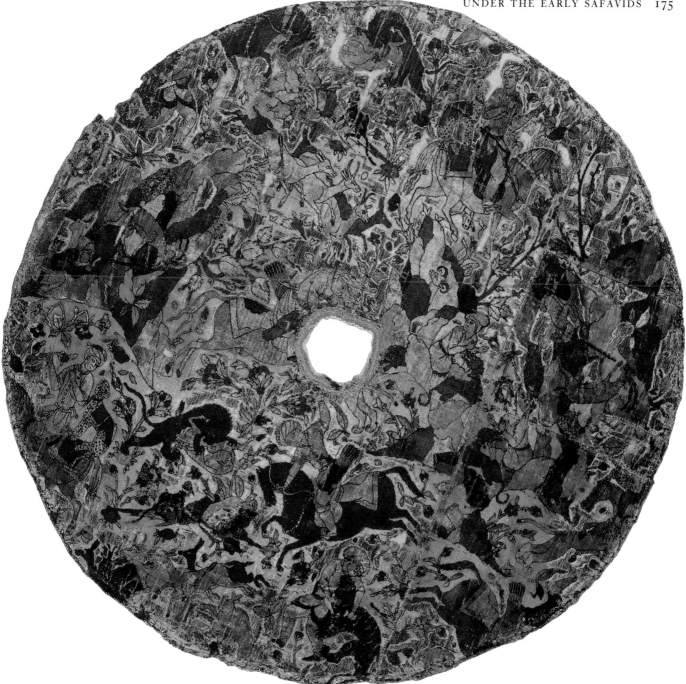

217. Tent medallion, Iran, sixteenth century. Cut and voided silk velvet.
Diameter 97 cm. Boston, Museum of Fine Arts

Tahmasp's military commanders,

> ...it was deemed necessary...to review and inspect the aforementioned tomes and specimens [of calligraphy]. Since they had not been arranged or organized, it was difficult, nay impossible, to locate any particular thing one wanted, and therefore it was seen as fitting to organize this album so that the confusion would be righted.[35]

The introductions to these planned albums, by such experts as Mir Sayyid-Ahmad, Dust Muhammad, and Malik Daylami, as well as the accounts of such contemporaries as Qazi Ahmad and Mir Munshi, are among the major sources for the history of the arts of the Persian book in the period.

They arc, furthermore, important evidence for a new and distinctly self-conscious awareness of the history of the art at this time.

Albums contained not only paintings from manuscripts but also drawings and sketches produced in the royal design studios for realization in other media. Indeed, narrative scenes predominate in sixteenth-century textiles, including pile rugs, lampas weaves, and velvets. A tent medallion [217] of cut and voided silk velvet on a satin weave foundation and faced with narrow strips of metal foil closely follows contemporary book illustration in its depiction of hunters fighting tigers and lions and shooting gazelles with arrows. One figure, crouched in the rocks at left, holds a musket, a new type of weapon introduced from the West during the reign of Tahmasp. This circular piece would have decorated the inside of a tent around the central pole; the loom width of 64 centimeters was not sufficient and the right side was carefully pieced together from scraps. Other fragments from the same velvet were made into lobed ogival medallions, which would have been disposed around the central one.[36] The technical sophistication of the weaving is matched by the ingenuity of the design, in which the confines of the repeat were avoided by placing figures in rows facing alternately left and right and varying the colors of the repeat.[37]

THE ARTS UNDER THE LATER SAFAVIDS (1576–1732) AND ZANDS (1750–94)

Following Tahmasp's death in 1576, the political situation in Iran fell into chaos under several weak and ineffectual rulers, and few major works of art were produced in the last part of the sixteenth century. Many painters emigrated to Bukhara and Delhi, where they found work for royal patrons (see Chapters 14 and 19), and although Isma'il II (r. 1576–8) apparently commissioned a large-size copy of the *Shāhnāma*, its illustrations never seem to have been completed.[38] The great revival of the arts took place under 'Abbas I (r. 1588–1629), and his transfer of the capital to Isfahan in 1591 signaled a major spurt in architectural patronage (see Chapter 13) and state-sponsored production of other arts.

The production of carpets was transformed under 'Abbas when they became a commercial commodity for domestic and foreign consumption. He had the Armenian population of Julfa on the Araxes river in Azerbayjan relocated to New Julfa, a new suburb to the south of Isfahan, and their monopoly of the silk trade became their main source of wealth and a crucial source of revenue for the Safavid state.[39] The figural designs popular in court carpets and textiles of the sixteenth century were increasingly superseded by floral patterns. The new type of carpet is exemplified by the so-called Polonaise carpets, of which some three hundred examples are known, many of them gifts to Europeans in Iran or commissions by the noble houses of Europe. Although most examples have now faded to a dusky rose tonality, they were knotted in bright green, blue, yellow, and pink silk on silk or cotton warps and enriched with silver and gold brocading. They were first called "Polonaise" when exhibited in the Paris Exhibition of 1878, for one example from Kraków bears the coat of arms then believed to be that of the Polish Czartoryski family. A flat-woven rug (*kilim, gelim*) in Munich with a similar design bears the arms of Sigismund Wasa III, King of Poland.[40] A document dated 12 September 1602 records that Sigismund sent an Armenian, Sefer Muratowicz, to buy silk carpets in Kashan. There he bought six pairs of carpets and paid five extra crowns to have the king's arms put on.[41]

Almost all Polonaise carpets share a similar arrangement, with several borders and guard bands of varying width enclosing a rectangular field. The field contains one or more central medallions and quarter medallions in the corners. The ground is an arabesque of flowers and leaves spiraling

218. Detail of the Doria Polonaise carpet, Iran, early seventeenth century. Silk pile with silver and gold brocade on cotton and silk foundation. 4.10 × 1.80 m. Tehran, Carpet Museum

219. Fragment of a vase carpet, Kirman, early seventeenth century. Wool. 2.44 × 1.44 m. Berlin, Museum für Islamische Kunst

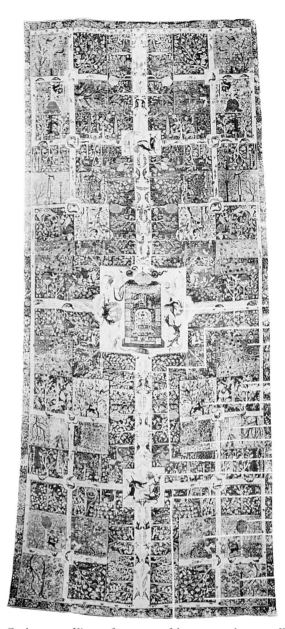

220. Garden carpet, Kirman, first quarter of the seventeenth century. Wool on cotton, wool and silk foundation. 8.75 × 3.75 m. Jaipur, Central Museum

in a stately rhythm over the field, making the anachronistic epithet oddly appropriate. One of a pair formerly owned by the Doria family [218] is particularly noteworthy, for the carpets retain their vivid palette of orange-red, pink, white, yellow, light green, green, light blue, blue, dark blue, lilac, light brown, dark brown, and black.[42] The Doria Polonaise carpets are unusual for their asymmetrical arrangement, for quarter medallions are found at only one end of each carpet and the central medallions are not centered. It is likely that they were designed to be laid end to end.[43]

Another group of carpets attributed to the time of 'Abbas are the so-called Vase carpets [219]. Their one-directional design is characterized by a lattice on three planes, one system made up of a ivory spiraling vine, the others of thicker red and blue stems. The stems issue from vases (hence the name) and bear an abundance of large and small

blossoms, sprays, and leaves. The rugs are worked in an exuberant palette of a dozen or more colors of dyed wool against a deep blue or red ground, although other ground colors are known. The type is distinguished technically by cotton warps and three weft shoots, of which the first and third are wool and the second silk or cotton. As this distinct structure is characteristic of carpets produced in the nineteenth and twentieth centuries at Kirman, Vase carpets are generally attributed to the same city.[44]

The technique characteristic of Vase carpets is also found in carpets with arabesque, landscape, and garden designs. The earliest examples in the group can be dated on the basis of the most splendid surviving of the garden carpets, a huge example (8.75 by 3.75 meters) discovered in 1937 in a sealed room in the palace of the Maharaja of Jaipur at Amber, India [220]. A label on the lining states that it was

221. Lampstand, Isfahan?, early seventeenth century. Engraved brass.
H 35 cm; diameter at bottom 18 cm. New York, Metropolitan Museum of
Art

inventoried in Amber fort near Jaipur on 29 August 1632.[45]
Like most examples of its type, it represents the plan of a
formal Persian garden divided into quadrants by streams; in
the center is a large pavilion with a blue dome and richly
decorated interior seen in elevation. Naturalistically drawn
fish, ducks, turtles, and such fabulous Chinese creatures as
dragons and *chi-lin* inhabit the waters; the plots are planted
with cypresses, planes, fruit trees, date palms, lilies, roses,
and carnations. Pheasants perch on the trees, feed their
young in nests, and sit on the grass. The design is worked
in blues, greens, yellows, and other vivid colors on a red
ground. It is unquestionably the finest and most sumptuous
garden carpet in existence and may well depict the style of
gardens built by 'Abbas in contemporary Isfahan and elsewhere in Iran (see Chapter 13).

Metalwares from the later sixteenth century also show a
new esthetic in their sleek tapered forms, the almost complete
disappearance of precious metal inlays, and the use of inscriptions in *nasta'līq* script. Figural decoration, which had
not been common in Iranian metalwares since the fourteenth
century, reemerged, although it remained secondary to vegetal and abstract ornament. The most distinctive new form is
the pillar-shaped lampstand, a tapered cylinder with a flared
base and a chamfered or faceted mid-section [221]. The
shape is emphasized by the allover decoration of zig-zag
bands or spiraling arabesques. Other common forms from
the period are wine bowls with shallow feet and flaring lips,
ewers with globular bodies and curved spouts, and buckets
with slender bases and upward-curving sides. They are
decorated with allover vegetal and arabesque patterns and
sometimes have animal and human figures enclosed by cartouches or polylobes set against a ground of vegetal scrolls.
In contrast to earlier wares which had been inscribed with
the maker's name and place of production, Safavid metalwares are inscribed with Persian poems and owners' names
in cartouches. On some pieces the cartouches are empty,
suggesting that they were made for the market. Others
have Armenian names, suggesting that they were made for
Armenian patrons, probably members of the Armenian community in New Julfa.

Although 'Abbas also ordered a large-size manuscript of
the *Shāhnāma*,[46] the importance of the book as a collective
work of art by several artists was increasingly supplanted by
the single page as a product of one individual. The leading
artist under 'Abbas was Riza (ca. 1565–1635), whose close
connection with the shah is demonstrated by his sobriquet
'Abbasi.[47] Thanks to contemporary chronicles and his own
signed works, his career can be established with a precision
impossible for artists a century or even a half-century earlier.
He was the son of 'Ali Asghar, an artist active in the court of
Tahmasp, and when Tahmasp renounced painting in the
1540s, Riza moved to Mashhad for ten years. There he
apparently developed his skill at portraits and genre scenes
appreciated by non-royal patrons. His early work, such as
the charming and sensitive *Young Man in a Blue Coat* [222],
continues the features of court painting in the 1570s and
1580s in its characteristic fine drawing, closed contours, and
large expanses of primary color, but Riza introduced a distinctive fluttering edge to the depiction of turbans and
sashes.[48] This fluttering drapery was developed in the fine,

222. Riza: *Young Man in a Blue Coat*, Qazvin, ca. 1587. Opaque watercolor on paper. 13 × 7.5 cm. Cambridge, MA, Harvard University Art Museums

223. Riza: *Nashmi the Archer*, Isfahan, 1622. Opaque watercolor on paper. 19 × 10 cm. Cambridge, MA, Harvard University Art Museums

calligraphic drawings he produced between 1591, his first dated work, and 1603, when he first signed a drawing *Riża-yi ʿAbbāsī*.[49] His standard subject matter expanded from courtly youths to include workers and mystics. Shortly after 1603 he appears to have undergone a mid-life crisis, for contemporary chronicles state that he took up with low-life characters and ceased painting court figures. The sympathetic portrait of *Nashmi the Archer* [223], dated 4 Rabiʿ II 1031/25 February 1622 exemplifies one of the low companions of Riza's middle years. The conventions of line and color Riza had used to depict languid youths are marshaled for the representation of a pot-bellied slipshod slob smoking an opium pipe. His appearance would have affronted the refined sensibilities of the court, but Riza's painting ironically alludes to the momentous change in

224. Mu'in: *Tiger Attacking a Youth*, Isfahan, 1672. Brown ink on paper.
13.7 × 20 cm. Boston, Museum of Fine Arts

225. Mu'in: *Portrait of Riza*, Isfahan, 1673. Opaque watercolor on paper.
18.7 × 10.5 cm. Princeton University Library, Garrett Collection

Safavid society brought about by 'Abbas's reorganization of
the army along functional, rather than tribal, lines and by the
acceptance of firearms. A traditional archer, such as Nashmi,
became superfluous in an army of musketeers, and this
pensioner would have sought solace in puffs of his opium
pipe.[50]

Riza's most gifted pupil was Mu'in *Musavvir* ("the
painter"), who was active throughout much of the seventeenth century.[51] Although he worked on manuscripts of the
Shāhnāma early in his career, he is primarily known for
single-page compositions which epitomize the esthetic of
seventeenth-century Iran. Brilliant draughtsmanship and a
keen sense of observation characterize his work. This is
evident in his brown-ink drawing of a *Tiger attacking a Youth*
[224].[52] A light red tint has been applied to the tiger and
the hats of three of the men who are trying to restrain the
animal. A long inscription across the top of the drawing
explains the subject:

> It was Monday, the day of the feast of the blessed Ramadan
> of the year 1082, when the ambassador of Bukhara had
> brought a tiger with a rhinoceros as gifts for his most exalted
> majesty Shah Sulayman. At *Darvaza-Dawlat*, the above-
> mentioned tiger jumped up suddenly and tore off half the
> face of a grocer's assistant, fifteen or sixteen years of age. He
> died within the hour. We heard about the grocer but did not
> see him. [This] was drawn in memory of it. And in that year
> from the beginning of the second half of the honourable
> month of Sha'ban until now, the eighth day of Shawwal,
> there have been eighteen heavy snowfalls of such magnitude
> that the trouble of shoveling snow has exasperated people.
> The price of most goods has gone up and firewood, one *man*
> at four *bisti*, and kindling, one *man* at six *bisti*, were still
> unobtainable. The cold was such that there were no glass
> bottles or rosewater bottles left. May God ... end it well. [It
> is] Monday the eighth of the month of Shawwal of the year
> 1082. Heavy snow is falling. We stayed at home because of
> the cold. It was drawn by Mu'in Musavvir.

Such immediacy of drawing and specificity of reference are
unique in Persian painting and can be explained by Mu'in's

unusual choice of subject. Unlike other painters, who tended
to work within such well-defined genres as illustrating the
Shāhnāma and the poems of Nizami, or portraiture, Mu'in
often represented events in his own time. Such representations have the immediacy of photojournalism and did not
belong to any established genre; they needed captions to
explain their subject. Although other seventeenth-century
artists also signed, dated, and inscribed their work, Mu'in's
inscriptions are far more detailed and informative and reveal
otherwise unrecorded aspects of daily life in contemporary
Isfahan. The long inscription also specifies when and where
Mu'in did the drawing: at home on Monday, 8 February

1672, when confined by an unusually long spell of cold weather.[53] This location confirms the growing independence of seventeenth-century painters from royal patronage and the court atelier.

One of Mu'in's best-known works is his affectionate and gentle portrait of his teacher Riza [225], completed on 24 December 1673 at the request of Mu'in's son. The aged artist, who sits surrounded by the tools of his trade, peers through his spectacles at the portrait on his lap of a man in European dress. Although the portrait shares some of the immediacy of Mu'in's drawing of the tiger, according to the inscription along the left side it was executed in two stages and may have been based on an earlier portrait Mu'in had drawn in 1635, a month before Riza's death. The portrait exists in two nearly identical versions,[54] suggesting that the portrait was not the spontaneous work it appears to be at first glance. One of the rare portraits of a Persian artist at work, the representation belongs to an established genre in Islamic, although not in specifically Persian, painting.[55] Mu'in depicted Riza drawing a figure in European dress, and, like his master, Mu'in himself drew some figures in European dress. Whether this familiarity with European dress extended to a knowledge of European modes of representation is a matter of debate; the immediacy of his drawings and their unusual subject matter may have been Persian interpretations of European ideas or hallmarks of a distinctly individual style.

European elements are more clearly seen in the work of Mu'in's contemporary Muhammad Zaman (fl. 1649–1704).[56] His work includes figures in European dress and even Biblical scenes based on Flemish and Italian prints, which circulated widely in Safavid Iran, and emphasize such foreign elements as atmosphere, night-scenes, and shadow. His work was so appreciated at court that he was asked to complete one of the most splendid manuscripts in the royal library, the *Khamsa* of Nizami that had been prepared for Tahmasp and illustrated by the leading artists of the middle of the sixteenth century [213]. Muhammad Zaman touched up figures in some paintings (e.g. the female faces in *Khusraw and Shirin Listening to Stories* on fol. 66v) and added four paintings of his own, including *Fitna Astonishing Bahram Gur* [226].[57] The painting illustrates an episode from Nizami's poem *Haft Paykar* ("Seven portraits"). King Bahram Gur took the maid Fitna (lit. "Mischief") out hunting, expecting that his prowess would win her admiration. Instead, she scoffed at his accomplishments, saying that it is nothing to excel when one has practiced so long. Infuriated, Bahram Gur ordered her put to death, but she escaped the sentence and reappeared two years later carrying an ox on her back. The painting depicts the climactic moment when Fitna appeared before the ruler. Asked how she was able to carry an ox, she replied that she had carried it every day since it was young; as it grew heavier she grew stronger: "Practice makes perfect."[58]

Muhammad Zaman's Europeanizing composition differs from traditional Persian manuscript painting in the use of single-point perspective to create a sense of space and focus attention on the figure of the ruler. Other spatial devices borrowed from the European traidition include the architectural elements in the lower corners and the figure of Fitna

226. Muhammad Zaman: *Fitna Astonishing Bahram Gur* added to the *Khamsa* made for Tahmasp, Isfahan, 1675. London, British Library, MS Or. 2265, f. 213r

and the ox dramatically seen from behind, which is used as a repoussoir in a manner not seen in Persian painting since the Great Mongol *Shāhnāma* [35]. Other three-dimensional effects are the use of cast shadows to suggest the depth of the niches, shading to suggest volume, as on the body of the cow, and transparency, as on Fitna's skirt and the wine-bottle. The tripartite composition can be traced to the early stages of Islamic manuscript painting and the subject matter is traditional, but the drawing and modeling combine traditional and European modes of representation in a novel and appealing style that sets the direction for later Iranian painting on both the small and the large scale. Indeed, at this very moment oil paintings on canvas in this style were first produced in Iran.[59] These European ideas could have reached Iran either directly from Europe or via India, for other Safavid artists, such as Shaykh 'Abbasi, were inspired by Indian painting.[60]

The most popular type of Safavid ceramic was undoubtedly that painted cobalt blue on white; this continues the infatuation with Chinese blue-and-white ceramics that had characterized the Islamic world for centuries [90]. The production is only provisionally dated and localized, although many of the pieces are associated with Mashhad, which had been an important center in the late fifteenth century. The most noteworthy group, however, is the lusterwares, a technique revived on a limited scale in the second half of the seventeenth century.[61] Although not as common as wares underglaze painted in blue, Safavid lusterwares were produced in a wide variety of shapes, including bottles, ewers, jars, jugs, hookah bases, spittoons, bowls, dishes, goblets, and cups. Most are very small: bottles are usually less than 28 centimeters high and dishes 22 centimeters in diameter. The white frit body was coated with a slip, possibly of pure ground quartz, which could be stained deep blue, or more rarely turquoise or lemon yellow. The vessel was then covered with a transparent glaze. The luster pigment is a coppery color, but can vary in tone. Unlike blue-and-white wares, whose shapes and designs were often taken from the Chinese repertory, the shapes and designs of Safavid lusterwares are derived from traditional Near Eastern models. The designs include floral sprays, trees, flowers, and leaves. They seem to have been produced in a single workshop or a closely related group, for the signature of only one potter, Khatim, is known.[62] A spouted jar [227] with three handles around the shoulder is one of several of the same shape known.[63] Its squat and rounded shape is typical of many of

228. Detail of Ja'far: *Court of Karim Khan Zand*, Shiraz, late eighteenth century. Oil on canvas. Shiraz, Pars Museum

227. Luster-painted spouted jar, Iran, seventeenth century. H 14.5 cm. Copenhagen, David Samling

the lusterware pieces produced, although such other shapes as bottles are characteristically elongated and sinuous.

The waning power of the Safavids was eventually extinguished by the Afghan invasions beginning in 1732. The horrors of the invasions and their chaotic aftermath were not conducive to patronage of the arts, and only with the relatively peaceful and prosperous reign of Karim Khan Zand (r. 1750–79), who ruled from Shiraz as *vakīl* ("regent") of Isma'il III, did the arts begin to flourish again in Persia.[64] Karim Khan was a notable builder, and palace walls were decorated with large oil paintings, such as one depicting his court [228]. The most important painter of the period was Sadiq, whose long career spanned the second half of the seventeenth century. He worked not only on a large scale in oil, but on a small scale in such media as lacquer and book illustration. In all these media, Western elements such as shading, modeling, drapery, and perspective were integrated into the Persian tradition of meticulous craftsmanship and rich color.

CHAPTER 13

Architecture in Iran under the Safavids and Zands

The buildings erected under the rule of the Safavid dynasty are perhaps the most alluring and attractive in all Iranian architecture. Their enveloping glittering web of glazed tile, soaring portals, bulbous domes, and slender minarets epitomize for many the essential qualities of Persian architecture. In part this is a matter of survival, for a large and impressive ensemble of buildings is easily accessible in Isfahan, the former Saljuq capital that became the third capital of the dynasty; but in part the attractiveness of Safavid architecture is due to its open and easy design, with simple compositions based on addition and symmetry. Safavid architecture shows little, if any, structural or formal innovation, for architects needed to build and decorate vast structures in the shortest time, and so colorful tile revetments often conceal structural banality. Its greatest strength lies in the planning and execution of large urban ensembles, which integrate a variety of commercial, religious, and political functions in harmonious compositions. Just as Safavid painters began to be interested in the history of their art, Safavid architects showed a distinct consciousness of their architectural heritage, be it the Timurid tradition of dynastic architecture in Khurasan or the local tradition of architecture in Isfahan and its region.

Whereas many examples of art survive from the first century of Safavid rule and attest to the dynasty's lavish patronage (see Chapter 12), almost no examples of Safavid architecture survive from the sixteenth century. Texts and scattered remains confirm the construction and restoration of mosques, shrines, and tombs throughout the country, and inscriptions on more than forty buildings state that work on them was carried out during the long reign of Tahmasp I (1524–76). His major efforts were probably concentrated at Qazvin, the city he made capital in 1555, but only a portal and a restored pavilion from his palace have survived the numerous earthquakes in the city.[1] Texts describe the wall paintings, which depicted famous scenes from literature,[2] and the walls of a ruined, two-story palace at Nayin are richly decorated with scenes typical of contemporary book-painting, such as events from Persian poetry, enthroned royal couples, polo matches, banquets, and the hunt, as well as chinoiserie themes of dragons, phoenixes, and flying ducks in the vaults.[3] These fragmentary remains do not allow much assessment of the architectural style of the early Safavid period, and it is only with the transfer of the capital to Isfahan by 'Abbas I (r. 1588–1629) in the 1590s that Safavid architecture found its true expression.

By the end of the sixteenth century the Safavids were in a sorry state. Following the death of Tahmasp, their legitimacy and power had been challenged internally and externally. The underpinnings of the Safavid state had been eroded by squabbles between members of the line about who was the rightful claimant to the throne. The theological basis that justified the legitimacy of the Safavid line rested on public acceptance of the ineffable authority of twelver Shi'ism and the role of the Safavids as its custodians. Yet already in the

1530s the Safavids had lost control of the major Shi'ite shrines at Najaf and Karbala' in Iraq to their rivals, the Sunni Ottomans, and in 1589 they lost the holy shrine at Mashhad in Khurasan to the Sunni Shibanids. Its recapture a decade later did not erase the stain on Safavid honor, and 'Abbas substantially reendowed the shrine after his penitent pilgrimage there in the winter of 1601–2. The relocation of the capital from the insecure borderlands to the center of the country was the central act of a deliberate policy to consolidate Safavid political and religious authority, develop state capitalism, and establish Safavid Iran as a world economic and diplomatic power.[4]

The most significant part of the urban program carried out by 'Abbas in his new capital was the relocation of the commercial, religious, and political center of the city south-southwest toward the Ziyanda river [229]. A two-kilometer

229. Plan of Isfahan as developed under 'Abbas I. 1) Old Maidan; 2) Friday Mosque; 3) Bazaar; 4) New maidan; 5) Bazaar portal; 6) Mosque of Shaykh Lutfallah; 7) 'Ali Qapu; 8) Shah Mosque; 9) Chahar Bagh avenue; 10) Si-o-se Pul

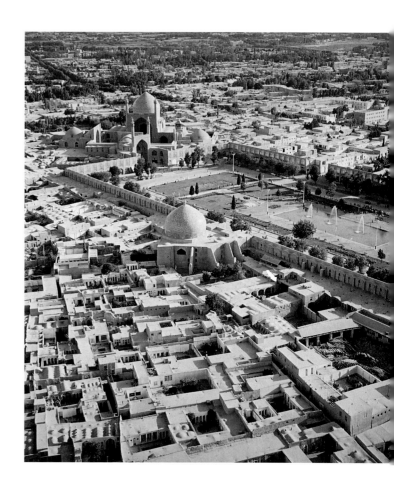

230. Isfahan, Maydan-i Shah, aerial view from north-east

231. Isfahan, Allahverdi Khan bridge (Si-o-se Pul), 1602

bazaar connected the maidan near the congregational mosque to a new one, the royal square called Naqsh-i Jahan ("Design of the World") [230]. An elongated rectangle (512 by 159 meters) which covered eight hectares, a space far larger than contemporary European plazas, the new maidan was conceived, designed, and constructed between 1590 and 1595 primarily for state ceremonies and sports. In a second phase, completed by 1602, it was redeveloped for commercial purposes, with two stories of shops around the perimeter, which were let at low rents to attract reluctant merchants from the old city center. The long modular façades, originally decorated with polychrome glazed tiles, are broken only by the monumental entrances to four buildings. On the north lies the dramatic portal to the bazaar which connected the new maidan with the old. On the east is the Mosque of Shaykh Lutfallah, and on the south is the monumental Shah Mosque (Pers. *Masjid-i shāh*), which was designed to replace the old Friday mosque as the locus of public worship. On the west is the entrance to the palace complex, the 'Ali Qapu ("Lofty gate" or "Sublime porte"), and to the west of the palace and its gardens, a long avenue, the Chahar Bagh ("Four[-fold] Garden"). This elegant boulevard, some four kilometers long, was flanked by the palaces of the nobles, who were encouraged by the shah to add fine buildings in the new capital, and divided into two lanes by a central canal punctuated by fountains and cascades and planted with flowers and trees. It is a realization on an enormous scale and in three dimensions of the typical garden carpet [220]. The southern end of the Chahar Bagh opens onto the Si-o-se Pul ("Bridge of Thirty-three [Arches]") [231], erected in 1602 by Allahvardi Khan, favorite and generalissimo of 'Abbas. Measuring a remarkable 300 meters long, it has a passage for beasts of burden flanked by raised lanes for pedestrians. At several points pavilions project from the main structure to allow pedestrians to stop and enjoy the splendid view of the river basin. Until the nineteenth century the interior was decorated with paintings, condemned as obscene by European observers. As in the Chahar Bagh itself, esthetics are joined to practical functions in a splendid ensemble, for the bridge crossed the Ziyanda river and linked the city to New Julfa, the economically important quarter of the Armenians, who had been recently relocated there from the war-torn borderlands, and to the great royal pleasance on the slopes of Takht-i Rustam, the Hazar Jarib ("Thousand Acres") or Bagh-i 'Abbasabad ("Garden of the Abode of 'Abbas").

The maidan represents an early example of a multifunctional space and was the most impressive feature of the new city for foreign travelers, who universally praised it for its sheer size and its architectural homogeneity and described it as a great square, overflowing with life from the bazaars, and a backdrop to pageantry and ceremonial splendor. A stone channel ran around the perimeter of the square at a short distance from the arcade and separated the space for walking from the central area, which was originally unpaved and covered with gravel. The covered walkway and the outer arcades served as a bazaar. The great central space housed the stalls of merchants, craftsmen, barbers, and entertainers, but could be cleared for military parades, drill by the shah's personal militia, archery contests, polo matches, and festivals.

At night fifty thousand earthenware lamps hanging from thin poles in front of the buildings illuminated the square.[5]

The majestic portal to the bazaar [232] consists of a high iwan flanked by arched galleries on two stories. The spandrels of the iwan are revetted with tile mosaics depicting Sagittarius, under whose astrological sign Isfahan was founded, set on a ground of floral arabesques. The interior faces of the iwan have faded frescoes depicting 'Abbas's victories over the Shibanids. The galleries housed the *naqqāra-khāna*, or music pavilion, where a consort of royal musicians played daily on trumpets and drums, somewhat cacophonously to European ears. The portal leads to a two-storied royal bazaar, the *qaisariyya*, in which fine textiles were sold. A domed node (Pers. *chahārsū*) gave access to the royal mint on the east and the royal caravanserai on the west. This was the largest caravanserai in the city and had 140 rooms, with space for cloth merchants on the ground floor and workshops and stores for jewelers, goldsmiths, and engravers on the second. A grid of lanes intersecting under domed spaces to the north and east opened onto more caravanserais, baths, and a hospital.[6]

The Mosque of Shaykh Lutfallah [234, 235] on the east side of the maidan is small but exquisite. The building is unique among Safavid mosques: it comprises a single domed room (19 meters on a side) surrounded by service areas and resting on another room of almost the same dimensions, covered with low vaults resting on four octagonal piers. The building lacks such standard accoutrements of mosques as a court, side galleries, iwans, or minarets; its form fits better within the long-established Iranian tradition of large domed mausoleums. The dome, which has a modest pointed-arch profile, is covered with an unusual design of ocher-colored arabesques and its center is displaced some 6.5 meters to the right of the entrance axis. As in the Shah Mosque, the portal is aligned with the maidan and the interior aligned with the direction of Mecca. To reach the prayer hall, one must pass through the portal iwan, ablaze with glittering tile, through a gloomy corridor around two sides of the sanctuary so as to enter it opposite the mihrab.[7]

The visual and psychological impact on entering the vast, glowing room [233] is stunning, for it is probably the most perfectly balanced interior in all of Persian architecture. The dome, one of the few single shells in Safavid architecture, is decorated with a sunburst at the apex; from it descend tiers of ogival medallions, which swell in size with the curve of the dome. The medallions are filled with floral motifs which play against the monochrome ground. The drum has sixteen arched panels alternating with windows, fitted with double ceramic grilles in arabesque patterns. The drum is supported by sixteen kite-shaped shields resting on four great squinches alternating with arched panels, all springing from the floor, outlined by light blue cable moldings, and framed by magnificent inscription bands in white on a dark blue ground. The structural system, a tripartite arrangement of square base, octagonal zone of transition, and dome, is simple and had been standard in Iranian architecture for centuries.[8] The integration of the two lower stories, however, creates an unusual sense of spaciousness and harmony. The inspiration for this novel feature may well have been local, for the only other example in Iranian architecture is in the north dome

232. Isfahan, Bazaar portal, 1619–20

233. Isfahan, Mosque of Shaykh Lutfallah, interior

234. Isfahan, Mosque of Shaykh Lutfallah, 1603–19, view from maidan

236. Isfahan, Shah Mosque, 1611–38

added to the Friday mosque in Isfahan in 1088.[9] The possibilities inherent in the early example seem to have remained unappreciated for centuries, until Isfahan again became the capital and center of a metropolitan building tradition. The interior surface of the Safavid room is enveloped in a web of color: the dado and some of the upper wall surfaces are revetted with tiles painted in carpet patterns; their flat surface is distinguished from the tile mosaic, whose uneven surfaces scatter light.

Inscriptions outline the chronology of building and name

235. Isfahan, Mosque of Shaykh Lutfallah, plan

the participants: the major foundation inscription on the portal dates the beginning of construction to 1012 (1603–4) and names the calligrapher 'Ali Riza al-'Abbasi, who later worked on the Shah Mosque; a second inscription at the base of the interior of the dome gives a date for the decoration (1025/1616); and a third inscription on the mihrab names the architect, Muhammad Riza son of the master Husayn, the builder from Isfahan, and gives the date of completion (1028/1618–19). The inscriptions identify the building as a mosque (*masjid*), but its function remains a mystery, although it is often considered to have been a royal chapel. The building is usually known as the Mosque of Shaykh Lutfallah after Shaykh Lutfallah Maysi al-'Amili, the distinguished scholar and teacher who came to Isfahan at 'Abbas's request and took up residence on the site, but the mosque only came to be called after him some time after his death in 1622– and he does not seem to have played any part in its construction.

On the south side of the maidan lies the Shah Mosque [236], whose entrance portal mirrors that of the bazaar on the north. Begun in the spring of 1611, construction of this monumental mosque was not finished until ca. 1630 under 'Abbas's successor Safi (r. 1629–42), and its marble dadoes were installed only by 1638.[10] Inscriptions and texts indicate that three individuals were involved in its design and construction: Badi' al-Zaman Tuni prepared the site and building plans; 'Ali Akbar al-Isfahani was the engineer in charge, and Muhibb 'Ali Beg was the general contractor. The building was endowed with agricultural and commercial properties in and around the city, and both the building and its generous endowment were another aspect of 'Abbas's plan to shift the city's commercial and religious center away from the area near the Friday mosque.[11]

The entrance vestibule is aligned with the maidan; the remainder of the building (100 by 130 meters) is turned 45° to face Mecca. The mosque follows the typical Iranian plan of a central court (70 meters on a side) surrounded by arcades, with an iwan in the middle of each of the four sides

237. Isfahan, Shah Mosque, courtyard and west iwan

[237] and a domed sanctuary beyond the iwan on the qibla side; but the plan is noteworthy in several ways. The lateral iwans also lead to domed chambers, as in the Mosque of Bibi Khanum at Samarqand [49]. The domed sanctuary is flanked by rectangular chambers, which are covered by eight domes and serve as winter prayer halls. These halls in turn lead to rectangular courts surrounded by arcades, which serve as madrasas. Paired minarets soar from both entrance portal and sanctuary iwan, although the call to prayer was given from an edicule (Pers. *guldasta*) over the west iwan. Another arcaded court containing latrines opens off the vestiule via a domed quincunx. The whole plan is marked by an extraordinary concern for symmetry, made possible by the unusual availability of virtually unlimited space.

Above the continuous marble dado, all vertical surfaces, both exterior and interior, are clad in polychrome glazed tile, most of which was replaced in the 1930s on the basis of extant remains. The tile revetment is predominantly blue, except in the covered halls, which were later revetted in tiles of cooler, yellowy-green shades. The exterior of the sanctuary

dome is covered with a spiraling beige arabesque on a light blue ground. The enormous dome (external diameter 25 meters; height 52 meters) is raised on a sixteen-sided zone of transition and a tall drum. It has a double shell, for the bulbous exterior dome rises some fourteen meters above the interior hemisphere, an arrangement also derived from Timurid prototypes. Despite its large size, it seems to float above the other domed roofs of the mosque, which are left plain.

The entrance portal [238] is the tour-de-force of the mosque's tile decoration and is entirely executed in tile mosaic in a full palette of colors. The outer edge of the iwan is framed by a wide inscription band with religious texts written in white *thuluth* script on a dark blue ground. The arch is framed by a triple cable molded in light blue tile and ascending from marble vases. The semidome is filled with glittering tiers of muqarnas which spring from a horizontal band across the back and sides of the iwan. The band is inscribed with the foundation text; like the framing band, it is executed in white letters on a dark blue ground, but the

238. Isfahan, Shah Mosque, portal, 1616

239. Isfahan, 'Ali Qapu, ca. 1597–1660

patron's name in the center, directly above the doorway, is highlighted in light blue letters. The inscription ends with the name of the master calligrapher who designed it, 'Ali Riza, and the date 1025 (1616). Panels in the balcony over the doorway are decorated with confronted peacocks, and other panels in the semidome are decorated with stars and vine scrolls issuing from vases. Magnificent panels laid out like prayer carpets flank the doorway, which is revetted with marble panels. The rest of the mosque is decorated with tiles of poorer quality, probably because money was short and the spaces to be covered vast. Most of it is done in multicolored glazed tiles (Pers. *haft rangi*), which can give a dazzling effect in strong sunlight but which are less effective in such dark interior spaces as the domed sanctuary and the winter prayer halls.

On the west side of the maidan opposite the Lutfallah mosque is the 'Ali Qapu [239]. Begun by 'Abbas to act as a modest atrium for the royal gardens, over the next sixty years it was repeatedly modified and extended upwards as it evolved from its simple origins to an audience hall to an official tribune from which to review the troops and games held in the maidan. The final building consists of a block (20 by 20 by 33 meters) preceded by an entrance complex itself surmounted by a columned porch (Pers. *talar*). This extension at the front brought the building into alignment with the arcades added around the maidan by 1602, and the porch

provided an elevated reviewing stand for royalty and guests. The ingenuity and playfulness of the court architects can be seen in the way they transformed the *talar*, a traditional Persian form found already in the Achaemenid *apadana* at Persepolis, from an earth-bound verandah into one towering two stories above the ground.

The main block of the 'Ali Qapu is subdivided into five main and one intermediate stories [240], which differ markedly in plan. Many of the supporting elements lack structural continuity from floor to floor, revealing the additive nature of the design, and the main supports, which are massive on the lower floors, become lighter and thinner at the top. From the third floor they turn into hollow pilasters and on the fifth floor they are a network of thin arches from which is suspended the fantastic plaster revetment over the "music room" [241]. The revetment consists of muqarnas niches which have been pierced in the shapes of the glass-wares and ceramics the Safavid rulers assiduously collected; the shell, which has also been painted with geometric and arabesque designs, played an acoustic as well as a decorative role. The functions of some rooms in the building, such as the reception hall with water tank and fountain on the level

240. Isfahan, 'Ali Qapu, section

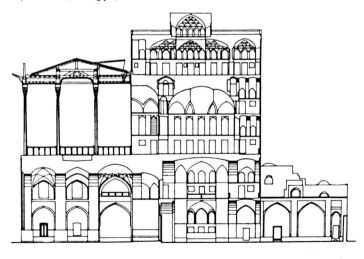

241. Isfahan, 'Ali Qapu, 'Music Room'

of the *talār*, can be easily determined, but the function of many small rooms is uncertain. They were once richly decorated with wall paintings, most only faintly visible, with scenes of a mildly erotic nature, such as the languid youths popularized in small paintings and drawings by Riza [222]. In design and decoration the 'Ali Qapu exemplifies the palatial architecture of the reign of 'Abbas.

The architectural endeavors of 'Abbas were not limited to Isfahan alone, for he built extensively throughout the country, visually reasserting the power of the monarchy. Perhaps the most important of his projects was the renovation of the shrine of Imam Riza at Mashhad. Work there culminated with another large endowment to the shrine in 1614, for the legitimacy of the Safavid state depended on venerating the tradition of the imams. As the "thresholds" of imams 'Ali, Hasan, and Husayn at Najaf, Kazimayn, and Karbala' in Iraq were outside the Safavid domain, the importance of Mashhad was all the greater. Preexisting structures at Mashhad, including the large four-iwan mosque added by Gawharshad and the two halls connecting it to the tomb (see Chapter 4), forced the Safavid architects to work on the north side of the shrine, where they monumentalized and regularized the structures behind a chain of courts linked by a watercourse. The ingenious transformation of exterior spaces into monumental interiors open to the sky and the central role of water recall earlier work at Isfahan.[12]

Another contemporary project of comparable scale is the complex built between 1596 and 1606 by Ganj 'Ali Khan, governor of Kirman under 'Abbas. Comprising a rectangular maidan (100 by 50 meters) lined with a continuous portico, the ensemble includes a large caravanserai and small mosque on the east, an unusually large and well-preserved bath on the south, a water tower on the north, and a market node (Pers. *chahārsū*) at the south-west corner. The caravanserai is remarkable for its size and tile decoration with chinoiserie motifs and other subjects also popular in arts such as carpets and textiles. The grand scale and functional diversity of the complex show it to be closely related to the work at Isfahan, although it is unclear whether it was the prototype for or a minor replica of its more famous cousin.

In addition to these single projects, 'Abbas systematically extended the road system that linked Isfahan with the cities of the realm and its major ports. To further facilitate trade, caravanserais were erected along these routes at intervals of thirty to forty kilometers, representing a day's journey. Caravanserais had long been a feature of Iranian architecture, but the number, size, and uniformity of examples erected during the Safavid period indicate that they must have been designed in a central government bureau. Indeed, so many were built during the reign of 'Abbas that virtually all examples built from the sixteenth century to the nineteenth are known as caravanserais of Shah 'Abbas.

The caravanserai at Bisutun on the road from Baghdad to Hamadan [242] is one of the larger Safavid examples to survive in good condition. It was erected by Shaykh 'Ali Khan Zangana, a local notable, between 1681 and 1685. Built of brick on a dressed stone socle, it is a rectangle measuring 80 by 90 meters, with rounded towers at the corners; at some other sites towers are set at intervals along the perimeter walls. The exterior is plain on three sides; the main façade with arched niches was marked by the portal, which was two stories high and projected several meters. Inside the portal lies a broad vestibule, here with an upper story containing a well-ventilated chamber (Pers. *balākhāna*) reserved for important guests. The interior court is a spacious rectangle (50 by 52 meters) with iwans in the middle of each of the four sides and beveled corners. The iwans are linked by a line of shallow arched porches, each of which leads to a small room for sleeping; the doorways are raised so that animals cannot stray from the court. Stables, accessible by passages from the court, run around the perimeter of the building behind the sleeping quarters. Divided into four sectors, they too had elevated platforms with fireplaces for accommodation. In hot weather the roof was also used for sleeping.

Within the type there is surprising variety: some examples are fancier, with such amenities as shops, bakeries, baths, or separate quarters for women. Some larger sites have rooms on two floors, while others have closed courtyards (against inclement weather) or are more heavily fortified. In general, however, security on the roads during the reign of 'Abbas was so good that some caravanserais are unfortified, such as the pavilion type found in the coastal lowlands along the Persian Gulf. In marked contrast to earlier examples, such as those of the Saljuq period in Iran, Syria, and Anatolia, which had superb vaulting and heavily decorated portals,[13] caravanserais of the Safavid period show their utilitarian character in the simplicity of their decoration. The large number of caravanserais needed and the speed with which they were erected left little room for elaborate decoration of the type that characterized other Safavid buildings.[14]

The expansive patronage of architecture under 'Abbas was not continued by his successors after his death in 1629, although Isfahan remained the capital and smaller civil structures continued to be built. The Khwaju bridge was erected in 1650 on the foundations of a fifteenth-century span under 'Abbas II (r. 1642–66). It lay astride the old road to Shiraz and linked the Khwaju quarter due south of the maidan with the Zoroastrian quarter on the south bank. Half the length of the earlier Si-o-se Pol, the bridge is far more complex: a central track for horses and wheeled traffic is flanked by vaulted pedestrian paths. The whole is raised on a high stone base, with contreforts on the upstream side to interrupt the current and steps on the downstream side. In the center is a raised octagonal pavilion, from which the ruler was able to enjoy the spectacles staged on the river below.[15]

Small palaces and pavilions were built, particularly in the royal park covering some seven hectares behind the 'Ali Qapu. The Chihil Sutun is aligned on the axis of the maidan and sits on a platform enclosed on three sides by stone channels with fountains and jets which flow into a long reflecting pool (110 by 20 meters) stretching before the main façade. The building consists of three discrete parts, all clearly visible from the exterior [243]. In the front is a *talār* supported on twenty columns and covered with a flat wooden roof. Behind it is a deep porch flanked by rectangular halls; at the rear of the porch is an iwan whose vault is revetted with muqarnas and mirror-work (Pers. *ā'ina-kārī*). From the iwan one passes into the main interior space, a large rectangular reception hall (23 by 11 meters) covered with

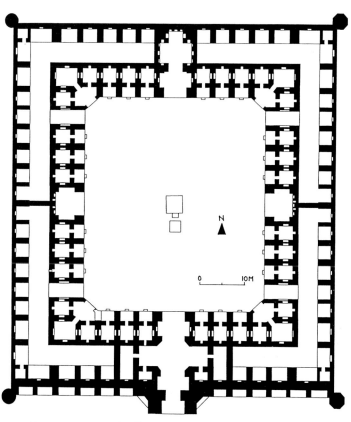

242. Bisutun, caravansarai, 1681–5, court

243. Isfahan, Chihil Sutun, begun 1647, view from north-west

244. Isfahan, Chihil Sutun, mural in side room (P4) showing picnickers,
ca. 1647

245. Isfahan, Chihil Sutun, mural in main hall showing Tahmasp
Receiving Humayun, late 1660s

transverse vaults supporting domes. Subsidiary rooms on two levels fill the corners; on the sides are shallow porches opening to the exterior. The plan is distinguished by the intermingling of interior and exterior spaces; one passes from open garden through sheltered and semi-enclosed spaces to an enclosed interior. The dissolution of the wall surface was enhanced by the extensive use of mirrors, not only in the small surfaces of the muqarnas vault but also in larger expanses of full-length mirrors of Venetian glass presented by the Doge. The building's name, Chihil Sutun ("Forty columns"), is popularly thought to derive from the combined effect of the twenty columns of the *talar* and their reflection in the long pool. This picturesque interpretation is probably inaccurate, as the word "forty" is used in Persian as "hundreds" in English, to refer to large numbers of things.

The Chihil Sutun was built by 'Abbas II in 1647, possibly around an earlier nucleus. Heavily damaged in a fire of 1705, it was substantially rebuilt in the following year, when the *talar* was added. Thus the building does not represent a particular moment, but rather shows, like the 'Ali Qapu, how Safavid palaces were continuously refurbished and enlarged to meet changing tastes and needs. Similarly, the wall paintings show differences in style and subject matter and were probably executed over time. Most of the small paintings seem to date from the late 1640s, while the four large ones that are the focus of the main hall were probably added twenty years later.[16]

The finest small paintings are found in the chambers east of the main hall on either side of the iwan, where they decorate the walls and lunettes below the ceiling. Enclosed in painted frames, they resemble paintings hung on a wall previously decorated with floral patterns. Well-preserved and beautifully restored, they represent the best of contemporary wall painting and show close affinities in subject matter and style to contemporary manuscript and album paintings. Indeed, some of the best have been attributed to Muhammad Qasim, one of the court painters at the time of Shah 'Abbas II and known for his work on several manuscripts.[17] One room (P4) is decorated with scenes of picnickers in the country [244], drinking, pouring wine, chatting with cup and bottle in hand, reclining on cushions, or seated side by side under trees in open landscapes. Landscape elements are only an artificial background to the subject, which is the detailed depiction of the leisure class. These languid youths, with their elegant dress, show how the style of Riza persisted well into the mid-seventeenth century. Another room (P3) has scenes from Persian literature, depicting Khusraw and Shirin or Yusuf and Zulaykha, as well as unidentified single figures; its iconographic program seems to have been a counterweight to that of the courtly pleasures depicted in the chamber opposite.

An entirely different style was used for the large historical murals in the main room. The four show the Safavid shahs engaged with their Muslim neighbors on the east: Isma'il battling the Uzbek Shibani Khan (often misidentified as the battle of Chaldiran), Tahmasp receiving the Mughal Emperor Humayun [245]; 'Abbas I receiving Vali Nadr Muhammad Khan (the ruler of Bukhara from 1605 to 1608); and 'Abbas II receiving an Indian ambassador (probably

Tarbiyat Khan, who was sent to the Safavid court on 12 November 1663 with a reply to 'Abbas II's embassy on the occasion of Awrangzib's accession in 1658). The composition and the use of chiaroscuro and atmospheric landscape show the impact of Western techniques of representation, although these features are superficially applied to a traditional Persian representational scheme. While overlapping figures have been used to suggest depth, the figures of the monarchs are centered in splendid isolation. Tahmasp, for example, is accorded the place of honor on the right. This Europeanizing style can also be seen in a dozen oil paintings on canvas as well as in the wall painting decorating the houses of the Armenians in New Julfa.[18] The program of historical murals in the main room of the Chihil Sutun establishes the official character of the building, which was used for receptions and audiences. In contrast to the paintings of the 'Ali Qapu, there are few erotic elements. These representations of official triumphs and embassies belong to the genre of wall decoration in palaces in the Islamic world and in western Central Asia, which can be traced back as early as the eighth century at Qusayr 'Amra in the Jordanian desert and the seventh century at Afrasiyab (old Samarqand).[19]

The other Safavid pavilion [246] to survive in Isfahan was erected under Sulayman I/Safi II (r. 1666–94) and is of an entirely different character. Known as the Hasht Bihisht ("Eight Paradises"), it is a two-storied square structure in the *Bagh-i bulbul* ("Garden of the Nightingale"), aligned with the axis of the Chahar Bagh avenue. Measuring some thirty meters on a side, the pavilion consists of a central hall roofed with a muqarnas vault supporting a lantern over the

246. Isfahan, Hasht Bihisht, 1669, plan

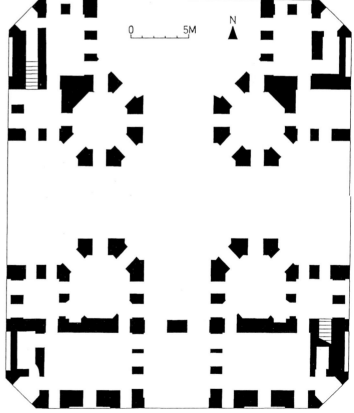

247. Isfahan, Hasht Bihisht, view of interior

central pool [247]. Large openings on four sides lead to porches facing the gardens, and small doors in the corners lead to groups of chambers on two stories. Historical sources state that the building was built in 1669; its name refers to a type of palace known since the fifteenth century in Herat and Tabriz (see Chapter 4). The type was imported by the Ottomans for the Çinili Kiosk at Istanbul [270] and developed by the Mughals in India for imperial tombs (see Chapter 18), but the name in this case seems to imply only that the palace was designed to bring the pleasures of Paradise down to earth.

Although some remains show the building to have been richly decorated with non-figural wall paintings, it is more important for its spatial rather than its decorative features. Interior and exterior spaces are hardly distinguished from one another, as one is always conscious of the outside from within and the inside from without. This interpenetration of volumes was enhanced by the use of water; hydraulic systems fed a fountain in the central basin and cascades in the south iwan and beyond the north side. The interior is lit from several sources; the original effect must have been splendid, with light reflected from the shimmering water and mirror-mosaic in the ceilings. Much of the tiled[20] and painted

revetment has disappeared, but Coste's drawing made in the nineteenth century shows that the surfaces were richly decorated. Most of the Safavid work, including the tiled panels in the spandrels of the exterior, seems to have been on a small scale commensurate with the private nature of the building, but Fath 'Ali Shah (r. 1797–1834) had large tile panels installed which depicted him enthroned and flanked by his sons.

Fath 'Ali Shah's figural tiles are of a type known from Safavid Isfahan. Several sets of cuerda seca tiles said to come from one or more of the pavilions behind the Chahar Bagh are preserved in European and American collections.[21] They all show male and female figures in garden settings. In one in New York [248], a reclining female figure with a wine-bottle in one hand is attended by a male figure holding a length of cloth and several other servants proffering food and drink. The female figure has distinctly non-Iranian features and hairstyle, and her male companion wears European dress. In the London example the main figures are familiar Persian types. In all cases the compositions have been assembled from stock figures, accessories, and landscape elements and rendered in six colors (green, light and dark blue, black, yellow, and white). The irregular shape of the upper edge of the large London and New York panels shows that they were made to fit a specific location; the left edge of the New York panel seems to have been cut at a later date, for the figure offering a fruit-bowl is largely missing. The New York panel has other peculiarities: the principal female figure has three curious marks on each forearm. These may correspond to the self-inflicted burns seen on the arms of male lovers in seventeenth-century Persian drawings, and the scarf her companion offers is already wound suggestively through her legs. This suggestive iconography would have been appropriate for the decoration of isolated pavilions for dalliance, and indeed a text from the mid-eighteenth century describes in lurid detail the goings-on in the gardens behind the Chahar Bagh.

The last major architectural achievement from the Safavid period is the complex of buildings erected by Husayn I (r. 1694–1722) on the Chahar Bagh.[22] The ensemble represents a return to the grandiose planning favored by 'Abbas I and includes a madrasa, known as the Madar-i Shah ("Mother of the Shah"), as well as a caravanserai, stables, and a bazaar, whose combined revenues supported the charitable foundation. The plan is characterized by rigid symmetry and axiality: the madrasa, caravanserai, and stables are aligned and connected by the bazaar, which runs along their north sides. The bazaar is a broad corridor 220 meters long, bordered on both sides by arcades: the 80 meters on the west along the madrasa have deep recesses for shops, while the central and eastern parts have shallower booths. The main entrance to the madrasa opens off the Chahar Bagh and leads to its open court [249]. Pathways and pools divide it into quadrants, a repetition on a smaller scale of the Chahar Bagh outside. The court is surrounded by two stories of rooms, and, as at the fifteenth-century madrasa at Khargird [62, 63], the corners are beveled. The dome chamber, set at right angles to the entrance and therefore not accurately aligned with the qibla, apes that of the Shah Mosque, although the tilework shows a notable decline from that of the

248. *Cuerda seca* tile panel showing figures in a garden, Isfahan, early seventeenth century. L 1.98 m. New York, Metropolitan Museum of Art

previous building. There are large bands of simple checker-work and almost no tile mosaic. The geometric designs are often coarse, and the palette includes a caustic yellow. Nevertheless, the courtyard of the Madar-i Shah madrasa, with its shaded walkways, whitewashed plaster with the vaulting lines picked out in blue, and shimmering tilework reflected in the pool, bestows an air of grace and serenity on the building far greater than its architecture might otherwise merit. The expansive scale and confident massing of forms in the complex set the style for architects in the following two centuries.

249. Isfahan, Madar-i Shah Madrasa, first quarter of the eighteenth century, courtyard

The grand development of Isfahan under 'Abbas I was repeated on a smaller scale at Shiraz under the patronage of Muhammad Karim Khan Zand, who was the Safavid regent there from 1750 to 1779.[23] He glorified his capital with broad avenues and more than twenty-five public buildings, including a mosque, a bazaar, and a palace. The most important were grouped around a great maidan, following the arrangement introduced by the Safavids at Isfahan and Kirman. Although it has been modernized and bisected by a boulevard, the original disposition of buildings can be reconstructed. On the north lies the citadel, or Arg, and some fragmentary remains of the palace grounds. On the south is the Regent's Mosque (Masjid-i Vakil), which was begun in 1766. It is a congregational mosque with a square court (60 meters to a side) surrounded by single-story arcades with iwans on the north and south. The north iwan connects to the deeply recessed entrance from the maidan, while the south iwan leads to the main prayer hall, a deep rectangle with five rows of vaulted bays supported on forty-eight fluted stone columns. The court façade has a stone dado and tiles painted with naturalistic flowers in distinctive rose and yellow tones [250]. The Vakil complex also included a public bath behind the mosque and a vaulted bazaar to its east.

250. Shiraz, Regent's Mosque, begun 1766, courtyard, detail of tilework

CHAPTER 14

Architecture and the Arts in Central Asia under the Uzbeks

Between the fall of the Timurid dynasty at Herat in the early sixteenth century and the coming of the Russians in the nineteenth, Transoxiana underwent a neo-Chingizid revival, and the political system was organized into appanages led by khans descended from Chingiz Khan through his eldest son Jochi. Sovereignty was corporate and embodied in the ruling clan, and succession was established by seniority. In the sixteenth century legitimacy was limited to agnates, or male descendants, of Jochi's youngest son Shiban (or Shayban), and the family that controlled Transoxiana from 1500 to 1598 is usually known as the Shibanids.[1] In the seventeenth and early eighteenth centuries, legitimacy was limited to agnates of another of Jochi's sons, Tuqay-timur, and the family that controlled the area is known as the Tuqay-timurids.[2] Even more important than the khans were the amirs, leading members of Turko-Mongol tribal groups who held both military and bureaucratic ranks. A third group of participants within the appanage framework was the learned class, which included traditional Muslim scholars and the shaykhs and members of Sufi brotherhoods. This group often served to mediate between the other two and between the disenfranchised and the ruling classes.[3] All three groups, commonly if somewhat inaccurately called Uzbeks, were important patrons of architecture and art, particularly book-painting. In form and style, the works of art produced under Uzbek patronage in Central Asia were dependent upon the models established in the fifteenth century under the Timurids (see Chapters 4 and 5), and the repetition of the same forms for more than two centuries means that these works of art, although copious in quantity (more than 350 public buildings, for example, are mentioned in contemporary sources), are often mediocre in quality, particularly when compared with contemporary works produced under the Safavids and Ottomans, who had far greater treasuries at their disposal.

ARCHITECTURE UNDER THE UZBEKS

The Shibanids and Tuqay-timurids were active builders.[4] They had broad international contacts, especially with Muscovy, and many commercial structures, such as bazaars, caravanserais, bridges, and underground reservoirs, were erected; but patronage of major buildings was concentrated in Bukhara, the capital, and such other large centers as Samarqand. The most characteristic civic structure was the *chārsū*, a type of retail market structure which had a central domed space surrounded by vaulted lanes and workshops. In general the architectural traditions established in the fifteenth century under the Timurids were continued, but bold vaults and domical systems that organized interior spaces in new ways were also used. Plans and forms became standardized, and the structural innovations of individual buildings are not as interesting as the organization and siting of architectural ensembles which reveal the economic and urban development of the area in this period.

The city of Bukhara replaced Samarqand as the political and religious center of Transoxiana. In the first half of the sixteenth century, the capital underwent radical reconstruction under the Shibanid 'Ubaydallah, who served as khan of Bukhara from 1512 and as supreme khan from 1533 until his death in 1540, and his son 'Abd al-'Aziz, who served as khan of Bukhara from 1540 to 1550 [251].[5] The city walls were rebuilt, and the remains of a huge fortified wall, ten meters high and five meters thick, with a crenellated parapet and semicircular towers, can still be seen. Like Fez in Morocco, Bukhara has preserved much of its traditional aspect, and it presents one of the best examples of a pre-modern Islamic city.

Several ensembles were built, including one in the center of Bukhara known as Pa-yi Kalan ("Foot of the Kalan"), which comprised a minaret, mosque, and madrasa. The forty-five-meter Kalan minaret had been built in 1127 by the Qarakhanid Arslan Khan and was one of the outstanding monuments in the city.[6] Adjacent to it was a large congregational mosque, which had been founded at the same time the minaret was built. One of the largest mosques in Central Asia, it measures 130 by 80 meters and accommodates 12,000 worshippers. During the fifteenth century the mosque was renovated, and according to an inscription the redecoration was completed in 1514 [252]. In the center of the main, or east, façade rises a slender entrance portal with beveled corners flanking a wide arched opening. The portal leads to a spacious court (77 by 40 meters) with iwans

251. Bukhara, plan in the sixteenth century. a) City walls, b) Citadel, c) Registan, d) Inner city, e) Rud-i Shah (Branch of the Zarafshan), f) Congregational mosque, g) Mir-i 'Arab madrasa, h) Road to Chahr Bakr, i) Goldsmiths' dome, j) Hatsellers' dome, k) Moneychangers' dome, l) Caravanserai, m) Warehouse, n) Qul Baba Kulkaltash madrasa, o) Lab-i Haws complex

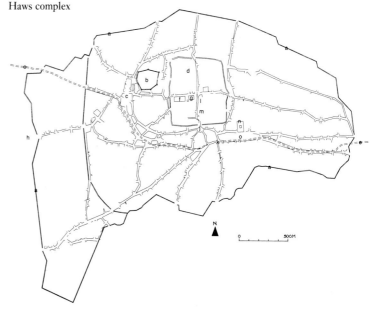

252. Bukhara, Kalan Mosque, redecorated 1514, courtyard

253. Bukhara, Mir-i Arab madrasa, 1535–6, façade

in the middle of the four sides linked by single-storied arcades. The long central axis is marked by a tall blue dome (30 meters in height) and a polychrome mihrab in the interior. The building is remarkable for its clear and simple form and restrained decoration, especially compared to that of the previous century. Most of the walls are of polished brick inset with glazed tiles, and only the portal is set off by more elaborate decoration in marble and glazed tile.

The third building in the Pa-yi Kalan ensemble, the large Mir-i ʿArab madrasa (1535–6) which stands opposite the Kalan Mosque, is named for its founder. Sayyid Mir ʿAbdallah was a Sufi shaykh known as Mir-i ʿArab who came from Sayram (Isfijab) to Bukhara sometime after 1515. The madrasa takes its simple, rectangular form (73 by 55 meters) from the adjacent mosque. It has a central court (37 by 33 meters) surrounded by iwans and two stories of rooms. Three sides of the building are blank, while the main façade, once covered with multicolored tile mosaic of high quality, contains a central iwan flanked by arcades and towers at the corner [253]. Two slender blue domes on tall drums rise behind the façade: one marks the cruciform lecture hall (Pers. *darskhāna*), the other the burial place of the founder. The interior rooms are covered by a distinctive system of four intersecting arches, flat pendentives, and a muqarnas frieze supporting a lantern drum and dome, all faced with white plaster and highlighted with polished brick and glazed insets around the edges of the design.

In the second half of the sixteenth century, Bukhara flourished under another branch of the Shibanid family and the leadership of ʿAbdallah b. Iskandar.[7] ʿAbdallah seized Bukhara in 1557 and four years later managed to have his father Iskandar proclaimed supreme khan. Iskandar remained a figurehead while ʿAbdallah served as actual ruler, and at his father's death in 1583, ʿAbdallah himself was proclaimed supreme khan with the help of the Sufi shaykh Khwaja Saʿd al-Din Juybari. Under the patronage of ʿAbdallah Khan (r. 1583–98), his chief confidant, the amir Qul Baba Kukaltash, and the Sufi Khwaja Saʿd, two large-scale projects were undertaken in the city of Bukhara [251]: a major east–west thoroughfare and a north–south artery. Both of these developments attest to the economic expansion of the city in the second half of the sixteenth century and mix commercial and cultural functions, as do other large-scale urban developments of the period, such as the Maydan-i Shah in Isfahan (see Chapter 13).[8]

The east–west thoroughfare in Bukhara ran from the Registan, an important retail district below the citadel, westward beyond the city walls for five kilometers to the shrine complex known as Char Bakr [254, 255]. The name was a shortened form of Chahar Bagh-i Imam Abu Bakr Ahmad b. Saʿd ["Four-fold garden of the Imam Abu Bakr Ahmad b. Saʿd"], and the site was the family cemetery of the Juybari shaykhs, the leading representatives of the Naqshbandi order of Sufis. It was a favorite area for outings by the Juybari family, and by the mid-sixteenth century already contained several tombs and shrines. In the decade 1559–69, ʿAbdallah Khan financed the construction of several new buildings, including a mosque (1 on plan), a madrasa (2), and a khanaqah or hospice for Sufis (3). The three buildings are set on a platform in a U-shape open to the east: the longer

254. Bukhara, Shrine of Char Bakr, 1559–69, plan. 1) Mosque; 2) Madrasa; 3) Khanaqah; 4) Gateway; 5) Park

255. Bukhara, Shrine of Char Bakr, 1559–69, view from south-east

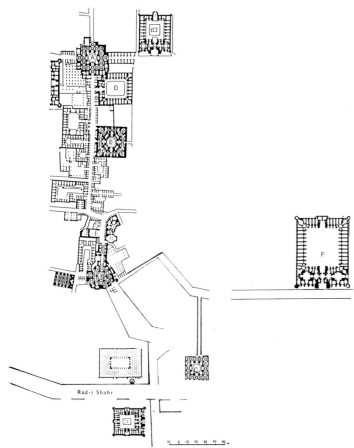

256. Bukhara, map showing the development of the central commercial district, second half of the sixteenth century. A) Goldsmiths' Dome; B) Hatsellers' Dome; C) Moneychangers' Dome, D) Caravanserai; E) Warehouse; F) Qul Baba Kukaltash madrasa

comprising a bath and two facing madrasas, the Madar-i Khan Madrasa, completed in 1566–7, and the 'Abdallah Khan madrasa, added twenty years later. To accommodate the residential and "green-belt" development that accompanied the new boulevard, the city walls were extended and the overall area enclosed within the walls increased by some twenty percent.

The development of the north–south artery through the center of Bukhara between 1562 and 1587 was more commercial in character [256]. Spaced along the center of this artery are three covered markets, called *chārsū* or *chahārsu* [257]. A shortened form of *chahar sūq* ("four markets"), the term refers to a building erected over the intersection of two major commercial streets or to the surrounding district that takes its name from the market. In Bukhara these *chārsū* are also called *ṭāqāt* ("arches") because of their domed roofs. The northernmost (A) is the Goldsmiths' Dome (*ṭāq-i zārgārān*), which, despite its name, was a retail emporium for textiles. Some 350 meters to the south (B) is the Hatsellers' Dome (*ṭāq-i tilpaq furūshān*); another 150 meters to the south-east (C) is the Moneychangers' Dome (*ṭāq-i sarrāfān*). These retail markets were surrounded by supporting commercial facilities and public institutions. Between the Goldsmiths' Dome and the Hatsellers' Dome, for example, there is a large caravanserai (D) and a warehouse for wholesale trading (Pers. *tīm*; E). The caravanserai is a rectangular building, whose plan is similar to that of a madrasa: a court surrounded with two floors of lodgings, storerooms, and stables. The warehouse, by contrast, is an enclosed and roofed building which can be locked at night and does not have stables or lodgings. To the east of the Moneychangers' Dome, the amir Qul Baba Kukaltash financed the construction of a madrasa in 1569 (F). Measuring 86 by 69 meters, it is one of the largest madrasas in Central Asia and could accommodate some three hundred students. Like earlier buildings in Bukhara, it has a simple plan and plain exterior [258], but the interior façades are more heavily decorated with glazed tile.

Following 'Abdallah's death in February 1598, Shibanid control of Transoxiana collapsed, and sovereignty in the area passed to the Tuqay-timurids. They controlled a smaller territory than their predecessors had, as the Tuqay-timurids had lost Herat and Khurasan and the northern province. Already in the first decade of their rule, squabbles erupted over the question of succession, and in 1612 the khanate was divided into a bipartite state ruled separately from two capitals: Imamquli ruled from Bukhara as great khan (r. 1612–42), and his younger brother Nadr (Nadhr) Muhammad ruled from Balkh as little khan. The construction boom that had characterized Bukhara in the second half of the sixteenth century was curtailed, although large complexes were still built. The major patron in the first half of the seventeenth century in Bukhara was Nadr Divanbegi Arlat, a high-ranking military administrator. One of his major works is the complex known as the Lab-i Haws ("Edge of the reservoir"). The area between Qul Baba Kukaltash's madrasa and the branch of the Zarafshan river that ran through the city center was developed by adding a rectangular stone reservoir (36 by 45.5 meters). On the west side of the tank, Nadr Divanbegi Arlat ordered a combined

and lower madrasa in the center connects the mosque and khanaqah, each with a large iwan in front of a tall dome. On the exterior, both mosque and khanaqah appear similar, with double domes set on drums pierced with windows, but their interiors are markedly different. The rectangular mosque has a single unified space ingeniously created by setting the three-tiered cupola between semidomes supported on horseshoe arches. The cruciform khanaqah has a more traditional arrangement of a dome resting on intersecting arches and a network of decorated pendentives. Several hundred yards to the east of the complex at the end of the road from Bukhara was an elaborate two-story gateway (4), and to the north of the shrine lay a twenty-five-hectare park (5) planted with flowering and fruit-bearing trees. The head of the Juybari family provided a substantial endowment for the shrine, with income from several parcels of land, a village, and two gristmills west of Bukhara. As late as 1914, the income supporting the madrasa still amounted to some six thousand rubles. The east-west thoroughfare served as the locus of development for a residential and cultural district in the south-west section of the city. At the east end, the thoroughfare was anchored by another public complex,

257. Bukhara, Hatsellers' Dome, 1580s

258. Bukhara, Qul Baba Kukaltash madrasa, 1569, façade

259. Bukhara, Lab-i Hawz complex, mosque-khanaqah, completed 1620

mosque-khanaqah [259] and on the east a madrasa. Work on the U-shaped complex was completed by 1620, and the arrangement may have inspired the final plan of the most famous complex from the period, the Registan in Samarqand.

The Registan, the town square of Samarqand, had been the site of a paired madrasa-khanaqah built by the Timurid ruler Ulughbeg in 1417–21 (see Chapter 4). During the fifteenth century other smaller buildings had been added around the square, and in the first decade of the sixteenth century the conqueror of Transoxiana and founder of the Shibanid line, Muhammad Shibani (r. 1501–10), had built a double madrasa on the east. It served as a funerary madrasa for the patron and thirty-three members of his dynasty and had a massive stone platform (four meters square and two meters high) for their cenotaphs. Other sixteenth-century buildings in the area included a congregational mosque and madrasa, built to the south of Ulughbeg's madrasa ca. 1528 by Alikah Kukaltash, an important military figure. The only one of these fifteenth- and sixteenth-century buildings to survive is Ulughbeg's madrasa [57–58], and it was the key to the Registan's development in the seventeenth century.

Work on the Registan [260] was renewed ca. 1618 by Yalangtush Bi Alchin, a military administrator who was governor of Samarqand, the center of his family's feudal territory. He had Ulughbeg's khanaqah demolished to make way for a new madrasa, known as the Shirdar ("Lion possessing") from the rampant lions decorating the spandrels of the entry portal [261]. Completed in 1635–6, the building was designed to complement Ulughbeg's madrasa opposite. It has the same massing and composition of the

260. Samarqand, Registan, first half of the seventeenth century, anoxometric view, surrounding buildings are conjectural

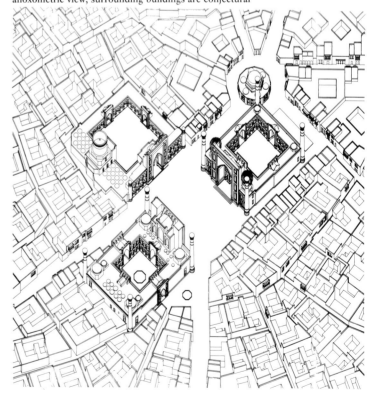

261. Samarqand, Shirdar madrasa, 1616–36, entrance portal

façade as the Timurid prototype: a huge iwan flanked by ribbed domes on tall drums, with slender minarets at the corners. On the interior, the court is surrounded by two stories of cells. The most striking feature of the building is its decoration. Both exterior and court façades are revetted in tile, and interior surfaces are painted with polychome vegetal themes. The spandrels on the main façade show deer being pursued by lions which have human-faced suns rising behind their backs, astrological figures recalling those over the entrance to the bazaar at Isfahan [232]. The figures are done in a full palette of tile mosaic, with a predominant use of yellow. Although striking from a distance, the drawing is less assured than the work of the fifteenth century.

The third and largest building on the Registan [262] is the madrasa known as the Tilakari ("Gold work"). Built between 1646 and 1660, it has a symmetrical façade with an arched portal flanked by minarets at the corners. The domed rooms for teaching and prayer found in the other two madrasas on the Registan are omitted, as the building includes a large congregational mosque on the west. The mosque comprises a ribbed dome set on a high drum, flanked by rectangular halls covered with fifteen vaults supported on piers. On the interior, a marble dado is surmounted by richly painted and gilded plaster. Despite the additive nature of construction, the Registan in Samarqand appears as a unified

ensemble because of the harmonious proportions, majestic volumes, and brightly colored revetment. It gives a good sense of the scale of work undertaken in Transoxiana during the seventeenth century. Forms were constantly repeated and less attention was paid to individual units than to the building of large urban ensembles with elaborate decoration.

The power of the Tuqay-timurid state continued to decline in the later seventeenth century. In 1642, on the death of his older brother, Nadr Muhammad assumed the khanate, which was briefly reunited during his reign (1642–5). Following his death, however, civil war and occupation by the Mughals of India meant that the khanate was divided again in 1651. The two khanates were once more held by brothers, although not on friendly terms: Bukhara was ruled by Nadr Muhammad's eldest son, 'Abd al-'Aziz, and Balkh was ruled by Nadr Muhammad's fifth son, Subhanquli. 'Abd al-'Aziz, who ruled as chief khan from 1651 to 1681, was considered a cultured man with a fondness for devotional poetry.[9] The sources praise his love of Islamic learning, which can be seen in his role as the major patron in Bukhara during the second half of the seventeenth century. In addition to a now destroyed madrasa on the Registan, he built a large (60 by 48 meters) madrasa in the city [263]. Completed in 1651–2, it forms an ensemble with the Ulughbeg madrasa near the Goldsmiths' Dome. The plan is based on that of the

263. Bukhara, Madrasa of 'Abd al-'Aziz, 1651–2, courtyard

Mir-i 'Arab madrasa, but the proportions are distorted and although smaller than its model it was meant to overshadow all previous buildings in scale and luxury. A rich variety of decorative devices is used. Domes and vaults are faced with a network of plaster muqarnas in fantastic combinations. A new type of muqarnas created the effect of a half-open fan through the play between star-shaped medallions and radial facets. Interior surfaces were richly painted with landscape scenes. The exterior is revetted in tile, with a heavy use of an acid green and yellow. The quality of the glaze is poor, and the limited and faded colors attest to the diminishing power of the Tuqay-timurid khanate, whose territory and political authority were considerably reduced during 'Abd al-'Aziz's reign.

Under 'Abd al-'Aziz's successor, his brother Subhanquli (r. 1681–1702), the khanate was reunited. He made Bukhara his capital and allowed Balkh to continue as the seat of the heir-apparent, while trying to control its administration. Subhanquli left a notable cultural legacy. He commissioned a world history, *Muḥīṭ al-tawārīkh* ("Envelope of histories"), written in 1697–8 by Muhammad Amin b. Mirza Muhammad Zaman, which mentions some of the artists active at his court (see below). Subhanquli built a madrasa opposite the shrine of Abu Nasr Parsa at Balkh, so that the two monumental portals (*pīshṭāq*) faced each other, and left a substantial endowment for a madrasa at the shrine of 'Ali b. Abi Talib at Mazar-i Sharif, some fifteen kilometers east of Balkh.[10] Despite Subhanquli's efforts, the Uzbek amirs became increasingly troublesome, and by the beginning of the eighteenth century Central Asia was in a state of deepening political and economic crisis as the khans steadily lost control to the resurgent tribal forces.

THE ARTS UNDER THE UZBEKS

Other than architecture, the major art form patronized by the Shibanids and Tuqay-timurids in Central Asia was the illustrated book. The production of luxury books had been a major feature of the Timurid patronage in Central Asia (see Chapter 5), and the tradition continued under the Uzbeks. Many of the calligraphers and painters captured in raids on Herat and other cities in Khurasan were brought to ateliers in Bukhara, Samarqand, and Tashkent. Nevertheless, in terms of both quality and quantity, book production declined from its fifteenth-century apogee. Books were produced in moderate quantity for local consumption. The repertory of subjects became increasingly limited, the range of compositions increasingly stereotyped, and the palette increasingly restricted. Unfinished manuscripts taken from Timurid libraries were often completed with illustrations modeled on Timurid prototypes. This updating of earlier manuscripts and the limited range of models makes it difficult to establish meaningful stylistic chronologies.

The Shibanids' debt to their Timurid predecessors is evident in the first illustrated manuscripts produced for them in the early sixteenth century, which have illustrations in the Timurid style.[11] The seven paintings in a copy of Muhammad Shadi's *Fathnāma* ("Book of conquests"), for example, have large figures with Mongol faces which could be taken for work of the mid-fifteenth century. The text, however, chronicles the exploits of Muhammad Shibani, the founder of the Shibani line.[12] Manuscripts illustrated in this retardataire style have been documented to Samarqand and Tashkent, and this provincial style was apparently abandoned soon after the death of its main patron, the ruler of Tashkent, Abu'l-Muzaffar Sultan Muhammad Bahadur, known as Keldi Muhammad, in 1532–3.

A finer style of painting developed in Bukhara, where 'Ubaydallah took calligraphers, painters, and manuscripts captured in Herat between 1512 and 1536. Contemporary chroniclers such as Vasifi and Mirza Haydar Dughlat praise the flowering of the arts that took place under his enlightened patronage. The earliest book that can be attributed to 'Ubaydallah's patronage at Bukhara is a manuscript of *Mihr*

264. *Prince Mihr Cutting off a Lion's Head at one Blow* from Assar, *Mihr and Mushtarī*, Bukhara, 1523. Washington, DC, Freer Gallery of Art

and Mushtarī, copied by Ibrahim Khalil at Bukhara in 1523.[13] The text is a mystical poem in rhyming couplets (Pers. *mathnavī*) composed by Muhammad Assar of Tabriz in 1377. The subjects chosen for the four paintings—a night scene with crescent moon and starry firmament, a school scene, a reception, and a hunt—are typical of the style associated with the school of Bihzad at Herat in the last decades of the fifteenth century, and the paintings retain the rounded figures, frontal buildings, and division into simple planes of the earlier style. The palette, however, has been reduced from the jewel-like modulated tones typical of the Bihzadian style to a few colors. The finest painting in the manuscript [264] shows Mihr hunting a lion. The illustration recalls the hunting scenes in the two famous manuscripts of Nizami's *Khamsa* ("Five poems") in the British Library that are attributed to Bihzad or his school,[14] but the composition has been altered to create a wider spacing of figures in two planes and the sensitively painted foliage in the foreground creates a sense of distance between the viewer and the painting.

This retardataire style modeled on the Bihzadian style continued to be in vogue in Bukhara until the middle of the sixteenth century. The continuing attachment of the Shibanids to their Timurid predecessors can be seen in a copy of Sa'di's *Gulistān* ("Rose-garden").[15] According to the colophon, the manuscript was copied by the famous Timurid scribe Sultan 'Ali Mashhadi at Herat in 906/1500, but a long dedicatory inscription recounts that the manuscript that had been transcribed for the Timurid Husayn Bayqara was "perfected and completed" for the Shibanid 'Abd al-'Aziz, and one of the eight paintings is dated 954/1547. The paintings reproduce the Herati canon, and the compositions and style are modeled on another illustrated copy of the *Gulistān* made for Husayn Bayqara at Herat in 1486.[16] Pictorial space, however, has been simplified, using larger figures and more open compositions, and the rich palette of saturated colors has been lightened and reduced.

In the 1530s a new style was introduced to the Bukharan atelier, probably by a new group of artists captured in 'Ubaydallah's seizure of Herat in 1529. They included the calligrapher Mir 'Ali and the artist Shaykhzada, one of Bihzad's most famous pupils. The impact of these new artists can be seen in a manuscript of the *Haft manzar* ("Seven countenances"), completed at Bukhara in January 1538.[17] The text, by the Persian poet Hatifi (d. 1521), a nephew of Jami, is a romantic poem modeled on Nizami's *Haft paykar* ("Seven portraits"). The copyist was the renowned master of *nasta'liq* script Mir 'Ali. Originally a protégé of the Timurid prince Husayn Bayqara, he continued to work at Herat during the Safavid occupation, but in 1529 he was taken by the Shibanids to Bukhara, where he remained until his death. His work became the model of *nasta'liq* and was eagerly collected, particularly by later Mughal rulers who incorporated it into superb imperial albums (see Chapter 19 and 371). The manuscript of the *Haft manzar* contains four full-page illustrations, and the rubrics around the double-page frontispiece name the Shibanid ruler 'Abd al-'Aziz and the artist Shaykhzada.[18] The painting of *Bahram Gur and the Princess in the Black Pavilion* [265] shows an elaborate setting with a flat architectural backdrop and ornate tile patterns. The same style of complex architectural setting can be seen in another painting ascribed to Shaykhzada, in a manuscript of the *Dīvān* of Hafiz done a decade earlier for the Safavid prince Sam Mirza, brother of Shah Tahmasp.[19] The figures in the *Haft Manzar* illustrations have puffy faces and heavy brows, and the women wear embroidered white headcloths, held in place by a tiara. The palette is restricted to a limited range of strong colors: crimson and deep blue are common, and dark green is often used for the outdoor setting of a meadow, which is sprinkled with plants bearing long-stemmed flowers.

This new style was continued, with diminishing artistic results, by Mahmud *mudhahhib* ("the gilder") and his contemporary 'Abdallah, who worked at Bukhara at least until 1575.[20] Illustrated copies of popular texts, such as Jami's *Tuhfat al-ahrār* ("Gift of the noble"), were often produced in these years. A manuscript with paintings dedicated to 'Abd al-'Aziz and the date 955/1547–8, for example, shows that artists closely repeated simple compositions and stylistic features drawn from a limited number of models.[21] In addition to manuscript paintings, these artists also did studies of single figures and couples, a genre which was taken up at the end of the sixteenth century at the Safavid court in Iran (see Chapter 12). Mahmud, for example, painted a portrait of the Timurid poet and statesman 'Alishir Nava'i [267].[22] It is

265. *Bahram Gur and the Princess in the Black Pavilion*, f. 22v, from Hatifi,
Haft Manzar, Bukhara, 1538. Washington, DC, Freer Gallery of Art

267. *Youth Declaring his Love to a Lady*, from Jami, *Tuḥfat al-aḥrār*, Bukhara, 1547–8. Dublin, Chester Beatty Library, MS. 215, f. 63v

Shīrīn dated 1568–9, maintain the figural types and costumes of contemporary Bukharan painting but incorporate typical features of Golconda painting, such as a tall narrow format, division of paintings into superimposed registers, and distinctive palette of inky blue and lilac pink.[24]

Illustrated manuscripts were still produced in Transoxiana during the seventeenth century, but as with architecture, the work became increasingly repetitive and the quality declined. Successive invasions of Khurasan brought a new infusion of Persian motifs, and paintings such as those in a copy of Sharaf al-Din ʿAli Yazdi's *Zafarnāma* ("Book of conquests") dated 1628–9, repeat features of the earlier style, such as elaborate rock formations, often outlined by smaller whitish rocks, and the prominent use of blue pigment.[25] The names of several seventeenth-century painters are known from signed works. Muhammad Murad Samarqandi (fl. 1600–25), for example, added the illustrations to a manuscript of the *Shāhnāma* copied in 1556–7 for ʿIsh Muhammad, the ruler of Khiva.[26] The painter worked in a distinctive but naive style in which satiric figures drawn with heavy, black lines are set against a single color ground, but the colors are somewhat dull. The names of several other painters and calligraphers who worked at the court atelier in Bukhara in the seventeenth century are recorded in the world history composed for the Tuqay-timurid ruler Subhanquli.[27]

Manuscripts were also made for other members of court, including amirs and members of the learned class. A *Court Scene* [266] from a manuscript of Saʿdi's *Būstān* ("Orchard"), for example, bears an inscription over the doorway stating that it was made for the library of Hidayat b. Mir Muʿin al-Din b. Khwaja ʿAbd al-Rahim b. Khwaja Saʿd in 1025 (1616).[28] The patron belonged to the powerful family of Juybari shaykhs who were the chief representatives of the Naqshbandi order of Sufis in Bukhara. His great-grandfather, Khwaja Saʿd, had been instrumental in the urban development undertaken in Bukhara in the second half of the sixteenth century under the Shibanid ruler ʿAbdallah b. Iskandar. The painting shows the conservative nature of manuscript illustration in seventeenth-century Central Asia: the large figures are seated in a generic interior composition of the type that had been standard in Bukhara for at least a century [265], but the elaborate tile patterns have been simplified. The large figures with heavy beards and tilted heads are set in stereotyped poses, often in pairs.

The Mughal occupation of Central Asia in 1646–7 meant that contacts with Indian painting increased, and manuscripts illustrated at Bukhara in the later seventeenth century, such as a copy of Nizami's *Khamsa* made in 1648, show that Bukharan painters were increasingly dependent on foreign models, particularly Indian ones, for the depiction of landscape and dress.[29] Traditional compositions were maintained, but buildings are surmounted by bulbous ribbed domes and women sport jeweled necklaces, feathered caps, and corkscrew curls. In the eighteenth century the quality of book production in Central Asia continued to decline, and the few illustrated manuscripts produced there are even more heavily indebted to the commercial style of illustration that flourished in Kashmir in the eighteenth and nineteenth centuries (see Chapter 19 and ill. 383).

based on an earlier study, perhaps by Bihzad, showing the poet resting his hands on a staff. According to a description by Vasifi, the earlier portrait was set in a garden set with blossoming trees with birds perched on their branches, running streams, and flowers everywhere. In Mahmud's copy, the poet stands against a plain gold ground.

Following the death of the Shibanid khan ʿAbd al-ʿAziz in 1550, royal patronage of illustrated manuscripts was apparently curtailed. Illustrated manuscripts produced for ʿAbdallah Khan, de facto ruler during most of the later seventeenth century, such as a *Shāhnāma* ("Book of kings") dated 1564, have rich but limited coloring, old-fashioned figures set in simple landscapes, and a curious mannerism of drawing female figures in which their heads are set at right angles to the axis of their bodies.[23] Some artists emigrated to Golconda in the Deccan, where they found work at the court of the Qutb Shahis (see Chapter 19). The manuscripts they illustrated there, such as a copy of Hatifi's *Khusraw and*

266. *Court Scene*, from Saʿdi, *Būstān*, Bukhara, 1616. Dublin, Chester Beatty Library, MS. Pers. 297

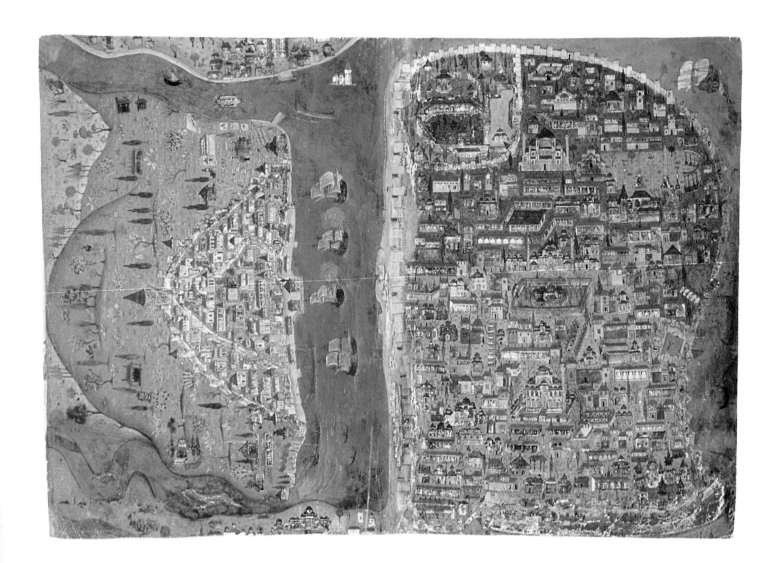

CHAPTER 15

Architecture under the Ottomans after the Conquest of Constantinople

Ottoman troops entered the Byzantine capital of Constantinople at dawn on 29 May 1453; fighting ended by mid-afternoon. The following day Mehmed II, the twenty-one-year-old sultan, made a ceremonial tour of the city. Entering the Church of Hagia Sophia, he decreed that it should be transformed into the city's congregational mosque (Arab. *jāmi'*; Turk. *cami*) and that henceforth the city would be his capital. His principal concern was to rebuild and repopulate it and foster its economic revival. Although the city would continue to be known in official Ottoman documents and on coins by its traditional Arabic, Persian, and Turkish name of Qustantiniyya ("The [city] of Constantine"), it was popularly called Istanbul. Mehmed's conquest of a city coveted by Islam since the seventh century gained him unprecedented charisma among Muslims, and he desired to complete his mission by establishing the rule of Islam over all the lands once held by the Eastern Roman Empire, particularly Italy. To this end he conducted an incessant series of campaigns against Venice and Hungary. In addition to establishing the territory of the Ottoman empire from the Danube to the Euphrates, Mehmed laid down its ideological basis in the absolute sovereignty of the ruler whose wishes were executed by an extensive bureaucracy.[1]

Ottoman architecture from the period before the conquest of Constantinople (see Chapter 10) had already shown a strong preference for cubic volumes covered by hemispherical domes, but the presence of Hagia Sophia, with its massive dome looming above the skyline, undoubtedly provided further inspiration and impetus in this direction. Ottoman architecture has at times been disparaged for apparently consisting of an endless set of variations on a Byzantine theme, but its true creativity lies in such self-imposed restrictions as maintaining the integrity between the inner and outer profiles of the dome, rather than separating them as in Iranian architecture. The canon of classical Ottoman architecture of the sixteenth century consists of a rather limited range of forms combined in a limited number of ways. As practiced by such masters as Sinan, the achievement of classical Ottoman architecture lies in the calculated solution of problems and the meticulous execution of details, with carefully controled harmonies and dissonances. When practiced by his less talented successors, Ottoman architecture often became repetitious and dull, as the classical canon was fossilized. Ottoman public buildings are imposing, important, deliberate, and reserved; rarely are they inventive or playful, for in the Ottoman scheme of things architecture was far too serious a business for levity.

As was the case elsewhere in the Islamic world, endowment deeds were drawn up to stipulate the ownership and support of charitable foundations, and an unusually large number of these has survived. Like all bureaucrats, Otto-

man functionaries protected themselves behind sheafs of documents, stored for reference and safety in the palace archives. Since the Ottoman empire lasted until the Turkish Republic was declared in 1923, the archives survived largely intact. This incomparable resource has provided scholars with vital information for the arts and architecture of the Ottoman period, such as names of artists, sources of materials, technical vocabulary, and prices, which is unknown for any other period of Islamic art. Nevertheless this data must be used with caution: the bureaucrat's view from the palace precincts did not necessarily reflect that of the artisan outside the palace walls or in a provincial center.

FROM THE CONQUEST OF CONSTANTINOPLE TO SINAN

Sultan Mehmed II (r. 1444–81, with interruption) was as eager to acquire learning as lands and was a noted patron of Turkish, Persian, and European writers and artists, who flocked to his court in Istanbul. He seems to have had a passion for building palaces; in addition to the one he completed in 1452–3 at Edirne, his old capital, he commissioned several in Istanbul. The first, built in 1455 and later known as the Old Palace (Eski Saray), was located in the center of the city on a site covering some eighty to one hundred hectares and presently occupied by Istanbul University and the Süleymaniye Mosque complex. The palace is shown in the center of a mid-sixteenth-century plan of Istanbul [268] as a large square enclosure with a single gate. Gardens surround an inner enclosure comprising several domed buildings. This undefended palace in the center of the city was complemented by the Yedikule Fortress, set astride the southern end of the city's land walls where they met the Sea of Marmara. Built according to Italian design theories in the shape of a five-pointed star, with a complement of seven distinctive towers, the fortress housed the royal treasury and royal residential quarters in the unlikely event of attack on the city.[2]

Mehmed's most important palace, begun in 1459, was located on a spectacular site covering sixty hectares at the tip of the Istanbul peninsula and overlooking two seas and two continents, the Ottoman arsenal, and the dockyards, as well as the European colony at Galata.[3] Known in its own time as the Yeni Saray or the Saray-i Cedīd ("New Palace") and since the nineteenth century as Topkapı Saray ("Cannon-Gate Palace"), it stood on the site of the acropolis of ancient Byzantium.[4] Mehmed's palace took almost a decade to complete, and it was often repaired, remodeled, and replaced to conform with changing fashions. Topkapı Palace represents an accretion of styles and tastes from several centuries, although the founder's initial concerns are still visible in the spatial organization of the palace precinct.

Unlike such European palaces as the Louvre or the Vatican, Topkapı Palace comprises a jumble of stables, kitchens, halls, pavilions, and kiosks arranged in a seemingly

268. *View of Istanbul* from Matrakçi Nasuh, *Bayān-i manāzil*, Istanbul, 1537–8. Istanbul, University Library, MS. 5964, ff. 8v–9r

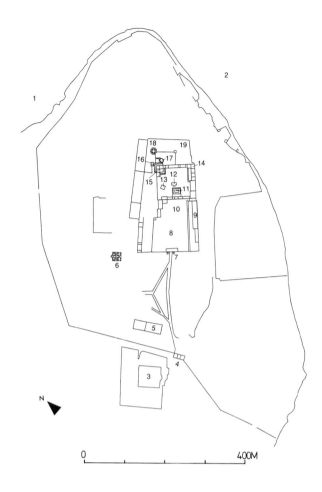

269. Istanbul, Topkapı Palace, begun 1459, plan: 1) Golden Horn; 2) Bosporus; 3) Hagia Sophia; 4) First Gate; 5) Hagia Eirene; 6) Çinili Kiosk; 7) Second Gate; 8) Second Court; 9) Kitchens; 10) Third Gate; 11) Chamber of Petitions; 12) Library of Ahmed III; 13) Mosque; 14) Treasury; 15) Privy Chamber; 16) Sünnet Odası; 17) Revan Kiosk; 18) Baghdad Kiosk; 19) Terraced garden

270. Istanbul, Çinili Kiosk, 1472

haphazard fashion within an outer wall punctuated with towers and gates [269]. Large areas of park-like open space were lushly planted and maintained by a battery of gardeners to provide both delight and food to the sultan and his enormous retinue. The palace functioned not only as the residence of the sultan and his family but also as the administrative center of the empire, with dormitories for functionaries and schools for trainees, and as a center of artistic production. The apparently casual formal arrangement belies a strict hierarchical organization of services and structures in three yards of increasing privacy. Only the sultan and his intimates were able to enjoy the innermost court. Although the power of the Ottoman sultans in the fifteenth and sixteenth centuries was no less than that of their European rivals, the Ottoman palace was designed to project the power of its owners not through massive piles of masonry but through the isolation of the ruler in a web of elaborate ceremonial and awesome silence.

In the outer gardens of the New Palace, Mehmed had three pavilions erected around a maidan: one, the Sırça Saray or Tiled Palace, was constructed in the mode of the ancient rulers of Persia, another was in the Ottoman style,

and a third was in the Greek mode. A fourth pavilion in an Italianate mode, with inlaid wooden paneling and murals by Gentile Bellini, seems to have been contemplated, but it was never built.[5] Only the Persianate pavilion, completed in September-October 1472 and now known as the Çinili Kiosk ("Tiled Pavilion;" 270), survives. Built into the slope of the ground and raised on a high basement, the brick building measures some twenty-eight by thirty-six meters and presents its main façade on the east. Two flights of steps approach a broad verandah supported on slender stone columns; the porch, an eighteenth-century reconstruction of the original, whose columns were of wood, is much like the *talār* of Iranian architecture [239]. A central iwan in the porch leads through a vestibule to a cruciform central hall covered with squinch-net vaulting and a dome some sixteen meters high. Opposite the entrance is an irregular hexagonal room projecting from the mass of the building; on the cross-axes are recessed porches opening to the outside. In each corner are rectangular rooms. The cruciform orientation is repeated, with some slight variation, on the lower story. The spatial organization of the building is that of the Iranian type of palace known as *hasht bihisht* ("Eight Paradises"), preserved only in later examples in Iran [246] and India [336], but known from a description of the contemporary example at Tabriz built by the Aqqoyunlu ruler Ya'qub. The network vaulting on the interior is similarly indebted to Iranian models.

The glory of the Çinili Kiosk is its revetment of ceramic tiles. The interior, transformed in the twentieth century into a museum of ceramics, has dadoes and niches faced with hexagonal and triangular tiles glazed turquoise, blue, and white, often highlighted with gold. The most lavish decoration is reserved for the porch, where a broad band in the *bannā'ī* technique crosses the façade and outlines its major divisions, and the iwan, which is lined with *bannā'ī* work, the first use of the technique in Istanbul. A horizontal band of tile mosaic crosses the vault below the springing. Executed in light and dark blue, white, yellow, and purple, the band

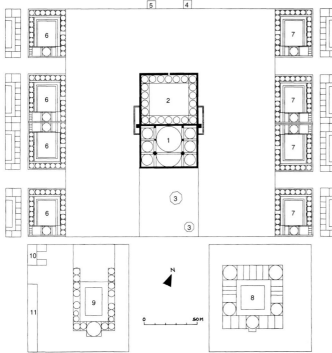

271. Istanbul, Fatih Complex, 1463–71, conjectural plan: 1) Mosque;
2) Court; 3) Tombs; 4) Primary school; 5) Book storage; 6) 'Mediterranean'
madrasas; 7) 'Black Sea' madrasas; 8) Hospital; 9) Hospice; 10) Soup-
kitchen; 11) Caravanserai

complexes in Bursa and Edirne, the plan of Mehmed's complex in Istanbul [271] is rigidly symmetrical and totally indifferent to the lay of the land or practical requirements. This scale and symmetry were undoubtedly made possible by the large tracts in the city that were available for construction. It has been argued that this new arrangement was due to the presence in Istanbul of the Italian architect Antonio Filarete, who is known to have intended to set out for Mehmed's court in 1465, but this date is two years after the project was initiated.[9] The vast, almost square area measured approximately 325 meters to a side. The mosque lay at the center of an enormous square court, approximately two hundred meters on a side, and was preceded by a forecourt and followed by a garden containing the tombs of the founder and his wife. The two types of ancillary buildings comprised charitable foundations (*khayrāt*) and buildings of public utility to provide income for the upkeep of the foundation. To the north of the court lay a small primary school and a book storage, and four large madrasas lay on either side. Each madrasa was a rectangular building with a porticoed court surrounded by some twenty small cells, a domed teaching room, and latrines. Eight subsidiary madrasas lay behind the large ones beyond a narrow street; they had only nine or ten cells facing a long narrow court. Outlying buildings included a hospice, caravanserai, hospital, and double bath, as well as residences for the ulema employed in the madrasas. The complex also included a great covered market, with 280 shops, and the saddlers' market, comprising 110 shops within a walled enclosure, as well as the ancillary horse-market, stables, and workshops of the stirrup-makers and farriers. In a period of military activity this district would have been thronged with troops equipping their mounts. To the south of the saddlers' market, Mehmed ordered new barracks (the *Yeni Odalar*) for the Janissaries; these barracks remained their quarters until the Janissaries were dissolved in the nineteenth century.

Much of Mehmed's complex was destroyed in the earthquake of 22 May 1766 and rebuilt by Mustafa III over the next five years, but the original mosque can be reconstructed from a variety of sources, including Melchior Lorichs' view of the city in 1559 [272].[10] The mosque was a rectangular

272. Melchior Lorichs: Panoramic View of Istanbul, 1559. Sepia on paper. Leiden, University Library, detail of mosque of Mehmed II

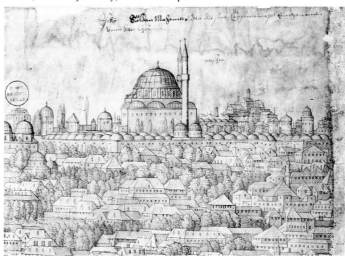

contains the foundation inscription in white *thuluth* script against a light blue arabesque scrolling on a dark ground. Like the plan and the vaulting, the decoration, which combines cut tile and tile mosaic, is deeply indebted to Iranian models. Although nothing is known of the builders, an undated petition in the Topkapı archives records the complaints of "Khurasani" (i.e. Iranian) tilecutters about the difficulties facing them after completing work on an imperial pavilion, undoubtedly this building.[6]

Although Mehmed could easily contemplate using Italian painters and Iranian tilecutters to decorate the pavilions of his new palace, he seems to have been far more conservative and less ecumenical in the design and execution of his major project of religious architecture in Istanbul, an imperial mosque with dependencies. In function it continued the long tradition, begun by his predecessors in Bursa, of commissioning a complex of buildings centered on a large mosque and the intended tomb of the sultan.[7] In form, the mosque at the center of the complex represents a conjunction of the tradition of erecting imperial mosques as developed in Bursa and Edirne with the new example of the Byzantine Church of Hagia Sophia. Often known as the Fatih complex after the epithet of its founder, the ensemble has given its name to an entire quarter of Istanbul. Work was ordered on 21 February 1463 and completed by December 1470/January 1471; the architect was Usta Sinan, known also as Sinan-i Atık or Sinan the Elder, to distinguish him from his more famous successor. The chosen site, covering about ten hectares, was the fourth hill of Istanbul, formerly occupied by the Church of the Holy Apostles, the second largest church in the city and the burial place of the Byzantine emperors.[8]

Unlike Mehmed's New Palace and Ottoman religious

domed structure (46 by 33 meters) preceded by an open court (21 by 30.5 meters interior) surrounded by arcades. The exterior walls, two massive piers, and two enormous porphyry columns supported a central dome some 26 meters in diameter (as compared to 31 meters at Hagia Sophia and 24.10 meters at the Üç Şerefeli Mosque in Edirne) with a half dome of the same diameter over the mihrab and three smaller domes arranged in a line on either side. The scheme is a logical sequel to that of the Üç Şerefeli Mosque [183], completed only sixteen years earlier, for both have integral courtyards and central domes flanked on either side by two smaller domes; indeed the main portal of the Fatih Mosque is an almost literal copy of that of the Üç Şerefeli Mosque. The major differences are that the dome is supported on four, rather than six, points and that the interior has been extended on the qibla axis by the introduction of a semidome. The use of a semidome, which would be the major focus of spatial experimentation in the design of mosques during the following century, was undoubtedly inspired by the example of Hagia Sophia standing before the architect's eyes.[11]

Two polychrome tile lunettes in the courtyard of the present mosque, attributed to the Tile Masters of Tabriz (see Chapter 10), are all that survive from the decoration of the mosque of Mehmed II. Underglaze-painted on a white frit body, they resemble the underglaze-painted tiles made for the Üç Şerefeli Mosque, except that the palette includes yellow.[12]

The Fatih Complex as a whole reveals several important developments in Ottoman society of the post-conquest period. In sharp contrast to earlier Ottoman complexes in Bursa, where spatial prominence was given to Sufi hospices (see Chapter 10), here the hospice was detached from the mosque and relegated to a relatively peripheral position. This undoubtedly reflects the declining role of the Sufi shaykhs and the increased importance of the ulema in the post-conquest Ottoman state. Indeed, the endowment deed stresses that the sultan built the numerous madrasas "to repair and fill with light the house of knowledge and to convert the imperial capital to a realm of learning."[13] In addition to serving as a religious and educational center, the complex functioned as a nucleus for the economic and social regeneration of this quarter of the city. Its income in 1489 and 1490 amounted to some one and a half million akçe (silver pieces), far exceeding the endowments to Hagia Sophia, by then transformed into a mosque. The income came from twelve baths in Istanbul and Galata, the poll or head tax on non-Muslims (Arab. jizya) of these two cities, the tax income from over fifty villages in Thrace, and various rents; half of it derived from outside the city and brought the wealth of the countryside into the city. Some sixty percent of the income went for salaries to the 383 employees (102 at the mosque, 168 at the madrasas, 45 at the hospice, 30 at the hospital, 21 agents and clerks to collect revenues, and 17 builders and workmen), and additional payments were made to indigent ulema, their children, and disabled soldiers. Some thirty percent of the income was spent on food at the hospice, which distributed 3300 loaves and fed two meals to 1117 individuals daily. The remainder went to support the hospital and pay for repairs.

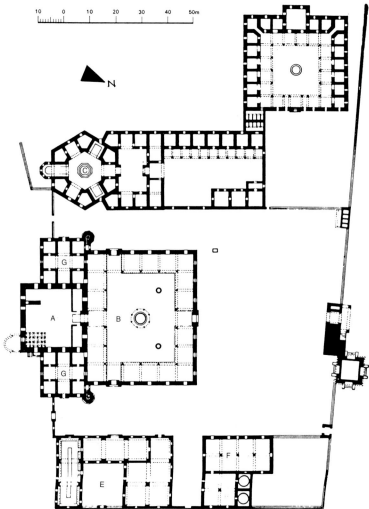

273. Edirne, Complex of Bayezid II, 1484–8, plan. A) mosque; B) Courtyard; C) Hospital; D) Medical school; E) Kitchen; F) Store; G) Hospice

Fraternal struggles framed the succession of Mehmed's son, Bayezid II (r. 1481–1512), and grandson, Selim I (r. 1512–20). Bayezid's accession was challenged by his younger brother, Cem (d. 1495), who sought alliances against Mehmed with both Muslim and Christian princes. Bayezid's policy against the Mamluks in Egypt, Syria, and northern Mesopotamia was not successful, and he was sorely challenged by the rise of the Safavids, who were Shi'ites, on the eastern frontiers of his empire. His European policy was more successful: in the summer of 1484 he established control of the land route to the Ottoman vassal state in the Crimea, and during his reign the economy expanded significantly. At the end of his life, Bayezid saw his sons Ahmed and Selim struggling to succeed him; Selim, appropriately known as "the Grim," won and forced the aged Bayezid to abdicate a month before his death. Selim's rule was marked by the expansion of the Ottoman state to the south and east: his conquests in Syria, Egypt, the Hijaz, Iraq, and Iran made the Ottoman sultan the undisputed power in the Levant and protector of the holy cities in Arabia, and brought him the title of caliph (Arab. khalīfa), or successor to the Prophet

274. Istanbul, Mosque of Bayezid II, 1500–5

Muhammad, which conferred undisputed prestige to the Ottoman sultan over other claimants to universal Islamic sovereignty.

Bayezid II was a major patron of architecture, commissioning religious complexes in Tokat (1485), Amasya (1486), where he had been governor before his accession, Edirne (1484–88), still the gateway to the European provinces, Manisa (1489), and Istanbul (1500–5). Members of his family and entourage were also responsible for buildings in several cities of the empire. The variety of plans and elevations used during the period shows that architectural practice was still largely a matter of local concern, although all of Bayezid's buildings fit within the standard Ottoman vocabulary.[14] His complex on the banks of the Tunca river at Edirne, for example, was designed by the royal architect Hayreddin Aga and financed with booty captured at the battle of Aqkirman (Belgorod) on the Dneistr estuary. The complex [273] includes a mosque, hospital, medical school, kitchen, foodstore, bakery, lavatories, refectories, and ample provision for itinerant dervishes. The mosque, a high walled structure 20.25 meters square covered by a single dome and preceded by a spacious forecourt, has a raised platform not

bonded into the fabric of the building to one side to serve as a private balcony (*mahfil*) for the sultan. The function undoubtedly derives from the royal loggia of the Yeşil Mosque at Bursa of nearly a century earlier [181], but the formal antecedents are a matter of some debate.[15]

The major monument of Bayezid's reign was his mosque complex in Istanbul. Located to the south of the Old Palace on the ancient Forum Tauri, the site needed extensive substructures to cover a major Byzantine cistern. The complex included an outer precinct with shops, a mosque, madrasa, school, hospice, hammam, and khan; it was the center of a district in the rapidly repopulating city. The old districts became more densely inhabited, with much new building; new districts were created in formerly deserted areas of the city, especially towards the land walls. In addition to the revenues generated locally, the income from several civil buildings in Bursa, including two great khans erected in 1490 and 1508, was used to support the sultan's foundation in Istanbul. The mosque [274] has a central dome (17.5 meters in diameter) and semidomes at either end; the spacious interior is expanded with aisles along either side covered with four small domes. Although the complex as a whole lacks unity of design in comparison with Bayezid's complex at Edirne or Mehmed's in Istanbul, the cascade of domes from the mosque to its courtyard shows a far greater sense of integration than does the Fatih Mosque. The expanded role of semidomes evidently derives from the examples of Hagia Sophia and the Mosque of Mehmed II, and Ottoman architects of the early sixteenth century were clearly grappling with the creative interpretation of earlier buildings. Two lateral wings, with minarets at their ends, are usually assumed to have served as hospices for traveling dervishes, although their function is still undetermined and their present condition, which shows no signs of alteration, is scarcely appropriate for that purpose. The beautifully finished stone construction exemplifies the fine materials and workmanship available to royal patrons and is characteristic of all later imperial mosques in the capital.

THE AGE OF SINAN

Selim I seems to have had little time or inclination for building; his mosque in Istanbul, which was completed in 1522 and closely modeled on the Mosque of Bayezid in Edirne, may actually have been built under his son Süleyman (r. 1520–66).[16] Selim's greatest contribution to the history of Ottoman architecture may have been quite inadvertent, for it was during his reign that the young Sinan (d. 1588), the greatest of Ottoman architects and one of the great architects of all times, was recruited in the *devşirme*, the Ottoman system of collecting subject Christian boys. The figure of Sinan and his role as director of the palace department of buildings (*khāṣṣa miʿmārlarɪ*) dominate Ottoman architecture in the middle and later years of the sixteenth century. In 1525 the department had thirteen architects, all Muslim; by 1604 it had tripled in size, employing twenty-three Muslims and sixteen Christians, testifying to its increased involvement in the architectural affairs of the entire empire.[17] Sinan's life and career have long been the stuff of legend, and his name has attracted buildings with the same power that George Washington's name has attracted beds.[18] He seems to have been born in Anatolia to a Christian family, recruited for Ottoman service as a boy, and trained in the science and art of building while serving in the campaigns of Selim I and Süleyman. By 1521 he had become a full-fledged Janissary, and his career as an architect became inextricably tied to the reign of Süleyman, arguably the greatest of Ottoman sultans.

In 1538 Sinan was appointed chief court architect (*mimar-başı*) and given the commission to design and build a mosque for Süleyman's wife Haseki Hürrem Sultan (Roxelane) at Aksaray in Istanbul. The complex of mosque, madrasa, hospital, hospice, and school was supported by a khan, bath, wood-store, slaughterhouse, shops, and warehouses which produced a combined annual revenue of half a million *akçe*. The single-domed mosque and U-shaped madrasa follow plans established in the early decades of the century and give little evidence of the architect's later genius. Sinan's first major commission was the Şehzade complex in Istanbul [275, 276]. It was built between 1545 and 1548 at the sultan's behest in memory of Mehmed, his son and heir-

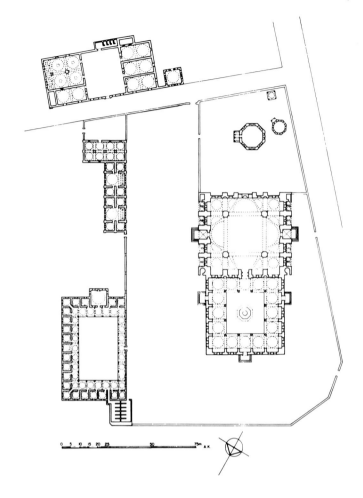

275. Istanbul, Şehzade mosque, 1545–8, plan

apparent (*şehzade*), who had died of smallpox at the age of twenty-two. Occupying a site on the city's third hill, the complex includes a mosque and its courtyard, as well as a madrasa, hospice, school, tomb, and caravanserai. The plan of the mosque is based on two adjoining squares (each approximately 38 meters to a side internally), which have been "riveted" together with two minarets.[19] One square, comprising the arcaded court, is open to the sky, while the other, comprising the prayer hall, is covered with a 19-meter dome, four semidomes, and four small domes in the corners. The plan is a logical development not only from such earlier buildings as the Mosque of Bayezid II but also from Sinan's mosque for Süleyman's daughter Mihrimah Sultan in Üsküdar, which the architect had planned a year earlier.[20]

Although Sinan later considered the Şehzade Mosque a work of his apprenticeship, several of its features show evidence of his sophisticated ability to innovate within the canons of the evolving Ottoman style. The loads of the superstructure have been concentrated on four massive piers beneath the central dome and the buttresses along the exterior walls. The bulk of the piers has been minimized by modulating their shape; the massiveness of the buttresses has been concealed by moving the exterior walls, except on the side of the mosque facing the court, towards the inner

276. Istanbul, Şehzade mosque

face of the buttresses. In that way most of their bulk lies outside the mosque. The concentration of loads allowed for thinner walls and more and larger windows. The exterior has been articulated to maximize its visual impact: the cascades of domes and semidomes eddy around the four contreforts which stabilize the piers. Loggias conceal the buttresses on the lateral sides of the mosque, superposed windows lighten the façades of the court, and delicate tracery enlivens the shafts of the minarets. The dramatic spaciousness and airiness of the Şehzade Mosque are apparent in comparison with the other imperial mosques standing in the city at that time.[21] The ostensible justification for this building, the tomb of Şehzade Mehmed, stands behind the mosque, slightly beside the axis. Modeled on the tomb of Selim I, it is a domed octagonal prism (diameter 9.20 meters) with a fluted dome and a tetrastyle portico of pink porphyry and verd-antique columns. Colorful cuerda seca tile panels flank the entrance; those on the interior cover the entire wall from the floor to the springing of the dome and depict an illusionistic arcade, with serrated leaves and blossoms, motifs popular in contemporary textiles and ceramics [301, 302]. In some of the tiles around the upper windows, the designers attempted to circumvent the inherent limitations of the cuerda seca technique, which required lines at the edge of

colored areas, by introducing an unusual white ground. These tiles are believed to be among the last works of a group of itinerant Iranian tile masters brought by Selim I from Tabriz nearly thirty years earlier.[22]

As a Janissary, as well as an architect and engineer who could assist in the design and construction of bridges and fortresses, Sinan accompanied Süleyman on campaigns in Europe and the Middle East and undoubtedly became familiar with the great architectural monuments of the Islamic and pre-Islamic past. He is credited with designing buildings from Buda in Hungary to Mecca in Arabia, and these structures, whether or not by the hand of the master, were instruments in a concerted Ottoman policy of establishing sovereignty through the erection of buildings in a distinctively Ottoman style with hemispheric domes and tall thin minarets. The design and supervision of these works in the provinces by court architects in the capital were made possible not only by the Ottoman system of central administration but also by the development of imperial standards and a system of architectural representation. Thus it could be expected that plans drawn up in the capital would be reasonably executed in the provinces by local talent or that materials could be ordered in one part of the empire for use elsewhere.

277. Jerusalem, Dome of the Rock, tile revetment, mid-16th century, restored 1960s

Many of these features can be seen in the work ordered by Süleyman at Jerusalem. Not surprisingly, the sultan considered himself the second Solomon, and it was only appropriate for him to order the refurbishment of the Dome of the Rock, the earliest example of Islamic architecture and the structure that stood on the site of the first Solomon's temple.[23] The refurbishment in the Ottoman style was further appropriate as the Dome of the Rock stands opposite the splendid Ashrafiyya madrasa [120], built some sixty years earlier in the finest Mamluk style. Sinan is said to have stopped in Jerusalem during his pilgrimage to Mecca and organized the restoration of the Dome of the Rock. The major impact of this work, whether or not Sinan was responsible, was the replacement of the Umayyad mosaics on the exterior of the drum and octagon with tiles executed in cuerda seca and polychrome underglaze, along with tile mosaic and blue-and-white tiles [277].[24] An inscription in tile mosaic bears the date 952/1545–6, while a tile on the north porch painted in blue, turquoise, and black on a white ground is signed 'Abdallah of Tabriz and dated 959/1552; work continued at least until the end of Süleyman's reign.[25] Unlike the lamps made at Iznik that Süleyman presented to the Dome of the Rock [303], the tiles appear to have been made locally, although there is no evidence for an indigenous and sophisticated pottery industry in Syria at that time. During the course of their work, the tile-makers seem to have developed a technique in which the glaze overflows the cuerda seca outlines. Although the total effect of the tile revetment (restored in the mid-twentieth century) remains

one of the most striking images in Islamic art, tiled exteriors were not repeated in Ottoman architecture, either because the technique was site-specific or because it was not considered particularly successful as design. The restoration of the Dome of the Rock, however, seems to have been instrumental in the development of a contemporary taste for large expanses of underglaze-painted tiles on the interior of buildings. This new style of tile, the main product of an expanded ceramic industry at Iznik, was characterized by large-scale compositions easily readable from a distance. The earlier soft palette of blues and greens was replaced with a brilliant one dominated by a distinctive tomato red, which seems to have been deemed more effective for the visual organization of large mural surfaces.[26]

Another of Sinan's projects for Süleyman outside the capital was a complex of buildings for pilgrims along the Barada river in Damascus. Although the pilgrimage route from Damascus had long been important, it gained prominence after the Ottomans took control of Syria in 1516, and facilities along the pilgrimage route there became increasingly a matter of imperial concern.[27] The Sulaymaniyya Complex, completed in 1554–5, was designed by Sinan, but executed by an assistant, to judge from the local materials and techniques used, particularly the alternating white and dark gray stone construction of its walls, a distinctly Syrian feature.[28] The complex is a symmetrical composition organized around a longitudinal axis: the mosque and the soup kitchen (Arab. *dār al-it'am*) stand at the ends of a rectangular court, flanked by pairs of caravanserais and hospices,

278. Damascus, Sulaymaniyya Complex, completed 1554–5, portico

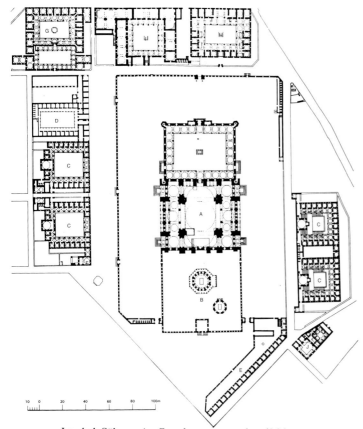

279. Istanbul, Süleymaniye Complex, 1550–7, plan. A) Mosque;
B) Mausoleum; C) Madrasa; D) Medical school; E) School for Traditions;
F) Koran school; G) Hospital; H) Hostel; I) Kitchen; J) Bath

the whole enclosed within a wall. The mosque is a single
domed structure, flanked by minarets and preceded by a
deep double porch [278]. The relatively small size of the
complex (one hectare) seems to have assured the successful
integration of parts. Tile lunettes over the mosque's windows
are executed in the underglaze technique currently fashionable at Iznik in Turkey, but repeat the traditional designs of
cuerda seca tiles. They differ from those produced at Iznik
in the absence of the brilliant white slip and bright red.[29]

The most ambitious of Süleyman's many projects in the
Balkans, Istanbul, Anatolia, Syria-Palestine, Arabia, and Iraq
was Sinan's complex for the sultan in the capital [279].[30] It
is a conscious restatement of the complex of Mehmed Fatih;
none of Bayezid's complexes nor that of Selim I approaches
its grand scheme. A sloping site of over seven hectares
overlooking the Golden Horn was made available when the
Old Palace was damaged in a fire. Work was begun in July
1550 and continued at least until October 1557. The first
task must have been terracing the site to provide foundations
for the complex, which was to comprise a congregational
mosque, two mausoleums, four general madrasas, two specialized madrasas (one for medicine and one for hadith), a
Koran school for children, a hospital, a hostel, a public
kitchen, a caravanserai, a hammam, and rows of small shops.
The presence of a solitary Sufi hostel contrasts sharply with
the six madrasas, an anomaly explained by the declining
power of the Sufi shaykhs, who had been instrumental in the
Ottomans' rise, in face of the increasing centralization of the
Ottoman state. The zaviye mosque, which had been charac-

teristic of early Ottoman imperial foundations, was gradually
abandoned after the conquest of Constantinople. Süleyman,
known in Turkish as Kanuni, or law-giver, entrusted Ebussuud Effendi, the leading religious figure of the day, with the
task of harmonizing traditional Islamic law with the administrative practices of the Ottoman state. The endowment deed
to the complex specifies its function as the most prestigious
center of religion and religious law in the empire, "to
elevate matters of religion and religious sciences in order
to strengthen the mechanisms of worldly sovereignty and to
reach happiness in the afterworld."[31]

The account books from the construction of the Süleymaniye Complex provide invaluable evidence for the pro-
cedures followed in such a major enterprise.[32] Materials and
craftsmen were assembled from Istanbul and other parts of
empire; indeed, most of the official correspondence and
court orders concern the acquisition of marble, porphyry,
and granite. The most expensive and time-consuming
operation was the search for four red granite columns for the
mosque and their transport to the building site. The court
orders agree with textual reports that one column came from
the Old Palace, in the gardens of which the complex
was being built, one from Baalbek in Lebanon, one from
Alexandria in Egypt, and one from the fifth hill of Istanbul
(Kiztasi Mahalle), but it is impossible that the four matched
columns in the mosque could have come from these four
disparate sources. Rather, the four columns assembled were
probably stored in the imperial warehouses for another use,
and a matched set of four columns found elsewhere. The
official record, no matter how attractive, does not always
have to be the truth.

The account books also record wholesale purchases of
Iznik tiles, lapis lazuli for blue pigment, assorted colors,
foreign gold coin for gilding, gold foil, gold leaf, mercury,
ostrich eggs, tin, timber, planks, sandarac resin, and petro-
leum thinner. The wide spectrum of hues reported is unparalleled in Ottoman architectural decoration or elsewhere
in Islamic art, so the varnishes, sizes, and pigments must
have been ordered for use on objects associated with the
complex. Of the 3523 workers assembled from throughout
the empire, half were Christian and half Muslim; all were
kept under strict discipline. When finished, the complex had
a staff of 748, whose stipends accounted for nearly one million akçe. The endowment of the complex was consolidated
into one deed, according to a rescript made during the reign
of Murad III (1574–95), when the annual income was over
five million akçe. Eighty-one percent of the income derived
from taxes on villages in the European part of the empire.

For this immense project, Sinan exploited the sloping site,
terracing the shops, innkeepers' rooms, and caravanserai
into the hillside, relaxing the absolute symmetry that characterizes such earlier complexes as the Fatih in Istanbul or the
Sulaymaniyya in Damascus, and more skillfully integrating
the complex into the urban fabric. The overall impression of
the complex is of an imposing pyramidal mass of domed
units punctuated by the four slender minarets of the mosque
[280]. The mosque itself stands in the middle of a huge
walled enclosure (216 by 144 meters) and is preceded by a
rectangular court (44 by 57 meters) with minarets at each of
its four corners. Although this arrangement had been intro-

280. Istanbul, Süleymaniye Mosque

281. Istanbul, Süleymaniye Mosque, interior

duced a century earlier at the Üç Şerefeli Mosque in Edirne [183], the relationships among the minarets and between the minarets and the mosque are more carefully controled in the Süleymaniye Mosque, for the two minarets at the juncture of mosque and court are taller and have three balconies, while those at the north end of the court have only two. The overall concept of the building is based closely on Hagia Sophia: it consists of a central domed space (diameter 26.20 meters) expanded along the qibla axis with semidomes, themselves expanded with semicircular exedrae, the whole flanked by subsidiary spaces covered with a series of smaller domes. The somber interior [281] is spatially different from Hagia Sophia, however, for the nave and screened aisles of the church have been opened to form a single space for prayer, interrupted only by the four massive piers supporting the central dome and the two great columns on either side. The exterior composition of gray, lead-covered domes and white stone walls is carefully orchestrated, lightened only by the arched openings of windows and arcades arranged in threes and fives. The mosque is a logical refinement of Sinan's earlier spatial experiments, in the Şehzade Mosque, for example, and exemplifies the classical Ottoman style, in which traditional forms are repeatedly honed to perfection.

The ornament on the interior of the mosque was also kept deliberately to a minimum, although it was the first of many mosques in Istanbul to receive extensive but discreet decoration in underglaze-painted tiles, particularly along the qibla wall.[33] The tiles flanking the mihrab are a single design painted on many tiles; when repeated they form a continuous pattern. The calligraphic roundels set in the large square panels above the mihrab are each composed of sixty-four square tiles surrounded by a border of narrower tiles. Stencils for them were designed by Ahmed Karahisari, the foremost calligrapher of the day, or one of his students.[34] Tiles in the techniques of cuerda seca and monochrome glazing, which were used for areas of secondary importance and minarets, continued to be produced in Istanbul, but underglaze-painted tiles were largely made in commercial establishments at Iznik, probably because they had the capacity to produce the large expanses of tile revetment that were becoming popular. This development brought about several changes: the use of underglaze painting allowed for a greater sense of draftsmanship, the new designs and large expanses to be covered seem to have encouraged the change from a hexagonal format, characteristic of the Iranian tile tradition dominant in the fifteenth and early sixteenth centuries, to a square format. The inscriptions in the mosque were prepared by Ebussuud Effendi; they are all Koranic except for the foundation inscription, which emphasizes the sultan's Ottoman lineage, his divine right to rule, and his role as the protector of orthodox Islam and the Shari'a against heterodoxy.

Süleyman died on 7 September 1566, during the siege of Szigetvár in Hungary; his embalmed body was brought to Istanbul later that year and buried in the cemetery behind the mosque. Süleyman's octagonal tomb, whose interior was modeled after that of the Dome of the Rock, was completed a year later. The walls and pendentives are sheathed with magnificent tiles below stained glass windows and a dome with designs painted over carved plaster. Curiously, any intended reference to the Dome of the Rock was not visible from the exterior.

The services of the chief court architect were also available to members of the upper echelons of the Ottoman court, represented by such figures as Rüstem Pasha (ca. 1500–1561). Born in Bosnia, he rose to be a general in the Ottoman army and married Süleyman's daughter Mihrimah in 1539. He was noted for his financial acumen and became increasingly involved in court intrigue. Appointed grand vizier in 1544, he was dismissed in 1553 for plotting, on behalf of his mother-in-law, Hürrem Sultan, the execution of Şehzade Mustafa, Süleyman's son and heir-apparent. After two years of voluntary retirement with his wife, Rüstem was reinstated as grand vizier and survived in the post until his death. He accumulated vast wealth during his career and at his death left a fortune in estates, cash, and luxuries; his wife is said to have received two thousand ducats a day from the tax-farms of the Bursa silk looms and the salt-pans at Clissa. His library contained thousands of calligraphed volumes, as well as innumerable chests of miscellaneous papers and books.[35]

The most famous of Rüstem Pasha's many pious foundations is the mosque built for him by Sinan near Eminönü, below the Süleymaniye Complex.[36] The building is located on one of the most valuable sites in a bustling market area of Istanbul, and even such a powerful patron had to go to great lengths to acquire it. The Byzantine church on the site had been converted into a mosque in the fifteenth century, and Rüstem had to obtain a legal opinion (Arab. fatwa) condemning the mosque as no longer adequate to meet the needs of the congregation. To appease the supervisors of the endowment of the earlier mosque, he was forced to use the materials salvaged from it to build a replacement elsewhere. Work on Rüstem's own mosque was incomplete at the patron's death, and his widow had to petition her father for funds to complete it. The mosque is built above a row of shops and a cross-vaulted warehouse which provided revenues for its upkeep. The substructure also served to raise the mosque so that it would offer a more monumental profile than might be expected from its size. The small mosque comprises a rectangular prayer hall with central dome (15.20 meters in diameter), preceded by a porch with five domes and flanked by two-storied aisles. The dome (22.8 meters high) rests on a high octagonal zone of transition supported by the exterior walls and four massive piers. Four semidomes fill the corner spaces.

The most notable feature of the Mosque of Rüstem Pasha, however, is the extensive revetment of Iznik tiles on the interior [282]. They cover the walls, piers, mihrab, and minbar in a web of stylized floral and foliate designs executed on a white slip in black, purple, dark blue, turquoise blue, and red under a transparent glaze. In this comparatively intimate setting, Sinan seems to have been experimenting with the lavish use of tiles, which he had used sparingly and to little effect in the grand Süleymaniye Mosque. The tiles, which show great diversity of design, include both large compositions spread over many tiles and designed to fit a specific surface and mass-produced modular tiles cut to fit the wall on which they were installed.[37] The designs com-

282. Istanbul, Mosque of Rüstem Pasha, ca. 1561–2, interior

283. Edirne, Selimiye Complex, 1568–75, axonometric view

bine elongated leaves with jagged edges with flowers and
leaves depicted on the contemporary textiles whose production had been encouraged by the vizier's fiscal policies (see
Chapter 16). The Mosque of Rüstem Pasha and the contemporary Mosque of the Ramazanoğlu in Adana set a
precedent for lavish tile revetments which continued to be
popular for the remainder of the century.[38]

Sinan's masterpiece is the complex at Edirne designed
and built for Süleyman's son and successor, Selim II (r.
1566–74) [283, 284]. Although the city was no longer
the capital, it remained important as the gateway to the
extensive Ottoman domains in Europe and staging-point for
campaigns to the west. As crown prince Selim had already
commissioned buildings, and funds for the new building
were supplied by the spoils from his campaign in Cyprus,
which amounted to 27,760 purses, according to the contemporary chronicler Evliya Čelebi. The Selimiye Complex
was begun in 1568 on a prominent site (190 by 130 meters)
in the center of the city which had once been occupied by a
palace constructed by Yıldırım Bayezid. The mosque is set
in the center of the site; a madrasa and a school for hadith
occupy the rear corners, and a covered market (Turk. *arasta*),
built somewhat later, runs along one flank.

According to Sinan's biography, the *Tezkiretü'l-Bünyan*,
written by Sa'i Mustafa Čelebi near the end of the architect's
life:

284. Edirne, Selimiye Complex

Sultan Selim Khan ordered the erection of a mosque in Edirne ... His humble servant prepared for him a drawing depicting, on a dominating site in the city, four minarets on the four corners of a dome. All four had three balconies, two of them with separate staircases leading to each balcony. The Üç Şerefeli minaret is like a thick tower, but the Selimiye minarets are slender. The difficulty of putting three staircases in shafts as slender as these should be obvious to all. Those who consider themselves architects among Christians say that in the realm of Islam no dome can equal that of the Hagia Sophia; they claim that no Muslim architect would be able to build such a large dome. In this mosque, with the help of God and the support of Sultan Selim Khan, I erected a dome six cubits higher and four cubits wider than the dome of the Hagia Sophia.[39]

Sinan's boast was carefully crafted: the dome is approximately the same diameter as the slightly elliptical one of Hagia Sophia and is indeed higher, although the entire baldachin is twelve meters shorter from pavement to crown. Contemporary eyes accepted the validity of the claim and believed that the architecture of the Ottomans had finally and demonstrably surpassed that of the Ancients.

Seen from afar, the Selimiye presents an unforgettable profile: the four pencil-shaped minarets, each grooved to accentuate its verticality, are some of the tallest ever built (70.89 meters from ground to finial). They frame the central mass and delimit it from its surroundings. Sinan's concern with building so high, however, makes the exterior less integrated than that of the Süleymaniye. There the minarets are set around the court and provide a counterpoint to the high central mass of the dome, and the domes and half-domes cascade to the ground without the interruption of the high drum of the Selimiye. Nevertheless, the careful articulation of the exterior of the Selimiye is exquisite. The system of support is delicately suggested by the slightly projecting buttresses; the detail of the window grilles and balustrades contrasts with the otherwise smooth walls; the discreet use of red sandstone and the dark gray of the lead roofs add a note of color to the honey-colored walls; and the carefully arranged voids and projections invite light to play across the surface of the building.

Like the Şehzade Mosque in Istanbul, the Selimiye Mosque comprises two equal parts, one open and one covered, but the squares of the Istanbul building have been replaced at Edirne by laterally set rectangles (60 by 44 meters). The spacious court, with an ablution fountain in the center, is surrounded by arcades on granite and marble columns supporting muqarnas capitals and arches with alternating voussoirs of red and white. The regularity apparent in plan is less apparent in elevation, where the domes of the arcade along the mosque are raised significantly higher than those of the other three sides to reflect its derivation from the domed porch in early Ottoman mosques [e.g. 181]. The dome in front of the central portal is higher still and distinguished by its fluted shape. The windows around the court are surmounted by lunettes of Iznik tiles, with inscriptions reserved in white against blue, green, and a bit of red, undoubtedly in acknowledgement of the tiled lunette panels in the nearby Üç Şerefeli Mosque [185].

The superb quality of the exterior does not adequately prepare one for the breathtaking spaciousness and sheer poetry of space and light within [285]. The octagonal system of supports is a much enlarged and more sophisticated version of the system used at the Mosque of Rüstem Pasha. The vertical loads are concentrated on eight massive piers of dodecahedral shape; the two (on either side of mihrab) are incorporated into the exterior wall, the other six are freestanding. The outward thrust of the dome is absorbed by additional buttresses concealed within the walls. This ingenious system creates an extraordinary sense of space by allowing the corners of the building to be opened, and the architect was able to pierce the walls to an unprecedented degree and flood the interior with light from every level. The effect, however, may have been somewhat diminished if the windows were originally glazed with colored glass. The dome rests on a crown of windows and the semidomes on tiaras; the tympana are pierced with double tiers of arched windows.

Under the center of the great dome stands a tribune supported by twelve marble columns two meters high; a small fountain stands underneath, although the major ablution areas were in the court and on either side of the building. The mihrab recess projects beyond the exterior; the mihrab itself and adjacent minbar are of finely worked

285. Edirne, Selimiye Mosque, interior

Marmara marble. This area of the mosque is decorated with superb Iznik tiles, as is the royal gallery (Turk. *hünkâr mahfili*), to the left of the mihrab. These tiles, with their delicate floral patterns, were made specifically for the project, and their superb quality was appreciated by the Russians, who removed some of them in 1878 during the Turco-Russian War. The mosque library stands in the corner to the right of the mihrab.

Sinan was probably in his late seventies when the Selimiye Mosque was completed in 1574. He continued as chief court architect until his death fourteen years later, but the commissions offered were more modest than in earlier times and the projects were increasingly executed by assistants. The relatively smaller works ascribed to Sinan in this period continue some themes seen in his classical works, but are more experimental and mannered.[40] A building such as the complex built for Sultan Murad III (r. 1574–95) at Manisa [286], where he had been governor, exemplifies Sinan's last works. Built to Sinan's plans by the architects Mahmud and Mehmed Aga between 1583 and 1585, the building has a five-domed porch preceding a T-shaped prayer hall. The interior is covered with a large central dome and three cloister vaults. The T-plan seems to have been inspired by the zaviye mosques of early Ottoman times, but the ribbed vaults and the verticality of the façades, which are further enlivened by polychrome arches and variations in texture, accentuate a distinctly anti-classical approach to mosque design.

Sinan died on 17 July 1588 and was buried in a small tomb he had designed for himself at the bottom of his garden near the Süleymaniye Mosque in Istanbul. He was described in the introduction to his endowment deed as "the eye of the illustrious engineers, the ornament of the great founders, the master of the learned men of his time, the Euclid of his century and of all times, the architect of the Sultan and the teacher to the empire," and his reputation remains justifiably great to this day.[41]

THE SEVENTEENTH AND EIGHTEENTH CENTURIES

The age of Süleyman marked the apogee of Ottoman military strength, and apart from the battle of Cyprus in 1570–1 the Ottomans incurred no great victories after his reign. Rather, they fought exhausting wars against the Persians in the east and the Hapsburgs in the west. The empire became too great to maintain, particularly in face of a Europe increasingly unified against them. The battle of Lepanto in October 1571 was the greatest combat ever fought on the Mediterranean. The Ottomans lost half their fleet, and although they were able to rebuild it, they never regained control of the Mediterranean, partly because they continued to use galleys while the Europeans introduced tall ships with sails which were able to fire broadsides. The Portuguese circumnavigation of Africa and opening of direct trade with India meant that the Levant no longer controlled the luxury trade from the Orient. Iran also expanded its international contacts under 'Abbas I (see Chapters 12 and 13), who was able to bypass the Ottomans by establishing direct European trade through the port of Bandar Abbas on the Gulf. By the seventeenth century the Ottoman empire had shrunk to a regional power confined to Asia Minor, the Balkans, and the Arab lands.

The string of military losses profoundly affected Ottoman society and the patronage of art. The earlier series of victories had enriched the royal coffers with booty, but now the sultans needed to spend more on munitions, men, and administration. The financial crunch was exacerbated by rampant inflation between 1585 and 1606, caused by the importation of massive quantities of silver from the New World. The cost of living escalated, but prices for materials and labor had been fixed by royal decree many decades before. Thus the palace paid the same price per tile in 1616 as it had in 1556, leading to a decrease in the quality of production for the court and preference of artisans to sell their work on the market. Edicts to prevent artisans from doing so were of no avail, as were government attempts to solve the problem with the traditional means of debasing the coinage. In retrospect, the Ottomans were unable or unwilling to integrate themselves into the new world economy dominated by European capitalism. Indeed they were repeatedly forced to grant concessions (capitulations) to the European states and kept looking back to the past, particularly the glorious reign of Süleyman, which was seen as an age of balance and perfection in society and the arts.

Ahmed I (r. 1603–17) was the first Ottoman sultan in three decades to erect a major imperial mosque in the capital. Whereas his predecessors had paid for their foundations with the booty captured in campaign, Ahmed's reign was devoid of notable victories, so the funds had to come from the treasury, provoking the anger of the religious establishment. Well known to modern tourists because of its prime location on the Hippodrome or Atmeydan, the mosque replaced several important residences, including that of Sokullu Mehmed Pasha, which had been built on the site of the Great Palace of the Byzantine emperors. The foundations of the mosque were laid in 1609 and opening ceremonies held in 1617. The architect was Mehmed Aga (d. 1622), who had been appointed in January 1586 to complete the Muradiye Mosque in Manisa [286] and promoted to chief imperial architect in October 1606.[42] Known as Mehmed Aga *Sedefkar* ("the worker in mother-of-pearl"), he also made a splendid walnut throne encrusted with mother-of-pearl and tortoiseshell.[43] According to his biographer Ca'fer Effendi, the mosque was the summation of Mehmed Aga's career.

Like other imperial foundations in Istanbul, the Mosque of Ahmed I is the centerpiece of an ensemble comprising the tomb of the founder, a madrasa, a hospice, a hospital, a bazaar, and a row of shops. Unlike them, the layout is

286. Manisa, Mosque of Murad III, 1583–5

irregular, as the complex had to be fitted within a preexistent urban fabric, and the major façade faced the Hippodrome. The mosque has a spacious court preceding a domed prayer hall, with ablution facilities arranged on either side. The four sides of the court have been successfully integrated into a continuous arcade at the expense of some monotony, and when seen from afar the dramatic profile of the mosque with its six minarets becomes a smooth succession of domes and semidomes from the court [287]. The prayer hall (64 by 72 meters) has a quatrefoil plan much like that of the Şehzade Mosque [275], but each semidome has been given

287. Istanbul, Mosque of Ahmed I, 1609–17, courtyard

three exedrae. The large central dome (23.5 meters in diameter) is supported on four cylindrical piers of massive size; their heaviness is only accentuated by their vertical grooves. This impression of weightiness is countered by the somewhat fussy decoration of the interior, with colored glass, tile, and paint in a palette dominated by blue, whence the building's popular epithet "the Blue Mosque." On close examination, however, many of the tiles have runny colors and dull glazes, especially when compared to the finest work of the mid-sixteenth century. The absence of imperial commissions during the preceding generation had greatly reduced the production of tiles; the decorators of Ahmed's mosque had to procure new tiles at old prices or rely on available stock. The best tiles, on the back balcony wall, were recycled products made for the Topkapı Palace in the 1570s and 1580s. As in the Mosque of Rüstem Pasha [282], disparate elements have been united by a characteristic border tile used throughout the building. Mehmed Aga's tutelage under Sinan and his long experience all over the empire undoubtedly familiarized him with the grand tradition of Ottoman architecture. In this complex he ably synthesized the lessons he had learned from the classical style, but as he was unable or unwilling to control the dissonances characteristic of Sinan's masterpieces, he avoided them altogether.

The best aspects of Ottoman architecture in the first half of the seventeenth century can be seen on a much smaller scale in two pavilions erected in the hanging terraced garden beyond the third court of Topkapı Palace. The Revan (1635–6) and Baghdad (1638–9) kiosks were erected to commemorate victories by Murad IV (r. 1623–40) at Yerevan in Armenia and Baghdad in Iraq. The Baghdad Kiosk is raised on the foundations of one of the towers of the original palace, to take advantage of the splendid view of the Istanbul skyline along the Golden Horn to the Süleymaniye and beyond. It is a small cruciform building with an outer gallery covered by broad eaves which protect a high dado of marble and porphyry panels, somewhat in the Mamluk style, surmounted by tile panels. Within [288], it is a central domed space, with four alcoves filled with low seats (Turk. *sofa*) from which one can enjoy the view to the exterior. A great bronze fireplace in one corner warmed the building. The interior is a showpiece of decorative arts: the walls are revetted with a mixture of re-used cuerda seca tiles and new underglaze-painted blue-and-white tiles, some of which are copies of early-sixteenth-century originals [298]. A stately inscription band encircles the walls above the dado: inscribed with the Throne Verse (Koran 2:255) extolling God's majesty over heaven and earth, the text hints at the sultan's semi-divine status. According to the historian Naima, the inscription was the work of the calligrapher Tophaneli Mahmud Čelebi. The tile revetment continues to the springing of the wooden dome, which is painted with arabesques against a red ground. The wooden shutters and doors are exquisitely inlaid with ivory, tortoiseshell, and mother-of-pearl, and double windows glazed with colored glass filtered the light. Soon after construction, the Baghdad Kiosk was transformed into one of the palace libraries, and the volumes it contained, now consolidated in a single palace library, are identified by the shelfmark Bağdat.[44]

In the later seventeenth and eighteenth centuries, funds

288. Istanbul, Topkapı Palace, Baghdad Kiosk, 1638–9, interior

for vast royal construction became increasingly scarce, particularly after 1683, the disastrous end of the second Ottoman siege of Vienna. The one exception, the Yeni Valide Complex at Üsküdar (1708–10), on the banks of the Golden Horn below the Süleymaniye Complex, was built by Ahmed III (r. 1703–30) to honor his mother. It was endowed with taxes from Cairo, and hence the great market adjacent to it is known as the Egyptian Bazaar. Commercial structures, often erected by great families who had profited from their government positions, were the main type of construction. The 1718 Treaty of Passarovitz with the Austrians and Venetians opened Ottoman society to European ideas and styles, and the last twelve years of Ahmed's reign, under the guidance of his vizier Nevşehirli Ibrahim Pasha, are known as the "Tulip Period," as the cultivation of this flower became somewhat of a craze. The secular spirit of the age is exemplified by the verse of the poet Nadim (d. 1730): "Let us laugh and play and enjoy the world!" Instead of mosques and charitable foundations, the sultan built pavilions and gardens, whose designs were imported from the West.

The architecture of the Tulip Period is epitomized by the seven grand fountains built in Istanbul between 1728 and 1732, two by Ahmed III and the others by his nephew and

289. Istanbul, Fountain of Ahmet III, 1728

successor Mahmud I (r. 1730–54). The first, erected by Ahmed III near the main entrance to Topkapı Palace [289], is an elegant square structure with rounded corners projecting slightly from the façades. The fountain is surmounted by a quincunx of domes, and projecting scalloped eaves protect the users from rain or sun. Fountains at the corners are concealed behind grillework, and there are additional fountains on each façade. The marble walls are decorated with naturalistic floral motifs in low relief and elegant calligraphic panels with verses praising the donor and offering blessings. Both walls and iron grilles were highlighted with color and gilding. Bronze cups, presumably chained to the fountain, allowed the passers-by to quench their thirst.

Enthusiastic dispatches describing life in France by Mehmed Yirmisekiz Čelebi Efendi (d. 1732), ambassador

290. Istanbul, Nur-u Osmaniye Mosque, 1748–55

291. Istanbul, Mosque of Mehmed Fatıh, rebuilt 1767

plenipotentiary to the court of Louis XV, had introduced the European Baroque to the Ottomans.[45] The first buildings in this imported style, including palace fantasies in plaster-and-lath, were destroyed by the mob that dethroned the sultan in 1730, and the first major monument in the Turkish Baroque style to survive is the Nur-u Osmaniye ("Light of the Ottomans") Mosque.[46] Begun under Mahmud I in 1748, it was completed under Osman III in 1755. Located adjacent to the covered market in a busy section of the city, the mosque [290] is raised on a high plinth to achieve monumentality, in much the same way Sinan had elevated the much smaller Mosque of Rüstem Pasha. A small D-shaped court precedes a single-domed prayer hall, covered with a baldachin of four massive arches supporting a dome 24 meters in diameter and 43 meters high. Major access to the mosque, however, is not through the court, which functions like an annex, but from the sides, approached by irregular flights of steps. The walls of the mosque, which are largely the tympana of the great arches, are pierced with many windows. On the qibla side, a semicylindrical exedra projects to house the mihrab, and an extensive royal *loge* occupies the south-east corner. The mosque maintains the traditional plan of single domed square, although some attempt was made to apply the spatial dynamics characteristic of European Baroque architecture by contrasting the constricted court and the open interior space. Most of the Baroque impact, however, is limited to the decoration. The enormously heavy and deeply profiled moldings that define the great arches are worlds apart from the austere simplicity of Sinan's great arches in the Süleymaniye [280], and the traditional muqarnas hoods over the doorways have been reworked into corbeled vegetal moldings. The slender, two-balcony minarets have tapering stone finials, rather than the traditional lead caps. This daring exercise remained an anomaly, and when Mustafa III had the mosque erected by Mehmed Fatıh rebuilt after the earthquake of 1766 [291], it was done in a frank revival of the style of the Şehzade Mosque [275, 276] of two centuries earlier, albeit with some moldings and decorative details in the new style.

The Arts under the Ottomans after the Conquest of Constantinople

Evidence for the patronage of the portable arts by members of the Ottoman dynasty before the conquest of Constantinople (see Chapter 10) is limited, but with the establishment of court ateliers there by Mehmed II (r. 1444–81, with interruption), a burst of activity ensued in a variety of media. Artists sought inspiration from a wide range of sources in the artistic traditions of the Islamic and Mediterranean lands, thanks to the new position of the Ottoman empire as heir to the Byzantine (Roman) empire and a major world power. By the mid-sixteenth century, during the reign of Süleyman (r. 1520–66), a classical Ottoman style had emerged, with a distinctive visual vocabulary which was applied equally to textiles, ceramics, and other media. This style struck an extraordinary balance between the geometric order underlying much of Islamic art and a lyric naturalism visible in the common representation of plants and flowers. By the end of the seventeenth century this style became increasingly codified and repetitious, and in the eighteenth century Ottoman society, beset by increasing economic, military, and political problems, turned back to the reign of Süleyman as a golden age.

THE FORMATIVE PERIOD: FROM MEHMED TO SELIM

Mehmed II Fatih seems to have had an unusual interest in the arts: one of the sketchbooks preserved from his childhood has a page with several portrait busts shaded with crosshatching. It shows that even at an early age Mehmed was familiar with Western conventions of representation, perhaps through the Florentine engravings he is known to have collected later in his life. Mehmed's private cultural activity was directed toward the figural arts and learning of Europe, Byzantium, and the Latin West, as well as toward the traditional arts and literature of Islam. He supported the works of eminent scholars and mastered the principles of Christianity, European history, and geography. He commissioned a biography in Greek from Kritovulos of Imbros and was extolled in Italian epic poetry. Mehmed visited Troy in 1462, and commissioned a copy of the *Iliad* soon thereafter. There was a widespread, if coincidental, belief in Europe that the Turks (*Turci*) were descendants of the Trojans (*Teucri*).[1]

Mehmed's interest in art and ancient history made him one of the foremost patrons of Italian medalists, whose medium had just been revived in Italy.[2] The first portrait medal, made by Pisanello in 1438, depicts John VIII Paleologus, the penultimate Byzantine emperor of Constantinople. Costanzo da Ferrara, a follower of Pisanello, spent several years in Istanbul in the 1470s, and his medal of the sultan [292] has been justly described as one of the finest portrait medals of the Renaissance. The obverse shows a bust of the sultan in profile; he is still plump-faced (he became gravely thin just before his death) and wears a turban with broad transverse folds and a caftan with a thick collar. The reverse shows him, dressed in a turban and heavy robes, riding through a wintry landscape. The scene appears to be a contemporary view of the aged ruler riding forth in triumph, but the composition is actually based on Roman imperial prototypes known from coins minted in coastal Asia Minor and showing the emperor's ceremonial *adventus*.[3]

Mehmed's patronage of Europeans, particularly painters and bronze-workers, increased at the end of the 1470s. Between the autumn of 1478 and spring of 1479 he concluded a truce with Venice, and in the two years before his death, the Venetians were free to respond to Mehmed's request for artists. Such artists as the Venetian painter Gentile Bellini and the Paduan sculptor Bartolommeo Bellano journeyed to the sultan's court in Istanbul. While in Istanbul, Bellini may have been commissioned to decorate a palace pavilion (see Chapter 15), and he produced sketches, oil paintings, and medals. The most famous product of this trip is his oil portrait of the sultan in the National Gallery, London. Bellano's dubious talents were less appreciated by the patron, and his two surviving medals are mediocre. In form, style, and technique, the medals made for Mehmed are entirely Italian; even the inscriptions are in Latin. Yet, as works designed for a Muslim patron in an Islamic land, the

292. Costanzo da Ferrara: Portrait medal of Mehmed II, Istanbul, 1470s. Bronze. Diameter 12.3 cm. Washington, DC, National Gallery of Art, Samuel H. Kress Collection

medals can also be considered to be "Islamic art," and they demonstrate the cosmopolitan nature of the Ottoman empire in the second half of the fifteenth century.

Mehmed also encouraged the development of more traditional media of Islamic art, such as the arts of the book, and at least seventy-five manuscripts can be attributed to his patronage.[4] These works represent a new stage in Ottoman book production, for the quality of the paper, illumination, and calligraphy improved dramatically. Early Ottoman books had been modeled on Mamluk examples (see Chapter 8), but gradually a more Persianate taste developed, particularly from the 1460s, when Istanbul began to enjoy a new role as a major center of book production. One noteworthy example is a copy of the *Fawā'iz al-ghiyāthiyya*, transcribed by Ahmad b. 'Ali al-Maraghi ("from Maragha") for the treasury of Mehmed II. The binding, painted and varnished ("lacquered") with chinoiserie flowers and elaborate arabesques in black and gold on a brown ground, is the earliest dated example of a type that became popular in Iran under the Timurids [86].[5] Iranian books were also prized: Mehmed asked for rare books and albums (*muraqqa'*) as part of the ransom for the Aqqoyunlu prince Yusuf Mirza, who was captured in 1472. These may have formed the basis of the collections of drawings and calligraphy later known as the "Fatih Albums." Following Mehmed's victory over the Turkomans in 1474, he forceably removed artisans from Tabriz to Istanbul.[6]

These Iranian artisans undoubtedly brought with them a repertory of floral motifs which formed part of the International Timurid style developed in book ateliers. The Ottoman variation of this style is found in a variety of other media, such as woodwork, ceramics, and textiles. The shared designs and motifs, together with the qualitative improvement in the minor arts produced under the Ottomans in the second half of the fifteenth century, suggest not only that the style was disseminated from the arts of the book, notably bindings and illumination, but also that there was some degree of central direction, probably from a court scriptorium in Istanbul. One of the leading artists in this scriptorium was Baba Nakkaş ("Venerable/Old Master Designer"). An Uzbek Turk, Baba Nakkaş enjoyed privileged status at court, to judge from endowments he received from Mehmed in 1466.[7] One example of the artist's work is an album in Istanbul University Library (F 1423), datable to the later years of Mehmed's reign. It contains decorative designs for square, rectangular, and crenellated borders in the chinoiserie floral style typical of fifteenth-century Persian art; these tile designs are similar to those found in the bindings and illuminations of manuscripts dedicated to Mehmed.

As in architecture, the 1460s and 1470s marked a major turning in the decorative arts of the Ottoman period, and works from these decades show a greater homogeneity of design and a higher standard of finish. The stylistic change can be ascribed partly to the appreciation of foreign models and presence of foreign artisans, and the change in quantity and quality can be ascribed to the pressing need to decorate and furnish the extensive buildings commissioned by the sultan. Both the New Palace and the vast Fatih Complex (see Chapter 15), for example, would have required enormous quantities of lamps, carpets, textiles, ceramic vessels, tiles,

293. Large-pattern Holbein carpet, Anatolia, late fifteenth century. Wool pile. 4.29 × 2.00 m. Berlin, Museum für Islamische Kunst

and other furnishings.[8] The new style can be seen most clearly in two media which were transformed under the patronage of Mehmed and the establishment of court ateliers: carpets and ceramics.

For several centuries woolen pile carpets had been made for domestic use and sale in Anatolia, but in the fifteenth century commercial production was expanded for export to Europe. A range of different designs were produced, but all types were knotted entirely in wool, with symmetrical knots of medium density in a limited range of colors. The designs are usually known after the names of the European painters in whose works the carpets were depicted, including Carlo Crivelli, Gentile Bellini, Hans Holbein the Younger, Hans Memling, and Lorenzo Lotto, or according to the towns in which they are thought to have been made, most notably Ushak in western Anatolia. Among the most distinctive types of carpet produced in Anatolia in the later fifteenth century are those known as large-pattern Holbein, or wheel, rugs [293].[9] The typical example has a field containing several large octagons inscribed in square frames which are separated and bordered by bands composed of smaller octagons. The octagons are usually decorated with strapwork patterns, and there are usually several borders of varying width which are often decorated with elegant pseudo-Kufic inscriptions with intertwined stems. Although the carpets are known from their appearance in the paintings of Hans Holbein the Younger (1497–1543), such as his *Ambassadors* (London, National Gallery), large-pattern Holbein carpets are actually depicted as early as ca. 1450 in northern European paintings and in the 1460s and 1470s in Italian works. The widespread popularity of these carpets in Europe testifies to the expanded commercial production in Anatolia in the later fifteenth century.

Under Mehmed's patronage, even larger and finer carpets were produced for the Ottoman court [294].[10] Known as Ushak medallion carpets, they are behemoth in comparison to export rugs, and the large size presupposes a significant investment in loom equipment, labor, and materials consonant with royal patronage. Ushak medallion carpets have traditionally been attributed to the sixteenth or seventeenth centuries, but a close analysis of their design structure and of such details as the shape of leaves suggests that a date in the third quarter of the fifteenth century is more appropriate.[11] The composition of these rugs shows a rhythmic balance of arabesques with small-scale tendrils; the same designs are found on other objects from the reign of Mehmed. The graphic conception and curvilinear design of Ushak medallion carpets also differ from the geometric conception of such earlier types as Holbeins or animal carpets [189], where the weavers could generate the designs directly at the loom. In contrast, these large-scale curvilinear compositions demanded the use of paper cartoons, which were undoubtedly furnished by the court design studio. The role of the court is further supported by the absence of transitional pieces, and the lack of contemporary European representations of this type of carpet argues for their specific production for the Ottoman court. By the mid-sixteenth century, when Ushak carpets were represented under the feet of such rulers as Henry VIII (1491–1547) or the Venetian Doge, Ottoman court taste had moved on to another type [311].

294. Ushak medallion carpet, Anatolia, third quarter of the fifteenth century. Wool pile. L. 7.23 m. Kuwait, National Museum on loan from the al-Sabah collection

295. Underglaze-painted blue-and-white charger, Iznik, ca. 1480.
Diameter 44.5 cm. The Hague, Gemeentemuseum

Ceramics, the other medium transformed by Ottoman patronage under Mehmed, were used as architectural revetments as well as tablewares. Coarse red-bodied earthenwares decorated on a white slip under a clear glaze had been produced in the fifteenth century at several centers, particularly Iznik in north-western Anatolia (see Chapter 10). From the 1470s, however, a distinctly new type of load-rich fritware with a lead-fluxed glaze began to be produced.[12] The earliest of these ceramics, which are known by various modern names, are exemplified by a deep dish decorated in blue and white and datable ca. 1480 [295]. These pieces are of a technical standard unmatched in Islamic ceramics since the Kashan wares of the thirteenth century and are often quite large, measuring over forty centimeters in diameter.[13] They have a hard and dense body, which has been covered with a brilliant white slip and painted in cobalt blue, often in reserve, with elaborate arabesques and floral scrolls. The colorless glaze shows no tendency to crackle and little tendency to pool.

In general concept these wares were inspired by Chinese blue-and-white porcelains, which were exported throughout the Islamic lands in the fifteenth century. The hard white body gives the impression of porcelain, and the shapes and designs on the exteriors of some dishes, with peony scrolls in blue on white, are also somewhat Chinese in flavor. The designs on the interiors, however, are an Ottoman variation of the International Timurid style: the rather languid rhythms of the prototype were transformed into a more forceful design, which has a greater sense of three-dimensionality and a more intense and contained quality. The disparity of scale among the various motifs was reduced; broad leaves were tightened into compact roundels by twisting their ends and turning them in on themselves, and buds on stems were

made to clasp the scrolls.[14] The few examples of precious metalwork that survive from the period show a similar combination of arabesques (Turk. *rumi*) and chinoiserie ornament (Turk. *hatayi*), suggesting once again that the designs originated in a central source, presumably the court atelier under the direction of Baba Nakkaş.[15] This hypothesis is supported by the superb quality of the ceramics and the enormous investment of time that would have been required for their intricate decoration in reserve. Despite their decorative origins in the International Timurid style, these exquisite Baba Nakkaş wares are technically distinct from contemporary Iranian ceramics [90] as well as from contemporary architectural ceramics, such as those on the Fatih Mosque or the Çinili Kiosk, suggesting that the technology to make these vessels was an invention of Ottoman ceramicists, who were encouraged by the expanded patronage of the court in Istanbul. As fragments of this ware have been discovered at Iznik, a site known earlier and later for its ceramics, it is assumed that they were made there.

Mehmed's private patronage had little effect on later developments, while his public patronage of such media as carpets and ceramics were essential stages in the formulation of the classical Ottoman style. His interest in Italian medals and naturalistic portraiture, for example, was not shared by other high officials at court. As his patronage failed to inspire others, his experiments in cultural eclecticism ended upon his death, and these elements were not integrated into the mainstream of Ottoman taste. The tastes of Mehmed's son Bayezid II (r. 1481–1512) did not run to Italian figural art, and he sold most of his father's collection for the benefit of the great mosque he established in Istanbul in 1505 [274]. He continued royal patronage of more traditional types of Islamic art, collecting and cataloguing his father's manuscripts and reorganizing the court studio.[16] The fourteenth-century copy of Ibn Bakhtishu's *Manāfi' al-ḥayawān* ("Benefits of animals") [31], for example, bears Bayezid's seal, and may have been rebound at this time. The sultan was an accomplished calligrapher, composer, and poet. While serving as governor of Amasya, he studied calligraphy with a local teacher, Shaykh (Şeyh) Hamdullah (1436–1520), and upon assuming the sultanate, Bayezid brought his master to Istanbul and assigned him a workroom in the palace. Shaykh Hamdullah became the most influential calligrapher of the entire Ottoman period and is credited with revising the six canonical scripts of Yaqut (see Chapter 3).

Shaykh Hamdullah designed the inscriptions for the sultan's mosques in Istanbul and Amasya and is said to have copied nearly fifty manuscripts of the Koran [296] as well as hundreds of single sheets with religious texts and prayers. These calligraphic specimens often juxtapose a line of large script with several lines of smaller script and include small panels of painting and marbled paper, all enclosed within a ruled frame. To give a rhythmic flow to his hand, the calligrapher elongated and exaggerated certain letters, such as the long *sīn* in the *basmala* at the upper left and the long scooped bowls of the *nūn*s on the first and third lines which extend to encompass the following word or rosette. His fluid and controlled calligraphy is often accompanied by a crisp and colorful style of illumination. Many of his characteristic motifs, such as cartouches and knotting, appear in contem-

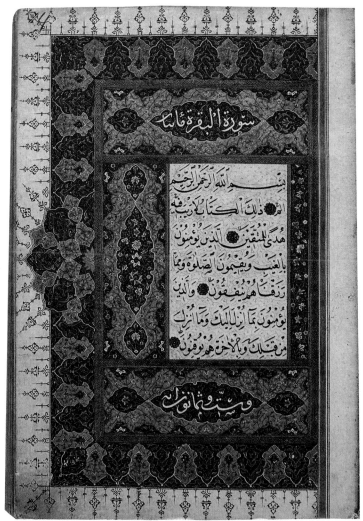

296. Left half of a double frontispiece to a Koran, Istanbul, 1491. Istanbul, Tokapı Palace Library, MS. Y. 913, f. 4r

which this chest was intended has not been identified, the oblong format suggests that it could have been an early Kufic Koran which Bayezid had restored. The Ottomans clearly prized early specimens of calligraphy, and manuscripts of the Koran copied by Yaqut or one of his followers were often refurbished in Ottoman times.[18] The style of the decoration on the Koran chest has some similarities with ivory carving in late-fifteenth-century Egypt under the Mamluks and also shares many features with contemporary North Italian work associated with the Embriachi workshops.[19] The wide geographical range of sources is no sur-

297. Hexagonal box for a manuscript of the Koran, Istanbul, 1505–6. Walnut veneered with ebony and encrusted with ivory. H 82 cm; diameter 56 cm. Istanbul, Türk ve Islam Eserleri Müsezi

porary ceramics, which are decorated in a variant of the Baba Nakkaş style with more open and spacious compositions. The use of these ceramics at court is documented by treasury inventories and kitchen registers, the first of which date from Bayezid's reign.[17]

Fine manuscripts of the Koran often formed part of the endowments to mosques. A magnificent walnut box [297] made for Bayezid by Ahmad b. Hasan *al-qālibī al-fānī* ["The ephemeral mould-, frame-, or block-maker"] in 1505–6 was probably commissioned for the sultan's mosque in Istanbul, which was completed in that year [274]. The hexagonal box, with a hinged lid surmounted by a twelve-sided pyramid and carved ebony and ivory finial, is the earliest example of a distinct Ottoman style of woodwork and one of the finest pieces extant. The exterior is veneered with ebony, encrusted with ivory panels, and inset with fine marquetry; the interior, with more restrained decoration of minute inlay in fine woods, ivory, and gilt brass, is divided into compartments to hold a thirty-volume Koran of oblong format. While the particular manuscript of the Koran for

prise, for the splendid court at Istanbul attracted artisans from all over the eastern Mediterranean lands who came together to create the new Ottoman style.

THE CLASSICAL OTTOMAN STYLE

A distinct Ottoman visual vocabulary emerged during the long and prosperous reign of Süleyman (r. 1520–66).[20] Already by Mehmed's time, objects were produced for the court in two different types of factories. There were royal factories, often in Istanbul, for carpets, silk textiles, ceramics (both vessels and tiles), and designs. Commercial factories in such provincial centers as Ushak, Bursa, or Iznik produced carpets, silk textiles, and ceramics of differing quality for various types of patrons. Some of their products were sold to the Ottoman court, while others were sold on the open market for use at home or abroad. Although some pieces for the court were made on commission from patterns prepared by court designers at the capital, others were purchased from among ready-made examples. In this manner the fashions of the court at Istanbul were synthesized with popular tastes.

Süleyman's predecessor, Selim the Grim (r. 1512–20), spent most of his reign on campaign, leaving him little time for royal patronage of the arts, although regular production seems not to have been interrupted. As with architecture, the effects of Selim's reign on the history of art are indirect, for his victory over the Safavids at Chaldiran in September 1514 led to the increased presence of Iranian artists and works of art at the Ottoman court. An unpublished inventory in the Topkapı Palace archives lists some of the booty taken, including gold and silver vessels, jades, porcelains, furs, rich brocades, and carpets, as well as craftsmen, including tailors, furriers, marquetry-workers, goldsmiths, and musicians.[21] Many of these craftsmen were put to work in the imperial studios at Istanbul. One of the most important artists was Shahquli (Şahkulu), mentioned in several registers of the imperial design studio. By 1526 he had become the head draftsman (ressam) of the twenty-nine artists and twelve apprentices employed there, and in that year he received the high salary of 22 akçe. He became popular with Süleyman: he gave a picture of a peri to the sultan and received gifts including 2000 akçe and brocaded caftans and velvets.[22]

The finest work during the early years of Süleyman's reign is epitomized by five enormous tiles, over one meter high, now installed on the façade of the Sünnet Odası (Circumcision Room) of Topkapı Palace in Istanbul [298]. These perfectly smooth slabs, larger even than the Fortuny Tablet of a century earlier (see Chapter 9), show an extraordinary technical command of fabrication and firing. The magnificent compositions in mirror reverse are superbly painted underglaze in blue and turquoise (a new addition to the palette), with birds and Chinese deer-like creatures (qilin) among a loose scroll of feathery leaves and fantastic composite flowers.[23] White chinoiserie clouds on a dark blue ground decorate the spandrels at the upper corners. The compositions are clearly based on pounced paper designs, undoubtedly supplied by the imperial design studio. The tiles have variously been dated from the 1530s to 1580 on

298. Istanbul, Topkapı Palace, Sünnet Odası, underglaze-painted tile panels, ca. 1527–8

stylistic comparisons with the album of Murad III (r. 1574–95) in Vienna, but a date in the late 1520s is more likely, for these tiles were probably made by the royal ceramics workshop in Istanbul to decorate Süleyman's New Kiosk, built ca. 1527–8 and destroyed by fire in 1633.[24] In 1638 the Baghdad Kiosk was built on the site of Süleyman's damaged building, and tiles, including these enormous slabs, must have been rescued from the ruins. They were reassembled in their present location when the Sünnet Odası was restored.[25]

The designs on the tiles epitomize the *saz* style, in which composite flowers are displayed on a gracefully curving armature of lanceolate leaves with feathered edges. The name of the style may derive from the *saz* (reed) pen, used for the drawing. Particularly associated with the work of Shahquli, the *saz* style represents the final flowering of the International Timurid style as it had been developed under Ottoman patronage by Persian artists from Tabriz and Herat. As the first generation of émigré artists and craftsmen retired and were replaced by locally trained artists, the Timurid esthetic was gradually replaced by a more distinctive Ottoman one. This development in the visual arts was parallel to the gradual replacement of Persian with Turkish as the literary language of the Ottomans during the second half of the sixteenth century.

It has been suggested that these tiles were produced in an imperial ceramic workshop at Tekfur Saray in Istanbul known through palace account books. This ceramic studio, which had five kilns and seven assistants, also produced vessels, for on religious holidays the ceramicists presented the sultan with special gifts, such as a ceramic rose and a large dish.[26] A fragmentary dish with a foliate rim in Vienna [299] may be one of their works, for it is decorated in

299. Underglaze-painted dish with foliate rim, Istanbul or Iznik, 1520s. Diameter 38 cm. Vienna, Österreichisches Museum für Angewandte Kunst

300. Yatagan with gold inlay and jewels, Istanbul, 1526–27. L 66 cm.
Istanbul, Topkapı Saray Museum

turquoise and cobalt blue with a bird amidst foliage in a style virtually identical to that of the Sünnet Odası tiles. The free quality of the design in the field of the dish is subtly distinct from the rather mechanical drawing of the cavetto and rim; this could be explained by the differentiation of labor in the shop or by the use of pounces for the field design. Without technical analysis, it is impossible to state whether this dish was made in Istanbul or Iznik, but the superb quality of the drawing sets it aside from most wares assigned to Iznik. Many of the largest and finest pieces of "Iznik" wares from the first half of the sixteenth century may have been made in the royal workshops at Istanbul.

The sultan in Istanbul increasingly surrounded himself with the trappings of imperial splendor, according to both European and Islamic traditions. Although traditional Muslim headgear for centuries had been the turban, Süleyman commissioned Venetian goldsmiths to make a fantastic golden helmet with four crowns decorated with pearls, diamonds, rubies, and a large turquoise; in 1532 it was sold to the sultan for the enormous sum of 144,400 ducats. The helmet was designed to show Süleyman's European audience that he was not only the superior of the Pope and the Holy Roman Emperor but also the successor to Alexander the Great.[27] The foreign iconography of the crown, however, meant that it had no real place at the Ottoman court, and it was eventually melted down for its precious materials.

Some of Süleyman's more traditional Islamic regalia, however, was preserved in the palace treasury, such as an extraordinary sword inlaid with gold by Ahmed Tekelü in 1526–7 [300]. The hilt is ivory, engraved with a blossom-scroll inlaid with black mastic and overlaid with a golden network of floral scrolls and chinoiserie cloud-bands. The golden network on the pommel is set with rubies and once had a large central gem, possibly a turquoise. Apart from the cutting edge itself, the damascened steel blade is lavishly decorated on both sides. The upper third was chased with scrolls and overlaid with representations of a dragon confronting either a simurgh or a phoenix. The creatures were cast separately and affixed to the surface, which was parcel gilt and inlaid with rubies for the animals' eyes. The middle third of the sword displays a scroll supporting composite flowers or animal heads. The lower third displays a beautiful *thuluth* inscription with Süleyman's names and titles; the spine of the blade is inscribed in *nasta'liq* script with Persian verses and the signature of the craftsman, probably a Turkoman brought from Tabriz by Selim. This virtuoso transformation of the International Timurid style into a distinctly Ottoman mode is characteristic of the finest products of the Ottoman court in the early part of Süleyman's reign.[28]

The pomp and ceremony surrounding the sultan and his distance from the general populace propelled his grand viziers into prominence as royal tastemakers, often at enormous profit to themselves. The sultan was forbidden by protocol from doing anything so practical as meeting with craftsmen, so that Ibrahim Pasha (1523–36), for example, was instrumental in procuring the Venetian commission for the crown, and luxury textiles were imported from Italy on a large scale during his vizierate. The opulence and European direction of patronage were reoriented under Rüstem Pasha (1544–53 and 1555–61), when domestic production of luxury textiles was encouraged. The splendor of Ottoman textiles from the middle of the sixteenth century is epitomized by a full-length ceremonial caftan with ankle-length decorative sleeves and pocket slits [301].[29] Woven of polychrome silk and gilt-metal thread in seven colors (blue, brown, green, peach, red, white, and gold) on a brown-black silk ground, it displays a scroll of chinoiserie composite flowers and leaves in a dazzling rendition of the *saz* style. The design, which must have been extraordinarily difficult to set up on the drawloom, is known in one other color range with a cream-colored ground.[30] Contrary to almost all other Ottoman textiles, the layout of the design does not repeat. This caftan is typical of the outer robes worn during ceremonial activities: the arms passed through slits at the shoulders, leaving the ankle-length sleeves to hang over the back. Although the design is carefully matched across the front opening, there are no fastenings to keep the robe closed, suggesting that the wearer stood still. The label is inscribed "Sultan Bayezid," which must refer not to Bayezid II, but to Süleyman's son Bayezid (d. 1562), as the pattern is typical of the mid-sixteenth century. This date accords well with the companion garment made of the cream-ground fabric, which belonged to Bayezid's brother Mustafa (d. 1553).

These Ottoman designs of the mid-sixteenth century, in which delicate scrolls of long serrated leaves act as the armature for composite flowers, are quite distinct from the tighter and more regular style of the late fifteenth century and epitomize the classical Ottoman style. These *saz* designs were transferred to other media, particularly to ceramics and to carpets, where they remained popular for decades. A deep dish with *saz* designs [302] is similar in size and shape to the fragmentary dish in Vienna [299], but the decorative scheme has been simplified so that the entire inner surface is covered by one continuous design.[31] The design is a simplified combination of the serrated leaves and composite flowers found on the caftan and was probably transmitted to the ceramic studio via paper patterns. The design is drawn in black on a white ground and colored with cobalt blue, turquoise, and sage green. A purply pink is often included

301. Caftan, Istanbul, ca. 1550. Polychrome silk and gilt-metal thread.
L 1.47 m. Istanbul, Topkapı Palace Museum

302. Underglaze-painted dish with slightly foliated rim, Iznik, ca. 1550.
Diameter 38.5 cm. London, British Museum

303. Underglaze-painted mosque lamp from the Dome of the Rock in
Jerusalem, Iznik, 1549. H 38.5 cm. London, British Museum

on other ceramics of this type, formerly known as Damascus wares because they were once thought to have been produced there.

The so-called Damascus wares are among the finest examples of Ottoman ceramics. Mainly vessels, these pieces have extraordinarily varied designs and brilliant glazes and use an unusually wide range of underglaze colors, although fine effects were often achieved with a limited palette. The group can be dated approximately by a unique lamp from the Dome of the Rock in Jerusalem [303], which has a fragmentary inscription around the footring mentioning the date 1549, the signature of the artisan, and the Iznik saint Eşrefzade Rumi.[32] The lamp has a pear-shaped body with a flaring neck; three handles at the shoulder would have allowed it to be suspended by chains. The shape is ultimately derived from Mamluk glass lamps [138], and several Ottoman examples are associated with the tomb of Bayezid.[33] The opaque ceramic body, however, would have rendered these lamps useless for illumination, and they must all have been intended for decoration. Unlike the earlier blue-and-white examples, the Jerusalem lamp is decorated with three bands of inscriptions reserved in white on a blue ground separated by two fields of arabesque ornament in two colors of blue on a white ground. Although some of the major motifs belong to the International Timurid vocabulary, other distinctive motifs, such as the cloud-bands, small black arabesques on a turquoise ground, and bands of cartouches containing white tulip buds, link the lamp to a group of large footed bowls in the *saz* style and show how Ottoman designers were successfully able to combine elements from various modes of decoration in a single piece.[34]

Another lamp [304], which was made for Süleyman's mosque in Istanbul [279–81] completed in 1557, shows how the Ottoman ceramic industry was transformed in the 1550s by the introduction of red bole pigment. The introduction of red coincides with the new direction of the Iznik ceramic industry as court patrons began to decorate their architectural foundations with extensive tile revetments and the production of pottery vessels increasingly became a by-product of the tile industry. In shape the Süleymaniye mosque lamp is similar to, but larger than, the one associated with the Dome of the Rock; inscriptions play a diminished role in the decoration, which has become increasingly complex. The design is delicately drawn in black on a white ground, which is almost entirely covered by the intricate pattern of serrated leaves and composite flowers painted in two colors of thin blue, red, and black. This piece, the earliest datable example with bole red, is experimental in color and pattern. The use of black as a field color was limited to this piece and a few other tiles. The bole red was applied unevenly, showing that the potters were still mastering the technical and esthetic demands of the pigment. In later examples it was applied much more thickly; indeed, the red often stands in relief on the surface, and its glazed surface catches the light. The distinctive hue also visually organized the decoration of vessels and tiles in a new way, for the minute detail and intricacy of design seen on this lamp were abandoned in favor of greater visual legibility, achieved through magnified scale and the contrast of leaves and flowers painted in bright red, blue, and green on a white

304. Underglaze-painted mosque lamp from the Süleymaniye complex in Istanbul, Iznik, ca. 1557. H 48.2 cm. London, Victoria & Albert Museum

ground. Ottoman ceramics from the second half of the sixteenth century are often delightful and charming, a welcome change from the sober imperial commissions of the earlier period.

The inauguration of the Süleymaniye Mosque in 1557 encouraged the court scriptorium to produce and refurbish fine manuscripts of the Koran and other works for endowment to the mosque and its teaching institutions; but few if any of these manuscripts have been identified.[35] The other major project of the scriptorium at this time was the composition, transcription, and illustration of the *Shāhnāma-yi Āl-i ʿUthmān* ("Book of kings of the Ottoman house"), a history of the Ottoman dynasty in the metre and Persian verse of Firdawsi's classic *Shāhnāma* ("Book of kings"). The Ottoman history was composed by the poet ʿArif Čelebī, known as ʿArifi (d. 969/1561–2). Although born to a Persian family, he probably came to the Ottoman court after Selim's capture of Egypt in 1517 and was eventually appointed *şahnamaci*, or court historian. A separate structure had to be added to his house as a studio for the calligraphers and five painters employed on this project, which was

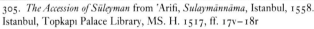

305. *The Accession of Süleyman* from 'Arifi, *Sulaymānnāma*, Istanbul, 1558. Istanbul, Topkapı Palace Library, MS. H. 1517, ff. 17v–18r

intended to be a masterpiece of poetry and the arts of the book.[36]

Only three of the original five volumes of 'Arifi's work have survived.[37] The presentation copy of the fifth volume, the *Sulaymānnāma* ("History of Süleyman"), transcribed in fine *nasta'līq* calligraphy by 'Ali b. Amir Beg Shirvani in 1558, is the first important history of Süleyman's reign.[38] It is a lavishly illustrated chronicle, with 617 folios of fine gold-speckled and polished paper, exquisite illumination, and sixty-nine large illustrations, of which four are double spreads. In the earlier years of Süleyman's reign the scriptorium had been occupied with the copying and illustration of such classic works as those written in Chaghatay Turkish by the celebrated Timurid poet 'Alishir Nava'i. Their illustrations are deeply indebted to Persian models; indeed, they are probably the work of painters brought from Tabriz and can be identified as Ottoman only by such details as the gold sky. In the *Sulaymānnāma*, however, the pictorial and spatial formulas of traditional Iranian book illustration have been combined with a distinctly Ottoman interest in topographical representation and portraiture quite unknown in the Iranian tradition.

A painting such as that showing Süleyman's accession in 1520 [305] is distinguishable from contemporary Iranian work by the specificity of the image, which frankly depicts a contemporary event in a way unknown in Iranian book-painting. The setting can be identified as the Topkapı Palace; the first court is depicted on the left, the second court on the right. The painting combines specific references to Ottoman buildings, such as the alternating joggled voussoirs of the arcade behind the sultan and the lead-sheathed roofs of the palace towers, with conventional features of Iranian book-painting, such as tiled exteriors and semé ground. The lush green foliage of the trees is typical of book-painting in the Turkoman style [91] and would have been known from manuscripts (or artisans) brought from Tabriz in 1514. The representations of the major figures, such as Süleyman, the grand vizier Piri Mehmed Pasha to the left, and below him the *shaykh al-islam* Zenbili Ali Effendi with a white beard, are portraits probably based on such likenesses as those prepared at approximately this date by Ra'is Haydar, known as Nigari.[39] The Ottoman preoccupation with status and rank is shown by the carefully choreographed procession of courtiers, each group wearing a distinctive headgear.

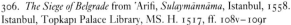

306. *The Siege of Belgrade* from 'Arifi, *Sulaymānnāma*, Istanbul, 1558.
Istanbul, Topkapı Palace Library, MS. H. 1517, ff. 108v–109r

Another double-page painting from the *Sulaymānnāma*, which shows Süleyman's siege of Belgrade in 1521 [306], clearly differentiates the Ottomans from the Europeans. These differences have been explained as expressing the calm of the Ottoman camp and the panic of the city's defenders, but they also show that the various traditions had not yet been entirely integrated into a unified style.[40] The extraordinary detail of the brocaded caftans worn by the larger Ottomans on the left contrasts sharply with the unpatterned clothes worn by the smaller Hungarians on the right. Although the two halves of the image were intended to depict a single event, the links of landscape are subsumed by the uneasy juxtaposition of traditional modes of spatial representation used in Persian painting with the rendering of perspective known from images in the European style. The tents of the Ottoman siege camp are depicted as overlapping planes, while the houses in the European city are depicted with shading and receding volumes.

An interest in topographical representation had already been evident in earlier manuscripts prepared for Süleyman, such as Matrakci Nasuh's *Bayān-i manāzil-i safar-i 'Irāqayn-*

i Sulṭān Sulaymān Khān, an account of Süleyman's campaign in Iraq and Iran against the Safavids in 1534–5.[41] The 128 illustrations in the manuscript, completed in 1537–8, show the towns through which the sultan passed and the shrines he visited. They draw upon the author's direct observation as well as Venetian bird's-eye views, engineers' siege plans, and other sources. The representation of the former Mongol capital at Sultaniyya in Iran [3], for example, shows many features of the site that are no longer visible, while the two-page representation of Istanbul [268], the most magnificent painting in the volume, is a valuable source for the urban history of the Ottoman capital.[42] The painting shows the Istanbul peninsula on the right page and Galata on the left, separated by the Golden Horn in the gutter. The painter has clearly depicted such Byzantine monuments as the Church of Hagia Sophia, the Hippodrome, with its columns and obelisks, and the aqueduct of Valens. New Ottoman monuments include Topkapı Palace with its three courts, the covered bazaar, the Old Palace in the center of the city, and the complex of Bayezid II below it. Nasuh's contribution to the illustration of his works is difficult to determine, but

an image lies not in its scale or topographical accuracy but in its enumeration of significant elements. The six minarets are correct in number for the time, although they have been slightly rearranged in position. Such pietistic images were repeated many times, not only in manuscripts but also on tiles, well into the nineteenth century.[44]

Although all the disparate sources are not entirely integrated, the manuscripts produced for Süleyman were the first in a distinctive classical Ottoman style. This style was developed throughout the rest of the sixteenth century in a series of manuscripts produced in the court scriptorium. The studio reached the peak of productivity during the reign of Murad III (r. 1574–95), when the historian Lokman cooperated with the new chief artist Osman in the composition and illustration of several historical and genealogical works. Increasingly the authors turned from Persian poetry to Turkish rhymed prose, and the illustrators repeated the compositional formulas established in the *Sulaymānnāma*, although they added many details of contemporary Ottoman court life. The manuscripts are thus particularly important for their documentary value. A copy of Ahmed Feridun Bey's account of Süleyman's Hungarian campaign, *Nuzhat asrār al-akhbār dar safar-i Sigitvār* (1568–9), for example, includes the first depiction of a type of gem-encrusted gold canteen, of which a spectacular example survives in Topkapı Palace.[45] Osman's illustration to a volume of Lokman's history of the Ottoman dynasty, *Shahnāma-yi Salīm Khan* (1581), shows the presentation of gifts by the Safavid ambassador to Selim II (r. 1566–74) at Edirne [308].[46] Shahquli, the governor of Erevan for the Safavid ruler Tahmasp, was sent at the head of an embassy to congratulate Selim II on his accession. The caravan, consisting of seven hundred men and nineteen thousand pack animals, arrived at Edirne early in 1567 and brought extraordinary gifts, including enormous woolen carpets and luxury manuscripts, one of which was the *Shāhnāma* made for Tahmasp earlier in his reign [209, 210]. The ambassador, who wears the distinctive Safavid baton, is held immobile before the sultan by two chamberlains, typical treatment before the great Ottoman sultan, and the gifts are carried by a retinue of servants. A large medallion Ushak carpet is spread before the sultan. The increasing repetition in Ottoman manuscript painting can be seen in the use of the same composition and figures for the depiction in Istanbul of another Persian embassy, by Toqmaq Khan in 1576 to congratulate Murad III on his accession.[47]

The court scriptorium also had to illustrate other kinds of texts, and the final project begun under Murad III was a six-volume copy of the biography of the Prophet Muhammad, composed by Mustafa Darir in the late fourteenth century. Four volumes of the *Kitāb siyar-i Nabī* ("Life of the Prophet") survive; one is fragmentary and one exists only as scattered pages.[48] The 814 illustrations seem to have been supervised by Hasan, who evidently worked on volume I and on some of volume VI (dated 1594–5). The style of illustration was dictated by the grandeur of the subject, for the paintings are strikingly different from those made for contemporary histories. Their size, bare landscapes, reduced cast, and suppression of detail contrast sharply with the panoply of Ottoman historical painting. *The Birth of the Prophet* [309], for example, has only five figures: the Prophet enveloped in

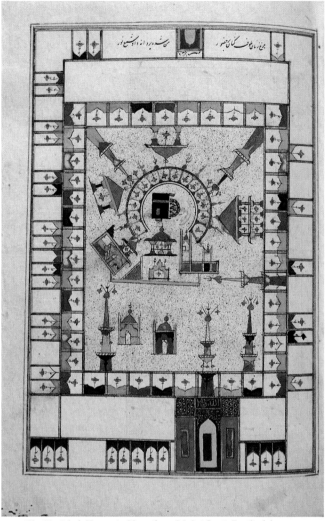

307. *The Masjid al-Haram in Mecca* from Muhyi Lari, *Futūḥ al-ḥaramayn*, Istanbul, ca. 1540. Istanbul, Topkapı Palace Library, MS. R. 917, f. 14r

this new interest in the accurate depiction of topography remained an important preoccupation in Ottoman illustrated books.

Another type of topographic representation used by Nasuh and perhaps more common in Ottoman times is represented by illustrations to the *Futūḥ al-ḥaramayn* ("Conquests of the two sanctuaries") of Muhyi Lari (d. 1526). It was written in Persian verse and dedicated in 1506 to the sultan of Gujerat, Muzaffar b. Mahmud (r. 1511–26), who is thought to have presented it in turn to Isma'il, the Safavid ruler of Iran. The first illustrated copy was produced ca. 1540 at Süleyman's court in Istanbul. It contains thirteen topographic scenes, with schematic representations of such essentials for pilgrims as the Mosque of the Prophet in Medina or the Masjid al-Haram in Mecca [307].[43] The image schematically shows the arcades surrounding the esplanade of the Haram. A lamp hangs in each bay, but because of the conventions of representation, some lamps hang to the right, left, or upside-down. The Kaaba stands in the upper center, with the *ḥijr*, a semicircular enclosure, to its right and the well of Zamzam below it. The value of such

308. *The Presentation of Gifts by the Safavid ambassador Shahquli to Selim II in 1567* from Loqman, *Shahnāma-yi Salīm Khān*, Istanbul, 1581. Field of each page 30 × 18 cm. Istanbul, Topkapı Palace Library, MS. A. 3595, ff. 53v–54r

309. *The Birth of the Prophet* from the first volume of Mustafa Darir, *Kitāb siyar-i Nabī*, Istanbul, 1594. 18.5 × 18 cm. Istanbul, Topkapı Palace Library, MS. H. 1221, f. 223v

a golden cloud, his veiled mother to the right, and three attendant angels. The setting is a schematic rendering of a tiled and marble interior; the floor is covered with matting. The origin of the style used in these religious paintings is unknown, for they are unlike most work produced in the scriptorium and show no familiarity with earlier illustrations relating to the life of Muhammad [33].

THE SEVENTEENTH AND EIGHTEENTH CENTURIES

As in architecture, the decline of Ottoman political and economic power resulted in a decline in the quality of the portable arts, as less money was available to pay for materials and craftsmen to transform them. The court scriptorium had been reduced in size under Mehmed III (r. 1595–1603), who had dismissed Lokman and Osman. Illustrated manuscripts continued to be produced, but they included new subjects made for a wider range of patrons and in a more folk style. For example, a large manuscript of the *Fālnāma*, a large illustrated book of divination, produced ca. 1610 for the master-of-works Kalender Pasha, has thirty-five folio-sized paintings combining folk themes and religious figures, executed in a bold style somewhat derived from that of the *Siyar-i Nabī*.[49] The last illustrated historical work by the official court biographer is Nadiri's *Shāhnāma* for Osman II (r. 1618–22); the text, about the conquest of Hotin, is illustrated with twenty paintings indebted in style to works of the previous century.[50] Rather than historical texts with many illustrations, most of the illustrations produced in the scriptorium were intimate figure studies and scenes from daily life for albums. Other centers of production also developed; although nothing remains from the workshop at Edirne, a provincial school developed at just this time in Baghdad, where religious and esoteric texts were often illustrated.[51]

A similar change took place in the production of ceramics. Beginning ca. 1610, the artistic and technical qualities of both tablewares and tiles declined perceptibly. The revetment for the Mosque of Ahmed I, opened in 1617 (see Chapter 15), had been cobbled together from available stock, cannibalized monuments, and specific commissions of far lower quality than those produced in the mid-sixteenth century. Ceramics attributed to the second quarter of the seventeenth century show the decline in technique and draftsmanship and a widened repertory, which ranges from figural and animal depictions to ships [310] and buildings, including pagoda-like pavilions and domed churches. The Ottoman system of fixed prices for materials and finished products left little room for artisans to make a profit in a period of rampant inflation, except by cutting the cost of labor. Designs become simplified and standardized: the characteristic border, ultimately derived from Chinese wave motifs, has become a pattern of alternating leaves and spirals, and the designs of the field are repeated in numerous examples. The dishes are approximately thirty centimeters across, three-quarters the diameter but only half the size of the standard pieces made a century earlier. The green underglaze painting is often uneven and thin and tended to

310. Underglaze-painted dish with sailing ship, Iznik, second quarter of the seventeenth century. Diameter 29.5 cm. Athens, Benaki Museum

run into the glaze. Evidence for the broadening of patronage can be seen in a series of tiles, probably made between 1640 and 1675 as pilgrimage souvenirs, that depict Mecca with the Kaaba at the center and a group of fifteen dishes with uncial Greek inscriptions that can be dated 1666–78. In 1648 the Ottoman traveler Evliya Çelebi visited Iznik and reported that there were only nine potteries left out of hundreds said to have been in operation earlier.[52] Some potters undoubtedly emigrated to other Mediterranean lands, taking with them the workshop traditions and paving the way for the emergence other centers of production in the eighteenth century such as Kutahya or Tunis.

Carpets had long been produced at many centers in the eastern Mediterranean, and the localization of carpets produced for the Ottoman court is still a matter of speculation. A group of carpets with floral patterns in the *saz* style is generally attributed to the second half of the sixteenth century; these rugs are usually known as Ottoman court carpets, to distinguish them from contemporary carpets thought to have been manufactured without royal patronage. Their designs, like those of the Ushak medallion carpets [294], derive from cartoons produced in the court studio, but the variety of materials and techniques used suggests that the carpets were manufactured at different times in different locales. The carpets all have an asymmetrical knot of cotton or wool, but the ground can be wool or silk and the yarn spun with an S or a Z twist. In 1585 Murad III is known to have ordered eleven carpet-weavers to move from Cairo to the court in Istanbul (see Chapter 8). Some of the artisans undoubtedly remained in Cairo, for the largest and best-preserved example of this type of carpet is the example in the Pitti Palace in Florence [311], made in Cairo. It was brought as a gift to Grand Duke Ferdinand II by admiral Da

311. Medici Ottoman carpet, Cairo, early seventeenth century. Wool pile. 3.30 × 9.95 m. Florence, Pitti Palace

Verrazzano, possibly a descendant of the great navigator, in 1623 and was described in contemporary inventories of the Medici wardrobe as *cairino*, the standard word in Italian inventories for Mamluk carpets. Its warps and wefts are S-spun, a technique associated with Egypt. It has 23 knots per square centimeter, or some 7.6 million knots in all, and is knotted in seven colors: white, light blue, crimson, green, light yellow, orange, and brown/black. The borders are perfectly matched and turn the corners effortlessly, showing that the sophisticated design had been worked out on paper, although the field consists of only three and a half repeats of the pattern.[53] Just as the potters of Iznik had sought to develop new markets for their products to counter the economic stagnation at the Ottoman court, the weavers in Cairo sold one of their most magnificent products on the open market to a European.

Calligraphy, the most traditional of all the Islamic arts, was the one art that continued to maintain high standards of quality in the seventeenth century. The finest calligrapher was Hafiz Osman (1642–98), who is known for his manuscripts of the Koran and calligraphic specimens. He evolved an apparently simple style of writing based on the principles of Yaqut and Shaykh Hamdullah. Hafiz Osman taught calligraphy to Mustafa II (r. 1695–1703) and his son Ahmed; money received from royal patrons allowed the master to devote one day each week to teaching indigent students. The clarity and elegance of his style is epitomized by a manuscript of the Koran in *naskh* (Turk. *nesih*) script, as well as in an album in Berlin [312].[54] The album comprises ten calligraphic specimens bound in accordion format, each leaf has a large line of majuscule script juxtaposed to four lines of naskh flanked by panels of exuberant floral decoration, the whole framed with marbled paper. The decoration has evolved from the dominant cartouches and arabesques typical of the International Timurid style to a more exclusively floral style, where flowers even invade the spaces between the lines of script. The style of Hafiz Osman remained the model for calligraphers of later generations; in the nineteenth century manuscripts of the Koran penned by him were lithographed at Istanbul and circulated throughout the Islamic world.

The floral style seen in the margins of Hafiz Osman's manuscript of the Koran became increasingly important in the reign of Ahmed III (r. 1703–30), during which time there was a self-conscious attempt to recreate the artistic glories of the past. Particularly after the peace with the Austrians in 1718, in the years retrospectively called the Tulip Period (see Chapter 15), familiar patterns and flowers – tulips, carnations, and hyacinths, for example – continued to be used, but floral forms became simplified and more stylized, as naturalism gave way to a more abstract vision. A pair of voided velvet cushion covers (Turk. *yastık*), presented by the commander-in-chief 'Abdi Pasha to King Frederick I of Sweden in 1731, are the only examples of their type that can be dated with precision.[55] The warp is silk, the weft silk and cotton, with details brocaded in silk thread wrapped with silver. The pile is green and red on a white satin ground. The organization of the pattern follows conventions established in the sixteenth century, with a central field and six lappets at either end, but the design combines familiar

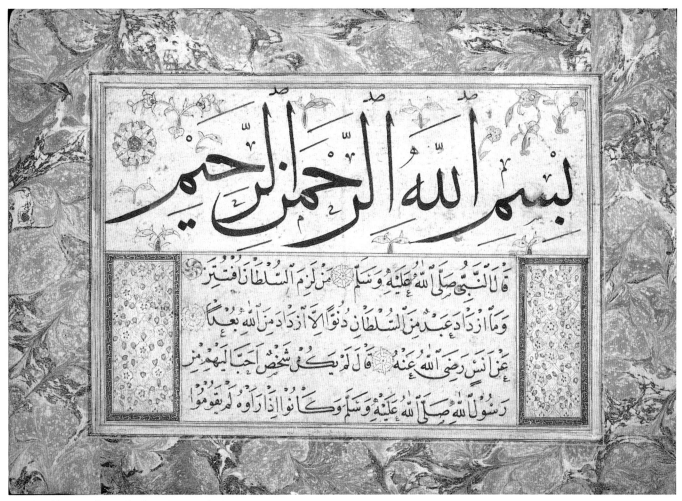

312. Leaf from an album of calligraphy by Hafiz Osman, Istanbul,
1693‒4. 21 × 15 cm. Berlin, Museum für Islamische Kunst, I.1983.11.1.

elements in new ways. The field has tulips in the spandrels
enclosing an ogival medallion [313], much like that on the
Ushak medallion carpet [294], but these curvilinear forms
contain an octagon formed of rotated squares, much in the
manner of Mamluk rugs [144], while the octagonal border
elements resemble those in Holbein carpets [293].

Ahmed III, who as a prince had studied calligraphy with
Hafiz Osman, was also an accomplished epistolarian and
poet. His interest in books is attested by his construction of a
new library in the Third Court of Topkapı Palace in 1719
(now the Topkapı Palace Library reading room) and the
cataloguing of the royal collection of manuscripts. During
his reign, in 1727, Ibrahim Müteferrika established a printing press at Istanbul; he had begun printing engraved maps
a decade or so earlier, using copper-plates and probably
techniques imported from Vienna. The royal scriptorium
was revived, and the most famous manuscript produced
there, also the most important illustrated manuscript of later
Ottoman painting, was the *Sūrnāmā* ("Book of festivals")
written by the court poet Vehbi to commemorate the circumcision festivities for Ahmed III's four sons in 1721.[56] Such
entertainments had long been celebrated at the Ottoman
court: great festivities surrounded the circumcision of

313. Detail of a voided velvet cushion cover, probably Bursa, first half of
the eighteenth century. Silk. Manchester, Whitworth Gallery

314. *Procession of the Confectioners with Candy-Gardens* from Vehbi, *Sūrnāma*, Istanbul, 1723. Istanbul, Topkapı Palace Library, MS. A 3593, f. 162b

Süleyman's sons in 1530, and invitations to the circumcision of Murad III's sons in 1582 were sent to the principal courts a year in advance. This latter event was officially illustrated in the *Sūrnāma-i humayūn*, which shows the various urban corporations on parade, and probably served as a libretto, or book of ceremonies, to guide the organization of the celebrations and participants.[57] Ahmed III's order for a new copy seems to have been a conscious revival of sixteenth-century models.

The illustrations to the text [314] are characterized by elaborate compositions, with a palette of pale colors and particular attention devoted to the popular types that attracted European travelers. The illustrations are associated with Levni, a court painter from Edirne, the second capital and preferred residence of the sultans during the late seventeenth and early eighteenth centuries. He began his career composing albums of fashionably dressed ladies and gentlemen.[58] Only two of the 137 paintings in the *Sūrnāma* are signed by him, both in inconspicious places,[59] but the illustrations are done in such a consistent style that all must have been executed under his close supervision. The volume was apparently unfinished when he died in 1732. A superb draftsman and colorist, Levni excelled in composing highly structured scenes, some with more than one hundred figures. The most elaborate, spread over sixteen consecutive double pages, show the circumcision procession, in which the princes are escorted from the Archery Ground (Okmeydan) festival grounds outside the city (the Hippodrome was no longer large enough since the Mosque of Ahmed I had been erected on its south side) to the Topkapı Palace, where the operation was performed. Each painting depicts a different social group with its leaders and corps in proper position and attire. The parade of the guilds is exemplified by the procession of the confectioners, who carry elaborate candy gardens containing pavilions, fountains, and trees. Other scenes depict entertainments and water parties on the Golden Horn, with costume plays, fireworks, acrobats on rafts, and even girls dancing on barrels submerged in the sea. The illustrations, which document every detail of the festivities, are important records for the study of Ottoman society in the eighteenth century.

CHAPTER 17

Architecture and the Arts in Egypt and North Africa

The expulsion of the Moors from the Iberian peninsula in 1492 by the Christian rulers of Aragon and Castile ended nearly eight centuries of Muslim presence there. The simultaneous discovery of the New World encouraged a reorientation of trade to the North Atlantic from the Mediterranean and its European and African coasts. North Africa had traditionally provided a route to supply Europe and the Mediterranean world with African gold and ivory, but the rounding of the Cape by the Portuguese mariner Vasco da Gama in 1497 rendered this overland route increasingly redundant and expensive. Cairo, which for centuries had been the major entrepot for eastern goods, received a serious blow when its lucrative Indian trade through the Red Sea was intercepted by the Portuguese. The Ottoman conquest of the Mamluk sultanate in January 1517 sealed the city's fate; it became a provincial capital in the Ottoman empire, a status it retained for three centuries. Political disintegration and economic disruption across North Africa resulted in the replacement of the regional powers of the preceding period (see Chapter 9) with Ottoman provincial governorates in city-states along the coast which were supported largely by piracy. Although Spanish concerns in the sixteenth century were largely focused on the New World, Spain was enticed to protect its rear by extending its power to the Moroccan and Algerian coasts of the Mediterranean. In response, the Ottomans extended their influence across the Libyan, Tunisian, and Algerian coasts through the intermediary of the corsairs. Despite the recognition of Ottoman suzerainty in Algiers (1529), Tripoli (1550s), and Tunis (1574) and the establishment of Ottoman governors there, the high culture of the Ottoman court at Istanbul was known largely at a distance. By the late seventeenth century local powers had usurped much of the governors' power.[1]

Architecture across North Africa presents a variety of responses by local traditions to the Ottoman domination and increased European power in the region. Egypt, the closest to the capital, was a valuable supplier of textiles and foodstuffs, and architecture there shows the strongest impact of imperial Ottoman styles. In Tunis and Algiers hybrid styles of building were evolved under the patronage of Ottoman governors, who looked not only to Istanbul for models but also to Italy for materials, particularly marbles. Only in Morocco, which remained independent of Ottoman or European domination under the Sharifan dynasties of the Sa'dis (r. 1511–1659) and 'Alawis (r. 1631–), were traditional styles of building continued, but the isolation of the region from developments elsewhere led to the repetition of traditional models to such a degree that they became hackneyed clichés. European paper had already replaced the Egyptian product by the fifteenth century, and after 1500 Ottoman and European manufactures increasingly replaced locally produced luxury goods throughout the north of Africa. Other than architecture and its fittings, the traditional arts of this period are represented only by a few illuminated manuscripts.

EGYPT, LIBYA, TUNISIA, AND ALGERIA

In the three centuries between the defeat of the last Mamluk sultan in 1517 and the arrival of Napoleon's expedition in 1798, Cairo was the capital of the Ottoman province of Egypt, and the city's finest products, such as large woolen carpets [311], were made primarily for export to the Ottoman and European courts. Although enormous amounts of information and many buildings survive from the period, only recently has its architecture been the focus of study, for the period has usually been considered one of decadence and stagnation.[2] Cairo was deemed a hardship post for the Turkish officials assigned there; mismanagement and taxfarming meant that Egyptian revenues fell substantially. The governors had neither the funds nor the time for large projects, for they did not serve there for extended periods. As they did not want to be buried in Cairo, they erected their funerary complexes in Istanbul, where, in contrast to Cairo, large parcels were still available for construction in the center of the city. Many of the Ottoman foundations that were established in Cairo are concentrated in Bulaq, the port that grew to the north of the old city as the Nile receded to the west.[3]

The Ottoman conquest of Egypt did not totally disrupt the vibrant tradition of Mamluk architecture (see Chapters 6 and 7), and architecture in Egypt under Ottoman rule shows strong continuities with the past, although patronage was more limited. Notable changes include the introduction of a provincial version of the Ottoman pencil-shaped minaret in place of the multistoried Mamluk type and a preference for domed rather than hypostyle mosques. By the late Mamluk period, stone domes were associated almost exclusively with funerary architecture, but within a decade of the Turkish conquest they were introduced into mosques, as in the Mosque of Sulayman Pasha (also known as Sidi Sarya) erected on the Citadel in 1528. Such features as its open court, slender minaret, and central dome flanked by three semidomes were directly inspired by the architecture of Istanbul, although the interior decoration with marble paneling follows local traditions. Indeed, these marble revetments were briefly in vogue at the Ottoman court in Turkey immediately following the conquest of Egypt.[4] In general, however, court taste was imitated in provincial capitals, and glazed tile became a common revetment in Egypt under Ottoman rule. The Mamluk Mosque of Aqsunqur (1347), for example, was redecorated in 1652 when the Janissary Ibrahim Aga Mustahfizan built his mausoleum next to the entrance; the extensive blue and green tiles along the qibla wall and in the mausoleum have given the building its sobriquet, the Blue Mosque.[5]

Ottoman provincial building in Egypt is exemplifed by the mosque built by Sinan Pasha at Bulaq in 1571 [315].[6] The patron, an Albanian who had been recruited as a boy in the *devşirme* and risen to become cup-bearer to the Ottoman sultan Süleyman, was twice governor of Cairo and

315. Cairo, Mosque of Sinan Pasha at Bulaq, 1571

316. Cairo, Fountain of 'Abd al-Rahman Katkhuda, 1744

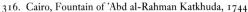

five times grand vizier. He was a notable patron of architecture, both in Istanbul, where he commissioned a mosque and madrasa, and in Cairo, where he commissioned a large complex in Bulaq (1567–73). In addition to a mosque, it included a large urban caravanserai (Arab. *wakāla*), public bath, fountain house, and several storage facilities. A free-standing building set in a walled enclosure, the mosque comprises a single-domed prayer hall with domed porches on three sides and a minaret in the south corner. The dome, fifteen meters in diameter, is the largest stone dome in Cairo and shows the continuation of the Mamluk tradition of masonry domes, although the exterior is no longer carved. The squat profile is carried on a two-tiered zone of transition: the lower octagonal story has two arched windows between buttresses; the upper sixteen-sided story has a single hourglass-shaped window between buttresses. On the interior the drum is supported on four arched squinches, each containing a trilobed arch with muqarnas in the upper portion. The squinch system is similar to that found in a series of late Mamluk domes, most notably the Qubbat al-Fadawiyya (1479–81).[7] Over the entrance to the mosque opposite the mihrab is a wooden balcony which served either as a *dikka* or as a viceregal box. The back wall of the balcony and the qibla wall are richly decorated with polychrome marble strips in the traditional manner.

In plan, the Mosque of Sinan Pasha belongs to the classical Ottoman type of single-domed mosque, of which literally hundreds were built throughout the empire (e.g. [280]). While most have a single portico of three or more domes across the main façade, some, such as that of Lari Čelebi built at Edirne in 1514, have U-shaped porticoes like this building. It confirms the standard Ottoman practice of sending plans, but neither elevations nor workmen, to the provinces, for the elevation of this structure is distinctly Cairene. The spaciousness of the setting in an enclosed garden also distinguishes this building from most Cairene foundations, which were shoehorned into a dense urban fabric, and such a broad open space would have been available, even to a rich patron, only in the new lands created when the Nile shifted to the west. The mosque was seen in Cairo as a successful type, for it was imitated in the eighteenth century by Muhammad Bey Abu Dhahhab in the mosque he erected opposite al-Azhar in 1774.

The most characteristic type of building erected under the Ottomans in Cairo was the *sabīl-kuttāb*, in which a water dispensary on the ground floor was combined with a primary school for boys on the upper floor. The type had developed at the end of the Mamluk period [119] and seems to have been introduced to the Ottoman capital on the Mamluk model.[8] More than one hundred such structures were erected in Cairo during the Ottoman period, and one of the most famous [316] is that built in 1744 by 'Abd al-Rahman Katkhuda (d. 1776) in a prominent position on the main north–south artery in the center of Fatimid Cairo.[9] The patron was an officer in the Janissary corps who rebuilt and restored many of the important shrines and mosques throughout the city. He also built several *sabīl-kuttāb*s, including this splendid example which stands where the *qaṣaba* bifurcates. On each of the three façades, an elaborate iron grille is enclosed in a round arch with polychrome joggled voussoirs resting on carved marble colonnettes. These arches, which are set within rectangular frames, are further enclosed within arches on colonnettes and rectangular frames. An elaborate muqarnas cornice supports the projecting wooden balcony of the school, which is reached from an elaborate portal on the east. The doorway is enclosed in a tall narrow composition of polychrome panels separated by raised double fillets and surmounted by a lobed arch containing muqarnas supporting a shell. The portal recreates the mature Mamluk style of two and a half centuries earlier [119], but the filling between the arches on the façades includes naturalistic depictions of peonies, asters, and chrysanthemums popular in Ottoman Turkey somewhat earlier in the century. The interior of the water dispensary also follows Ottoman styles, for it is revetted with tiles underglaze-painted in blue and green with flowers, inscriptions, and stylized depictions of Mecca.

Throughout the middle ages Tripoli had been a entrepot of modest importance on the land and sea routes between Egypt and North Africa; the city reached its apogee under the Qaramanli dynasty, a family of Turkish origin that ruled the region between 1711 and 1835.[10] The founder of the dynasty, Ahmad Bey (r. 1711–45), extended his power over Barqa and Fezzan and made Tripoli an important staging post in eastern Mediterranean trade. He established many endowments in favor of the city and constructed numerous buildings there. The most notable is a mosque complex (1736–8), nestled to the south-west of the citadel into the orthogonal grid pattern remaining from Roman times. The congregational mosque is a square hypostyle structure, with twenty-five domed bays supported on sixteen marble columns. It is enclosed on two sides by a covered gallery whose walls are revetted in glazed tile. The interior of the prayer hall is elaborately decorated with carved stucco above the tile dado. The complex includes ablution facilities, a stubby octagonal minaret of the provincial Ottoman type, an irregularly shaped tomb chamber for the patron and his family, and a madrasa with an open court. In many respects, the complex conforms to the provincial Ottoman style more familiar from monuments in Tunisia.

Hafsid rule in Tunisia was already on the wane in the fifteenth century, as the towns in the interior often threw off Hafsid control, and rival contestants in different cities claimed the throne. By the beginning of the sixteenth century, only the region of Tunis remained under Hafsid dominion, but the proliferation of piracy led the Emperor Charles V of Spain to plant a garrison there in 1535. With Spanish support, the Hafsids managed to contain the Turks until 1574, when Tunis was seized by the Ottomans for the third and final time and the last Hafsid sovereign was taken as captive to Istanbul. Turkish authority in Tunisia was first maintained by an army of occupation of four thousand Janissaries, who collected rural taxes; but by the early seventeenth century the Muradid family of beys had emerged as rulers under nominal Ottoman authority. Their regency from 1612 to 1702 began as a period of prosperity in Tunisia, for the arrival of the Moriscos following their expulsion from Spain in 1609 stimulated the development of agriculture and industry. Trade with Europe increased in the first half of the seventeenth century, with leather, cereals, and coral as major exports. In the second half of the century, increasing attacks by the Algerians and Bedouin tribes

317. Kairouan, Mosque of the Barber, 1629–85, arcaded gallery

showed up the weakness of the Muradids, and in 1705 a new family of beys, the Husaynids, assumed control, which they maintained until the French occupation in the nineteenth century.

The economy flourished during the Muradid regency, as the agricultural surplus from the large productive plain in the northern half of the country was readily collected by the army. Public and charitable works were erected throughout the country: bridges were built over the Mejerda river, fountains decorated the city of Tunis, and mosques and madrasas were restored and constructed. For example, Hammuda Pasha (r. 1631–65) began the restoration of the zāwiya of Abu'l-Balawi in Kairouan, the traditional capital and center of religious learning in the country which had long been superseded as a commercial and political center by Tunis. The zāwiya had been founded in the fourteenth century over the tomb of a companion of the Prophet, Abu'l-Balawi. He reputedly wore three hairs of the Prophet's beard, hence the building's common names, "Mosque of the Barber" or "Mosque of Sidi Sahib." Hammuda began by reconstructing the cupola of the mausoleum, and rooms for the poor and pilgrims, lodgings for staff, and a prayer hall were added. Muhammad Bey (r. 1675–96) had a minaret and madrasa built between 1690 and 1695. The building has been restored in modern times and much of its original fabric has been replaced, but the arcaded gallery [317]

318. Tunis, Mosque of Hammuda Pasha, 1655

319. Algiers, Mosque of the Fishermen, 1660–1

leading to the third courtyard with the tomb of the saint is particularly evocative of seventeenth-century taste. The columns and surrounds around the windows and doors are made of Italian white marble. The upper walls are revetted with stucco carved with stylized trees and geometric motifs, while the lower walls are covered with glazed tiles arranged in large compositions of arched frames, structures, vases, and vegetal motifs. The heavy use of a strong yellow distinguishes the work from Ottoman examples, from which these tile revetments, mostly made in the Qallalin quarter of Tunis, are ultimately derived.[11]

In 1655 Hammuda Pasha commissioned a mosque [318] in the heart of the medina of Tunis, not far from the congregational mosque. The second ruler of the Muradid family, he was the real founder of the dynasty, and the mosque and adjacent tomb for the Muradid family are set in a walled enclosure with a minaret at the corner. Built of stone, the mosque consists of a rectangular prayer hall five bays deep and seven bays wide. The bays are covered with barrel or cross-vaults, except for the domed bay in front of the mihrab. The dome has a square drum, octagonal zone of transition, and slightly pointed profile. Many features, such as the hypostyle hall enclosed on three sides by courts, the mausoleum with a pyramidal roof of green tiles, and the octagonal minaret, repeat those found in the nearby mosque built by Yusuf Dey in 1616 and continue the long Tunisian tradition of hypostyle stone mosques. In contrast, many features of the decoration, such as the capitals and the polychrome revetment around the mihrab, are clearly Italian products adapted to Tunisian taste.

Until the sixteenth century Algiers had been a small town opposite several islets (Arab. *al-jazā'ir*, hence its name). Its most notable monument was the Almoravid congregational mosque (*jāmi' al-kabīr*), with an elaborately carved wooden minbar dated 1097.[12] In the fifteenth century many Muslim

refugees from Spain established themselves there as corsairs, and in the early sixteenth century the Spanish occupied the islets to suppress them. The inhabitants appealed for help from the Turkish corsair 'Aruj, who established his base of operations there in 1510. After his death in 1518, his brother, Khayr al-Din (Barbarossa), assumed power but was pushed back by the Spanish. In 1529 he finally captured the town, dismantled the Spanish fortress on the largest of the islets, and used the materials to construct a breakwater connecting the islets with the mainland. After Khayr al-Din bequeathed his territories to the Ottoman empire, Algiers became the major Ottoman center of power in the Maghrib and the seat of the most important Janissary force outside Istanbul.[13] Although nominally the capital of a Turkish province, Algiers increasingly enjoyed de facto independence from Istanbul, and its rulers, known successively as beys, pashas, aghas, and finally deys, maintained direct relations with European states.

As Algiers expanded, the city was embellished with mosques and palaces. The most important mosque is the new congregational mosque (*jāmi' al-jadīd*; commonly known as the Mosque of the Fishermen, from the fishmarket that once was nearby) erected some fifty metres south-west of the Almoravid mosque.[14] An inscription states that it was built in 1070/1660–1 by al-Hajj Habib, a member of the Janissary corps sent from Istanbul to govern. Funds for construction were provided by the Janissaries to an institution created to collect and administer offerings made to the Hanafis, the school of law favored by the Ottomans. From the exterior [319] the building appears to be a low whitewashed structure with a square minaret in the north-east corner and a prominent ovoid dome in the center. The dome is surrounded by barrel vaults alternating with small gored domes; on the north opposite the mihrab the vaults are extended by two additional bays to create a nave-like extension flanked by aisles. The minaret, originally standing 30 meters high (the pavement has risen some five meters), has a straight square shaft crowned with a tiled band and surmounted by a small edicule. The lower story is plain, the middle story is decorated on all sides with oval panels, and the upper story is decorated with rectangular panels, now set with clock-faces. The edicule is an open kiosk with coupled windows surmounted by an oculus on all four sides.

The main entrance to the spacious interior [320] is from the north down a flight of stairs from the present level of the street. The high central nave is flanked by cloister-vaulted aisles, with mezzanines inserted at the level of the present street. In the center stands the dome, 23 meters high, supported on four massive piers, arches, and pendentives. Under it stands a raised wooden rostrum reached by a flight of steps with a canopy. The actual minbar, of marble, is set in the traditional location to the right of the mihrab. The minbar preserves the standard articulation of parts but is executed with frankly Italianate swags, balusters, and scrolls. The mihrab, in contrast, is a deep seven-sided niche with a horseshoe arch, a type typical of western Islamic mosques since the Great Mosque of Córdoba.[15] The square surround and faceted hood are executed in stucco carved with geometric and epigraphic motifs. The arch is supported on marble colonnettes, and the dado is revetted with underglaze-painted tiles and crowned with an inscribed band.

320. Algiers, Mosque of the Fishermen, interior

It is no surprise that the mosque exhibits a mélange of Ottoman, North African, and European forms and motifs. The plan and spatial organization are completely different from traditional mosques in North Africa and have often been compared to Ottoman mosques in Bursa, Byzantine churches in Turkey, or European churches. Rather than any single source for this unusual plan, the building suggests that the builder started with the standard plan of an Ottoman mosque having a central dome buttressed by four semi-domes, such as that of the Şehzade Mosque in Istanbul [275]. As he understood the model imperfectly, having no first-hand experience of it, he transformed the semidomes into barrel vaults and replaced the open court with a covered nave. The shape and proportions of the dome are as distinctly at odds with Ottoman models as they are with North African ones, where domes were usually concealed behind green tiled roofs and are rarely visible from the exterior of a building. The Algiers mosque was meant to appear "Ottoman," and for seventeenth-century viewers, who did not have photographs and ready access to representations, it did. The minaret, by contrast, is frankly Maghribi in shape and proportions and bears no relation to the pencil-shaft minarets of Ottoman mosques elsewhere. The marbles for the mosque were imported from Italy. Although marble had been quarried across all North Africa in Antiquity, it was not quarried there in Islamic times. Minbars were usually made of wood, and the use of marble for the minbar is distinctly an Ottoman taste. Unable to meet the demand locally, the builder had to look to Italy for marble fittings. While elements such as capitals, columns, and colonnettes must have been produced commercially for sale on the market, the minbar must have been a specific commission.

MOROCCO

The situation in Morocco was entirely different from else-where in North Africa, for the Ottoman navy was never able to extend its power into the Atlantic and the Ottoman government did not implant itself along the Mediterranean coast or in the mountains and plateaux of Morocco. Power there was concentrated in the hands of figures whose authority derived from affiliation with Sufi fraternities orga-nized around the veneration of local saints. The Christian reconquest of Spain and the expulsion of the Muslims in 1492 increased the appeal of leaders who would defend the frontiers of Islam. In 1511, the Sa'dian family of sharifs, who claimed descent from the Prophet, founded a state in southern Morocco and took control of Marrakesh. This was a time of increasing prosperity: in the northern cities the Andalusian emigrants brought industrial skills and inter-national contacts, and in the south the Sa'dians extended their power over the Saharan trade routes bringing gold and slaves. The Sa'dian sharifs, however, were unable to firmly establish control, and by the mid-seventeenth century they were replaced by another family of sharifs from the Tafilalt oasis, the Filalis or 'Alawis, whose descendants are still the Kings of Morocco.

In this period Morocco became increasingly isolated from developments in the rest of the Islamic world and in Europe. The Muslim refugees from Spain encouraged indigenous tendencies towards conservatism and traditionalism, and only a few Moroccans traveled to the central Islamic lands, primarily as pilgrims, while even fewer visitors came to Morocco from the east. Fez remained a regional center of learning, but it was less than half the size of Tunis and much smaller than Cairo.[16] The patronage of art and architecture was restricted, and traditional models were repeated with far less innovation than elsewhere in North Africa. In contrast to the Marinid period, when Fez had been the center of artistic life, under the Sa'dians Marrakesh became the center, and under the 'Alawis it was supplanted by Meknes, although the sultan and his court made regular progressions from one capital to another to collect taxes and reaffirm their sovereignty.

The finest example of Sa'dian architecture is the Ben Yusuf madrasa in Marrakesh [321], the largest madrasa in the Maghrib and the only surviving example of those built under Sa'dian patronage. It is not, as is usually said, a restoration of a Marinid madrasa, but a new building ordered by 'Abdallah al-Ghalib (r. 1557–74) which is dated by inscription to 972/1564–5. The building takes its name from the nearby mosque erected by the Almoravid 'Ali b. Yusuf (r. 1106–42) as the first congregational mosque of Marrakesh, which 'Abdallah al-Ghalib had restored in the mid-sixteenth century. The madrasa is announced by a deep vaulted porch which bridges the street to the west, an arrangement recalling that of the Bu 'Inaniya madrasa in Fez [156] of some two centuries earlier. The exterior faces of the portal are lavishly decorated in cut tile and carved stucco with cusped arches, arabesques, inscriptions, floral motifs, and muqarnas. The interior is covered by an elaborate vault of stucco muqarnas like the one over the entrance to the Mosque of Abu Madyan near Tlemcen [154]. An unusually long and narrow corridor, dramatically lit by skylights, leads

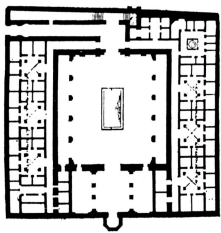

321. Marrakesh, Ben Yusuf Madrasa, 1564–5, plan

to a square vestibule, which housed a marble basin made in Spain in the first decade of the eleventh century.[17] On the left, stairs lead to the upper floor; on the right, corridors lead to cells and service areas on the sides and a central door opens into the spacious courtyard [322]. In the center is a large rectangular pool; on either side are deep galleries behind heavy piers which support carved wooden consoles and beams. Opposite the entrance stands the prayer hall, a rectangular room divided into three by two rows of columns. The central space, in front of the deep pentagonal mihrab, is covered with a splendid octagonal wooden vault. The sides of the building have square lightwells surrounded by more than a hundred cells on two floors for students and teachers. An ablution facility stands in the north-east corner.

Much of the interior is enveloped in a web of exuberant decoration in tile mosaic, carved stucco, and carved and painted wood. The arrangement of tiled dadoes and in-scription bands, stuccoed walls, and wooden cornices con-tinues a tradition already established in the region two centuries earlier. The overall effect is stunning, creating one of the most charming ensembles in Morocco, but on close examination the individual elements are somewhat dry and monotonous, particularly in comparison to their fourteenth-century models. The symmetry, regularity, and spaciousness of the square plan are unusual, for by this date most large foundations had to be shoehorned into a densely built urban fabric.

Far more typical is the irregular plan of the *zāwiya* for the Sufi saint Sidi'l-Jazuli (Ben Sliman al-Jazuli) in the Riyad al-'Arus quarter of Marrakesh. Al-Jazuli (d. 1465?) belonged to the Berber tribe of Jazula in the Moroccan Sus and was the author of the *Dalā'il al-khayrāt* ("Proofs of the blessings"), a collection of prayers for the Prophet and description of his tomb and names. After al-Jazuli's death he became the focus of a popular religious brotherhood, which believed in repeated recitation of his celebrated work for spiritual benefit.[18] Al-Jazuli's followers had been instru-mental in bringing the Sa'dian sharifs to power, and one of the first acts by Ahmad al-A'raj (r. 1517–57) was to have his

322. Marrakesh, Ben Yusuf Madrasa, view of courtyard

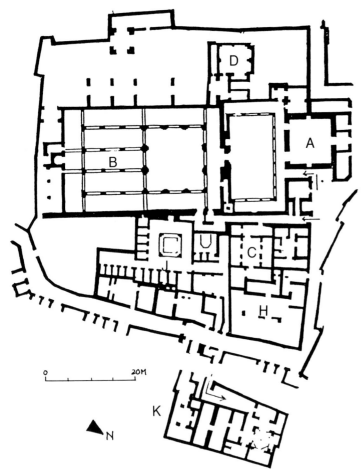

323. Marrakesh, Zāwiya of Sidi'l-Jazuli, plan, 1529–57. A) Tomb;
B) Mosque; C) Cemetery; D) Tomb of the Black Sultan; E) School;
F) Fountain; G) Superintendent's residence; H) Hospice; J) Ablution

324. Marrakesh, Saʿdian tombs, 1557–1603, courtyard

father buried beside al-Jazuli's tomb at Afughal. In 1529 the sultan had both bodies transferred to Marrakesh to celebrate the dynastic connection with the order and to designate the city as capital. Al-Jazuli became one of the seven patron saints (Arab. *sabʿa rijāl*) of the city, and his tomb became a major place of visitation there.

Al-Jazuli's *zāwiya* in Marrakesh [323] is an agglomeration of elements similar to such Marinid foundations as the funerary complex for Abu Madyan outside Tlemcen [153–55] or such earlier foundations as the shrine complex of ʿAbd al-Samad at Natanz [8–11]. It differs from the others in continuing to be a center of maraboutism, the distinctive form of Moroccan Islam, and its component buildings have been repeatedly renovated and restored over the centuries.[19] Al-Jazuli's tomb (A) is a small square (five meters on a side) surmounted by a pyramidal tiled roof, rather than the dome typical in the eastern Islamic world. A rectangular court with an arcade connects the tomb to a rectangular mosque (B). Like the mosque at Tlemcen, it has a square court surrounded by arcades and a prayer hall with five aisles parallel to the qibla; the arcades stop one bay short of the qibla wall and the pentagonal mihrab projects beyond it into a narrow court. The space (C) around the mosque and tomb is a cemetery for the saint's disciples and includes the square tomb (D) for the unidentified "Black Sultan." The northeast corner of the complex contains other dependencies, including a school (E) with a fountain (F) adjacent to the

principal entrance, the residence of the superintendent, who also served as leader of the order (G), a hospice for pilgrims and members of the order (H), and ablution facility and latrines (J). The bath (K) lies across a small street.[20] This architectural ensemble provided a center of urban services not only for the immediate neighborhood but also for a broader geographical region linked by pilgrimage to the shrine.

After 1557 Saʿdian rulers were buried in a walled garden [324] set against the south wall of the Almohad Mosque of the Qasba. The cemetery seems to have existed as early as the Almohad period, and the Saʿdians may have made it their dynastic necropolis because of its holiness and affiliation with the Almohads, the great messianic reformers of North Africa who had ruled from Marrakesh in the twelfth and thirteenth centuries. The garden was sealed off from the adjacent Badiʿa palace by the Mulay Ismaʿil (r. 1672–1727), the ʿAlawi sultan who plundered Marrakesh and destroyed the palaces in the Qasba for materials for his buildings in Meknes (see ills. 328–30), and the Saʿdian tombs were "rediscovered" only in 1917.

The magnificent vaults over the Saʿdian tombs were constructed at two different times. The tomb on the east, built by ʿAbdallah al-Ghalib for his predecessor Muhammad al-Shaykh (d. 1557), originally had the typical form of a square funerary structure, but it was enlarged in 1590 when Ahmad al-Mansur (r. 1578–1603) buried his mother there. The more ambitious tomb on the west was also erected by Ahmad al-Mansur and serves as his own tomb. A central room with twelve columns [325] contains the cenotaphs. It is flanked by a three-aisled mosque on the south or qibla side and a lecture room on the north, an arrangement probably inspired by the now lost Nasrid mausoleum (Arab. *rawda*) at the Alhambra in Granada. The rich decoration in stucco, marble, tile mosaic, and wood epitomizes the finest of Saʿdian craftsmanship, and the organization of materials repeats Marinid and Nasrid precedents.

The garden setting of the Saʿdian tombs can be seen on a

325. Marrakesh, Saʿdian tombs, interior of west tomb showing central room with cenotaphs, 1590s

326. Marrakesh, ruins of the Badi'a palace in the Kasba, 1578–93

327. Fez, Qarawiyyin mosque, fountain pavilion in the courtyard, 1613–24

far grander scale in the contemporary Badi'a palace, which was built by Ahmad al-Mansur between 1578 and 1593. Although the palace is largely destroyed, its plan is clear from the ruins of the rammed earth walls [326], which would have originally been concealed behind elaborate revetments of stucco and tile. In the center was a vast open court (135 by 110 meters), which contained a huge pool (21.7 by 90.4 meters) flanked on each side by sunken parterres planted with fruit trees and flowers. Smaller basins were dug on the sides of the parterres in the four corners. Raised walkways paved with tiles allowed one to stroll among the pools and gardens, as if on a living carpet. Four large pavilions projected from the middle of the short sides of the enclosure at either end of the long central pool and between the corner basins. One of them, although ruined, gives an idea of the typical pavilion: measuring 14.7 by 16 meters, it too was built of rammed earth and has a joined wooden (artesonado) ceiling. It contains remnants of an elaborate fountain. Celebrated for its size and splendor, the Badi'a palace was sometimes known as the Alhambra. Like the prototype, the Sa'dian palace was based on cross-axial planning and the interpenetration of water and space, but the scale of the original was vastly inflated.

Marrakesh was the center of Sa'dian patronage, but a rare example of Sa'dian architecture outside the city can be seen in two pavilions added between 1613 and 1624 to the courtyard of the ancient Qarawiyyin Mosque in Fez [327].[21] The two kiosks project from the short sides of the rectangular courtyard. Each pavilion is supported on eight marble columns arranged in a rectangle. The upper walls are decorated with carved stucco and contain large lambrequin arches in the centers. A richly decorated wooden cornice of inscriptions, muqarnas, and corbels supports the pyramidal tiled roof. Under each kiosk is a basin, and according to a contemporary source the western one had been sent to the mosque in 1587 by Ahmad al-Mansur. The interiors of the pavilions are also richly decorated with tile mosaic, carved stucco, and carved wood. The geometric patterns are rather crude when compared to earlier work, and many of the marbles were imported from Italy. As at the Badi'a palace, the pavilions evoke Andalusian models, but the pavilions in the Qarawiyyin Mosque rest on single columns rather than the clusters of thin colonnettes used at the Alhambra

[163]. Although this type of projecting pavilion had long been common in secular architecture, this is the first known example of its use in a religious building. The mosque already had ablution rooms and a basin in the center of the court, so the kiosks must have been primarily ornamental, particularly as their disposition on an axis perpendicular to the qibla has no specific liturgical meaning. The construction of fountains, however, recalls the Sa'dian practice in Marrakesh of endowing public fountains.

By the seventeenth century the Sa'dian dynasty was showing signs of trouble, as the three sons of Ahmad al-Mansur vied for power while the country lapsed into a period of strife. Order was restored only in the middle of the century under the 'Alawi sharifs. The founder of the dynasty, Mawlay Rashid (r. 1667–72), sent his brother Isma'il to Meknes, a pleasant town in a fertile agricultural region near Fez. Mawlay Isma'il succeeded his brother in 1672 and became the greatest of the early 'Alawi rulers. Under him the government assumed the form it retained until the twentieth century, with a royal household of black slaves, a ministry drawn from the leading families of Fez or the Jaysh tribes, and an army of European converts, former black slaves, and Jaysh tribesmen. Mawlay Isma'il's policies extended far beyond Morocco: he established diplomatic relations with Louis XIV, whom he wanted to enlist against the Spanish, and tried to cement the alliance by marriage. In return for great commercial benefits, French merchants supplied arms and munitions, including the artillery used against the Berbers and the rulers of Algiers, the other major power in the western Mediterranean. The French also

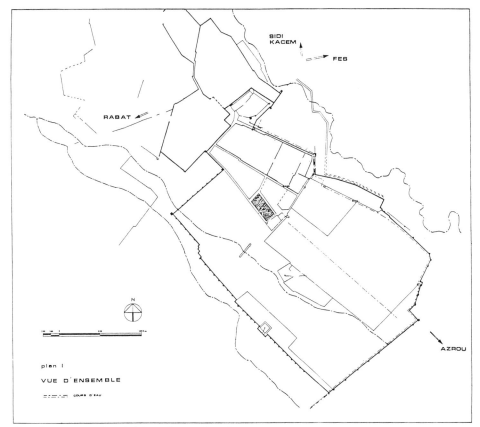

328. Meknes, Palace Complex, seventeenth and eighteenth centuries, plan

329. Meknes, palace granaries

assisted in Mawlay Isma'il's grand building program, which included roads, forts, and palaces. These projects were supported by brutal taxation, a levy on the corsairs, ransoms from European captives, and generous gifts from foreign ambassadors, who were received with a mixture of buffoonery and splendor.

Mawlay Isma'il made Meknes the capital and scene of his architectural extravagances. To the south of the medina, he created an extended and complex royal city of palaces, mosques, military and commercial quarters, and vast gardens, all enclosed within seven kilometers of ramparts [328, 329].[22] This royal city shares a general affiliation with the Alhambra in having several grand palaces, each comprising several smaller palaces, but its scale is far greater. Largely constructed of pisé, the walls were decorated with tile, terracotta, and carved plaster, but only the ruins remain. In addition to waterwheels, artificial pools, stables, and silos to supply the enormous court, there were three palaces. The first of them is known as the Grand Palace (Dar al-Kabira). Measuring 320 by 420 meters, it is set off from the adjacent medina by three walls. Monumental gateways led to the interior, which contained several ensembles, arranged somewhat haphazardly and connected by narrow passageways. Each unit had an open rectangular court surrounded by reception rooms, baths, kitchens, and storerooms. Other buildings within the palace include the relatively private tomb of the founder, built on the site of the grave of a local saint, a congregational mosque, known as the Mosque of Lalla 'Awda, and the mashwar, where the sultan reviewed his troops. This first palace was finished in 1679, and its combination of private and public spaces suggests that it was the residence of the sultan.

330. Meknes, Bab al-Mansur, 1732

The second palace, known as the Dar al-Madrasa after a nearby madrasa, is entirely different in conception. It comprises a huge garden (700 by 400 meters) enclosed by high walls. In contrast to the separate and haphazardly arranged units in the first palace, the interior of the second is strictly orthogonal and represents one architectural conception. A monumental entrance on the north led to apartments arranged around small courts and a long rectangular court with many small rooms on the east. Other buildings include a prayer hall, minaret, slaughterhouse, kitchens, and several baths, but the palace lacks any provision for the public life of the sovereign. Rather, it resembles a Moroccan private house inflated to a royal scale and probably served as the residence of the sultan's enormous harem. (He reportedly had five hundred concubines and several hundred children.)

Remains of the third palace, known as the Palace of the Labyrinth (Qasr al-Muhannasha) from the serpentine design of a fountain in the interior, lie to the south-east of the second palace. Measuring 400 by 240 meters, it consists of a series of large square or rectangular courts with rooms and pavilions and extensive gardens. The tunnel entrance on the south-east leads to a court, in the center of which stands a square mosque, added between 1792 and 1822. Although contemporary sources describe it as being in "the style of Istanbul," its massive plain exterior and tiled pyramidal roof are more reminiscent of traditional mausoleums in Morocco. Beyond the treasury lies a large court of honor (74 by 71

meters), with axial reception rooms and a pool fed by channels in the center. The Marble Garden behind is divided into parterres like those at the Badi'a palace at Marrakesh. The hierarchical organization and range of spaces, from rows of rooms to elaborate pavilions, suggest that this palace was designed for official functions and receptions.

The grandiose scheme at Meknes invites comparison with imperial palaces at Istanbul, Isfahan, and Fatehpur Sikri.[23] The plan evolved as it was being built, but the royal city was so large that it remained unfinished at the end of the sovereign's long reign. Although pisé, made from the ever-available earth, was the main material of construction, other materials were collected wherever available: Roman sites such as Volubulis and Islamic sites such as Chella and Marrakesh were plundered, and marbles were imported from Pisa. Labor was extracted from the tribes under the sultan's control, and Christian slaves and renegades were also put to work, although their numbers are often wildly exaggerated, particularly by tourist guides.

Meknes suffered during the succession crisis following Mawlay Isma'il's death, and one-quarter of the royal city was razed. Nevertheless, work on the palace city continued, and the decoration of some monumental façades, such as that of the Bab Mansur [330], were completed. This ponderous imposing gateway, which links the medina with the Dar al-Kabira, had been begun by Mawlay Isma'il and was completed by his son Mawlay 'Abdallah in 1732. The grandest gate of the city, it has a horseshoe-arched opening flanked by salients, an arrangement which goes back to Almohad times, although the proportions and decoration have changed. The towers are raised on arcades and columns, giving them a curiously insubstantial quality, and the façade is covered with elaborate lattice decoration in green and black tile, a motif more typical of minarets.[24] The sumptuous decoration underscores the ceremonial function of the gate, which was meant to impress by its size and richness rather than its defensive potential.

These grandiose architectural ensembles were elaborately embellished and furnished.[25] Fine-quality woodwork, both carved and turned, continued to be produced from wood cut in the Moroccan forests, and many beautiful ceilings survive. In general, the Marinid style (see Chapter 9) was continued, but the carving became shallower until it was gradually abandoned in favor of painting, a faster (and cheaper) technique of decoration. In comparison to the superb tiles and tablewares made in Iran and Turkey, Moroccan ceramics are relatively coarse, although many examples made in the eighteenth and nineteenth centuries have an undeniable charm.[26]

Distinctive woven and embroidered textiles continued to be produced throughout the region, such as the superb Algiers embroideries of the seventeenth and eighteenth centuries, although the most sophisticated patrons often preferred imported pieces and many of the designs followed Ottoman models.[27] A large banner woven of silk with metallic thread [331] follows the *sanjak* type known in Ottoman Turkey, with its shield shape and depiction of ʿAli's legendary two-bladed sword. Its inscription, in the distinctive Maghribi script, and date (1094/1683) indicate that it was made for members of the Qadiriyya, a Sufi order which flourished in North Africa.[28] It was designed to be carried on the pilgrimage to Mecca. Its technique and design represent the continuation of the superb silk-weaving traditions of Nasrid Spain [166].

Illuminated and illustrated manuscripts also continued Maghribi traditions of script and decoration. Such texts as al-Jazuli's *Dalāʾil al-khayrāt* were perennially popular, and these manuscripts were often decorated with representations of places or objects attached to the Prophet. A seventeenth-century manuscript containing several religious texts, including that of al-Jazuli, has, among others, illustrations of the Mosque of the Prophet, with the minbar and mihrab, and his grave and those of the two first caliphs at Medina [332]. In addition to its typical Maghribi square format (13.5 by 13.8 cm), the text is written in Maghribi script and the decorations are a late (and simplified) example of the western Islamic style of decoration.[29] This manuscript was acquired in the 1960s in a bazaar in Kabul, Afghanistan; this provenance, in conjunction with the Devanagri script on paper re-used to bind the manuscript, suggests that this distinctively Moroccan manuscript had been taken to Mecca, where it was later acquired by another pilgrim from India.

Other manuscripts were made by and for royal patrons. An ʿAlawi sultan himself is known to have copied a collection of hadith in 1789–90, following the old tradition of calligraphy as an appropriately royal art.[30] Luxury copies of the Koran were also produced for the royal family to use and

331. Pilgrimage banner, probably Morocco, 1683. Brocaded maroon silk with metallic thread. 3.61 × 1.88 m. Cambridge, MA, Harvard University Art Museums

332. *The Tomb of the Prophet in Medina*, from a Collection of Prayers,
Morocco, sixteenth century. Each page 13.5 × 13.8 cm. Berlin, Museum
für Islamische Kunst

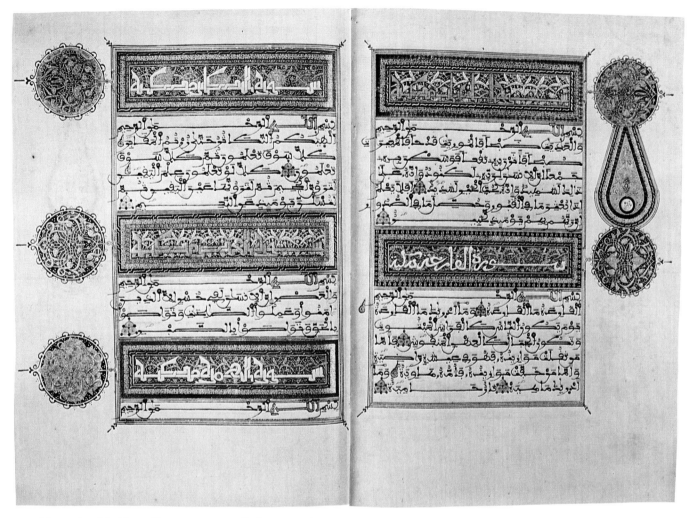

333. Manuscript of the Koran, Morocco, 1729–30. Each page 31.5 by 19.5 cm. Cairo, National Library, MS. 2.5, ff. 258v–259r

give. One example [333], copied for a Sharifan prince in 1142/1729–30, is remarkable for its extensive use of color, including bright red, green, blue, and gold.[31] With 263 folios measuring 31.5 by 19.5 cm, the manuscript has twenty lines of text per page in the vertical format standard outside the far Maghrib. The text is written in a somewhat spindly Maghribi hand, the chapter headings in an archaizing knotted Kufic. Other panels of decorative script, such as the one on the middle right of the illustrated page, are in a stylized cursive hand. The large *thuluth* inscription in the lower margin of folio 261r states that the manuscript was endowed by Muhammad Bey to his congregational mosque, and suggests that the manuscript was eventually presented to one of the Beys of Egypt.

Architecture in India under the Mughals and their Contemporaries in the Deccan

The Mughals (r. 1526–1858) were the greatest, richest, and longest-lasting Muslim dynasty to rule India. Their enormous wealth, which dwarfed that of their contemporaries in Iran and Turkey, derived ultimately from agriculture, for in this well-watered subtropical land a very large number of crops could profitably be raised, ranging from foodstuffs to fibers for an extensive textile industry. Babur (r. 1526–30), the founder of the dynasty, was a Chaghatay Turk descended on his father's side from Timur and on his mother's from Chingiz Khan. Babur's father, 'Umar Shaykh, had ruled a small Timurid principality in the Farghana Valley in Central Asia, but the rising power of the Uzbek Turks forced Babur to the east. In 1504 he took Kabul and swiftly began raids on India, defeating the Lodi sultan at Panipat in 1526 and the Rajput chiefs at Kanwa near Agra in the following year.

With these victories, the Mughal line gained a foothold in northern India, but Babur's son Humayun (r. 1530–56, with interruption) was dislodged by insurrections of the nobles from the old Lodi regime, particularly Farid Khan Sur. Operating from Bihar, the Afghan chief defeated Humayun at Kannawj in 1540 and drove the Mughal ruler from India until 1555. The Mughal domains passed to the control of Farid Khan, who assumed the regnal name Shir Shah Sur (r. 1540–55). He was not only a fine general but an able ruler, introducing important fiscal and monetary reforms, which were incorporated into the Mughal system of administration. During Shir Shah's interregnum, Humayun spent fifteen years in exile in Sind, Iran, and Afghanistan, but the squabbling for succession among Shir Shah's successors enabled the Mughal to regain the throne in 1555. Humayun died unexpectedly a year later after falling down the stairs of his library in Delhi and was succeeded by his son Akbar (r. 1556–1605). During Akbar's long reign the dynasty extended its power over northern and central India, and under his successor, Jahangir (r. 1605–27), the policy of subjugating outlying areas of the Indian subcontinent was continued. Shahjahan (r. 1628–58) undertook an ambitious program of uniting Central Asia and India in a grand empire of Sunni Islam (to counter the Shi'ite Safavids), but this ended in failure in 1647, and a conservative reaction ensued under Awrangzib (r. 1658–1707). Notables and provincial officials, both Muslim and non-Muslim, became increasing powerful, and by the eighteenth century the Mughal emperors in Delhi were only shadows of their former selves, as power devolved to provincial rulers and Europeans, particularly the British.

More monuments survive from the period of Mughal rule than from any other, for the Mughal state was well aware of the declamatory power of architecture and used it as a means of self-representation and an instrument of royalty.[1] In the later part of the period, royal patronage of architecture and the arts was curtailed, but the great monuments of the past continued to provide inspiration for patrons with shallower pockets. Under Mughal patronage there developed a distinctive and elegant style of architecture, in which indigenous traditions of Indo-Islamic architecture (see Chapter 11) were combined with forms and techniques imported from Iran and Central Asia (see Chapters 2 and 4). A similar composite style drawing on local and Iranian traditions developed in the Deccan. In general, the solid three-dimensional massing typical of earlier sultanate buildings gave way to a linear approach, in which flat surfaces were divided into panels. The brick and tile typical of earlier times were replaced by stone, particularly red sandstone and white marble, but the application of color was restrained in favour of high polish and meticulous finish. While trabeate construction continued to be used in secular buildings, such new forms as the ogee arch and the bulbous dome became standard features of the Mughal style. Large congregational mosques were built by rulers who wished to emphasize their Muslim piety, but the most famous buildings associated with the Mughals are monumental tombs set on platforms amidst pools and formal gardens and magnificent forts and fortified palaces constructed throughout the empire, particularly in the capitals at Delhi, Fatehpur Sikri, Lahore, and Agra.

ARCHITECTURE UNDER THE EARLY MUGHALS (1526–1628) AND THEIR CONTEMPORARIES

Little remains of the architectural works by the first Mughal emperors, Babur and Humayun, although Babur is credited with introducing to India the Persian style of four-fold garden (*chahārbāgh*), and Humayun founded Din Panah, Delhi's sixth city, in 1533.[2] Shir Shah was a notable patron of architecture. He restored the old pilgrimage road across his territory from Bengal to the Punjab; taken over by Akbar, it became the Grand Trunk Road later immortalized by Rudyard Kipling. Shir Shah also fortified the Purana Qal'a ("Old Fort") in Din Panah and added the Qal'a-i Kuhna Mosque (1540–5) there [334]. The mosque, which provides the link between sultanate architecture and the emerging Mughal style, combines features of Lodi buildings, such as the single-aisle plan and red sandstone inlaid with white marble, with traditional Hindu ones, such as projecting balconies, slab eaves, and corbels. His most ambitious constructions were at Sasaram, the Sur family landhold (Pers. *jāgīr*) in Bihar, where he commissioned a monumental tomb, built between 1538 and 1545 [335].[3] Octagonal in plan and three stories in elevation, it continues the type of tomb already erected in Delhi by the Lodis, but on a far grander scale. Measuring 41.5 meters in diameter, Shir Shah's mausoleum is several times larger than any Lodi tomb. The tomb is set on a stepped foundation and a tall terrace

334. Delhi, Purana Qal'a, Qal'a-i Kuhna mosque, 1540–5, view from the east

335. Sasaram, Tomb of Shir Shah Sur, 1538–45

with domed pavilions (chatris) at the corners, creating an immense pyramidal pile of ordered masonry which rises 45.7 meters in five distinct stages. The three stories of the model tomb are also articulated: the lowest story takes the form of a verandah with triple arches on each side, the second story is enlivened by crenellated parapets and domed pavilions at the corners, and the third story is relieved by a series of kiosks which break into the circular base of the dome and carry the eye upward to the ascending curves of the dome and its massive finial. The mausoleum is set in the middle of a great artificial lake, whose concreted sides measure 416 meters, and the building's reflection in the water enhances its grandeur. Constructed of fine sandstone obtained from the nearby quarries at Chunar, the tomb is now a uniform gray but was originally brightly painted in red, blue, yellow, and white. Located close to the Grand Trunk Road for maximum visibility, it was designed to promote the idea of Shir Shah as a just ruler with an elevated genealogy. To boost his lineage, Shir Shah also built a second tomb at Sasaram for his father, Hasan Sur, and another (1542–3) at Narnaul, 120 kilometers south-west of Delhi, for his grandfather, Ibrahim Sur, a minor notable who had died ca. 1488.[4]

Much controversy surrounds Humayun's architectural patronage, and much of the work in the Purana Qal'a should probably be attributed to Shir Shah. One small exception is the small octagonal pavilion known as the Sher Mandal and identified as the library where the emperor fell to his death. The monument most closely associated with Humayun, his tomb at Delhi [336, 337], was only begun six years later, under his son Akbar, and completed a decade later in 1571–2.[5] Humayun's tomb lies on the flat plain of Delhi near the

336. Delhi, Tomb of Humayun, 1562–72, view from south

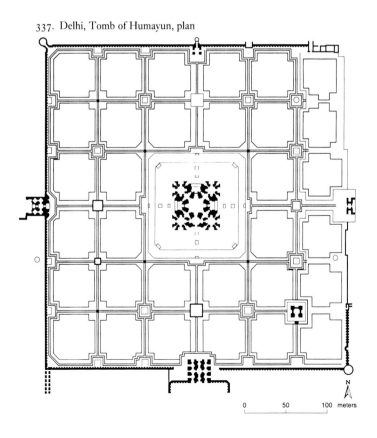

337. Delhi, Tomb of Humayun, plan

0   50   100 meters

banks of the Yamuna river, 1500 meters south of the rubble walls of Din Panah. The tomb is set to the east of the shrine of Nizam al-Din Awliya' (1236–1325), one of India's most revered Sufi saints; he was the successor of Shaykh Farid Shakarganj in the Chistiyya, the mystical order held in high esteem by the Mughals, who legitimized their rule by association with Sufis. Humayun's tomb is set in the center of a large garden (348 metres square), which is divided into 36 squares by cross-axially arranged water channels and pathways. The tomb sits on a large podium (99 meters square) with 56 cells containing more than a hundred cenotaphs, and the height of the podium (6.5 meters) enhances the massiveness of the tomb, which measures 47.5 meters on a side and towers 42.5 meters above the ground. The flat surfaces and the restrained combination of red sandstone and white marble in flat panels create an impression of sobriety. On the interior, the central space contains Humayun's cenotaph; two stories of octagonal chambers, containing cenotaphs for various members of Humayun's family, fill the corners. This type of plan, often called by the Persian expression *hasht bihisht* ("Eight Paradises"), is known to have been used in Timurid Iran (see Chapter 4). According to the contemporary historian 'Abd al-Qadir Bada'uni, the tomb was designed by Mirak Mirza Ghiyath, an architect of Iranian descent who had worked in Herat, Bukhara, and India before undertaking this project.

The architect of Humayun's tomb drew upon a wide range of sources. The building employed many of the same materials and techniques of construction used nearby in the sultanate period and Sur interregnum. The immediate inspiration for constructing a monumental tomb was undoubtedly Shir Shah's slightly smaller tomb at Sasaram,

338. Agra, Red Fort, Jahangiri Mahal, 1565

and like it, the building may well have been intended as a dynastic monument, although in both cases, for different reasons, this was not to be. The garden setting for Humayun's tomb also paraphrases the pool at Sasaram, but the garden setting may be understood as another paradisiacal reference implicit in the choice of the *hasht bihisht* form. Furthermore, Humayun's tomb fits squarely into the Iranian tradition of imperial mausoleums, seen for example in Uljaytu's tomb at Sultaniyya [4–6] and Timur's at Samarqand [53, 54], and such features as a radially symmetrical plan and elongated drum with bulbous double dome show specific knowledge of the Timurid architectural repertory.[6]

The Timurid features would have been readily known to the architect and desirable to the patron. Mirak Mirza Ghiyath is representative of craftsmen trained in the Timurid traditions of Iran and Central Asia who emigrated to India in the sixteenth century in search of patrons, bringing with them the International Timurid style, as it had been carried somewhat earlier to the Ottoman court. This taste for things Timurid may also show that already in the mid-sixteenth century Mughal rulers attempted to connect their line in India with its forebears in Iran by using forms identified with the Timurids. The Timurid architectural legacy, however, was substantially changed under the Mughals. Whereas Timurid architects had played with innovative vaulting and varied the interior spaces, the interior spaces of Humayun's tomb have been regularized and made somewhat predictable as exterior monumentality became the overriding concern, and later the standard feature of imperial Mughal architecture.

Akbar originally ruled from Delhi, but two years after his accession he moved his capital to Agra, 200 kilometers to the south-east. The city was renamed Akbarabad in his honor and became the greatest in his empire. The main part lay on the west bank of the Yamuna and was provided with a drainage system to control the flow of rainwater. A new city wall was erected, and the old mud-brick fortress used by the Lodis was rebuilt in 1565 of sandstone, whose red color gives rise to its modern name, the Red Fort. The fort follows the irregular semicircular plan of its predecessor. On the city side it is enclosed by a moat and a double wall, broken by the Delhi Gate on the west and the Amar Singh Gate on the south. The two massive gates are distinguished by rows of arched niches and stunning veneer in red sandstone and white marble, with highlights in blue glazed tile. According to the contemporary historian Abu'l-Fazl, construction of the fort was supervised by Muhammad Qasim Khan, who is credited with various feats of civil engineering and who bore the dual titles Master of the Land and Sea Routes (*mīr-i barr u bahr*) and Master of Pyrotechnics (*mīr-i ātish*).[7]

Despite extensive remodeling to the interior of the Red Fort, two palaces in its south-east corner can be dated to the period of Akbar's restoration. Both are trabeated structures organized around central courts. The Akbari Mahal is partially destroyed, and the Jahangiri Mahal, which despite its name belongs to Akbar's restoration, is the earliest Mughal palace extant.[8] Like the gates, the outer façade [338] is articulated with an orderly series of blind niches and panels filled with geometric motifs. The interior is divided into a complex set of apartments. In contrast to the calm austerity of the exterior, many interior surfaces [339] are extravagantly decorated in carved stone, painted and carved stucco, and

339. Agra, Red Fort, Jahangiri Mahal, corbels in interior court

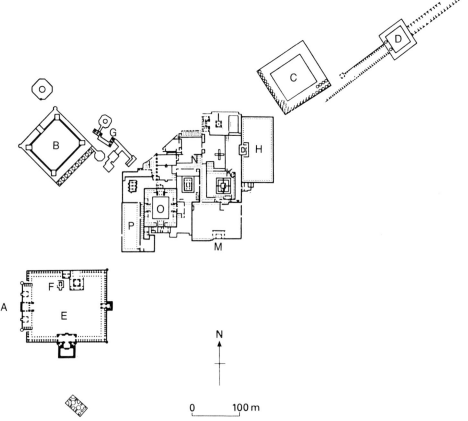

340. Fatehpur Sikri, 1571–9, plan. A) Hermitage of Salim Chisti;
B) Caravanserai; C) Mint or factory; D) Bazaar; E) Congregational
Mosque; F) Tomb of Salim Chishti; G) Elephant Gate; H) Divan-i 'Am;
I) Divan-i Khass; J) Anup Talau; K) House of the Turkish Sultana;
L) Khwabgah; M) Daftarkhana; N) Panj Mahal; O) Jodh Bai's Palace;
P) Harem

tile. Brackets and struts are richly carved, and many of the motifs, such as the crocodile-like creatures emitting scrolls of foliage from their mouths, are adapted from the Hindu palaces at Gwalior, suggesting that masons were brought from this town 100 kilometers south, which had an imposing fort dating from the period of Tomar rule (1398–1517). Nevertheless, the geometric patterns on screens and flat panels in the Jahangiri Mahal derive from Timurid designs, particularly from the vocabulary of book ornament, for Timurid books were a rich source for Mughal ateliers (see Chapter 19). The flat paneling and juxtaposition of materials of different colors recall earlier architecture in Delhi.

The same synthesis of diverse architectural traditions can be seen on a grander and more regular scale at Fatehpur Sikri [340], the new capital that Akbar founded in 1571.[9] Located forty kilometers west of Agra along the five-hundred-kilometer royal corridor that linked Agra to Ajmer, the city is set in the midst of a vast plain on a long (four-kilometer) narrow ridge overlooking a large lake, now dry. Babur had constructed a garden and octagonal pavilion at the site in 1527, and since 1561 Akbar had made an annual pilgrimage along this route to the tomb of the shaykh Mu'in al-Din Chishti (d. 1236), the founder of the Chishtiyya, at Ajmer. Sikri was a day's journey from Agra and the site of the hermitage of the shaykh Salim Chishti (1479–1572). In 1568 he presciently predicted that the sonless Akbar would soon have three sons, and in the following year Akbar's Rajput wife Maryam al-Zamani gave birth to Prince Salim (later Jahangir) at Sikri. To commemorate the event, two

years later Akbar ordered the construction of a new city known as Fathabad (City of Victory), a Persian name which was soon supplanted in popular usage by the Indianized form Fatehpur Sikri and which became particularly apposite after Akbar's conquest of Gujerat in 1573. Construction of the major elements in the new capital was finished within a decade, but the emperor left for Lahore in the Punjab in 1585 and seldom returned. The common explanation for Akbar's abrupt departure is that the city's water supply dried up, but this fact is not mentioned by any contemporary source and there was extensive provision for collecting, storing, and draining water in stepwells, reservoirs, pools, tanks, and channels. A more likely explanation is that Akbar departed to deal with the military and political upheaval following the death of his half-brother Mirza Hakim Muhammad, the governor of Kabul.

Most of the major constructions at Fatehpur Sikri can be dated to the fourteen years when the city served as Akbar's principal residence. In contrast to such other imperial centers as Delhi, Agra, or Isfahan (see Chapter 13), it was built in a relatively short time by a single patron, and its plan is marked by a unity of design based on proportional modules and ratios.[10] Akbar's constructions at Fatehpur Sikri are an interrelated series of modules set beside each other on the ridge, which provided the fine red sandstone used for the new buildings there and at Agra. The city is inserted between the old town of Sikri to the north-east and the hermitage of Salim Chishti (A on the plan) to the south-west. Eleven kilometers of massive stone walls with parapets

341. Fatehpur Sikri, Tomb of Salim Chishti, 1573–4, marble screen

and gateways (not shown on the plan) surrounded the city, except on the north-west, where the lakeshore once extended. The urban settlement formerly spread beyond the walls for a radius of twenty kilometers, and the environs contained imperial gardens and resthouses, residences for the nobility, a drinking and gambling zone, and even an experimental school dedicated to the study of language acquisition in children. Within the city the buildings are set in two distinct ways: service buildings such as the caravan-serai (B), the mint or factory (C), and a long bazaar with a service node (Pers. *chahār-sūq*, D) are set perpendicular to the south-west–north-east axis of the ridge, while the imperial section of the city, including the congregational mosque (E) and a residential and administrative area known as the palace (Pers. *dawlatkhāna*), is set at an angle to the ridge and aligns with the qibla.

The congregational mosque at Fatehpur Sikri (1573–4), one of the biggest in India, is a huge rectangular building set on a high podium. The vast central court (95 by 118 meters) is surrounded by multi-domed arcades. A line of domed pavilions crowns the prayer hall on the west; its façade is

divided by a tall iwan which screens the sanctuary dome. Opposite the mihrab in the east wall is the Imperial Gate (Badshahi Darvaza), which provided access to the Palace. The gate and sanctuary dome are aligned with the hermitage of Salim Chishti to the west and form the east–west axis of the mosque. A north–south axis is marked by a monumental gateway (height 34 meters) in the south wall, the Lofty Gate (Buland Darvaza), which is approached from below by a steep flight of steps. On the north side of the court stands the white marble tomb of Salim Chishti (F), a small square (14.63 meters on a side) with a front porch carried on extraordinary serpentine brackets. The central chamber is surrounded by a verandah whose intricate lattice screens (Pers. *jālī*) [341] are some of the finest examples of their type. The tomb is visually distinct as the only building in the city not constructed of red sandstone, for white marble was reserved in this period for saints' tombs.[11] These tombs are also distinguished by interior wooden canopies overlaid with mother-of-pearl, a technique associated with Gujerat in the seventeenth and eighteenth centuries [382].[12]

The palace at Fatehpur Sikri was a large complex (340 by 275 meters) with public areas to the north-east and private ones to the south-west. The main entrance from the ridge lay to the north-west through the Elephant Gate (G), now destroyed, but well known from contemporary representations in books [365]. The nobility seems to have lived just inside the gate in the triangular area formed by the caravan-serai, the north wall of the congregational mosque, and the west wall of the palace. The visitor passed from the Elephant Gate through a series of walkways and gates, now destroyed or walled up, to the court on the extreme north-east known as the State Hall (Divan-i 'Am; H on the plan). This large court (100 by 50 meters) was surrounded by colonnades; a five-bay loggia with beautifully carved sandstone screens projects from the center of the west side. The court was used for public receptions, ceremonies, and congregational prayer, and the emperor apparently sat in the royal *loge* facing east.

A small door in the north-west corner of the State Hall gave access to a second court [342], which was apparently

342. Fatehpur Sikri, palace, second court

343. Fatehpur Sikri, Divan-i Khass, central pillar

used for semi-public functions. At the north side is a small two-story pavilion (I), popularly known as the Divan-i Khass ("Private Hall"). Inside the pavilion, a central column with curvilinear brackets supports a circular platform with railings of pierced stone screens [343]. It apparently served as a throne. Screened bridges in the corners connect the platform to a screened walkway encircling the room. At the same level on the exterior is a balcony supported on brackets. At the south end of the court is a man-sized game board, where Akbar and his courtiers played a game like pachisi, and a small tank (J), known as the Anup Talau, which Akbar had filled with coins in 1579–80 during a spree of largesse to the poor and needy. The small building known as the "House of the Turkish Sultana" (K) has exquisite scenes of animals and birds carved in low relief on the interior dadoes; the scenes derive from Persian book covers [e.g. 87] and are another example of the popularity of the International Timurid style at the Mughal court. At the south end of the Anup Talau is the Khwabgah (L), Akbar's sleeping-chamber, and further south is yet another court, with a building (M) in the center of the south side called the Daftarkhana (Office).

A five-story pavilion topped by a domed kiosk (N) rises above the west side of the second court. Now known as the Panj Mahal ("Palace of Five [Levels]"), it is the tallest building in the palace complex. Its balanced pyramidal form overlooks the courtyard to the east, around which the civic structures were positioned, and it marks the transition from the public areas on the north-east to the private apartments on the south-west. These include several large courts and pavilions, whose fanciful names bear no relation to their function in the sixteenth century. Jodh Bai's palace (O), for example, may have served as Akbar's residence, and the long, open structure adjoining it to the south-west (P) may have been the harem. Most of these buildings are trabeate structures, whose severe lines would have been modified by awnings and screens of cloth. Tents may also have been set up in the court.

Contemporary chroniclers are reticent in describing Akbar's palace at Fatehpur Sikri, and the paucity of historical and epigraphic evidence makes it difficult to put the buildings into context, leading to wild speculation and fanciful theories. Interpretations of the palace's function and identification of the individual units rest on formal analysis of the architecture. The palace precinct was clearly situated to take advantage of the site, and the Panj Mahal (N) towers over the other buildings. In Istanbul the Ottoman sultans inserted their palace and mosque into a preexisting urban matrix (see Chapter 15), whereas at Fatehpur Sikri the contours of the land and the location of the old town and

Salim Chishti's hermitage created the matrix into which the palace was fitted. At Topkapı Palace, there was a clear linear progression from public to private, as the honored guest was led through a series of increasingly secluded courts to reach the sultan. The palace precinct at Fatehpur Sikri was a group of abutting functional areas which were loosely arranged from public to private, from Divan-i Khass (H) to Harem (Q). There was no need to accommodate procession, for the Mughals followed the Persian tradition of protocol, in which the ruler rode out to meet the honored guest. Rather, there was an axis of imperial appearances running north–south through the Divan-i Khass (I), the court with a game board, the projecting bay overlooking the tank known as Anup Talau (J), and the small window projecting from the south façade of the Daftarkhana (M). The window may well be the *jharoka*, the canopied throne seen in such other Mughal palaces as the fort at Lahore and well known from contemporary painting [375]. The important nodes at Fatehpur Sikri were the elevated and framed spots where the emperor sat for royal appearance.

Mughal architecture achieved its distinct character during the reign of Akbar, when the intense architectural activity surpassed even the building frenzy that had taken place two centuries earlier under the Tughluqs (see Chapter 11). The expansion of the Mughal empire was reflected in its architecture, as craftsmen emigrated from the new provinces to the Mughal court. Heterogeneous elements from earlier Indian, Central Asian, and Persian styles were unified by the ubiquitous building material, red sandstone, which was not only readily available, easily carved, and attractive but had the added advantage of being of the color reserved for imperial tents. Trabeated construction was the norm for palaces; arcuate forms were less common but used in mosques, tombs, and large entrances.

At the same time that the Mughal style was established in northern India, another composite style combining features from Iranian and Indian traditions developed in the Deccan. By the late fifteenth century increasing rivalry between native Deccani Muslims and outsiders had sapped the power of the Bahmanids, the powerful sultanate that had ruled the northern Deccan from Gulbarga since 1347 (see Chapter 11 and ills. 197, 198). They were succeeded by five local dynasties, all springing from former servants. The successor states were constantly at war with each other, but they banded together temporarily in 1564 to crush Vijayanagar, the Hindu state to the immediate south, and sack its wealthy capital at Talikota. Their successes attracted the attention of the Mughals, but it was only under Awrangzib in the 1680s that the Deccan passed definitively under Mughal authority.

The two successor states of the Bahmanids that lasted the longest were the 'Adil Shahis (1490–1686), descended from Yusuf 'Adil Khan, a Turk who served as governor of Bijapur for the Bahmanids, and the Qutb Shahis (1512–1687), descended from a Qaraqoyunlu Turkoman commander who served as governor of Telingana, the easternmost domain of the Bahmanids. Both dynasties were Shi'ite and maintained close ties with the Safavids in Iran. Both states were great centers for the patronage of literature, painting, and architecture. The 'Adil Shahis ruled from Bijapur, which preserves more significant buildings than any other city in India

344. Hyderabad, Char Minar, 1590–1

except Delhi, and the fifth ruler, Ibrahim II (r. 1579–1627), was probably the most brilliant patron in the Deccan (for his portrait, see 373). The local style of architecture there is the most harmonious of all the Deccani styles, both structurally and esthetically, and is epitomized in the tomb of Ibrahim's son, Muhammad (r. 1627–56; see ill. 356).

The Qutb Shahis ruled first from Golconda, but their distinctive style of architecture can better be seen at Hyderabad, which was planned in 1590–1 by the fifth Qutb Shahi ruler, Muhammad Quli (r. 1580–1612), as a suburb of the Golconda fort. Travelers and historians describe its gardens, bazaars, and palaces, but the most impressive monument to survive is the Char Minar [344], the triumphal archway in the center of the city. In position and function, it recalls the Tin Darvaza built nearly one hundred and seventy years earlier at Ahmadabad [202], but the Hyderabad gate is considerably larger: the ground story measures thirty meters square, each of the four great ogee arches oriented to the cardinal points has a 10.8-meter span, and the four lofty minarets at the corners rise 55.8 meters above the ground. The ascending stories of the minarets are marked by arcaded balconies, a feature characteristic of Qutb Shahi architecture, and the minarets are crowned by round kiosks with ogee domes foliated at the base, like those built by the 'Adil Shahis in Bijapur [356]. The gateway is dignified yet spirited; the upper structure displays a graceful inventiveness and the minarets add appropriate verticality.

In the Mughal domains the thrust of architectural activity shifted under Akbar's son and successor Jahangir (r. 1605–27) from public projects to work of a more private nature, such as hunting palaces, formal gardens, and ornamental retreats, of which little has survived. The first quarter of the

345. Sikandra, Tomb of Akbar, 1605–13

seventeenth century was a period of transition and experimentation, in which buildings are distinguished by highly decorated surfaces in a variety of materials, ranging from the familiar sandstone to white marble, stone intarsia, painted stucco, and tile. The most important work carried out at the beginning of Jahangir's reign was the construction of his father's tomb [345] at Sikandra, eight kilometers north-west of Agra. The site had been developed under Sikandar Lodi (r. 1489–1517), after whom it was named, and Akbar selected it for a garden named Bihishtabad ("Abode of Paradise"); but the actual construction of the tomb seems to have been begun only after the emperor's death on 16 October 1605. Inscriptions on the gateway indicate that the complex was finished by 1613, eight years after Jahangir's accession.

Like Humayun's tomb at Delhi, Akbar's tomb at Sikandra is set in a vast garden (765 meters square) enclosed by a high wall and divided by water channels. The red sandstone gateway on the south side is crowned by four white marble minarets and boldly decorated in white, gray, and black marble, set in panels with geometric designs and large-scale floral arabesques which resemble the patterns on textiles. The numerous Persian verses in the frame around the arch compare the tomb and its garden to Paradise and were designed by ʿAbd al-Haqq Shirazi, who was later awarded the title Amanat Khan ("Trustworthy Noble") and was responsible for many of the inscriptions on the Taj Mahal.[13] Akbar's tomb sits on a massive plastered and painted podium

(104 meters square; 9.14 meters high) with arcades and projecting portals on the four sides. The sandstone portals, set within rectangular frames following the classical Iranian form of the *pīshṭāq*, are inlaid with marble.

The tomb (52 meters square) is a pyramidal arrangment of three tiers of red sandstone pavilions with domed pavilions (chatris) at the corners. A vestibule, exquisitely decorated with painted plaster in a Persianate mode [346], gives access to a descending ramp to the plain domed tomb chamber at the heart of the structure. On the top is an open court containing the emperor's marble cenotaph surrounded by pierced marble screens; the white color of the marble contrasts sharply with the red sandstone used elsewhere. The play of light and shadow over the increasingly delicate superstructure contrasts with the powerful massing of the basement. The structure is a marked departure from the conventional domed tomb, such as that made for Humayun [336] almost a half-century earlier. With its receding stories of pillared galleries, Akbar's tomb belongs to the indigenous tradition of trabeate construction used for palaces, while the podium, with its vaulted bays, vestibule decorated with painted plaster, and high portals whose stone intarsia reproduces the effect of tile, maintains the Timurid tradition of vaulted masonry.

346. Sikandra, Tomb of Akbar, detail of mural in vestibule

347. Agra, Tomb of I'timad al-Dawla, 1622–8

The emphasis on exquisite finish and colorful decoration seen on the gateway at Sikandra is further developed at a small tomb on the east bank of the Yamuna opposite Agra [347]. It houses the remains of Jahangir's minister of finance, Mirza Ghiyath Beg, usually known by his title I'timad al-Dawla ("Pillar of the State"). His daughter, Mihr al-Nisa ("Sun of Women"), who became Jahangir's wife Nurjahan ("Light of the World"), directed construction of the tomb during the six years after her father's death in 1622. The tomb stands in a quadripartite garden. The enclosure walls, a guesthouse on the Yamuna, and the podium are made of the traditional red sandstone inlaid with colored marble, but the tomb itself is the first structure in India in which white marble replaces red sandstone as the ground for polychrome pietra dura inlay. The structure, measuring twenty-one meters on a side, contains a central tomb chamber surrounded by square and rectangular rooms decorated with carved and painted plaster in the Persianate style. Broad octagonal towers, like minarets, mark the corners, and a small pavilion or upper story rises above the roof. Three arched openings on each side provide shadows which contrast with the gleaming surface, and the cornice and eaves mark strong horizontal lines.

The modest, jewel-like building is remarkable for its delicate but exuberant decoration and warm tonality. The traditional technique of inlay has changed: *opus sectile*, marble intarsia of various colors, has been replaced by pietra dura, in which hard and rare stones such as lapis, onyx, jasper,

topaz, cornelian, agate, and jasper were embedded in the marble. Traditional geometric designs and arabesques are combined with representational motifs of wine cups, vases with flowers, and cypress trees, visual allusions to the descriptions of Paradise in the Koran. The intricate inlay in yellow, brown, gray, and black, contrasting with the smooth white marble, prefigures the later phase of white marble garnished with gold and precious stones that marks the most sumptuous buildings erected under later Mughal patronage.

ARCHITECTURE UNDER THE LATER MUGHALS (1628–1858) AND THEIR CONTEMPORARIES

Mughal architecture achieved its classical moment under Jahangir's son and successor Shahjahan (r. 1628–58), who was also the most prolific patron of the Mughal emperors. During his reign centralized planning gave way to bilateral symmetry, and the repertory of forms became more standardized and limited. The lobate or cusped arch, for example, was ubiquitous, and white marble or fine stucco replaced red sandstone as the preferred facing material. These materials were highly polished and exquisitely finished with relief carving and colored inlay. As in the Ottoman empire, uniformity of style was achieved though the institution of a court bureau of architects who worked closely under the supervision of the emperor.

In the seven years following Jahangir's death in 1627,

348. Lahore, Tomb of Jahangir, 1627–34

349. Agra, Taj Mahal, 1631–47, plan. 1) Tomb; 2) Mosque;
3) Guesthouse; 4) Gatehouse

Shahjahan had a tomb built for his father at Shadera, outside of Lahore. The city was an important crossroads for caravans from Delhi, Multan, Kashmir, and Kabul, and visitors praised the handsome appearance of its mosques, bazaars, palaces, gardens, and mansions, few of which remain today. Following the Mughal model, Jahangir's tomb is set in a quadripartite garden, which had been laid out during his lifetime. On the east the enclosure (500 meters square) is bounded by the Ravi river; to the west is a large forecourt with a mosque. As at Akbar's tomb at Sikandra, the garden is divided into sixteen squares and the tomb is set on a large podium (85 meters square). Unlike its predecessors, the tomb is a single story, with towering minarets at the corners [348]. The cenotaph on the top, which has been removed, was once surrounded by carved stone screens and was left open, as at Akbar's tomb at Sikandra [345]. In keeping with the style of the period, the red sandstone surface is decorated with white marble set in the shape of wine vessels and flower vases.

The Taj Mahal [349, 350], the tomb Shahjahan built in memory of his favorite wife Mumtaz Mahal, is more famous than the one he built for his father; indeed this structure is probably the best-known building in all Islamic architecture and one of the most memorable works of man. The distinctive profile of this building, like those of the Pyramids, the Eiffel Tower, or the Tower of Pisa, has become an icon for the country in which it stands. Work on the tomb began soon after Mumtaz Mahal's unexpected

350. Agra, Taj Mahal

death in 1631, and the building was completed by 1647. Three architects were involved, but Ahmad Lahawri (from Lahore) apparently dominated 'Abd al-Karim Ma'mur Khan and Makramat Khan. Following the standard arrangement, the tomb is set in a large quadripartite garden (308 by 554 meters), but unlike earlier examples, it stands not at the center but at the north end along the riverbank, balanced by a large gateway on the south [349]. The tomb and the platform on which it is set are of polished white marble [350], a crystalline and translucent material that presents an intense contrast to the opaque red sandstone used for the outlying structures and the two buildings flanking the tomb, a guesthouse on the east and a mosque on the west. In plan and massing, the tomb refines the model provided by Humayun's tomb at Delhi [336]: the great bulbous tomb is set on a higher drum, the small pavilions at the corners are pulled in close to the drum, the octagonal rooms in the corners are more logically connected, and four tall minarets frame the building. This carefully balanced image, reflected in the water channel dividing the garden, is enhanced by the superb polish and detailed carving of the marbles.

Unlike the tomb for I'timad al-Dawla [347], the Taj Mahal has only restrained pietra dura decoration in the form of slender arabesques and extensive inscriptions. Most of the texts are short chapters from the Koran emphasizing eschatological themes, particularly the Day of Judgment, and it has been suggested that the epigraphic program, which was designed by Amanat Khan, was meant to drive home the message implicit in the building's form and location, that the tomb was an allegorical representation of the Throne of God above the gardens of Paradise on the Day of Judgment.[14] On both interior and exterior of the tomb, there is a continuous dado showing flowering plants in low relief [351]; the same motif is repeated in pietra dura on the two cenotaphs for Shahjahan and his wife and in red sandstone on the surrounding structures. The motif of the flowering plant was taken from engravings in European herbals and first appeared in Mughal art in a manuscript made for Jahangir ca. 1620; from the period of Shahjahan the motif became ubiquitous in all the arts produced for the Mughals.[15]

Shahjahan was also an active patron of palaces and mosques. Upon his accession, he ordered the fort at Agra renovated. The work, which was completed by 1637, included three major courts: a public space for audience (Divan-i Khass wa 'Am), an area for treasures and private audience, known today as the Machhi Bhavan, and a residential court, known today as the Garden of Grapes (Anguri Bagh). The first court is close to the entrance, while the latter two courts, used by the emperor and his entourage, overlook the river. The congregational mosque within the fort, known today as the Moti ("Pearl") Mosque from the translucent white marble used on the interior, was not

351. Agra, Taj Mahal, detail of dado

completed until 1653, after Shahjahan had moved the capital to Delhi. The mosque comprises a rectangular prayer hall (49 by 17 meters) divided by cruciform piers into three aisles of seven bays supported on cusped arches and surmounted by three bulbous domes. A larger version of the mosque built at Ajmer in 1636–7, the Moti Mosque at Agra uses an additive system of vaulted bays, the type of plan favoured for smaller mosques built under imperial patronage.

The single-aisled plan that had been used already for Shir Shah's mosque in Delhi [334] was preferred for large, urban congregational mosques, which have immense courtyards with narrow prayer halls fronted by *pīshṭāq*s and surmounted by three or five domes. The Mosque of Vazir Khan at Lahore [352, 353], built by the court physician Hakim ʿAli of Chiniot in 1634–5, is but one example of this group.[16] The paved rectangular court (51 by 39 meters) has four octagonal minarets in the corners and is surrounded on three sides by single-aisled arcades and on the fourth, or qibla, side by a triple-domed prayer hall with a monumental portal. The main entrance on the west is enlarged to house the domed octagonal chamber of a bazaar street. The mosque is constructed of brick, glazed tile, and stucco, and these traditional building materials of the Punjab set it apart from other Mughal mosques in northern India. The congregational mosque at Agra, for example, was built of red sandstone, with white marble used sparingly for calligraphic bands. Completed in 1648, under the patronage of the emperor's daughter Jahanara, the mosque has a similar but enlarged plan, where the bays of the wings of the prayer hall are doubled. Similarly, the congregational mosque built between 1650 and 1656 by the emperor at his new capital in Delhi, Shahjahanabad, is faced with red sandstone. There the prayer hall is flanked by slender minarets.

351. Agra, Taj Mahal, detail of dado

352. Lahore, Vazir Khan Mosque, 1634–5, plan and section

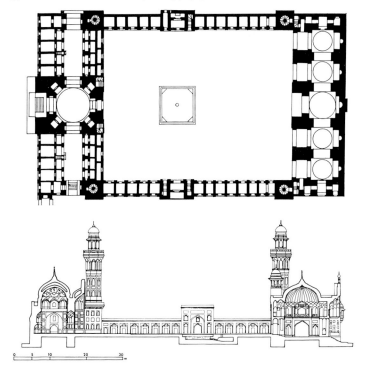

353. Lahore, Vazir Khan mosque

Shahjahanabad was laid out under the emperor's auspices from 1639 to 1648. An irregular semicircle set on high ground along the west bank of the Yamuna river, it covered much of the area of the fourteenth-century city of Firuzabad. The massive project was designed by Ahmad Lahawri, the chief architect of the Taj Mahal, and another architect, Hamid; Ghayrat Khan and later Makramat Khan, who also worked on the Taj Mahal, supervised construction. The walled city included broad avenues with water channels, markets, mosques, gardens, the houses of the nobility, and a fortified palace called Lal Qal'a ("Red Fort") after the high red sandstone wall that surrounded the white marble palaces and gardens on all but the river side. The fort, twice the size of the one at Agra, was laid out on a strict axial plan. A covered bazaar led from the Lahore Gate, the main entrance on the west, to a court in front of the hall for public audience (Divan-i 'Am). A pillared pavilion (57 by 21 meters) of red sandstone, it resembles the hall of public audience in the fort at Agra, but has a covered marble throne with baluster columns supporting a curved stone canopy. The wall behind

354. Delhi, Red Fort, 1639–48, Divan-i Khass

the throne is decorated with panels of black marble inlaid with colored stones in vegetal and floral patterns. The small panel behind and above the throne depicts *Orpheus Playing his Lyre* and is apparently of Florentine origin.[17] Further to the east in the fort, overlooking the river is a row of residential and administrative chambers arranged along a water channel. Most are flat-roofed, single-storied pavilions, built of marble or brick masonry covered with polished white plaster. They have small edicules at the corners of the roofs, and the façades consist of a row of cusped arches of equal size, supported by piers or pillars and protected by a broad eave. The most sumptuous are the women's quarters, originally known as the Imtiyaz Mahal but now called the Rang Mahal ("Painted Palace"), and the Divan-i Khass ("Private Audience Hall") [354]. These are decorated with paintings, pietra-dura inlay in gold and precious stones, and sumptuously carved marble.

Shahjahan, like his father, was a notable patron of gardens. Jahangir had developed Kashmir as a summer residence for the court: one of his first acts as emperor was to found a garden around the natural spring at Vernag south of Srinagar, and his visit there in 1620–1 initiated a flurry of garden construction. He ordered his son, Prince Khurram (later Shahjahan), to dam the stream around Shalimar on Lake Dal at Srinigar; the site, known as Farah Bakhsh ("Joy Giving"), became the lower garden of Shahjahan's famed Shalimar Garden. In 1634 Shahjahan added another quadripartite garden, named Fazd Bakhsh ("Bounty Giving"), to the north-east. The Mughal gardens in Kashmir are said to have numbered (an apocryphal) 777 in the time of Jahangir. Most have a central pavilion, the superb one at the Fazd Bakhsh built of the local black stone, over a spring whose water is collected in a canal forming the main axis of the garden. Terraces, ponds, branch canals, and pavilions are set along the waterway to take advantage of the sloping sites. The gardens contained nearly one hundred species of plants, including evergreens, screwpines and other trees, roses, violets, sunflowers, cockscombs, and several varieties of jasmine. They were not only enchanting places of repose but also yielded a substantial revenue in roses and musk mallow. In the eyes of contemporary French travelers, they were the equal of Versailles.[18]

Shahjahan's biggest garden foundation was the Bagh-i Fayd Bakhsh wa Farah Bakhsh, now known as the Shalimar Garden, at Lahore [355], completed in 1642–3. Inspired by its namesake in Kashmir, it is distinguished by its size and scale. Water was supplied by a canal linking the Ravi river to the city; it had been dug under 'Ali Mardan Khan, an Iranian nobleman and engineer who had defected to the Mughal court in 1638. The earlier scheme of two quadripartite gardens set along a central waterway was expanded by the insertion of a third terrace in the middle. The terrace contains a stupendous tank, more than sixty meters wide, which sparkles with jets from more than one hundred fountains. Cascades, nearly five meters high, link the units, and the visitor enters at the lowest terrace to progress, as in Mughal palaces, through successively private areas.

During Shahjahan's reign the Mughals penetrated deeper into the Deccan, and their successful campaign in 1636 forced the 'Adil Shahis to acknowledge Mughal suzerainty.

355. Lahore, Shalimar Gardens, completed 1642-3

357. Delhi, Moti Mosque, 1662, interior

Shahjahan then returned north to concentrate his attentions on his new capital at Shahjahanabad, and the young prince Awrangzib was appointed viceroy and commander-in-chief of Mughal forces in the Deccan. During the next two decades, the 'Adil Shahis at Bijapur enjoyed peace, and the dynasty's prosperity in the mid-seventeenth century is exemplified by the tomb for Muhammad 'Adil Shah [356]. Known as the Gol Gumbaz, it is the largest building constructed by the 'Adil Shahis and is striking for its formal simplicity. A gigantic hemispherical dome (exterior diameter 43.9 meters) rests on an almost cubical mass (47.4 meters square) with a staged octagonal turret at each corner. The dome is supported internally by arches set in intersecting squares. The floor area covered (1693 square meters) exceeds that of the Pantheon in Rome and at the time of its construction was the largest space in the world covered by a single dome. Such an elephantine construction was made possible in part by the exceptional tenacity of local mortar, used to hold together first rubble-and-plaster and then masonry of local stone, a very brittle trap. The main decora-

356. Bijapur, Tomb of Muhammad 'Adil Shah, 1656

tion on the exterior of the tomb is the great cornice (3.5 meters wide) supported by four courses of brackets and the ring of lotus petals at the base of the dome. Decoration apparently stopped at the patron's death in 1656, for the plastering is incomplete.

Awrangzib spent most of his reign (1658–1707) at war in the Deccan, and although Delhi remained the seat of Mughal administration in northern India, few buildings were constructed there. Shortly after his accession, the emperor ordered a small mosque added to the fort. It is known today as the Moti ("Pearl") Mosque, after the white marble used. The building follows the traditional form of small mosque and is a virtual copy of the Nagina Mosque that Shahjahan had built in the fort at Agra. Its decoration, however, is innovative, for the plain surfaces favored for religious buildings constructed under Shahjahan have been replaced by exuberant floral decor carved in relief [357]. Vases with stems of

358. Lahore, Badshahi Mosque, 1673–4

flowers fill the spandrels; spreading tendrils echo the cusps of the arches, which culminate in a fleur-de-lys. The decoration of this exquisite building shows that the realistic floral motif that had been typical of the Shahjahan period became increasingly abstract.

The most impressive building of Awrangzib's reign is the Badshahi ("Imperial") Mosque adjacent to the fort at Lahore [358]. Built under the supervision of his foster-brother Fida'i Khan Koka in 1673–4, it is the last in the series of great congregational mosques in red sandstone and is closely modeled on the congregational mosque that Shahjahan had built at Shahjahanabad. The red sandstone of the walls contrasts with the white marble of the domes and the subtle intarsia decoration. The materials depart from the local tradition of tile revetment, seen in the Mosque of Vizier Khan [352], and the cusped arches and arabesque floral patterns inlaid in white marble give the building, despite its vast proportions, a lighter appearance than the prototype.[19]

In the eighteenth century the patronage of architecture became increasingly independent of the Mughal court. The major new patrons were provincial rulers who proclaimed their defiance of the Mughals by copying their lifestyle and architecture. The Hindu Rajput princes of Amber, for example, had been allied militarily and through marriage to the Mughals since the time of Akbar, and their palace in the hilltop fortress incorporated such Mughal features as the Divan-i 'Am. With Mughal power on the wane, Maharaja Jai Singh II (r. 1699–1727) decided to expand from the cramped quarters to the dry lakebed on the plain below. The splendid new city was called Jaipur after its founder. The architect was Vidyadhar Chakravarti, a Bengali Brahmin who worked in the department of revenue and had already assisted in renovating the waterworks in nearby cities. The new city was laid out as a rectangle with seven unequal sectors arranged in a grid pattern with intersecting avenues, roads, lanes, and alleys. The main roads or bazaars are lined on each side with an equal number of shops of uniform size, shape, and façade. The central sector houses the palace complex with seven stories and multiple courts on the southern edge of a quadripartite garden, which housed the temple of the ruler's personal deity, Govinda Deva. In addition to public buildings, residential quarters, ateliers, and offices, the palace includes an astronomical observatory [359] called Jantar Mantar, from the Sanskrit Yantrasala, literally storehouse of machines. The observatory, built

359. Jaipur, Jantar Mantar, 1734

360. Delhi, Tomb of Safdarjang, 1754

in 1734, is an assemblage of thirteen structures of rather futuristic appearance, which are actually complex astronomical instruments built of stone and masonry, including a hemispherical and an equinoctial sundial. Like the Timurid ruler Ulughbeg (see Chapter 4) Jai Singh used these huge instruments to construct astronomical tables.

The best example of architecture in the late Mughal period is the tomb of Safdarjang [360], built at Delhi in 1753–4 for the second ruler (*nawāb*) of Oudh (Avadh). The nawabs, of Iranian origin, had entered the service of the Mughals in 1713; within ten years they were appointed governors of the province of Avadh, and by 1775 they had made it the most important principality in north India.[20] Loosely modeled on the tomb of Humayun [336], it is the last great example of the classical type of Mughal mausoleum, in which a walled quadripartite garden contains a podium supporting a building of the *hasht-bihisht* type. The proportions of the model have been changed in favor of a new esthetic, in which the small pointed dome with a constricted neck emphasizes the sense of verticality and attenuation. The building is revetted on the exterior with small panels of fawn and rose sandstone and white marble and on the interior with sculpted plaster. The increased attention to inlaid decoration, for example on the corner towers, with diminutive designs of white marble cut in intricate shapes, tends to overwhelm the structural massing. The trend towards florid ornamentation, the preference for bulbous shapes, and the increased use of stucco is characteristic of the late eighteenth century. This style was adopted throughout the Indian subcontinent from the Himalyas to Mysore and from the Punjab to Bengal, and even traveled as far as England [387].

369. Fragment of a animal carpet, Lahore, ca. 1600. Wool pile on cotton foundation. The Burrell Collection, Glasgow

Mughal period, and their designs were often copied in many of the other arts produced in royal ateliers. A network of imperial workshops (Pers. *kārkhāna*) produced everything from coins to textiles and funishings for the imperial household. In 1562–3 Akbar reintroduced gold coins to India, after a hiatus of more than a century. In 1577 the mint was reorganized, and the artist 'Abd al-Samad was made supervisor of the mint at Fatehpur. Square coins were introduced, and they supplanted round ones within two years. Akbar's standard gold coin, the mohur [368], weighs eleven grams and has the profession of faith on the obverse and the emperor's name, the mint, and the date on the reverse. Finely cut dies for striking gold coins were prepared by skilled engravers who even included poetic texts. The large flowing calligraphy, with deeply cut letters carefully piled on top of each other, attests to the art of the die-cutters.[25]

Many of the workshops, which were administered as part of the emperor's extensive household, produced textiles, furnishings, and carpets. Carpet-weaving is not native to India, as the hot damp climate makes woolen pile rugs both impractical and unnecessary as floor coverings, and this Iranian and Central Asian art was introduced there only under the Mughals. The first documentary evidence of carpet production dates to the reign of Akbar, who probably imported weavers from Herat. One of the earliest pieces attributed to Mughal patronage is an animal carpet with a red ground [369].[26] Coarsely woven on a cotton warp with wool weft, it has some six knots to the square centimeter. Rather than an overall pattern, the fragments show such recurring elements as a six-headed bird and a leopard mask with menacing fangs loosely connected to an arabesque. On the basis of technical and stylistical similarities to imperial carpets produced at Lahore in the seventeenth century, the carpet has been attributed there.[27] The coarse weaving might suggest that it was the product of a workshop set up after Akbar's move there in 1585, although its enormous size indicates that it was by no means the first product. The unusual design of this animal carpet may have been inspired by a similar design visible on an inhabited scroll depicted behind Timur's head in a painting showing *Timur Granting Audience* from the copy of the *Ẓafarnāma* made for Husayn Bayqara and later in Akbar's library.[28] The quality of carpets

produced in India soon improved, for a similar carpet with a more conventional arrangement of scrolling arabesques, whose leaves and bracts are replaced by animal heads, is more finely woven.[29]

Akbar's love of illustrated books spurred other court patrons to establish ateliers and commission luxury manuscripts. 'Abd al-Rahim Khan-i Khanan (1561–1626/7), commander-in-chief of the Mughal armies under Akbar and Jahangir, employed some twenty artists over nearly three decades, and at least seven manuscripts can be attributed to his atelier.[30] In 1597 he commissioned a splendid illustrated copy of the Hindu epic, the *Rāmāyana*, in imitation of the one that Akbar had ordered.[31] The manuscript was completed in 1605. Of the 130 paintings, the ones at the beginning of the manuscript are close in style to those produced in the imperial workshops, although 'Abd al-Rahim's artists used the simpler compositions and brighter colors of traditional Indian painting. The depiction of *Rama and Lakshonana Fighting the Demoness Taraka* by the artist Mushfiq [370],

370. Mushfiq: *Rama and Lakshman Fight the Demoness Taraka* from a *Rāmāyana*, 1597–1605. Washington, DC, Freer Gallery of Art, MS. 07.271, f. 35v

for example, shows the two heroes confronting the giant demoness in an elaborate landscape setting. The pink rocky outcroppings and cloud-streaked sky relate to imperial work, but the demoness is painted a vibrant combination of blue and orange and the two heroes are shown in profile and wear skirts of bright yellow and red.

Akbar's son Salim, the future Jahangir, was another prominent patron of illustrated manuscripts at the end of the sixteenth century. According to Salim's memoirs, the Iranian painter Aqa Riza joined the prince's service when the painter emigrated to India sometime before his son Abu'l-Hasan was born in the palace in 1588–9.[32] When Salim went into exile at Allahabad at the beginning of the seventeenth century, he took his atelier with him, and at least three fine manuscripts are known to have been produced for him there.[33] Like the poetic texts made for Akbar in the late 1590s [367], these works show Salim's preference for small books with fewer and finer illustrations, often by a single artist. They also show the new interest in portraiture, for there are several portraits of the prince, who is shown witnessing a polo game and hunting deer. This interest was shared by Akbar, for his biographer Abu'l-Fazl reported that the emperor had the likenesses taken of his chief nobles and bound in albums. The practice of collecting specimens of calligraphy and painting in albums was already well established under the Safavids (see Chapter 12), and the Mughal emperors continued and refined the art.

While only a few of the imperial portraits commissioned by Akbar are known, two of Salim's albums have survived and are the earliest and greatest of Mughal albums. The Gulshan Album in the Imperial Library, Tehran, contains works dated between 1600 and 1609, and the album in the Staatsbibliothek, Berlin, contains works dated between 1609 and 1618.[34] Both albums contain portraits, genre scenes, animal and flower studies, Persian and Deccani works, European paintings and prints, and Mughal versions of them. The paintings are uniformly high in quality, although Jahangir's atelier was smaller than his father's. Lesser painters went to seek work elsewhere, and the remaining masters were more specialized. Such artists as Manohar, Dawlat, and Bishan Das did portraits, Abu'l-Hasan large court scenes, and Mansur nature subjects. As in earlier albums, two facing pages of calligraphy, mainly by the renowned Persian calligraphers Mir 'Ali (d. 1558) and Sultan 'Ali Mashhadi (d. 1520), were succeeded by two pages with illustrations. All the folios are bordered by extraordinary marginal decoration painted in gold with polychrome washes: the calligraphic pages have figural borders, and the illustrated pages have floral or abstract motifs. Fine gold-painted borders had already been used in manuscripts made in the 1590s [367], but in the borders of the Jahangir albums, figures became increasingly prominent and are emphasized with color and modeling. These borders contain many of the greatest Mughal portraits and are often signed. The album borders include a wide range of subjects, such as animals and hunting scenes, European themes, and studies of shaykhs and holy men, courtiers, and workmen. Some of the scenes were copied from earlier works: the Gulshan Album, for example, includes Dawlat's copy of Bihzad's portrait of the Persian mystical poet Jami on folio 140. One of the finest

371. Page from an album made for Jahangir, 1608–18. 26.8 by 15.8 cm. Washington, DC, Freer Gallery of Art

372. Bichitr: *Jahangir Preferring a Sufi to Kings*, from an album made for Jahangir, ca. 1615–20. 27.5 × 18.1 cm. Washington, DC, Freer Gallery of Art

pages in the Berlin Album shows the young Akbar presenting a book to Humayun in a tree-platform; it is a copy of ʿAbd al-Samad's painting in the same album [361].[35] Other scenes were drawn from palace life. The recto of a detached folio [371], for example, has calligraphy by Mir ʿAli and marginal drawings depicting six artists preparing books in a landscape with hills, trees, and flowers.[36] The marginal paintings on the detached page show different stages in the production of books and related objects, and the Berlin Album contains a verso page (folio 18) whose margins show that it would have been the facing page.

The interest in portraiture continued throughout Jahangir's reign, as did a growing interest in European techniques and motifs. The English were frequent visitors to the Mughal court after 1600, the year the East India Company was granted a charter, and English examples provided the general prototypes for Mughal allegorical portraits. Bichitr's painting of *Jahangir Preferring a Sufi Shaykh to Kings* [372], removed from a sumptuous album in St Petersburg, shows

the emperor presenting a book to the aged Shaykh Husayn, descendant of Muʿin al-Din Chishti and superintendent of his shrine at Ajmer, where Jahangir lived from 1613 to 1616. Three men crowd into the lower left: a Turkish sultan, who seems to be a general type drawn from a European representation rather than a specific portrait by an Ottoman painter; King James I of England, who is copied from an English painting by John de Critz, which was probably presented to the Mughal court by the English ambassador, Sir Thomas Roe; and a Hindu who is holding a painting of himself bowing. This third and smallest figure seems to be a self-portrait of the painter, a well-known portraitist. Such self-portraits were an established visual conceit in Mughal painting [cf. 361]. Many of the motifs in the painting, such as the putti, hourglass, and halo, are allegorical elements assimilated from European painting. The painting is thought to symbolize the emperor's choice of spiritual life over worldly power and allude to the source of Mughal dynastic power by association with mystical orders.[37] In the second

373. *Sultan Ibrahim 'Adil Shah II in a Fantastic Landscape*, Bijapur, ca. 1610. 17 × 10.2 cm. London, British Museum

uce an atmosphere of languor and lyricism. The earliest, most original, and briefest flowering of painting took place in the northern Deccan at Ahmadnagar, capital of the Nizam Shahi sultans. A second school of painting flourished at Golconda under the Qutb Shahis (1512–1687), who were descended from a Qaraqoyunlu Turkoman commander. The Iranian antecedents of the dynasty and the close contacts they maintained with Iran serve to explain the Persianate style of many of the works produced there in the sixteenth century. A third school of painting flourished at Bijapur, and the large body of surviving work allows a reconstruction of its development from the mid-sixteenth century to the late seventeenth. The finest work was made for Ibrahim 'Adil Shah II (r. 1579–1627), probably the most brilliant patron in the Deccan. A portrait done in the 1610s [373] depicts the sultan in a fantastic landscape.[39] The castanets in his left hand signify his devotion to music. He wears pink breeches cut in Portuguese style and a transparent robe which flutters in the breeze. His hooked nose, known from other portraits, has been straightened to produce a sensual and idealized image. The expressive power and technical refinement in such a painting rival work made at the Safavid and Mughal courts.

THE ARTS UNDER THE LATER MUGHALS (1628–1858) AND THEIR CONTEMPORARIES

During the reign of Shahjahan (1628–58), much of the court's attention and artistic interest shifted to the patronage of architecture (see Chapter 18), and the royal painting atelier continued to shrink in size from its apogee under Akbar. Although a few copies of poetic texts were illustrated, the paintings are restricted to narrow horizontal bands in the middle of the page. Full-page paintings were still made for albums. One compiled early in the reign of Shahjahan is known as the Minto Album, after its former owner, the Earl of Minto, Governor General of India from 1807 to 1813.[40] A somewhat later one, known as the Late Shahjahan Album, was dispersed in the early twentieth century.[41] Other albums were broken up in the nineteenth century, and both the Wantage and Kevorkian Albums have paintings from the early part of Shahjahan's reign reassembled alongside later Mughal works.[42]

The great painters from the beginning of the century, such as Bichitr and Balchand, were still active in the 1640s, and most of the works in these albums done in the beginning of Shahjahan's reign are portraits, which are usually mounted within illuminated borders decorated with flowers with heavy gold outlining. The naturalism that had been apparent in the borders of the Jahangir albums [371] became increasingly stiff and formal, especially in the Late Shahjahan Album, which contains paintings mainly from the 1650s, mounted in borders decorated with full-colored figures set against a background of flowers done in lightly brushed gold. Unlike the albums made for Jahangir, in which figural borders were limited to calligraphic pages, in the Late Shahjahan Album the figures in the borders are often associated with the personality or accomplishments of the sitter in the main portrait. In this page from the Late Shahjahan Album,

half of Jahangir's reign, the narrative context of earlier portraits showing darbars and other contemporary events was often replaced by such allegorical portraits of majestic figures isolated against lavish symbols of their wealth and power. Another painting detached from the album in St Petersburg depicts an imaginary meeting between Jahangir and the Safavid 'Abbas I.[38]

The model furnished by the Mughals in northern India was copied elsewhere in the subcontinent, particularly in the Deccan, where a parallel but independent style of painting developed. Many of the works identified as Deccani are single paintings and portraits destined for albums, but unlike Mughal paintings, few Deccani works record historical events or portray their subjects realistically. Princely portraits predominate. They show conventional poses, but are distinguished by fantastic color and distorted forms, which prod-

374. *Shahjahan Holding a Jewel*, f. 23v from the Late Shah Jahan Album, ca. 1645. 36.7 × 23.8 cm. Los Angeles County Museum of Art

375. Balchand: *Jahangir Bids Farwell to Khurram at the Beginning of a Military Campaign* from a *Pādshāhnāma*, 1656–57. Windsor, Royal Library, MS. HB 149, f. 43v

the central portrait of *Shahjahan Holding a Jewel* [374] is echoed in the marginal figures of his courtiers, who are also shown in strict profile. The application of color and line to paper is immensely controled, but the warmth and sympathy of the earlier portraits have given way to a glittering jewel-like surface.

The finest paintings from the reign of Shahjahan are found in an imperial copy of the *Pādshāhnāma* ("History of the Emperor").[43] The single extant volume, covering the first decade of the emperor's reign and illustrated with forty-four full-page paintings, was copied by Muhammad Amin al-Mashhadi in 1656–7. Another dozen paintings may have been prepared for subsequent volumes which were never completed because of the emperor's deposition in 1658, but the complicated history of the text and the paintings remains to be unraveled.[44] The paintings, like the text, emphasize formal occasions, and many of the illustrations, such as Balchand's depiction on folio 43v of *Jahangir Bidding Farewell to his Son Khurram [later the Emperor Shahjahan] at the Beginning of a Military Campaign* [375], are formal court scenes in which the emperor is depicted as a superior being: he is shown in profile, haloed, and placed high on his throne platform above his courtiers, who stare across the empty space in the lower register. Faces were often drawn from

studies kept on file, and the necessity for accurate depiction is underscored by the labels identifying the participants. Some sections were done with pounces of perforated gazelle skin over which a fine charcoal dust was sprinkled. These records of formal occasions are static and stylized compositions, but the battle scenes, by contrast, show a greater technical development in the depiction of landscape and crowds. The artists were able to overcome the awkward spatial discontinuities seen in earlier work and control spatial recession by painterly means, blurring the figures in the distance so that they merge into background. The Windsor Castle copy of the *Pādshāhnāma* is the last great manuscript made for the Mughal emperors; in it the technique of portraiture is at its most brilliant, and disparate Indian and European elements are blended into a harmonious whole.

The same unity of disparate elements drawn from a wide variety of sources can be seen in *objets d'art* made during the reign of Shahjahan, such as a splendid wine cup carved of white nephrite [377].[45] It is inscribed with the date

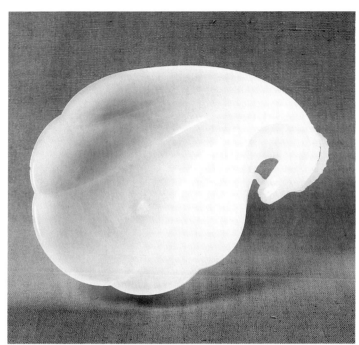

377. Wine cup, 1656–7. White nephrite. L 18.7 cm; W 14 cm. London, Victoria and Albert Museum

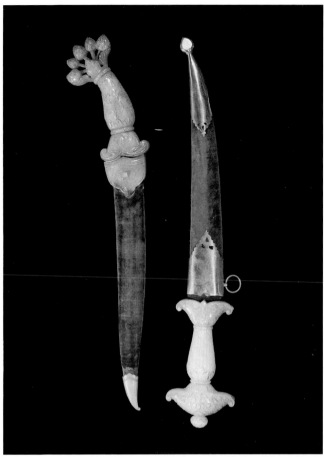

378. Dagger and scabbard, late seventeenth century. National Trust, Powis Castle

1067 (1656–7) and the emperor's title "Second Lord of the Conjunction," an epithet taken in homage to his illustrious ancestor Timur, who was "Lord of the Conjunction." The wine cup is probably the most exquisite hardstone object made for the Mughals and is notable for its superb design and craftsmanship. The basic form of the cup, a halved fruit or gourd, is borrowed from the Chinese repertory, while such features as the scroll handle ending in a goat's head, acanthus leaf decoration, and prominent foot are European in origin. The flowering lotus blossom at the base is characteristic of Hindu art, while the realistic portrayal of natural forms is typical of Mughal art.

Equally fine craftsmanship can be seen in the best textiles and rugs produced under Shahjahan. The Aynard prayer rug [376] has the deep coloring typical of Mughal carpets and the design of a large flowering plant within a lobed niche.[46] Its fine workmanship has been identified as representing the kind of imperial work produced at Lahore.[47] The rug is knotted of woolen pile on silk warps and wefts and has 174 asymmetrical knots per square centimeter, nearly thirty times as many as in the earlier woolen carpet with animal designs [369]. Such fine weaving, combined with the lustrous wool, the same type used in making Kashmir shawls, gives the effect of a sumptuous velvet rather than a wool rug. The piece (90 by 125 cm) was possibly part of a larger prayer rug with multiple arches, as it has been repaired at the center with pieces of identical make and similar design, and the width and pattern of the borders are consistent

376. Aynard prayer rug, Lahore, second quarter of the seventeenth century. Wool pile on silk foundation. 125 × 90 cm. Lugano, Thyssen-Bornemisza Collection

with a multiple prayer rug. Like the wine cup made for the emperor, the design incorporates chinoiserie motifs, such as the stylized rocks and ground at the bottom of the niche and the clouds inserted as space fillers between the flowers and the edge of the field. Floral designs were probably taken from European herbals, which circulated at the Mughal court in the early seventeenth century. As in Ottoman art of the mid-sixteenth century, the flowering plant became an important motif in Mughal art and crafts from the mid-seventeenth century and can be traced in many media from architectural revetment (e.g. the marble friezes on the Taj Mahal [351] and the fort at Agra Fort) to carpets and textiles.

The great age of imperial patronage came to an end under Awrangzib (r. 1658–1707), who withdrew from active patronage of the arts. Book illustration reached a technical and stylistic plateau, as artists retreated from realism, reverted to more traditional concepts of composition, and produced simplified, rather lifeless portraits. In 1680, when the orthodox ruler banned music and painting at his court, many Mughal painters moved to the employ of provincial governors and nobles. The floral naturalism typical of Shahjahan's reign became more stylized, and objects became increasingly showy rather than practical. Gemstones, cut and polished as cabuchons or carved, were lavishly inset into objects of precious metal or jade. Daggers and their scabbards [378]

379. Covered jar, ca. 1700. Cloisonné enamel on gold. H 14.3 cm. Cleveland Museum of Art

Other techniques popular in the later Mughal period, such as pietra dura inlay and the cutting of cameos, were also introduced by Europeans, but there is one technique peculiar to India. Bidri ware is a type of metalware whose name is derived from Bidar in the Deccan, where the technique is thought to have originated. Objects are cast from an alloy of zinc with an admixture of copper, tin, and lead. They are then inlaid with silver or brass, occasionally with gold, and subsequently coated with a paste of mud containing sal ammoniac. When the coating is removed and the piece polished, the base metal is left a rich matte black which provides a foil to the shiny inlay. The technique was developed by the early seventeenth century, for Bidri wares are commonly depicted in Deccani paintings from the second half of the century. By the eighteenth century, the technique had spread from Bidar to several centers in northern India such as Purnea, Lucknow, and Murshidabad.[51] It was used for a wide variety of forms, including bowls, ewers, covered boxes, and salvers, but one of the most common is the base for a water pipe or huqqa [380]. These bottles could be spherical or bell-shaped and were often decorated with floral designs. The design, of four cusped cartouches enclosing flowering plants with silver flowers and brass leaves, follows the general style of Mughal floral motifs, but the plants are stiff and formalized compared with the naturalistic ones favored under Shahjahan.

380. Huqqa base, Deccan or north India, second half of the seventeenth century. Zinc alloy inlaid with silver. H 18.6 cm; diameter 16.8 cm. London, Victoria and Albert Museum

were particularly elaborate. The blades are watered steel, sometimes decorated with several colors of gold. The hilts are crystal or jade and are inset with rubies, emeralds, and diamonds in gold. The scabbards are covered with red velvet with lockets and chapes of jeweled jade or gilt.

New decorative techniques were introduced to India by European craftsmen. European jewelers such as Augustin of Bordeaux served the Mughal court, and these Europeans probably introduced such new techniques as enameling. One of the few early pieces to survive is a gold thumb ring chased and inset with rubies, with enameled decoration in white, blue, pale green, and black on the interior.[48] The ring can be dated to the beginning of the seventeenth century, for it is identical in shape to the jade thumb ring made for Jahangir.[49] Indian craftsmen soon learned the technique of enameling and expanded the repertory. A gold jar and cover made ca. 1700 [379] has decoration in champlevé/basse-taille enamel showing a white trellis against a translucent green ground, with details in translucent yellow. The white flowers on the lid are highlighted in pink, an early example of pink painted enamel.[50]

381. Wall panel from Tipu Sultan's chintz tent, Burhanpur, mid-eighteenth century. Coarse cotton, printed, painted and dyed. 6.30 m square. National Trust, Powis Castle

Of all the arts produced in India, probably the best-known and most varied is textiles. India had been famed since Antiquity as a source for fine textiles, but under the Mughals production of luxury fabrics was encouraged. The finest pieces from the early Mughal period are plain, but in textiles, as in the other arts, the naturalistic flowering plant motif became the dominant theme from the mid-seventeenth century, and the sumptuous gold- and silver-ground textiles with embroidered or woven flowering plants produced under Shahjahan are often taken to epitomize the culture of the Mughal court. Paintings from the late seventeenth century show that "cloth of gold" ground textiles were lavishly used for furnishings and costume. Garments in the imperial wardrobe or store (Pers. *tushkhāna*) were classified according to the date of entry, which was recorded, sometimes with other information, on a label tacked onto the piece. Such rich textiles were also used for furnishings. According to a description by François Bernier, who accompanied a progress of Awrangzib from Delhi to Lahore and Kashmir in 1665, the royal apartments consisted of large and elaborate tents, some with an upper story. They were set in a great square and walled in by textile panels or screens (Pers. *qanat*) two to three meters high. On the outside these screens were usually red, the imperial color, and on the inside they were lined with printed chintz representing vases of flowers.[52]

The trappings and ceremonial of the imperial court was often copied by princes and provincial patrons, whether Muslim or Hindu. The Rajput princes of Amber and Jaipur in Rajasthan, who took service with the Mughals, emulated their way of life and established workshops and stores. A number of tent-hangings of cotton embroidered with silk and silver-gilt thread and of velvet stenciled and painted with gum and gold leaf are said to belonged to the store there in the seventeenth or eighteenth century.[53] Tipu Sahib, sultan of Mysore from 1782 to 1799, also had a large wardrobe/store, which included a tent of fine chintz. It was made at Burhanpur (Madhya Pradesh), a city in central India to the south of Malwa, which, along with Agra and Sironj in northern India, was known for the finest tent-hangings. The complete tent includes wall panels and a roof of printed, painted, and dyed cotton. The wall panels [381], approximately 6.30 meters square, have a white ground with a row of niches enclosing vases of flowers, executed mainly in reds and greens. A band of black and white merlons runs along the top, and other leaf and floral borders divide the compartments. The roof segments are painted with similar vases and flowers and edged with a band of red and white patchwork. The outside of the tent is a separate layer of coarse whitish cotton. It is probably the "tent of fine chintz" in which Lord Cornwallis and his entourage were received by Tipu's two small sons, the hostage princes, on 27 February 1792.[54]

Painting flourished in the independent states established in the Deccan, Bengal, and Oudh after the collapse of effective Mughal rule following Awrangzib's death in 1707. Nadir Shah's sack of Delhi in 1739 meant that many of the imperial treasures, including such fine manuscripts as the Gulshan Album, were taken to Iran, and many of the artists still in the imperial atelier sought work in the provinces. Nevertheless, the imperial studio was not entirely abolished, for during the twilight of the Mughal empire in the early nineteenth century the remains of the imperial studio in Delhi produced illustrated manuscripts in luxury format. Many were copies of the histories of Shahjahan's reign, and it was at this time that earlier copies of the same texts, such as one of the manuscripts of the *Bāburnāma* made for Àbkar and the Windsor Castle copy of *Pādshāhnāma*, were refurbished. These manuscripts were apparently designed for presentation to Europeans, who were fascinated by the pomp and state of the Mughals and their buildings. Paintings in the nineteenth-century copies of the *Pādshāhnāma* depict such great architectural monuments commissioned by Shahjahan as the Taj Mahal and the Red Fort, and later manuscripts of this type, such as a copy of Muhammad Salih Kanbu's history of Shahjahan known as '*Amal-i ṣāliḥ*, even depict Europeans admiring Mughal monuments.[55]

Some commercial centers became identified with specific exports, and thus Kashmir was famed for its shawls, Golconda for its chintzes, Gujarat for its overlaid mother-of-pearl wares [382] and carved wood, and Cambay for its hardstone carving.[56] A distinctive style of illustrated manuscripts, apparently produced for export, developed in Kashmir.[57] A copy of the *Shāhnāma* copied at Rajur in 1719 has been identified as an early example of the folk style of illustrated manuscripts that flourished in the eighteenth and nineteenth centuries.[58] Most of the texts are the classics of Persian poetry, such as Nizami, Sa'di, and Hafiz. Kashmir was famed for its production of paper, and the manuscripts are copied on fine paper, which is burnished and sprinkled with gold. The folios are decorated with lavish floral borders in gold, blue, and pink, some of the richest illumination

382. Storage chest, Gujerat, early seventeenth century. Wood overlaid with mother-of-pearl and black lacquer. H. 54 cm, L. 109 cm. Copenhagen, David Sammlung

383. *Hafiz and the Beauty* from Hafiz, *Dīvān*, Kashmir, 1796–7. 6.7 × 5.4 cm. St. Petersburg, Saltykov-Shchedrin State Public Library, MS. 386, f. 108r

found in India. The many small paintings [383] are usually enclosed by the text. The simple but busy compositions often include a group of people in front of a white pavilion set in a landscape. Persian figures, such as the figure of Hafiz on the left, are set in three-quarter profile, while Indian figures, such as the Beauty on the right, are set in full profile. Details of dress and textiles are often picked out in bright red or orange, a series of colored hills is used to show recession in space, and the horizon is often dotted with tall fir trees set against a slate-blue sky. Finally, the books were bound in finely patterned leather or painted and varnished bindings. This style of illustrated manuscript had a direct impact on the arts of the book in Central Asia, as illustrated books from Kashmir were commonly exported there.

CHAPTER 20

The Legacies of Later Islamic Art

The European conquests that end the period this volume covers are sometimes marked by precise events, such as Napoleon's expedition to Egypt in 1798 or the French seizure of Algeria in 1832. In other areas, European political and economic domination was more gradual, as in India, where Clive's victory at the battle of Plassey in Bengal in 1757 led to a slow consolidation of power by the British East India Company and eventually to the establishment of direct colonial rule in 1858. The power of traditional patrons to commission works of art was severely limited, and the colonial masters appropriated Mughal traditions for their own imperial ends.[1] In Turkey, the Ottoman sultans retained ostensible political power into the twentieth century, although for centuries European powers had forced them to make economic concessions (the capitulations) and carved off pieces of the Empire (Greece, for example, declared its independence in 1822). In Iran, despite the increasing impact of Western technologies, such as lithography and photography, a distinctive artistic tradition was maintained under the patronage of the Qajar rulers well into the twentieth century.[2]

The West's discovery of the art and architecture of the Islamic lands, its impact there in the nineteenth and twentieth centuries, and the integration and substitution of European ideas and materials for indigenous ones in the same period are important and interrelated subjects which this book can only briefly address. The wealth of information available has just begun to be studied, and these topics demand full and independent treatment elsewhere. In the present context the topics discussed and illustrated should be seen merely as possible directions for future research.

THE IMPACT OF ISLAMIC ART ON THE WEST

The idea of a tradition of Islamic architecture and art which began in Syria in the seventh century and grew to encompass the architecture and art of the lands from the Atlantic to the Indian Ocean is a creation of late-nineteenth- and twentieth-century Western thought, for there is no evidence that any artist or patron mentioned in the preceding chapters ever thought of his art as Islamic.[3] Such all-embracing terms as "Mohammedan" or "Islamic" and "Moslem/Muslim" came to be applied commonly to the culture only in the nineteenth century, when they increasingly replaced such restrictive geographic or ethnic terms as "Indian" (or "Hindoo"), "Persian," "Turkish," "Arab," and "Moorish," which had been applied to styles previously thought distinct. In the twentieth century the tradition of an Islamic art has been increasingly elaborated, not least with the encouragement

or under the sponsorship of a re-empowered region and religion. In addition to the taxonomic tasks of description and classification, much recent work has been devoted to searching for and explaining the unifying principles behind this art, be they geometry or arabesque. At the close of the twentieth century, scholarly opinion has come not quite full circle from the early nineteenth, for in addition to recognizing the common heritage of much, if not all, Islamic civilization, it is also increasingly cognizant of the distinct regional variations. It is, therefore, meaningless to seek to explain the Alhambra and the Taj Mahal in one breath.

The invention of a tradition of Islamic art was a product of European interest in the region where Islam held (and holds) sway. An interest in European diplomatic history led scholars, particularly continental ones, into Ottoman studies; the British interest in India encouraged a scholarly interest in Islam in the subcontinent and then in neighboring Persia, while in the nineteenth century French colonial interest in North Africa (French) led French scholars in that direction. Semitists were interested largely in Cairo, capital city of the Arab world, but also in neighboring Syria.[4] Until the nineteenth century European familiarity with the Islamic world, and particularly its architecture and art, was limited by the relatively few images available.

Islamic manuscripts had been collected in the West with a view to recovering lost classical texts, and there was a sporadic acquaintanceship there with Islamic architecture and art. A painting such as *The Reception of a Venetian Embassy in Damascus* (Paris, Louvre), attributed to the school of Bellini in the early sixteenth century, was undoubtedly the work of someone familiar with the topography and monuments of Damascus, but it had no discernible impact on the history of Western architecture.[5] Similarly, Rembrandt owned a collection of some two dozen Mughal and Deccani paintings, which he copied before being forced to sell them in 1656, but it can hardly be said that Indian miniatures had an appreciable impact on the course of European painting.[6]

The circulation of images of Islamic architecture in the first half of the eighteenth century increased the West's awareness of the tradition. The publication of Johann Bernhard Fischer von Erlach's general history of architecture, *Entwurff einer historischen Architektur* (Vienna, 1721), with representations of Arab, Turkish, and Persian architecture [384] taken from coins and the writings of travelers and archaeologists, spurred the design of several structures in a quasi-Oriental manner. Although Fischer von Erlach's sources were such public monuments as mosques, the resulting designs were almost exclusively for such civil structures as kiosks, pavilions, palaces, and theaters, all pertaining to an architecture of leisure with which the Orient was invariably associated. Frederick, Prince of Wales, commissioned the English architect Sir William Chambers (1723-

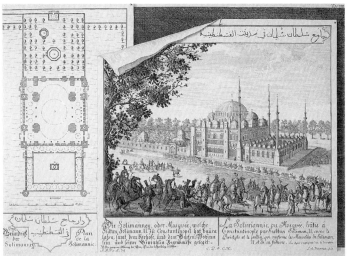

384. Ground plan of the Solimanny, or Moskee built at Constantinople by Sultan Soliman II, from Johann Bernhard Fischer von Erlach, *Entwurff einer historischen Architektur* (Vienna, 1721)

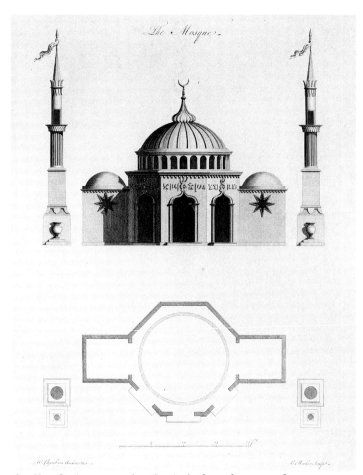

385. Kew Garden, octagonal pavilion in the form of a mosque, from William Chambers, *Plans, Elevations, Sections and Perspective Views of the Gardens and Buildings at Kew in Surrey* (London, 1763)

96) to design an "Alhambra" for the gardens at Kew in 1750. His rococo Gothic design of 1758 has absolutely nothing in common with its namesake save the paired slender columns that support it; they derive from a design for the pavilion submitted to the prince in 1750 by Johann Heinrich Muntz (1727-98), a Swiss artist who had actually visited Spain before setting in England.[7] In 1761 Chambers followed his Alhambra with an octagonal pavilion in the form of a mosque [385]; it was based on a free improvisation on the domed Ottoman mosques flanked by minarets illustrated by Fischer von Erlach. A pagoda completed the trio of exotic buildings in the Wilderness at Kew.[8] Chambers's designs were followed by such other architects as William Wrighte in his designs for Hartwell House in Buckinghamshire and Nikolaus von Pigage, who built a mosque-shaped pavilion in the gardens at Schwetzingen near Mannheim ca. 1780.[9] On a more common level, European visitors to Turkey became familiar with kiosks in public gardens where coffee and other beverages were served. Writing in 1717, Lady Mary Wortley Montagu, for example, described a kiosk raised on nine or ten steps and enclosed with gilded lattices, but other examples were more modest bowers, with shutters serving as walls in winter but removable in warm weather. From such descriptions a taste for kiosks developed in Europe, where they served not only in their original function as garden pavilions but also as refreshment, band- and news-stands.

The monuments of Muslim India provided inspiration for many British artists and architects. Tilly Kettle (1735–86), the first British artist in India, returned home with a sizable fortune, a fact that undoubtedly encouraged others to follow his tracks there. William Hodges (1746–97), in India between 1780 and 1783, was the first British artist to visit Agra, where he was smitten by the beauties of the Taj Mahal, which he drew and painted. Perhaps most influential was the English landscape painter Thomas Daniell (1749–1840), who went to India in 1784 accompanied by his nephew

William (1769–1837). Thomas Daniell returned a decade later and published *Oriental Scenery* in six folio-sized parts between 1795 and 1808. Each part has twenty-four hand-colored aquatint plates, which brought the unfamiliar and exotic scenes to a wide if not universal audience.[10] The popularity of these volumes led Daniell to publish a separate one with views of the Taj Mahal [386]. Even those who could not afford such books learned about the monuments of India from the views combined and reproduced on blue-and-white Staffordshire crockery and wallpaper.[11] Daniell's representations had an immediate and profound effect on the taste for orientalism: in 1803, when Samuel Pepys Cockerell designed Sezincote House in Gloucestershire for his brother Charles, a nabob in the East India Company who had known the Daniells in India, he employed Thomas Daniell as a consultant, and the house has such Oriental features as a bulbous dome with corner chatris and over-hanging eaves, cusped arches, and pinnacles.

Far more important were the Prince Regent's commissions at Brighton. Around 1803 the future George IV commissioned William Porden (ca. 1755–1822) to build royal stables and a riding house, which were finished five years later. In 1797 Porden had exhibited at the Royal Academy

386. The Taje Mahel, Agra, Taken in the Garden, from Thomas and William Daniell, *Views of the Taje Mahel at the City of Agra in Hindoostan taken in 1789*. Aquatint. London, India Office Library

"a design for a place of amusement in the style of the Mahometan architecture of Hindostan." In his design for Brighton, he offset the great mass of the central rotunda with angle pavilions crowned by chatris. For the Royal Pavilion [387], the Prince Regent commissioned the architect John Nash (1752–1835) to remodel an unfinished Palladian structure in an imaginative combination of Gothic, Chinese, and Indian elements. Nash borrowed four volumes of Daniell's *Oriental Scenery* for inspiration. Built between 1815 and 1822, the pavilion has a large central ogival dome offset by four subsidiary domes. The Oriental fantasy extended as far as the kitchens, where iron palm trees with copper fronds support the roof, but Nash used the latest technology, such as cast-iron ceiling frames and columns. In addition to giving the royal nod to the Oriental mode, the building set the style for glazed conservatories with bulbous domes.

Spain was the most accessible country with exotic buildings. Already in the second half of the eighteenth century, the Real Academia de San Fernando had sent the architects Juan de Villanueva and Pedro Arnal to make drawings of

387. Brighton, Royal Pavilion, 1815–22

Granada and Córdoba under the direction of Joseph de Hermosilla; they were published in 1780 as *Antiguedades árabes de Espana*.[12] As the country was increasingly visited by seekers of the picturesque, the Alhambra penetrated into the verbal and visual imagination of the West.[13] James Cavanah Murphy, who was in Spain from 1802 to 1809, published *The Arabian Antiquities of Spain* (London, 1813), based on the *Antiguedades*, and he was soon followed there by such European and American literati and aristocrats as Chateaubriand, Victor Hugo, Washington Irving, and Théophile Gautier, who wrote glowingly of their travels. These verbal accounts were paralleled by visual ones: Girault de Prangey visited Spain in 1832–3 and four years later published his *Souvenirs de Grenade et de l'Alhambra* (Paris, 1836–7), followed by *Monuments arabes et moresques de Cordoue, Séville et Grenade* (Paris, 1839), which actually deals only with Córdoba and Seville. A few years later he produced *Essai sur l'architecture des Arabes et des Mores, en Espagne, en Sicile, et en Barbarie* (Paris, 1841), which introduced North African monuments in Tunis, Algiers, and Bône. Jules Goury and Owen Jones drew the Alhambra in 1834; Goury died, leaving Jones to continue, and he returned alone in 1837. Their work *Plans, Elevations, Sections, and Details of the Alhambra* (London, 1836–45) in two atlas folios was conceived as a pattern book for architects.[14]

Owen Jones designed two palatial houses in Kensington Palace Gardens, London, in the Moorish style, and in 1854 he created an Alhambra Court, following the Court of the Lions, for the reconstructed Crystal Palace at Sydenham. It featured individual elements at full scale, although the whole was somewhat smaller than the original. In 1856 the Royal Panopticon, designed by Thomas Hayter Lewis (1818–96), opened on Leicester Square in London. Designed in a Moorish style, with two (vaguely Mamluk) minarets flanking a polychrome façade and an interior enlivened with polychromy and horseshoe arcades, the building was transformed two years later into the "Alhambra" music-hall, which it remained for some twenty-five years, undoubtedly setting the style for a host of other theaters and music-halls in an orientalizing mode in Britain and North America.[15]

Orientalism in architecture was paralleled in painting, particularly in France.[16] Some of the earliest and finest examples of this genre were produced by Eugène Delacroix (1798–1863), who had been to Morocco in 1832 with the Comte de Mornay, whom Louis Philippe had sent as ambassador extraordinary to the sultan after France occupied Algiers. Delacroix's seven sketchbooks record his six-month trip from Tangiers to Meknes and provided material for his later works.[17] His opportunity to visit a harem, apparently the dream of almost every nineteenth-century man, resulted in a picture such as his *Femmes d'Alger*, painted two years later in 1834 [388]. It combines first-hand knowledge with an imaginative facility to evoke an idealized and languorous Orient. Twenty years after his trip, Delacroix noted in his journal that he "began making something passing out of my trip to [North] Africa only after I had forgotten all the little details and, in my pictures, retained only the striking and poetic side."[18] By contrast, his contemporary J. A. D. Ingres (1780–1867), who never ventured beyond Rome, appropriated details gleaned from publications to create a more

388. Eugene Delacroix: *Les Femmes d'Alger*, 1834. Oil on canvas. 1.8 × 2.3 m. Paris, Louvre

explicit, but ultimately less sensuous, image of the imaginary East.[19]

Frederic Church (1826–1900), the foremost American landscape painter of the mid-nineteenth century, developed a reputation from the mid-1840s for precisely detailed New World landscapes on an epic scale. Following his only tour to Europe, Palestine, and Syria in 1867–9, Church complemented his paintings of the western hemisphere with a sequence of Mediterranean compositions, including scenes of Jerusalem and Petra. His trip filled him with enthusiasm for Islamic architecture, and after 1870 he devoted most of his life to the design, construction, and furnishing of his mansion at Greendale-on-Hudson, New York [389]. Built between 1870 and 1872, with additions over the next decade and a studio wing constructed in 1888–9, the residence was called Olana, from the Arabic ῾alānā, "our [place] on high". Calvert Vaux served as consulting architect. Church did not rely on his own experience but also culled inspiration from published works on Islamic architecture, and the house combined Alhambra motifs, simplified Hindu detail, and

Persian tilework. He owned a copy of *Monuments modernes de la Perse* (Paris, 1867) by Pascal Xavier Coste (1787–1879), and such features at Olana as the piazza columns and the stencils in the Court Hall are based on Persian motifs known through Coste's work.

In addition to books and paintings, the international exhibitions which proliferated in the second half of the nineteenth century were a primary means for disseminating knowledge about the arts and crafts of the Islamic lands.[20] The Great Exhibition of 1851 had been held by the Society of Arts under the presidency of the Prince Consort at the Crystal Palace erected in Hyde Park, London. More than one hundred thousand exhibits were assembled from all over the world, including raw materials, handtools and handicrafts, and machines and their products, to celebrate the industrial revolution as well as Europe's continuing colonial expansion. Persian exhibits included carpets and carpet designs which were pastiches of many styles, both national and historical. Some used flowers, shaded naturalistically to give the impression of a third dimension. These pastiches

389. Olana, Greendale-on-Hudson, New York, 1870–2; detail of window

Bullerwood carpet [390] woven in 1889 for the Sanderson family. The rich colors, coherent pattern, and planar surface show the impact of Persian Vase carpets [219] on the design.[21] Morris had extensive knowledge of Persian, Turkish, and Chinese carpets, amassing his own collection and acting as adviser to the South Kensington Museum (now the Victoria and Albert Museum). In 1893 Morris strongly supported the museum's acquisition of the Ardabil carpet [214], which had been brought from Iran.

Ceramics from the Islamic world also became popular among discerning collectors, particularly in Britain. Ottoman ceramics, then known as "Damascus" or "Rhodian" wares (see Chapter 16), were avidly collected by such men as F. DuCane Godman, whose sizable collection was eventually acquired by the British Museum.[22] Persian luster tiles and vessels, as well as many other types of Persian art, were collected by Major-General Sir Robert Murdoch Smith, director of the Persian telegraph department and consultant to the South Kensington Museum, where an exhibition of Persian art was held in 1876.[23] Godman and George Salting were also prominent in the collecting of early examples of Hispano-Moresque lusterware. In 1885 the Burlington Fine Arts Club in London held an exhibition of over six hundred examples of Persian and Arab art, primarily ceramics.

Interest in Islamic ceramics seems to have encouraged the revival of the luster technique in Europe.[24] The production of iridescent lusterwares, both in Iran and in Spain and Italy, where it had spread from the Islamic world, had declined in the late sixteenth and seventeenth centuries. By 1700 the taste for iridescent luster had been superseded by a taste for gilded surfaces achieved by using powdered gold or gold leaf, and the traditional technique of reduced-pigment

were, however, condemned by many critics, including William Morris (1834–96), the poet, designer, and theorist of the Arts and Crafts movement.

Morris, who owned a copy of Owen Jones's *Grammar of Ornament* (1856), which was notable for the attempt to differentiate such national types of "Mohammedan" design as Turkish, Moresque, Persian, and Indian, was not predisposed to Islamic art as such, but responded to the geometric structure as the basis of patternmaking as well as the role of the craftsman as artist in Islamic art. Morris condemned the imported carpets which were coming to the West in large numbers from Tabriz (see below), but he appreciated traditional Persian carpets: he used them exclusively at the Red House, Bexleyheath, his new home, in 1860 and soon he was designing carpets inspired by, rather than imitating, Persian examples.

Morris's first hand-knotted carpets were made in 1878 at Kelmscott House, his home in Hammersmith on Thames, where he had the coach-house and adjoining stable converted into weaving sheds. His first designs took the classic form of a central medallion with quartered medallions in the corners, but from 1887 carpets woven at the Morris & Co. factory had directional patterns. The most famous is the

390. Detail of the Bullerswood Carpet, Hammersmith, 1899. Wool pile. 7.64 × 4 m. London, Victoria and Albert Museum

391. William De Morgan: red luster-painted ceramic, 1880s. H 40 cm.
Chicago, private collection

luster, the method used for almost all lusterware made before 1800, was replaced by resinate luster, in which dissolved gold, platinum, and later other metals were suspended with fluxes in a resin-balsam. These noble-metal preparations produced bright and reliable glazes and were extensively used in industrial manufacture at such studios as Wedgwood and Minton. While the manufacturers were able to obtain a range of golds, silvers, pinks, grays, and plums, they could not achieve a rich deep red, one of the most elusive ceramic colors but one that had become particularly popular in the mid-nineteenth century. In order to achieve such a ruby red, several potters, working as individual artist-ceramicists rather than for industrial firms, experimented with methods which revived the traditional technique of reduced-pigment luster.

One of the most famous designers was William De Morgan (1839–1917), who produced striking ruby red luster-wares in his workshops at Fulham and Sands End in the 1880s [391]. De Morgan prepared elaborate designs for luster tiles and pottery, although he left the potting and painting to others. His designs exemplify the Islamic mood that began to appear in luster wares in the 1880s, partly as an expression of the Near Eastern romanticism that had entered European taste and partly because of the affinity of the arabesque with the sinuous forms favored by the Art Nouveau movement. Gradually, his interest in dramatic red was replaced by the poetic overtones of silver-yellow luster on grounds of green and blue, which were inspired by Otto-man "Damascus" wares [302], and one of his major strengths was his controled use of varied concentrations to produce different tones of luster.[25]

The numerous international exhibitions of Islamic art brought it to the attention not only of collectors and crafts-men but also of painters. The French painter Henri Matisse (1869–1954) was the first, and probably the greatest, artist to integrate into his own work the West's growing familiarity with Islamic art. As early as 1893, he had attended the exhibition of twenty-five hundred items of Islamic art shown at the Palais de l'Industrie. Organized by Georges Marye, keeper of the Musée d'Alger, it was accompanied by an exhibition of works by the Peintres Orientalistes Français. Matisse also attended the Exposition Universelle 1900, which had Turkish, Persian, Moroccan, Tunisian, Algerian, and Egyptian pavilions, and the 1903 exhibition at the Union Central des Arts Décoratifs, organized by Gaston Migeon and Raymond Koechlin. In May 1906, Matisse visited Algeria for two weeks, quickly passing through Algiers, Biskra, Constantine, and Batna. Apart from his painting *Blue Nude: Souvenir of Biskra* (1907, Baltimore, Museum of Art), the only impact of the trip was the purchase of a small black ewer with camels, seen in several paintings, including *Pink Onions* (1906?, Copenhagen, Statens Museum for Kunst) and *Still Life with Asphodels* (1907, Essen, Museum Folk-wang). His interest in Islamic art increased dramatically after he went with Marquet in early October 1910 to see the extraordinary exhibition of Islamic art in Munich. Matisse was particularly taken with the textiles, ceramics, metal-wares, and book illustrations and in November went to Spain, where he visited Madrid, Córdoba, Seville, and Granada and brought home ceramic tiles.

Whereas his predecessors had added Oriental motifs to

392. Henri Matisse: *The Painter's Family*, 1911. Oil on canvas. 1.43 ×
1.94 m. St. Petersburg, Hermitage

give an exotic flavor and justify otherwise inappropriate subjects, Matisse incorporated some of the lessons he had learned from looking at Islamic art into his paintings. A work such as *The Painter's Family* [392], done in the spring of 1911, was inspired by the works of Islamic art he had just seen in Munich. Objects such as the carpet on the floor or the divans with cushions at the rear are obvious borrowings from Islamic art. The tripartite composition and flattened perspective, in which the floor and the wall are set in the same plane, are well known from Persian manuscript painting, as are the figures that apparently float in space, the use of purely local color, and the application of patterns, such as the four dots on the fireplace or the flowers on the wallpaper, to planar surfaces. Matisse's trips to Morocco in early 1912 and the winter of 1912–13 produced some of his most memorable works, which are also some of the most evocative images of Maghribi architecture.[26] His interest in Islamic art continued throughout his long life, and such works as his illustrated book *Jazz*, published in 1947, combine text and image in ways inspired by, if not based directly on, Persian illustrated manuscripts. "With Matisse Orientalism gave way to orientality."[27]

THE IMPACT OF ISLAMIC ART
ON THE ISLAMIC WORLD

In the nineteenth and twentieth centuries while Europe enjoyed an Oriental obsession and knowledge about Islamic art increased there enormously, the Islamic lands participated in an Occidental obsession. As Europeanization progressed, such new kinds of buildings as barracks, train stations, post offices, banks, and museums were needed, and traditional local techniques and styles of building were deemed inappropriate. Such European-manufactured goods as textiles and ceramics replaced local handicrafts, except for carpets, which were increasingly manufactured for a European clien

tele. Paradoxically, only after the orientalist taste had been established in Europe were "Islamic" decorative motifs brought back to the Islamic lands and grafted, often quite incongruously, onto Beaux-Arts armatures.

The French Empire style was received enthusiastically during the reigns of the Ottoman sultans Mahmud II (r. 1808–39) and his son Abdülmecid (r. 1839–61). The Armenian Krikor Balyan (1767–1831) was the first Ottoman architect to study in Europe. After his return from the Ecole des Beaux-Arts in Paris, he was appointed chief royal architect and in 1826 he designed the Nusretiye (Victory) Mosque at Tophane in Istanbul to commemorate Mahmud II's victory over the Janissaries.[28] The traditional courtyard was replaced by a two-story block of state apartments, but the prayer hall remained a traditional domed square. Balyan's European training is most visible in the Baroque moldings and bulbous forms which support two very slender and tall minarets. Balyan also designed the Selimiye barracks at Haydarpaşa, an enormous and imposing four-towered structure raised on a high basement above the Sea of Marmara. It owes its name to wooden barracks built on the site by Selim III in 1799 to house his new army, which had been burned in the Janissary insurrection of 1808. The first wing of the new stone building was added by Mahmud II in 1828; three others added by Abdülmecid I between 1842 and 1853 completed the structure, which served as Florence Nightingale's hospital during the Crimean War.

In 1853 Krikor's son Garabed (1800–66) and grandson Nicoğos (1826–58), who had studied in Paris under the architect Henri Labrouste, designed the immense palace and mosque at Dolmabahçe on the shores of the Bosphorus [393]. The site had originally housed a royal garden during the reign of Mehmed II and a seaside kiosk for Selim I. The garden was extended under Ahmed I and Osman II by filling in a small harbor, whence its name, the "filled-in garden." Designed with a neo-Baroque façade and a long marble terrace along the waterfront, the palace has a vast throne room (44 by 46 meters), two stories high, lit by a four-and-a-half ton British chandelier.[29] A grand staircase, with a double flight and balusters of rock crystal, leads to an ornate oval gallery. Elsewhere in the building are cruciform apartments, loosely based on the tradition of the Çinili Kiosk, for the sultan, his harem, and the heir-apparent. Outside the palace gates, themselves decorated to excess with convoluted foliage, stands the Valide Bezmialem Mosque, which has a domed prayer hall behind a medium-sized Renaissance-style palace flanked by two slender minarets in the form of Corinthian columns.

Similarly, European institutions and architectural styles were introduced in Egypt by Muhammad 'Ali, the Ottoman soldier of Albanian origin who became governor-general and effective ruler from 1805 to 1848. He tried to revive the Egyptian economy, which was based on agriculture and trade, and integrated the country into the world economy of the nineteenth century. He founded military academies and schools for medicine, veterinary medicine, pharmacy, applied chemistry, midwifery, agriculture, arts and crafts, civil engineering, administration, and languages and translation. At the suggestion of Muhammad 'Ali, the Marseillais architect Pascal Xavier Coste, who had lived in Egypt since 1818,

393. Istanbul, Dolmabahçe Palace, 1853, view from the sea

394. Cairo, Mosque of Muhammad 'Ali, 1820–57

rebuilt the fortress at Abukir. By the 1830s a new Ottoman-Mediterranean architectural style combining Greek, Italian, and Spanish elements began to replace the Mamluk and Ottoman styles favored earlier. New buildings included barracks, dockyards, office buildings, schools, hospitals, palaces, and mansions; the *mashrabiyya* windows of earlier structures were replaced by sashes of framed glass panes with shutters. Nevertheless, for his mosque in Cairo [394], Muhammad 'Ali chose a version of the Ottoman style of Istanbul rather than the Beaux-Arts style current in Egypt.

Muhammad 'Ali's mosque was erected in the citadel on the site of the Qasr al-Ablaq, a palace erected by the Mamluk sultan al-Nasir Muhammad in 1313–14 and later known as the Palace of Joseph. The palace and neighboring structures had been damaged in 1824, when a powder magazine had exploded, and in 1828 the remains were removed to make room for the mosque.[30] Muhammad 'Ali had broached the idea of building a new mosque on the site as early as 1820 with Coste, and construction continued under Muhammad 'Ali's successor Sa'id until 1857. The design was not based on the traditional Islamic architecture of Egypt (see Chapters 6 and 7), but on a rather vague knowledge of Ottoman imperial architecture. Considering the patron's role in establishing Egyptian independence from Ottoman domination, this choice is somewhat surprising, but by 1840 Muhammad 'Ali had been forced by the European powers to recognize the suzerainty of the Ottoman sultan in return for hereditary rule in Egypt. It may, however, be anachronistic to see architecture in national terms: for an Egyptian in the early nineteenth century, the Ottoman style of building was virtually the only one appropriate for the design of a monumental mosque; for a European, Ottoman architecture would have been the most familiar. Indeed, even the Ottomans, who had readily adopted Western architectural styles, continued to commission domed mosques and only decorated them with Classical or Baroque features.

The Mosque of Muhammad ʿAli, which covers over five thousand square meters, is the largest mosque built in the first half of the nineteenth century. The design is often attributed to Yusuf Bushnaq, a Greek from Istanbul, but all that can be said about the architect is that he was somewhat familiar with both Ottoman and contemporary European architectural practice. The general scheme – a square forecourt (55 by 57 meters) preceding a square prayer hall (45 by 46 meters) covered by a central dome and four semidomes resting on four great supports – repeats that of the Şehzade [275], Ahmed [287], or Fatih [291] mosques in Istanbul, but few if any of the subtleties in the models were understood. For example, the massing and articulation are comparatively crude and uninspired, for the blocklike walls contrast sharply with the rounded forms of the roof, without the mitigation of arched windows and tympana typical of Istanbul mosques. The corner turrets are elongated and fussy versions of Mamluk *mabkhara* ("incense-burner") minarets, while the 84-meter minarets are themselves unusually attenuated. The marble (or alabaster) revetment on the lower walls has yellowed and pitted, and the structure was poorly engineered. The domes showed cracks by the end of the century and were replaced in the 1930s. Nevertheless, the building is one of the most popular tourist sites in Cairo. The orientalist painter Eugène Fromentin (1820–76) said that it was "Baroque in style, but very luxurious ... The interior [is] utterly sumptuous."[31] On the north-west side of the court is a stubby tower surmounted by a pavilion decorated with Gothic tracery and Moorish arabesques. It houses a clock presented to the sovereign by Louis Philippe in 1846 in exchange for the obelisk erected in the Place de la Concorde in Paris. Muhammad ʿAli's white marble cenotaph lies to the right of the entrance in the west corner of the mosque behind a gilded bronze grille.[32]

The process of Europeanization in Egypt accelerated after Khedive Ismaʿil (r. 1865–79) – visited the Paris Exposition Universelle of 1867 and engaged the Egyptian engineer ʿAli Mubarak to transform Cairo into a modern city as Baron Haussmann had transformed Paris.[33] The distinctive Mamluk style was not revived in Egypt until later in the century with the Mosque of al-Rifaʿi (1869–1912). Ordered by the Princess Khushyar, mother of Khedive Ismaʿil, the building was designed by the architect Husayn Pasha Fahmy. It replaced a *zāwiya* of the Sufi shaykh al-Rifaʿi (d. 1180) and included the tomb of ʿAbdallah al-Ansari, a companion of the Prophet, as well as tombs for the founder and her descendants.[34] Work was suspended ca. 1880 for financial reasons and resumed in 1905. Although the planning reveals the strong symmetries of the Beaux-Arts tradition and is quite foreign to any Egyptian style, the decoration, completed under the direction of Max Herz, an Austrian member of the Committee for the Conservation of Monuments of Arab Art, was based on examples taken directly from Cairene buildings, and the minarets and crenellations copy those of the fourteenth-century Mosque of Sultan Hasan opposite.[35] It is somewhat ironic that the conservation and preservation of the incomparable heritage

of Islamic Cairo were assumed by Europeans, to the exclusion, whether systematic or not, of most Egyptians.[36]

Egypt, which had relied on Turkish export goods since the Ottoman conquest in 1517, was flooded by European manufactures in the nineteenth century. The French traveler Maxime du Camp commented in 1854 that "Egyptian art is not even in decadence, it simply no longer exists."[37] The increased presence of European tourists, particularly after the opening of the Suez Canal in 1869, created a new demand for souvenirs, and local craftsmen were encouraged to recreate the glorious works of the past that tourists could see in the Arab Museum (originally housed in the Mosque of al-Hakim). While passing through Cairo, the Governor-General of India Lord Curzon (1859–1925), for example, ordered a copy of an inlaid bronze lamp (which had been made for Baybars II in 1309) to be given as a gift to the Taj Mahal. The pair of bronze doors of Barquq's madrasa (1384–6) were copied for exhibition at the Street of Cairo at the Midway Plaisance in the Chicago 1893 Columbian Exposition.[38] One of the most popular works copied was the octagonal stand made in 1327 by Muhammad b. Sunqur al-Baghdadi for al-Nasir Muhammad, of which some six copies are known.[39] European travelers also encouraged the revival of inlaid metalwork in Damascus, where mostly Jewish craftsmen did free interpretations of Mamluk models. A large brass tray inlaid with silver and copper [395], for example, combines Mamluk-style arabesques with seven Old Testament scenes rendered in a neo-Ancient Near Eastern style. Such objects are a provocative counterpoint to metalwares of the thirteenth century which were made by Muslims but decorated with specifically Christian scenes, probably for Christian patrons.[40]

The commercial development of carpet manufacture in

395. Tray, Damascus, ca. 1925. Brass inlaid with silver and copper. Diameter 65.6 cm. New York, Jewish Museum

396. Ziegler carpet, Sultanabad, late nineteenth century. Peter Pap
Oriental Rugs, Dublin, NH and San Francisco

Iran was similarly tied to European taste. As early as 1858, Persian carpet manufacturers had begun to alter traditional designs and dimensions to suit a new European demand for their products. Whereas Turkish rugs had been popular in Europe for centuries (see Chapter 16), Persian carpets were hardly known there. The first known enterprise to organize rug manufacture in Persia with foreign capital was the Manchester-based firm of Ziegler. Its initial involvement was limited to importing European cottons to Iran and exporting new and used rugs available on the market to Europe. The most famous antique rugs handled by the firm were the Ardabil carpets, one of which [214] was acquired by the South Kensington Museum in 1893. Ziegler's need to find a dependable supply to meet the ever-increasing Western demand for carpets led to the establishment of an agency in Sultanabad (now Arak) in central Iran between 1877 and 1882. The firm provided weavers with ready-dyed wools and charts of the required designs, which were based on small repeating floral patterns of Persian origin but adapted to the taste and interior spaces of the growing European middle class [396]. Ziegler and Co. were soon joined by a second generation of manufacturers, such as the Oriental Carpet Manufacturers, Nearco Castelli & Brothers, and Persische Teppichgesellschaft-AG, who estabished their own weaving factories for greater quality control. Carpets were produced in standard dimensions of 3 by 5, 4 by 6, 8 by 10, and 9 by 12 feet, and synthetic dyes, which had been developed in Europe in the 1850s, were introduced by the 1870s. Cheaper and easier to apply than natural dyes, these vivid colors were often unstable in light and not colorfast when washed.[41]

The traditional technique of luster pottery was also revived in Persia about this time, probably as a result of European interest in the technique and in collecting early examples.[42] In addition to collecting antiques, Sir Robert Murdoch Smith patronized contemporary Persian potters, such as 'Ali Muhammad, a young potter who emigrated from Isfahan to Tehran in 1884.[43] Most of 'Ali Muhammad's work follows the florid, European-inspired style popular in nineteenth-century Iran, but several pieces imitate medieval wares [397] and may have been made either to replace damaged or destroyed originals or to deceive. At the request of Murdoch Smith, 'Ali Muhammad composed a technical treatise describing his working methods, which was published in Edinburgh in 1888 under the title *On the Manufacture of Modern Kashi Earthenware Tiles and Vases*.[44] Curiously, the potter concentrates on underglaze-painted wares and omits any mention of luster, perhaps to preserve the secret of the technique.

European notions and techniques of fine art were also imported into the Islamic lands. Oil painting on canvas, for example, had been introduced into Iran in the seventeenth century (see Chapter 12), where it continued to enjoy a certain vogue. The most famous practitioner of the technique in Turkey was Osman Hamdi (1842–1910), son of the

397. 'Ali Muhammad: Luster-painted border tile, Tehran, 1887. 34.4 ×
19.8 cm. London, Victoria and Albert Museum

Ottoman grand vizier and ambassador Ibrahim Edhem
Pasha. In 1857 Hamdi was sent to Paris, where he trained
under the academician Gustav Boulanger (1824–88) and
the orientalist painter Jean-Léon Gérôme (1824–1904).
Returning to Istanbul in 1868, Hamdi served in several
official positions, becoming director of the new Imperial
Ottoman Museum at the Çinili Kiosk in 1881 and founding
the Fine Arts Academy in 1883. His works, which he regularly exhibited in Paris, were inspired by European orientalist
paintings, and like them were often executed with the aid of
photographs. *Mihrab* [398], one of his best-known works,
painted in 1901, shows a buxom woman in a tight-fitting
European-styled dress seated on a *rahle*, or folding stand for
manuscripts of the Koran, in front of a tiled mihrab. Spread
about her feet is a jumble of manuscripts – many of them
identifiably copies of the Koran – on an old rug. The artist's
sympathies clearly lie with the woman, who represents
European progress and gazes with contempt at the musty
traditions of Islam and Islamic art, represented by the accoutrements spread about her. The devices of European
orientalism, which had been used in Europe to depict a
strange and exotic world of escape, have been adopted
somewhat paradoxically by the very Orient depicted for a
more trenchant social purpose.

   At virtually the same time, the frankly European style of
building practiced at the Ottoman court by European-trained
Armenians was being replaced by an eclectic orientalism
brought to Istanbul by Europeans. The German architect A.
Jachmund (d. 1927) was either sent or invited to Istanbul in
1890, where he designed the Sirkeci Railroad Terminus
for the Orient Express [399]. Its combination of Moorish
horseshoe arches, neo-Mamluk striped masonry and rose
windows, and Indian chatris perfectly exemplifies the eclectic
orientalism of the day. The Ottoman elite enthusiastically
received the building as a real and symbolic gateway to
Europe and modernity.[45] The French architect Alexandre
Vallaury, chief instructor at the School of Fine Arts and
architect to the imperial palace, designed banks and public
buildings in Istanbul in a variety of European and orientalist
styles. One of his most important commissions was the
Archaeological Museum erected on the grounds of Topkapı
Palace between 1891 and 1907. Standing opposite the
delicate Çinili Kiosk [270], this long U-shaped building in

398. Osman Hamdi: *Mihrab*, 1901. Oil on canvas. 2.1 × 1.08 m. Private
collection

399. Istanbul, Sirkeci Railroad Terminal, 1890

an austere Neoclassical style was designed to exhibit the extraordinary collection of Graeco-Roman art excavated under European impetus throughout the empire. Vallaury and Jachmund, director of the architectural program at the new Civil Service School of Engineering, were able to inculcate a young generation of Turkish architects.

Jachmund's students included Kemalettin (1870–1927), who designed the Fourth Vakif Han in Bahçekapı between 1912 and 1926 [400].[46] The Vakif Han, an immense seven-story block on an irregular site, was one of seven office buildings designed by Kemalettin and planned by the Ministry of Pious Foundations (Vakif) to generate rental income. The traditional façade of cut stone conceals the steel skeleton that supports the building and the high and narrow central court. Such elements of classical Ottoman architecture as the carefully controled fenestration, deeply projecting eaves, lead-sheathed domes, tile panels, geometric carving, and rich moldings give an attractive Ottoman guise to a standard turn-of-the-century office block.[47]

Architects followed this first, but rather superficial, national style with one in which inspiration was sought in the traditions of domestic and vernacular building, rather than in the urban and monumental tradition of architecture with which this book has been largely concerned.[48] Instead of looking at Sinan, they looked at the anonymous wooden houses of Turkey with projecting balconies and overhanging eaves. This search for authenticity in the vernacular tradition was not limited to Turkey, and it has enjoyed favor in many countries of the Islamic world in the second half of the twentieth century. The greatest representative of this tradition was the Egyptian architect and theorist Hassan Fathy (1900–89), whose village of New Gourna (1945) near Luxor turned to the vernacular mud-brick traditions of the countryside rather than the masonry architecture of Cairo.[49] Forced to evacuate Old Gourna, which lay in the Antiquities Zone, the villagers themselves erected the buildings, which abandoned such universal "Islamic" symbols as the tower

400. Istanbul, Fourth Vakif Han, 1912–26

minaret in favor of such local ones as the staircase minaret.

It would be somewhat ironic if the vibrant and noble traditions of architecture and art in the Islamic world were to meet such a modest end. Twentieth-century life has wreaked havoc on the traditional matrices of craft production and offered new and very different opportunities to people whose opportunities had previously been restricted by access to education, travel, and the like. In the second half of the twentieth century, however, the increased power and wealth of countries in the Islamic world have broadened knowledge about the history of cultural traditions, not only architecture and art. Sophisticated patrons are no longer content to commission pastiches of earlier times, and architects are increasingly looking at the great buildings of the past for more than decorative motifs. In the portable arts the situation is not so hopeful. Although calligraphers are rarely called upon to produce manuscripts, some artists have been inspired by the traditions of Arabic and Persian calligraphy for work in other media, such as sculpture and painting in oils. Many of the traditional crafts are dying, and carpet factories continue to produce thousands of repetitive examples of earlier work. In Turkey a modest attempt has been made to combine traditional carpet craftsmanship with twentieth-century approaches to design, and one hopes similar approaches in the other arts will be fruitful elsewhere.

Notes

PRINCIPAL ABBREVIATIONS

EI/2	*Encyclopaedia of Islam*, 2nd ed.
Ettinghausen and Grabar	Richard Ettinghausen and Oleg Grabar, *The Art and Architecture of Islam: 650–1250* (Harmondsworth, 1987)
Lentz and Lowry	Thomas W. Lentz and Glenn D. Lowry, *Timur and the Princely Vision: Persian Art and Culture in the Fifteenth Century* (Los Angeles, 1989)
Pinner and Denny	Robert Pinner and Walter B. Denny, eds, *Oriental Carpet and Textile Studies II: Carpets of the Mediterranean Countries 1400–1600* (London, 1986)
RCEA	Étienne Combe, Jean Sauvaget, and Gaston Wiet, *Répertoire chronologique d'épigraphie arabe*, 18 vols. (Cairo, 1931 ff.)
SPA	A. U. Pope and P. Ackerman, eds, *A Survey of Persian Art from Prehistoric Times to the Present*, 8 vols. (London and New York, 1938 ff.)
Thackston	Wheeler M. Thackston, trans., *A Century of Princes* (Cambridge, MA, 1989)

CHAPTER 1: INTRODUCTION

1. Ibn Khaldun, *The Muqaddimah: An Introduction to History*, trans. Franz Rosenthal, 2nd ed. (Princeton, 1967), 2:347.

CHAPTER 2: ARCHITECTURE IN IRAN AND CENTRAL ASIA UNDER THE ILKHANIDS AND THEIR SUCCESSORS

1. The basic work on Ilkhanid architecture is Donald M. Wilber, *The Architecture of Islamic Iran: The Il-Khānid Period* (Princeton, 1955, repr. New York, 1969). It contains general essays on architectural style and a catalogue of 119 monuments in Iran proper. The notes here will only cite subsequent publications.

2. Most of these features are discussed in Ettinghausen and Grabar, Ch. 7, pp. 256–91.

3. P. Vardjavand, "La Découverte archéologique du complexe scientifique de l'observatoire de Maraqé," *Akten des VII. internationalen Kongresses für iranische Kunst und Archäologie, München 7.–10. September 1976* (Berlin, 1979), pp. 527–36.

4. Rudolf Naumann, *Die Ruinen von Tacht-e Suleiman und Zendan-e Suleiman* (Berlin, 1977); Ulrich Harb, *Ilkhanidische Stalaktitengewölbe: Beiträge zu Entwurf und Bautechnik* (Berlin, 1978); Jonathan M. Bloom, "On the Transmission of Designs in Early Islamic Architecture," *Muqarnas* 10 (1993): 21–8.

5. Assadullah Souren Melikian-Chirvani, "Le Shāh-nāme, la gnose soufie et le pouvoir mongol," *Journal asiatique* 222 (1984): 249–338; idem, "Le livre des rois, miroir du destin, I," *Studia Iranica* 17/i (1988): 7–46; idem, "Le livre des rois, miroir du destin, II: Takht-e Soleymān et la symbolique du *Shāh-nāme*," *Studia Iranica* 20/i (1991): 33–148.

6. Sheila S. Blair, "Ilkhanid Architecture and Society: an Analysis of the Endowment Deed of the Rab'-i Rashīdī," *Iran* 22 (1984): 67–90.

7. Sheila S. Blair, "The Mongol Capital of Sulṭāniyya, 'the Imperial,'" *Iran* 24 (1986): 139–51. See also the studies published in *Soltāniye III. Quaderni del Seminario di Iranistica, Uralo-Altaistica e Caucasologia dell'Università degli Studi di Venezia*, 9 (Venice, 1982). For Matrakci Nasuh, see Chapter 16.

8. Sheila S. Blair, "The Epigraphic Program of the Tomb of Uljaytu at Sultaniyya: Meaning in Mongol Architecture," *Islamic Art* 2 (1987): 43–96; Eleanor Sims, "The 'Iconography' of the Internal Decoration in the Mausoleum of Uljaytu at Sultaniyya," *Content and Context of Visual Arts in the Islamic World*, ed. P. P. Soucek (University Park, PA, and London, 1988), pp. 139–76.

9. The grave itself has been the focus of June Taboroff's doctoral dissertation and excavations (in progress) by Chahryar Adle on the site in the *Encyclopaedia Iranica*, whose work is summarized in a brief article on the site in the *Encyclopaedia Iranica*, s.v. "Bestam." The flanged tomb tower has been studied by Robert Hillenbrand, "The Flanged Tomb Tower at Bastam," and Sheila S. Blair, "The Inscription from the Tomb Tower at Bastâm: an Analysis of Ilkhanid Epigraphy," in *Art et société dans le monde iranien*, ed. Chahryar Adle (Paris, 1982), pp. 237–61 and 263–86. Blair (as in Note 6 above) has hypothesized that Rashid al-Din's tomb also stood behind the qibla iwan of his mosque at the Rab'-i Rashidi.

10. A. S. Melikian-Chirvani, "The Lights of Sufi Shrines," *Islamic Art* 2 (1987): 117–48.

11. Sheila S. Blair, *The Ilkhanid Shrine Complex at Natanz, Iran* (Cambridge, MA, 1986).

12. Max van Berchem, "Une inscription du sultan mongol Uldjaitu," *Mélanges Hartwig Derenbourg* (Paris, 1909), pp. 367–78; *RCEA* 5279; Luṭfallah Hunarfar, *Ganjīna-yi āthār-i tārīkhī-yi Isfahān*, 2nd ed. (Tehran, 1350/1977), pp. 115–20.

13. George C. Miles, "The Inscriptions of the Masjid-i Jami' at Ashtarjan," *Iran* 12 (1974): 89–98.

14. See Renata Holod, "Text, Plan and Building: On the Transmission of Architectural Knowledge," *Theories and Principles of Design in the Architecture of Islamic Societies* (Cambridge, MA, 1988), pp. 1–12.

15. R. Paone, "The Mongol Colonization of the Isfahān Region," *Isfahan. Quaderni del Seminario di Iranistica, Uralo-Altaistica e Caucasologia dell'Università degli Studi di Venezia*, 10 (Venice, 1981), pp. 1–30.

16. Lionel Bier, *Sarvistan: A Study in Early Iranian Architecture* (University Park, PA, and London, 1986), especially pp. 31–9.

CHAPTER 3: THE ARTS IN IRAN AND CENTRAL ASIA UNDER THE ILKHANIDS AND THEIR SUCCESSORS

1. Ettinghausen and Grabar, p. 328.

2. Sheila S. Blair, "Artists and patronage in late fourteenth century Iran in light of two catalogues of Islamic metalwork," *Bulletin of the School of Oriental and African Studies* 48/1 (1985): 53–9.

3. Vienna, Erzbischöfliches Dom- und Diözesan Museum. It was made into the burial robe of Duke Rudolf IV of Austria (d. Milan, 1365). It may have been acquired by an Italian merchant in Iran after Abu Sa'id's death, when textiles with the sultan's name would no longer have been of value. See Anne E. Wardwell, "*Panni Tartarici*: Eastern Islamic Silks woven with Gold and Silver (13th and 14th centuries)," *Islamic Art* 3 (1988–9): 95–173, and *SPA*, p. 2049 and pl. 1003.

4. Richard Ettinghausen, "New Light on Early Animal Carpets," *Aus der Welt der islamischen Kunst: Festschrift für Ernst Kühnel*, ed. R. Ettinghausen (Berlin, 1959), pp. 93–116. See also Chapter 10.

5. The technique of luster decoration was not lost, as shown by a series of tombstones and frieze tiles from the fifteenth and sixteenth centuries and a large number of bowls and other objects from the seventeenth century [227].

6. The genealogy of the Abu Tahir family is given in Oliver Watson, *Persian Lustre Ware* (London, 1985), pp. 178–9. Sheila Blair, "A Medieval Persian Builder," *Journal of the Society of Architectural Historians* 45 (1986): 389–95, discusses the three brothers. J. W. Allan, "Abu'l Qasim's Treatise on Ceramics," *Iran* 11 (1973): 111–20, translates the treatise into English with commentary.

7. Formerly in the collection of Richard Ettinghausen. See Richard Ettinghausen, "New Affiliations for a Classical Persian Pottery Type," *Parnassus* 8 (March 1936), p. 10, and Arthur Lane, *Early Islamic Pottery* (London, 1947), p. 43.

8. Berlin, Museum für Islamische Kunst, no. I. 24/66; no. 459 in *Museum für Islamische Kunst Berlin, Katalog 1971*, Berlin, Staatliche Museen Preussischer Kulturbesitz, 1971.

9. Similar wares were excavated at Sarai Berke, some 64 kilometers east of Volgograd, the capital of the Golden Horde. It was founded by Berke Khan (r. 1257–66), became the capital under Uzbek Khan (1312–40), and was destroyed by Timur in 1395. The ceramics of Sarai Berke are similar to A. Lane's subgroup 2 of Sultanabad wares, but the shapes are different and the drawing is stiffer. Arthur Lane, *Later Islamic Pottery* (London, 1957), pp. 10–15.

10. E. Atil, *Ceramics from the World of Islam* (Washington, 1973), no. 70.

11. London, British Museum, 91.6-23.5. The piece is illustrated in Douglas Barrett, *Islamic Metalwork in the British Museum* (London, 1949), pls. 32–3. Mahmud is believed to have been the brother of Muhammad b. Sunqur al-

Baghdadi (from Baghdad), who signed a hexagonal *kursi* (table) dated 728/1327 in Cairo (Museum of Islamic Art, 139). The penbox is attributed to Baghdad because it continues many features of Mesopotamian metalwork in the earlier part of the century.

12. Boston, Museum of Fine Arts 55.106, ex-Stora coll. See A. S. Melikian-Chirvani, "The Lights of Sufi Shrines," *Islamic Art* 2 (1987): 117-48.

13. Jessica Rawson, *Chinese Ornament: The Lotus and the Dragon* (London, 1984), pp. 149-98.

14. See Chapter 10, Note 29.

15. The pieces were formerly in the Harari Collection. One is illustrated in *SPA*, pl. 1357a.

16. Richmond, Surrey, Keir Collection, no. 132. Geza Fehérvári, *Islamic Metalwork of the Eighth Century to the Fifteenth Century in the Keir Collection* (London, 1976), pp. 110-11 and color pl. J.

17. St Petersburg, Hermitage Museum, IR-1484. *SPA*, pl. 1363b, and *Masterpieces of Islamic Art in the Hermitage Museum*, exh. cat., Kuwait, Dar al-Athar al-Islamiyyah, 1990, no. 51.

18. A. S. Melikian-Chirvani, "Bronzes et cuivres iraniens du Louvre: I. L'École du Fars au XIVᵉ siècle," *Journal Asiatique* 257 (1969): 20-36; idem, "Nouvelles remarques sur l'école du Fars à propos des bassins iraniens du xivᵉ s. au Musée des Beaux-Arts," *Bulletin des Musées et Monuments Lyonnais* iv/3 (1971): 361-91; idem, *Islamic Metalwork from the Iranian World, 8th-18th Centuries* (London, 1982), pp. 147-52.

19. Galleria Estense, 8082. Eva Baer, "'Fish-Pond' Ornaments on Persian and Mamluk Metal Vessels," *Bulletin of the School of Oriental and African Studies* 31 (1968): 14-27.

20. Only one piece of metalwork can be attributed to the patronage of the Jalayirids, the successors to the Ilkhanids in the second half of the fourteenth century: a large water basin in the sanctuary at Ardabil. See Yedda A. Godard, "Bassin de cuivre au nom de Shaikh Uwais," *Athar-é Iran* 1 (1936): 21-35.

21. M. B. Smith and P. Wittek, "The Wood Minbar in the Masdjid-i Djami', Nain," *Ars Islamica* 5 (1938): 21-35.

22. New York, Metropolitan Museum of Art, 10-218. The inscription is published in *RCEA* 6337; see also Lentz and Lowry, no. 9.

23. Giovanni Curatola, "Some Ilkhanid Woodwork from the Area of Sultaniyya," *Islamic Art* 2 (1987): 97-116.

24. Sheila S. Blair, "The Development of the Illustrated Book in Iran," *Muqarnas* 10 (1993): 266-74.

25. New York, Pierpont Morgan Library, M 500; Richard Ettinghausen: "The Covers of the Morgan Manafi' Manuscript and other early Persian Book-bindings," *Studies in Art and Literature for Belle da Costa Greene* (Princeton, 1954), pp. 459-73. The manuscript was once in the possession of the Ottoman sultan Bayezid II (r. 1481-1512), for it bears his oval seal. E. J. Grube, *Persian Painting in the Fourteenth Century. A Research Report*, Supplemento no. 17 agli Annali, Instituto Orientale di Napoli, 38, 1978, fasc. 4, pl. 1. The binding, however, may date to the time of Bayezid II, for it corresponds to the size of the trimmed pages. For the new dating, see Barbara Schmitz's forthcoming catalogue of Islamic manuscripts in the Morgan Library.

26. Two generally accepted examples are in Tehran, Iran Bastan Museum 4277, dated 1286-7, and Istanbul, Topkapi Palace Library, E. H. 74, dated 1294. Both are illustrated in Martin Lings, *The Qur'ānic Art of Calligraphy and Illumination* (London, 1976), pls. 23, 26-7.

27. E.g. a Koran copied in *thuluth* script refurbished with splendid illumination in the Ottoman court style of the mid-sixteenth century. See Esin Atil, *The Age of Sultan Süleyman the Magnificent* (Washington, DC, and New York, 1987), no. 13, and J. M. Rogers and R. M. Ward, *Süleyman the Magnificent* (London, 1988), no. 19. According to Rogers and Ward, the signature and date are later additions, perhaps by the later calligrapher Ahmad Karahisari, although the manuscript may well be what it claims to be.

28. David James, *Qur'ans of the Mamluks* (London, 1988), nos. 39, 40, 42, 45, and 46.

29. The few surviving volumes and fragments are now widely dispersed. James, *Qur'ans*, no. 39.

30. Istanbul, Süleymaniye Mosque Library, Esad Efendi 3638, fols. 3v-4r. Richard Ettinghausen, *Arab Painting* (Geneva, 1962), pp. 98-102.

31. New York, Pierpont Morgan Library, M. 500. The manuscript has been retouched and several large paintings depicting scenes from the *Shāhnāma* or the poems of Nizami have been painted directly over the text, but it is still possible to distinguish several different styles in the original illustrations.

32. Edinburgh, University Library, Arab 161.

33. Priscilla Soucek, "An Illustrated Manuscript of al-Bīrūnī's *Chronology of Ancient Nations*," *The Scholar and the Saint*, ed. Peter Chelkowski (New York, 1975), pp. 103-65; eadem, "The Life of the Prophet: Illustrated Versions," *Content and Context of Visual Arts in the Islamic World*, ed. P. P. Soucek (University Park, PA, and London, 1988), pp. 193-218.

34. Sheila S. Blair, "Ilkhanid Architecture and Society: an Analysis of the Endowment deed of the Rab'-i Rashidi," *Iran* 22 (1984): 67-90.

35. The Koran fragment, dated Safar 715/April 1315, is in Istanbul (Topkapi Palace Library, EH 248); the religious tracts are in Paris (Bibliothèque Nationale, Arabe 2324). Two manuscripts of the Persian edition of the author's history are preserved in Istanbul (Topkapi Palace Library H. 1653 and 1654); both bear the library seal of the Timurid ruler Shahrukh. H. 1653 is a fourteenth-century manuscript of Rashid al-Din's *Universal History*, to which Hafiz-i Abru added replacement pages (see Chapter 5, note 13). H. 1654 was copied for Rashid al-Din and finished on 3 Jumada I, 717/14 July 1317. The manuscript has 118 illustrations and 21 pages with portraits of Chinese emperors, most of a later date. Albums in Berlin also have illustrations which could have been detached from a volume on the history of the Mongols.

36. The fragment is now divided between the Edinburgh University Library (Arab 20) and the Khalili Collection in London. It has often been thought that these two fragments were from separate manuscripts, but collation of the text, pagination, catchwords, and numbering of illustrations indicates that they were once part of the same volume. See Blair (forthcoming).

37. See, for example, the type of thirteenth-century handscroll discussed in Julia K. Murray, "The *Ladies' Classic of Filial Piety* and Sung Textual Illustration: Problems of Reconstruction and Artistic Context," *Ars Orientalis* 18 (1988): 95-130. Although handscrolls with text and paintings had become somewhat old-fashioned, copies of classical works were popular with some of the southern Sung emperors as souvenirs of imperial beneficence.

38. Terry Allen, "Byzantine Sources for the *Jami' al-Tawarikh* of Rashid al-Din," *Ars Orientalis* 15 (1985): 121-36.

39. Oleg Grabar and Sheila Blair, *Epic Images and Contemporary History: The Illustrations of the Great Mongol Shahnama*, Chicago, 1980; Sheila S. Blair, "On the Track of the 'Demotte' *Shâhnama* Manuscript," *Les Manuscrits du Moyen-Orient: Essais de codicologie et de paléographie*, ed. François Déroche (Istanbul/Paris, 1989), pp. 125-31; Sheila S. Blair and Jonathan M. Bloom, "Epic Images and Contemporary History: the Legacy of the Great Mongol *Shah-nama*," *Islamic Art* 5 (forthcoming).

40. Eric Schroeder, "Ahmad Musa and Shams al-Din: a review of fourteenth-century painting," *Ars Islamica* 6 (1939): 113-42.

41. The dates December 1335-May 1336 given by Grabar and Blair (p. 48) hardly allow enough time for the conception, preparation, and execution of such a large project, so the broader range of 1328-36 seems more likely.

42. Translated by Thackston, p. 345.

43. Istanbul, Topkapi Palace Library, H. 2154. See Richard Ettinghausen, "Persian Ascension Miniatures of the Fourteenth Century," *Accademia Nazionale dei Lincei* 12 (1957): 360-83.

44. Istanbul University Library, F. 1422. Jill Sanchia Cowen, *Kalila wa Dimna: an Animal Allegory of the Mongol Court* (New York and Oxford, 1989), who attributed them to the patronage of Ghiyath al-Din. She assumed that the manuscript was the model for another copy of *Kalila and Dimna* dated 1343-4 (Cairo, Egyptian National Library, Adab Farsi 61, for which see Ernst Kühnel, "A Bidpai Manuscript of 1343-44 in Cairo," *Bulletin of the American Institute of Iranian Art and Archaeology* 5 (1937): 137-41), but such a linear view of manuscript production is unwarranted. See also Ernst J. Grube, "Prolegomena for a Corpus Publication of Illustrated *Kalilah wa Dimnah* Manuscripts," *Islamic Art* IV (1991), pp. 301-482.

45. Istanbul, Topkapi Palace Library, Hazine 654. Richard Ettinghausen, "On Some Mongol Miniatures," *Kunst des Orients* 3 (1959): 56-65.

46. An album in Istanbul (Topkapi Palace Library, H. 2153) contains many *Shāhnāma* illustrations; other albums in Berlin contain related images. See Richard Ettinghausen, "Some Paintings in Four Istanbul Albums," *Ars Orientalis* 1 (1954): 91-103, and M. Ipşiroğlu, *Saray-Alben: Diez'sche Klebebände aus den Berliner Sammlungen* (Wiesbaden, 1964).

47. London, British Library, Or. 13297, for which see Norah Titley, "A Fourteenth-Century Khamseh of Nizami," *British Museum Quarterly* 36 (1972): 8-11; and Paris, Bibliothèque Nationale, Supp. pers. 332.

48. London, British Library, Add. 18113. See B. W. Robinson, *Persian Miniature Painting from Collections in the British Isles* (London, 1967), p. 40, and Lentz and Lowry, no. 13. For a biography of the poet, see Teresa Fitzherbert, "Khwājū Kirmānī (689-753/1290-1352): An Eminence Grise of Fourteenth-Century Persian Painting," *Iran* 29 (1991): 137-52.

49. The text describes the events of the marriage, including lovemaking, drinking, music, and Humay pouring gold and jewels at Humayun's feet. The scene to the left in the painting apparently shows Humay's handmaidens presenting her with the gold objects from Humayun, while in the scene to the right Humay is being showered with gold coins, an event not mentioned in the text and perhaps one of contemporary interest.

50. Topkapi Palace Library, Hazine 2154, fol. 20v. See Verna Prentice, "A Detached Miniature from the *Masnavis* of Khwaju Kermani," *Oriental Art* 27 (1981): 60-66. Fitzherbert has shown that the painting depicts a scene from the poet's youth in which he dreamed of an angel.

51. The Timurid chronicler Ibn 'Arabshah mentioned 'Abd al-Hayy as a skilled painter working for Timur and the wall paintings on Timurid palaces,

although he does not expressly connect the two. Several black-and-white drawings attributed to the late fourteenth century bear notations that they were copied from 'Abd al-Hayy's drawings by Muhammad b. Mahmud Shah Khayyam. Priscilla P. Soucek, "'Abd al-Hayy, Khwaja," *Encyclopaedia Iranica*.

52. Washington, DC, Freer Gallery of Art, a manuscript of 337 folios from which nine folios have been detached as FGA nos. 32.29-37. The manuscript lacks a colophon, but a note on the last page states that it was completed in "the month of Ramadan in the year eight and five hundred," which would correspond to the unlikely date 1114. If the note was intended to read "five and eight hundred," the date would correspond to March-April 1403, well within Sultan Ahmad's reign. Another note on the same folio says that the scribe was Mir 'Ali, the same calligrapher who penned Khwaju Kirmani's *Divan* in London. Indeed, the handwriting is the same. See Esin Atıl, *Brush of the Masters: Drawings from Iran and India* (Washington, DC, 1978), pp. 14-27.

53. Deborah Klimberg-Salter, "A Sufi Theme in Persian Painting: the *Divan* of Sultan Ahmad Ğalair in the Freer Gallery of Art, Washington, DC," *Kunst des Orients* 11 (1976-7): 43-84.

54. Marianna Shreve Simpson, *The Illustration of an Epic: the Earliest Shahnama Manuscripts* (New York and London, 1979).

55. Four manuscripts are dated between 1330 and 1352. One in Istanbul (Topkapı Palace Library, Hazine 1479) is dated 1330; another in St Petersburg (Public Library, Dorn 329) is dated 1333. There are two dispersed copies, one dedicated in 1341 to an Injuid vizier, the second known as the "Stephens" *Shāhnāma*, which bears a note in a later hand giving the date of 1352. Several other manuscripts, such as the dispersed *Kalīla and Dimna* dated 1333, *Kitāb-i Samak-i 'Ayyār* (Oxford, Bodleian Library, Ouseley 379-81), and the Persian translation of Tabari's *Annals* (*Tarjama-yi Tārākh-i Tabarī*, Washington, DC, 30.21, 47.19, 56.16), can be attributed to the same school on stylistic grounds.

56. London, British Library, Or. 13506. The manuscript, which was copied by [Abu'l]-Makārim Hasan, has 209 folios measuring 22 by 10 cm, an unusually elongated format. It has a double-page frontispiece and 66 smaller illustrations. See P. Waley and Norah M. Titley, "An Illustrated Persian Text of Kalila and Dimna dated 707/1307-8," *British Library Journal* 1 (1975): 42-60.

57. Istanbul, Topkapı Palace Library, Hazine 1511. Mehmet Aga-Oglu, "Preliminary Notes on some Persian Illustrated Mss. in the Topkapu Sarayi Müzesi - Part I," *Ars Islamica* 1 (1934): 183-99.

58. Cairo, National Library, Adab Farsi no. 6. Ivan Stchoukine, *Les Peintures des manuscrits Tīmūrides* (Paris, 1954), no. iii.

CHAPTER 4: ARCHITECTURE IN IRAN AND CENTRAL ASIA UNDER THE TIMURIDS AND THEIR CONTEMPORARIES

1. The basic source for Timurid architecture is Lisa Golombek and Donald Wilber, *The Timurid Architecture of Iran and Turan*, 2 vols. (Princeton, 1988). Modeled on Wilber's monograph on Ilkhanid architecture (see Chapter 2, Note 1), it also contains essays on the architectural style of the period and a catalogue of 229 buildings in Iran and Transoxiana. Monuments in the province of Khurasan in Iran are treated more fully in Bernard O'Kane, *Timurid Architecture in Khurasan* (Costa Mesa, CA, 1987), which has a similar format. These works contains complete bibliographies for each building, so the notes here are limited to substantial monographs for the individual sites.

2. Beatrice Manz, "Tamerlane and the Symbolism of Sovereignty," *Iranian Studies* 21 (1988): 105-22; Beatrice Forbes Manz, *The Rise and Rule of Tamerlane* (Cambridge, 1989); and Lisa Golombek, "Tamerlane, Scourge of God," *Asian Art* 2 (1989): 31-61.

3. See M. E. Masson and G. A. Pugachenkova, "Shahrisiabz pri Timure i Ulugbeke," trans. J. M. Rogers, "Shahr-i Sabz from Timur to Ulugh Beg," *Iran*, 16 (1978): 103-26 and 18 (1980): 121-43.

4. For the biography of Ahmad Yasavi, see *EI/2*.

5. Lisa Golombek, *The Timurid Shrine at Gazur Gah*, Royal Ontario Museum Art and Archaeology Occasional Paper 15 (Toronto, 1969), pp. 54-6; Golombek and Wilber, *Timurid Architecture*, pp. 193-4.

6. In addition to the references given in Golombek and Wilber, p. 288, see L. Iu. Man'kovskaia, "Towards the Study of Forms in Central Asian Architecture at the End of the Fourteenth Century: the Mausoleum of Khvāja Ahmad Yasavī," trans. Lisa Golombek, *Iran* 23 (1985): 109-28.

7. Jonathan M. Bloom, "On the Transmission of Designs in Early Islamic Architecture," *Muqarnas* 10 (1993): 21-8. Fourteenth-century sources already mention that plans for Shams al-Din's tomb complex in Yazd were sent there from Tabriz, the capital, and a recently discovered design scroll may date from the Timurid period; see Gülru Necipoğlu, "Geometric Design in Timurid/Turkmen Architectural Practice: Thoughts on a recently Discovered Scroll and its Late Gothic Parallels," *Timurid Art and Culture: Iran and Central Asia in the Fifteenth Century*, ed. Lisa Golombek and Maria Subtelny (Leiden, 1992), pp.

48-66. Ottoman builders seem to have been trained to realize standard plans with local materials and workmen; see Chapter 15.

8. Donald Wilber, "The Timurid Court: Life in Gardens and Tents," *Iran* 17 (1979): 127-33.

9. Although the lateral domes have been reconstructed with ribs, Man'kovskaia has challenged this assumption.

10. Sheila S. Blair, "The Mongol Capital of Sultāniyya, 'the Imperial'," *Iran* 24 (1986): 139-51.

11. It is often erroneously reported that 480 columns were brought to Samarqand from India, but Yazdi's text, translated in Golombek and Wilber, pp. 258-9, leaves no doubt that the stones were quarried locally.

12. *EI/2*, s.v. "Kuthām b. al-'Abbās."

13. N. B. Nemtseva and Iu. Z. Shvab, *Ansambl' Shakh-i Zinda* ["Ensemble of Shah-i Zinda"] (Tashkent, 1979).

14. V. A. Shishkin, "Nadpisi v Ansamble Shakhi-Zinda [Inscriptions in the Ensemble of Shah-i Zinda]," *Zodchestvo Uzbekistana* 2 (1970): 7-71.

15. The shrine remains one of the most venerated sites in Iran and scholarly access is limited, so much of its architecture and decoration remains to be studied.

16. For the city of Herat under the Timurids, see also Terry Allen, *A Catalogue of Toponyms and Monuments of Timurid Herat* (Cambridge, MA, 1981) and *Timurid Herat* (Wiesbaden, 1983).

17. Lisa Golombek, *Timurid Shrine at Gazur-Gah*.

18. Bernard O'Kane, "The Madrasa al-Ghiyasiyya at Khargird," *Iran* 14 (1976): 79-92.

19. Bernard O'Kane, "The Tiled Minbars of Iran," *Annales islamologiques* 22 (1986): 133-55.

20. G. A. Pugachenkova, *Ishrat Khane* ["The 'Ishrat Khana"] (Tashkent, 1958) and "Ishrat-Khaneh and Ak-Saray - Two Timurid Mausoleums in Samarkand," *Ars Orientalis* 5 (1963): 177-89.

21. Other examples are at Gazargah (Golombek, *Timurid Shrine at Gazur Gah*, figs. 124-7), Boston, Gardner Museum, S12W2; and Paris, Louvre, MAO 342.

22. See Chapter 2 and Sheila S. Blair, "Ilkhanid Architecture and Society: an Analysis of the Endowment Deed of the Rab'-i Rashidi," *Iran* 22 (1984): 67-90. It could also have been modeled, as was the Rashidiyya complex, on the complex of Ghazan Khan, whose architecture is virtually unknown.

23. The adjectives in the fragmentary foundation inscription are in the feminine and cannot refer to a mosque, which is masculine in Arabic, but a more general (and feminine) term, such as '*imāra* (building) could have been used. See Golombek and Wilber, no. 214.

24. Lisa Golombek, "From Tamerlane to the Taj Mahal," *Essays in Islamic Art and Architecture in Honor of Katharina Otto-Dorn*, ed. A. Daneshvari (Malibu, 1981), pp. 43-50.

25. Bernard O'Kane, "Tiled Minbars of Iran."

CHAPTER 5: THE ARTS IN IRAN AND CENTRAL ASIA UNDER THE TIMURIDS AND THEIR CONTEMPORARIES

1. Timurid art was the subject of an exhibition held in 1989, and many of the objects discussed here can be found in the catalogue, Thomas W. Lentz and Glenn D. Lowry, *Timur and the Princely Vision: Persian Art and Culture in the Fifteenth Century* (Los Angeles, 1989); in addition, see the selected papers from the symposium "Timurid and Turkmen Societies in Transition: Iran in the Fifteenth Century," published in *Timurid Art and Culture: Iran and Central Asia in the Fifteenth Century*, ed. Lisa Golombek and Maria Subtelny (Leiden, 1992).

2. One possible exception is an anthology of epics, dated 1397-8, now divided between the Chester Beatty Library in Dublin (Pers. MS. 114) and the British Library (Or. 2780); see Lentz and Lowry, no. 16.

3. The piece is now in the Bukhara Museum.

4. The doorknocker from the tomb chamber is also dated in *abjad* (alphabetic numbering) equivalent to 751 or 780 (1350-1 or 1378-9). Ivanov explained this early date with the suggestion that 'Izz al-Din had brought an early piece with him from Isfahan. See A. A. Ivanov, "O bronzovykh izdeliiakh kontsa XIV v. iz mavzoleia Khodzha Ahmeda Iasevi [On the bronze objects of the end of the 14th century from the mausoleum of Ahmad Yasavi]," *Sredniaia Aziia i ee sosedi v drevnosti i srednevekov'e*, ed. B. A. Litvinskii (Moscow, 1981), pp. 68-84; Boris Deniké, "Quelques monuments de bois sculpté au Turkestan Occidental," *Ars Islamica* 2 (1935): 69-83; Golombek and Wilber, *Timurid Architecture*, no. 53.

5. Measuring 1.75 meters in diameter, the basin, which is still *in situ*, lacks the high foot of the Turkestan example. It is signed by Hasan b. 'Ali b. Hasan b. 'Ali Isfahani. See A. S. Melikian-Chirvani, "Un bassin iranien de l'an 1375," *Gazette des Beaux-Arts* 78 (1969): 5-18. Melikian-Chirvani has also noted the existence of a third basin in the shrine built over 'Ali's tomb at Mazar-i Sharif in Afghanistan. See A. S. Melikian-Chirvani, *Islamic Metalwork from the Iranian*

World, 8th–18th Centuries (London, 1982), p. 232. For Timurid metalwork in general, see Linda Komaroff, *The Golden Disk of Heaven: Metalwork of Timurid Iran* (Costa Mesa and New York, 1992).

6. Three of the lampstands have been dismembered; two of them and several parts of another were taken from the shrine and are now either in St Petersburg (Hermitage SA-15931, 15932) or Paris (Louvre, Inv. 7079, 7080). Three bear crude inscriptions on their bases with the same name and date as on the doorknockers, but Ivanov has questioned the authenticity of these inscriptions, which were probably added at a later date. The dedicatory inscriptions themselves use formulas and titles typical of Mamluk metalwork, which has led Komaroff, *Golden Disk of Heaven*, to suggest that the craftsmen brought from Damascus after Timur captured the city were involved in the production of these lamps.

7. Folios and fragments from this manuscript are widely dispersed. Eight folios are in Mashhad (Shrine of Imam Reza Museum); two folios are in the A. Soudavar Collection; see Lentz and Lowry, no. 6. The complicated history of this manuscript and its nineteenth-century copy have been elucidated by David James, *Qur'ans of the 15th and 16th Centuries*. The Nasser D. Khalili Collection of Islamic Art, iii (London, 1992), no. 2.

8. Priscilla P. Soucek, "The Manuscripts of Iskandar Sultan: Structure and Content," *Timurid Art and Culture*, ed. Golombek and Subtelny, pp. 116-31.

9. Norah Titley, "Persian Miniature Painting: The Repetition of Compositions during the 15th Century," *Akten des VII. Internationalen Kongresses für Iranische Kunst und Archäologie. 1976* (Berlin, 1979), pp. 471-91; Lentz and Lowry, appendix III.

10. Istanbul, Topkapı Palace Library, H. 796. Ivan Stchoukine, "La Peinture à Yazd au début du XVe siècle," *Syria* 43 (1966): 99-104.

11. Istanbul, Topkapı Palace Library, B. 282.

12. The Historical Style was first identified and discussed by Richard Ettinghausen, "An Illuminated Manuscript of Hâfiz-i Abrû in Istanbul. Part I," *Kunst des Orients* 2 (1955): 30-44; it was also discussed by Güner Inal, "Miniatures in Historical Manuscripts from the Time of Shahrukh in the Topkapi Palace Museum," in *Timurid Art and Culture*, ed. Golombek and Subtelny, pp. 103-15.

13. Istanbul, Topkapı Palace Library, Hazine 1653. The Historical Style can also be seen in a dispersed copy of the replacement volume and a copy of the *Jâmi' al-tawârikh* (Paris, Bibliothèque Nationale, Supp. Pers. 1113). For further discussion about 14th- and 15th-century manuscripts of the works of Rashid al-Din and replacement volumes by Hafiz-i Abru, see Abolala Soudavar, *Art of the Persian Courts: Selections from the Art and History Trust Collection* (New York, 1992), no. 22.

14. See Chapter 3, Note 35.

15. Washington, DC, Freer Gallery of Art, 31.32-37. Mehmet Aga-Oglu, "The Khusrau wa Shirin Manuscript in the Freer Gallery," *Ars Islamica* 4 (1937): 479-81.

16. Istanbul, Topkapi Palace Library, Hazine 2153, fol. 98a; the text has been translated by Thackston, pp. 323-7.

17. The seven are (1) Sa'di's *Gulistān* ("Rose-garden"); 1426-7; Dublin, Chester Beatty Library, P119; (2) an anthology of poetry and treatises on music and chess; 1426-7; Settignano, Villa I Tatti; (3) Khwaju Kirmani's *Humay and Humayūn*; 1427-8; Vienna, Nationalbibliothek, N. F. 382; (4 and 5) two copies of *Kalīla and Dimna*; 1429 and 1431; Istanbul, Topkapı Palace Library, Revan 1022 and Hazine 362; (6) *Shāhnāma*; completed 1430; Tehran, Gulistan Palace Library, 61; and (7) Nizami Arudi's *Chahār Maqāla*; 1431; Istanbul, Museum of Turkish and Islamic Art, 1954.

18. Robert Hillenbrand, "The Uses of Space in Timurid Painting," *Timurid Art and Culture*, ed. Golombek and Subtelny, pp. 76-102.

19. In most *Shāhnāma* manuscripts, the scene chosen to illustrate the reign of Bahram Gur shows the hero as king while hunting; in this manuscript, however, the scene shows scholars convincing the young prince's father, the evil Yazdigird, to entrust the prince to the care of a tutor. Similarly, Kay Khusraw is typically depicted defeating Afrasiyab, the great enemy of Iran, or appointing Prince Luhrasp his successor. In this manuscript, however, the emphasis is shifted to Prince Luhrasp, who hears of his father's disappearance in a snowstorm. See also Eleanor Sims, "The Illustrated Manuscripts of Firdausi's *Shāhnāma* Commissioned by Princes of the House of Tīmūr," *Ars Orientalis* 22 (1992), pp. 43-68.

20. Berlin, Staatliche Museen Preussischer Kulturbesitz, Museum für Islamische Kunst, I.4628. Some of the illustrated folios have been detached. The manuscript was originally published by Ernst Kühnel, "Die Baysonghor-Handschrift der Islamische Abteilung," *Jahrbuch der Preussischen Kunstsammlungen*, 52 (1931): 133-52.

21. Oxford, Bodleian Library, Ouseley Add. 176. 28.7 by 19.8 cm. B. W. Robinson, *A Descriptive Catalogue of the Persian Paintings in the Bodleian Library* (Oxford, 1958), pp. 16-22.

22. Eleanor Sims, "Ibrahim-Sultan's Illustrated *Zafarnama* of 1436 and its Impact in the Muslim East," *Timurid Art and Culture*, ed. Golombek and

Subtelny, pp. 132-43, and aedem, "Ibrāhīm-Sultān's illustrated *Zafar-nāmeh* of 839/1436," *Islamic Art* 4 (1991), pp. 175-218.

23. Paris, Bibliothèque Nationale, Supp. pers. 494.

24. Cleveland Museum of Art, 45.169 and 56.10, illustrated in Basil Gray, *Persian Painting* (Geneva, 1961), pp. 102-3.

25. Paris, Bibliothèque Nationale, Supp. turc 190. See Marie-Rose Séguy, *The Miraculous Journey of Mahomet/Mirâj Nâmeh* (New York, 1977).

26. These paintings were the subject of a colloquy held by the Percival David Foundation in London. The proceedings were edited by Ernst J. Grube and E. Sims and published as *Islamic Art* 1 (1981).

27. Although the manuscript is undated and unsigned, Muhammad Juki's name and titles appear on a banner illustrated on folio 296a. London, Royal Asiatic Society, ms. 239; 34 by 22 cm. See B. W. Robinson, "The Shahnama of Muhammad Juki," in *The Royal Asiatic Society: Its History and Treasures*, ed. Stuart Simmonds and Simon Digby (Leiden, 1979), pp. 83-102; J. V. S. Wilkinson, *The Shah-nameh … with 24 illustrations from a fifteenth-century Persian Manuscript*, Introduction by Laurence Binyon (London, 1931).

28. Maria Eva Subtelny, *The Poetic Circle at the Court of the Timurid Sultan Husain Baiqara, and Its Political Significance* (Ph.D. dissertation, Harvard University, 1979).

29. Baltimore, Johns Hopkins University, Milton S. Eisenhower Library, John Work Garrett Collection. Eleanor Sims, *The Garrett Manuscript of the Zafar-Name: A Study in Fifteenth-Century Timurid Patronage*, (Ph.D. dissertation, Institute of Fine Arts, New York University, 1973).

30. "Behzād, Kamāl al-Dīn," by Priscilla P. Soucek in *Encyclopaedia Iranica*; "Bihzād, Kamāl al-Dīn, Ustād," by Richard Ettinghausen, in *EI/2*; and Thomas W. Lentz, "Changing Worlds: Bihzad and the New Painting," in *Persian Masters: Five Centuries of Painting*, ed. Sheila R. Canby (Bombay, 1990), pp. 39-54.

31. Lisa Golombek, "Toward a Classification of Islamic Painting," *Islamic Art in the Metropolitan Museum of Art*, ed. R. Ettinghausen (New York, 1972), pp. 23-34.

32. Annemarie Schimmel, *Mystical Dimensions of Islam* (Chapel Hill, NC, 1975), p. 429.

33. Ettinghausen, "Bihzad," *EI/2*.

34. A. Adamova has suggested that painters deliberately copied earlier illustrations executed in various styles in the same manuscript to show their virtuosity and mastery. See "Repetition of Compositions in Manuscripts: The *Khamsa* of Nizami in Leningrad," *Timurid Art and Culture*, ed. Golombek and Subtelny, pp. 67-75.

35. Ettinghausen's list also includes a *Khamsa* of 'Alishir Nava'i dated 890/1485 (Oxford, Bodleian Library, Elliot Ms. 287, 408, 317, 339; Manchester, John Rylands Library, Turk. Ms. 3); a *Khamsa* of Amir Khusraw Dihlavi dated 890/1485 (Dublin, Chester Beatty Library, Pers. ms. 156); a *Gulistan* of Sa'di dated Muharram 891/January 1486 (Soudavar Collection); a *Khamsa* of Nizami, text dated 846/1442 (London, British Library, Add. 25900, with one miniature dated 898/1493); a *Khamsa* of Nizami with one painting dated 900/1494-5 (London, British Library, Or. 6810); and several single paintings.

36. Istanbul, Museum of Turkish and Islamic Art, no. 1905.

37. Istanbul, Museum of Turkish and Islamic Art, no. 2046. Almost contemporary is an anthology made at Yazd in 810/1407 (Istanbul, Topkapı Palace Library, H. 796). See Oktay Aslanapa, "The Art of Bookbinding," *The Arts of the Book in Central Asia: 14th to 16th Centuries*, ed. Basil Gray (Boulder, CO, 1979), p. 61.

38. Thackston, p. 346.

39. A carpet fragment in Athens (Benaki Museum, inv. no. 16147) has recently been attributed to the fifteenth century by Lentz and Lowry, no. 119, but questions about it still remain. See Louise Mackie, "A Piece of the Puzzle: A 14th-15th Century Persian Carpet Fragment Revealed," *Hali* (1989): 16-23. The standard study of Timurid carpets is still Amy Briggs, "Timurid carpets," *Ars Islamica* 7 (1940): 20-54.

40. Melikian-Chirvani, *Islamic Metalwork*, no. 109.

41. London, British Museum, 1962.7-18.1; Lentz and Lowry, no. 151.

42. Melikian-Chirvani, *Islamic Metalwork*, p. 248.

43. Lisbon, Gulbenkian Foundation, inv. 328; and London, British Museum, no. OA 1950.4-3.1 (57). See Lentz and Lowry, no. 125.

44. G. A. Bailey, "The Dynamics of Chinoiserie in Timurid and Early Safavid Ceramics," *Timurid Art and Culture*, ed. Golombek and Subtelny, pp. 179-90.

45. St Petersburg, State Hermitage, VG-2650. Ernst Grube, "Notes on the Decorative Arts of the Timurid Period," *Gururajamanjarika: Studi in onore di Giuseppe Tucci*, 1 (Naples, 1974), 235, figs. 1 and 2; idem, "Notes on the Decorative Arts of the Timurid Period, ii," *Islamic Art* 3 (1989): 175-208; A. A. Ivanov, "Fayansovoe blyudo XV veka iz Mashkhada [A 878/1473-4 earthenware dish from Mashhad]," *Soobscheniya Gosudarstvennogo Ordena Lenina Ermitazha*, 45 (1980): 64-6, 79-80. The Royal Ontario Museum in Toronto has undertaken a major reassessment of these ceramics, which may modify current

opinion; see Bailey, "Dynamics of Chinoiserie," *Timurid Art and Culture*, ed. Golombek and Subtelny.

46. Istanbul, Topkapı Palace Library, H. 762.

47. I. Stchoukine, "Les peintures turcomanes et safavies d'une *Khamseh* de Nizâmî, achevée à Tabriz en 886/1481," *Arts Asiatiques* 44 (1966): 1–16, and I. Stchoukine, *Les peintures des manuscrits de la "Khamseh" de Nizami au Topkapı Sarayı Müzesi d'Istanbul* (Paris, 1977), pp. 70–81. The amusing and detailed colophon has been translated by Thackston, pp. 333–4.

48. The manuscript, originally containing 155 illustrations, is in the Museum of Decorative Arts, Tehran, but some of its illustrations were removed after 1953 and are now in various public and private collections, including Cambridge, MA, Harvard University Art Museums, Dublin, Chester Beatty Library, New York, Metropolitan Museum of Art, and the collection of Sadruddin Aga Khan in Geneva.

49. For the identification and enumeration of the Turkoman manuscripts, see B. W. Robinson, "The Turkman school to 1503," *Arts of the Book in Central Asia*, pp. 215–48.

CHAPTER 6: ARCHITECTURE IN EGYPT UNDER THE BAHRI
MAMLUKS (1260–1389)

1. On the Mamluks to 1382, see Robert Irwin, *The Middle East in the Middle Ages: The Early Mamluk Sultanate 1250–1382* (London and Sydney, 1986) and *EI/2*, s.v. "Mamlūks." The standard survey of Mamluk architecture in Egypt to 1326 is K. A. C. Creswell, *The Muslim Architecture of Egypt*, 2 (Oxford, 1959; repr. New York, 1979). Creswell's survey is now supplemented by Michael Meinecke, *Die mamlukische Architektur in Ägypten und Syrien*, 2 vols (Glückstadt, 1992).

2. Christel Kessler, "Funerary Architecture within the City," *Colloque Internationale sur l'histoire du Caire* (Gräfenheinichen, 1972), pp. 257–68.

3. This and the following chapter deal largely with the buildings of Cairo. For Mamluk architecture in other cities see Michael Meinecke, "Mamluk Architecture. Regional Architectural Traditions: Evolution and Interrelations," *Damaszener Mitteilungen* 2 (1985): 163–75, with extensive bibliography and Meinecke, *Mamlukische Architektur*, to which should be added Michael Hamilton Burgoyne, *Mamluk Jerusalem, an Architectural Study*, with additional historical research by D. S. Richards (n.p., 1987); Mohamed-Moain Sadek, *Die mamlukische Architektur der Stadt Gaza* (Berlin, 1991); Hayat Salam-Lieblich, *The Architecture of the Mamluk City of Tripoli* (Cambridge, MA, 1983); Jean Sauvaget, *Alep: Essai sur le développement d'une grande ville syrienne des origines au milieu du xixe siècle* (Paris, 1941); and Ernst Herefeld, *Inscriptions et monuments d'Alep*, 2 vols. (Cairo, 1954–5).

4. Jonathan M. Bloom, "The Mosque of Baybars al-Bunduqdari in Cairo," *Annales islamologiques* 18 (1982): 45–78; on al-Husayniyya, see Doris Behrens-Abouseif, "The North-Eastern Extension of Cairo under the Mamluks," *Annales islamologiques* 17 (1981): 157–89.

5. Michael Meinecke, "Das Mausoleum des Qala'un in Kairo: Untersuchungen zur Genese der mamlukischen Architekturdekoration," *Mitteilungen des Deutschen Archäologischen Instituts: Abteilung Kairo* 27/1 (1971): 63–7, and Janine Sourdel-Thomine and Bertold Spuler, *Die Kunst des Islam* (Berlin, 1973), p. 332, no. 298.

6. Ettinghausen and Grabar, p. 43.

7. The basic publication is Creswell, *Muslim Architecture of Egypt*, 2: 190–212.

8. For the decoration of the mausoleum, see Michael Meinecke, "Das Mausoleum des Qala'un in Kairo: Untersuchungen zur Genese der mamlukischen Architekturdekoration," *Mitteilungen des Deutschen Archäologischen Instituts: Abteilung Kairo* 27/1 (1971): 47–80.

9. See J. Michael Rogers, "Evidence for Mamluk-Mongol Relations, 1260–1360," *Colloque International sur l'Histoire du Caire* (Gräfenheinichen, 1972), pp. 387–8. Similar applied hollow bosses are subsequently found elsewhere in Cairo but they are not nearly as fine. See Layla Aly Ibrahim, "Four Cairene Mihrabs and their Dating," *Kunst des Orients* 7 (1970–1): 30–9.

10. Salar was the son of a Turkish master of the hunt for a Saljuq sultan of Anatolia. He was captured in 1276 during the expedition to Asia Minor of Baybars I al-Bunduqdari; he was later purchased by Qala'un and then passed to the service of his sons Khalil and Muhammad. See D. S. Rice, *The Baptistère de Saint-Louis* (Paris, 1953), pp. 16–17. Sanjar was a former mamluk of Jawli, one of the amirs of Baybars I. After Jawli's death, Sanjar first served Qala'un and then, under al-Ashraf Khalil, he was posted to Kerak, the fortress in Palestine, where he remained during the reign of al-Adil Kitbugha. According to the historian al-Maqrizi, he befriended the amir Salar like a brother and advanced in service to become a minor *üstādār* (major-domo) in the time of Baybars II al-Jashangir and Salar. See al-Maqrīzī, *al-Mawā'iz wa'l-i'tibār bi-dhikr al-khitāz wa'l-āthār* (Cairo, 1853), 2: 398.

11. On the term *khushdāshiyya*, see Irwin, *The Middle East in the Middle Ages*, pp. 88–90, with reference to David Ayalon, *L'Esclavage du mamelouk* (Jerusalem, 1951), pp. 29–37, and Donald Little, *An Introduction to Mamluk Historiography* (Wiesbaden, 1970), pp. 125–6.

12. Creswell, *Muslim Architecture of Egypt*, 2: 242–5.

13. On the building, see Leonor Fernandes, "The Foundation of Baybars al-Jashankir: Its Waqf, History, and Architecture," *Muqarnas* 4 (1987): 21–42, and Creswell, *Muslim Architecture of Egypt*, 2: 249–53.

14. Creswell, *Muslim Architecture of Egypt*, 2, pp. 260–4, and more recently, Nasser Rabbat, "Mamluk Throne Halls: Qubba or Iwan?," *Ars Orientalis* 23 (1993): 201–9.

15. Michael Meinecke, "Die mamlukischen Fayencemosaikdekorationen: eine Werkstätte aus Tabriz in Kairo (1330–1350)," *Kunst des Orients* 11 (1976–7): 85–144.

16. J. Michael Rogers, "Evidence for Mamluk-Mongol Relations, 1260–1360," *Colloque International sur l'Histoire du Caire* (Gräfenheinichen, 1972), pp. 385–404.

17. In addition to the mosque of Altinbugha, others founded in the area during al-Nasir Muhammad's reign include the mosques of Almalik al-Chukandar (1319), Ahmad al-Mihmandar (1324–5), Almas/Yilmaz (1329–30), Qusun/Qawsun (1329–30), and Beshtak (1335). The mosques of Aslam al-Baha'i/al-Silahdar (1344), Aqsunqur (1346–8), and Shaykhu al-'Umari (1349) belong to the general type but are slightly later.

18. According to Maqrizi, *Khitat*, 2:284, Ibn al-Suyufi was also responsible in 1340 for the madrasa that Aqbugha added to the Azhar mosque and its minaret.

19. Michael W. Dols, *The Black Death in the Middle East* (Princeton, 1977), and André Raymond, "Cairo's Area and Population in the Early Fifteenth Century," *Muqarnas* 2 (1984): 21–32.

20. Meinecke, "Mamluk Architecture. Regional Architectural Traditions", pp. 173–4.

21. According to Friedrich Sarre and Ernst Herzfeld, *Archäologische Reise im Euphrat- und Tigris-Gebiet* (Berlin, 1911–20), 2:74, the arch at Ctesiphon measures 25.63 meters wide, 43.72 meters deep, and 25.62 meters high, with a total height of 29.28 meters.

22. For the inscriptions, see Erica Cruikshank Dodd and Shereen Khairallah, *The Image of the Word: A Study of Quranic Verses in Islamic Architecture* (Beirut, 1981), pp. 43–60, a revised version of Erica Cruikshank Dodd, "The Image of the Word (Notes on the religious iconography of Islam)," *Berytus* 18 (1969): 35–62.

23. Ibn Khaldun, *The Muqaddimah: An Introduction to History*, trans. Franz Rosenthal, 2nd ed. (Princeton, 1967), 2:238–9.

24. Michael Meinecke, "Die mamlukischen Fayencemosaikdekorationen," 131 ff., and Christel Kessler, *The Carved Masonry Domes of Mediaeval Cairo* (London, 1976), pp. 9–10.

25. The earliest extant example of a double dome in Iran is the second tomb tower at Kharraqan (1093) in north-west Iran, for which see Ettinghausen and Grabar, pp. 268–9, but Nizam al-Mulk, the vizier to the Saljuk Malikshah, describes one of the Buyid tombs at Rayy (tenth century) as having two covers (*bi dū pūshish*). See Nizam al-Mulk, *The Book of Government or Rules for Kings*, trans. Hubert Darke (London, 1978), p. 167.

26. K. A. C. Creswell, "A Brief Chronology of the Muhammadan Monuments of Egypt to A.D. 1517," *Bulletin de l'Institut français d'archéologie orientale* 16 (1919): 114–15; Richard B. Parker, Robin Sabin, and Caroline Williams, *Islamic Monuments in Cairo: A Practical Guide* (Cairo, 1985), pp. 90–2; Kessler, *Carved Masonry Domes of Mediaeval Cairo*, pl. 15.

CHAPTER 7: ARCHITECTURE IN EGYPT, SYRIA, AND ARABIA
UNDER THE CIRCASSIAN MAMLUKS (1389–1517)

1. Jean Sauvaget, *Alep: Essai sur le développement d'une grande ville syrienne des origines au milieu du XIXe siècle* (Paris, 1941).

2. Ernst Herzfeld, *Inscriptions et monuments d'Alep*, 2 vols. (Cairo, 1954–5), pp. 362–66.

3. Jean Aubin, "Comment Tamerlan prenait les villes," *Studia Islamica* 19 (1963): 83–122, and Beatrice Forbes Manz, *The Rise and Rule of Tamerlane* (Cambridge, 1989).

4. Michael Meinecke, "Mamluk Architecture. Regional Architectural Traditions: Evolution and Interrelations," *Damaszener Mitteilungen* 2 (1985): 163–75.

5. [J.] Michael Rogers, "The Stones of Barquq: Building materials and architectural decoration in late fourteenth-century Cairo," *Apollo* 103, no. 170 (1976): 307–13, and Saleh Lamei Mostafa, "Madrasa, Hanqa und Mausoleum des Barquq in Kairo, mit einem Beitrag von Felicitas Jaritz," *Abhandlungen des Deutschen Archäologischen Instituts, Abteilung Kairo, Islamische Reihe* 4 (1982): 118 ff.

6. Saleh Lamei Mostafa, *Kloster und Mausoleum des Farag ibn Barquq in Kairo* (Glückstadt, 1968).

7. al-Maqrizi, *Khitat*, 2: 328.

8. Michael Hamilton Burgoyne, *Mamluk Jerusalem, an Architectural Study* (n.p., 1987), p. 90. Simpler folded groined vaults appear in Cairo at the complexes of Barquq and Faraj.

9. Or some 35 meters above the roof. Compare this to the minarets of Faraj, which extend 30 meters above the roof for a total height of 46 meters.

10. Doris Behrens-Abouseif, *The Minarets of Cairo* (Cairo, 1985), p. 116.

11. Amy W. Newhall, "The Patronage of the Mamluk Sultan Qa'it Bay, 872–901/1468–1496" (Ph.D. dissertation, Harvard University, 1987).

12. See Michael Meinecke, *Die Restaurierung der Madrasa des Amirs Sabiq ad-Din Mitqal al-Anuki und die Sanierung des Darb Qirmiz in Kairo* (Mainz, 1980).

13. L. A. Mayer, *The Buildings of Qaytbay, as Described in his Endowment Deed* [in Arabic] (London, 1938).

14. Doris Behrens-Abouseif, *Islamic Architecture in Cairo, an Introduction* (Leiden, 1989), p. 147; Newhall, *Patronage*, pp. 157–63.

15. Newhall, *Patronage*, Ch. 7.

16. Burgoyne, *Mamluk Jerusalem*, pp. 589–605.

17. Archie G. Walls, *Geometry and Architecture in Islamic Jerusalem: A Study of the Ashrafiyya* (Buckhurst Hill, 1990).

18. Burgoyne, *Mamluk Jerusalem*, p. 97.

19. It is dated Shawal 887/November–December 1482. Burgoyne, *Mamluk Jerusalem*, no. 64, pp. 606–12, and Christel Kessler and M. Burgoyne, "The Fountain of Sultan Qaytbay in the Sacred Precinct of Jerusalem," *Archaeology in the Levant: Essays for Kathleen Kenyon*, ed. R. Moorey and P. Parr (Warminster, Wilts, 1978), pp. 250–69.

20. J. M. Rogers, "Innovation and Continuity in Islamic Urbanism," *The Arab City, its Character and Islamic Cultural Heritage*, a symposium held in Medina, ed. Ismail Serageldin and Samir El-Sadek (n.p., 1982), pp. 53–61.

21. See Jacques Revault and Bernard Maury, *Palais et maisons du Caire du XIVe au XVIIIe siècle*, 3 vols. (Cairo, 1975–); Laila 'Ali Ibrahim, "Residential Architecture in Mamluk Cairo," *Muqarnas* 2 (1984): 47–60; Jean-Claude Garcin, Bernard Maury, Jacques Revault, and Mona Zakariya, *Palais et maisons du Caire, I. Epoque Mamelouke* (Paris, 1982).

22. Garcin et al., *Palais et maisons*, pp. 51–9; Revault and Maury, *Palais et maisons*, 2:31–48.

23. The enormous extent of Qawsun's wealth is indicated by the economic effects when his palace was looted in 1342. Before the palace was looted, the ratio of silver to gold was twenty to one, the standard ratio in the Islamic middle ages. The incredible quantity of gold coin found there and put into circulation violently upset the ratio, and it briefly fell to eleven to one. See Michael W. Dols, *The Black Death in the Middle East* (Princeton, 1977), p. 257, n. 7.

24. It is signed by the artist, Muḥammad b. Aḥmad Zaghlish al-Shāmī ("from Syria"). See Revault and Maury, *Palais et maisons*, 2:31–48.

25. Behrens-Abouseif, *Islamic Architecture*, pp. 39–40, and Laila 'Ali Ibrahim, "Middle-class Living Units in Mamluk Cairo: Architecture and Terminology," *Art and Archaeology Research Papers* 14 (1978): 24–30.

26. D. Brandenburg, *Islamische Baukunst in Ägypten* (Berlin, 1966), pp. 197–200.

27. Mohamed Scharabi, "Drei traditionelle Handelsanlagen in Kairo: Wakalat al-Bazara, Wakalat Du l-Fiqar und Wakalat al-Qutn," *Mitteilungen des Deutschen Archäologischen Instituts: Abteilung Kairo* 34 (1978): 127–64.

28. Nuha Sadek, "Rasulid women: Power and Patronage," *Proceedings of the Seminar for Arabian Studies* 19 (1989): 121–36; Barbara Finster, "An Outline of the History of Islamic Religious Architecture in Yemen," *Muqarnas* 9 (1992): 124–47.

29. R. B. Lewcock and G. R. Smith, "Three Medieval Mosques in the Yemen," *Oriental Art* 20 (1974): 75–86 and 192–203.

CHAPTER 8: THE ARTS IN EGYPT AND SYRIA UNDER THE MAMLUKS

1. Michael W. Dols, *The Black Death in the Middle East* (Princeton, 1977), p. 263.

2. James W. Allan, "The Survival of Precious and Base Metal Objects from the Medieval Islamic World," in *Pots and Pans: A Colloquium on Precious Metals and Ceramics* (Oxford Studies in Islamic Art, 7; Oxford, 1985), pp. 57–70.

3. Cairo, Museum of Islamic Art, 1657 (diam. 25 cm; h. 22.5 cm); see Esin Atıl, *Renaissance of Islam: Art of the Mamluks* (Washington, DC, 1981), no. 10. A similar, although slightly smaller candlestick (diam. 19.5 cm; h. 17.9 cm) is in a private collection, for which see James W. Allan, *Islamic Metalwork: The Nuhad Es-Said Collection* (London, 1982), no. 13. He notes similar decoration on several other pieces.

4. Ettinghausen and Grabar, pp. 362–73.

5. From the epithet *al-mawṣulī* it is difficult to determine whether the individual or his family actually came from Mosul or whether he used it to identify the style of his work. See Atıl, *Renaissance*, p. 58.

6. Allan, *Islamic Metalwork*, pp. 82–3, citing al-Maqrizi, *Kitāb al-sulūk*, ed. Ziada (Cairo, 1942), vol. 2, pt. 2, pp. 345–6.

7. Paris, Louvre, LP 16. See D. S. Rice, *The Baptistère de Saint-Louis* (Paris, 1953); Atıl, *Renaissance*, no. 21.

8. Freer Gallery of Art, 55.10.

9. As, for example, the set made before 1341 for Sayf al-Din Toqto, cup-bearer to al-Malik al-Ashraf, which was found at Qus in Upper Egypt. See Amal A. El-Emery, "Studies in Some Islamic Objects Newly Discovered at Qus," *Annales islamologiques* 7 (1967): 121–38, and *The Arts of Islam* (London, 1976), nos. 219 and 220.

10. Rice, *Baptistère*, pp. 13–17.

11. Elfriede R. Knauer, "Einige trachtgeschichtliche Beobachtungen am Werke Giottos," *Scritti in Onore di Roberto Salvini* (Florence, 1984), pp. 173–81, has suggested that the scenes depict an exchange of embassies between Berke Khan and Baybars I which culminated in the circumcision of Baybars' son on 10 Dhu'l-Qa'da 662/3 September 1264. Similarly Doris Behrens-Abouseif, "The Baptistère de Saint Louis: A Reinterpretation," *Islamic Art* 3 (1988–9): 3–9, has attributed it to the patronage of Baybars. Both of these attributions would put the basin some thirty years earlier than the date proposed by Rice and disregard the stylistic evidence so carefully elucidated by him. For contemporary narrative, see Marianna Shreve Simpson, "Narrative Allusion and Metaphor in the Decoration of Medieval Islamic Objects," Herbert L. Kessler and Marianna Shreve Simpson, eds, *Pictorial Narrative in Antiquity and the Middle Ages* (Washington, 1985), pp. 131–49.

12. London, British Museum, BM 51–4 1. See Atıl, *Renaissance*, no. 26.

13. Jonathan M. Bloom, "A Mamluk Basin in the L. A. Mayer Memorial Institute," *Islamic Art* 2 (1987): 15–26.

14. Paris, Louvre, MAO 331, the Vasselot bowl. See Atıl, *Renaissance*, no. 20.

15. Istanbul, Topkapı Palace Museum, 2/1796. See Çengiz Köseoğlu, *The Topkapı Saray Museum: The Treasury*, trans., expanded, and ed. J. M. Rogers (Boston, 1987), no. 109, which gives the correct reading of the inscription (RCEA 6105).

16. Jerusalem, L. A. Mayer Memorial Institute, M 58. Bloom, "Mamluk Basin."

17. El-Emery, "Studies," pp. 123–7, and *The Arts of Islam*, no. 218. See also Atıl, *Renaissance*, p. 75. The Is'ardiyya Madrasa in Jerusalem preserves a screen of forged iron inscribed "Muhammad b. al-Zayn, the servant of the humble servant of the one in need of God, who hopes for the pardon of his Lord, His Excellency . . ." The date of the madrasa is uncertain: although it is mentioned as early as 1345, its endowment deed dates only from 1359. The relationship of this screen to the work of the master craftsman who produced the Baptistère is uncertain, for this is not the way he signed other pieces and this screen may not have been made for its present location. For the Is'ardiyya Madrasa and the screen, see M. H. Burgoyne, *Mamluk Jerusalem, an Architectural Study*, with additional historical research by D. S. Richards (n.p., 1987), pp. 368–79.

18. See Gaston Wiet, *Catalogue générale du Musée Arabe du Caire: Objets en cuivre* (Cairo, 1932); Atıl, *Renaissance*, nos. 18–27; Allan, *Islamic Metalwork*, nos. 14, 15.

19. Cairo, Museum of Islamic Art, 15125; h. 31 cm. *The Arts of Islam*, no. 223. Tuquztimur was a typical Mamluk amir who grew wealthy during the peaceful reign of al-Nasir Muhammad; following the sultan's death in 1340 he participated unsuccessfully in the squabbles for succession and died in disgrace in 1345. Three of his daughters married future Mamluk sultans. See Robert Irwin, *The Middle East in the Middle Ages: The Early Mamluk Sultanate 1250–1382* (London and Sydney, 1986), pp. 125–7.

20. Cairo, Museum of Islamic Art, 183, for which see Atıl, *Renaissance*, no. 25; Cairo, Al-Azhar Library, for which see Wiet, *Objets en cuivre*, app. no. 180, and *Islamic Art in Egypt: 969–1517 AD* (exh. cat., Ministry of Culture, U.A.R., Cairo, 1969), no. 60; Berlin, Museum für Islamische Kunst, no. I.886, see *The Arts of Islam*, no. 214, and *Museum für Islamische Kunst Berlin: Katalog 1971*, no. 19.

21. Cairo, Museum of Islamic Art, no. 139, dated 728/1327–8; see *Islamic Art in Egypt*, no. 61.

22. *The Travels of Ibn Battuta, A.D. 1325–1354*, trans. H. A. R. Gibb (London, 1958), 1:44, and David James, *Qur'ans of the Mamluks* (London, 1988), pp. 32–3.

23. London, British Library, Add. 22406–12.

24. Leonor Fernandes, "The Foundation of Baybars al-Jashankir: Its Waqf, History, and Architecture," *Muqarnas* 4 (1987): 27.

25. James, *Qur'ans*, pp. 36–7, citing Ibn Iyas, I, i, 418–19. The relative cost of the Koran manuscript can be established by comparison with the salary of the shaykh in charge of the entire khanaqah, which was 100 dirhams, or 5 dinars, a month. The Koran manuscript cost more than 26 times his annual salary.

26. James, *Qur'ans*, Ch. 3.

27. One of the manuscripts was ordered by Baybars al-Jashangir when he was an amir, two by al-Nasir Muhammad as sultan, and a fourth by one of his former slaves, a woman. See James, *Qur'ans*, nos. 1, 11, 12, and 19.

28. Abu Sa'id Sayf al-Din Bakhtimur b. 'Abdallah was cup-bearer to al-Nasir Muhammad; see James, *Qur'ans*, pp. 103–10 and cat. no. 45.

29. For example, a *Kitāb al-Zardaq*, a veterinary manual with eleven paintings or diagrams (Istanbul University Library, A.4689), was produced for Yalbay, a mamluk of Qanibay al-Hamzawi (d. 1458), probably in Damascus ca. 1435. Yalbay was keeper of the horse for the commander-in-chief of Damascus during the reign of Barsbay (r. 1422–37). A two-volume Turkish translation of the *Shāhnāma* was transcribed by Husayn b. Hasan b. Muhammad al-Husayni al-Hanafi for Qansuh al-Ghawri (r. 1501–17; Istanbul, Topkapı Palace Museum, H. 1519); it contains 62 paintings. It is the only illustrated manuscript known to have been commissioned by a Mamluk sultan. See Esin Atıl, "Mamluk Painting in the Late Fifteenth Century," *Muqarnas* 2 (1984): 163–9.

30. Atıl, *Renaissance*, pp. 255–7.

31. Paris, Bibliothèque Nationale, MS. arabe 5847. See Oleg Grabar, *The Illustrations of the Maqamat* (Chicago, 1984), no. 3.

32. Escorial, Ar. 898, dated 1354; London, British Library, Or. 9718; Vienna, Nationalbibliothek, A. F. 9, with 195 folios measuring 37 by 25.5 cm, containing 70 illustrations; see Duncan Haldane, *Mamluk Painting* (Warminster, 1978), pp. 50, 100.

33. Richard Ettinghausen, *Arab Painting* (Geneva, 1962), p. 154.

34. Ettinghausen, *Arab Painting*, p. 65.

35. Homaizi Collection, Kuwait; four detached folios are in the Freer Gallery (54.1–2), Sadruddin Aga Khan and al-Sabah collections; facsimile with translation by M. Amari and commentary by A.S. Melikian-Chirvani, *Muhammad Ibn Zafar al-Siqilli's Sulwan al-Muta' [Prescription for Pleasure]* (Kuwait, 1985).

36. Two manuscripts can be associated with the sons of Mamluk officials. The first is a copy (Oxford, Bodleian Library, Marsh 458) of the *Maqāmāt* made in 1337 for Nasir al-Din Muhammad, the free-born son of Turuntay (d. 1290), who served as viceroy of Egypt under Qala'un. A copy of Isma'il b. al-Razzaz al-Jazari's *Kitāb fī ma'rifat al-hiyāl al-handasiyya* ("Treatise on automata") was transcribed in 1354 by Muhammad b. Ahmad al-Ismiri for the amir Nasr al-Din Muhammad, the son of Tulak al-Harrani, a military judge in the service of sultans Salah al-Din Salih (r. 1351–54) and his brother Hasan. Most of the manuscript is in Istanbul, Süleymaniye, 3606. Both of these patrons were therefore members of the *awlād al-nās*, the descendants of Mamluks who presumably could have read Arabic fluently and would have enjoyed doing it. See *The Arts of Islam*, no. 535; Haldane, *Mamluk Painting*, p. 55.

37. London, British Library, Add. 7293.

38. Haldane, *Mamluk Painting*, p. 50.

39. See James, *Qur'ans*, Ch. 8.

40. Cairo, National Library, nos. 6, 7, and 54.

41. David James, *The Master Scribes: Qur'ans of the 10th to the 14th centuries AD* (London, 1992), pp. 172–5.

42. Ibrahim al-Amidi signed one manuscript (Cairo, National Library, 10), and three others (Cairo, National Library, 9, 15, and a dispersed manuscript) can be attributed to him. See James, *Qur'ans*, nos. 32, 31, 34, and 35.

43. James W. Allan, "Sha'ban, Barquq, and the Decline of the Mamluk Metalworking Industry," *Muqarnas* 2 (1984): 85–94.

44. European patrons included Hugh IV of Lusignan, King of Cyprus 1324–59. A basin in Paris (Louvre, MAO 101) is inscribed with his name. See Anthony Welch, *Calligraphy in the Arts of the Muslim World* (Austin, 1979), no. 23.

45. Florence, Museo Nazionale del Bargello, 357C. See *The Arts of Islam*, no. 216.

46. Paris, Musée des Arts Décoratifs. *RCEA* 4705. Other Egyptian brasses made for the Rasulids are discussed in Max van Berchem, "Notes d'archéologie arabe," *Journal asiatique*, 10e sér. 3 (1904): 5–96, and Atıl, *Renaissance*, p. 62.

47. Atıl, *Renaissance*, no. 19, and *The Arts of Islam*, no. 220.

48. Atıl, *Renaissance*, pp. 146–92; Marilyn Jenkins, "Mamluk Underglaze Painted Pottery: Foundations for Further Study," *Muqarnas* 2 (1984): 95–114; for the Fustat evidence, see the many articles by George Scanlon, including "Mamluk Pottery: More Evidence from Fustat," *Muqarnas* 2 (1984): 115–261; Lane, *Later Islamic Pottery*, pp. 31.

49. *Arts of Islam*, no. 311; the piece was acquired by the al-Sabah Collection (LNS 188C), for which see Marilyn Jenkins, ed., *Islamic Art in the Kuwait National Museum: The al-Sabah Collection* (London, 1983), p. 84.

50. See Ettinghausen and Grabar, pp. 346, 362.

51. Atıl, *Art of the Arab World*, no. 75.

52. Gaston Wiet, *Lampes et bouteilles en verre émaillé* (Cairo, 1929), pp. 167–73.

53. Koran 24:35. This passage is commonly translated as "The likeness of His Light is as a niche wherein is a lamp...", thereby leading to the erroneous comparison to a mihrab, but instead it is clearly describing a floating lamp in a glass. This juxtaposition of the sultan's name in reserve with the Light Verse in enamel occurs already on lamps made for the madrasa of al-Nasir Muhammad. See Wiet, *Lampes*, no. 313.

54. Wiet, *Lampes*, nos. 332 and 333; E. Ashtor, *A Social and Economic History of the Near East in the Middle Ages* (Berkeley and Los Angeles, 1976), p. 309.

55. Louise W. Mackie, "Toward an Understanding of Mamluk Silks: National and International Considerations," *Muqarnas* 2 (1984): 128.

56. M. A. Marzouk, "The Tiraz Institutions in Mediaeval Egypt," *Studies in Islamic Art and Architecture in Honour of Professor K. A. C. Creswell* (Cairo, 1975), p. 161.

57. Ashtor, *Social and Economic History*, p. 310.

58. Robert G. Irwin, "Egypt, Syria and their Trading Partners 1450–1550," in Pinner and Denny, p. 79.

59. London, Victoria and Albert Museum, 753–1904, made into an orphrey.

60. Three other sultans bore the title al-Ashraf before 1430: al-Ashraf Sha'ban II (r. 1363–76) is also a possibility, but the other two, al-Ashraf Khalil (r. 1290–4) and al-Ashraf Kujuk, who reigned only in 1341, both seem too early.

61. Allan, "Sha'ban, Barquq," p. 91.

62. Amy W. Newhall, *The Patronage of the Mamluk Sultan Qa'it Bay, 872–901/1468–1496* (Ph.D. dissertation, Harvard University, 1987), Ch. 6.

63. Wiet, *Objets*, p. 35, nos. 1–5, and Atıl, *Renaissance*, no. 34. Cairo, Museum of Islamic Art, 4072, 4297; Athens, Benaki Museum, 13040; ex-'Ali Pasha Ibrahim and ex-Harari collections.

64. Some two dozen objects bear Qa'itbay's name. See Wiet, *Objets*, nos. 355–77, and A. S. Melikian-Chirvani, "Cuivres inédits de l'époque de Qa'itbay," *Kunst des Orients* 6 (1969): 99–133.

65. Istanbul, Museum of Turkish and Islamic Art; Zahir Güvemli and Can Kerametli, *Türk ve İslam Eserleri Müzesi* (Istanbul, 1974), p. 48.

66. One in New York, Metropolitan Museum of Art, 91.1.565, has only engraved decoration; another in London, Victoria and Albert Museum, 1525.1856, has a raised design on the bottom of lanceolate forms. It was originally inlaid but much of the inlay has fallen out.

67. Victoria and Albert Museum, 1050–1869; h. 7.30 m. *Die Kunst des Islam*, no. 309; Stanley Lane-Poole, *The Art of the Saracens in Egypt* (London, 1886), pp. 111–44.

68. Newhall, *Patronage*, 235, citing Sakhawi and Wustenfeld, III: 224.

69. Metropolitan Museum of Art, 07.236.26, 28–31, and 46. See Atıl, *Renaissance*, no. 104.

70. Atıl, *Renaissance*, pp. 195–6.

71. Chester Beatty Library, Arab. 4169. Three other undated manuscripts with similar *takhmis* were executed during the reign of Qa'itbay. See Atıl, *Renaissance*, pp. 46–7.

72. The largest and most comprehensive collection of these is in the Textile Museum in Washington, DC, for which see E. Kühnel and L. Bellinger, *Cairene Rugs and Others Technically Related* (Washington, DC, 1957). See also Pinner and Denny.

73. Vienna, Österreichisches Museum für angewandte Kunst, T 8332. S. Troll, *Altorientalische Teppiche* (Vienna, 1951), pl. 40.

74. The unique example with five octagons is the "Simonetti" Mamluk carpet, New York, Metropolitan Museum, inv. no. 1970.105. It measures 8.97 by 2.39 m. See M. S. Dimand and Jean Mailey, *Oriental Rugs in the Metropolitan Museum of Art* (New York, 1973), fig. 181. The largest surviving example is the Medici Mamluk carpet, which measures 10.88 by 4 meters, recently discovered in a storeroom in the Pitti Palace. Documents record that it was acquired in 1567 during the reign of Grand Duke Cosimo I. See Alberto Boralevi, "Three Egyptian Carpets in Italy," in Pinner and Denny, pp. 205–20.

75. Robert G. Irwin, "Egypt, Syria and their Trading Partners 1450–1550," in Pinner and Denny, p. 79.

CHAPTER 9: ARCHITECTURE AND THE ARTS IN THE MAGHRIB UNDER THE HAFSIDS, MARINIDS, AND NASRIDS

1. G. Marçais, *Architecture musulmane d'occident* (Paris, 1954), pp. 294–5, and Abdelaziz Daoulatli, *Tunis sous les Hafsides. Evolution urbaine et activité architecturale* (Tunis, 1976). For general bibliography, *see* Chapter 17 note 1.

2. Jonathan M. Bloom, "The Origins of Fatimid Art," *Muqarnas* 3 (1985), pl. 1.

3. On the earlier history of the madrasa, see Ettinghausen and Grabar, pp. 255 and 266.

4. Paris, Bibliothèque Nationale, Arabe 389–392. François Déroche, *Les Manuscrits du Koran du Maghreb à l'Insulinde*, pt. 2 (Paris, 1985), pp. 36–7.

5. Jonathan M. Bloom, "Al-Ma'mūn's Blue Koran?," *Revue des Études Islamiques* 54 (1986): 61–5.

6. Ibrahim Shabbūh, "Sijil qadīm li-maktaba jāmi' al-qayrawān [An old register of the library of the Great Mosque of Kairouan]," *Revue de l'institut des manuscrits arabes* 2 (1956): 345.

7. Georges Marçais and Louis Poinssot, *Objets Kairouanais IXe au XIIIe siecle* (Tunis, 1948), pl. 46.

8. The basic study of the mosque is Henri Terrasse, *La Grande Mosquée de Taza* (Paris, 1943). Despite the evidence of the inscription, Terrasse recon-

structed the original Almohad mosque as nine bays wide and felt that the side bays were only rebuilt by the Marinids.

9. See Ettinghausen and Grabar, pp. 128 ff.

10. Rachid Bourouiba, *L'Art religieux musulmane en Algérie* (Algiers, 1973), pp. 85–6.

11. On the tradition of minbars in Morocco, see Jonathan M. Bloom in Jerrilynn D. Dodds, ed., *Al-Andalus: The Art of Islamic Spain* (New York, 1992), pp. 249–51 and 362–7.

12. The basic work on Tlemcen remains William and Georges Marçais, *Les Monuments arabes de Tlemcen* (Paris, 1903).

13. Ettinghausen and Grabar, pp. 141–3.

14. Ettinghausen and Grabar, fig. 123.

15. See Sheila S. Blair, "Sufi Saints and Shrine Architecture," *Muqarnas* 7 (1990): 35–49.

16. Charles Terrasse, *Médersas du Maroc* (Paris, n.d.).

17. Henri Basset and E. Lévi-Provençal, *Chella: une necropole mérinide* (Paris, 1922), extract from *Hesperis* (1922).

18. Oleg Grabar, *The Alhambra* (London and Cambridge, MA, 1978), with extensive bibliography, and James Dickie, "The Alhambra: Some Reflections Prompted by a Recent Study by Oleg Grabar," *Studia Arabica et Islamica: Festschrift for Ihsan 'Abbas on his Sixtieth Birthday*, ed. Widad al-Qadi (Beirut, 1981), pp. 127–49; Dodds, *Al-Andalus*, pp. 127–72.

19. Antonio Fernández Puertas, *The Facade of the Palace of Comares* (Granada, 1980).

20. Jerrilynn D. Dodds, "The Paintings in the Sala de Justicia of the Alhambra: Iconography and Iconology," *Art Bulletin* 61 (1979): 186–97.

21. Summer S. Kenesson, "Nasrid Luster Pottery: The Alhambra Vases," *Muqarnas* 9 (1992): 93–115; Alan Caiger-Smith, *Lustre Pottery: Technique, Tradition and Innovation in Islam and the Western World* (London, 1985), pp. 84–99; Balbina Martinez Caviró, *La Loza dorada* (Madrid, 1983), pp. 52–88; Richard Ettinghausen, "Notes on the Lusterware of Spain," *Ars Orientalis* I (1954): 145–48; A. W. Frothingham, *Lusterware of Spain* (New York, 1951), pp. 21–4. The major fragment is in the Freer Gallery of Art, Washington, DC (03.206), for which see Esin Atıl, *Ceramics from the World of Islam* (Washington, DC, 1973), no. 78; Dodds, *Al-Andalus*, nos. 110–12.

22. Antonio Almagro Cárdenas, *Estudio sobre las inscripciones árabes de Granada* (Granada, 1879), pp. 47–8, and Grabar, *Alhambra*, p. 141.

23. Frothingham, *Lusterware of Spain*, pp. 21–4.

24. Madrid, Instituto de Valencia de Don Juan. It is known for the painter Mariano Fortuny who purchased it from a carman in the Albaicín near the Alhambra in the middle of the nineteenth century. Caiger-Smith, fig. 57 and pp. 96–9; Dodds, *Al-Andalus*, no. 113.

25. Caiger-Smith, p. 127.

26. Cleveland Museum of Art, 82.16. The other two are in New York, at the Metropolitan Museum of Art and the Cooper-Hewitt Museum. See Anne Wardwell, "A Fifteenth-Century Silk Curtain from Muslim Spain," *Bulletin of the Cleveland Museum of Art*, 70 (1983): 58–72; Dodds, *Al-Andalus*, no. 99. The Cleveland curtain was first published by Cristina Partearroyo, "Spanish-Muslim Textile," *Bulletin de liaison du Centre International d'Etude des Textiles Anciens* 45 (1977): 78–81.

27. Dorothy G. Sheperd, "A Treasury from a Thirteenth-Century Spanish Tomb," *Bulletin of the Cleveland Museum of Art* 65 (1978): 111–29.

CHAPTER 10: ARCHITECTURE AND THE ARTS IN ANATOLIA UNDER THE BEYLIKS AND EARLY OTTOMANS

1. For example, the mosque of 'Ala al-Din at Konya, built between 1156 and 1220; see Ettinghausen and Grabar, p. 314 and ill. 338.

2. J. M. Rogers, "The Date of the Çifte Minare Medrese at Erzurum," *Kunst des Orients* 8 (1974): 77–149.

3. R. H. Ünal, *Les Monuments islamiques anciens de la ville d'Erzurum et de sa région* (Istanbul, 1968), pp. 32–51.

4. The foundation inscription, including the text of the endowment, is prominently engraved in the south iwan (*RCEA* 5277 and Ünal, pp. 49–51); a briefer text with the patron's name and date is inscribed over the main portal (*RCEA* 5276 and Ünal, p. 48).

5. See Ettinghausen and Grabar, p. 317 and ills. 344–6, where the date is incorrectly given as 1253.

6. An example of dynastic history is Oktay Aslanapa, *Turkish Art and Architecture* (New York, 1971); a typological analysis is provided by M. Oluş Arık, "Turkish Architecture in Asia Minor in the Period of the Turkish Emirates," in Ekrem Akurgal, ed., *The Art and Architecture of Turkey* (New York, 1980), pp. 111–36.

7. Katharina Otto-Dorn, *Das Islamische Iznik* (Berlin, 1941); the foundation inscription is published in *RCEA* 5659.

8. Ettinghausen and Grabar, ill. 350.

9. Aptullah Kuran, *The Mosque in Early Ottoman Architecture* (Chicago, 1967), pp. 78–9. Oktay Aslanapa, "Iznik'te Sultan Orhan Imaret Camii Kazisi (Die Ausgrabungen der Sultan Orhan Imaret Moschee von Iznik)," *Sanat Tarihi Yıllığı* I (1964–5): 16–31 (Turkish), 32–8 (German).

10. Semavi Eyice, "Zaviyeler ve Zaviyeli Camiler [Sufi convents and mosques containing them]," *Iktisat Fakültesi Mecmuası* 23 (1962–3): 3–80.

11. The fundamental study of the city and its monuments is Albert Gabriel, *Une capitale turque, Brousse (Bursa)* (Paris, 1958).

12. Kuran, *Mosque*, pp. 98–101.

13. Katharina Otto-Dorn, "Die Isa Bey Moschee in Ephesus," *Istanbuler Forschungen* 17 (1950): 115–31, and *RCEA*, vol. 17, no. 776 013.

14. See Ettinghausen and Grabar, pp. 37–45 and ills. 11–15.

15. *RCEA* 768 006 cites the date in the foundation inscription over the portal as 768 (1366–7), but other sources report the date as 776 (1374–5) or 778 (1376–7).

16. Karl Wulzinger, "Die Piruz-Moschee zu Milas," *Festschrift anlässlich der 100 jährigen Bestens der Technischen Hochschule Fridericiana zu Karlsruhe* (Karlsruhe, 1925), pp. 161–87, and Aslanapa, *Turkish Art and Architecture*, p. 186.

17. An Ottoman source states that the same Hajji 'Iwad was subaşi, or prefect, of Bursa in 1413, when the Karamanids besieged the town. His brave conduct led to his promotion first to governor of Bursa and later to vizier. He was dismissed by Murad II in 1426–7 and died the following year. See Robert Mantran, "Les inscriptions arabes de Brousse," *Bulletin d'études orientales* 14 (1952–4): 92–4.

18. Nurhan Atasoy and Julian Raby, *Iznik: The Pottery of Ottoman Turkey* (London, 1989), p. 82.

19. Mantran, "Inscriptions," pp. 105–8.

20. Rudolf M. Riefstahl, "Early Turkish tile revetments in Edirne," *Ars Islamica* 4 (1937): 249–81.

21. Atasoy and Raby, *Iznik*, p. 88, and John Carswell, "Six Tiles," *Islamic Art in the Metropolitan Museum of Art*, ed. Richard Ettinghausen (New York, 1972), pp. 99–124.

22. Both of these features appear, however, in the Mosque of Güzelce Hasan Bey in Hayrabolu, Tekirdağ, built in 1406, for which see Kuran, *Mosque*, p. 182.

23. Atasoy and Raby, *Iznik*, pp. 83–9.

24. Friedrich Sarre, "Die Keramik der islamischer Zeit," *Das islamische Milet*, ed. K. Wulzinger and P. Wittek (Berlin, 1935).

25. Oktay Aslanapa, *Türkische Fliesen und Keramik in Anatolien* (Istanbul, 1965). "Miletus ware" was also produced at Kütahya and at Akcaalan near Ezine.

26. Arthur Lane, *Later Islamic Pottery* (London, 1957), pl. 17B.

27. M. Zeki Oral, "Anadolu'da san'at degeri olan ahsap minberler, kitabewrleri ve tarihçeleri [Wooden minbars of artistic value in Anatolia, with their inscriptions and histories]," *Vakiflar Dergisi* 5 (1962): 23–77.

28. Illustrated in Akurgal, *Art and Architecture of Turkey*, fig. 124.

29. See Ettinghausen and Grabar, p. 383. A group of bell-shaped candlesticks cast in bronze with hollow cores and inlaid with silver and occasionally gold has traditionally been attributed to Azerbayjan under the Ilkhanids, but recent opinion suggests that they were produced in Anatolia under the Saljuqs. They share common decorative schemes and vocabulary; two-thirds have princely themes, one-third show the labors of the month. See D. S. Rice, "The Seasons and Labours of the Months," *Ars Orientalis* I (1954): 1–39; Esin Atıl, "Two Il-Hânid Candlesticks at the University of Michigan," *Kunst des Orients* 8 (1972): 1–34; J. S. Allan, "From Tabrîz to Siirt – Relocation of a thirteenth-Century Metalworking School," *Iran* 16 (1978): 182–3; A. S. Melikian-Chirvani, *Islamic Metalwork from the Iranian World, 8th-18th Centuries* (London, 1982), pp. 356–68.

30. They include a small bronze vase in the Louvre dated 1329 with the name of sultan Orhan (published in the catalogue of the exhibition at the Musée des Arts Décoratifs, *Splendeur de l'art turc* (Paris, 1953), cat. no. 138) and a bowl in the Hermitage with the name and titles of Murad II, which is more closely related to Mamluk work (illustrated in Yanni Petsopoulos, ed., *Tulips, Arabesques & Turbans* (New York, 1982), p. 37).

31. The copy of *Warqa and Gulshah* in Istanbul (Topkapı Palace Library, Hazine 841; Ettinghausen and Grabar, pp. 360–1 and ills. 381–3) can be attributed to early-thirteenth-century Konya, as the scribe 'Abd al-Mumin b. Muhammad of Khoy was also mentioned in the endowment deed for the Karatay Madrasa built in Konya in 1251 (see M. K. Özergin, "Selçuklu Sanatçisi Nakkaş Abdülmü'min el-Hoyi Hakkinda," *Belleten* 34 (1970): 219–30). Another manuscript produced under the patronage of the Saljuqs of Rum is a three-part *Treatise on Astrology and Divination* (Paris, Bibliothèque Nationale, Persan 174) copied for Sultan Ghiyath al-Din Kaykhusraw III at Aksaray and Kayseri by Nasr al-Din Sivasi in 1271–2 (E. Blochet, *Les Enluminures des Manuscrits orientaux, turcs, arabes, persans* (Paris, 1926), pp. 70–2 and pls. XVIII–2XIX).

32. New York Public Library, Spencer, Arab. MS 3; see Barbara Schmitz, *Islamic Manuscripts in The New York Public Library*, with contributions by Latif

Khayyat, Svat Soucek, and Massoud Pourfarrokh (New York and Oxford, 1992), V. 8.

33. Paris, Bibliothèque Nationale, Suppl. turc 309; see Esin Atıl, "Ottoman Miniature Painting under Sultan Mehmed II," *Ars Orientalis* 9 (1973): 106 and fig. 1.

34. See also Ernst J. Grube, "Notes on Ottoman Painting in the 15th Century," *Essays in Islamic Art and Architecture in Honor of Katharina Otto-Dorn*, ed. Abbas Daneshvari (Malibu, 1981), pp. 51–62.

35. Istanbul, Topkapı Palace Museum Library, R. 1726 (Karatay F. 279). See *The Anatolian Civilisations III, Seljuk/Ottoman.* (Istanbul, 1983), p. 107, E. 2.

36. Other examples were found at Beyşehir in 1925, and further fragments were excavated at Fustat in Cairo.

37. These early carpets are discussed in Ettinghausen and Grabar, pp. 383–4 and ill. 402; see also Kurt Erdmann, *Seven Hundred Years of Oriental Carpets*, ed. Hanna Erdmann, trans. M. H. Beattie and H. Herzog (Berkeley and Los Angeles, 1970), pp. 41–6 and figs. 23–30; for the fourteenth-century dating, see Agnes Geijer, "Some thoughts on the problems of early Oriental carpets," *Ars Orientalis* 5 (1963): 83 and figs. 1–2.

38. There is, however, a unique Spanish copy of a Konya-type carpet in the Textile Museum, Washington (1976.10.3). See Louise W. Mackie, "Two Remarkable Fifteenth Century Carpets from Spain," *Textile Museum Journal* 4 (1977): 15–32, and Jerrilynn Dodds, ed., *Al-Andalus: The Art of Islamic Spain* (New York, 1992), no. 102.

39. C. J. Lamm, "The Marby Rug and some fragments of carpets found in Egypt," *Svenska Orientsällskapets Arsbok* (Stockholm, 1937), pp. 51–130; 'An Early Animal Rug at the Metropolitan Museum', *Hali* 53 (1990): 154–5.

40. The fresco is illustrated in Erdmann, *Seven Hundred Years*, fig. 2; *The Marriage of the Virgin* (London, National Gallery, 1317) in *Hali* 53 (1990): 155.

41. Washington, DC, Freer Gallery of Art, 23.5; see Richard Ettinghausen, "New Light on Early Animal Carpets," *Aus der Welt der islamischen Kunst: Festschrift für Ernst Kuhnel*, ed. R. Ettinghausen (Berlin, 1959), pp. 93–116.

42. Washington, DC, Smithsonian Institution, Sackler Gallery S86.0100; illustrated in color in Glenn D. Lowry with Susan Nemazee, *A Jeweler's Eye: Islamic Arts of the Book from the Vever Collection* (Washington, 1988), p. 79.

CHAPTER 11: ARCHITECTURE AND THE ARTS IN INDIA UNDER THE SULTANATES

1. The term India is used here to designate the geographical land mass of the subcontinent, known to medieval Muslims as Hindustan. This encompasses the present countries of Pakistan, India, and Bangladesh.

2. F. A. Khan, *Banbhore* (Karachi, n.d.). Inscriptions on stone slabs found during excavations of the mosque should probably be read as 209/824–5 and 294/907. See Sheila S. Blair, *The Monumental Inscriptions from Early Islamic Iran and Transoxiana* (Leiden, 1991), p. 15, n. 10. Another inscription, written in Arabic and Sanskrit, records the construction of a building, probably another mosque, in 243/857. Found in the Tochi Valley in Waziristan, the inscription is now in the Peshawar Museum. See G. Yazdani, ed., *Epigraphica Indo-Moslemica* (Calcutta, 1925–6), pp. 27–8, and C. E. Bosworth, "Notes on the pre-Ghaznavid History of Eastern Afghanistan," *Islamic Quarterly* 9 (1965): 22–3. Twelfth-century buildings at Bhadresvar have recently been published by Mehrdad Shokoohy, *Bhadresvar: The Oldest Islamic Monuments in India* (Leiden, 1988); for buildings built ca. 1200 in Bayana, see Mehrdad Shokoohy and Natalie H. Shokoohy, "The Architecture of Baha al-Din Tughril in the Region of Bayana, Rajasthan," *Muqarnas* 4 (1987): 114–32.

3. Ettinghausen and Grabar, pp. 291–3, and J. C. Harle, *The Art and Architecture of the Indian Subcontinent* (Harmondsworth, 1986), pp. 421–6. For sultanate architecture in general, see R. Nath, *History of Sultanate Architecture* (New Delhi, 1978); for Delhi in particular, see T. Yamamoto, M. Ara, and T. Tsukinowa, *Delhi: Architectural Remains of the Sultanate Period*, 3 vols. (Tokyo, 1968–70). The exact date when construction of the mosque began is somewhat ambiguous. An inscription still *in situ*, which may have been added later, gives a date of 587/1191–2; another gives a date of 592/1195–6, and a third one on the screen itself gives the date 20 Dhu'l-Qa'da 594/23 September 1198.

4. Iltutmish built a third mosque in Budaun (Uttar Pradesh), some 200 kilometers south-east of Delhi on the Sot river, in 1223, twenty-five years after the city was taken. Unlike the other two, it is a true four-iwan mosque built without temple spolia. See *EI/2*, s.v. "Bad'aun," and Tokifusa Tsukinowa, "The Influence of Seljuk Architecture on the Earliest Mosques of the Delhi Sultanate Period in India," *Acta Asiatica* 43 (1982): 37–60.

5. Robert Hillenbrand, "Political Symbolism in Early Indo-Islamic Mosque Architecture: The Case of Ajmir," *Iran* 26 (1988): 105–17, and Michael W. Meister, "The 'Two-and-a-half-day' Mosque," *Oriental Art*, N.S. 18/1 (1972): 57–63.

6. The relatively poor survival of so many buildings in Afghanistan and Iran means that the *pishtaq* surmounted by twin towers is a feature that survives only in contemporary Anatolia, as at the Çifte Minare madrasa (1243) in Erzurum. See Ettinghausen and Grabar, ill. 346, where the date is incorrect.

7. A. B. M. Husain, *The Manara in Indo-Muslim Architecture* (Dacca, 1970), p. 52.

8. Anthony Welch and Howard Crane, "The Tughluqs: Master Builders of the Delhi Sultanate," *Muqarnas* 1 (1983): 123–66.

9. J. Burton-Page, "The Tomb of Rukn-i Alam in Multan," *Splendors of the East*, ed. M. Wheeler (London and New York, 1965), pp. 72–91; Kamil Khan Mumtaz, *Architecture in Pakistan* (Singapore, 1985), pp. 45–6; Sherban Cantacuzino, ed., *Architecture in Continuity: Building in the Islamic World Today*, the Aga Khan Award for Architecture. (New York, 1985), pp. 170–7; and Robert Hillenbrand, "Turco-Iranian Elements in the Medieval Architecture of Pakistan: the Case of the Tomb of Rukn-i 'Alam at Multan," *Muqarnas* 9 (1992): 148–74.

10. See Holly Edwards, "The Ribat of 'Ali b. Karmakh," *Iran* 29 (1991): 85–94.

11. Sheila S. Blair, "The Octagonal Pavilion at Natanz: A Reexamination of Early Islamic Architecture in Iran," *Muqarnas* 1 (1983): 69–94.

12. Mehrdad Shokoohy and Natalie H. Shokoohy, *Hisar-i Firuza: Sultanate and Early Mughal Architecture in the District of Hisar, India* (London, 1988).

13. The word *manār* is usually pronounced *minār* in India, although the short vowel is not normally written. The use of the word does not mean that the structure was designed for the call to prayer. See Jonathan Bloom, *Minaret: Symbol of Islam* (Oxford, 1989).

14. J. A. Page, *A Memoir on the Kotla Firoz Shah* (Delhi, 1937), p. 42, quoted by Welch and Crane, p. 133.

15. See W. Jeffrey McKibben's forthcoming article in *Ars Orientalis*.

16. *The Travels of Ibn Battuta, A.D. 1325–1354*, trans. H. A. R. Gibb, (Cambridge, 1971), p. 624.

17. Although the reservoir is now dry, the district has become a chic quarter in Delhi with boutiques and secluded residences.

18. For the architecture of the Lodis, see Matsuo Ara, "The Lodi Rulers and the Construction of Tomb-Buildings in Delhi," *Acta Asiatica* 43 (1982), and Catherine B. Asher, "From Anomaly to Homogeneity: The Mosque in 14th- to 16th-Century Bihar," in *Studies in Art and Archaeology of Bihar and Bengal*, ed. G. Bhattacharya and Debala Mitra (Delhi, 1989).

19. Elizabeth S. Merklinger, *Indian Islamic Architecture: The Deccan 1347–1686* (Warminster, Wilts, 1981) and "Gulbarga," *Marg* 37 (1986): 27–39. See also George Michell and Richard Gaton, *Firuzabad: Palace City of the Deccan* (Oxford, 1992).

20. The inscription, published in *RCEA*, 17 (Cairo, 1982), no. 769 013, states that Rafi' built (Arab. *banā*) the mosque; this has led to the erroneous assumption that he was the architect. The form of the inscription implies that he was the patron.

21. Ahmad Hasan Dani, *Muslim Architecture in Bengal* (Dacca, 1961), and George Michell, ed., *The Islamic Heritage of Bengal* (Paris, 1984).

22. Yolande Crowe, "Reflections on the Adina Mosque at Pandua," *Islamic Heritage of Bengal*, pp. 155–64.

23. Shamsuddin Ahmed, *Inscriptions of Bengal*, 4 (Rajshahi, 1960), p. 38. Perween Hasan, "Sultanate Mosques and Continuity in Bengal Architecture," *Muqarnas* 6 (1989): 58–74. It has been suggested that the unusual plan of the building was modeled on the Great Mosque of Damascus, but no explanation of the method of transfer has yet been proposed. See Jonathan M. Bloom, "On the Transmission of Designs in Early Islamic Architecture," *Muqarnas* 10 (1993): 21–8.

24. See, for example, the view in Percy Brown, *Indian Architecture (Islamic Period)* (Bombay, 1956), pl. xxxii, fig. 2.

25. J. Burgess, *The Muhammadan Architecture of Ahmadabad 1412–1520*, 2. vols. (London, 1900–5) = *Archaeological Survey of India (New Imperial Series)*, vols. xxiv and xxxiii, or *Western India*, vols. vii and viii; George Michell and Snehal Shah, eds, *Ahmadabad* (Bombay, 1988).

26. See *EI/2*, s.v. "Mandu" by Yolande Crowe.

27. Paris, Bibliothèque Nationale, Cabinet des Médailles, Chabouillet 3271; Ernst Kühnel, *Die islamischen Elfenbeinskulpturen VIII–XIII Jh.* (Berlin, 1971), no. 17; one of the latest publications, S. C. Welch, *India: Art and Culture 1300–1900* (New York, 1985), no. 72, with bibliography, attributes the piece to the late eleventh or early twelfth century.

28. A rare exception is a pair of brass stirrups attributed to the thirteenth century; see A. S. Melikian-Chirvani, "Studies in Hindustani Metalwork: I – On Some Sultanate Stirrups," *Art et société dans le monde iranien*, ed. C. Adle (Paris, 1982), pp. 177–95.

29. Geneva, Sadruddin Aga Khan Collection, MS 32; see *Arts of Islam*, no. 635; Welch, *Calligraphy in the Arts of the Muslim World*, no. 75; and Jeremiah P. Losty, *The Art of the Book in India* (London, 1982), no. 18. Two manuscripts of the Koran in the Nour Collection, London, bear thirteenth-century dates but no places of production. The proto-Bihari style of script in one and the "Ghurid"-style illumination in the other have led to attributions to India.

30. The group includes two larger copies of the Koran, one dated 1447

(Karachi, National Museum of Pakistan, 1957–1033) and another dated 1453 (London, India Office Library, Arabic 4142). Another anthology (London, British Library, Or. 4110) whose decoration follows the same tradition was compiled in the reign of Mubarak Shah (r. 1399–1402), Sharqi sultan of Jaunpur.

31. Bijapur, Archaeological Museum, 912. In this particular manuscript two sizes of Bihari script are juxtaposed. Text pages have two lines of larger script alternating with three lines of smaller. This juxtaposition of scripts was already used for copying Korans in Iran and the central Islamic world, where scribes juxtaposed different scripts such as *thuluth* and *naskh*, but here the scribe has restricted himself to two sizes of the same script. See Welch, *India: Art and Culture 1300–1900*, pp. 71–2 and no. 71.

32. Losty, *Art of the Book in India*, p. 39 and no. 20, a Koran manuscript attributed to Gujarat before 1488.

33. Irma L. Fraad and Richard Ettinghausen, "Sultanate Painting in Persian Style, Primarily from the First Half of the Fifteenth Century: A Preliminary Study," *Chhavi, Golden Jubilee volume of the Bharat Kala Bhavan, Benares* (1972): 48–66.

34. Karin Adahl, for example, argues that the Uppsala Nizami dated 1439 was produced in southern Iran (*A Khamsa of Nizami of 1439*, Uppsala, 1981), and Glenn Lowry and Milo Beach note that three paintings in a dispersed *Anthology* dated 1417 relate to late Muzaffarid and early Timurid painting; but the closest parallels are in wall paintings decorating the 1404 tomb of Tuman-Aqa at the Shah-i Zinda in Samarqand (*An Annotated and Illustrated Checklist of the Vever Collection*, Washington, DC, 1988), nos. 48–50, pp. 37–8).

35. London, British Library, Or. 1403; it is known as the "Mohl *Shāhnāma*" after its former owner Jules Mohl, one of the first European editors and translators of the Persian national epic. Jules Mohl, *Le Livre des Rois*, text and French translation, 7 vols. (Paris, 1838–78).

36. Losty, *Art of the Book in India*, no. 22.

37. London, India Office Library, Pers. MS 149; Robert Skelton, "The Ni'mat-nama: A Landmark in Malwa Painting," *Marg* 12 (1959): 44–50; Losty, *Art of the Book in India*, no. 41; Welch, *India: Art and Culture 1300–1900*, no. 78.

38. New Delhi, National Museum, 48.6/4; Richard Ettinghausen, "The Bustan Manuscript of Sultan Nasir-Shah Khalji," *Marg* 12 (1959): 40–3; Losty, *Art of the Book in India*, no. 42; Welch, *India: Art and Culture 1300–1900*, no. 79.

39. K. Khandalavala and Moti Chandra, "A consideration of an illustrated MS from Mandapadurga (Mandu) dated 1439 AD," *Lalit Kala* 6 (1959): 8–29; Pramod Chandra, "Notes on Mandu Kalpasutra of A.D. 1439," *Marg* 12 (1959): 51–4; Losty, *Art of the Book in India*, no. 28.

CHAPTER 12: THE ARTS IN IRAN UNDER THE SAFAVIDS AND ZANDS

1. For the Safavids, see Roger Savory, *Iran under the Safavids* (Cambridge, 1980), and *The Cambridge History of Iran*, vol. 6: *The Timurid and Safavid Periods*, ed. Peter Jackson and Laurence Lockhart (Cambridge, 1986).

2. Three illustrated folios were detached from the manuscript in Istanbul (Topkapı Palace Library, H. 762), perhaps about fifty years ago, and are now in the Kier Collection, Richmond, Surrey. See B. W. Robinson et al., *Islamic Painting and the Arts of the Book* (London, 1976), pp. 178–9, nos. 207–9, and Priscilla Soucek, "Sultan Muhammad Tabrizi: Painter at the Safavid Court," *Persian Masters: Five Centuries of Painting* (Bombay, 1990), p. 58.

3. Uppsala University Library, O Nova 2. See K. V. Zetterstéen and C. J. Lamm, *Mohammad 'Asafi: The Story of Jamal and Jalal* (Uppsala, 1948).

4. Figures in the first illustration do not wear the distinctive Safavid headgear, but all the illustrations are done in the same style. Stuart Cary Welch (*Wonders of the Age, Masterpieces of Early Safavid Painting, 1501–1576* [Cambridge, MA, 1979], p. 34) suggested that the manuscript and its Herati artist trained in the Turkoman style changed hands after the first illustration was completed and that it was carried from Herat in 1504 by Muhammad Husayn, one of Husayn Bayqara's son, when he defected to the Safavids. It is simpler to imagine that the unillustrated manuscript was taken to Tabriz, where all the illustrations were added in the Turkoman style. The absence of Safavid headgear in the first illustration may simply have been the product of the artist's initial ignorance of the new style of dress.

5. B. W. Robinson, "Origin and Date of Three Famous *Shāh-nāmeh* Illustrations," *Ars Orientalis* 1 (1954): 105–12.

6. London, British Museum, 1948.12.11.023. Illustrated in Welch, *Wonders of the Age*, pp. 36–7.

7. Any statement about this monumental work must begin with the monumental study by Martin B. Dickson and Stuart Cary Welch, *The Houghton Shahnameh* (Cambridge, MA, 1982). See also Priscilla P. Soucek's review in *Ars Orientalis* 14 (1984): 133–8.

8. A copy of 'Arifi's *Guy u Chawgan*, dated 931/1524–5; St Petersburg,

Saltykov-Shchedrin Public Library, Dorn 441.

9. Was the Mongol copy in the Safavid royal library at Tabriz? There is no evidence that it was ever in the Timurid libraries, for its compositions were never repeated in Timurid painting, unlike those of other fourteenth-century manuscripts, such as the Khwaju Kirmani in London. Nor did it ever go to India like so many other Persian manuscripts from the library of the Timurids in Herat. The illustrated manuscript of Rashid al-Din's *Jāmi' al-tawarīkh* (see Chapter 3), for example, first passed to the Timurid court, as it bears a seal of Shahrukh (see Chapter 5) and then to the Mughal court. The Mongol *Shāhnāma* must have remained in Iran, as it is known to have been in the Qajar royal library at the end of the nineteenth century. See Sheila S. Blair and Jonathan M. Bloom, "Epic Images and Contemporary History: the Legacy of the Great Mongol *Shahnama*," *Islamic Art* 5 forthcoming.

10. Now in the collection of Prince Sadruddin Aga Khan, Geneva.

11. Thackston, p. 348.

12. The other is Aqa Mirak.

13. The manuscript, formerly in the Cartier Collection, survived intact until recently, when it, like the Tahmasp *Shāhnāma*, was brutally dismembered. The text, the double frontispiece, and the painted and varnished covers are now in the Harvard University Art Museums. Of the five paintings, a polo scene has been lost (illustrated in S. C. Welch, *Persian Painting: Five Royal Safavid Manuscripts* (New York, 1976), fig. C). *The Allegory of Drunkenness* is owned jointly by the Harvard University Art Museums, the Metropolitan Museum of Art and S. C. Welch. The other three paintings, the *Lovers Picknicking, Episode in a Mosque*, and the *Celebration of 'Id*, are now in private collections. The last is signed on a panel under the enthroned figure, who can be identified as the patron of the manuscript. The painting is illustrated in Welch, *Wonders of the Age*, no. 43, and Abolala Soudevar, *Art of the Persian Courts: Selections from the Art and History Trust Collection* (New York, 1992), no. 59.

14. Robinson has suggested that it might have been a rejected drawing for Shah Tahmasp's *Khamsa* (British Library, Or. 2265). See B. W. Robinson, *Persian Miniature Painting from Collections in the British Isles* (London, 1967), p. 55. Another preliminary drawing perhaps for the same manuscript shows *Khusraw watching Shirin Hunting* (Istanbul, Topkapi Palace Library, H. 2161, fol. 143b); illustrated in Titley, *Persian Miniature Painting* (Austin, 1984), fig. 73.

15. Titley, *Persian Miniature Painting*, Ch. 14: "Methods and Materials."

16. London, British Library, Or. 2265. Although the paintings were published as early as 1928 (Laurence Binyon, *The Poems of Nizami* [London, 1928]) and the manuscript is constantly cited in the literature as one of the masterpieces of Persian book-painting, the manuscript as a whole has not yet been studied.

17. Another painting of *The Battle between Khusraw and Bahram Chubina* (Edinburgh, Royal Scottish Museum, 1896–70) was probably detached from the manuscript. Two other paintings in the Harvard University Art Museums, *Nomadic Encampment* (1958.75) and *Night-time in a Palace* (1958.76), are often said to have come from the same manuscript, but as the text-blocks were removed when these folios were trimmed, split, and bound in an album, it has not yet been determined which stories these paintings illustrated and whether the British Library manuscript has gaps at these particular points.

18. Welch, *Wonders of the Age*, p. 139. This painting illustrates the complexities and problems of attributing early Safavid book-paintings to individual hands. S. C. Welch has suggested that it was designed and largely executed by Aqa Mirak and finished by Mir Sayyid 'Ali, whose father, Mir Musavvir, inscribed the walls in tribute to his son's unclaimed but superb accomplishment in this painting. See Welch, *Persian Painting*, p. 72, and *Wonders of the Age*, p. 78. A simpler explanation is that the painting is actually the work of Mir Musavvir, who wittily signed his work in a graffito on the walls of the ruined palace and complimented himself on a job well done. This would also concur with information provided by Dust Muhammad, who said that two painters, Aqa Mirak and Mir Musavvir, worked on the manuscript. Thackston, p. 348.

19. See n. 58, below.

20. Eskandar Beg Monshi, *History of Shah 'Abbas the Great*, trans. Roger Savory (Boulder, CO, 1978), pp. 270–1.

21. For the early history in Anatolia, see Chapter 10; for a carpet fragment attributed to fifteenth-century Iran, see Chapter 5, note 39.

22. Amy Briggs, "Timurid Carpets," *Ars Islamica* 7 (1940): 20–54.

23. London, Victoria and Albert Museum, 272–1893, 10.5 by 5.3 m; Los Angeles, County Museum, 53.50.2; 7.3 by 4.1 m. The outer borders and lower field of the Los Angeles carpet were cut down, probably in the late nineteenth century, and used to repair the carpet now in London. See Rexford Stead, *The Ardabil Carpets* (Malibu, 1974), and *Encyclopaedia Iranica*, s.v. "Ardabīl Carpet" by M. Beattie.

24. Milan, Poldi Pezzoli Museum, inv. no. 154. It has silk warps and three shoots of cotton weft after each row of asymmetrical knots. There are approximately 41 knots per square centimeter, or some 8.5 million knots in all. The basic publication is by F. Sarre and H. Trenkwald, *Old Oriental Carpets* (Vienna and Leipzig, 1929).

25. The date has also been read as 929 (1522–3), but the later date is preferable.

26. An issue of the Boston Museum *Bulletin* (69 [1971])was devoted to this carpet, with articles by S. C. Welch, Maurice Dimand, William Hanaway, and Richard Ettinghausen and a technical appendix by Larry Salmon. It has three shoots of silk weft after each row of knots. The other two carpets are in Vienna (Österreichisches Museum für angewandte Kunst) and Stockholm (Royal Palace Collection).

27. Ehsan Echraghi, "Description contemporain des peintures murales disparues des palais de Sâh Tahmâsp à Qazvin," *Art et société dans le monde iranien*, ed. C. Adle (Paris, 1982), pp. 117–26.

28. Eskandar Monshi, *History of Shah 'Abbas*, p. 311 and Massumeh Farhad and Marianna Shrere Simpson, "Sources for the Study of Safavid Painting and Patronage, or *Méfiez-vous de Qazi Ahmad*," *Muqarnas* 10 (1993): 286–91.

29. Washington, DC, Freer Gallery of Art, 46.12. Marianna Shreve Simpson, "The Production and Patronage of the *Haft Aurang* by Jāmī in the Freer Gallery of Art," *Ars Orientalis* 13 (1982): 93–119.

30. Folio 235r, for example, lacks the text verses and the gold decoration in the margins.

31. Simpson, "Production and Patronage," p. 110, has noted that one illustrated folio has been removed from the story of Layla and Majnun.

32. See Simpson, "Production and Patronage," p. 101, fn. 2, for a list of the earlier discussions of the attributions.

33. The fifteenth-century calligraphic album is exemplified by Istanbul, Topkapı Palace Library, H. 2310, which was prepared in Herat for Baysunghur (d. 1433). It contains specimens of the work of fourteenth-century master calligraphers. Scrapbook albums are exemplified by Istanbul, Topkapı Palace Library, H. 2152, H. 2153, and H. 2160.

34. There are three important "planned" albums surviving in Istanbul. In 951/1544–5 Dust Muhammad prepared an album for Bahram Mirza (1517–49), the brother of Tahmasp (Istanbul, Topkapı Palace Library, H. 2154). Malik Daylami prepared one in 968/1560–1 for Amir Husayn Beg, Tahmasp's treasurer (Istanbul, Topkapı Palace Library, H. 2151). The calligrapher Mir Sayyid Ahmad Mashhadi, who was the teacher of Qazi Ahmad, the biographer of calligraphers and painters, prepared an album in 972/1564–5 for Amir Ghayb Beg (Istanbul, Topkapı Palace Library, H. 2161). The introductions to all three albums are translated in Thackston.

35. Thackston, p. 356.

36. Carol Bier, ed., *Woven from the Soul, Spun from the Heart: Textile Arts of Safavid and Qajar Iran 16th–19th Centuries* (Washington, DC, 1987), pp. 194–7, nos. 30–32, and J. Algrove McDowell, "Textiles," *The Arts of Persia*, ed. R. W. Ferrier (New Haven and London, 1989), p. 162.

37. Milton Sonday, "Pattern and Weaves: Safavid Lampas and Velvet," Bier, ed., *Woven from the Soul, Spun from the Heart*, pp. 57–83.

38. B. W. Robinson, "Isma'il II's Copy of the *Shahnama*," *Iran* 14 (1976): 1–8.

39. Vartan Gregorian, "Minorities of Isfahan: The Armenian Community of Isfahan 1587–1722," *Studies on Isfahan*, ed. R. Holod, *Iranian Studies* 7 (1974), pp. 652–80.

40. Munich, Residenz Museum, no. WC3; it measures 2.4 by 1.3 meters.

41. Tadeusz Mankowski, "Some Documents from Polish Sources Relating to Carpet Making in the Time of Shah 'Abbas I," *Survey of Persian Art*, pp. 2431–6.

42. One of the pair was sold by the Doria family to John D. Rockefeller, from whom it passed to the Metropolitan Museum, 50.190.5. See Maurice Dimand and Jean Mailey, *Oriental Rugs in the Metropolitan Museum of Art* (New York, 1973), no. 18. The other was sold in 1976 at Colnaghi, London, to the Tehran Carpet Museum. See Donald King, "The Doria Polonaise Carpet," *Persian and Mughal Art* (London, 1976), pp. 301–10.

43. Jenny Housego, "Carpets," *The Arts of Persia*, ed. Ferrier, pp. 130–2.

44. May H. Beatty, *Carpets of Central Persia* (London, 1976).

45. M. S. Dimand, "A Persian Garden Carpet in the Jaipur Museum," *Ars Islamica* 7 (1940): 93–96.

46. Dublin, Chester Beatty Library, Pers. MS 277. See Anthony Welch, *Artists for the Shah* (New Haven, 1976), pp. 106–25.

47. He signed his work in various ways and is named differently in various chronicles (e.g. Riza, Riza-yi 'Abbasi, Aqa Riza, etc.); but see I. Stchoukine, *Les Peintures des manuscrits de Shah 'Abbas Ier à la fin des Safavis* (Paris, 1964), pp. 84–133.

48. See Marianna Shreve Simpson, *Arab and Persian Painting in the Fogg Art Museum* (Cambridge, MA, 1980), no. 29.

49. St Petersburg, Hermitage, *Kneeling Woman*.

50. Sheila R. Canby, "Age and Time in the Work of Riza," *Persian Masters: Five Centuries of Painting* (Bombay, 1990), pp. 71–84.

51. According to Anthony Welch (*Shah 'Abbas & the Arts of Isfahan* [New York, 1973], p. 147), Mu'in was born ca. 1617; his first dated work is 1635, and his last 1707. He reportedly died the following year. This extraordinarily long career has been questioned by, among others, Massumeh Farhad, "The Art of Mu'in Musavvir: A Mirror of His Time," *Persian Masters: Five Centuries of Painting* (Bombay, 1990), p. 114. She suggests that his career ended earlier, probably in the 1690s.

52. Massumeh Farhad, "An Artist's Impression: Mu'in Musavvir's *Tiger Attacking a Youth*," *Muqarnas* 9 (1992): 116–24.

53. The date has caused much confusion. See Farhad, "Artist's Impression." The cold weather may be related to the Little Ice Age in northern Europe, when in the winter of 1683–4 the River Thames froze solid and a fair was held on the ice.

54. One version is in the Princeton University Library, Garrett Collection, 96G; the other, formerly in the Parish-Watson Collection, was exhibited in London in 1931 (Laurence Binyon, J. V. S. Wilkinson, and Basil Gray, *Persian Miniature Painting* (London, 1933), no. 374 and pl. CXII A).

55. The genre is exemplified by three similar paintings of a seated artist at work. This tradition of representing artists at work has a European source. The earliest example, a European portrait of a Turkish painter poised to begin work (Boston, Isabella Stuart Gardner Museum, P15e 18-3), was once attributed to Bellini but is probably the work of Costanzo da Ferrara. It seems to have been the model for a Turkish portrait of a Turkish artist (Washington, DC, Freer Gallery of Art, 32.28), which shows the artist painting a portrait of a figure in Turkish dress. The image seems to have traveled as far as India, possibly via Iran, for it was used in mirror reverse for an Indian painting showing a Turkish artist painting the portrait of a Turk (Kuwait, Dar al-Athar al-Islamiyyah, LNS 57 MS). See Esin Atıl, ed., *Islamic Art and Patronage: Treasures from Kuwait* (New York, 1990), figs. 29, 30 and no. 79. One of the few other paintings of a Persian artist, although not depicted at work, is Mir Sayyid 'Ali's portrait of his aged father, Mir Musavvir, presenting a petition ca. 1565, presumably to the Mughal ruler Akbar (Paris, Musée Guimet, on extended loan from the Musée du Louvre, 3.619I,b). See S. C. Welch, *Wonders of the Age*, no. 81.

56. A. A. Ivanov, "The Life of Muhammad Zaman: A Reconsideration," *Iran* 17 (1979): 65–70, and Eleanor Sims, "The European Print Sources of Paintings by the Seventeenth-Century Persian Painter, Muhammad-Zaman ibn Haji Yusuf of Qum," in Henri Zerner, ed., *Le Stampe e la diffusione delle immagini e degli stili* (Bologna, 1983), pp. 73–83.

57. Fol. 203b: *Bahram Gur Killing a Dragon*; fol. 213a: *Fitna Astonishing Bahram Gur*; fol. 221b: *Bahram Gur and the Indian Princess*. A fourth painting, depicting *Majnun and the Animals*, formerly owned by Edwin Binney, 3rd (see A. Welch, *Shah 'Abbas*, no. 71), is now in the Art and History Trust Collection. See Abolala Soudavar, *Art of the Persian Courts* (New York, 1992), no. 151. Muhammad Zaman's signatures on the paintings copy the signature of his predecessor Mir Musavvir on fol. 15v, for they are written like graffiti on the back walls of architecture and include a couplet followed by his name and date.

58. Fitna replaces Azada in Firdawsi's version of the story in the *Shāhnāma*.

59. Eleanor G. Sims, "Five Seventeenth-Century Persian Oil Paintings," *Persian and Mughal Art* (London, 1976), pp. 223–32.

60. For a biography of this artist, see Robert Skelton, "'Abbasi, Shaykh," in *Encyclopaedia Iranica*.

61. The only dated piece is a small bottle (height 21.5 cm) whose present whereabouts are unknown; the lithographed illustration (published by H. Wallis, *Typical Examples of Persian and Oriental Art*, I (London, 1893); reproduced in Oliver Watson, *Persian Lustre Ware* (London, 1985), fig. 136) shows the mark on the base, but the reading is unclear and both 1062/1651 and 1084/1673 are possible.

62. I. Rapoport, "K voprosu o pozdney lyustrovoy keramike Irana [Objects of late Iranian ceramics signed by the master Hatim]," *Soobshcheniya Gosudarstvennogo Ermitazha* 31 (1970): 54–6.

63. E.g. British Museum, 91, 6-17.5, for which see Watson, *Persian Lustre Ware*, fig. 140.

64. See J. R. Perry, *Karim Khan Zand: A History of Iran, 1747–1779* (Chicago and London, 1979).

CHAPTER 13: ARCHITECTURE IN IRAN UNDER THE SAFAVIDS AND ZANDS

1. W. Kleiss, "Der safavidische Pavillon in Qazvin," *Archäologische Mitteilungen aus Iran*, n.s. 9 (1976): 290–8.

2. See Chapter 12, Note 27.

3. Ingeborg Luschey-Schmeisser, "Der Wand- und Deckenschmuck eines safavidischen Palastes in Nayin," *Archäologische Mitteilungen aus Iran*, n.s. 2 (1969): 183–92, and eadem, "Ein neuer Raum in Nayin," *Archäologische Mitteilungen aus Iran*, n.s. 5 (1972): 309–14.

4. Robert D. McChesney, "Waqf and Public Policy: The Waqfs of Shah 'Abbas, 1011–1023/1602–1614," *Asian and African Studies* 15 (1981): 165–90; idem, "Four Sources on Shah 'Abbas's Building of Isfahan," *Muqarnas* 5 (1988):

103-34; idem, "Postscript to 'Four Sources on Shah 'Abbas's Building of Isfahan'," *Muqarnas* 8 (1991): 137-8.

5. For the architectural history of the maidan, see E. Galdieri and R. Orazi, *Progetto di sistemazione del Maydan-i Sah* (Rome, 1969), and E. Galdieri, "Two Building Phases of the Time of Šah 'Abbas I in the Maydan-i Šah of Isfahan. Preliminary Note," *East and West*, n.s. 20 (1970): 60-9. On the travelers to Isfahan, see Roger Stevens, "European Visitors to the Safavid Court," *Iranian Studies* 7 (1974): 421-57.

6. Heinz Gaube and Eugen Wirth, *Der Bazar von Isfahan* (Wiesbaden, 1978), and Heinz Gaube, *Iranian Cities* (New York, 1979), pp. 87-92, have reconstructed much of the original layout.

7. The glittering tile beyond the cable molding of the iwan is modern and was added during renovations under Rizashah Pahlavi in 1929; compare the photographs taken by Pope for the *Survey of Persian Art* (pls. 481 and 482) with ill. 234.

8. See, for example, the tenth-century Mausoleum of the Samanids at Bukhara, illustrated in Ettinghausen and Grabar, ills. 219-21.

9. Ettinghausen and Grabar, ill. 274.

10. The endowment inscription for the mosque has been lost.

11. McChesney, "Four Sources on the Building of Isfahan," *Muqarnas* 5 (1988): 120-3.

12. The most convenient discussion of the work at Mashhad is found in Robert Hillenbrand, "Safavid Architecture," *Cambridge History of Iran*, vol. 6 (1986), pp. 789-92.

13. Ettinghausen and Grabar, pp. 276-8, 309, 323.

14. Maxime Siroux, *Caravansérails d'Iran et petites constructions routières* (Cairo, 1949); idem, *Anciennes voies et monuments routiers de la région d'Isfahan* (Cairo, 1971); idem, "Les caravansérais routiers safavides," *Iranian Studies* 7 (1974): 348-79; Muhammad-Yusuf Kiani, *Iranian Caravanserais with Particular Reference to the Safavid Period* (Tokyo, 1978).

15. Hillenbrand, "Safavid Architecture," *Cambridge History of Iran*, vol. 6, pp. 801-3.

16. Ernst Grube, "Wall Paintings in the Seventeenth Century Monuments of Isfahan," *Iranian Studies* 7 (1974): 511-42.

17. Basil Gray, "The Arts in the Safavid Period," *Cambridge History of Iran*, vol. 6, pp. 903-4 with other references.

18. Eleanor Sims, "Late Safavid Painting: The Chehel Sutun, The Armenian Houses, the Oil Paintings," *Akten des VII. Internationalen Kongresses für Iranische Kunst und Archäologie. 1976* (Berlin, 1979), pp. 408-18.

19. Ettinghausen and Grabar, pp. 58-62; for Afrasiyab, see G. Azarpay, *Soghdian Painting* (Berkeley, 1981).

20. Ingeborg Luschey-Schmeisser, *The Pictorial Tile Cycle of Hašt Behešt in Isfahān and its Iconographic Tradition* (Rome, 1978).

21. E.g. Victoria and Albert Museum (illustrated in Basil Gray, "The Arts in the Safavid Period," *Cambridge History of Iran*, vol. 6, p. 905 and pl. 69), Metropolitan Museum of Art, 1903.9a, b, and c (a panel composed of thirty-two tiles and measuring 1.98 m long), and Paris, Musée des Arts Décoratifs. An old photograph by Sarre shows a now destroyed pavilion at the north end of the Chahar Bagh with similar tile panels *in situ*. See Luschey-Schmeisser, p. 187 and fig. 201.

22. Hillenbrand, "Safavid Architecture," *Cambridge History of Iran*, vol. 6, pp. 808-11; *Survey of Persian Art*, pp. 1213-15.

23. 'Alī Bihrūzī, *Julga-yi Shīrāz* ["The plain of Shiraz"] (Shiraz, 1347 solar/1969), pp. 125-267.

CHAPTER 14: ARCHITECTURE AND THE ARTS IN CENTRAL ASIA UNDER THE UZBEKS

1. They are sometimes called the Abu'-Khayrids, after the agnate Abu'l-Khayr who took Khwarazm from the Timurids in 1447 and whose grandson Muhammad Shibani (r. 1500-10) conquered Transoxiana from the last Timurids in 1500.

2. They are also called the Janids, after the founder of the line in Transoxiana, or Astarkhanids, after the family's purported origins in the town of Hajji Tarkhan (Astrakahan) on the Volga. For the preferred form Tuqay-timurid, see Robert D. McChesney, "The Reforms of Bāqī Muhammad Khān," *Central Asiatic Journal* 24 (1980): 69-84.

3. The best introduction to the political system of the period is Robert McChesney's article "Central Asia. VI. In the 10th-12th/16th-18th Centuries" in the *Encyclopaedia Iranica*, vol. 5, fasc. 2.

4. These buildings are often inaccessible and poorly published, and there is no general survey of the architecture of this period.

5. 'Ubaydallah was a nephew of Muhammad Shibani and the great-grandson of Abu'l-Khayr.

6. See Ettinghausen and Grabar, ill. 290.

7. For a brief biography, see *Encyclopaedia Iranica*, vol. 1. fasc. 2, pp. 198-9,

s.v. "'Abdallāh Khān b. Eskandar." Like 'Ubaydallah, 'Abdallah's father Iskandar was a great-grandson of Abu'-Khayr.

8. Robert D. McChesney, "Economic and Social Aspects of the Public Architecture of Bukhara in the 1560's and 1570's," *Islamic Art* 2 (1987): 217-42.

9. For a brief biography, see *Encyclopaedia Iranica*, vol. 1, p. 99.

10. For the evolution of the endowments to the shrine, see R. D. McChesney, *Waqf in Central Asia: Four Hundred Years in the History of a Muslim Shrine, 1480-1889* (Princeton, 1991).

11. For a general introduction, see M. M. Ashrafi-Aini, "The School of Bukhara to c. 1550," *Arts of the Book in Central Asia*, ed. Basil Gray (Boulder, CO, 1979), pp. 249-73; on the question of the Timurid legacy, see Lentz and Lowry, Ch. V.

12. Tashkent, Oriental Library of the Academy of Sciences of the Uzbek SSR, MS. 5369; see Olympiada Galerkina, *Mawarannahr Book Painting* (Leningrad, 1980), pls. 3-4.

13. Washington, DC, Freer Gallery of Art, 32.5/8; the medium-sized manuscript (26.5 by 17 cm) has a varnished binding and four full-page paintings. See Laurence Binyon, J. V. S. Wilkinson and Basil Gray, *Persian Miniature Painting* (Oxford, 1933; reprint New York, 1971), no. 106, with black-and-white illustrations of all four paintings, and Gray, *Arts of the Book in Central Asia*, with color plates of two and black-and-white illustrations of the other two. See also Ivan Stchoukine, "Un manuscrit de Mehr et Moshtari illustré à Herat, vers 1430," *Arts Asiatiques* 8 (1961): 83-5.

14. British Library, Or. 6810 and Add. 25900; see Chapter 5.

15. Geneva, Bodmer Foundation, Pers. Ms. 30. See Basil Robinson, "An Unpublished Manuscript of the Gulistan of Sa'di," *Beiträge zur Kunstgeschichte Asiens. In Memoriam Ernst Diez*, ed. O. Aslanapa (Istanbul, 1963), pp. 223-36; Lentz and Lowry, p. 307 and fig. 101; two of the paintings are reproduced in color in Gray, *Arts of the Book in Central Asia*, pls. LXXVI-LXXVII.

16. Houston, Art and History Trust Collection; see Lentz and Lowry, no. 157 and A. Soudavar, *Art of the Persian Courts: Selections from The Art and History Trust Collection* (New York, 1992), no. 36.

17. Washington, DC, Freer Gallery of Art, 56.14.

18. The double-page frontispiece depicting a youth reading and a picnic scene is reproduced in black and white in M. Dickson and S. C. Welch, *The Houghton Shahnameh* (Cambridge, MA, 1982), figs. 41-2.

19. The painting, depicting an *Episode in a Mosque*, has been detached from the manuscript (ex-Cartier Collection) and is now in a private collection; see Stuart Cary Welch, *Wonders of the Age, Masterpieces of Early Safavid Painting, 1501-1576* (Cambridge, MA, 1979), fig. 42. Folio 135r from the manuscript, showing an *Allegory of Drunkenness*, is signed by Sultan-Muhammad (see ill. 211).

20. See the biography of the latter by Priscilla Soucek, "'Abdallāh Bokārī," *Encyclopaedia Iranica*, vol. 1, fasc. 2, pp. 193-5.

21. Dublin, Chester Beatty Library, Pers. MS. 215; see Binyon, Wilkinson, and Gray, *Persian Miniature Painting*, no. 110 and pl. LXXXI; color reproduction in Gray, *Arts of the Book in Central Asia*, pl. LXXVIII.

22. Several examples bound in an album presented to the shrine library at Mashhad are illustrated in Binyon, Wilkinson, and Gray, *Persian Miniature Painting*, pls. LXXXVI and LXXVII.

23. Istanbul, Topkapı Palace Library, Revan 1549; see Güner Inal, "Topkapı Sarayı Koleksiyonundaki Sultanî Bir Özbek Şehnamesi," *Sanat Tarihi Yıllığı* 6 (1974-5): 303-22 (with English summary).

24. The paintings from the manuscript, Patna, Khudabakhsh Library, MS. 229, are unpublished. See Mark Zebrowski, *Deccani Painting* (London, 1983), pp. 155-6.

25. Tashkent, Institute for Oriental Studies, MS. 4472; color illustrations in Galerkina, *Mawarannahr Book Painting*, pls. 42-6; A. M. Ismailova, *Oriental Miniatures* (Tashkent, 1980), pls. 35-7.

26. Tashkent, Institute for Oriental Studies, MS. 1811; color illustrations in M. M. Ashrafi, *Persian-Tajik Poetry in XIV-XVII Centuries Miniatures* (Dushanbe, 1974), figs. 78-85; Galerkina, *Mawarannahr Book Painting*, pls, 21-8; and Ismailova, *Oriental Miniatures*, pls. 44-5.

27. O. F. Akimushkin and A. A. Ivanov, "Une école artistique méconnue: Boxara au XVIIe siècle," *Art et société dans le monde iranien*, ed. C. Adle (Paris, 1982), pp. 127-39.

28. Dublin, Chester Beatty Library, Pers. MS. 297. See A. J. Arberry and others, *The Chester Beatty Library. A Catalogue of the Persian Manuscripts and Miniatures*, 3 vols. (Dublin, 1959-62), no. 297.

29. St Petersburg, State Public Library, MS 66; colour illustrations in Ashrafi, *Persian-Tajik Poetry*, pls. 86-91; Galerkina, *Mawarannahr Book Painting*, pls. 47-8.

CHAPTER 15: ARCHITECTURE UNDER THE OTTOMANS
AFTER THE CONQUEST OF CONSTANTINOPLE

1. For Mehmed, see Franz Babinger, *Mehmed the Conqueror and His Time* (Princeton, 1978). For the architecture of the Ottoman period in general, see Aptullah Kuran, *The Mosque in Early Ottoman Architecture* (Chicago, 1967); Godfrey Goodwin, *A History of Ottoman Architecture* (London and Baltimore, 1971); and Doğan Kuban, "Architecture of the Ottoman period," *The Art and Architecture of Turkey*, ed. Ekrem Akurgal (New York, 1980). On the impact of Hagia Sophia, see Gülru Necipoğlu, "The Life of an Imperial Monument: Hagia Sophia after Byzantium," in *Hagia Sophia: From the Age of Justinian to the Present*, ed. Robert Mark and Ahmet Ş. Çakmak (Cambridge, 1992), pp. 195−225.

2. Gülru Necipoğlu, *Architecture, Ceremonial, and Power: The Topkapı Palace in the Fifteenth and Sixteenth Centuries* (New York and Cambridge, MA, 1991), p. 10.

3. For the origin and development of this extraordinary complex group of structures, see Necipoğlu, *Topkapı Palace*.

4. The Top kapu or Top kapusı ("Cannon Gate") of the outer palace precinct stood at the tip of the peninsula (Seraglio Point) near the emplacement of cannon Mehmed II positioned to control the Bosphorus and the Golden Horn. In the late eighteenth century, a seaside residential structure (Topkapı Palace) was erected near it, and this building subsequently gave its name to the entire palace complex of the Ottoman sultans.

5. Necipoğlu, *Topkapı Palace*, pp. 210 ff., which now supersedes E. H. Ayverdi, *Osmanlı Mimarisinde Fatih Devri* ["The period of the Conqueror in Ottoman architecture"], pp. 4, 736−55; S. H. Eldem, *Köşkler ve Kasırlar* ["Kiosks and pavilions"], 1 (Istanbul, 1969), pp. 61−79.

6. Gülru Necipoğlu, "From International Timurid to Ottoman: A Change of Taste in Sixteenth-Century Ceramic Tiles," *Muqarnas* 7 (1990): 137.

7. In modern Turkish these complexes are often called *külliye*s, but this is a modern term developed when the traditional term *'imārat* came to mean only one part of the complex, the soup kitchen. This idea of a funerary complex already existed in Ilkhanid Iran; see Chapter 2.

8. Their porphyry sarcophagi were transported to Mehmed's New Palace, and many can still be seen in the grounds between the Çinili Kiosk and the Archaeological Museum. Following the conquest and the transformation of Hagia Sophia into a mosque, the Church of the Holy Apostles had briefly served as the Patriarchal cathedral.

9. On Filarete's visit to Istanbul, see Marcell Restle, "Bauplanung und Baugesinnung unter Mehmed II Fātih," *Pantheon* 39 (1981): 361−67, and Julian Raby, "Pride and Prejudice: Mehmed the Conqueror and the Italian Portrait Medal," *Italian Medals: Studies in the History of Art*, 21, ed. Graham Pollard (Washington, DC, 1987), pp. 171−94, esp. Appendix 3.

10. Mehmet Aga-Oglu, "The Fatih Mosque at Constantinople," *Art Bulletin* 12 (1930): 179−95.

11. The first semidome in Ottoman architecture before the conquest of Constantinople is found in the Mosque of Yahşi Bey at Tire near Aydın. A semidome with a diameter of about 11 meters also appears in the small, zaviye-type Mosque of Rum Mehmed Paşa in Üsküdar, Istanbul, built in 1471, and thus contemporary with the Fatih Mosque. The founder, second vizier of Mehmed II from 1466 and grand vizier from 1468 to 1471, was a Byzantine. See Kuran, *Mosque in Early Ottoman Architecture*, pp. 91, 96−7; Goodwin, *Ottoman Architecture*, pp. 114−15, with the wrong date. The relationship between Hagia Sophia and classical Ottoman mosque design has been the subject of much controversy, for some authors have attempted to show that there was little if any filiation. See Aptullah Kuran, *Sinan: The Grand Old Master of Ottoman Architecture* (Washington, DC and Istanbul, 1987), p. 19; Albert Gabriel, "Les Mosquées de Constantinople," *Syria* 7 (1927): 359−491; Martin A. Charles, "Haghia Sophia and the Great Imperial Mosques," *Art Bulletin* 12 (1930): 321−44 etc.

12. Necipoğlu, "From International Timurid to Ottoman."

13. *Fatih Mehmet II Vakfiyeleri* ["Endowment deeds of Mehmed II the Conqueror"] (Ankara, 1938); Ekrem Hakkı Ayverdi, *Osmanlı Mimarisinde Fatih Devri (855−886/1451−1581)* ["The Fatih period of Ottoman Architecture"], 4 vols. (Istanbul, 1973), 3:385−87. See Gülru Necipoğlu-Kafadar, "The Süleymaniye Complex in Istanbul: An Interpretation," *Muqarnas* 3 (1985): 92−117.

14. For architecture under Bayezid II, see Goodwin, *Ottoman Architecture*, pp. 143−95.

15. The balcony is sometimes said to have been built after an attempt on the sultan's life, but this seems to be an anecdotal explanation for an unfamiliar feature. It can be compared to a similar example at the Eşrefoğlu Mosque in Beyşehir [167], although it might also reflect a lost model in Mehmed II's mosque in Istanbul.

16. The most notable development of Selim's reign was a brief vogue in Istanbul and its environs for architectural decoration in the Mamluk mode, with dadoes composed of thin strips of colored marbles. Used in the new council hall behind the grand vizier's seat in the New Palace, on the structure now known as

the Pavilion of the Holy Mantle, and at the Marble Kiosk on shore, these marble revetments were also found in the palace of Čoban Mustafa Pasha, who had been viceroy of Egypt in 1522, in Istanbul as well as in his complex at Gebze. See Necipoğlu, *Topkapı Palace*, p. 83.

17. Şerafettin Turan, "Osmanli teşkilâtında hassa mimarları" ["Royal Architects in Ottoman Administration"], *Tarih Araştırmaları Dergisi* 1 (1963): 157−202; Italian summary in 2. *Cong. int. arte turca 1963*, pp. 259−63.

18. See most recently Kuran, *Sinan*; Doğan Kuban, "The Style of Sinan's Domed Structures," *Muqarnas* 4 (1987): 72−97; and Arthur Stratton, *Sinan* (London, 1972).

19. Kuran, *Sinan*, p. 64.

20. Kuran, *Sinan*, pp. 55−60.

21. Kuran, *Sinan*, p. 68.

22. Filiz Yenişehirlioğlu, "Les grandes lignes de l'évolution du programme décoratif en céramique des monuments ottomans au cours du XVIème siècle," *Erdem* 1 (1985): 456−65, and Necipoğlu, "From International Timurid to Ottoman," 142−3.

23. See Ettinghausen and Grabar, pp. 26−34, Priscilla P. Soucek, "The Temple of Solomon in Islamic Legend and Art," *Temple of Solomon*, ed. J. Gutmann (Missoula, MN, 1976), and Necipoğlu-Kafadar, "The Süleymaniye Complex in Istanbul," 100−1.

24. Necipoğlu, "From International Timurid to Ottoman," 137.

25. Max van Berchem, *Matériaux pour un Corpus Inscriptionum Arabicarum*, pt 2: Syrie du Sud; vol. 2, Jerusalem "Haram" (Cairo, 1927), pp. 329 ff., nos. 238 ff.

26. Arthur Lane, "The Ottoman Pottery of Isnik," *Ars Orientalis* 2 (1954): 247−81.

27. Jean Sauvaget, "Les Caravansérails syriens de ḥadjdj de Constantinople," *Ars Islamica* 4 (1934): 98−121.

28. Kuran, *Sinan*, pp. 74−8.

29. Necipoğlu, "From International Timurid to Ottoman," 157.

30. Necipoğlu-Kafadar, "The Süleymaniye Complex in Istanbul," 92−117.

31. Kemal Edib Kürkçüoğlu, *Süleymaniye Vakfiyesi* ["The Endowment Deed of the Süleymaniye"] (Ankara, 1962), pp. 33−7.

32. Ömer Lutfi Barkan, "L'Organisation du travail dans le chantier d'une grande mosquée à Istanbul au XVIe siècle," *Annales* 17 (1962): 1093−1106; idem, *Süleymaniye Camii ve Imareti Insaati (1550−1557)* ["The Construction of the Süleymaniye Mosque and its Adjoining Buildings (1550−1557)"], 2 vols. (Ankara, 1972−9); J. M. Rogers, "The State and the Arts in Ottoman Turkey: The Stones of Süleymaniye," *International Journal of Middle East Studies* 14 (1982): 71−86, 283−313.

33. A passage in the endowment deed says that the mosque would have been decorated with pearls and rubies, "if decorating sanctuaries with precious stones, gold, and silver had been required by the Prophet's Shari'a. Since it was not required, gilding and precious stones were not used and instead the mosque's services were increased and its structure strengthened." Kürkçüoğlu, *Süleymaniye Vakfiyesi*, p. 22, quoted in Necipoğlu-Kafadar, "The Süleymaniye Complex in Istanbul," 107.

34. Nurhan Atasoy and Julian Raby, *Iznik: The Pottery of Ottoman Turkey* (London, 1989), p. 220.

35. J. M. Rogers and R. M. Ward, *Süleyman the Magnificent* (London, 1988), p. 11.

36. Kuran, *Sinan*, pp. 138−48; Goodwin, *Ottoman Architecture*, pp. 249−52; Walter B. Denny, "Ceramics," in *Turkish Art*, ed. Esin Atıl (Washington, DC, 1980), pp. 239−98; and Walter B. Denny, *The Ceramics of the Mosque of Rüstem Pasha and the Environment of Change* (New York, 1977).

37. Atasoy and Raby, *Iznik*, p. 228.

38. Walter B. Denny, "Ceramic revetments of the mosque of the Ramazan Oğlu in Adana," *IVème Congrès international d'art turc* (Aix-en-Provence, 1976), pp. 57−66.

39. Adapted from Kuran, *Sinan*, pp. 168−9.

40. Jale Erzen, "Sinan as Anti-Classicist," *Muqarnas* 5 (1988): 70−86.

41. Doğan Kuban, "Sinan," *The Macmillan Encyclopedia of Architects*, ed. A. K. Placzek, 4 vols. (New York, 1982).

42. For Mehmed's biography and role in Manisa, see Howard Crane, *Risāle-i Mi'māriyye: An Early Seventeenth-Century Ottoman Treatise on Architecture* (Leiden, 1987), p. 8.

43. Topkapı Palace Museum, no. 1652. See Cengiz Köseoğlu, *The Topkapı Saray Museum: The Treasury*, trans, expanded and ed. J. M. Rogers (Boston, 1987), no. 1.

44. Kemal Çiğ, Sabahattin Batur, and Cengiz Köseoğlu, *The Topkapı Saray Museum, Architecture: The Harem and Other Buildings*, trans. and ed. J. M. Rogers (Boston, 1988), pp. 44−5.

45. For a biography, see *EI/2*, s.v. "Mehmed Yirmisekiz."

46. See Doğan Kuban, *Osmanlı Barok Mimarisi Hakkında bir Deneme* (Istanbul, 1954).

CHAPTER 16: THE ARTS UNDER THE OTTOMANS AFTER
THE CONQUEST OF CONSTANTINOPLE

1. Julian Raby, "East and West in Mehmed the Conqueror's Library," *Bulletin du Bibliophile* 3 (1987): 297–321.

2. Julian Raby, "Pride and Prejudice: Mehmed the Conqueror and the Italian Portrait Medal," *Italian Medals*, ed. J. Graham Pollard (Washington, DC, 1987), pp. 171–96.

3. Cornelius C. Vermeule III, "Graeco-Roman Asia Minor to Renaissance Italy: Medallic and Related Arts," *Italian Medals*, ed. Pollard, pp. 263–82.

4. Considering Mehmed's interest in European artists and techniques, it is surprising that he does not seem to have introduced printing with moveable type. The first book printed in Arabic in Europe is believed to be the Koran printed in Venice by Paganino de' Paganini in 1538. All copies were thought to have been destroyed by fire until 1987, when a single copy was discovered in a monastery library there. See Arthur Clark, "London's Oriental Bookshops," *Aramco World* 43/2 (March-April 1992), p. 6.

5. Istanbul, Topkapı Palace Museum Library, A. 1672 (Karatay A. 8150), measuring 27 by 16.5 cm. See *The Anatolian Civilisations III, Seljuk/Ottoman* (Istanbul, 1983), pp. 108–9 and E. 3.

6. Raby, "East and West in Mehmed the Conqueror's Library,' idem, "Mehmed II Fatih and the Fatih Album," *Islamic Art* 1 (1981): 42–9.

7. Süheyl Ünver, "Baba Nakkaş," *Fatih ve Istanbul* 2 (1954): 7–12 and 169–88; idem, *Fatih Devri Saray Nakışhanesi ve Baba Nakkaş Çalışmaları* ["The palace design studio in the Conqueror's time and the works of Baba Nakkaş"] (Istanbul, 1958).

8. One of the few pieces that can be specifically identified with the Fatih Mosque is a silver lantern (Istanbul, Museum of Turkish and Islamic Art, no. 167), which was found there. It exemplifies the new decorative vocabulary, with ogival medallions on a ground of scrolling stems supporting lotus palmettes, trilobed leaves, and petaled rosettes. See *Anatolian Civilisations III*, p. 118 and E. 21, and Jay A. Levenson, ed., *Circa 1492: Art in the Age of Exploration* (Washington, DC, 1991), no. 80.

9. Berlin, Museum für Islamische Kunst; inv. no. I.5526; 4.29 by 2.00 m; 920 knots per square decimeter. See Museum für Islamische Kunst Berlin, *Katalog 1971* (Berlin, 1971), no. 585, and Charles Grant Ellis, "On 'Holbein' and 'Lotto' Rugs," in Pinner and Denny, pp. 163–76.

10. Marilyn Jenkins, ed., *Islamic Art in the Kuwait National Museum: The al-Sabah Collection* (London, 1983), p. 146; a comparable, but slightly smaller piece (5.44 by 2.61 m) is in the Thyssen-Bornemisza Collection, Lugano. For a color illustration, see David Black, ed., *The Macmillan Atlas of Rugs and Carpets* (New York, 1985), p. 54a.

11. Julian Raby, "Court and Export: Part 2. The Uşak Carpets," in Pinner and Denny, pp. 177–88.

12. Nurhan Atasoy and Julian Raby, *Iznik: The Pottery of Ottoman Turkey* (London, 1989).

13. For the Kashan wares, see Ettinghausen and Grabar, pp. 343–53.

14. Atasoy and Raby, *Iznik*, p. 76.

15. Such as a parcel-gilt silver jug (h. 12 cm) in the Victoria and Albert Museum, 158–1894.

16. There are several illustrated manuscripts that can be attributed to his reign. A *Khamsa* of Amir Khusraw Dihlavi (Istanbul, Topkapı Palace Library, H. 799) is dated 1498; some of the illustrations show Western conventions of architectural representation, while others are in a simplified Herat style. See Filiz Çağman and Zeren Tanındı, *The Topkapı Saray Museum: The Albums and Illustrated Manuscripts*, ed., expanded and trans. J. M. Rogers (Boston, 1986), pp. 184–6.

17. Atasoy and Raby, *Iznik*, Ch. III.

18. For example, a copy of the Koran transcribed by Yaqut in 1282–3 was refurbished in the mid-sixteenth century (Istanbul, Topkapı Palace Library, E. H. 227), and another transcribed by 'Abdallah Sayrafi in 1344–5 was illuminated by Kara Memi in 1554–5 and bound by Mehmed Çelebi in 1555–6 (Istanbul, Topkapı Palace Library, E. H. 49). See Esin Atıl, *The Age of Sultan Süleyman the Magnificent* (Washington, DC, and New York, 1987), nos. 13 and 14.

19. J. M. Rogers in *Circa 1492: Art in the Age of Exploration*, ed. Jay A. Levenson (Washington, DC, 1991), no. 83, and *The Dictionary of Art*, s.v. "Embriachi."

20. Gülru Necipoğlu, "A Ḳānūn for the State, A Canon for the Arts: Conceptualizing the Classical Synthesis of Ottoman Art and Architecture," *Soliman le Magnifique et son Temps*, ed. Gilles Veinstein (Paris, 1990), pp. 195–216.

21. Çağman and Tanındı, *The Topkapı Saray Museum: The Albums and Illustrated Manuscripts*, pp. 184–5. A pot of dark green jade (nephrite) with a silvergilt handle, inlaid with gold and inscribed on the neck to the Safavid ruler Isma'il (r. 1501–24) and now in the Topkapı Palace Treasury (no. 1844), must have been part of the booty. See Cengiz Küseoğlu, *The Topkapı Saray Museum: The Treasury*, trans., expanded and ed. J. M. Rogers (Boston, 1987), no. 48.

22. Walter B. Denny, "Dating Ottoman Turkish Works in the Saz Style,"

Muqarnas 1 (1983): 103–22; Atıl, *Age of Sultan Süleyman*, pp. 289–97.

23. The fifth, unmatched tile shows vegetation growing from a vase. All five tiles can be see in photograph 109 in Kemal Çiğ, Sabahattin Batur, and Cengiz Köseoğlu, *The Topkapı Saray Museum, Architecture: The Harem and Other Buildings*, trans. and ed. J. M. Rogers (Boston, 1988). See also Jessica Rawson, *Chinese Ornament: The Lotus and the Dragon* (London, 1984), pp. 186–8.

24. This domed pavilion is represented in Melchior Lorichs' panoramic view of Istanbul [272]. The early date is discussed by Denny, "Dating Ottoman Turkish Works in the Saz Style," p. 104.

25. Gülru Necipoğlu ("From International Timurid to Ottoman: A Change of Taste in Sixteenth-Century Ceramic Tiles," *Muqarnas* 7 (1990), esp. pp. 148–53) dates the installation of the tiles to 1641, but a late-nineteenth-century photograph of the building (reproduced in Barnette Miller, *Beyond the Sublime Porte*, New Haven, 1931) is quite different.

26. Necipoğlu, "From International Timurid to Ottoman," *Muqarnas* 7 (1990): 136–70.

27. Gülru Necipoğlu, "Süleyman the Magnificent and the Representation of Power in the Context of Ottoman-Hapsburg-Papal Rivalry," *Art Bulletin* 71 (1989): 401–27.

28. Atıl, *Age of Sultan Süleyman*, no. 86, and J. M. Rogers and R. M. Ward, *Süleyman the Magnificent* (London, 1988), no. 83.

29. Atıl, *Age of Sultan Süleyman*, no. 116; Rogers and Ward, *Süleyman the Magnificent*, no. 106.

30. The piece, Topkapı Palace Museum, 13/529, is illustrated in Louise Mackie, "Rugs and Textiles," in Esin Atıl, *Turkish Art* (Washington, DC, 1980), pl. 59.

31. London, British Museum, Inv. no. G 1983.37; see Rogers and Ward, *Süleyman the Magnificent*, no. 142.

32. The signature has been read as Muslī, Muṣallī, or even Muṣt[af]a. London, British Museum, 87.5–16.1; see Atasoy and Raby, *Iznik*, no. 355, and Atıl, *Age of Sultan Süleyman*, pp. 238–9; Rogers and Ward, *Süleyman the Magnificent*, no. 148.

33. Atasoy and Raby, *Iznik*, figs. 88–91; but see also Levenson, ed., *Circa 1492*, nos. 103–4.

34. Floral motifs found on the lamp are exemplified in the floral esthetic associated with the artist Kara Memi, who illuminated royal manuscripts between the 1540s and 1560s and became head of the court designers in 1552. See, for example, a copy of Süleyman's poetry, the *Dīvān-i Muhibbī*, which was illuminated by Kara Memi in 1566 and is now in the Istanbul University Library (T. 5467). See Atıl, *Age of Sultan Süleyman*, no. 26, and Rogers and Ward, *Süleyman the Magnificent*, no. 31.

35. The question is discussed by J. M. Rogers, "The State and the Arts in Ottoman Turkey: The Stones of Süleymaniye," *International Journal of Middle East Studies* 14 (1982): 304–5.

36. See *Encyclopaedia Iranica*, s.v. "Čelebī, Fath-Āllāh 'Āref."

37. The first volume (private collection, sold in 1976 at Christie's, London) concerns the Creation and the early prophets; the second (lost except for a single folio in Los Angeles, County Museum of Art, M. 73.5.446), the appearance and rise of Islam; the third (lost), ancient Turkish rulers and the Saljuqs; the fourth (formerly New York, Kraus Collection), the foundation of the Ottoman empire; and the fifth (Istanbul, Topkapı Palace Library, H. 1517), the reign of Süleyman.

38. Istanbul, Topkapı Palace Library, H. 1517. The first volume was transcribed by Yusuf al-Haravi in 1558 and the fourth by Mirza Huy-i Shirazi. All three were apparently Iranians, to judge from their names.

39. These include Nigari's portraits of Süleyman as an old man ca. 1560, Selim II ca. 1570, and the admiral Babaros Hayreddin Paşa (Khayr al-Dīn Barbarossa; d. 1546); Istanbul, Topkapı Palace Library, H. 2134, fols. 8, 3, and 9.

40. Esin Atıl, *Süleymanname: The Illustrated History of Süleyman the Magnificent* (Washington, DC, 1986), p. 110.

41. Istanbul University Library, 5964. Originally entitled *Mecmü-i Menazil*, the manuscript has been edited in facsimile by H. G. Yurdaydin: *Naṣūḥü's-Silāḥī (Matrakçī): Beyān-i menāzil-i sefer-i 'Irāḳeyn-i Sulṭān Süleymān Khān* (Ankara, 1976).

42. Sheila S. Blair, "The Mongol Capital of Sulṭāniyya, 'the Imperial'," *Iran* 24 (1986): 139–51, and Walter B. Denny, "A Sixteenth-Century Architectural Plan of Istanbul," *Ars Orientalis* 8 (1970): 49–63.

43. Istanbul, Topkapı Palace Library, R. 917; see Atıl, *Age of Sultan Süleyman*, pp. 63–5. See also Richard Ettinghausen, "Die bildliche Darstellung der Ka'ba im islamischen Kulturkreis," *Zeitschrift der Deutschen Morgenländischen Gesellschaft* 87 (1934): 111–37, and Hassan El-Basha, "Ottoman Pictures of the Mosque of the Prophet in Madīna as Historical and Documentary Sources," *Islamic Art* 3 (1988–9): 227–44.

44. See, for example, Sheila S. Blair and Jonathan M. Bloom, eds, *Images of Paradise in Islamic Art* (Hanover, NH, 1991), nos. 9b and 10b.

45. Topkapı Palace Library, H. 1339; the canteen is no. 2/3825. See Atıl, *Age of Sultan Süleyman*, no. 54; Rogers and Ward, *Süleyman the Magnificent*, no. 63.

46. The manuscript, which covers the reign of Selim, is the second of a multi-volume history of the Ottomans commissioned by Murad III. One volume (Dublin, Chester Beatty Library, T. 413) covers the reign of Süleyman; another volume is entitled the *Shāhanshāhnāma* (1581–2; Istanbul University Library, F. 1404) and covers 1574–82 of the reign of Murad III. There is also a second volume of the *Shāhanshāhnāma* (Topkapı Palace Library, B. 200) and another unidentified volume in the series (Göttingen, MS Pers 67). See Çağman and Tanındı, *The Topkapı Saray Museum: The Albums and Illustrated Manuscripts*, pp. 211–12.

47. It is in vol. 1 of the *Shāhanshāhnāma* (Istanbul University Library, F. 1404, fol. 41b–42a); illustrated in color in Nurhan Atasoy and Filiz Çağman, *Turkish Miniature Painting*, trans. Esin Atıl (Istanbul, 1974), pl. 18.

48. Volumes 1, 2, and 6 are in Istanbul (Topkapı Palace Library, H. 1221–23); volume 3 is in New York (New York Public Library, Spencer MS. 157) and volume 4 is mostly in Dublin (Chester Beatty Library, Turk. MS. 419). See Carol Garrett Fisher, "A Reconstruction of the Pictorial Cycle of the *Siyar-i Nabī* of Murad III," *Ars Orientalis*, 14 (1984): 75–94.

49. Istanbul, Topkapı Palace Library, MS. 1703.

50. Istanbul, Topkapı Palace Library, H. 1124; see Atasoy and Çağman, *Turkish Miniature Painting*, pls. 45 and 46.

51. Rachel Milstein, *Miniature Painting in Ottoman Baghdad* (Costa Mesa, CA, 1990).

52. Atasoy and Raby, *Iznik*, p. 273.

53. Alberto Boralevi, "Three Egyptian carpets in Italy," in Pinner and Denny, pp. 205–20.

54. E.g. a manuscript of the Koran in Istanbul University Library, A. 6549, with 458 folios; dated 1663–4. See *The Anatolian Civilisations III*, no. E 309. For other work of Hafiz Osman, see Elke Niewöhner-Eberhard, "Die Berliner Murakka von Hafiz Osman," *Jahrbuch der Berliner Museen* 31 (1989): 41–59.

55. Stockholm, Royal Armoury, no. 3661. See *The Arts of Islam* (London, 1976), no. 30, and Agnes Geijer, *Oriental Textiles in Sweden* (Copenhagen, 1951), p. 111, no. 69. The example illustrated is identical.

56. Istanbul, Topkapı Palace Library, A. 3593. See Esin Atıl, "The Surname-i Vehbi: An Eighteenth-Century Ottoman Book of Festivals" (Ph.D. dissertation, University of Michigan, Ann Arbor, 1969).

57. Çağman and Tanındı, *Topkapı Saray Museum: The Albums and Illustrated Manuscripts*, pp. 252–3.

58. An album in Istanbul (Topkapı Palace Library, H. 2164) contains 43 studies of men and women; color illustration of folios 17a and 18a in Çağman and Tanındı, *The Topkapı Saray Museum: The Albums and Illustrated Manuscripts*, pls. 171–2.

59. An imperial reception on fol. 17b is signed on the footstool beneath the sultan's feet, and fol. 171a is signed beneath a courtly rider in a parade and was possibly intended as a self-portrait.

CHAPTER 17: ARCHITECTURE AND THE ARTS IN EGYPT AND NORTH AFRICA

1. For a general survey of the period, see Charles-André Julien, *History of North Africa from the Arab Conquest to 1830*, revised and ed. R. Le Tourneau, trans. John Petrie, ed. C. C. Steward (New York and Washington, 1970), Abdallah Laroui, *The History of the Maghrib, an Interpretive Essay*, trans. Ralph Manheim (Princeton, 1977), and Jamil M. Abun-Nasr, *A History of the Maghrib in the Islamic Period* (Cambridge, 1987).

2. André Raymond, *Grandes villes arabes à l'époque ottoman* (Paris, 1985).

3. Nelly Hanna, *An Urban History of Būlāq in the Mamluk and Ottoman Periods* (Cairo, 1983).

4. The mosque of Čoban Mustafa Pasha at Gebze (ca. 1522–3), for example, has marble revetments in the Mamluk style, as does the Baghdad Kiosk at Topkapı Palace. See Michael Meinecke, "Mamlukische Marmordekorationen in der osmanischen Turkei," *Mitteilungen des Deutschen Archäologischen Instituts: Abteilung Kairo* 27/2 (1971): 207–20, and Chapter 15 above.

5. Viktoria Meinecke-Berg, "Die osmanische Fliesendekoration der Āqsunqur-Moschee in Cairo," *Mitteilungen des Deutschen Archäologischen Instituts: Abteilung Kairo* 29 (1973): 39–62.

6. John Alden Williams, "The Monuments of Ottoman Cairo," *Colloque International sur l'Histoire du Caire* (Cairo, 1969), pp. 453–65; Doris Behrens-Abouseif, *Islamic Architecture in Cairo, an Introduction* (Leiden, 1989), pp. 161–2 with plan and view.

7. On these late Mamluk domes, see Doris Behrens-Abouseif, "Four Domes of the Late Mamluk Period," *Annales islamologiques* 17 (1981): 191–202; eadem, "The *Qubba*, an Aristocratic type of *Zāwiya*," *Annales islamologiques* 19 (1983): 1–7.

8. J. M. Rogers, "Innovation and Continuity in Islamic Urbanism," *The Arab City, its Character and Islamic Cultural Heritage*, ed. Ismail Sedrageldin and Samir El-Sadek (n.p., 1982), pp. 53–61.

9. Doris Behrens-Abouseif, "The 'Abd al-Raḥmān Katkhudā Style in 18th Century Cairo," *Annales islamologiques* 26 (1992): 117–26.

10. *Islamic Art and Architecture in Libya* (London, 1976).

11. See for example the panel of fifty tiles with a keyhole arch enclosing a vase and flowers in Paris (Musée des Arts Africains et Océaniens, no. MN.AM 1962.723), illustrated in *L'Islam dans les collections nationales* (Paris, 1977), no. 508.

12. See Ettinghausen and Grabar, pp. 140, 155 and ill. 136.

13. For Nigari's portrait of Khayr al-Din as an old man (Istanbul, Topkapı Palace Library, H. 2134, fol. 9), see Esin Atıl, *Turkish Art* (Washington, DC, 1980), p. 193, fig. 86. For a biography, see *EI*, s.v. "Khayr al-Dīn Pasha."

14. Georges Marçais, *L'Architecture musulmane d'occident* (Paris, 1954), pp. 433–4, and Rachid Dokali, *Les mosquées de la période turque à Alger* (Algiers, 1974).

15. See Ettinghausen and Grabar, pp. 128–37.

16. Albert Hourani, *A History of the Arab Peoples* (Cambridge, 1991), pp. 243–8.

17. Jerrilynn D. Dodds, ed., *Al-Andalus: The Art of Islamic Spain* (New York, 1992), no. 43.

18. *EI/2*, s.v. "al-Djazūlī," and J. Spencer Trimingham, *The Sufi Orders in Islam* (Oxford, 1971), pp. 84–6.

19. On maraboutism, see Dale F. Eickelman, *Moroccan Islam: Tradition and Society in a Pilgrimage Center* (Austin and London, 1976).

20. Marçais, *Architecture musulmane d'occident*, pp. 386–7. The principal entrance is shown in Derek Hill and Lucien Golvin, *Islamic Architecture in North Africa* (London, 1976), fig. 467. The continuing veneration of al-Jazuli has meant that the shrine has not yet been the subject of a detailed architectural study.

21. Henri Terrasse, *La Mosquée al-Qaraouiyn à Fès* (Paris, 1968), pp. 70–2, and Marçais, *Architecture musulmane d'occident*, p. 387.

22. Marianne Barrucand, *L'Architecture de la qasba de Moulay Ismaïl à Meknès*, 2 vols. (Casablanca, 1976), and eadem, *Urbanisme princier en Islam: Meknès et les villes royales islamiques post-médiévales* (Paris, 1985).

23. Barrucand, *Urbanisme princier*, pp. 107–69.

24. See, for example, the Oudaia Gate and the minaret of the Mosque of Hasan, both at Rabat and illustrated in Ettinghausen and Grabar, ills. 122–3.

25. Many of these objects were illustrated in the catalogue, *De l'Empire romain aux Villes impériales: 6000 ans d'art au Maroc*, Musée du Petit Palais (Paris, 1990).

26. See *L'Islam dans les collections nationales*, nos. 539–43, for examples.

27. The Rabat type of knotted carpet, for example, first appeared in the eighteenth century and was based on Anatolian models. See *From the Far West: Carpets and Textiles of Morocco*, ed. Patricia L. Fiske, W. Russell Pickering, and Ralph S. Yohe (Washington, DC, 1980), pp. 79–82. Algiers embroideries also often followed Ottoman patterns. See *L'Islam dans les collections nationales*, no. 527. Similarly, when 'Abdi Pasha of Algiers wanted a present for the King of Sweden, he chose velvet cushion covers in the metropolitan Ottoman style [16.22].

28. *EI/2*, s.v. "Ḳādiriyya," and Sheila S. Blair and Jonathan M. Bloom, eds, *Images of Paradise in Islamic Art* (Hanover, NH, 1991), no. 8a, and Walter B. Denny, "A Group of Silk Islamic Banners," *Textile Museum Journal* 4/1 (1974): 67–81.

29. E.g. a manuscript of the Koran (Paris, Bibliothèque Nationale, MS arabe 385, probably copied at Granada in 1303. See Martin Lings, *The Qur'anic Art of Calligraphy and Illumination* (London, 1976), nos. 104–5.

30. *De l'Empire romain*, no. 542.

31. Cairo, National Library, 2.5, published in Lings, *Qur'anic Art*, nos. 112–14; and Martin Lings and Yasin Safadi, *The Qur'an* (London, 1976), no. 53.

CHAPTER 18: ARCHITECTURE IN INDIA UNDER THE MUGHALS AND THEIR CONTEMPORARIES IN THE DECCAN

1. The most recent survey of Mughal architecture is Catherine B. Asher, *Architecture of Mughal India* (Cambridge, 1992). Good plans and plates are also available in Ebba Koch, *Mughal Architecture: An Outline of its History and Development (1526–1858)* (Munich, 1991).

2. Elizabeth B. Moynihan, *Paradise as a Garden in Persia and Mughal India* (New York, 1980). The most extensive example of Babur's garden architecture is his lotus garden at Dholpur between Agra and Gwalior. See Elizabeth B. Moynihan, "The Lotus Garden Palace of Zahir al-Din Muhammad Babur," *Muqarnas* 5 (1988): 135–52. See also Howard Crane, "The Patronage of Zahir al-Din Babur and the Origins of Mughal Architecture," *Bulletin of the Asia Institute*, 1 (1987): 95–110.

3. Catherine B. Asher, "The Mausoleum of Sher Shah Suri," *Artibus Asiae* 39 (1977): 273–98.

4. Catherine B. Asher, "Legacy and Legitimacy: Sher Shāh's Patronage of Imperial Mausolea," *Sharī'at and Ambiguity in South Asian Islam*, ed. Katherine P. Ewing (Berkeley, 1988), pp. 79–97.

5. Glenn D. Lowry, "Humayun's Tomb: Form, Function, and Meaning in Early Mughal Architecture," *Muqarnas* 4 (1987): 133–48.

6. For the links between Timurid and Mughal architecture, see Lisa Golombek, "From Tamerlane to the Taj Mahal," *Essays in Islamic Art and Architecture in Honor of Katharina Otto-Dorn*, ed. A. Daneshvari (Malibu, 1981), pp. 43–50.

7. Abu'l-Fazl, *Akbarnama*, ii, 73, cited in *Fatehpur Sikri: A Sourcebook*, ed. Michael Brand and Glenn D. Lowry (Cambridge, MA, 1985), p. 10 and note 25.

8. William G. Klingelhofer, "The Jahangiri Mahal of the Agra Fort: Expression and Experience in Early Mughal Architecture," *Muqarnas* 5 (1988): 153–69.

9. The site was the focus of a conference held during the Festival of India in 1985; many of the papers were later published in *Fatehpur-Sikri*, ed. Michael Brand and Glenn D. Lowry (Bombay, 1987). Many of the sources relating to the city were collected in *Fatehpur Sikri: A Sourcebook*. See also the catalogue for the exhibition held at the Asia Society in New York, Michael Brand and Glenn D. Lowry, *Akbar's India: Art from the Mughal City of Victory* (New York, 1985).

10. Attilio Petruccioli, "The Process Evolved by the Control Systems of Urban Design in the Moghul Epoch in India: The Case of Fathpur Sikri," *Environmental Design* 1 (1984): 18–27; idem, "The Geometry of Power: The City's Planning," in *Fatehpur-Sikri*, pp. 49–64.

11. In addition to the tombs of Nizam al-Din in Delhi and Mu'in al-Din at Ajmer, an early example is the tomb of Shah Alam in Ahmadabad, for which see Ebba Koch, "Influence on Mughal Architecture," in *Ahmedabad*, ed. George Michell and Snehal Shah (Bombay, 1988), pp. 168–72.

12. Simon Digby, "The Mother-of-Pearl Overlaid Furniture of Gujarat: the Holdings of the Victoria and Albert Museum," in *Facets of Indian Art, A symposium held at the Victoria and Albert Museum on 26, 27, 28 April and 1 May 1982*, ed. Robert Skelton, Andrew Topsfield, Susan Stronge, and Rosemary Crill (London, 1986), pp. 213–22.

13. Wayne E. Begley, "Amānat Khān and the Calligraphy on the Tāj Maḥal," *Kunst des Orients* 12 (1978–9): 5–60.

14. Wayne E. Begley, "The Myth of the Taj Mahal and a New Theory of Its Symbolic Meaning," *Art Bulletin* 56/1 (1979): 7–37.

15. Robert Skelton, "A Decorative Motif in Mughal Art," *Aspects of Indian Art*, ed. P. Pal (Leiden, 1972), pp. 147–52.

16. M. A. Chaghatai, *The Wazir Khan Mosque, Lahore* (Lahore, 1975).

17. Ebba Koch, *Shah Jahan and Orpheus* (Graz, 1988).

18. On Mughal gardens in general, see Y. Crowe, S. Haywood, and S. Jellicoe, *The Gardens of Mughal India* (London, 1972); Susan Jellicoe, "The Development of the Mughal Garden," *The Islamic Garden*, ed. Elisabeth B. Macdougall and Richard Ettinghausen (Washington, DC, 1976), pp. 107–30; and E. B. Moynihan, *Paradise as a Garden in Persia and Mughal India* (London, 1980).

19. M. A. Chaghtai, *The Badshahi Masjid* (Lahore, 1975).

20. B. Tandan, "The Architecture of the Nawabs of Avadh, 1722–1856," in *Facets of Indian Art*, ed. Skelton et al., pp. 66–75.

CHAPTER 19: THE ARTS IN INDIA UNDER THE MUGHALS AND THEIR CONTEMPORARIES IN THE DECCAN

1. Stephen Markel, "Fit for an Emperor: Inscribed Works of Decorative Art Acquired by the Great Mughals," *Orientations* 21/8 (August 1990): 22–36.

2. *Qalam-i turkī*, Rampur, State Library, no. 19. The colophon is dated 23 Safar 935/6 November 1528. See E. Denison Ross, "The poems of the Emperor Babur," *Journal of the Asiatic Society of Bengal* 6, extra. no. (October 1910): 1–43.

3. W. M. Thackston's new translation of the text will appear soon. Babur's son Kamran was thought to have commissioned illustrated manuscripts, to judge from a copy of Jami's *Yūsuf and Zulaykhā*, but the six illustrations in a poor version of the Bukhara style were pasted into the text at a later date. See Barbara Schmitz, *Islamic Manuscripts in the New York Public Library* (New York, 1992), no. II-15.

4. For example, a large painting on cotton depicting *The Princes of the House of Timur* (London, British Museum, 1913.2–8.1), for which see Stuart Cary Welch, *India: Art and Culture 1300–1900* (New York, 1985), no. 84; or a painting of *A Young Scribe* inscribed "Sayyid 'Ali, who is the rarity of the realm of Humayun Shah, painted this," for which see Michael Brand and Glenn D. Lowry, *Akbar's India: Art from the Mughal City of Victory* (New York, 1985), no. 6.

5. John Seyller, "Scribal Notes on Mughal Manuscript Illustrations," *Artibus Asiae* 48 (1987): 247–77.

6. Gulshan Album, Tehran, Gulistan Palace Library. See Laurence Binyon, J. V. S. Wilkinson, and Basil Gray, *Persian Miniature Painting* (Oxford, 1933), no. 230, pl. CIV; *SPA*, pl. 912; *Encyclopaedia Iranica*, s.v. "'Abd-al-Ṣamad."

7. Cleveland Museum of Art, 62.279. The major study of the *Tūṭīnāma* is Pramod Chandra, *The Tuti-Nama of the Cleveland Museum of Art and the Origins of Mughal Painting* (Graz, 1976), but the close examination of the paintings by John Seyller, *Ars Orientalis* (forthcoming), has forced a reevaluation of the date of the original manuscript and its history.

8. Most of the surviving pages came to Europe from Tehran, where they were

probably taken in Iranian raids on the Mughal empire after 1739. Sixty folios in the Museum für angewandte Kunst, Vienna, were purchased from the Persian Pavilion at the Vienna World's Fair. Of the twenty-seven folios in the Victoria and Albert Museum, twenty-four were found at Srinigar in 1881 tacked inside a wooden house to protect it from the weather. Most of those in American collections belong to a group of twenty-six purchased in 1912 by General Riza Khan Monif from the sister of the Qajar shah Ahmad. See Milo Cleveland Beach, *The Imperial Image: Paintings for the Mughal Court* (Washington, 1981), pp. 58–68. A new study by John Seyller, "A Dated *Ḥamzanāma* Illustration" *Artibus Asiae* 53 (1993) puts the date of the project ca. 1557–72.

9. Illustration 84 from book 11; see Pramod Chandra, "The Brooklyn Museum Folios of the *Hamza-nama*," *Orientations* 20/7 (July 1989): 39–45.

10. University of London, School of Oriental and African Studies Library, MS. 10102; see Welch, *India: Art and Culture*, no. 93; Jeremiah P. Losty, *The Art of the Book in India* (London, 1982), no. 57; John Seyller, "The School of Oriental and African Studies *Anvār-i Suhaylī*: The Illustration of a De Luxe Mughal Manuscript," *Ars Orientalis* 16 (1986): 119–52; Karl Khandalavala and Kalpana Desai, "Indian Illustrated Manuscripts of the *Kalilah wa Dimnah, Anvar-i Suhayli*, and *Iyar-i Danish*," *A Mirror for Princes from India*, ed. E. J. Grube (Bombay, 1991), pp. 128–44.

11. London, British Library, Or. 4615; see Losty, *Art of the Book in India*, no. 59. The manuscript is undated, but its 157 paintings are usually dated ca. 1580.

12. London, British Library, Add. 18497; see Losty, *Art of the Book in India*, no. 53; Brand and Lowry, *Akbar's India*, no. 21.

13. Jaipur, Maharaja Sawai Man Singh II Museum, MS. AG. 1683–1850.

14. Ellen Smart ("Paintings from the Babur-nama: A Study of 16th-Century Mughal Historical Manuscript Illustrations," Ph.D. dissertation, SOAS, University of London, 1977) has traced the relationships among the four major illustrated versions of the *Bāburnāma* produced in the Akbar period and used iconographic grounds to establish the sequence of manuscripts. In the earliest manuscript, done ca. 1589 (dispersed and V & A), the paintings followed the text closely; while paintings in three later manuscripts produced in the 1590s (British Library, Or. 3714, ca. 1590–1; a second copy divided between Baltimore, Walters Art Gallery, W. 596, and Moscow, State Museum of Eastern Cultures, no. 63; and a third copy dated 1597–9 in the National Museum, New Delhi) were based on earlier models with consequent misunderstanding of details.

15. London, Victoria and Albert Museum, MS. IS. 2–1896; see Beach, *Imperial Image*, pp. 83–90; for the recent redating of the paintings, see John Seyller, "Codicological Aspects of the Victoria and Albert Museum *Akbarnmma* and Their Historical Implications," *Art Journal* 49/4 (Winter 1990): 379–87.

16. *The Indian Heritage: Court Life and Arts under Mughal Rule* (London, 1982), no. 29; Brand and Lowry, *Akbar's India*, no. 15.

17. London, British Library, Or. 12988; Dublin, Chester Beatty Library, Ind. MS. 3; and dispersed. See Beach, *Imperial Image*, no. 12, pp. 102–22, and Losty, *Art of the Book in India*, nos 70–71. For the recent redating of the manuscript from 1604 to 1596–7, see Seyller, "Scribal Notes on Mughal Manuscript Illustrations" and "Codicological Aspects."

18. See Milo Cleveland Beach, *The Grand Mogul: Imperial Painting in India 1600–1660* (Williamstown, MA, 1978), pp. 118–25.

19. Oxford, Bodleian Library, MS. Elliot 254. See Beach, *Imperial Image*, p. 223, and Losty, *Art of the Book in India*, no. 64.

20. Most of the manuscript, with thirty-seven of the original forty-four paintings, is in the British Library (Or. 12208), but thirty-nine folios with five paintings are in the Walters Art Gallery, Baltimore, and two paintings have disappeared. See Beach, *Imperial Image*, p. 223; Losty, *Art of the Book in India*, no. 65.

21. Baltimore, Walters Art Gallery, W.624. See Beach, *Imperial Image*, p. 227; Losty, *Art of the Book in India*, no. 66; and Barbara Brend, "Akbar's *Khamsah* of Amir Khusraw Dihlavi – A Reconstruction of the Cycle of Illustration," *Artibus Asiae* 49, nos. 3/4 (1988–89): 281–315.

22. He apparently also transcribed the second copy of the *Akbarnāma*.

23. Fol. 80v; illustrated in Losty, *Art of the Book in India*, p. 91.

24. The covers are illustrated in Welch, *India*, no. 111, p. 179. On the development of borders, see J. P. Losty, "The 'Bute Hafiz' and the Development of Border Decoration in the Manuscript Studio of the Mughals," *Burlington Magazine* 127 (1985): 855–71.

25. Brand and Lowry, *Akbar's India*, nos. 77–9 and pp. 119–20.

26. Fragments of the rug are in many collections; see *Indian Heritage*, no. 191; Welch, *India*, no. 95, and Brand and Lowry, *Akbar's India*, no. 71.

27. Daniel Walker, "Classical Indian Rugs," *Hali* 4 (1982): 252–6.

28. Illustrated in Lentz and Lowry, p. 265.

29. Paris, Musée des Arts Décoratifs, Inv. 5212 and elsewhere; see *Indian Heritage*, no. 193.

30. He was also responsible for a Persian translation of Babur's memoirs from the Chaghatay Turkish original.

31. Akbar's copy is in Jaipur, Maharaja Sawai Man Singh II Museum, MS. AG. 1851–2026. The copy for Khan-i Khanan is in Washington, Freer Gallery

of Art, 07.271; see Beach, *Imperial Image*, pp. 128–55, and John Seyller, "The Freer Rāmāyana and the Atelier of ʿAbd al-Rahīm" (Ph.D. dissertation, Harvard University, 1986). Many of the paintings are reproduced in color in Swami Bhaktipada, *The Illustrated Ramayana* (New Vrindaban, WV, 1989).

32. *Tūzuk-i Jahāngīrī*, vol. II, p. 20, cited in Beach, "Aqa Riza," *Grand Mogul*, p. 92.

33. The three manuscripts made for Prince Salim at Allahabad are a copy of the collected poems of Hasan Dihlavi dated 17 July 1602 (Baltimore, Walters Art Gallery, W. 650); a Persian romance entitled *Rāj Kunvār* dated 1603–4 (Dublin, Chester Beatty Library, Ind. MS. 37); and a copy (London, British Library, Add. 18579) of *Anvār-i Suhaylī*, with a colophon dated 1019/1610–11 and two paintings dated 1013/1604. Another manuscript, a copy of the collected poems of Hafiz (London, British Library, Grenville XLI), may well have been made for him too. See Beach, *Grand Mogul*, pp. 33–41, and Losty, *Art of the Book in India*, nos. 72–5.

34. On the albums, see Ernst Kühnel and Hermann Goetz, *Indian Book Painting from Jahangir's Album in the State Library, Berlin* (London, 1926); Yedda A. Godard, "Les Marges du Muraḳḳaʿ Gulshan," *Āthār-é Īrān* 1 (1936): 11–35; Milo Beach, "The Gulshan Album and its European Sources," *Bulletin of the Museum of Fine Arts, Boston* 332 (1965): 63–91; Beach, *Grand Mogul*, pp. 43–60, and Losty, *Art of the Book in India*, no. 78.

35. Folio 24v; illustrated in Losty, *Art of the Book in India*, p. 97.

36. Washington, DC, Freer Gallery of Art, 54.116; see Esin Atil, *The Brush of the Masters: Drawings from Iran and India* (Washington, DC, 1978), no. 63; Beach, *Imperial Image*, no. 16b.

37. Richard Ettinghausen, "The Emperor's Choice," *De Artibus Opuscula XL: Essays in Honor of Erwin Panofsky*, ed. Millard Meiss (New York, 1961), pp. 98–120, reprinted in *Richard Ettinghausen: Islamic Art and Archeology Collected Papers*, ed. M. Rosen-Ayalon (Berlin, 1984), pp. 642–74; Beach, *Imperial Image*, no. 17a.

38. Washington, DC, Freer Gallery of Art, 42.16; Beach, *Imperial Image*, no. 17c.

39. Mark Zebrowski, *Deccani Painting* (London, 1983), no. 59; Welch, *India*, no. 195.

40. The Minto Album is divided between the Victoria and Albert Museum, London (IM. 8–1925 to 28–1925), and the Chester Beatty Library, Dublin (MS. 7).

41. The Late Shahjahan Album was apparently broken up in Paris in 1909; see Beach, *Grand Mogul*, pp. 76–7, for a list of known pages and several examples.

42. The Wantage Album is in the Victoria and Albert Museum, London; the Kevorkian Album is divided between the Metropolitan Museum in New York and the Freer Gallery of Art in Washington, DC; see S. C. Welch et al., *The Emperors' Album: Images of Mughal India* (New York, 1987). On the making of these later Mughal albums, see Vishakha N. Desai, "Reflections of the Past in the Present: Copying Processes in Indian Painting" (forthcoming).

43. Windsor Castle, Royal Library, MS. HB 149.

44. The varying quality of the paintings has led some authors to claim that some of them were added when the manuscript was remargined and rebound in the eighteenth century, but this view has recently been disputed. See Wayne Begley, "Illustrated Histories of Shah Jahan: New Identifications of some Dispersed Paintings and Problems of the Windsor Castle Padshahnama," *Facets of Indian Art, A Symposium held at the Victoria and Albert Museum on 26, 27, 28 April and 1 May 1982* ed. Robert Skelton, Andrew Topsfield, Susan Stronge, and Rosemary Crill (London, 1986), pp. 139–52.

45. Robert Skelton, *Shah Jahan's Jade Cup* (London, 1978); *Indian Heritage*, no. 356; Welch, *India*, no. 167; Markel, "Fit for an Emperor," fig. 11.

46. May Beattie, *The Thyssen-Bornemisza Collection of Oriental Rugs* (Castagnola, 1972), pp. 67–72; *Arts of Islam*, no. 100; *Indian Heritage*, no. 199; Welch, *India*, no. 138.

47. Walker, "Classical Indian Rugs."

48. London, Victoria and Albert Museum, I.M. 207–1920; see *Indian Heritage*, no. 303, and Welch, *India*, no. 129.

49. London, Victoria and Albert Museum, 1023–1871; see *Indian Heritage*, no. 355.

50. Cleveland Museum of Art, 62.206; *Indian Heritage*, no. 324; Welch, *India*, no. 181.

51. Susan Stronge, *Bidri Ware: Inlaid Metalwork from India* (London, 1985).

52. François Bernier, *Travels in the Mogul Empire*, trans. A. Constable (London, 1891, reprint New Delhi, 1968), p. 360, cited in *Indian Heritage*, p. 79.

53. See *Indian Heritage*, nos. 207–8.

54. See *Indian Heritage*, no. 213. The complete tent is part of Tipu's relics which were acquired by the second Lord Clive, son of Clive of India, and his connoisseur-collector wife, the Powis heiress, when he served as Governor of Madras from 1798 to 1803.

55. Nineteenth-century copies of the *Pādshāhnāma* include London, British Library, Add. 20734, and Patna, Khudabakhsh Library; see Losty, *Art of the*

Book in India, no. 107. The copy of the *ʿAmal-i ṣāliḥ* done ca. 1830 is in the British Library (Or. 2157); see Losty, no. 137.

56. Simon Digby, "The Mother-of-Pearl Overlaid Furniture of Gujarat: the Holdings of the Victoria and Albert Museum," in *Facets of Indian Art*, ed. Skelton et al., pp. 213–22.

57. For earlier painting in Kashmir, see Linda York Leach, "Painting in Kashmir from 1600 to 1650," in *Facets of Indian Art*, pp. 124–31.

58. London, British Library, Add. 18804; see Losty, *Art of the Book in India*, no. 125; A. Adamova and T. Greck, *Miniatures from Kashmirian Manuscripts* (Leningrad, 1976).

CHAPTER 20: THE LEGACIES OF LATER ISLAMIC ART

1. Bernard S. Cohn, "Representing Authority in Victorian India," in Eric Hobsbawm and Terence Ranger, eds, *The Invention of Tradition* (Cambridge, 1992), pp. 165–210.

2. For the arts of Qajar Iran, see B. W. Robinson, "Persian Painting under the Zand and Qājār Dynasties," and Jennifer Scarce, "The Arts of the Eighteenth to Twentieth Centuries: Architecture, Ceramics, Metalwork, Textiles," in Peter Avery, Gavin Hambly, and Charles Melville, eds, *From Nadir Shah to the Islamic Republic, The Cambridge History of Iran, VII* (Cambridge, 1991), pp. 870–90 and 890–958.

3. Mohamed Al-Asad, "The Re-invention of Tradition: Neo-Islamic Architecture," *Proceedings of the XXVIII International Congress of the History of Art* (Berlin, 1992).

4. Other traditions should be mentioned, such as the Spanish interest in the Islamic heritage in Iberia and Russian interest in Central Asia. For the history of European interest in the Islamic world, see Edward Said, *Orientalism* (New York, 1979), among others.

5. For this painting, see Julian Raby, *Venice, Dürer and the Oriental Mode* (London, 1982).

6. Richard Ettinghausen, "The Impact of Muslim Decorative Arts and Painting on the Arts of Europe," *The Legacy of Islam*, ed. Joseph Schacht and C. E. Bosworth (Oxford, 1974), pp. 290–320; F. Sarre, "Rembrants Zeichnungen nach indisch-islamischen Miniaturen," *Jahrbuch der Königl. Preussischen Kunstsammlungen*, 25 (1904): 143–58; idem, "Ein neues Blatt von Rembrandts indischen Zeichnungen," *Jahrbuch der Konigl. Preussischen Kunstsammlungen*, 30 (1909): 283–90.

7. John Sweetman, *The Oriental Obsession: Islamic Inspiration in British and American Art and Architecture 1500–1920* (Cambridge, 1987), pp. 70–2.

8. William Chambers, *Plans, Elevations, Sections, and Perspective Views of the Gardens and Buildings at Kew in Surrey* (London, 1763).

9. John Harris, *Sir William Chambers, Knight of the Polar Star* (London, 1970), p. 37, and Kurt Martin, *Die Kunstdenkmäler des Amtsbezirks Mannheim: Stadt Schwetzingen* (Karlsruhe/Baden, 1933), p. 290.

10. Sweetman, *Oriental Obsession*, pp. 101–11.

11. Pratapaditya Pal and others, *Romance of the Taj Mahal* (Los Angeles and London, 1989), pp. 199–203.

12. Michael Scholz-Hänsel, "'Antiguedades Arabes de Espana', Wie die einst vertriebene Mauren Spanien zu einer wiederentdeckung im 19. Jahrhundert verhalfen," *Europa und der Orient 800–1900* (Berlin, 1989), pp. 368–82.

13. Oleg Grabar, *The Alhambra* (London and Cambridge, MA, 1978), pp. 17–19.

14. For some connoisseurs a copy was not as good as the real thing: in 1866 the banker Arthur Gwinner Dreiss acquired, with the permission of the Spanish crown, the Torre de las Damas at the Alhambra. He later sold the building but retained its magnificent wooden ceiling, which he dismantled and installed in his house in Berlin. The ceiling was purchased by the Museum für Islamische Kunst, Berlin, in 1978. See Jerrilynn D. Dodds, ed., *Al-Andalus: The Art of Islamic Spain* (New York, 1992), no. 116.

15. Sweetman, *Oriental Obsession*, pp. 160 and 254.

16. Mary Anne Stevens, ed., *The Orientalists: Delacroix to Matisse* (London, 1984).

17. Guy Dumur, *Delacroix et le Maroc* (Paris, 1988).

18. Jack Cowart et al., *Matisse in Morocco: The Paintings and Drawings 1912–1913* (Washington, DC, 1990), p. 23.

19. Linda Nochlin, "The Imaginary Orient," *Art in America*, 71 (1983): 118–31 and 187–91. See, for example, the two versions of Ingres' *Odalisque and Slave*, that of 1839 in Cambridge, MA (Harvard University Art Museums), and that of 1842 in Baltimore (Walters Art Gallery).

20. Zeynep Celik, *Displaying the Orient: Architecture of Islam at Nineteenth-century World's Fairs* (Berkeley, 1992).

21. David Black, ed., *The Macmillan Atlas of Rugs and Carpets* (New York, 1985), pp. 218–21.

22. F. DuCane Godman, *The Godman Collection of Oriental and Spanish Pottery and Glass* (London, 1901); the collection is now in the British Museum.

23. His pieces formed the basis of the Victoria and Albert Museum's collection of Persian art.

24. Oliver Watson, *Persian Lustre Ware* (London, 1985), pp. 169–75.

25. Alan Caiger-Smith, *Lustre Pottery* (London, 1985), Ch. 9, "Revival," and Sweetman, *Oriental Obsession*, pp. 183–5.

26. Cowart, *Matisse in Morocco*.

27. Pierre Schneider, *Matisse* (New York, 1984), p. 158.

28. Godfrey Goodwin, *A History of Ottoman Architecture* (London and Baltimore, 1971), pp. 417–18.

29. Goodwin, *History of Ottoman Architecture*, pp. 421–3.

30. K. A. C. Creswell, *The Muslim Architecture of Egypt* (Oxford, 1959), 2, p. 262. Was it only coincidental that in 1811 Muhammad 'Ali had invited the Mamluk leaders to a ceremony in the citadel at which they were murdered? See Mohammad Al-Asad, "The Mosque of Muhammad 'Ali, Cairo," *Muqarnas* 9 (1992): 39–55.

31. Gaston Wiet, *The Mosques of Cairo* (Paris, 1966), p. 110.

32. Gaston Wiet, *Mohammed Ali et les beaux-arts* (Cairo, 1949), pp. 265–88.

33. Donald Malcolm Reid, "Cultural Imperialism and Nationalism: The Struggle to Define and Control the Heritage of Arab Art in Egypt," *International Journal of Middle East Studies* 24 (1992): 57–76.

34. These include not only King Fuad (r. 1917–36), but also Muhammad Reza Shah Pahlevi, the last Shah of Iran.

35. Mohammad Al-Asad, "The Mosque of al-Rifa'i in Cairo," *Muqarnas* 10 (1993): 108–24, and Max Herz Bey, *La Mosquée el-Rifaï au Caire paru á l'occasion de la consécration de la mosquée* (Milan, ca. 1912).

36. Reid, "Cultural Imperialism."

37. Maxime du Camp, *Le Nil, Egypte et Nubie* (Paris, 1854).

38. The doors, acquired by the Hispanic Society of America in New York, have never been published.

39. Cairo, Museum of Islamic Art, no. 1 139. Copies exist in Cambridge, MA (Harvard University, Semitic Museum, 8494.1), Philadelphia (University Museum, NE-P-69), Istanbul (Topkapı Palace Museum), and several private collections.

40. Ettinghausen and Grabar, ill. 392: the Freer Basin. See Eva Baer, *Ayyubid Metalwork with Christian Images* (Leiden, 1989). Jews were the greatest practitioners of metal inlay in Damascus, and in 1909 A. Bar-Adon, head of the copper department of the new Bezalel craft school in Jerusalem, went to Damascus to learn the craft of inlay. The workshop he founded in Jerusalem became known for inlaid objects, often with representational and religious decoration. M. S. al-Qasimi, *Dictionnaire des métiers damascains* (in Arabic, 2 vols.; Paris, 1960); Estelle Whelan, *The Mamluk Revival: Metalwork for Religious and Domestic Use* (New York, Jewish Museum, 1981).

41. *Encyclopaedia Iranica*, s.v. "Carpets. xi. Qajar Period."

42. Watson, *Persian Lustre Ware*, pp. 169–75.

43. Jennifer Scarce, "'Ali Mohammad Isfahani, Tile maker of Tehran," *Oriental Art* n.s. XXII/3 (1976): 278–88.

44. Translated by John Fargues, also printed in W. J. Furnival, *Leadless Decorative Tiles, Faience and Mosaic* (Stone, 1904).

45. Renata Holod and Ahmet Evin, eds, *Modern Turkish Architecture* (Philadelphia, 1984), p. 36.

46. Gülsüm Baydar Nalbantoğlu, "The Professionalization of the Ottoman-Turkish Architect" (Ph.D. dissertation, University of California, Berkeley, 1989), pp. 54–5, and Zeynep Çelik, *The Remaking of Istanbul: Portrait of an Ottoman City in the Nineteenth Century* (Seattle and London, 1986).

47. Holod and Evin, *Modern Turkish Architecture*, p. 47.

48. Sibel Bozdoğan, "Modernity in the Margins: Architecture and Ideology in Early Republican Turkey," *Proceedings of the XVIII International Congress of the History of Art* (Berlin, 1993).

49. D. Rastofer, J. M. Richards, and I. Serageldin, *Hassan Fathy* (Singapore, 1985).

Bibliography

I. ISLAMIC ART: GENERAL

The Arts of Islam. Exhibition catalogue. Hayward Gallery, London, 1976.

ASLANAPA, OKTAY. *Turkish Art and Architecture*. New York, 1971.

ATASOY, NURHAN et al., ed. *The Art of Islam*. Paris, 1990.

ATIL, ESIN. *The Age of Sultan Süleyman the Magnificent*. Washington, DC, 1987.

——. *Art of the Arab World*. Washington, DC, 1973.

——. *Islamic Art and Patronage: Treasures from Kuwait*. New York, 1990.

——. *Renaissance of Islam: Art of the Mamluks*. Washington, DC, 1981.

——. *Turkish Art*. Washington, DC, 1980.

BLAIR, SHEILA S., and JONATHAN M. BLOOM, eds. *Images of Paradise in Islamic Art*. Hanover, NH, 1991.

BRAND, MICHAEL, and GLENN D. LOWRY. *Akbar's India: Art from the Mughal City of Victory*. New York, 1985.

BREND, BARBARA. *Islamic Art*. Cambridge, MA, 1991.

BURCKHARDT, T. *L'Art de l'Islam: Langue et signification*. Paris, 1985.

DODDS, JERRILYNN D., ed. *Al-Andalus: The Art of Islamic Spain*. New York, 1992.

ETTINGHAUSEN, RICHARD, and OLEG GRABAR. *The Art and Architecture of Islam: 650–1250*. Harmondsworth, 1987.

ETTINGHAUSEN, RICHARD, and EHSAN YARSHATER, eds. *Highlights of Persian Art*. Boulder, 1979.

FALK, TOBY, ed. *Treasures of Islam*. London, 1985.

FERRIER, R. W. *The Arts of Persia*. New Haven and London, 1989.

GRABAR, OLEG. *The Mediation of Ornament*. A. W. Mellon Lectures in the Fine Arts, 1989. Princeton, 1992.

GRUBE, ERNST J. *The World of Islam*. Landmarks of the World's Art. New York and Toronto, 1966.

Islamic Art in Egypt: 969–1517 AD. Exhibition catalogue. Cairo, 1969.

LENTZ, THOMAS W., and GLENN D. LOWRY. *Timur and the Princely Vision: Persian Art and Culture in the Fifteenth Century*. Los Angeles, 1989.

LEVENSON, JAY A., ed. *Circa 1492: Art in the Age of Exploration*. Washington, 1991.

PAPADOPOULO, ALEXANDRE. *L'Islam et l'art musulman*. Paris, 1976.

POPE, A. U., and P. ACKERMAN, eds. *A Survey of Persian Art from Prehistoric Times to the Present*. London and New York, 1938–9; repr. 16 vols. Tokyo, 1977.

ROGERS, J. M. *Islamic Art and Design: 1500–1700*. London, 1983.

——. *The Spread of Islam*. Oxford, 1976.

SOURDEL-THOMINE, JANINE, and BERTOLD SPULER. *Die Kunst des Islam*. Propyläen Kunstgeschichte. Berlin, 1973.

WELCH, ANTHONY. *Calligraphy in the Arts of the Muslim World*. Austin, TX, 1979.

——. *Shah 'Abbas & the Arts of Isfahan*. New York, 1973.

WELCH, STUART CARY. *India: Art and Culture 1300–1900*. New York, 1988.

II. ARCHITECTURE

1. *General*

AL-ASAD, MOHAMMAD. "The Re-invention of Tradition: Neo-Islamic Architecture." In *Proceedings of the XXVIII International Congress of the History of Art*. Berlin, 1993.

BLAIR, SHEILA S. "Sufi Saints and Shrine Architecture." *Muqarnas* 7 (1990): 35–49.

CANTACUZINO, SHERBAN, ed. *Architecture in Continuity: Building in the Islamic World Today, the Aga Khan Award for Architecture*. New York, 1985.

ÇELIK, ZEYNEP. *Displaying the Orient: Architecture of Islam at Nineteenth-century World's Fairs*. Berkeley, 1992.

CONNER, PATRICK. *Oriental Architecture in the West*. London, 1979.

DODD, ERICA CRUIKSHANK, and SHEREEN KHAIRALLAH. *The Image of the Word: A Study of Quranic Verses in Islamic Architecture*. 2 vols. Beirut, 1981.

ETTINGHAUSEN, RICHARD, and OLEG GRABAR. *The Art and Architecture of Islam: 650–1250*. Harmondsworth: 1987.

GOLOMBEK, LISA. "From Tamerlane to the Taj Mahal." In *Essays in Islamic Art and Architecture in Honor of Katharina Otto-Dorn*, ed. Abbas Daneshvari. Malibu, CA, 1981. Pp. 43–50.

HOAG, JOHN D. *Islamic Architecture*. New York, 1977.

HOLOD, RENATA. "Text, Plan and Building: On the Transmission of Architectural Knowledge." In *Theories and Principles of Design in the Architecture of Islamic Societies*, ed. Margaret Bentley Ševčenko. Cambridge, MA, 1988. Pp. 1–12.

MICHELL, GEORGE, ed. *Architecture of the Islamic World: Its History and Social Meaning*. New York, 1978.

SWEETMAN, JOHN. *The Oriental Obsession: Islamic Inspiration in British and American Art and Architecture 1500–1920*. Cambridge Studies in the History of Art. Cambridge, 1987.

2. *Egypt, Syria, and the Yemen*

AMIN, M. M., and LAILA A. IBRAHIM. *Architectural Terms in Mamluk Documents*. Cairo, 1990.

AL-ASAD, MOHAMMAD. "The Mosque of al-Rifa'i in Cairo." *Muqarnas* 10 (1993): 108–24.

——. "The Mosque of Muhammad 'Ali in Cairo." *Muqarnas* 9 (1992): 39–55.

BEHRENS-ABOUSEIF, DORIS. "Four Domes of the Late Mamluk Period." *Annales islamologiques* 17 (1981): 191–202.

——. *Islamic Architecture in Cairo, an Introduction*. Supplements to Muqarnas. Leiden, 1989.

——. *The Minarets of Cairo*, 1985.

——. "The North-Eastern Extension of Cairo Under the Mamluks." *Annales islamologiques* 17 (1981): 157–89.

——. "The *Qubba*, an Aristocratic Type of *Zāwiya*." *Annales islamologiques* 19 (1983): 1–7.

BLOOM, JONATHAN M. "The Mosque of Baybars Al-Bunduqdārī in Cairo." *Annales islamologiques* 18 (1982): 45–78.

BRANDENBURG, DIETRICH. *Islamische Baukunst in Ägypten*. Berlin, 1966.

BURGOYNE, MICHAEL HAMILTON. *Mamluk Jerusalem, an Architectural Study*. Additional historical research by D. S. Richards, n.p., 1987.

CRESWELL, K. A. C. "A Brief Chronology of the Muhammadan Monuments of Egypt to A.D. 1517." *Bulletin de l'Institut français d'archéologie orientale*. Cairo, 1919.

——. *Early Muslim Architecture*. 2 vols. Oxford, 1932–40; 2nd edition of vol. 1 in 2 parts: Oxford, 1969; reprint New York, 1980.

——. *The Muslim Architecture of Egypt*. 2 vols. Oxford, 1952–9; reprint New York, 1979.

DODD, ERICA CRUIKSHANK. "The Image of the Word (Notes on the Religious Iconography of Islam)." *Berytus* 18 (1969): 35–62.

FERNANDES, LEONOR. "The Foundation of Baybars Al-Jashankir: Its Waqf, History, and Architecture." *Muqarnas* 4 (1987): 21–42.

FINSTER, BARBARA. "An Outline of Religious Architecture in the Yemen." *Muqarnas* 9 (1992): 124–47.

GARCIN, JEAN-CLAUDE, BERNARD MAURY, JACQUES REVAULT, and MONA ZAKARIYA. *Palais et maisons du Caire, I. Epoque mamelouke*. Paris, 1982.

HERZ BEY, MAX. *La Mosquée el-Rifaï au Caire paru à l'occasion de la consécration de la mosquée*. Milan, ca. 1912.

HERZFELD, ERNST. *Inscriptions et monuments d'Alep*. Cairo, 1954–5.

IBRAHIM, LAILA 'ALI. "Four Cairene Mihrabs and Their Dating." *Kunst des Orients* (1970–1): 30–9.

——. "Middle-class Living Units in Mamluk Cairo: Architecture and Terminology." *Art and Archaeology Research Papers* 14 (1978): 24–30.

——. "Residential Architecture in Mamluk Cairo." *Muqarnas* 2 (1984): 47–60.

KESSLER, CHRISTEL. *The Carved Masonry Domes of Medieval Cairo*. London, 1976.

——. "Funerary Architecture Within the City." In *Colloque internationale sur l'histoire du Caire*. Gräfenheinichen, 1972. Pp. 257–68.

KESSLER, CHRISTEL, and M. BURGOYNE. "The Fountain of Sultan Qaytbay in the Sacred Precinct of Jerusalem." In *Archaeology in the Levant: Essays for Kathleen Kenyon*, ed. R. Moorey and P. Parr. Warminster, Wilts, 1978. Pp. 250–69.

LEWCOCK, R. B., and G. R. SMITH. "Three Medieval Mosques in the Yemen." *Oriental Art* 20 (1974): 75–86, 192–203.

AL-MAQRĪZĪ. *Al-mawā'iz wa'l-i'tibār bi-dhikr al-khiṭaṭ wa'l-āthār*. 2 vols. Cairo, 1853.

MAYER, L. A. *The Buildings of Qaytbay, as Described in his Endowment Deed* [in Arabic]. London, 1938.

MEINECKE, MICHAEL. "Mamluk Architecture. Regional Architectural Traditions: Evolution and Interrelations." *Damaszener Mitteilungen* 2 (1985): 163–75.

——. "Die Mamlukischen Faiencemosaikdekorationen: Eine Werkstätte aus Tabriz in Kairo (1330–1350)." *Kunst des Orients* 11 (1976–77): 85–144.

——. "Das Mausoleum des Qala'un in Kairo: Untersuchungen zur Genese der Mamlukischen Architekturdekoration." *Mitteilungen des Deutschen Archäologischen Instituts: Abteilung Kairo* 26 (1970): 47–80.

——. *Die mamlukische Architektur in Ägypten und Syrien*, 2 vols. Glückstadt, 1992.

——. *Die Restaurierung der Madrasa des Amīrs Sābiq Al-Dīn Miṭqāl Al-Ānūkī und die Sanierung des Darb Qirmiz in Kairo*. Mainz, 1980.

MEINECKE-BERG, VIKTORIA. "Die osmanische Fliesendekorationen der Äqsunqur-Moschee in Cairo." *Mitteilungen des Deutschen Archäologischen Institut: Abteilung Kairo* 29 (1973): 39–62.

MOSTAFA, SALEH LAMEI. *Kloster und Mausoleum des Farağ ibn Barqūq in Kairo*. Glückstadt, 1968.

NEWHALL, AMY W. *The Patronage of the Mamluk Sultan Qa'it Bay, 872–901/ 1468*. Ph.D. dissertation, Harvard University. 1987.

RABBAT, NASSER. "Mamluk Throne Halls: Qubba or Iwan?" *Ars Orientalis* 23 (1993): 201–9.

RAYMOND, ANDRÉ. "Cairo's Area and Population in the Early Fifteenth Century." *Muqarnas* 2 (1984): 21–32.

REID, DONALD MALCOLM. "Cultural Imperialism and Nationalism: The Struggle to Define and Control the Heritage of Arab Art in Egypt." *International Journal of Middle East Studies* 24 (1992): 57–76.

REVAULT, JACQUES, and BERNARD MAURY. *Palais et maisons du Caire du XIVe au XVIIIe siècle*. 4 vols. Cairo, 1975–83.

ROGERS, J. M. "Innovation and Continuity in Islamic Urbanism." In *The Arab City, its Character and Islamic Cultural Heritage*, ed. Ismail Serageldin and Samir El-Sadek, n.p., 1982. Pp. 53–61.

——. "Evidence for Mamluk-Mongol Relations, 1260–1360." In *Colloque internationale sur l'histoire du Caire*. Gräfenheinichen, 1972. Pp. 385–404.

SADEK, MOHAMED-MOAIN. *Die mamlukische Architektur der Stadt Gaza*. Berlin, 1991.

SADEK, NOHA. "Rasulid Women: Power and Patronage." *Proceedings of the Seminar for Arabian Studies* 19 (1989): 121–36.

SALAM-LEIBLICH, HAYAT. *The Architecture of the Mamluk City of Tripoli*. Cambridge, MA, 1983.

SAUVAGET, JEAN. *Alep: Essai sur le développement d'une grande ville syrienne des origines au milieu du XIXe siècle*. Paris, 1941.

SCHARABI, MOHAMED. "Drei traditionelle Handelsanlagen in Kairo: Wakalat Al-Bazara, Wakalat Ḏu l-Fiqar und Wakalat Al-Qutn." *Mitteilungen des Deutschen Archäologischen Instituts: Abteilung Kairo* 34 (1978): 127–64.

SERJEANT, R. B., and R. LEWCOCK, eds. *Ṣan'ā': An Arabian Islamic City*. London, 1983.

WALLS, ARCHIE G. *Geometry and Architecture in Islamic Jerusalem: A Study of the Ashrafiyya*. Buckhurst Hill, Essex, 1990.

WIET, GASTON. *Mohammed Ali et les beaux-arts*. Cairo, 1949.

——. *The Mosques of Cairo*. Paris, 1966.

WILLIAMS, JOHN ALDEN. "The Monuments of Ottoman Cairo." In *Colloque internationale sur l'histoire du Caire*. Gräfenheinichen, 1972. Pp. 453–65.

3. India

AHMED, SHAMSUDDIN. *Inscriptions of Bengal*. Rajshahi, 1960.

ARA, MATSUO. "The Lodi Rulers and the Construction of Tomb-Buildings in Delhi." *Acta Asiatica* 43 (1982): 61–80.

ASHER, CATHERINE B. *Architecture of Mughal India*. New Cambridge History of India. Cambridge, 1992.

——. "From Anomaly to Homogeneity: The Mosque in 14th- to 16th-Century Bihar." In *Studies in Art and Archaeology of Bihar and Bengal*, ed. G. Bhattacharya and Debala Mitra. Delhi, 1989. Pp. 67–84.

——. "Legacy and Legitimacy: Sher Shāh's Patronage of Imperial Mausolea." In *Sharī'at and Ambiguity in South Asian Islam*, ed. Katherine P. Ewing. Berkeley, 1988. Pp. 79–97.

——. "The Mausoleum of Sher Shah Suri." *Artibus Asiae* 39 (1977): 273–98.

BEGLEY, WAYNE E. "Amānat Khān and the Calligraphy on the Tāj Maḥal." *Kunst des Orients* 12 (1978–9): 5–60.

——. "The Myth of the Taj Mahal and a New Theory of Its Symbolic Meaning." *Art Bulletin* 56/1 (1979): 7–37.

BRAND, MICHAEL, and GLENN D. LOWRY, eds. *Fatehpur-Sikri: A Sourcebook*. Cambridge, MA, 1985.

——, eds. *Fatehpur-Sikri*. Bombay, 1987.

——. *Akbar's India: Art from the Mughal City of Victory*. New York, 1985.

BROWN, PERCY. *Indian Architecture (Islamic Period)*. Bombay, 1956.

BURGESS, J. *The Muhammadan Architecture of Ahmadabad 1412–1520*. 2 vols. London, 1900–5.

CANTACUZINO, SHERBAN, ed. *Architecture in Continuity: Building in the Islamic World Today, the Aga Khan Award for Architecture*. New York, 1985.

CHAGHTAI, M. A. *The Badshahi Masjid*. Lahore, 1975.

——. *The Wazir Khan Mosque, Lahore*. Lahore, 1975.

COHN, BERNARD S. "Representing Authority in Victorian India." In *The Invention of Tradition*, ed. Eric Hobsbawm and Terence Ranger. Cambridge, 1992. Pp. 165–210.

CRANE, HOWARD. "The Patronage of Zahir al-Din Babur and the Origins of Mughal Architecture." *Bulletin of the Asia Institute* 1 (1987): 95–110.

CROWE, Y., S. HAYWOOD, and S. JELLICOE. *The Gardens of Mughal India*. London, 1972.

CROWE, YOLANDE. "Reflections on the Adina Mosque at Pandua." In *The Islamic Heritage of Bengal*, ed. George Michell. Paris, 1984. Pp. 155–64.

DANI, AHMAD HASAN. *Muslim Architecture in Bengal*. Dacca, 1961.

EDWARDS, HOLLY. "The Ribat of 'Ali b. Karmakh." *Iran* 29 (1991): 85–94.

HARLE, J. C. *The Art and Architecture of the Indian Subcontinent*. Harmondsworth, 1986.

HASAN, PERWEEN. "Sultanate Mosques and Continuity in Bengal Architecture." *Muqarnas* 6 (1989): 58–74.

HILLENBRAND, ROBERT. "Political Symbolism in Early Indo-Islamic Mosque Architecture: The Case of Ajmir." *Iran* 26 (1988): 105–17.

——. "Turco-Iranian Elements in the Medieval Architecture of Pakistan: the Case of the Tomb of Rukn-i 'Alam at Multan," *Muqarnas* 9 (1992): 148–74.

HUSAIN, A. B. M. *The Manara in Indo-Muslim Architecture*. Dacca, 1970.

JELLICOE, SUSAN. "The Development of the Mughal Garden." In *The Islamic Garden*, ed. Elisabeth B. Macdougall and Richard Ettinghausen. Washington, DC, 1976. Pp. 107–30.

KLINGELHOFER, WILLIAM G. "The Jahangiri Mahal of the Agra Fort: Expression and Experience in Early Mughal Architecture." *Muqarnas* 5 (1988): 153–69.

KOCH, EBBA. *Mughal Architecture: An Outline of its History and Development (1526–1858)*. Munich, 1991.

——. *Shah Jahan and Orpheus*. Graz, 1988.

LOWRY, GLENN D. "Humayun's Tomb: Form, Function, and Meaning in Early Mughal Architecture." *Muqarnas* 4 (1987): 133–48.

MEISTER, MICHAEL W. "The 'Two-and-a-half-day' Mosque." *Oriental Art*, N.S. 18, no. 1 (1972): 57–63.

MERKLINGER, ELIZABETH S. *Indian Islamic Architecture: The Deccan 1347–1686*. Warminster, Wilts, 1981.

MICHELL, GEORGE, ed. *The Islamic Heritage of Bengal*. Paris, 1984.

MICHELL, GEORGE, and RICHARD EATON. *Firuzabad: Palace City of the Deccan*. Oxford, 1992.

MOYNIHAN, E. B. *Paradise as a Garden in Persia and Mughal India*. London, 1980.

——. "The Lotus Garden Palace of Zahir al-Din Muhammad Babur." *Muqarnas* 5 (1988): 135–52.

MUMTAZ, KAMIL KHAN. *Architecture in Pakistan*. Singapore, 1985.

PAGE, J. A. *A Memoir on the Kotla Firoz Shah*. Delhi, 1937.

PAL, PRATAPADITYA, JANICE LEOSHKO, JOSEPH M. DYE, III, and STEPHEN MARKEL. *Romance of the Taj Mahal*. Los Angeles and London, 1989.

PETRUCCIOLI, ATTILIO. "The Process Evolved by the Control Systems of Urban Design in the Moghul Epoch in India: The Case of Fathpur Sikri." *Environmental Design* 1 (1984): 18–27.

SHOKOOHY, MEHRDAD. *Bhadresvar: The Oldest Islamic Monuments in India*. Leiden, 1988.

SHOKOOHY, MEHRDAD and NATALIE H. "The Architecture of Baha Al-Din Tughril in the Region of Bayana, Rajasthan." *Muqarnas* 4 (1987): 114–32.

——. *Hisar-i Firuza: Sultanate and Early Mughal Architecture in the District of Hisar, India*. London, 1988.

TANDAN, B. "The Architecture of the Nawabs of Avadh, 1722–1856." In *Facets of Indian Art, A symposium held at the Victoria and Albert Museum on 26, 27, 28 April and 1 May 1982*, ed. Robert Skelton, Andrew Topsfield, Susan Stronge, and Rosemary Crill. London, 1986. Pp. 66–75.

TSUKINOWA, TOKIFUSA. "The Influence of Seljuk Architecture on the Earliest Mosques of the Delhi Sultanate Period in India." *Acta Asiatica* 43 (1982): 37–60.

WELCH, ANTHONY, and HOWARD CRANE. "The Tughluqs: Master Builders of the Delhi Sultanate." *Muqarnas* 1 (1983): 123–66.

YAMAMOTO, T., M. ARA, and T. TSUKINOWA. *Delhi: Architectural Remains of the Sultanate Period*. 3 vols. Tokyo, 1968–70.

YAZDANI, G., ed. *Epigraphica Indo Moslemica*. Calcutta, 1925–6.

4. Iran and Central Asia

ALLEN, TERRY. *A Catalogue of Toponyms and Monuments of Timurid Herat*. Cambridge, MA, 1981.

——. *Timurid Herat*. Wiesbaden, 1983.

BERCHEM, MAX VAN. "Une inscription du sultan mongol Uldjaitu." In *Mélanges Hartwig Derenbourg*. Paris, 1909. Pp. 367–78.

BLAIR, SHEILA S. "Ilkhanid Architecture and Society: an Analysis of the Endowment Deed of the Rab'-i Rashīdī." *Iran* 22 (1984): 67–90.

——. *The Ilkhanid Shrine Complex at Natanz, Iran*. Cambridge, MA, 1986.

——. "The Inscription from the Tomb Tower at Bastām: An Analysis of Ilkhanid Epigraphy." In *Art et société dans le monde iranien*, ed. Chahriyar Adle. Paris, 1982. Pp. 263–86.

——. "The Mongol Capital of Sulṭāniyya, 'the Imperial'." *Iran* 24 (1986): 139–51.

GALDIERI, EUGENIO. "Two Building Phases of the Time of Šah 'Abbas I in the Maydan-i Šah of Isfahan. Preliminary Note." *East and West* n.s. 20 (1970): 60–9.

GALDIERI, EUGENIO, and R. ORAZI. *Progetto di sistemazione del Maydan-i Šah*. Rome, 1969.

GAUBE, HEINZ. *Iranian Cities*. New York, 1979.

GAUBE, HEINZ, and EUGEN WIRTH. *Der Bazar von Isfahan*. Tübinger Atlas des Vorderen Orients, Beihefte, Reihe B, nr. 22. Wiesbaden, 1978.

GOLOMBEK, LISA. *The Timurid Shrine at Gazur Gah*. Art and Archaeology Occasional Paper 15. Toronto, 1969.

GOLOMBEK, LISA, and DONALD WILBER. *The Timurid Architecture of Iran and Turan*. 2 vols. Princeton, 1988.

GRUBE, ERNST. "Wall Paintings in the Seventeenth Century Monuments of Isfahan." *Iranian Studies* 7 (1974): 511–42.

HARB, ULRICH. *Ilkhanidische Stalaktitengewölbe: Beiträge zu Entwurf und Bautechnik*. Berlin, 1978.

HERDEG, KLAUS. *Formal Structure in Islamic Architecture of Iran and Turkistan*. New York: 1990.

HILLENBRAND, ROBERT. "The Flanged Tomb Tower at Bastām." In *Art et société dans le monde iranien*, ed. Chahriyar Adle. Paris, 1982. Pp. 237–61.

——. "Safavid Architecture." In *The Timurid and Safavid Periods*, ed. P. Jackson. Cambridge History of Iran, vol. 6. Cambridge, 1986. Pp. 789–92.

HUNARFAR, LUṬFALLAH. *Ganjīna-yi āthār-i tārīkhī-yi Isfahan*. 2nd ed. Tehran, 1350/1977.

KIANI, MUHAMMAD-YUSUF. *Iranian Caravanserails with Particular Reference to the Safavid Period*. Tokyo, 1978.

KLEISS, W. "Der Safavidische Pavillon in Qazvin." *Archäeologische Mitteilungen aus Iran*, n.s. 9 (1976): 290–8.

LUSCHEY-SCHMEISSER, INGEBORG. "Ein Neuer Raum in Nayin." *Archäeologische Mitteilungen aus Iran*, n.s. 5 (1972): 309–14.

——. *The Pictorial Tile Cycles of Hašt Behešt in Isfahan and Its Iconographic Tradition*. Rome, 1978.

——. "Der Wand- und Deckenschmuck eines Safavidischen Palastes in Nayin." *Archäeologische Mitteilungen aus Iran*, n.s. 2 (1969): 183–92.

McCHESNEY, ROBERT [D.]. "Central Asia. VI. In the 10th–12th/16th–18th Centuries." In *Encyclopaedia Iranica*, V.

——. "Economic and Social Aspects of the Public Architecture of Bukhara in the 1560's and 1570's." *Islamic Art* 2 (1987): 217–42.

——. "Four Sources on Shah 'Abbas's Building of Isfahan." *Muqarnas* 5 (1988): 103–34.

——. "Postscript to 'Four Sources on Shah 'Abbas's Building of Isfahan'." *Muqarnas* 8 (1991): 137–8.

——. "Waqf and Public Policy: The Waqfs of Shah 'Abbas, 1011–1023/1602–1614." *Asian and African Studies* 15 (1981): 165–90.

——. *Waqf in Central Asia: Four Hundred Years in the History of a Muslim Shrine, 1480–1889*. Princeton, 1991.

MAN'KOVSKAIA, L. Iu. "Towards the Study of Forms in Central Asian Architecture at the End of the Fourteenth Century: The Mausoleum of Khvāja Ahmad Yasavī," trans. Lisa Golombek. *Iran* 23 (1985): 109–28.

MASSON, M. E., and G. A. PUGACHENKOVA. "Shakhri Syabz pri Timure I Ulug Beke [Shahr-i Sabz from Tīmūr to Ūlūgh Beg] – I," trans. J. M. Rogers. *Iran* 16 (1978): 103–26.

——. "Shakhri Syabz pri Timure I Ulug Beke [Shahr-i Sabz from Tīmūr to Ūlūgh Beg] – II," trans. J. M. Rogers. *Iran* 18 (1980): 121–43.

MILES, GEORGE C. "The Inscriptions of the Masjid-i Jami' at Ashtarjan." *Iran* 12 (1974): 89–98.

NAUMANN, RUDOLF. *Die Ruinen von Tacht-e Suleiman und Zendan-e Suleiman*. Berlin, 1977.

NECIPOĞLU, GÜLRU. "Geometric Design in Timurid/Turkmen Architectural Practice: Thoughts on a Recently Discovered Scroll and Its Late Gothic Parallels." In *Timurid Art and Culture: Iran and Central Asia in the Fifteenth Century*, eds Lisa Golombek and Maria Subtelny. Supplements to Muqarnas. Leiden, 1992. Pp. 48–66.

NEMTSEVA, N. B., and IU. Z. SHVAB. *Ansambl' Shakh-i Zinda*. Tashkent, 1979.

O'KANE, BERNARD. "The Madrasa al-Ghiyasiyya at Khargird." *Iran* 14 (1976): 79–92.

——. "The Tiled Minbars of Iran." *Annales islamologiques* 22 (1986): 133–55.

——. *Timurid Architecture in Khurasan*. Costa Mesa, 1987.

PAONE, R. "The Mongol Colonization of the Isfahān Region." In *Isfahan. Quaderni del Seminario di Iranistica, Uralo-Altaistica e Caucasologia dell'Universitá degli studi di Venezia, 10*. Venice, 1981. Pp. 1–30.

PUGACHENKOVA, G. A. "Ishrat-Khaneh and Ak-Saray – Two Timurid Mausoleums in Samarkand." *Ars Orientalis* 5 (1963): 177–89.

——. *Ishrat Khane*. Tashkent, 1958.

SCARCE, JENNIFER. "The Arts of the Eighteenth to Twentieth Centuries: Architecture, Ceramics, Metalwork, Textiles." In *From Nadir Shah to the Islamic Republic*, ed. Peter Avery, Gavin Hambly, and Charles Melville. Cambridge History of Iran, vol. 7. Cambridge, 1991. Pp. 890–958.

SHISHKIN, V. A. "Nadpisi v ansamble Shakhi-Zinda." *Zodchestvo Uzbekistana* 2 (1970): 7–71.

SIMS, ELEANOR. "The 'Iconography' of the Internal Decoration in the Mausoleum of Uljaytu at Sultaniyya." In *Content and Context of Visual Arts in the Islamic World*, ed. P. P. Soucek. University Park, PA, and London, 1988. Pp. 139–76.

SIROUX, MAXIME. *Anciennes voies et monuments routiers de la région d'Isfahan*. Cairo, 1971.

——. *Caravansérails d'Iran et petites constructions routières*. Cairo, 1949.

——. "Les caravansérails routiers safavides." *Iranian Studies* 7 (1974): 348–79.

Solṭaniye III. Quaderni del Seminario di Iranistica, Uralo-Altaistica e Caucasologia dell'Universitá degli Studi di Venezia, 9. Venice, 1982.

WILBER, DONALD M. *The Architecture of Islamic Iran: The Il-Khānid Period*. Princeton, 1955; reprint New York, 1969.

——. "The Timurid Court: Life in Gardens and Tents." *Iran* 17 (1979): 127–33.

5. *Spain and the Maghrib*

ALMAGRO CÁRDENAS, ANTONIO. *Estudio sobre las inscripciones árabes de Granada*. Granada, 1879.

BARRUCAND, MARIANNE. *L'architecture de la qasba de Moulay Ismaïl à Meknès*. 2 vols. Casablanca, 1976.

——. *Urbanisme princier en Islam: Meknès et les villes royales islamiques post-médiévales*. Paris, 1985.

BASSET, HENRI, and E. LÉVI-PROVENÇAL. *Chella: une nécropole mérinide*. Paris, 1923.

BOUROUIBA, RACHID. *L'Art religieux musulmane en Algérie*. Algiers, 1973.

DAOULATLI, ABDELAZIZ. *Tunis sous les Hafsides. Evolution urbaine et activité architecturale*. Tunis, 1976.

DICKIE, JAMES. "The Alhambra: Some Reflections Prompted by a Recent Study by Oleg Grabar." In *Studia Arabica et Islamica: Festschrift for Ihsan 'Abbas on his Sixtieth Birthday*, ed. Widad al-Qadi. Beirut, 1981. Pp. 127–49.

DODDS, JERRILYNN D., ed. *Al-Andalus: The Art of Islamic Spain*. New York, 1992.

——. "The Paintings in the Sala de Justicia of the Alhambra: Iconography and Iconology." *Art Bulletin* 61 (1979): 186–97.

DOKALI, RACHID. *Les Mosquées de la période turque à Alger*. Algiers, 1974.

FERNÁNDEZ PUERTAS, ANTONIO. *The Facade of the Palace of Comares*. Granada, 1980.

GRABAR, OLEG. *The Alhambra*. Cambridge, MA, 1978.

HILL, DEREK, and LUCIEN GOLVIN. *Islamic Architecture in North Africa*. Introduction by Robert Hillenbrand. London, 1976.

Islamic Art and Architecture in Libya. Exhibition catalogue. London, 1976.

MARÇAIS, GEORGES. *Architecture musulmane d'occident*. Paris, 1954.

MARÇAIS, GEORGES and WILLIAM. *Les Monuments arabes de Tlemcen*. Paris, 1903.

RAYMOND, ANDRÉ. *Grandes villes arabes à l'époque ottoman*. Paris, 1985.

TERRASSE, CHARLES. *Médersas du Maroc*. Paris, n.d.

TERRASSE, HENRI. *La Grande Mosquée de Taza*. Paris, 1943.

——. *La Mosquée al-Qaraouiyin à Fès*. Paris, 1968.

6. *Turkey and the Balkans*

AKURGAL, EKREM, ed. *The Art and Architecture of Turkey*. New York, 1980.

ASLANAPA, OKTAY. "Iznik'te Sultan Orhan Imaret Camii Kazisi (Die Ausgrabungen der Sultan Orhan Imaret Moschee von Iznik)." *Sanat Tarihi Yıllığı* 1 (1964–5): 16–31 (Turkish); 32–8 (German).

——. *Turkish Art and Architecture*. New York, 1971.

BARKAN, ÖMER LUTFI. "L'Organisation du travail dans le chantier d'une grande mosquée à Istanbul au XVIe siècle." *Annales* 17 (1962): 1093–106.

——. *Süleymaniye Camii ve Imareti Insaati (1550–1557)*, 2 vols. Ankara, 1972–9.

BOZDOĞAN, SIBEL. "Modernity in the Margins: Architecture and Ideology in Early Republican Turkey." *Proceedings of the XVIII International Congress of the History of Art*. Berlin, 1993.

ÇELIK, ZEYNEP. *The Remaking of Istanbul: Portrait of an Ottoman City in the Nineteenth Century*. Seattle and London, 1986.

ÇIĞ, KEMAL, SABAHATTIN BATUR, and CENGIZ KÖSEOĞLU. *The Topkapı Saray Museum, Architecture: The Harem and Other Buildings*, trans. and ed. J. M. Rogers. Boston, 1988.

CRANE, HOWARD. *Risāle-i Mi'māriyye: An Early Seventeenth-Century Ottoman Treatise on Architecture*. Facsimile with translation and notes. Supplements to Muqarnas. Leiden, 1987.

DENNY, WALTER B. "Ceramic Revetments of the Mosque of the Ramazan Oğlu in Adana." In *IVème Congrès international d'art turc*. Aix-en-Provence, 1976. Pp. 57–66.

——. *The Ceramics of the Mosque of Rüstem Pasha and the Environment of Change*. New York, 1977.

ERZEN, JALE. "Sinan as Anti-Classicist." *Muqarnas* 5 (1988): 70–86.

EYICE, SEMAVI. "Zaviyeler ve zaviyeli camiler." *İktisat Fakültesi Mecmuasi* 23 (1962–3): 3–80.

GABRIEL, ALBERT. *Une Capitale turque, Brousse (Bursa)*. Paris, 1958.

GOODWIN, GODFREY. *A History of Ottoman Architecture*. London, Baltimore, 1971.

HOLOD, RENATA, and AHMET EVIN, eds. *Modern Turkish Architecture*. Philadelphia, 1984.

KUBAN, DOĞAN. "Architecture of the Ottoman period." In *The Art and Architecture of Turkey*, ed. Ekrem Akurgal. New York, 1980. Pp. 137–69.

——. "The Style of Sinan's Domed Structures." *Muqarnas* 4 (1987): 72–97.

KURAN, APTULLAH. *The Mosque in Early Ottoman Architecture*. Chicago, 1967.

——. *Sinan: The Grand Old Master of Ottoman Architecture*. Washington, DC and Istanbul, 1987.

KÜRKÇÜOĞLU, KEMAL EDIB. *Süleymaniye Vakfiyesi*. Ankara, 1962.

MANTRAN, ROBERT. "Les Inscriptions Arabes de Brousse." *Bulletin D'études Orientales* 14 (1952–54): 87–114.

NECIPOĞLU, GÜLRU. *Architecture, Ceremonial, and Power: The Topkapı Palace in the Fifteenth and Sixteenth Centuries*. New York and Cambridge, MA, 1991.

——. "The Life of an Imperial Monument: Hagia Sophia after Byzantium." In *Hagia Sophia: From the Age of Justinian to the Present*, ed. Robert Mark and Ahmet Ş. Çakmak. Cambridge, 1992. Pp. 195–225.

——. "The Süleymaniye Complex in Istanbul: An Interpretation." *Muqarnas* 3 (1985): 92–117.

OTTO-DORN, KATHARINA. "Die Isa Bey Moschee in Ephesus." *Istanbuler Forschungen* 17 (1950): 115–31.

——. *Das Islamische Iznik*. Berlin, 1941.

ÖZERGIN, M. K. "Selçuklu Sanatçisi Nakkaş Abdülmü'min El-Hoyi Hakkinda." *Belleten* 34 (1970): 219–30.

RIEFSTAHL, RUDOLF M. "Early Turkish Tile Revetments in Edirne." *Ars Islamica* 4 (1937): 249–81.

ROGERS, J. M. "The Date of the Çifte Minare Medrese at Erzurum." *Kunst des Orients* 8 (1974): 77–149.

——. "The State and the Arts in Ottoman Turkey: The Stones of Süleymaniye." *International Journal of Middle East Studies* 14 (1982): 71–86, 283–313.

SAUVAGET, JEAN. "Les Caravansérails syriens du ḥadjdj de Constantinople." *Ars Islamica* 4 (1934): 98–121.

ÜNAL, R. H. *Les Monuments islamiques anciens de la ville d'Erzurum et de sa région*. Bibliothèque archéologique de l'Institut français d'archéologie d'Istanbul. Istanbul, 1968.

WULZINGER, KARL. "Die Piruz-Moschee zu Milas." In *Festschrift anlässlich der 100 jährigen Bestens der technischen Hochschule Fridericiana zu Karlsruhe*. Karlsruhe, 1925. Pp. 161–87.

YENIŞEHIRLIOĞLU, FILIZ. "Les grandes lignes de l'évolution du programme décoratif en céramique des monuments ottomans au cours du XVIème siècle." *Erdem* 1 (1985): 456–65.

III. ARTS OF THE BOOK

ADAHL, KARIN. *A Khamsa of Nizami of 1439*. Uppsala, 1981.

ADAMOVA, A. "Repetition of Compositions in Manuscripts: The Khamsa of Nizami in Leningrad." In *Timurid Art and Culture: Iran and Central Asia in the Fifteenth Century*, ed. Lisa Golombek and Maria Subtelny. Supplements to Muqarnas. Leiden, 1992. Pp. 67–75.

ADAMOVA, A. T., and L. T. GUZALIAN. *Minyaturi Rukopisi Poemy 'Shakhnama' 1333 Goda*. Leningrad, 1985.

ADAMOVA, A., and T. GRECK. *Miniatures from Kashmirian Manuscripts*. Leningrad, 1976.

AGA-OGLU, MEHMET. "The Khusrau Wa Shirin Manuscript in the Freer Gallery." *Ars Islamica* 4 (1937): 479–81.

——. "Preliminary Notes on Some Persian Illustrated Mss. in the Topkapu Sarayi Müzesi – Part I." *Ars Islamica* 1 (1934): 183–99.

AKIMUSHKIN, O. F., and A. A. IVANOV. "Une école artistique méconnue: Boxara au XVIIe siècle." In *Art et société dans le monde iranien*, ed. Chahriyar Adle. Paris, 1982. Pp. 127–39.

ALLEN, TERRY. "Byzantine Sources for the *Jami' al-Tawarikh* of Rashid Al-Din." *Ars Orientalis* 15 (1985): 121–36.

ARBERRY, A. J., et al., eds. *The Chester Beatty Library: A Catalogue of the Persian Manuscripts and Miniatures*. 3 vols. Dublin, 1959–62.

ASHRAFI, M. M. *Persian-Tajik Poetry in XIV–XVII Centuries Miniatures*. Dushanbe, 1974.

ASHRAFI-AINI, M. M. "The School of Bukhara to C. 1550." In *Arts of the Book in Central Asia*, ed. Basil Gray. Boulder, CO, 1979. Pp. 249–73.

ASLANAPA, OKTAY. "The Art of Bookbinding." Ibid. Pp. 59–91.

ATASOY, NURHAN, and FILIZ ÇAĞMAN. *Turkish Miniature Painting*, trans. Esin Atıl. Istanbul, 1974.

ATIL, ESIN. *The Brush of the Masters: Drawings from Iran and India*. Washington, DC, 1978.

——. "Mamluk Painting in the Late Fifteenth Century." *Muqarnas* (1984): 163–9.

——. "Ottoman Miniature Painting Under Sultan Mehmed II." *Ars Orientalis* 9 (1973): 103–20.

BAYĀNĪ, M. *Aḥvāl-o āthār-i khushnivīsān*, 2nd ed. in 4 vols. Tehran, 1363/1985.

BEACH, MILO CLEVELAND. *The Grand Mogul: Imperial Painting in India 1600–1660*. Exhibition catalogue. Williamstown, MA, 1978.

——. "The Gulshan Album and Its European Sources." *Bulletin of the Museum of Fine Arts, Boston* 332 (1962): 63–91.

——. *The Imperial Image: Paintings for the Mughal Court*. Washington, DC, 1981.

——. *Mughal and Rajput Painting*. New Cambridge History of India. Cambridge, 1992.

BEGLEY, WAYNE. "Illustrated Histories of Shah Jahan: New Identifications of Some Dispersed Paintings and Problems of the Windsor Castle Padshahnama." In *Facets of Indian Art*, ed. Robert Skelton et al. London, 1986. Pp. 139–52.

BINYON, LAURENCE. *The Poems of Nizami*. London, 1928.

BINYON, LAURENCE, J. V. S. WILKINSON, and BASIL GRAY. *Persian Miniature Painting*. New York, 1971.

BLAIR, SHEILA S. "The Development of the Illustrated Book in Iran." *Muqarnas* 10 (1993): 266–74.

——. "On the Track of the 'Demotte' *Shāhnāma* Manuscript." In *Les Manuscrits du Moyen-Orient: Essais de Codicologie et de Paléographie*, ed. François Déroche. Istanbul/Paris, 1989. Pp. 125–31.

BLAIR, SHEILA S., and JONATHAN M. BLOOM. "Epic Images and Contemporary History: The Legacy of the Great Mongol *Shahnama*." *Islamic Art* 5 (1994).

BOSCH, GULNAR, JOHN CARSWELL, and GUY PETHERBRIDGE. *Islamic Bindings and Bookmaking*. Exhibition catalogue. Chicago, 1981.

CANBY, SHEILA R. "Age and Time in the Work of Riza." In *Persian Masters: Five Centuries of Painting*, ed. Sheila R. Canby. Bombay, 1990. Pp. 71–84.

ÇAĞMAN, FILIZ, and ZEREN TANINDI. *The Topkapı Saray Museum: The Albums and Illustrated Manuscripts*. ed. and trans. J. M. Rogers. Boston, 1986.

CHANDRA, PRAMOD. "The Brooklyn Museum Folios of the *Hamza-nama*." *Orientations* 20 (July 1989): 39–45.

——. *The Tuti-Nama of the Cleveland Museum of Art and the Origins of Mughal Painting*. Graz, 1976.

COWEN, JILL SANCHIA. *Kalila wa Dimna: an Animal Allegory of the Mongol Court*. New York and Oxford, 1989.

DENNY, WALTER B. "Dating Ottoman Turkish Works in the Saz Style." *Muqarnas* 1 (1983): 103–22.

DÉROCHE, FRANÇOIS. *Les Manuscrits du Coran, du maghrib à l'insulinde*. Bibliothèque Nationale, Département des manuscrits, Catalogue des manuscrits arabes. Paris, 1985.

DICKSON, MARTIN B., and STUART CARY WELCH. *The Houghton Shahnama*. 2 vols. Cambridge, MA, 1982.

ENDERLEIN, VOLKMAR. *Die Miniaturen der Berliner Baisonqur-Handschrift*. Bilderhefte der Staatlichen Museen zu Berlin, Heft 1. Berlin, 1991.

ETTINGHAUSEN, RICHARD. *Arab Painting*. Geneva, 1962.

——. "The Bustan Manuscript of Sultan Nasir-Shah Khalji." *Marg* 12 (1959): 40–3.

——. "The Covers of the Morgan Manafi' Manuscript and Other Early Persian Bookbindings." In *Studies in Art and Literature for Belle Da Costa Greene*. Princeton, 1954. Pp. 459–73.

——. "The Emperor's Choice." In *De Artibus Opuscula XL: Essays in Honor of Erwin Panofsky*, ed. Millard Meiss. New York, 1961. Pp. 98–120.

——. "An Illuminated Manuscript of Hâfiz-i Abrû in Istanbul. Part I." *Kunst des Orients* 2 (1955): 30–44.

——. "The Impact of Muslim Decorative Arts and Painting on the Arts of Europe." In *The Legacy of Islam*, ed. Joseph Schacht and C. E. Bosworth. Oxford, 1974. Pp. 290–320.

——. "On Some Mongol Miniatures." *Kunst des Orients* 3 (1959): 56–65.

——. "Persian Ascension Miniatures of the Fourteenth Century." *Accademia Nazionale dei Lincei* 12 (1957): 360–83.

——. "Some Paintings in Four Istanbul Albums." *Ars Orientalis* 1 (1954): 91–103.

FARHAD, MASSUMEH. "An Artist's Impression: Mu'in Musavvir's *Tiger Attacking a Youth*." *Muqarnas* 9 (1992): 116–23.

——. "The Art of Mu'in Musavvir: A Mirror of His Times." In *Persian Masters: Five Centuries of Painting*, ed. Sheila R. Canby. Bombay, 1990. Pp. 113–28.

FARHAD, MASSUMEH, and MARIANNA SHREVE SIMPSON, "Sources for the Study of Safavid Painting and Patronage, or *Méfiez-vous de Qazi Ahmad*." *Muqarnas* 10 (1993): 286–91.

FISHER, A. W. and C. G. "A Note on the Location of the Royal Ottoman Ateliers." *Muqarnas* 3 (1985): 118–20.

FISHER, CAROL G., ed. *Brocade of the Pen: The Art of Islamic Writing*. Exhibition catalogue. East Lansing, MI, 1991.

——. "A Reconstruction of the Pictorial Cycle of the *Siyar-i Nabī* of Murad III," *Ars Orientalis* 14 (1984): 75–94.

FITZHERBERT, TERESA. "Khwājū Kirmānī (689–753/1290–1352): An Eminence Grise of Fourteenth-Century Persian Painting." *Iran* 29 (1991): 137–52.

FRAAD, IRMA L., and RICHARD ETTINGHAUSEN. "Sultanate Painting in Persian Style, Primarily from the First Half of the Fifteenth Century: A Preliminary Study." *Chhavi* (1972): 48–66.

GALERKINA, OLYMPIADA. *Mawarannahr Book Painting*. Leningrad, 1980.

GODARD, YEDDA. "Les Marges du Muraḳḳa' Gulshan." *Āthār-é Īrān* 1 (1936): 11–35.

GOLOMBEK, LISA. "Toward a Classification of Islamic Painting." In *Islamic Art in the Metropolitan Museum of Art*, ed. Richard Ettinghausen. New York, 1972. Pp. 23–34.

GRABAR, OLEG. *The Illustrations of the Maqamat*. Chicago, 1984.

GRABAR, OLEG, and SHEILA [S.] BLAIR. *Epic Images and Contemporary History: The Illustrations of the Great Mongol Shah-nama*. Chicago, 1980.

GRAY, BASIL. *Persian Painting*. Geneva, 1961.

GRUBE, E. J. *Persian Painting in the Fourteenth Century. A Research Report*, Supplemento no. 17 agli Annali, Instituto Orientale di Napoli, 38, 1978, fasc. 4.

——. *The Classical Style in Islamic Painting, The Early School of Herat and Its Impact on Islamic Painting of the Later 15th, 16th and 17th Centuries: Some Examples in American Collections*. [New York], 1968.

——. "Notes on Ottoman Painting in the 15th Century." In *Essays in Islamic Art and Architecture in Honor of Katharina Otto-Dorn*, ed. Abbas Daneshvari. Malibu, CA, 1981. Pp. 51–62.

——. "Prolegomena for a Corpus Publication of Illustrated *Kalīla Wa Dimna* Manuscripts." *Islamic Art* 4 (1990–1): 301–482.

GUEST, GRACE R. *Shiraz Painting in the Sixteenth Century*. Washington, DC, 1949.

HALDANE, DUNCAN. *Islamic Bookbindings in the Victoria and Albert Museum*. London, 1983.

——. *Mamluk Painting*. Warminster, Wilts, 1978.

HILLENBRAND, ROBERT. *Imperial Images in Persian Painting*. Edinburgh, 1977.

——. "The Uses of Space in Timurid Painting." In *Timurid Art and Culture: Iran and Central Asia in the Fifteenth Century*, ed. Lisa Golombek and Maria Subtelny. Supplements to Muqarnas. Leiden, 1992. Pp. 76–102.

INAL, GÜNER. "Miniatures in Historical Manuscripts from the Time of Shahrukh in the Topkapi Palace Museum." Ibid. Pp. 103–15.

——. "Topkapi Sarayi Koleksiyonundaki Sultani Bir Özbek Şehnamesi." *Sanat Tarihi Yilliği* 6 (1974–5): 303–22.

IPŞIROĞLU, M. *Saray-Alben: Diez'sche Klebebände aus den Berliner Sammlungen*. Wiesbaden, 1964.

Islamic Art 1 (1981). Percival David Foundation Colloquies on Art and Archaeology in Asia, ed. Ernst Grube and Eleanor Sims.

ISMAILOVA, A. M. *Oriental Miniatures*. Tashkent, 1980.

IVANOV, A. A. "The Life of Muhammad Zaman: A Reconsideration." *Iran* 17 (1979): 65–70.

JAMES, DAVID. *After Timur: Qur'ans of the 15th and 16th Centuries*, ed. Julian Raby. The Nasser D. Khalili Collection of Islamic Art. London, 1992.

——. *The Master Scribes: Qur'ans of the 10th to the 14th Centuries AD*, ed. Julian Raby. The Nasser D. Khalili Collection of Islamic Art. London, 1992.

——. *Qur'ans of the Mamluks*. London, 1988.

KARĪMZĀDA TABRĪZĪ, M. A. *Aḥvāl u āthār-i naqqāshān-i qadīm-i īrān*, 3 vols. London, 1985.

KHANDALAVALA, KARL, and KALPANA DESAI. "Indian Illustrated Manuscripts of the *Kalilah wa Dimnah, Anvar-i Suhayli*, and *Iyar-i Danish*." In *A Mirror for Princes from India*, ed. Ernst J. Grube. Bombay, 1991. Pp. 128–44.

KLIMBERG-SALTER, DEBORAH. "A Sufi Theme in Persian Painting: the *Divan* of Sultan Ahmad Galair in the Freer Gallery of Art, Washington, D.C." *Kunst des Orients* 11 (1976–7): 43–84.

KÜHNEL, ERNST. "Die Baysonghor-Handschrift der Islamischen Kunstabteilung." *Jahrbuch der Preussischen Kunstsammlungen* 52 (1931): 133–52.

——. "A Bidpai Manuscript of 1343–44 in Cairo." *Bulletin of the American Institute of Iranian Art and Archaeology* 5 (1937): 137–41.

KÜHNEL, ERNST, and HERMANN GOETZ. *Indian Book Painting from Jahangir's Album in the State Library, Berlin*. London, 1926.

LEACH, LINDA YORK. "Painting in Kashmir from 1600 to 1650." In *Facets of Indian Art, A symposium held at the Victoria and Albert Museum on 26, 27, 28 April and 1 May 1982*, ed. Robert Skelton, Andrew Topsfield, Susan Stronge, and Rosemary Crill. London, 1986. Pp. 124–31.

LENTZ, THOMAS W. "Changing Worlds: Bihzad and the New Painting." In *Persian Masters: Five Centuries of Painting*, ed. Sheila R. Canby. Bombay, 1990. Pp. 39–54.

LENTZ, THOMAS W., and GLENN D. LOWRY. *Timur and the Princely Vision: Persian Art and Culture in the Fifteenth Century*. Los Angeles, 1989.

LINGS, MARTIN. *The Qur'anic Art of Calligraphy and Illumination*. London, 1976.

LINGS, MARTIN, and YASIN SAFADI. *The Qur'an*. London, 1976.

LOSTY, J. P. "The 'Bute Hafiz' and the Development of Border Decoration in the Manuscript Studio of the Mughals." *Burlington Magazine* 127 (1985): 855–71.

——. *The Art of the Book in India*. London, 1982.

LOWRY, GLENN D., with SUSAN NEMAZEE. *A Jeweler's Eye: Islamic Arts of the Book from the Vever Collection*. Washington, DC, 1988.

MELIKIAN-CHIRVANI, A. S. "Le Roman de Varqe et Golšâh." *Arts Asiatiques* 22 (1970).

MILLSTEIN, RACHEL. *Islamic Painting in the Israel Museum*. Jerusalem, 1984.

——. *Miniature Painting in Ottoman Baghdad*. Costa Mesa, CA, 1990.

PINAR, S., ed. *A History of Ottoman Painting*. Seattle, and London, 1989.

PRENTICE, VERNA. "A Detached Miniature from the *Masnavis* of Khwaju Kermani." *Oriental Art* 27 (1981): 60–6.

RABY, JULIAN. "East and West in Mehmed the Conqueror's Library." *Bulletin du Bibliophile* 3 (1987): 297–321.

——. "Mehmed II Fatih and the Fatih Album." *Islamic Art* 1 (1981): 42–9.

RENDA, GÜNSEL, et al. *A History of Turkish Painting*. Seattle, and London, 1988.

ROBINSON, B. W. *A Descriptive Catalogue of the Persian Paintings in the Bodleian Library*. Oxford, 1958.

——. *Islamic Painting and the Arts of the Book*. Catalogue of the Keir Collection. London, 1976.

——. "Isma'il II's Copy of the *Shahnama*." *Iran* 14 (1976): 1–8.

——. "Origin and Date of Three Famous *Shâhnâma* Illustrations." *Ars Orientalis* 1 (1954): 105–12.

——. *Persian Paintings in the India Office Library, A Descriptive Catalogue*. London, 1976.

——. *Persian Paintings in the John Rylands Library: A Descriptive Catalogue*. London, 1980.

——. "Persian Painting Under the Zand and Qājār Dynasties." In *From Nadir Shah to the Islamic Republic*, ed. Peter Avery, Gavin Hambly, and Charles Melville. Cambridge History of Iran, vol. 7. Cambridge, 1991. Pp. 870–90.

——. "The Shahnama of Muhammad Juki." In *The Royal Asiatic Society: Its History and Treasures*, ed. Stuart Simonds and Simon Digby. Leiden, 1979.

——. "The Turkman School to 1503." In *Arts of the Book in Central Asia*, ed. Basil Gray. Boulder, 1979. Pp. 215–48.

——. "An Unpublished Manuscript of the Gulistan of Sa'di." In *Beiträge zur Kunstgeschichte Asiens. In Memoriam Ernst Diez*, ed. O. Aslanapa. Istanbul, 1963. Pp. 223–36.

——. *Persian Miniature Painting from Collections in the British Isles*. London, 1967.

ROHANI, NASRIN. *A Bibliography of Persian Miniature Painting*. Cambridge, MA, 1982.

SAFADI, Y. H. *Islamic Calligraphy*. Boulder, 1978.

SCHIMMEL, ANNEMARIE. *Calligraphy and Islamic Culture*. New York, 1984.

SCHMITZ, BARBARA. *Islamic Manuscripts in The New York Public Library*. Contributions by Latif Khayyat, Svat Soucek, and Massoud Pourfarrokh. New York and Oxford, 1992.

SCHROEDER, ERIC. "Ahmed Musa and Shams Al-Din: A Review of Fourteenth-Century Painting." *Ars Islamica* 6 (1939): 113–42.

——. *Persian Miniatures in the Fogg Museum of Art*. Cambridge, MA, 1942.

SÉGUY, MARIE-ROSE. *The Miraculous Journey of Mahomet/Mirâj Nameh*. New York, 1977.

SEYLLER, JOHN. "Codicological Aspects of the Victoria and Albert Museum *Akbarnama* and Their Historical Implications." *Art Journal* 49 (1990): 379–87.

——. "A Dated *Hamzanāma* Illustration." *Artibus Asiae* 53 (1993).

——. "The School of Oriental and African Studies *Anvar-i Suhaylī*: The Illustration of a *De Luxe Mughal* Manuscript." *Ars Orientalis* 16 (1986): 119–52.

——. "Scribal Notes on Mughal Manuscript Illustrations." *Artibus Asia* 48 (1987): 247–77.

SIMPSON, MARIANNA SHREVE. *Arab and Persian Painting in the Fogg Art Museum*. Cambridge, MA, 1980.

——. *The Illustration of an Epic: the Earliest Shahnama Manuscripts*. New York and London, 1979.

——. "The Production and Patronage of the *Haft Aurang* by Jāmī in the Freer Gallery of Art." *Ars Orientalis* 13 (1982): 93–119.

SIMS, ELEANOR. "The European Print Sources of Paintings by the Seventeenth-Century Persian Painter, Muhammad-Zaman Ibn Haji Yusuf of Qum." In *Le Stampe e la diffusione delle immagini e degli stili*, ed. Henri Zerner. Bologna, 1983. Pp. 73–83.

——. *The Garrett Manuscript of the Zafar-Name: A Study in Fifteenth-Century Timurid Patronage*. Ph.D. dissertation, New York University, Institute of Fine Arts. 1973.

——. "Ibrahim-Sultan's Illustrated *Zafarnama* of 1436 and Its Impact in the Muslim East." In *Timurid Art and Culture: Iran and Central Asia in the Fifteenth Century*, ed. Lisa Golombek and Maria Subtelny. Supplements to Muqarnas. Leiden, 1992. Pp. 132–43.

——. "Ibrāhīm-Sultān's Illustrated *Zafar-Nāmeh* of 839/1436." *Islamic Art* 4 (1990–1): 175–218.

——. "The Illustrated Manuscripts of Firdausī's *Shāhnāma* Commissioned by Princes of the House of Tīmūr." *Ars Orientalis*, 22 (1992), pp. 43–68.

SKELTON, ROBERT. "The Ni'mat-nama: A Landmark in Malwa Painting." *Marg* 12 (1959): 44–50.

SMART, ELLEN. *Paintings from the Babur-nama: A Study of 16th-Century Mughal Historical Manuscript Illustrations*. Ph.D. dissertation, SOAS, University of London, 1977.

SOUCEK, PRISCILLA P. "Dickson and Welch: *The Houghton Shahnameh*." Review. *Ars Orientalis* 14 (1984): 133–8.

——. "An Illustrated Manuscript of Al-Bîrûnî's *Chronology of Ancient Nations*." In *The Scholar and the Saint*, ed. Peter Chelkowski. New York, 1975. Pp. 103–65.

——. "The New York Public Library *Makhzan Al-asrār* and Its Importance." *Ars Orientalis* 18 (1988 [1990]): 1–38.

——. "The Life of the Prophet: Illustrated Versions." In *Content and Context of Visual Arts in the Islamic World*, ed. Priscilla P. Soucek. University Park, PA, and London, 1988. Pp. 193–218.

——. "The Manuscripts of Iskandar Sultan: Structure and Content." In *Timurid Art and Culture: Iran and Central Asia in the Fifteenth Century*, ed. Lisa Golombek and Maria Subtelny. Supplements to Muqarnas. Leiden, 1992. Pp. 116–31.

——. "Sultan Muhammad Tabrizi: Painter at the Safavid Court." In *Persian Masters: Five Centuries of Painting*, ed. Sheila R. Canby. Bombay, 1990. Pp. 55–70.

SOUDAVAR, ABOLALA. *Art of the Persian Courts: Selections from the Art and History Trust Collection*. Contribution by Milo Cleveland Beach. New York, 1992.

STCHOUKINE, IVAN. "Un Manuscrit de Mehr et Moshtari Illustré à Herat, Vers 1430." *Arts asiatiques* 8 (1961): 83–92.

——. "La Peinture à Yazd au début du XVe siècle." *Syria* 43 (1966): 99–104.

——. *La Peinture iranienne sous les derniers Abbasides et les Il-Khans*. Bruges, 1936.

——. *Les Peintures des manuscrits de Shah 'Abbas Ier à la fin des Safavis*. Paris, 1964.

——. *Les Peintures des manuscrits de la "Khamseh" de Nizami au Topkapid Sarayi Müzesi d'Istanbul*. Paris, 1977.

——. *Les Peintures des manuscrits safavies de 1502 à 1587*. Paris, 1959.

——. *Les Peintures des manuscrits Tîmûrides*. Paris, 1954.

——. "Les Peintures turcomanes et safavies d'une *Khamseh* de Nizâmî, achevée à Tabriz en 886/1481." *Arts asiatiques* 44 (1966): 1–16.

SWIETOCHOWSKI, M. L. "The Language of the Birds: The Fifteenth Century Miniatures." *Bulletin of the Metropolitan Museum of Art* 25 (May 1967): 317–38.

SWIETOCHOWSKI, MARIE LUKENS, and SUSSAN BABAIE. *Persian Drawings in The Metropolitan Museum of Art*. New York, 1989.

TITLEY, NORAH M. "A Fourteenth-Century Khamseh of Nizami." *British Museum Quarterly* 36 (1972): 8–11.

——. *Persian Miniature Painting and Its Influence on the Art of Turkey and India: The British Library Collections*. Austin, TX, 1984.

——. "Persian Miniature Painting: The Repetition of Compositions during the Fifteenth Century." In *Akten des VII. Internationalen Kongresses für Iranische Kunst und Archäologie, 1976*. Berlin, 1979. Pp. 471–91.

WALEY, P., and NORAH M. TITLEY. "An Illustrated Persian Text of Kalila and Dimna dated 707/1307–8." *British Library Journal* 1 (1975): 42–60.

WELCH, ANTHONY. *Artists for the Shah*. New Haven, 1976.

——. *Calligraphy in the Arts of the Muslim World*. Austin, TX, 1979.

WELCH, ANTHONY, and STUART CARY WELCH. *Arts of the Islamic Book: The Collection of Prince Sadruddin Aga Khan*. Exhibition catalogue. Ithaca, NY, and London, 1982.

WELCH, STUART CARY. *A King's Book of Kings*. New York, 1972.

——. *Persian Painting: Five Royal Safavid Manuscripts*. New York, 1976.

——. *Wonders of the Age: Masterpieces of Early Safavid Painting, 1501–1576*. Contributions by Sheila R. Canby and Nora Titley. Cambridge, MA, 1979.

WELCH, STUART CARY, ANNEMARIE SCHIMMEL, MARIE L. SWIETOCHOWSKI, and WHEELER M. THACKSTON. *The Emperors' Album: Images of Mughal India*. New York, 1987.

WILKINSON, J. V. S. *The Shah-nameh . . . with 24 Illustrations from a Fifteenth-century Persian Manuscript*. With an introduction by Laurence Binyon. London, 1931.

YURDAYDIN, H. G. *Naṣūḥü's-Silāḥī (Maṭrāḳçī), Beyān-i Menāzil-i Sefer-i 'Irāḳeyn-i Sulṭān Süleymān Hān* ["Maṭrāḳçī Naṣūḥ and His 'The Description of the Stages of Sulṭān Süleymān Hān's Campaign in the Two 'Irāḳs'"]. Ankara, 1976.

ZEBROWSKI, MARK. *Deccani Painting*. Berkeley and Los Angeles, 1983.

IV. DECORATIVE ARTS

1. *Ceramics*

ALLAN, J. W. "Abu'l-Qasim's Treatise on Ceramics." *Iran* 11 (1973): 111–20.

ATASOY, NURHAN, and JULIAN RABY. *Iznik: The Pottery of Ottoman Turkey*. London, 1989.

ATIL, ESIN. *Ceramics from the World of Islam* [in the Freer Gallery of Art]. Washington, DC, 1973.

BAILEY, G. A. "The Dynamics of Chinoiserie in Timurid and Early Safavid Ceramics." In *Timurid Art and Culture: Iran and Central Asia in the Fifteenth Century*, ed. Lisa Golombek and Maria Subtelny. Supplements to Muqarnas. Leiden, 1992. Pp. 179–90.

CAIGER-SMITH, ALAN. *Lustre Pottery: Technique, Tradition and Innovation in Islam and the Western World*. London, 1985.

CARSWELL, JOHN. *Blue and White: Chinese Porcelain and Its Impact on the Western World*. Exhibition catalogue. Chicago, 1985.

——. "Six Tiles." In *Islamic Art in the Metropolitan Museum of Art*, ed. Richard Ettinghausen. New York, 1976. Pp. 99–124.

DENNY, WALTER B. "Ceramic Revetments of the Mosque of the Ramazan Oğlu in Adana." In *IVème Congrès international d'art turc*. Aix-en-Provence, 1976. Pp. 57–66.

——. *The Ceramics of the Mosque of Rüstem Pasha and the Environment of Change*. New York, 1977.

——. "Ceramics." In *Turkish Art*, ed. Esin Atıl. Washington, DC, 1980. Pp. 239–98.

ETTINGHAUSEN, RICHARD. "New Affiliations for a Classical Persian Pottery Type." *Parnassus* 8 (1936): 10.

——. "Notes on the Lusterware of Spain." *Ars Orientalis* 1 (1954): 145–8.

FROTHINGHAM, ALICE WILSON. *Catalogue of Hispano-Moresque Pottery in the Collection of the Hispanic Society of America*. New York, 1936.

GODMAN, F. DuCANE. *The Godman Collection of Oriental and Spanish Pottery and Glass*. London, 1901.

GRUBE, ERNST J. "Notes on the Decorative Arts of the Timurid Period." In *Gururajamanjarika: Studi in Onore di Giuseppe Tucci, i*. Naples, 1974. Pp. 233–79.

——. "Notes on the Decorative Arts of the Timurid Period, II." *Islamic Art* 3 (1989): 175–208.

HAKENJOS, BERND. *Marokkanische Keramik*. Exhibition catalogue. Stuttgart and London, 1988.

IVANOV, A. A. "Fayansovoe Blyudo XV Veka Iz Mashkhada." *Soobscheniya Gosudarstvennogo Ordena Lenina Ermitazha* 45 (1980): 64–66, 79–80.

JENKINS, MARILYN. "Mamluk Underglaze Painted Pottery: Foundations for Further Study." *Muqarnas* 2 (1984): 95–114.

KENESSON, SUMMER S. "Nasrid Luster Pottery: The Alhambra Vases." *Muqarnas* 9 (1992): 93–115.

LANE, ARTHUR. *Early Islamic Pottery*. London, 1947.

——. *Later Islamic Pottery*. London, 1957.

——. "The Ottoman Pottery of Isnik." *Ars Orientalis* 2 (1954): 247–81.

LUSCHEY-SCHMEISSER, INGEBORG. *The Pictorial Tile Cycles of Hašt Behešt in Isfahan and Its Iconographic Tradition*. Rome, 1978.

MARTI NEZ CAVIR, BALBINA. *La Loza Dorada*. Madrid, 1983.

NECIPOĞLU, GÜLRU. "From International Timurid to Ottoman: A Change of Taste in Sixteenth-Century Ceramic Tiles." *Muqarnas* 7 (1990): 136–70.

O'KANE, BERNARD. "The Tiled Minbars of Iran." *Annales islamologiques* 22 (1986): 133–55.

ÖNEY, GÖNÜL. *Ceramic Tiles in Islamic Architecture.* Istanbul, n.d.

RAPOPORT, I. "K Voprosu O Pozdney Lyustrovoy Keramike Irana." *Soob-schcheniya Gosudarstvennogo Ermitazha* 31 (1970): 54–6.

RIEFSTAHL, RUDOLF M. "Early Turkish Tile Revetments in Edirne." *Ars Islamica* 4 (1937): 249–81.

SCANLON, GEORGE. "Mamluk Pottery: More Evidence from Fustat." *Muqarnas* 2 (1984): 115–26.

SCARCE, JENNIFER. "'Ali Mohammad Isfahani, Tile Maker of Tehran." *Oriental Art* 22 (1976): 278–88.

——. "The Arts of the Eighteenth to Twentieth Centuries: Architecture, Ceramics, Metalwork, Textiles." In *From Nadir Shah to the Islamic Republic*, ed. Peter Avery, Gavin Hambly, and Charles Melville. Cambridge History of Iran, vol. 7. Cambridge, 1991. Pp. 890–958.

SOUSTIEL, JEAN. *La Céramique Islamique: Le Guide du Connaisseur.* Fribourg, 1985.

ÜNVER, SÜHEYL. "Baba Nakkaş." *Fatih Ve Istanbul* 2 (1954): 7–12 and 169–88.

WATSON, OLIVER. *Persian Lustre Ware.* London, 1985.

2. Metalwork

ALLAN, J. W. "From Tabrîz to Siirt – Relocation of a Thirteenth-Century Metalworking School." *Iran* 16 (1978): 182–3.

——. *Islamic Metalwork: The Nuhad Es-Said Collection.* London, 1982.

——. "Sha'ban, Barquq, and the Decline of the Mamluk Metalworking Industry." *Muqarnas* 2 (1984): 85–94.

——. "The Survival of Precious and Base Metal Objects from the Medieval Islamic World." In *Pots and Pans: A Colloquium on Precious Metals and Ceramics.* Oxford Studies in Islamic Art. Oxford, 1985. Pp. 57–70.

BAER, EVA. "'Fish-Pond' Ornaments on Persian and Mamluk Metal Vessels." *Bulletin of the School of Oriental and African Studies* 31 (1968): 14–27.

BARRETT, DOUGLAS. *Islamic Metalwork in the British Museum.* London, 1949.

BLAIR, SHEILA S. "Artists and Patronage in Late Fourteenth-Century Iran in Light of Two Catalogues of Islamic Metalwork." *Bulletin of the School of Oriental and African Studies* 48, no. 1 (1985): 53–9.

FEHÉRVÁRI, GEZA. *Islamic Metalwork of the Eighth Century to the Fifteenth Century in the Kier Collection.* London, 1976.

GODARD, YEDDA A. "Bassin de cuivre au nom de Shaikh Uwais." *Āthār-é Īrān* 1 (1936): 371–3.

HAUPTMANN VON GLADISS, ALMUT, and JENS KRÖGER. "Metall, Stein, Stuck, Holz, Elfenbein, Stoffe." Berlin, Staatliche Museen Preussischer Kulturbesitz, Museum für Islamische Kunst. In *Islamische Kunst: Loseblatt-katalog unpublizierte Werke aus Deutschen Museen*, 2, ed. Klaus Brisch. Mainz/Rhein, 1985.

IVANOV, A. A. "O Bronzovykh Izdeliiakh Kontsa XIV V. Iz Mavzoleia Khodzha Ahmeda Iasevi." In *Sredniaia Aziia I Ee Sosedi V Drevnosti I Srednevekov'e*, ed. B. A. Litvinskii. Moscow, 1981. Pp. 68–89.

KOMAROFF, LINDA. *The Golden Disk of Heaven: Metalwork of Timurid Iran.* Costa Mesa and New York, 1992.

——. "Persian Verses of Gold and Silver: The Inscriptions on Timurid Metalwork." In *Timurid Art and Culture: Iran and Central Asia in the Fifteenth Century*, ed. Lisa Golombek and Maria Subtelny. Supplements to Muqarnas. Leiden, 1992. Pp. 144–57.

MELIKIAN-CHIRVANI, A. S. "Bronzes et cuivres iraniens du Louvre: I. L'École du Fars au XIVe siècle." *Journal Asiatique* 257 (1969): 20–36.

——. "Cuivres inédits de l'époque de Qa'itbay." *Kunst des Orients* 6 (1969): 99–133.

——. "Studies in Hindustani Metalwork: I – On Some Sultanate Stirrups." In *Art et société dans le monde iranien*, ed. Chahriyar Adle. Paris, 1982. Pp. 177–95.

——. *Islamic Metalwork from the Iranian World, 8th–18th Centuries.* London, 1982.

SCARCE, JENNIFER. "The Arts of the Eighteenth to Twentieth Centuries: Architecture, Ceramics, Metalwork, Textiles." In *From Nadir Shah to the Islamic Republic*, ed. Peter Avery, Gavin Hambly, and Charles Melville. Cambridge History of Iran, vol. 7. Cambridge, 1991. Pp. 890–958.

STRONGE, SUSAN. *Bidri Ware: Inlaid Metalwork from India.* London, 1985.

WIET, GASTON. *Objects en cuivre.* Catalogue générale du musée arabe du Caire. Cairo, 1932.

3. Textiles

BEATTIE, MAY. *The Thyssen-Bornemisza Collection of Oriental Rugs.* Castagnola, 1972.

——. *Carpets of Central Persia.* London, 1976.

BLACK, DAVID, ed. *The Macmillan Atlas of Rugs and Carpets.* New York, 1985.

BORALEVI, ALBERTO. "Three Egyptian Carpets in Italy." In *Oriental Carpet and Textile Studies II: Carpets of the Mediterranean Countries 1400–1600*, ed. Robert Pinner and Walter B. Denny. London, 1986. Pp. 205–20.

BRIGGS, AMY. "Timurid Carpets." *Ars Islamica* 7 (1940): 20–54.

Carpets of the Mediterranean Countries 1400–1600. ed. Robert Pinner and Walter B. Denny. Oriental Carpet and Textile Studies. 2 (1986).

DIMAND, M. S. "A Persian Garden Carpet in Jaipur Museum." *Ars Islamica* 7 (1940): 93–6.

DIMAND, M. S., and JEAN MAILEY. *Oriental Rugs in the Metropolitan Museum of Art.* New York, 1973.

ERDMANN, KURT. *Seven Hundred Years of Oriental Carpets*, ed. Hanna Erdmann. trans. M. H. Beatty and H. Herzog. Berkeley and Los Angeles, 1970.

ETTINGHAUSEN, RICHARD. "New Light on Early Animal Carpets." In *Aus der Welt der Islamischen Kunst: Festschrift für Ernst Kühnel*, ed. R. Ettinghausen. Berlin, 1959. Pp. 93–116.

FISKE, PATRICIA L., W. RUSSELL PICKERING, and RALPH S. YOHE, eds. *From the Far West: Carpets and Textiles of Morocco.* Exhibition Catalogue. Washington, DC, 1980.

GEIJER, AGNES. "Some Thoughts on the Problems of Early Oriental Carpets." *Ars Orientalis* 5 (1963): 79–87.

HOUSEGO, JENNY. "Carpets." In *The Arts of Persia*, ed. R. W. Ferrier. New Haven and London, 1989. Pp. 118–56.

IRWIN, ROBERT G. "Egypt, Syria and Their Trading Partners 1450–1550." In *Oriental Carpet and Textile Studies II: Carpets of the Mediterranean Countries 1400–1600*, ed. Robert Pinner and Walter B. Denny. London, 1986. Pp. 73–82.

KING, DONALD. "The Doria Polonaise Carpet." In *Persian and Mughal Art.* London, 1976. Pp. 301–12.

KÜHNEL, ERNST, and LOUISA BELLINGER. *Cairene Rugs and Others Technically Related.* Washington, DC, 1957.

LAMM, C. J. "The Marby Rug and Some Fragments of Carpets Found in Egypt." In *Svenska Orientsällskapets Arsbok.* Stockholm, 1937. Pp. 51–130.

LOMBARD, MAURICE. *Les Textiles dans le Monde Musulman VIIe-XIIe Siècle.* Civilisations et Sociétés 61. Paris-La Haye-New York, 1978.

McDOWELL, J. ALGROVE. "Textiles." In *The Arts of Persia*, ed. R. W. Ferrier. New Haven and London, 1989. Pp. 157–70.

MACKIE, LOUISE W. "A Piece of the Puzzle: A 14th–15th Century Persian Carpet Fragment Revealed." *Hali* 11, no. 47 (1989): 16–23.

MANKOWSKI, TADEUSZ. "Some Documents from Polish Sources Relating to Carpet Making in the Time of Shah 'Abbas I." In *Survey of Persian Art*, ed. A. U. Pope and P. Ackerman. London and New York, 1939. Pp. 2431–6.

PARTEARROYO, CRISTINA. "Spanish-Muslim Textile." *Bulletin de liaion du Centre internationale d'étude des textiles anciens* 45 (1977): 78–81.

RABY, JULIAN. "Court and Export: Part 1. Market Demands in Ottoman Carpets 1450–1550." In *Oriental Carpet and Textile Studies II: Carpets of the Mediterranean Countries 1400–1600*, ed. Robert Pinner and Walter B. Denny. London, 1986. Pp. 29–38.

——. "Court and Export: Part 2. The Uşak Carpets." Ibid. Pp. 177–88.

RESWICK, IRMTRAUD. *Traditional Textiles of Tunisia and Related North African Weavings.* Los Angeles, 1985.

SARRE, F., and H. TRENKWALD. *Old Oriental Carpets.* Vienna and Leipzig, 1929.

SCARCE, JENNIFER. "The Arts of the Eighteenth to Twentieth Centuries: Architecture, Ceramics, Metalwork, Textiles." In *From Nadir Shah to the Islamic Republic*, ed. Peter Avery, Gavin Hambly, and Charles Melville. Cambridge History of Iran, vol. 7. Cambridge, 1991. Pp. 890–958.

STEAD, REXFORD. *The Ardabil Carpets.* Malibu, CA, 1974.

WALKER, DANIEL. "Classical Indian Rugs." *Hali* 4 (1982): 252–6.

Glossary

= Arabic; P = Persian; T = Turkish

Abbasid	dynasty of caliphs who ruled from Iraq 749–1258
amir	prince or commander
arabesque	geometricized vegetal ornament
'anaza (A)	wooden screen in the form of a mihrab erected in the courtyard of a North African mosque
b.	son of (Arab, ibn/bin)
beveled style	style of carving stucco and wood with a slanted cut; developed under the Abbasid dynasty in Iraq, it spread throughout the Islamic lands
chatri	a rooftop pavilion in Indian architecture
chinoiserie	motifs and ornament derived from Chinese prototypes
cuerda seca	("dry cord") technique of glazing ceramics with several colors simultaneously by separating them with a greasy substance mixed with manganese; it left a matte black line between the colors after firing
dikka (A)	tribune for the official charged with repeating the daily prayers
Hanafi	follower of Abu Hanifa (d. 767), founder of a school of law particularly popular in the Ottoman empire
imam	(1) descendant of the Prophet Muhammad; (2) the leader of prayer in the mosque
imāmzāda (P)	literally, a descendant of an imam (1); by extension, the tomb where he is buried
iwan	barrel-vaulted space open at one end
khan	caravanserai
khānaqāh (A/P)	hospice for Sufis
Kufic	style of writing characterized by angular shapes
lambrequin arch	arch with pendant forms when seen in profile
lampas	textile weave with two sets of warps and two sets of wefts
lājvardīna (P)	literally, having the quality of lapis lazuli; used to describe a deep blue ceramic glaze
madrasa (T medrese)	theological college; sometimes called medersa in North Africa
maidan (A maydān)	open square or plaza
minaret	tower attached to a mosque, often used for the call to prayer
minbar (T mimber)	pulpit, usually of wood but sometimes of stone or decorated with glazed ceramic, from which the sermon is given during communal worship in the congregational mosque on Friday
mosque	Muslim house of worship, from the Arabic masjid, "place of prostration"; also masjid al-jāmi' (A: "congregational mosque"), masjid-i jum'a (P: "Friday mosque"); ulu cami (T: "great mosque"); jami' masjid (in India)
muḥaqqaq (A)	style of cursive script characterized by a narrow zone below the base line, shallow bowls on descending letters, and straight, sharp tips
muqarnas (A)	architectural device composed of serried tiers of niche-like elements, sometimes likened to stalactite or honeycomb vaulting
naqqāsh (A)	scribe; designer; painter
naskh	the common cursive hand for copying books; "minuscule" form of thuluth (q.v.)
opus sectile	ornamental paving or wall revetment made from colored marble slabs cut in geometric shapes
pisé	rammed earth
pīshṭāq (P)	high and formal gateway composed of an arch set within a rectangular frame and functioning like a shallow iwan
qanāt (P)	underground aqueduct
qibla (T kible)	direction of prayer towards the Kaaba in Mecca
rayḥān	"minuscule" form of muḥaqqaq (q.v.)
riqā'	"minuscule" form of tawqī' (q.v.)
sayyid	descendant of the Prophet Muhammad
semé	elements scattered on a plain ground
Shafi'i	follower of al-Shafi'i (d. 820), founder of a school of law particularly popular in Egypt and Syria
Shāhnāma (P)	literally "Book of Kings"; the Persian national epic written down by Firdawsi ca. 1010
Shi'ite	from the Arabic shī'a, literally "party"; those who believe that the caliphate passed to the Prophet's son-in-law 'Ali and his descendants
simurgh (P)	mythical phoenix-like bird
squinch	an arch thrown diagonally across the corner of a room to support a circular or polygonal superstructure
Sufi	mystic
tawqī'	cursive script characterized by distended final forms and numerous unorthodox connections between letters
thuluth	"majuscule" form of naskh (q.v.), often used in headings and inscriptions
Umayyad	first Islamic dynasty of caliphs, who ruled from Damascus 661–750; another branch ruled in Spain 756–1031
zāwiya (A), zaviye (T)	hospice for Sufis